C. C. Seaman

41st Congress, } HOUSE OF REPRESENTATIVES. { Ex. Doc.
2d Session. } { No. 27.

REPORT OF SPECIAL COMMISSIONER OF THE REVENUE.

LETTER

FROM

THE SECRETARY OF THE TREASURY,

TRANSMITTING

The report of the Special Commissioner of the Revenue upon the industry, trade, commerce, &c., of the United States for the year 1869.

December 20, 1869.—Referred to the Committee of Ways and Means and ordered to be printed.

Treasury Department,
December 17, 1869.

Sir: I have the honor to transmit herewith the report of the Special Commissioner of the Revenue.

I am, yours, respectfully,

GEORGE S. BOUTWELL,
Secretary.

Hon. James G. Blaine,
Speaker of the House of Representatives.

REPORT

OF

THE SPECIAL COMMISSIONER OF THE REVENUE.

TREASURY DEPARTMENT,
OFFICE SPECIAL COMMISSIONER OF THE REVENUE,
Washington, D. C., December, 1869.

SIR: In accordance with the provision of law creating the office of Special Commissioner of the Revenue, I have the honor to submit my fourth annual report in respect to the industry, trade, commerce, and revenues of the country; and would request that the same may be transmitted to Congress for consideration.

REVIEW OF THE PROGRESS OF THE NATION FOR THE YEAR 1869.

To review the main features of our national experience in respect to capital and industry for the past year, is but to chronicle and affirm anew the apparent continuance of that same wonderful rate of progress and development which, with the exception of a period of war, has especially characterized the history of the nation for the last quarter of a century.

The revenue receipts of the national exchequer, as in every other year since the termination of the war, have been largely in excess of national expenditures; the tide of labor-seeking, wealth-producing immigration continues to flow with increasing volume upon our shores of the West as upon those of the East; the aggregate of the crops has been bountiful in quantity, excellent in quality, and in excess of any recent average; the circle of settlement has been so rapidly extended, that millions of acres are now included in its area which twelve months ago were uncultivated wilderness; the number of miles of railway constructed has been greater than that of any preceding year, and a regular daily routine of travel and traffic has for the first time been established thereon across the continent; the restoration of the South to a condition of prosperity, equal or greater than that which prevailed antecedent to the war, is a work well-nigh accomplished; peace reigns in all our borders; and from the Atlantic to the Pacific, from the St. John's to the Rio Grande, there are few who, exempt from physical ailment, need hunger from scarcity of food, or be idle for lack of some opportunity for remunerative employment. In short, the experience of another year reaffirms the principle before announced, that the progress and growth of the country, through its elements of vitality, viz., great national resources and an inherent spirit of energy and enterprise in the people, are in a great degree independent of legislation, and of the impoverishment and disorder which the occurrence of a long war has necessarily occasioned.

In support of the above generalizations, the Commissioner would next ask attention to the following specific evidence:

EXCESS OF NATIONAL REVENUE OVER NATIONAL EXPENDITURES.

The national revenue for the fiscal year ending June 30, 1869, was $370,943,747 21. The national expenditure for the same period was $321,490,597 75, leaving an excess of revenue over expenditure of $49,453,149 46.

The following table shows the relation of receipts to expenditures for each fiscal year since the termination of the war:

Years.	Receipts.	Expenditures.	Excess of receipts.
1865-'66	$558, 032, 620 06	$520, 750, 940 48	$37, 281, 679 58
1866-'67	490, 634, 010 27	346, 729, 129 33	143, 905, 880 94
1867-'68	405, 638, 083 32	377, 340, 284 86	28, 297, 798 46
1868-'69	370, 943, 747 21	321, 490, 597 75	49, 453, 149 46

REDUCTION OF THE NATIONAL DEBT.

On the 1st of September, 1865, the amount of the public debt, then at its maximum, was, less cash in the treasury, $2,757,689,571 43. At the commencement of the present fiscal year, July 1, 1869, the amount of the public debt, less cash and sinking fund in the treasury, was $2,489,002,480 58, showing a reduction to that date of $268,687,090 85. Within the same period, taxes which if continued to the present time would have yielded, in the aggregate, upwards of $200,000,000 per annum, have also been abated or relinquished. To find a parallel to such results, the financial history of other nations will be searched to no purpose.

The amount of the public debt on the 1st of December, 1869, less cash and sinking fund in the treasury, was $2,453,559,735 23, making a total reduction since the 1st of September, 1865, of $304,129,836 20, and for the current calendar year, of $87,147,466 02.

TOTAL COST OF THE WAR.

It would seem to be desirable at this point, now that all feeling in regard to the subject from its bearing on political questions has apparently passed away, to place upon record the exact cost of the war, as nearly as the same can be determined. With this object, attention is asked to the following exhibit:

The amount of outstanding national indebtedness March 7, 1861, was $76, 455, 299 28

During the four years of war which terminated in April, 1865, (April 1, 1861, to April 1, 1865,) the actual receipts of the treasury were as follows:

From internal revenue	$314, 337, 317 01
From customs	280, 861, 618 45
From lands	1, 812, 083 80
From direct tax	4, 668, 259 31
From miscellaneous sources	74, 120, 413 37
Total receipts	675, 799, 691 94

The receipts of revenue from April 1, 1865, to June 30, 1869, inclusive, during which period the larger portion of the expenditures has been directly in consequence of the war, were as follows:

From internal revenue	$967, 207, 221 41
From customs	729, 991, 875 97
From lands	7, 402, 188 28
From direct tax	9, 017, 217 30
From miscellaneous sources	194, 949, 122 13
Total receipts	1, 908, 567, 625 09

The amount of outstanding indebtedness, less cash and sinking fund in treasury, June 30, 1869, was	$2, 489, 002, 480 58
Deducting from this the amount of outstanding indebtedness at the outbreak of the war ($76,455,299 28,) we have, as the sum borrowed for war purposes and not repaid out of the receipts above indicated	2, 412, 547, 181 30
Making the total expenditure (loans and receipts) in eight and a quarter years of war and its effects	4, 996, 914, 498 33
Deducting the amount which, but for the war, might be taken as the average expenditure of the government during this period, say one hundred millions per annum	825, 000, 000 00
We shall have	4, 171, 914, 498 33

which sum represents the cost of the war to the United States government down to June 30, 1869.

To this sum should be added the value of the pensions now paid by the Government on account of the war, if the same were capitalized. This, at eight years' purchase of the present annual payment, would amount to about *two hundred millions.*

But this aggregate, however large, must still further be increased by other items if we would reach the true cost of the war to us as a people, the above representing only the expenditures of the national government.

These additional charges are substantially as follows:

Increase of State debts, mainly on war account........	$123,000,000
County, city, and town indebtedness increased on account of the war, (estimated) *	200,000,000
Expenditures of States, counties, cities, and towns, on account of the war, not represented by funded debt, (estimated)	600,000,000
Estimated loss to the loyal States from the diversion and suspension of industry, and the reduction of the American marine and carrying trade	1,200,000,000
Estimated direct expenditures and loss of property by the Confederate States by reason of the war †	2,700,000,000

These estimates, which are believed to be moderate and reasonable, show an aggregate destruction of wealth, or diversion of industry which would have produced wealth, in the United States since 1861, approximating *nine thousand millions* of dollars—a sum nominally in excess of the entire increase of wealth, as returned by the census, for the whole country from 1850 to 1860.

This, then, was the cost of the destruction of slavery; the cost of compromise; the cost of the unfaithfulness of those who founded this nation to the idea by which the nation lives. What does it measure? It is substantially a thousand millions a year for nine years; or, at the wages of five hundred dollars a year, the labor of two millions of men exerted continuously during the whole of that period. It is three times as much as the slave property of the country was ever worth. It is a sum which at interest would yield to the end of time twice as much as the annual slave product of the South in its best estate.

"The places of those who sleep in their graves have been filled by new laborers; the incubus of slavery, which was slowly but surely making the fertile South a desert scorched as by a consuming fire, has been removed; thousands of miles of new railroads; inventions never before excelled in their labor-saving character; millions of acres of the richest lands opened to settlement, now render labor easy and product large." Without faltering, and without tampering with the public faith, it is now the duty of this people to undertake the far easier task of payment for the service already rendered. If we hesitate or falter, dishonor,

* The report of the comptroller of the State of New York for 1869 states the bounty debt of the State to have been $26,862,000 in 1867; and the amount of local debt for war expenditures to have aggregated in 1868 the sum of $34,765,746 10. The war debt of the State of Massachusetts is at present $16,573,244; the local war debt of the State is not known. The amount paid by this State for bounties and to soldiers' families up to January, 1869, is returned at $26,801,000.

† In making this estimate of the loss by the war to the States in rebellion, a standard of value has been taken which is between the gold standard on the one hand, and the standard of the depreciated confederate currency on the other. The intention has been to take these losses at a standard of value conforming in general to that of the northern States during the same period.

second only to that which tolerated slavery, will overwhelm the land, and the idea of a free people governing themselves will become a scorn and a by-word among nations.

IMMIGRATION.

The following is a revised and the most accurate attainable statement of the course of alien immigration into the United States since and including the year 1856:

Year	Number	Year	Number
1856	200, 436	1863	176, 282
1857	251, 306	1864	193, 418
1858	123, 126	1865	248, 120
1859	121, 282	1866	318, 554
1860	153, 640	1867	298, 358
1861	91, 9	1868	297, 215
1862	91, 987	1869	352, 569
Total in fourteen years			2, 918, 213

Total from July 1, 1865, to June 30, 1869, *five years*, 1,514,816.

CHINESE IMMIGRATION.

The following table shows the course of Chinese immigration since and including the year 1856:

Year	Number	Year	Number
1856	4, 733	1863	7, 214
1857	5, 944	1864	2, 975
1858	5, 128	1865	2, 942
1859	3, 457	1866	2, 385
1860	5, 467	1867	3, 863
1861	7, 518	1868	10, 684
1862	3, 633	1869	12, 874
Total in fourteen years			78, 817

The present increment of population of the United States, from the natural increase of births over deaths and from immigration, is, probably, at the rate of 1,100,000 per annum as a minimum.

RAILWAY EXTENSION.

The number of miles of new railway constructed in the United States during the past year will, it is believed, approximate to five thousand; making a total construction since and including the year 1865, the year of the termination of the war, of about thirteen thousand. If it is assumed that a line of railway gives access to fifteen square miles of country on each side of it, or thirty square miles altogether, then the thirteen thousand miles of railway, which it is estimated have been constructed during the five years from 1865 to 1870, will have opened up three hundred and ninety thousand square miles of what, for the purposes of general production, may be considered new territory—a tract of country larger than the whole area of France and nearly three and a half times larger than the whole area of Great Britain.

TELEGRAPHIC EXTENSION.

The telegraph system of the United States has been extended during the past year by at least seven thousand miles of new wire, as compared with an estimated extension of six thousand in 1868; three thousand in 1867; and two thousand in 1866.

INDUSTRIAL RESUSCITATION AND DEVELOPMENT OF THE SOUTH.

But no one circumstance pertaining to the history of the past more strikingly illustrates the extent of the resources of the country and the energy of its population than the recent industrial resuscitation and development of the South. In 1865 this section of our country, which in 1860 represented nearly one-third of the entire population, and, omitting the value of the slaves, nearly two-sevenths of the aggregate wealth of the nation, found itself, as the result of four years of civil war, entirely prostrate; without industry, without tools, without money, credit, or crops; deprived of local self-government, and, to a great extent, of all political privileges; the flower of its youth in the hospitals, or dead upon the battle-fields, with society disorganized, and starvation imminent or actually present. Furthermore, the first efforts of the people of the South to improve their condition were also in the highest degree discouraging. During the years 1866 and 1867 the crops, both of cotton and grain, were, to a very great extent, failures. The freedmen were not disposed to work for hire; demanded excessive wages, and after accepting them, too often rendered poor service. The general result of all attempts to revive production seemed, therefore, up to 1868, to leave both freedman and planter in a condition more destitute and discouraged even than at the close of the war. But the year 1868, the third year of the free-labor experiment, at last brought an improvement. The harvest was sufficiently abundant to furnish the people with cheap food and to produce a large surplus for the future and for export, while the value returned from the sale of the exportable product of that year, in the form of cotton, grain, sugar, tobacco, and naval stores, and the like, amounted to an aggregate of at least three hundred millions of dollars in currency. Such a result of effort and industry, which in its very statement assumes the character of the marvellous, has brought to the people of the South, before so enfeebled, poor, and discouraged, a large measure of strength and prosperity. It has restored the broken and exhausted lines of railway intercommunication, and is creating many additional ones; it is enriching the soil and increasing the quality and quantity of the great staple per acre, through the extensive purchase and use of fertilizers and improved tools and implements; it is planting that distributor of comforts and necessities—the country store—at the cross-roads; and has led to a truer independence than could ever have been purchased through a victory at arms. The year 1869 has also closed auspiciously. The aggregate of the crops has almost uniformly been greater, while prices have continued to prove highly renumerative.

The general testimony of northern manufacturers is, that the new cotton is far superior in cleanliness, strength, and uniformity of fiber and absence of waste, than any ever before sent to market, while "a new variety, originating in Mississippi, the 'Peeler,' has also been introduced and brought to market, which commands a price from twenty-five to thirty per cent. higher than any other green-seed cotton of the same grade, because of the superior staple." The estimated product of rice for the Carolinas and Georgia is 55,000 tierces as compared with 35,000 for the previous year; and that of sugar 80,000 to 85,000 hogsheads as compared with 37,647 hogsheads in 1867. Before the war a large proportion of the net annual profit of the South was expended in the purchase of labor. It is now found that laborers can be obtained without expending anything for them, and that the capital thus formerly diverted can be saved and applied for the purchase of some other form of productive power, such as tools, machinery, and animals, while the value of manual labor can be supplemented and increased.* At present the supply of labor to the South is not sufficient to meet the demands of its various industries; but to doubt that with an assurance of profit, peace, personal freedom, and security of property for the future, such a supply cannot be obtained, is to doubt that the influences which have heretofore proved sufficient to control human action and direct the movement of population will continue to operate. But supposing the supply of labor to remain as it is, and the circumstances attending production to be only moderately favorable, the South gives fair promise of deriving annually a greater amount of active surplus capital as the results of its industry than any other section of the Union, and of thereby attaining to a degree of prosperity which will enable its population to become large consumers of the products of other States and countries.† This in turn must tend to increase the general prosperity of the whole country, to extend trade and commerce, to lighten, through wider distribution, the necessary burden of taxation, and to make certain the extinguishment of the national debt at a comparatively early period.

*Report upon cotton, United States Commissioners, Paris Exposition.

†"Since the war, experiments made to ascertain how much cotton can be produced upon a single acre have exhibited remarkable and gratifying results. When made with spade culture, stirring the soil deeply and often, after enriching it with phosphates and guano, the product has been very large. In one case reported, upon what seems to be good authority, the product of one acre was *four* bales, or over one thousand six hundred pounds of clean cotton. In past times one bale to the acre has been regarded as a fair crop, and two bales a very large one, on the very richest lands; while half a bale, or about two hundred and fifty pounds, was for many years a satisfactory result in Georgia and the Carolinas, where the lands were badly worn."—Report of United States Commissioners, Paris Exposition, 1867.

Furthermore, the large amount of capital thus becoming annually available at the South will, undoubtedly, seek in great part investment in domestic and local enterprises, and speedly lead to the establishment of manufactures on an extensive scale. The true diversity of employment which results from freedom has now, therefore, become to the South, for the first time, possible; and southern capital can soon be advantageously applied to the manufacture of agricultural tools and implements, leather, wagons, wooden-ware, soap, starch, clothing, and similar articles. These are manufactures in which iron, steel, and cloth are raw materials. They employ the largest amount of labor in proportion to product and capital, and warrant the payment of high wages. On the other hand, what are commonly called manufactures, viz., iron and steel, and cotton and woolen cloth, are examples of concentration. They require large capital, employ but few hands, and would naturally come much later. We already have in the United States an excess of cotton and woolen spindles, and to invest capital in more would be simply a waste, when there are vast needs at the South requiring far less capital, and warranting much greater compensation for labor than can be paid in textile fabrics.

THE TRUE TESTS OF MATERIAL PROSPERITY.

A presentation of evidence like that above given, touching the record of national production and development, naturally suggests a line of inquiry, which we propose to anticipate and answer. It is this: If the statements thus presented are not exaggerations; if the power of the country to repair its waste and extend its production is as great as is represented, what need of further investigation and legislation? Why talk of the burdens of the tariff, of the necessity of reforms in the internal revenue, or of the evils of an irredeemable paper currency? All these questions are certainly most pertinent to the subject; but in asking them let us not unintentionally deceive ourselves.

The aggregate production of a nation of forty millions, possessing the most fertile territory, with such varied conditions of climate and culture as to render the general failure of an annual harvest an impossibility, must necessarily be very great; while the annual increment of population from natural causes, superadded to an annual foreign immigration of over three hundred thousand, of necessity greatly expands the cultivated area of the State, requires an additional food product, augments the supply of labor and consequently of capital; which last in turn finds its expression and use most noticeably in the construction of houses and shops, and in the extension of the means of inter-communication.

QUESTIONS OF THE HOUR.

Not to increase, therefore, is to retrograde; and a realization of this truth makes it evident that the matter of vital interest to the nation in all these investigations is not the mere ascertainment and enumeration of the aggregates of production; but rather, first, *of the existing relations between national production and national consumption or expenditure;* second, *the determination of the question whether the resources and privileges which have accrued to the nation through its inheritance of soil, climate, race, and government, have been utilized to the best advantage;* and third, and most especially, *whether the influence of existing laws tends to promote such a distribution of the annual products of labor and capital as best subserves the interests of the whole people.*

To construct an inventory of the national wealth without reference to these questions would be equivalent to presenting merely the credit side of an account as evidence of the success of a business transaction, and of ignoring entirely the *per contra*, as it may appear in the form of interest on capital, wages of labor, or the cost of material; and although, in the institution of any fair and thorough comparison of things favorable with those unfavorable, we may feel assured that the balance in favor of the United States would be greater than that afforded by a similar investigation into the affairs of any other country, yet this fact renders it none the less desirable that we should earnestly endeavor to ascertain the elements of national weakness and the methods of remedy, as well as the elements of national strength; inasmuch as in a State or nation, as in a structure, the weakest point may be, and often is, the measure of the strength of the whole.

To a discussion, therefore, of the questions above suggested, with special reference to the results which the investigations and experience of another year have afforded, the Commissioner would next invite attention.

RELATION OF NATIONAL PRODUCTION TO NATIONAL CONSUMPTION OR EXPENDITURE.

In respect to the relation which the aggregate of national production sustains to the aggregate of national consumption or expenditure, it is difficult to arrive at any altogether definite or satisfactory conclusions.

PRESENT VALUE OF REAL AND PERSONAL PROPERTY OF THE UNITED STATES.

The value of the real and personal property of the United States, as deduced from the census returns of 1860, subtracting the value of the then slaves, and considering them, for the purpose of the inquiry, as producers and consumers of wealth and not property, was estimated in round numbers at fourteen thousand millions ($14,183,215,628;)* the value of the annual product at $3,804,000,000; the value of the annual product of each person at $121 03, and the average property of each person in the nation at $451 26.

A valuation of Great Britain for 1868–'69, which has undoubtedly claim

* Dr. William Elder.

to close approximative accuracy,* gives the following results: gross property of the nation $30,000,000,000, (£6,000,000,000.) Gross annual income, $4,070,000,000, (£814,000,000;) net income, or original earnings, $2,750,000,000 to $3,000,000,000, (£550,000,000 to £600,000,000.) The present population of the United Kingdom being 30,380,000, we have, according to the above valuation, a fraction less than $1,000 as the average value of property to each individual; and $134 as the proportion of the gross value of the annual product to each person.

Assuming the present population of the United States to be 39,000,000, and the average value of the property held by each person to have nominally increased from $451 26 gold in 1860, to $600 currency in 1869–'70, the present valuation of the United States would be $23,400,000,000, an increase since 1860 of $9,216,784,372 or 65.8 per cent.

This estimate the Commissioner believes to be as large as the evidence available on this subject will warrant, unless an estimate be given to land in excess of its real value as productive capital, or what it would exchange for in money or other marketable products.† He would further remind those who may be inclined to regard this aggregate as an underestimate, that the national valuation of $14,183,215,628, as deduced from the census returns of 1860, represents the surplus of accumulation over expenditure which had resulted up to that date from all the labor and economy of all the people who have inhabited the territory of the United States since its first discovery and settlement by Europeans, *plus* whatever of capital has been sent to it by other nations; and it is not reasonable to suppose that in the single decade which has elapsed since 1860, during nearly one-half of which time the nation was convulsed with war, that an actual increase of wealth has been attained in excess of sixty-five per cent. (including the enhancement of price from the premium on gold) of the accumulation of all the years previous, during which the United States has been a country and a nation.

A confirmation of this result, furthermore, may be reached by another and independent method of reasoning. The increase of property from 1850 to 1860, according to the estimates of the census, was from 6,174,000,000 to 14,183,000,000, or 129 per cent. Much of this large increase, however, is known to have been due to more accurate methods of enumeration, and to the inclusion of many elements previously left unnoticed. A careful review and comparison of the material of these two censuses, made during the past summer, at the request of the Secretary of the Treasury, by the Commissioner, in connection with certain

---

* R. Dudley Baxter.

† Land in general is valuable as an instrument of production, and its true measure of value is what it produces. Land to the agriculturist is worth most when it brings him the most and best of the commodities needed, and the largest surplus. It is worth the least to him when it brings him the least of these, with no surplus at all. The real value of land, therefore, is a very different thing from its nominal value for speculative purposes; and the appraisement of land at a value greater than its value for production, adds nothing whatever to the real wealth or capital of a country.

of the experts who prepared the census of 1860, resulted in the conclusion that the true rate of increase during the decade was about sixty-five per cent., or, allowing to the fullest extent for omissions and under-stimates, certainly not in excess of eighty per cent. This last, if continued, would give a total valuation in 1870 of $25,529,000,000, by the natural, uninterrupted gain of population and industry; adding thirty per cent. to this amount for the premium on gold, the currency valuation at the present time, according to this rate, would be $33,188,000,000. Deducting the estimated cost of the war to the government and to the people, from direct expenditure and from the diversion of industry and the destruction of property, as given above, $9,000,000,000, we should have left $24,188,000,000 as the accumulated wealth of the country at the close of the present decade.

VALUE OF THE GROSS ANNUAL PRODUCT OF THE NATION.

In respect to the value of the *annual product* of the nation, the data available for the formation of an opinion are also exceedingly limited, being mainly deductions from the census of 1860; a comparison of the results of similar investigations recently undertaken in Great Britain; and the estimated value of the products moved annually upon the railways of the country.

As has been already stated, the gross value of the annual product of the United States, as deduced from the census returns of 1860, was $3,804,000,000, and the gross value of the product of the year to each person $121 03. The corresponding figures for Great Britain for 1868–'69, are $4,070,000,000, and $134, respectively.

If we now assume $175 (currency) as the present value of the annual *per capita* product of the whole nation, and the population as 39,000,000, the gross value of the annual product becomes $6,825,000,000. Large as is this estimate, it is confirmed in general by the results afforded by investigations which have been recently made in respect to the quantity and value of the freight moved annually upon American railways.

If the estimate of $175 currency, as the present average value of the annual *per capita* product of the nation, as compared with $121 in 1860, should appear too small, it may be well to consider for a moment the components of the nation who by their labor create this value. Thus, of the present estimated population of 39,000,000, about one-half,* or

* According to the deductions of the last census and the standard tables of life insurance companies, the present assumed population of the United States—39,000,000—would be exactly proportioned between the two sexes as follows:

Males		19,951,100
Females		19,048,900
Proportions below the age of 16:		
Males	8,461,261	
Females	8,162,453	
Total	16,623,714, or 42.61 per cent.	

Whole number of population above 60 years, 1,675,097, or 4½ per cent.

19,000,000, are females; 42 per cent. of the whole number of both sexes are below the age of 16; while 4½ per cent. are over 60. Of the proportion of the whole population between the ages of 18 and 65 who are incapacitated for labor, no accurate determination can be made; but adopting the data afforded by the experience of the friendly societies of England—subject to certain local qualifications—the number in our present population undoubtedly approximates 500,000.*

In Great Britain, the results of investigation show that out of a population of 30,000,000, 54 per cent. of the whole number are without income or wages; or, in other words, for every five persons who support themselves, six are dependent. In the United States, where there is less disposition and less necessity for women and children, or the aged, to engage in remunerative employments, the Commissioner believes that the above ratio as ascertained for Great Britain will be greatly exceeded, and that 33 per cent., or 12,870,000, will fairly represent that portion of our population who are in receipt of income. Now, the persons thus enumerated as in receipt of income may be divided into two classes, viz: 1st, those whose income is the earnings of absolute production, and as such constitutes a direct addition to the nation's property; and 2d, those whose income is paid out of the income of the first class for the use of capital, or for services not directly productive. To ascertain, therefore, the number of those whose income is a direct addition to the wealth of the nation, we must deduct from the 12,870,000 above mentioned the following persons, viz: those who live on the interest of fixed investments; members of the learned professions, and those engaged in educational employments; civil officers of the government—national and State—and members of the army and navy; all those engaged in the amusement of the people; in disseminating news; in conveying persons or things for pleasure or for mere change from one place to another; artists; domestic servants; manufacturers and transporters of drinks and stimulants; agents, superintendents, and watchmen; and if it is assumed that product has contributed its maximum of wealth to the nation when it is lodged for distribution in the hands of the wholesale dealer, there must be further added to the number of those whose incomes are not independent sources of wealth to the country, all retail dealers, clerks, and distributors generally. Making allowance for these classes, it seems probable that the whole number of persons who by their labor add directly to the wealth of the country is not in excess of 10,000,000, and this number, it is to be noted, sustains as great a ratio to the present population of 39,000,000 as did the whole number of persons returned in 1860 as following all the various occupations of the country, whether engaged in original production or otherwise. Dividing, now, the assumed total value of the annual product, $6,825,000,000,

* For further information in respect to this topic, reference is made to an appendix to this Report, containing a communication made to the Commission by Dr. Edward Jarvis, marked A.

among the assumed number of the directly productive class, we have a *per capita* product of $682 50; which sum undoubtedly approximately represents the first hand average annual income of the direct producers of wealth in the nation, out of which the whole population have to live, provide food and clothing, pay taxes and all other expenses, and accumulate a surplus of future productive capital.

GROSS ANNUAL VALUE OF THE PRODUCTS OF LEADING INDUSTRIES.

It will be interesting to inquire at this point what proportion of the annual aggregate product of the nation results from the labor of the persons engaged in the various industrial occupations productive of direct wealth.

AGRICULTURE.

Among these that of agriculture ranks first; forty-one per cent., (or one in every two and a half persons,) exclusive of the slave population, of all whose occupations were specified according to the census of 1860, being engaged in this pursuit. Making allowance for the above exception, it is reasonable to suppose that of the whole number of persons in the United States who are in the receipt of income from some industrial occupation or the investment of capital, fully fifty per cent., or 6,435,000, are agriculturists. The value of their *per capita* product must, it would seem, be sufficient to make up for the following requirements:

Wages, $275; subsistence, $125; amount available to supply waste in animals, implements, and land, $50; interest on capital, $60; total, $510. This sum multiplied into the whole number of agriculturists would give $3,282,000,000 as the proportion of their contribution of the total gross value of the national product per annum.

ANNUAL VALUE OF THE PRINCIPAL AGRICULTURAL PRODUCTS OF THE NATION.

An estimate of the value of the leading agricultural products of the country for the present year may also tend to assist in forming a judgment in regard to the total annual value of the product in this department of national industry. The details of such an estimate would be somewhat as follows:

Cotton, 2,700,000 bales, 450 pounds each, at 25 cents	$303,750,000
Corn, 900,000,000 bushels, at 50 cents	450,000,000
Wheat, 300,000,000 bushels, at $1 25	375,000,000
Oats, 275,000,000 bushels, at 50 cents	137,500,000
Wool, 177,000,000 pounds, (estimated clip of 1868,) at 42½ cents	75,225,000
Tobacco, 225,000,000 pounds, at 16½ cents	37,125,000
Barley, 25,000,000 bushels, at $1 20	30,000,000

Hay, 25,000,000 tons, at $10	$250,000,000
Rye, 25,000,000 bushels, at $1 10	27,500,000
Hides, 6,700,000, at $5 50	36,850,000
Potatoes, 150,000,000 bushels, at 60 cents	90,000,000
Buckwheat, 20,000,000 bushels, at $1	20,000,000
Flesh of animals, deducting value of hay and grain consumed	*400,000,000
Dairy products, deducting value consumed of farm products previously enumerated	†400,000,000
All other products of agriculture, including the annual increase in the value of cattle and horses, the value of fruits, seeds, and garden products, the annual addition to the value of farms and farm buildings, and implements made by farm labor not classed as mechanical, (fences, drainage, &c., &c.)	650,000,000
Total	3,282,950,000

* The usual dietary of prisons in the United States allows about one pound of fresh meat, or its equivalent in salt meats or fish, for the subsistence of the inmates. In hospitals for the insane the allowance of meat or its equivalent is about one-half pound. The ration of the United States army is one and one-quarter pounds or its equivalent. An estimate of twenty dollars per head per annum as the cost of the meat food of the present population would yield a total of $780,000,000. When it is considered meat is consumed in the United States by the laboring as well as by the well-to-do classes, this will not seem an exaggerated estimate. A very careful examination into the dietary of one of the best-conducted factory boarding-houses in New-England shows a consumption of three and one-fifth pounds of meat, mostly fresh beef, per week for each person, at an expense per head of a little above twenty-eight dollars a year. Of the forty persons in this enumeration fourteen were females and four children.

† The dietary of the same factory boarding-house heretofore quoted, where the operatives were in large part French Canadians, notoriously frugal and simple in their habits, and in which they were furnished to their own satisfaction, shows an average consumption of butter amounting to about $16 51 a year for each person, including women and children. An average consumption for the entire population, taken at one-half of this sum, or $8 25 a head, would result in an expenditure on this account of $321,750,000. A consumption of milk to the value of one cent per day for each person would give an additional sum of $143,350,000, making a total for these two items of $464,100,000. To this must be added the value of cheese and eggs consumed. Any one who is acquainted with the manner in which milk, and more especially butter, are consumed in the families of American laboring men, as well as in the houses of the wealthy and well-to-do classes, will acknowledge that these estimates of consumption fall considerably within the mark. In further illustration of the several points indicated, we append the results (see appendix B) in full of the inquiry into the quantity and cost of food and other necessaries of life consumed in the New England factory boarding-house thus referred to. The investigation was made at the request of the Commissioner, and the results are undoubtedly correct to ounces and cents. In fact, it is believed that no similar investigation, as respects accuracy, has ever before been instituted in the United States.

PRODUCTS OF OTHER INDUSTRIES.

In respect to the other wealth-producing industries, the statistics of the manufacture of cotton, wool, iron, boots and shoes, and paper are sufficiently available and exact to allow of the very accurate determination of the increased value which accrues from the labor employed in these several departments.

MANUFACTURE OF COTTON.

Estimated number of spindles in the United States, from the latest returns to the Cotton Manufacturers' Association		6,930,346
Capital represented, at an average of $20 per spindle		$138,606,920
Estimated capacity of cotton, in pounds, per annum		450,000,000
Average number of yarn		28
Product of cloth, allowing one-sixth for waste, pounds		375,000,000
Value of product, on basis of twenty-five cents per pound for cotton—		
Cotton	$112,500,000	
Supplies and repairs	21,000,000	
Labor	42,000,000	
Profits on capital, say	8,500,000	
		$184,000,000
Estimated expenses of transportation and distribution		$31,415,000
Hands employed, mostly female, estimated		125,000
Value added to material by each hand		$404
Value of the manufactured product ready for transportation and distribution, exclusive of cost of raw cotton		$71,500,000

MANUFACTURES OF WOOL.

Estimated amount of machinery in carding and combing, equivalent to 6,000 sets of cards. Estimated consumption of wool and substitutes, 1868, in condition as marketed, pounds		235,000,000
Equivalent in pounds of scoured wool		125,000,000
Value of product:		
Wool	$90,000,000	
Supplies and repairs	25,000,000	
Labor	35,000,000	
Profits on capital, 1868–'69, estimated at six per cent	6,000,000	
		156,000,000
Estimated expense of transportation and distribution		$25,000,000
Number of hands employed, mostly males, at fifteen to each set of cards		90,000
Value added to material by each hand		$455

II

PIG AND BAR IRON.

Present annual product of pig iron, tons	1,725,000
Value at furnace, at $36 per ton	$62,100,000
Present annual product of rolling mills and bloomeries, tons	1,222,000
Value of product of rolling mills, 1,200,000 tons, at $90.	$108,000,000
Deducting value at rolling mills of pig and scrap iron used as raw material, say 1,416,000 tons, at $37 50	53,100,000
Added value of rolling-mill industry	54,900,000
Product of bloomeries, 22,000 tons, at $180	$3,960,000
Deduct value of pig metal used as raw material, say 26,400 tons, at $38	1,003,200
Added value of bloomery industry	2,956,800
Recapitulation:	
Pig metal	$62,100,000
Rolling-mill industry, added value	54,900,000
Bloomeries, added value	2,956,800
Total	119,956,800

The following is an estimate of the number of hands employed in the primary production of iron, viz: pig and bar iron, as returned by the Secretary of the American Iron and Steel Association:

At blast furnaces	12,500
Preparation of ore and fuel	42,000
At forges and bloomeries	2,500
In rolling mills	58,000
Total	115,000

There are no accessible data for estimating the royalty paid for ores, or the cost of the transportation of ores to the coal, or *vice versa*. It may also be noted that the profits of iron production, be they large or small, are included in this sum of $119,956,800. If it be all credited to the actual laborers, the value of the work of each hand is $1,043; but a fair deduction for labor of persons not enumerated, and for profits above six per cent., would probably reduce this average to $700 or $750.

LEATHER MANUFACTURES.

Value of leather tanned and dressed in United States	$124,760,069
Deducting value of hides and skins used as raw material	66,531,114
Value added by labor	58,228,955

Value of boots and shoes produced	$246, 252, 000
Deduct value of all materials used, including leather	130, 169, 608
Added value of boot and shoe industry	116, 082, 392

Value of other manufactures of leather, harness, hose, belting, bags, portemonnaies, &c	$63, 300, 000
Deduct value of materials, including leather	15, 000, 000
Added value of above industries	48, 300, 000

Number of hands employed in the manufacture of leather	30, 000
Employed in manufacture of boots and shoes	131, 333
Employed in other manufactures from leather	19, 000
	180, 333

Recapitulation:

Value added to hides and skins in the manufacture of leather	$58, 228, 955
Value added in manufacture of boots and shoes	116, 082, 392
Value added in other manufactures from leather	48, 300, 000
	222, 611, 347

The total value of product in the manufacture of leather is apportioned as follows:

Raw material	$66, 531, 114
Supplies and repairs	24, 328, 955
Labor	20, 000, 000
Capital *	13, 900, 000
	124, 760, 069

Value added to material by each hand, (excluding cost of "supplies and repairs")	$1, 130
Average wages	666⅔

The total value of the product of the boot and shoe industry is apportioned as follows:

Raw material	$130, 169, 608
Supplies and repairs	9, 373, 959
Capital	24, 625, 000
Labor	82, 083, 433
	246, 250, 000
Value added to material by each hand	812
Average wages	625

* The capital employed in making leather is much larger in proportion to product than in making boots and shoes.

For a more complete exhibit of the industry of the United States engaged in the production of leather and in the manufacture of articles from leather, reference is made to the appendix to this report marked B.

MANUFACTURERS OF PAPER.

The quantity annually manufactured in the United States is estimated for the Commissioner by the trade, at 780,000,000 pounds, valued at	$72,000,000
Number of hands employed	25,000

The Commissioner, however, has not the data requisite for separating the value of the labor from the material used.

VALUE ADDED TO PRODUCT BY RAILWAY TRANSPORTATION.

The addition made to the annual product of the country through the service rendered by capital and labor employed in railway transportation has recently been shown by competent authority to be at the rate of about three hundred and sixty millions of dollars, on an investment of capital of nearly one thousand eight hundred millions.

FISHERIES.

Unfortunately, and almost inexcusably, the products of our national fisheries have never been enumerated with any such completeness as to enable an estimate of the annual value of the production of this industry to be made with any great degree of assurance or satisfaction. But a recent canvass of certain fishing fields justifies the conclusion that the value of all the fisheries of the country—including sea-coast, lake, and river fisheries—is not less than one hundred millions of dollars per annum.

RECAPITULATION.

A summary statement of the values created by the leading industries of the country would therefore appear to be substantially as follows:

Agriculture	$3,282,950,000
Cotton manufacture	71,500,000
Woolen manufacture	66,000,000
Iron production, pig and bar	119,950,000
Leather manufactures	222,600,000
Railway service	360,000,000
Fisheries	100,000,000
	4,223,000,000

This aggregate, deducted from the estimated gross product of the country, viz., $6,825,000,000, gives $2,602,000,000 as the product of all the industrial classes remaining unenumerated. If we suppose the classes enumerated to embrace 7,165,000 producers, (6,435,000 agriculturists and 730,000 engaged in railway service, fisheries, and the manufactures specified,) this will leave a product of $2,602,000,000, divided among 5,705,000 producers, (the total number of producers having been taken at 12,870,000,) giving an average value of the labor of each one of $455 per annum. This large body of producers includes persons of the most various occupations and the most diverse character as regards the capacity of production, embracing as it does many highly skilled and highly paid artisans, as well as all the distributors of the country, and also great numbers of domestic servants, women and children, contributing in but a small degree to production, and receiving minimum wages.

So far as any estimate can be made of the proportionate number employed in mechanical employments, from the imperfect data of the census of 1860, there are in this remainder at least 1,000,000 skilled artisans, machinists, carpenters, blacksmiths, masons, and the like, whose average wages are at least $2 50 per day, or about $750 per year, and the value of whose labor in the work of manufacture or production must be estimated at the sum of their wages, with a fair rate of profit to the employer, and the wear of tools and apparatus—say $1,000 per annum—thus making them the most valuable producing class, and consequently the largest consuming class, in the community.

If we deduct $1,000,000,000 as the value of their labor, we have a remainder of $1,602,000,000 as the result of the work of the 4,705,000 common laborers, domestic servants, and of all distributors, or an average of $340 per annum to each person. This final result would indicate that the total estimate of annual product is an under rather than an over estimate.

It will be obvious, furthermore, that this estimate has been made upon a currency basis, or at a depreciation of the currency in relation to gold of from twenty-five to thirty per cent.; and, also, that the prices of many commodities included in these estimates are represented at a much higher rate in relation to gold than the nominal depreciation would indicate. What abatement should be made on this account from the total estimate as above given it is impossible to tell. The machinery and tools of production, transportation, and distribution were never before so ample or so effective; and so soon as the evil effect of a vicious currency and a burdensome tariff shall be removed, it will not be too much to expect that the present aggregate value of annual production will be maintained—not, of course, by maintenance ofprices, but from the vastly greater abundance, with its resulting comfort to the people.

ANNUAL INCREASE OF THE NATIONAL VALUATION.

If the estimate before given of the present value of the real and personal property of the United States, viz: $23,400,000,000, (currency,) be correct, the nominal increase in valuation, since 1860, has been at the rate of $921,700,000 per annum, or 13.4 per cent. of the value of the annual product. In this, however, is included an increase in the valuation of land, consequent upon the increasing density of population in the older sections of the country, and the annual rapid extension of settlement and civilization over territory before possessed of but nominal or no value. But such a rapid increase in the valuation of this description of property, gratifying as it certainly is in the abstract, does not represent to an equal extent an increase of capital available for reproduction and an active increase of wealth. On the contrary, in all the large cities in the country, especially where the increase experienced in the valuation of land since 1860 has been the greatest, much of the property thus appreciated not only subserves no higher or more useful purpose than before, but the increased value, as represented in increased rents, really becomes a tax upon some classes of production, and decreases the capital available for such purposes.

Making allowance for this element of unproductive land valuation, the Commissioner has been led to the conclusion that the annual increase of active capital in the United States, arising from the excess of production over expenditure, cannot at the present time be considered as in excess of eight per cent. of the gross annual product, or $546,000,000 per annum*.

In presenting this analysis of the valuation, annual product, and annual surplus of the country, the Commissioner has simply responded to a desire, of late most frequently expressed, that some exhibit should be made of the information available on these subjects. For the preparation of an exact statement the requisite data are not at present attainable. Certain elements can, however, undoubtedly be obtained which may be regarded as approximately accurate; such as the aggregate valuation, according to the census of 1860, and the *per capita* property and the *per capita* product of the nation at that period. The estimates

* If this estimate of the annual surplus of national production over national consumption, available as active capital for reproduction, should appear too small and disproportionate, it should be borne in mind that while the aggregate of the national product is proved by incontrovertible statistics to be very great, there is also no other fact better proved by comparison and observation than that the *per capita* consumption of the people of the United States is larger than that of the people of any other civilized nation. The habits of economy and frugality which necessity has forced upon the masses of the people in other countries are, in general, neither known nor practised in the United States; and all foreigners who visit the United States for the purpose of studying its social economy are particularly impressed with what, judging from their home standpoint of view, seems an enormous waste both in domestic living and domestic manufacturing. As showing, however, that this profusion in consumption is not wholly an unmixed evil, reference is here made to a recent report of M. Mantegazza, a member of the Italian Parliament, on the condition of Italy, in which the opinion is expressed, that one great reason for the physical, commercial, and financial depression of the masses of the Italian people is that they are not sufficiently well fed. "A nation which thinks only far enough ahead to keep body and soul lazily together, has no energy to spare for enterprise, no money for public purposes, no superfluity of heart and strength to put into war or defense."

which may be adopted of the increase upon these amounts which has occurred in the ten years which have elapsed since 1860, also admit of verification, to some extent, by comparison with the valuations and estimates arrived at in Great Britain during the past year, where density of population, limited area, and almost perfect machinery for investigation on the part of the government and voluntary associations, allow of the attainment of results far more worthy of confidence than those which can be deduced from similar investigations in the United States, under much less favorable conditions. On such a basis the Commissioner has conducted his investigations, and, without claiming to speak with authority, he submits his conclusions as the best result of much time and labor expended, in which he has been assisted by experts in many of the leading departments of production and industry.

RETARDATION OF NATIONAL DEVELOPMENT.

There are, however, certain departments of this inquiry where we may leave the field of estimate and assumption and deal with what seem to be exact and positive data; and these data, the Commissioner is sorry to say, are not calculated to afford much support to those who are accustomed to indulge in flattering estimates respecting the present amount and existing rate of increase of the national wealth. For example, he would ask attention to the following table, showing the

Total polls, houses, real and personal estate, and taxation in Massachusetts, from May 1, 1861, *to May* 1, 1868, *inclusive, as per statistics prepared by Hon. Oliver Warner, Secretary of the Commonwealth, and published by the legislature.*

	Polls.	Houses.	Personal.	Real estate.	Total value.	Taxation.
1861	280, 855	178, 194	$309, 397, 669	$552, 087, 749	$861, 485, 418	$7, 600, 501
1862	276, 443	178, 450	315, 311, 213	543, 669, 113	858, 980, 326	8, 605, 511
1863	275, 758	183, 528	343, 500, 267	553, 650, 716	897, 150, 983	10, 599, 097
1864	281, 220	185, 232	324, 584, 847	577, 298, 256	901, 883, 103	12, 876, 850
1865	287, 655	188, 005	386, 079, 955	605, 761, 946	991, 841, 901	16, 800, 332
1866	306, 993	190, 439	430, 272, 298	651, 043, 703	1, 081, 316, 001	15, 694, 039
1867	315, 742	195, 388	457, 728, 296	708, 165, 117	1, 165, 893, 413	19, 104, 074
1868	332, 759	200, 267	469, 775, 322	750, 723, 617	1, 220, 498, 939	16, 056, 193

By an analysis of the above table (which we have every reason to presume is comparatively accurate, errors of valuation at one period compensating for those of another) we find that the value of the real and personal property of Massachusetts, subject to taxation in 1861, was $3,069 to each poll, while in 1868 it was $3,668, a nominal increase of $600 per head, or close upon twenty per cent. on the valuation of 1861. But the valuation of 1861 was at gold rates, and, therefore, simply to make good the individual average of wealth, the *per capita* of 1868 should have been $4,142, (taking 35 as the average premium of gold for the year for which the last valuation was made,) a gain of $1,074.

The difference ($474) between this, the gain in price necessary simply to make good the depreciation of the currency and the sum of $600, the whole increase actually realized, marks the falling off in the valuation of the State *per capita*, during the eight years covered by the table. In other words, for every $100 (gold) of property possessed in 1861, there should have been $135 (currency) in 1868, on the supposition that real values had remained stationary. There was, in fact, however, but $119 56.

But an even more noticeable and significant fact, revealed by the above statement, is that the increase in the number of houses in Massachusetts does not keep pace with the increase of population. Thus, in 1861, there were one hundred and fifty-seven polls for every one hundred houses; but in 1868 the ratio was one hundred and sixty-six polls to every one hundred houses; or, in other words, the course of affairs in Massachusetts for the eight years, 1861 to 1868, inclusive, has been such that nine polls, or possibly as many heads of families, in every hundred, have been crowded out of houses—deprived by industrial causes o that degree of independence and comfort which is involved in the maintenance of a separate household. Surely, then, in this State, which a recent foreign economist has characterized as the head of the industrial army, we have an apparently unanswerable testimony to the effect that, whatever may be the condition of the rich, the poorer part of the community have certainly grown poorer. A comparison of the valuation of Massachusetts with the whole population leads substantially to the same conclusions.

Thus, the valuation of Massachusetts for 1850 was $597,936,995; the population 994,514—making a *per capita* valuation of about $600. In 1860 the valuation was $897,795,326; the population 1,231,066—making a *per capita* valuation of $729.

In 1865 the valuation was $991,841,901, currency; the population, 1,267,031—making a *per capita* valuation of $783, currency.

In 1868 the valuation was $1,220,498,939, currency; the population, (estimated,) 1,289,000; making a *per capita* valuation of $947, currency.*

This exhibit is the more noticeable because Massachusetts is preeminently a State dependent upon manufactures, and it would fairly be supposed that its prosperity might be secured, if that of any State could, by the high degree of protection afforded to its industry by the existing tariff, one of the most severe and rigorous ever enacted for the purpose of creating and endowing a diversified industry.

---

* The note accompanying the above statement, forwarded to the Commissioner from the office of the auditor of the State, adds:

"It will be observed from the above that the increase from 1850 to 1860 was natural and legitimate, while that from 1860 to 1865 was less than would be expected, but for the fact that to that date the prices of our real estate had not risen as they have since, and not at all in proportion to the prices of products. At present, our fixed property is perhaps priced as high as the personal estate, and all should be taken down at least one-fourth to reach the gold standard, making the total $915,374,204, and the *per capita* $700—which is less than in 1860."

Without going into so much of detail relative to the facts of appraisement in other States of the Union, the Commissioner would invite attention to the general effect of the following table, which exhibits the assessed value of real and personal property in the States of Rhode Island, Connecticut, Ohio, and Indiana, for the two years 1861 and 1868, and the State of Pennsylvania for the years 1861 and 1865, at which latter date the State tax was taken off from real property, which accordingly is no longer assessed for State purposes. With the exception of the State of Illinois, where, as is generally known, appraisement is habitually kept down by the provision in the State constitution requiring a yearly tax on all property for a purpose which is practically obsolete, these are the only States for which the Commissioner has obtained the figures. As his object merely is to rebut the presumption of an enormous general increase of wealth between 1860 and 1870, a larger collection of facts is plainly not necessary:

State.	Total value of real and personal property, by assessment of 1861.	Total value of real and personal property, by assessment of 1865.	Total value of real and personal property by assessment of 1868.	Increase. Per cent. of value, in 1861.	Gold premium taken.
Rhode Island	$121,118,126	....	$187,697,591	55	35
Connecticut	224,962,514	....	312,574,408	39	35
Ohio	892,850,084	....	1,143,461,386	28	35
Indiana	441,562,339	....	587,970,549	33	35
Pennsylvania	569,049,867	$595,591,994	....	4¾	35
New York	1,441,769,430	....	1,766,089,140	22½	35

From this table it would appear that, so far as the appraised value of real and personal property was concerned, the advance in only two of the States enumerated had been equal to the assumed premium on gold; while, had the exact average of the gold premium for 1868 (39.6) been taken for comparison, only one of these six States would have been found to make good the gold values of 1861—and that the small and rich State of Rhode Island. This calculation, however, has been made without regard to any increase that may have taken place in population during the period. If the latter element were taken into account, probably not one of these States would exhibit any increase in assessed values, while some would fail not only, as above, to make good the values of 1861 in gold, but even to sustain a *per capita* valuation in currency equal to the gold valuation of the period before the war.

At this point it may be proper to remark that the totals of State and local taxes exhibit no such incapacity to make good the figures of 1861. In the three important States of Massachusetts, Ohio, and New York, of which alone the Commissioner has full reports at hand, the totals of all State and local taxes levied in 1868 were, respectively, $16,056,143, $20,489,148, and $44,298,436, against $7,600,501, $11,071,127, and

$20,402,276; an increase of 111 per cent. in Massachusetts, 85 per cent. in Ohio, and 112 per cent. in New York.

The Commissioner has not cited these figures of State valuations with the idea that they prove a positive, or even a proportionate, decline in wealth throughout the country during the decade now closing. Something of the remarkable and even paradoxical result exhibited is due to inherent defects in the American system of appraisement, and to the withdrawal of large classes of personal property from taxation; but these statistics, while they would not justify the inference of a decline in wealth, certainly refute the common opinion of an enormous increase during the period in question. Whatever they may not prove, they clearly are sufficient to show that the large estimates so commonly made of the present value of property in the United States, as a whole, will not bear the test of an examination in detail. However defective the system of appraisement in most of the States of the Union may be, the same tendency to error certainly existed before the war as now. Indeed, the motives to a full appraisement are evidently stronger to-day than formerly, inasmuch as with the vast increase of taxation which has been shown, it becomes necessary for officials in charge either to obtain a larger aggregate of taxable property in the community, or to permit the rate of taxation to rise to such a degree as to excite animadversion and resistance.

EXISTING AGENCIES TENDING TO IMPAIR THE RAPIDITY OF NATIONAL ACCUMULATION.

But assign whatever of weight we may to the evidence thus presented respecting the retardation of national development during the past decade, there are many circumstances which seem to indicate with certainty that the present accumulation of new capital in the United States, available for the further creation of wealth and values—the result of the annual surplus of national production over national consumption or expenditure—is at a much slower rate than it ought to be, and than it necessarily would be under entirely healthy and natural conditions.

Some of the circumstances which seem to afford such indications are as follows:

1. *The condition of the foreign trade of the country.*

At the breaking out of the war, in 1861, the distrust felt by nearly all foreigners in the future of the United States was so great that the larger portion of American securities—national, State, and corporate—held in foreign countries, were returned for sale at almost any sacrifice; and to such an extent was this the case that the country in 1863 may be said to have exhibited a clean national ledger in respect to foreign indebtedness. Since this date there have been transferred from the United States to foreign countries obligations which have raised the total of foreign indebtedness to an estimated amount of about $1,400,000,000, which may be classified somewhat as follows:

NATIONAL SECURITIES.

In regard to the amount of national securities which have been transferred to *foreign* ownership since 1862–'3, the Commissioner finds a wide difference of opinion among American and European bankers best capable from experience of forming an estimate; the minimum being, however, from *seven* to *eight hundred millions.* The following estimate, prepared for the Commissioner by the house of Jay Cooke & Co., has not only received the approval of some of the largest purchasers of national securities on foreign account in New York, but has also been checked from various other and independent sources:

Fives of 1871 and 1874	$15,000,000
Sixes of 1881	90,000,000
Five-twenties of 1862	380,000,000
Five-twenties of 1864	30,000,000
Five-twenties of 1865, May and November	120,000,000
Five-twenties of 1865, January and July	200,000,000
Five-twenties of 1867	120,000,000
Ten-forties	25,000,000
Registered bonds of all issues	20,000,000
Total	1,000,000,000

As substantiating the accuracy of the above estimate, it is to be noted that the earlier issues of United States securities have almost entirely disappeared from the American market, and that transactions are now limited mainly to the issues of July, 1865, 1867, and 1868.

OTHER SECURITIES.

State.—Of State securities held abroad or on *foreign* account the investigations of the Commissioner indicate a sum in excess of *one hundred millions.* The following amounts are returned as positively known to the State authorities:

Alabama	$1,483,260
Georgia	72,000
Illinois	1,400,000
Louisiana	5,235,933
Massachusetts	12,277,500
Michigan	800,000
Missouri	1,500,000
New York	2,440,999
Ohio	3,500,000
Pennsylvania	9,458,600
Virginia	7,523,500
Total	45,691,792

This amount, it is to be noted, only includes those issues which have been "placed" abroad originally through distinct State agencies. To it must be added the larger amount which has been from year to year purchased in the American market, and either sent abroad or held here on foreign account.

Railway bonds and shares.—Of railway bonds and shares held abroad or on foreign account, the investigations of the Commissioner indicate a total of $130,000,000 of bonds and $113,000,000 of shares.

Of the amount of bonds specified, an aggregate of $61,350,349 has been positively reported to the Commissioner in behalf of fourteen companies.

Of the amount of railway stocks specified, seven companies return an aggregate of $83,449,800. A detailed statement of this element of our foreign indebtedness would be given had not the information been communicated under a pledge that the details should not be made public.

For the companies which have not reported the amount of their stocks and bonds held abroad, estimates have been carefully prepared for the Commissioner by the best authorities on this subject. The character of these statements and the representations which accompanied them is such as to satisfy the Commissioner that the aggregate given above, namely $243,000,000 of stocks and bonds, is not an over estimate.

Miscellaneous securities, (partially known and partially estimated.)

Municipal bonds	$7,500,000
Canal bonds	5,063,967
Mining shares and bonds	10,000,000

A careful estimate of other forms of foreign indebtedness on November 1, 1869, gives the following additional elements:

Capital lying in the United States in consequence of the comparatively low rate of interest in Europe—credits, bills of exchange, &c	$50,000,000
Cuban moneys temporarily transferred in consequence of the revolution	25,000,000
Foreign capital invested in mortgages of real estate, &c.	25,000,000

Recapitulation.

State bonds	$100,000,000
Railway bonds	130,000,000
Railway shares	113,000,000
Mining bonds and shares	10,000,000
Municipal bonds	7,500,000
Miscellaneous bonds and shares	5,000,000
Capital temporarily invested	50,000,000
Cuban moneys	25,000,000
Real estate mortgages, &c	25,000,000
Total	465,500,000

Adding $1,000,000,000 of federal securities held abroad, as before estimated, we have, as the total of the present foreign indebtedness of the United States, the sum of $1,465,500,000; on which, at an average of 6 per cent., an annual payment of interest accrues to the amount of $87,930,000; and of which $80,000,000 may be estimated as paid regularly.

ADVERSE FOREIGN BALANCE FOR 1868–'69.

But enormous as is this sum, the process of incurring indebtedness still continues as actively as ever. The account of the United States with foreign countries for the fiscal year ending June 30, 1869, may be exhibited substantially as follows:

Imports of merchandise, gold value		$417, 371, 765
Exports, (gold values)	$275, 611, 591	
Re-exports, &c	10, 907, 753	
		286, 519, 344
		130, 852, 421
Less excess of foreign goods, in bond, 1869 over 1868		14, 702, 079
Adverse balance 1868–'9 merchandise account		116, 150, 342

Movement of specie and bullion.

Exports	$42, 915, 966
Re-exports	14, 222, 414
Total	57, 138, 380
Imports	19, 654, 776
Loss of specie and bullion	37, 483, 604

If we suppose the excess of specie and bullion exports to have been devoted exclusively to the liquidation of balances incurred on the merchandise account, the remaining balance on this account to be settled for in some other manner would be $78,666,738.

To this sum must be added the following other items:

Obligations for interest, (paid,) estimated	$80, 000, 000
Excess of freights carried in foreign bottoms*	24, 000, 000
Expenditures of Americans in foreign countries†	25, 000, 000

Assuming that the sums chargeable to smuggling and undervaluation of imports are counterbalanced by the undervaluation of exports,‡ the sum total of the adverse balance of indebtedness of the United States to foreign countries will, at the present time, probably average about $210,000,000 per annum.

To meet and settle this constantly increasing and adverse balance

* The following table exhibits the proportions of the total trade of the country for each year, 1859–1869, inclusive, carried in American and in foreign vessels, respectively,

there would seem to be, under the present condition of prices and cost of production in the United States, but one resource, viz: to remit certificates of indebtedness—national, State, or corporate. And this process is undoubtedly adopted, and goes on, month after month and year after year, without occasioning thus far any marked disturbance in the trade and commerce of the country.

Now, whether so great an exchange of evidences of indebtedness for foreign commodities or foreign services is advantageous to the country at large, or how long such a method of liquidating balances can continue, are questions which it is not necessary to immediately consider, inasmuch as we would rather direct attention at this point to the fact that, while before the war we were able to wholly pay for our foreign imports and services with the products of our own industry, including, after the discovery of California, and up to the beginning of the war, such a proportion only of our product of gold as it would have been practically

---

with the gain to the United States or to foreign nations from the excess of freights carried in each year:

Year.	Imports, exports, and re-exports.				
	Total trade.	American vessels.	Foreign vessels.	Preponderance of foreign.	Gain to foreigners, calculated at 8 per cent. on gross excess.
1859	$695, 557, 592	$465, 741, 381	$229, 816, 211	*a*$235, 925, 170	*c*$18, 874, 014
1860	762, 288, 550	507, 247, 757	255, 040, 793	*a*252, 206, 964	*c*20, 176, 557
1861	530, 569, 412	350, 827, 256	179, 742, 156	*a*171, 085, 100	*c*13, 686, 808
1862	435, 710, 714	217, 695, 418	218, 015, 296	319, 878	25, 590
1863	584, 928, 502	241, 872, 471	343, 056, 031	101, 183, 560	8, 094, 685
1864	669, 855, 034	184, 061, 486	485, 793, 548	301, 732, 062	24, 138, 565
1865	571, 131, 290	146, 067, 245	425, 064, 045	278, 996, 800	22, 319, 744
1866	1, 003, 066, 748	324, 141, 463	678, 925, 285	354, 783, 822	28, 382, 705
1867	873, 064, 840	*b*296, 120, 912	*b*576, 943, 928	280, 823, 016	22, 465, 841
1868	848, 527, 647	297, 981, 573	550, 546, 074	252, 564, 501	20, 205, 160
1869	876, 364, 060	288, 916, 927	587, 447, 133	298, 530, 206	23, 882, 416
				1, 868, 933, 845	149, 514, 706

a Excess of American over foreign. *b* Partly estimated. *c* American gain.

The proportion which the cost of freights sustains to the value of goods transported varies of course greatly with the kinds and qualities of goods, and the distance over which they are moved. On tea and coffee, bought with foreign bills of exchange, the estimate prepared for the Commissioner by experts is 5 per cent.; on sugars and molasses the average is given at 12 per cent.; on general dry goods and merchandise 8 per cent.; on wool and hemp, 10 per cent.; on pig iron and coal, 15 to 20 per cent.

In this connection the Commissioner would state that the estimates made for him by experts of the loss to the country from the almost complete annihilation of the large carrying trade formerly enjoyed by American vessels between foreign ports, as from the East Indies and other ports to Europe, and from our non-participation in the

useless and even mischievous for us to retain, we are not now so doing; and this latter circumstance would seem to prove beyond question that the aggregate of national production does not maintain the same proportion as formerly to the aggregate of national consumption.

It must not be forgotten, furthermore, that by the remittance of bonds we have simply deferred payment, and must hereafter export products to meet these obligations; and whenever such export of products in payment for past imports shall be made, it will of necessity be in addition to the export then made to pay for current imports. Product for product is the absolute condition on which alone commerce is possible.

DIVERSION AND DEMORALIZATION OF INDUSTRY.

Another circumstance which indicates a change in the ratio that formerly existed between national production and national consumption is to be found in the fact that during the last few years large numbers of our population, under the influence and example of high profits realized in trading during the period of monetary expansion, have abandoned pursuits directly productive of national wealth, and sought employments connected with commerce, trading, or speculation. As a consequence we everywhere find large additions to the population of our commercial cities, an increase in the number and cost of buildings devoted to banking, brokerage, insurance, commission business, and agencies of all kinds, the spirit of trading and speculation pervading the whole community, as distinguished from the spirit of production, and all the external appearances of healthful activity. These things, however, are not to be regarded as the legitimate growth of a really sound commerce, but rather as the results of influences which have originated almost exclusively in currency inflation. But be the cause what it may, one thing is certain, viz: that national production has suffered in consequence; *directly* by the withdrawal of labor from productive to unpro-

---

emigrant and other passenger-carrying trade, reach nearly twenty-four millions of dollars additional.

† The average number of citizens of the United States who arrived as passengers in the country for the four years 1865 to 1868, inclusive, was in round numbers thirty-seven thousand. The present average number of foreigners arriving in the United States, and not intending to remain, is about twelve thousand per annum, leaving an apparent excess of Americans over foreign absentees of about twenty-five thousand. If we assume one thousand dollars as the average expenditure of each from the time of leaving the United States to the time of returning, the total annual expenditure thus incurred by citizens of the United States in foreign countries would be, approximately, twenty-five millions of dollars.

‡ If we confine ourselves to the comparison of the values given to imports and exports, respectively, in previous years, this may be considered a reasonable estimate; but for the last fiscal year it is certainly not the case. Under the present organization of the Bureau of Statistics, the values given to the exports of the country have been scrutinized and verified to such an extent as to leave but little doubt that the statement for the last year is substantially accurate and complete. The fraudulent undervaluation of imports, however, it is not within the power of such an agency to prevent.

ductive or less productive employment, and *indirectly* by infusing a spirit of discontent among those who, by the force of circumstances, are compelled to earn subsistence in agriculture or the mechanic arts, thereby impairing both the quantity and quality of the products of their industry. A most intelligent observer, the superintendent of one of the largest manufacturing establishments in the middle States, thus writes to the Commissioner:

Those who observe the laborer find that he shows less and less interest in the work he performs, his only anxiety being to hear the bell announce the hour of his discharge from labor.

Another, superintendent of an extensive manufacturing company, in answer to a question as to the comparative amount of work performed by mechanics and laborers in 1860 and 1869, submits the following statement:

"OCTOBER 1, 1869.

"In reply to your favor of the 29th, I would say that I now employ seventy-eight men as mechanics, some of them in building, (new machinery,) but most of them in the way of ordinary repairs. It is impossible for me to state accurately the quantity of work done by them as compared with what would have been accomplished by an equal number of mechanics in 1860, but I think it quite safe to say it is *twenty-five* per cent. less. This difference is occasioned in part by a feeling that they are less favored regarding the hours of labor than mechanics who are employed by the government, but chiefly because many of them are not really mechanics, having never served as apprentices, and lack the skill which would have secured such employment when help was more abundant."

With a view of obtaining further information concerning the relative product of labor in 1869 as compared with 1860, the following question was appended to a circular (relative to wages) extensively forwarded by the Commissioner to the largest and most intelligent employers of laborin different sections of the country: "*Please state whether in your opinion mechanics and laborers perform as much work in a day now as formerly.*"

The following is an abstract of the answers returned, the names of the parties or firms making the same being omitted:

Maine, Portland.—"No, surely;" "and yet they do all they get pay for"—"the row the mechanic now hoes is a hard one."

New Hampshire, Manchester.—"Only about two-thirds as much."

Connecticut, Bridgeport.—"Mechanics perform more, on account of the improved machinery, and laborers less."

Massachusetts, Worcester.—"I think we don't get as much work as formerly by fifteen per cent." *Milford.*—"I think five men did more work in 1860 than six men do now." "Good hands more scarce now than at that time."

New York, New York City.—"I think they perform from one-fourth to one-third less work since than before the war." *Buffalo.*—"Twenty-five per cent. discount." *Troy.*—"No, not by fifteen per cent. in the average." *Albany.*—"Three stone-masons or bricklayers will not do as much as two did formerly."

New Jersey, Jersey City.—"They do not perform more than two-thirds as much as formerly."

Pennsylvania, Lancaster.—"As much as before, since the ten-hour system has begun." *Philadelphia.*—"Three men do the work of two."

Ohio, Cleveland.—Three responded in the negative, and one to this effect: "We think they do now, but there was a time, for two to six years, when they did not." *Cincinnati.*—"No." *Dayton.*—"No."

Missouri, St. Louis.—"No, by fifteen to twenty per cent."

Illinois, Chicago.—"One-eighth less."

The Commissioner would further add, that of the answers received, as above, about one in nine indicated that the amount of work performed in a given time, in 1869, compared favorably with that performed at former periods."

The following statement, furnished to the Commissioner by the proprietor of the Morgan Iron Works of the city of New York, also indicates a change in the productiveness of labor in this department of industry which it is to be hoped is somewhat exceptional. Thus, in 1858, a marine engine was built at the above works, at a cost of $23,000, (including profit to the builder,) which required 2,323 days' labor. In 1869 another engine, precisely similar as respects pattern and weight, was constructed at the same works on contract, for $40,000. The result was a loss to the builder of $5,000 and a necessary expenditure of 3,538 days' labor, or 1,215 more days' labor than was required for the performance of the same work eleven years previously.

Here, then, are certain facts which the Commissioner, in the discharge of his duty, is bound to make public. The laborer appears to be less worthy of his hire than heretofore, and to have lost his interest in his work. If an explanation of the cause is demanded of the Commissioner, he can return but this general answer: because a vicious currency and unequal taxation take from the laborer a portion of the result of his work, and give him no return. The laborer feels this, but knows not the cause, and seeks in strikes, in eight-hour laws, and trades' unions the artificial remedy, where the natural remedy would be simply to restore to him good money, an honest measure of value, and such laws as will secure equitable distribution of the surplus of annual wealth which results from the excess of production over expenditure.

Again, the general result of the business of the last fiscal year to the merchants and manufacturers of the country is thus expressed by a recognized industrial authority:

"Those who, at the end of the fiscal year, have made a living and have their capital unimpaired, should be content, for they will be doing better than the majority."—Iron Age, June 24, 1869.

LOCAL DECREASE IN FARM STOCK AND ANIMAL PRODUCTS.

The undoubted decrease in farm stock and animal products in certain sections of the country also indicates a change, to at least a limited extent, in the relations which production formerly sustained to consumption and population. Thus, in the State of Ohio, for whose domestic statistics a greater degree of accuracy has been claimed than for those of any other State, the official report for 1869 states that, comparing this latter year with 1868, the whole number of sheep has decreased 1,416,205, or from 7,688,845 to 6,272,640; the hogs 356,629, or from 1,812,572 to 1,455,943; the cattle from 1,512,666 to 1,492,581; and the mules from 25,411 to 25,020. In respect to sheep generally, extensive returns published by the Department of Agriculture, conclusively prove a very large decrease in almost every section of the country. This decrease for the year 1868–'69 is estimated by the Bureau at not less than 4,000,000; while others competent to judge report to the Commissioner that the reduction in the whole number of sheep in the United States within the last two years has been at least twenty-five per cent. In one of the leading wool-growing States of the West, the wool clip for 1869 is estimated at thirty-five per cent. less than that of the previous year, 1868.

RELATION OF CAPITAL TO PRODUCT.

Another agency which has powerfully contributed to impair the productive forces of the country, and is still most influential, has been the great increase which has taken place since the commencement of the war in the amount of capital and cost of the instruments requisite for the prosecution and development of industry. It is not necessary to here inquire as to the causes which have contributed to produce this result; but to simply recognize the fact, which, however, is so patent as to hardly need demonstration. Nevertheless, the demonstration is afforded by the experience of every business man, who knows that the employment of capital to the value of two dollars currency is necessary to return the same product which in 1860 was afforded by the employment of one-half of that amount.

For example, in the case of the cotton manufacture, the mill and machinery which could have been put in operation at a cost of $15 to $17 per spindle, in gold, in 1859–'60, would now cost $30 to $33 in currency. If we deduct twenty-five per cent for the depreciation in the currency, we have the ratio of real or specie capital now required, viz: $22 50 to $24 75 per spindle, or an advance of fifty per cent. The direct tax, therefore, upon the community, from the required increase of capital in this department, estimated at seven per cent. per annum, is from fifty-two to fifty-three cents per spindle each year, or a sum which would have paid more than three per cent. per annum profit upon cost per spindles in 1859–'60. Indirectly a still greater loss to production is caused by the fact that the additional capital thus employed is taken away, or kept away, from other and perhaps equally important industries, which are thereby limited in growth.

A further illustration of the injurious influence of the increased cost of a given product of industry, thereby necessitating the employment of a largely increased capital, neutralizing the influence of improved machinery, diminishing exports and restricting home consumption, is to be found in the manufacture of boots and shoes. Thus, in 1858, the average price per case of one-half dozen men's "standard legged" boots was $27 25—six months' credit. In 1868, notwithstanding the introduction and employment of new and improved machinery and processes, whereby the *per capita* product of each workman, with a given amount of manual labor, has been increased upwards of twenty-five per cent., the price of this number and style of boots is $41 net cash, or fifty per cent. greater.

But in addition to the direct influence exerted in impairing the productive forces of the country, the recent unnatural increase in the cost of capital requisite for the prosecution and development of industry has also been productive of another effect, which cannot be regarded as other than prejudicial to the interest of a people living under a democratic form of government, and also to the very existence of such a government itself. This is, in short, the greater subordination of labor to capital, through the hindrances which increased cost interposes to the speedy attainment on the part of the laborer of that amount of capital which is necessary to enable him to take a position as an independent producer. Hence the rapid concentration of the business of manufacturing and of exchanging into single and vast establishments, and the utter annihilation of thousands of little separate industries, whose existence was formerly a characteristic of all the older sections of the country. To a certain extent, concentration of industrial production, by promoting method, system and division of labor, and thereby reducing the cost of product, is undoubtedly beneficial; but when the growth of such a system is unnaturally fostered through the necessities rather than the free will of the laborer, the result cannot be otherwise than to render the many dependent for all the elements of their livelihood upon the will of a few rather than upon their own.

One word further is needed to present this influence of the increased requirement and cost of capital in its true light, and it is this: that it makes no difference for the time being to a community, whether the diminution of the power of capital—meaning thereby tools, food, clothing, building material, as well as money—to develop industry is effected through the agency of fire, flood, earthquake or other physical disaster, or by the agency of legislation which so operates as to augment the value and cost of all the instrumentalities through which the aggregate of production is facilitated and cheapened. The evil of the increased cost of all capital involved in production, or, what is the same thing, the direct increased cost of production, is one, moreover, that is not limited in its influence to the immediate present, but inevitably entails a heavy burden upon the future.

A pertinent illustration of the manner in which circumstances at present increase the cost and requirements of capital, and also tend to convert active into fixed capital, is afforded by the following incident recently brought to the attention of the Commissioner. In a block of stores now erecting in one of the leading seaboard cities the expense of the glass (imported) used in the same is $29,000 (currency.) An analysis of this expenditure shows that one-fourth of it, $7,250, represents simply depreciation of the currency; one-third of the remaining cost, or $7,250, represents the duties imposed on its import; leaving $14,500 as the foreign cost of the material, plus the expenses of transportation, profits, &c. Now, without discussing the propriety of levying a tax upon this article to meet the necessities of the government, it unquestionably remains true that the whole of this increase of price, amounting to one hundred per cent., will remain, so long as these stores stand, a tax on all the industry to which they are made subservient, and also indirectly upon other industries, by diminishing the general supply of capital available in the country, and hence increasing its cost.

UTILIZATION OF NATIONAL RESOURCES AND ADVANTAGES.

A sufficient answer to the question whether the resources and privileges which have accrued to the United States through its inheritance of soil, climate, race, and government, have been utilized to the best advantage, is to be found in the fact; that, while as a nation we possess the greatest area of fertile and cheap land, unrivalled means of intercommunication, and the freest and most popular form of government, domestic production, as measured in price, is nevertheless carried on and maintained on terms of less advantage to the consumer than is the case in any other kindred and competing nation; a few articles, for which through natural circumstances or peculiar inventive skill a marked advantage has been acquired, like cotton, petroleum, the precious metals, sewing-machines, and fire-arms, being excepted.

The United States was formerly, and is likely soon again, to be the main source of the supply of that fibre essential for the cheap clothing of all nations, and its transportation in a crude form to the seats of European manufacture involves nearly as much labor and capital as are requsite for its home manufacture in localities contiguous to the points of its production. Yet the export of American manufactured cotton to other countries does not increase but diminishes, being for the fiscal year 1869 only $5,871,000, currency, as compared with a gold value of $10,934,000 in 1860, nominally one-half, but really one-quarter in quantity. In his last report the Commissioner stated that the opinion of experts communicated to him on the subject was to the effect that if the American manufacturer could be put upon the same basis as his foreign competitor, as regards direct and indirect taxation, cost, and excellence of machinery, and would bring to his business the same skill and economy, he would be enabled to produce cotton cloth, and yarn of No. 25 and under, at a cost which would enable him to undersell all other producers. A revision of these data, made for the Commissioner during the past year by a different but equally trustworthy authority, leads to the more definite conclusion that the export of cotton goods and yarns of low numbers, the staple of consumption, could be immediately and greatly enlarged if a reduction of cost equivalent to fifteen per cent. in the prices of labor could be effected; but, at the same time, it was added "that as the laborer now received but little more than was sufficient for his bare subsistence, owing to the high prices exacted from him for his food, fuel, clothing, and rent, to talk of such a reduction of wages would be both inhuman and useless." But the Commissioner sees that the high prices of food, fuel, clothing, and rent are due to causes which can in a great degree be removed by legislation, and until some steps are taken in this direction the resources of the country, in respect to this one great industry, are certainly not used to the best advantage.

Again, the country desires, and believes it expedient, that another great leading branch of manufacturing industry, viz, that of wool, should be extended, diversified, and cheapened; and men in the possession of the required skill and capital stand ready to engage in new enterprises, and enlarge the varieties of production did circumstances favor. But circumstances do not favor, mainly because a paternal government has seen fit to ordain that the American manufacturer shall not have that which the manufacturers of all other nations enjoy, and which the chairman of the commissioners of the United States to the wool and woolen department of the Paris exposition of 1867 has officially declared to be of "immeasurable advantage," viz, "an unlimited supply of every variety" of the raw material. The manufacture of woolens in the United States, therefore, from this and other obstructions created by legislation, so far from being encouraged, is depressed; wool returns to the grower a lower price in gold than has almost ever before been experienced; the exports of manufactured goods declined sixty per cent. within the last fiscal year, and amounted in the aggregate to the paltry sum of only $160,000, as compared with a British export of the same commodities of $129,000,000; while the importations of woolens into the United States for the same period increased from $32,458,884 to $34,620,943, mainly in the very descriptions of goods which Congress has practically declared the American workman shall not attempt to manufacture.

Let us inquire further in this direction. A boot or a shoe could be manufactured quicker, cheaper, and better in the United States in 1858 than in any other country; and since this period, the improvements in machinery and processes have been such that twenty-five per cent. more product results from the labor of each workman; and to such a degree of rapidity and perfection has the process of manufacturing been systematized that a man or woman may be measured and fitted with a pair of shoes, and made expressly for them, during the time taken for an inspection of the machinery and working of the factory. Boots and shoes, however, cost more in gold, under the new system, in 1869, than in 1858, under the old; and other nations not producing but consuming these products exchange the products of their own labor for boots and shoes manufactured elsewhere, thus depriving the American shipowner of his carrying trade, the American manufacturer of his profit, and the American workman of his employment. The manufacture of boots and shoes, therefore, so far from being encouraged, is limited; the export value declined from $1,329,000 in 1863, to $681,706, in 1867, and $475,050 in 1869. There being, moreover, more workmen desirous of manufacturing boots and shoes than are necessary to supply a consumption limited to our own country, steady and constant employment is not afforded for the whole number. Trade, therefore, is irregular; production stops short of its most profitable maximum, while the cost of manufacture is maintained, from this cause alone, above its most profitable minimum.*

If we turn next to one of the smaller branches of domestic industry, we shall find that the United States is in the exclusive possession of machinery which can manufacture combs, piano-keys, and other articles from ivory cheaper than can be done elsewhere. But the United States does not sell these products of their own industry to other nations, and mainly because the price by which ivory has been increased in accordance with certain supposed national necessities has been sufficent to counterbalance all the advantages which would otherwise have accrued from the exercise of American skill and ingenuity.

A multitude of other similar illustrations might be given; but those presented which sufficiently prove that in many respects the United States does not use the advantages it possesses in the best possible manner, and that if we annually increase in national wealth, it is rather by reason of our great natural resources, than from the intelligent direction through legislation of our national economy. If in the above statements too much significance should appear to be attached to the possession of an export trade, it should be remembered that *no country can export an article or product to any extent unless it is prepared to sell the same as cheap as other nations; and therefore, the ability or inability to export becomes a true test of the ability or inability profitably to produce for the domestic market.*

---

* Reference is here made to the detailed statement in another part of this report, by which it appears that the cost of boots and shoes is enhanced eight per cent. by the taxes on the materials actually entering into the production; to say nothing of the indirect taxes on the food, fuel, clothing, and shelter of the work-people, which must of necessity be made good to them in their wages, and hence appear again in the cost of their product.

DISTRIBUTION OF THE ANNUAL NET PRODUCT OF LABOR AND CAPITAL.

We come next to the consideration of the question whether the influence of existing laws tends to promote such a distribution of the annual products of labor and capital, as best subserves the interests of the whole people; but before endeavoring to apply to this subject anything in the nature of an immediate practical test, it seems desirable to review briefly the theory and practice of the past.

Production and consumption are the conditions of terrestrial existence; but it is not necessary, owing to the bounty of nature, that all who consume should take upon themselves the labor of direct and original production in order that all should exist. Humanity, therefore, from the first has spontaneously divided into two classes, whom we may designate as "producers" and "non-producers."*

Of all those who are in the receipt of any form of income from capital or wages, the original producers include the larger number and the slower minds; the non-producers the smaller number and the more active minds.

The proper field of labor for the so-called non-producers lies between production, and consumption; their labor is in fact the complement of the labor of production, exchange of products being necessary to the full fruition of productive labor, and beneficial to both producers and consumers. Up to this point there is unity of interest in the labor of the two classes, but here their interests separate and lead to antagonism.

The gains of the producers are derived directly from their own labor; but the gains of the non-producers, it is to be noted, are derived from the labor of the producers also. The producers create the property, and the non-producers come in to share it. One class naturally strives to keep and the other to get as much of the results of original production as it can; and in this struggle the more active minds get the better of the more sluggish, and the few grow rich, while the multitude remain poor.

In the *first stage* of society, property can hardly be said to exist, or exists in common. In the second stage, individual rights appear, but property is to a great extent transferred by force, and laws are devised to suppress force and prevent robbery. In the third stage, violence being checked, theft and fraud appear, and laws are made to prevent fraud. Robbery and plunder at first were more honorable than labor; they were the chief glories of the ancient heroes whom we are taught to admire before we are old enough to have attained to any clear perceptions of the principles of morality. Theft and fraud in turn became more honorable than plunder.

We come now to the fourth stage of society, where the grosser methods of transferring property diminish, and cunning comes in to take their place. This is the stage we now occupy. We have advanced no

* More properly, "indirect producers."

further, and have yet no laws to prevent transfers of property by cunning, artifice or trickery. These methods indeed begin to be opposed by public opinion, but that tribunal still applauds as often as it condemns; just as formerly it sanctioned oftener than it censured violence.

There is, however, some progress; and at this stage, let it be observed, the labor of the non-producers becomes the complement of the labor of the productives in a higher degree; more fully adding to the value of their products, and benefiting both producer and consumer by improved methods of transport and conversion, and by more just and reasonable methods of exchange and transfer. The unproductives are still animated by their ancient spirit, and being the chief makers of the laws and institutions for the protection of labor and ingenuity, the increase of products and the exchange and transfer of property, they shape all their devices so cunningly, and work them so cleverly, that they, the non-producers, continue to grow rich faster than the producers. Whoever at this day watches the subject and course of legislation, and appreciates the spirit of the laws, cannot fail to perceive how more and more the idea of the "*transfer*" of the surplus product of society, and the creation of facilities for it, available to the cunning and quick as against the dull and slow, has come to pervade the whole fabric of that which we call government, and how large a number of the most progressive minds of the nation have been led to accept as a fundamental truth in political doctrine, that the best way to take care of the many is to commence by taking care of the few; that all which is necessary to secure the well-being of the workman is to provide a satisfactory rate of profit for his employer. The agitation which now pervades all civilized countries (fourth stage) touching the relations of labor and capital, is but the instinctive uprising of the great productive classes against the institutions, methods, and devices of the non-productives. In short, the ancient combat, old as the dawn of civilization, still goes on; animated on the one side by the desire to keep, and on the other by the desire to get; the producers combining rather blindly and clumsily against the schemes of the unproductives, as they combined at successive stages in all past history against violence, robbery, plunder, theft, fraud, and the grosser acts whereby property was transferred from the hands of the many into those of the few.

PRACTICAL ILLUSTRATIONS.

Let us now see how far experience, in the form of positive facts, furnishes support to the general statements above presented; for there can be no *true* theoretic conclusions which will not be proved by the facts whenever the theory can be subjected to practical and actual application.

In a former report (January, 1869) the Commissioner stated, as the result of extensive investigations into the industrial and social condition of the people, that the tendency of affairs in the United States was toward an inequitable distribution of the annual surplus of production over expenditure, and to impair the power of the masses to accumulate property and better their condition. These conclusions were supported by a large amount of evidence drawn mainly from the older and more densely populated sections of the country, and contributed in great part at the cost of no little time and trouble, by extensive employers of labor occupying situations which afforded especial advantages for eliciting and determining the truth. The results arrived at, although often questioned, and denied on the floor of Congress and elsewhere, have never been refuted by the presentation of any corresponding rebutting evidence; but on the contrary have been strengthened in the time which has since elapsed by a large amount of additional testimony. Some of the difficulties which may seem to stand in the way of the acceptance of the assertion heretofore made, and which the Commissioner now repeats and again asserts, viz, that the poor of the United States, under and in consequence of the existing system of taxation and currency condition combined, tend to grow poorer, may possibly be cleared away by remembering, that the poor of this country are not, and never have been, the same as a class as the poor of Great Britain and Continental Europe. Here, poverty, as a general thing, means deprivation of comforts and luxuries; there, on the other hand, poverty reaches a lower depth and implies the deprivation of necessities and the possibility of starvation. Now the expression "the poor of the United States under the existing system tend to grow poorer," in its widest signification means this: that the great majority of professional men, of clerks, shopmen, and accountants, of whole classes of mechanics whose products, the results of constant employment, would naturally tend to be in excess of a consumption limited by legislation to an exclusively domestic market, and even there restricted by price, such as shoemakers, tailors, hatters, and miners, and at the present time paper-makers, and wool and cotton-spinners and weavers; all females who earn a livelihood in factories, in shoe-binding and stitching, and in ordinary sewing; and finally all those who have only unskilled labor in its rudest forms to sell—it means that all of these, who constitute a large proportion of the population, find their expenses for rent, fuel, food, and clothing maintaining a greater ratio to their receipts than formerly. As an inevitable result, accumulation is impaired and comfort diminished. Appearances, however, are maintained; hence the illusion of apparently undiminished prosperity. Yet there is no escaping the conclusions before arrived at if we pay any regard to the weight of evidence. Of this evidence a few examples may be cited.

In Massachusetts, as we have already shown, nine more polls were crowded into every hundred houses in 1868 than was the case in 1861.

Those conversant with the manufacture of cotton, of boots and shoes, and of hats, in the United States, state that the former average per capita, and even the average absolute domestic consumption of these products, is not maintained; and, if we except the southern portion of the country, that their consumption during the past year has noticeably diminished.

In the frequent fluctuations in the prices of cotton cloth which have taken place since the termination of the war, it is seen that the moment price falls below a certain point consumption enlarges to such an extent as to immediately relieve the market of all surplus; thus proving that millions of our people, for the greater portion of the time, are constantly restricting themselves in the use of what is the cheapest and most indispensable of all fabrics. And the same is true, also, of woolen goods, boots and shoes, coal, and lumber. If the existing machinery of production is worked to its most profitable maximum, the community, at present prices, cannot use the product; so that it becomes the alternative either to restrict consumption within limits most undesirable, or else to break down the market at short intervals through an excess of products which cannot be disposed of except at a sacrifice, which involves severe and often permanent injury to capital, from which, by its necessary relations, labor in turn must suffer.

The answers to a large number of circulars sent out by the Commissioner during the past year to clergymen, teachers, and other professional men, lead to the conclusion that, while their salaries or incomes have, as a general rule, been advanced since 1861, the advance has not been equal by any means in extent to the advance in the prices of commodities. The evidence, therefore, is conclusive as regards this large and important class of our population, that the comforts and luxuries of livelihood have seriously diminished.

Again, the returns of savings banks are often referred to as showing a highly prosperous condition of the masses. Properly considered, however, they indicate a very different state of things. Thus, the first and almost the only fact which attracts the attention of a mere superficial observer in examining these statistics, is a large apparent increase in deposits from 1860 to 1868 or 1869. But an intelligent examination will at once show that a very great part of the apparent accumulation referred to is mere inflation. For example, let us take the case of Massachusetts, where the conditions for increase would seem to be most favorable:

In 1860 the savings banks deposits in this State were, in round numbers	$45, 000, 000
In January, 1869, in currency, $95,000,000, or in gold at 133	71, 000, 000
Increase in eight years	26, 000, 000

or six millions less than the aggregate deposits of 1860 would have amounted to, in the same time, at a compound interest of seven per cent.; or, in other words, the deposits of 1860 were not made good in 1869 without reference to the increase of population, even if we reckon only their natural increase at compound interest. It is evident, therefore, that some cause has eaten into the accumulation which existed eight years previously, and has occasioned the withdrawal of a portion of that accumulation. Of course it was to be expected that withdrawals would take place; but in an ordinary condition of affairs the new deposits would certainly equal the withdrawals, and, in an advancing condition, would greatly exceed them. Now in Massachusetts, certainly, we do not find this to be the case. On the contrary, the laboring classes, so far as they are represented by the depositors of 1860, have not been able to keep at interest the sum (reckoned in gold) which at that time they had earned and laid by. They have either been less frugal or more unfortunate than was in 1860 fairly to have been expected.

In the State of New York the returns of the savings banks indicate a condition of affairs not substantially different from that which has been shown to exist in Massachusetts. Thus,

In 1861 the savings banks deposits of this State were, in round numbers	$67, 000, 000
In 1869, in currency, $169,000,000, or in gold at 133	127, 000, 000

or only $12,000,000 more in eight years than what the aggregate of the deposits of 1861 would have amounted to had they been simply left undisturbed, for the same period, to accumulate at compound interest. And notwithstanding the exhibit of the census of that State for 1865, no intelligent person can doubt that the population of New York has increased in a still greater ratio during the period refered to.

If it be objected that it is not fair in this comparison to reduce currency to gold, or that a dollar is always a dollar, the Commissioner would call attention to the fact that if the comparison were to be drawn between the *purchasing power* of these deposits in 1860 and 1868–'69, respectively; that is, as to the amount of comforts and luxuries which they would command at ordinary retail prices, the comparison would be found still less favorable than is obtained by reducing currency to gold.

But interesting and conclusive as are the statements submitted in respect to savings banks, the story is yet but half told. Formerly the deposits in these institutions represented in great part the hard-earned accumulations of persons who were entirely dependent for support upon the wages received for the performance of daily routine labor—such as operatives in factories, day laborers, mechanics, needle-women, clerks, and small traders. Now, on the contrary, all the evidence tends to show that exactly the contrary condition of affairs has been established.

In short, the recent increase of savings-bank deposits in the eastern States is chiefly due to the fact that they are more lightly taxed than any other kind of invested property.*

* This point is well illustrated by the case of Massachusetts. Until recently the tax on the savings-bank deposits in that State was only one-half of one per cent., and as the investments of these institutions were profitable, being very largely in United States bonds and bank stocks, the depositor received a net increase of seven per cent. without risk or trouble. The consequence was, that a new class of people, for whom

Another circumstance which has tended abnormally to increase the capital of savings banks is the dearness of real estate and of such stocks as were generally within the reach of this class of investors. Once a few hundred dollars would purchase for a mechanic or laborer a decent house; but such has been the increase of prices, resulting from a depreciated currency and high taxation, that a far larger sum is now required to purchase a home, and, when it is obtained, the taxes and repairs on it are a heavy burden. Thus the savings bank has become the depository of funds waiting for the return of better times—of lower prices and settled values. It certainly cannot be regarded as a symptom of healthy social condition when the laborers of the country are in this manner prevented from acquiring homes for their families and an established interest in the country and its prosperity.

The following representation of the condition of operatives engaged in the boot and shoe industry of Massachusetts, copied from the columns of the American Workman of July 3, 1869, is indorsed by the chief officer of the Crispin organization of Massachusests as "true, every word of it:"

"We know full well that the boot and shoe workmen as a class are, and have been for several years, suffering at certain seasons of the year from a lack of steady employment, and from a rate of wages that can scarcely be called remunerative. That their condition is one that calls for relief no one that is acquainted with it will deny; a few individuals, favored by peculiar circumstances, have been able to earn at times four, five, and six dollars per day; but for every one who has earned four dollars per day, there have been ten equally deserving workmen who earned less than half that sum. We know of towns where improved tools and the gang system have not

---

the savings banks were never designed, and who had no right to avail themselves of their eleemosynary character, began to use them, and to deposit the largest sums which are permitted to draw interest. That amount in Massachusetts is required to be less than $1,000 standing to the credit of one person. But to avoid this, deposits are made in the names of the wife and minor children, until they often amount to several thousand dollars. More palpable violations of the law than this are also resorted to or permitted by some institutions which, when the depositor's account reached the legal limit, allowed him to open another, and still another, in his own name, the pass-books being numbered 1, 2, 3, &c. The single fact, therefore, of a recent rapid accumulation in the deposits of savings banks "does not of itself," to use the language of the bank commissioners of Massachusetts, in their report for 1867, "afford any evidence that they are performing the beneficial work expected of them."

An instance may be given of one savings bank in the interior of that State, which having four or five years ago some $200,000 of deposits, was taken in hand by a retired capitalist, anxious to develop its possibilities, and in the short space of three years carried up to a capital of $700,000, the accumulations being all drawn from the population of an agricultural district. This result was accomplished by a process of active solicitation, through the press and by printed circulars, calling on the people to bring in their money, and promising to pay seven per cent. for it, free of taxes. The whole neighborhood was absolutely drained; mortgages, loans to mechanics and small manufacturers were called in, and an extreme stringency occurred in the local money market.

Now, what has thus been found to be true of Massachusetts will undoubtedly be found to be true of every other State where a system of savings banks has been established.

been introduced, where intelligent American workmen are unable to earn by twelve hours' labor more than $1 50 per day. Ten years ago, the shoemakers of New England, as a class, were well fed, well clothed, well housed, and had their pockets well supplied with spending money; now they have less surplus money, are more poorly clothed, and are crowding themselves into smaller tenements, while many of them who formerly saw meat and butter daily upon their tables, now see those articles there but seldom. During these ten years their food and family supplies have nearly doubled in prices, while the wages have increased but half."

The attention of the Commissioner has also been called to the following evidence, showing an increase of pauperism in the fourth collection district of the State of Maine.

Table showing the amounts expended by certain towns in the fourth district of the State of Maine for the support of the poor during the years 1861 *and* 1868, *and the number of polls on the tax lists of said towns in the same years.*

Towns.	Amounts expended.		Polls.	
	1861.	1868.	1861.	1868.
1. Brewer	$577 45	$1,573 00	532	609
2. Dover	782 00	1,367 00	401	421
3. Cornish	610 42	1,057 10	Not returned.	Not returned.
4. Dexter	476 16	1,166 74	514	536
5. Orono	1,000 00	1,500 00	Not returned.	Not returned.
6. Houlton	613 32	1,630 97	387	431
7. Lincoln	600 00	800 00	Not returned.	Not returned.
8. Presque Isle	45 00	300 96	Not returned.	Not returned.
9. Oldtown	1,636 83	4,087 39	645	688
10. Bangor	11,204 05	13,931 62	3,335	3,336
Total	17,545 23	27,417 69		

REMARKS.—Dover manufactures wool and iron—shire town, Piscataqua County; Orono, lumber manufacturing town; Dexter manufactures wool; Houlton, shire town of Aroostook County; Oldtown manufactures more lumber than any town in New England.

The official who communicates the above statements adds, "The state of things it discloses is by no means confined to the fourth district of Maine."

AGENCIES WHICH DISTURB THE EQUITABLE DISTRIBUTION OF NATIONAL WEALTH.

Having thus presented some evidences tending to show the want of equity in the distribution of the surplus product of the nation, let us next consider the agencies which have been instrumental in producing this result, and which further tend to perpetuate it. The general financial result of the war was toward impoverishment, and that to a degree which popular judgment has thus far not accepted. Hitherto, under the influence of currency inflation and the industrial activity which the necessity of supplying the waste of the war stimulated, the effect of the enormous destruction of property which occurred continuously from 1861 to 1865, added to the almost equally enormous waste resulting from the diversion of industry, has been disguised and rendered less apparent than it would have been under different circumstances. But with the return of affairs to their normal condition, many influences before unappreciated begin to make themselves felt. Enforced economy begins to supplant extravagance and restrict consumption, and restricted consumption in turn has left an unconsumed surplus upon the market of a great variety of products. Production, therefore, to a very great extent has ceased to be profitable; hence the anomalous spectacle which has been presented during the past year of representatives of great industries—coal miners, paper-makers, cotton and wool manufacturers, brick-makers, lumbermen, and others—resolving that it was expedient to diminish production; and then carrying the resolution into effect either by suspending work entirely, or by reducing the hours of employment to their operatives, and running machinery but half time.

A patriotic desire to magnify the prosperity of the country on the part of some, or zeal in behalf of party or policy on the part of others, may tempt to a denial of these conclusions. But it will be to no purpose in the face of the stern logic of events present and to come. Indeed, when we attempt to reduce to figures the cost and consequences of the war, the wonder will not be at any present disaster, but that the disaster has not been greater and did not come earlier. But the impoverishment which has resulted from the war is something which is neither to be apologized for nor lamented. The expenditure accomplished the result for which it was incurred, and that, for all loyal men, is sufficient; but the perpetuation of agencies since the termination of the war, either through legislation or the neglect of legislation, which tend to continue the impoverishment of the people and to transfer unequally the gains from the producers into the hands of non-producers, is a matter which is entitled to no apology or extenuation. Two agencies are at the present time in the United States conspicuously engaged in this work, and with an effect which becomes more marked as the period of their operations is extended through the lack of remedial measures, viz: *An inflated irredeemable currency, and excessive and unequal taxation.* How these agencies tend to distribute the surplus of production over consumption unequally; to impoverish the masses; to interrupt the natural course and development of industry, and effectually destroy all profitable commercial relations with foreign countries, the Commissioner next proposes to discuss, avoiding in so doing, to the greatest extent possible, any repetition of the facts and arguments which have before been presented.

HOW AN INFLATED, IRREDEEMABLE CURRENCY AND UNEQUAL TAXATION AFFECT THE FARMER.

We propose to inquire, first, how an inflated and irredeemable currency and unequal taxation affect the agriculturists of the country, who with their families constitute fully fifty per cent. of our whole population.

More wheat and other agricultural produce is and must be annually raised in the United States than is needed for home consumption, and the surplus, if disposed of at all, must find a market in foreign countries. But we can sell wheat in the markets of the world on the single condition of selling as cheap as others, inasmuch as, notwithstanding our magnificent natural advantages, the comparative nearness to the markets of Europe of the wheat-growing regions of the Baltic, the Danube, and the Crimea, reduce our superiority within very narrow limits.* The American agriculturist does not, therefore, command his own price, but the price commands him; and what wheat is worth in Mark Lane, London, the central market of the world, is what the United States must sell it for if it sells at all. And about selling, or not, we have practically but very little discretion. With an immense wheat-raising area we shall raise wheat, even if at the end of the year half the individual farmers find that they have not been able to pay their expenses.

Within certain limits even manufacturing does not depend upon temporary profit, much less farming. Men must live, and work in the occupations in which they have invested their capital, and upon which they have been accustomed to rely for a livelihood. It is only within considerable periods that a general change of industry can be effected. Nor, after the crop has been planted and harvested, has the farming community any more discretion as to the time or the price at which they will sell. Efforts have been made in the past to hold crops back from the market in order to secure an advance, but in general it must be said that such enterprises have only resulted in failure, and even in a greater loss. The fall of breadstuffs in 1868 was only made more certain and more disastrous by the ill-advised attempt to hold back the very abundant crop of that year. Where producers are numbered by hundreds of thousands, concert and discipline in such matters are absolutely hopeless; and with anything like a good season, it is morally certain that the United States will produce more of breadstuffs than the home demand, even when stimulated by the cheapness of food for men and for cattle, can absorb. That surplus will be sold abroad, whatever it may bring.†

* A continuous line of railroad now connects the great and fertile plains of Hungary and the wheat region of the Danube with Paris and other principal centers of distribution in Western Europe, and wheat and cattle are now carried from Buda-Pesth to Paris without change of cars.

† Unquestionably, it would be better for the farming community, considered apart from the interests of the whole country, if that surplus could be *destroyed*, as the surplus coffee of Java was destroyed by the Dutch Company for the purpose of securing a higher price for the remainder; but such a disposition of the surplus wheat of this country is impossible. Remove the tail-board of a cart loaded with potatoes, to use a homely illustration, and it is of course true that if the potatoes nearest would not tumble out the remainder need not; but, as the first potatoes have no choice whether they will obey the law of gravitation or not, the rest must take the chance all the same as if their falling did not depend on the action of others. In precisely the same way, with our own production of wheat, some must go abroad, and if the movement does not start at one point it will at another.

THE RELATION OF AGRICULTURE TO CERTAIN SPECIAL INDUSTRIES.

It is worth while to say a word at this point in reference to an opinion which is somewhat general, that the agricultural interests of the country are greatly dependent upon certain special domestic industries for a market for their products. It needs, however, but a slight examination of the subject to show the foundation upon which this opinion rests, and the tendency there is to an exaggeration of its importance. According to the statement before presented, the gross value of the annual agricultural product of the country approximates *three thousand three hundred millions of dollars*, ($3,282,950,000.)

The very careful investigations made within the last few years into the condition of the woolen and cotton manufacture of the United States, admit of a very accurate determination of the number of operatives directly employed in these branches of production, viz., about 90,000 in the manufacture of wool, and 125,000 in the manufacture of cotton. The price of board for operatives in these two industries in the United States at the present time will not exceed *three* dollars per week, or one hundred and fifty-six dollars per annum. Supposing the whole amount to be expended on the purchase and consumption of agricultural produce, the aggregate annual value of the product consumed would be $33,540,000. If we add an equal sum for the value of the agricultural produce consumed in the pig and bar iron industry, and double the total of the whole to cover the value of indirect consumption attributable to these industries, we have the sum of $134,160,000, or *four and a tenth per cent.* of the value of the annual agricultural product of the country; making it evident, therefore, that the great consumers of agricultural produce are the artisans, the unskilled laborers, and the professional men of the country, with their families, who do not class themselves with any of the more conspicuous manufactures.

We will add but one other item of evidence bearing upon this same question, and that is, that a statement has been made to the Commissioner during the past year, by one well qualified by information and experience to speak as authority, that the State of Illinois alone, if cultivated to the degree of the average of lands in Great Britain or Belgium, can produce annually a food supply ample for the subsistence of *all* the population now living upon the territory of the United States. There are even counties in some of the States of the Union, composed wholly of the finest wheat-growing lands in the world, that are larger in area than that portion of Hungary which, as the Buda-Pesth region, has come to be regarded as one of the granaries of Europe.

An ordinary good crop, therefore, in the United States cannot be held at home. The surplus must find a market abroad, and whatever it is worth for exportation measures the price of the whole crop, inasmuch as there cannot be two prices for the same article, one for the home and another for the foreign market.

But the value of the surplus for exportation is much less than it would be were the currency brought to a specie standard and taxation reduced and equalized, and to this extent the American agriculturist is placed at a disadvantage with his foreign competitor, from the very outset. Let us explain. It cannot be doubted that the cost of transportation, elevating, storing, and managing is at least ten per cent. greater than it would be under a normal condition of currency and taxation. It is also certain that the exporter of the grain will not give at the time of his purchase an exact equivalent in currency to the gold price at the place of sale in Europe, less commissions, transportation, and profits, inasmuch as it is always doubtful whether the gold received sixty or ninety days hence will then exchange for as much currency as it would at the time the grain was first purchased. The exporter, therefore, of necessity insures himself to the extent of one, two, or four per cent., as the case may be. But whatever these charges may amount to, and, differ as we may in reference to particulars it must be agreed that they are considerable, they are all reflected back and borne by the producer, and not charged to the foreign consumer, for the latter can at all ordinary times buy wheat from the Baltic or the Crimea which is not subject to such charges; and this loss, furthermore, is not limited merely to the surplus available for export, but, in accordance with the law above explained, is multiplied by the whole product, and diminishes the price for which every bushel is sold, whether the same be intended for domestic or foreign consumption.

We have thus stated the position of the American agriculturist in respect to what he has to sell. Let us next consider his position in regard to that which he wishes to buy. And here it is necessary to bear in mind that what the grower of food and other agricultural products wants is not money, but that which money will buy.

We will therefore assume that the farmer has turned say one hundred bushels of wheat into one hundred specie dollars, and next endeavor to trace this sum of money through its course in procuring for its possessor the satisfaction of the wants under the stimulus of which he has performed the labor of guiding the powers of nature to the production of the wheat.

He has need of salt, and he finds that he can purchase it in Liverpool or Cadiz and lay it down in the United States at from fifteen to twenty cents per bushel; but the government, through its currency and its tariff, has imposed such a tax upon it as to make it better for him to pay from forty to forty-five cents per bushel for American salt; or, in other words, to take less than half the quantity for the same money; the government, at the same time, receiving but little revenue—the ostensible object for which a tax on salt, through the medium of the tariff, was in the first instance imposed.

Or, perhaps, he lives in Maine, and wants coal, and could get twenty tons from Nova Scotia for his hundred dollars. But the government having imposed a tax of one dollar and twenty-five cents per ton of two thousand pounds, in gold, upon its importation, he finds it better for him to expend one dollar and a half per ton more for transportation of coal from Pennsylvania. Thus, thirty dollars' worth of unnecessary transportation has been performed, the government has no more revenue, and he has less coal.

Or, perhaps, he wishes to carpet his rooms. In London the specie dollar received for a bushel of his wheat would purchase of "tapestry Brussels," a yard and a third; but in New York he would find that government, through its currency and tariff, had so taxed carpets that his specie dollar, even converted into currency, will purchase only about four-sixths of a yard of the same style and quality. If, however, his means do not allow of the purchase of tapestry Brussels, and he should endeavor to satisfy his wants with a coarse drugget or bocking, he would find that the price of his grain would purchase less comparatively than of even the more expensive and costly article. If he wishes to invest the proceeds of his wheat in blankets, he will find that one hundred bushels sold in Liverpool will buy him over seven hundred pounds of this article; but if sold in New York, at present prices, it will not bring him an excess of three hundred and fifty pounds. If he should endeavor to console himself with the reflection that the treasury gains to the extent that he loses, and that through his sacrifices the period for the extinguishment of the national debt is shortened, he will find the receipts from the duties on blankets under the tariff to have been as follows: 1862, $612,283; 1866, $485,978; 1867, $207,598; 1868, $25,288.

In fact, in almost any direction in which he attempts to expend his one hundred dollars in specie—or, in other words, for whatever article he attempts to exchange his one hundred bushels of wheat—he finds that the government has interposed and has dictated to him that at this present time he must either buy what he might not have chosen, or take less than what he might otherwise obtain.

The following table shows the purchasing power of a hundred bushels of wheat as measured by the price of various articles in the city of New York in the years 1859 *and* 1869, *respectively.*

Commodities.	Prices in 1859.	Quantities which 100 bushels of wheat would purchase in 1859.	Prices in 1869.	Quantities which 100 bushels of wheat would purchase in 1869.	Decrease per cent.
Wheat	$1 45 per bus.	100 bushels	$1 35 per bus.	100 bushels	......
English bar iron, com'n.	2⅛ c. per lb.	6, 824 pounds	3¼ c. per lb.	4, 154 pounds	39
Collins's axes	9 00 per doz.	16 1-9 dozen	12 00 per doz.	11¼ dozen	30
Ingrain two-ply Lowell carpeting	75 c. per yd.	193⅓ yards	1 30 per yd.	103 11-13 yards	46
Cut nails	3 c. per lb.	4, 833 pounds	5 c. per lb.	2, 700 pounds	43
Blankets, 10-4	3 50 per pair.	41½ pairs	5 50 per pair.	26½ pairs	36
Liverpool salt, in bags.	90 c. per bag	161 1-9 bags	2 60 per bag.	51 12-13 bags	68
Men's ordinary boots	21 50 per doz.	6¾ dozen	112 00 per doz.	3 1-7 dozen	53
Waxed-legged boots	4 50 per pair	32 pairs	6 83 per pair.	20¼ pairs	37
Black alpaca	24 c. per yd	604 1-6 yards	40 c. per yd.	337½ yards	44
Steel, Sheffield cast steel	14 c. per lb.	1, 035 5-7 pounds	19 c. per lb.	710 10-19 pounds	31
Stoves, five holes	6 00 each	24 1-6 stoves	9 50 each	14 1-5 stoves	41
Mackerel, No. 1	11 00 per bbl.	13 1-5 barrels	27 00 per bbl.	5 barrels	62
Mackerel, No. 2	10 00 per bbl.	14½ barrels	16 00 per bbl.	8½ barrels	41
Codfish, large	4 00 pr. 100 lbs.	3, 625 pounds	7 50 pr. 100 lbs.	1, 800 pounds	50

THE FARMER AS A PRODUCER.

It remains but to consider the position which the farmer holds distinctively as a producer. He raises his wheat and other produce, under a system of currency which unsettles values, inflates prices, enhances the cost of labor and all the elements of production, and affords daily opportunities to speculators for plunder. He raises his wheat and other produce under a tariff which, without affording him any sufficient compensation, unnecessarily increases the cost of his tools, his clothing, his fuel, his fencing and his shelter.

Wheat produced under these circumstances costs a great deal more than it does in countries free from such embarrassments, but it does not sell for more. On the contrary, it has to compete in the market with wheat produced by the so-called "pauper labor" of Europe, and returns to the farmer no more than the price of real pauper labor in America. Nor does it cheer the grower of wheat to reflect, that while he suffers from a depreciated currency, and competes with the stable conditions, metallic values, cheap materials, and cheaper labor of other countries, contributing at the same time his share to the public revenues, he also makes much heavier contributions on his clothing, iron, lumber, coal, salt, and the like, not for revenue, but for the profit of industries more favored than his own, that they may be screened from the competition to which he is forced to submit.*

RELATION OF SPECIAL TAXES TO THE NET SAVINGS OF THE COUNTRY.

But it is not necessary that we should confine our illustrations of the inequality of the distribution of the net products of industry, resulting from the present system of currency and taxation, to any particular class of the community. The evil is general; the illustrations can be made general also.

Thus, we have heretofore indicated that the present net saving, or addition to the productive capital of the country, does not exceed $600,000,000 per annum. It is interesting to inquire what agencies affect the distribution of this surplus, and what is the relation borne to it by any bounty which may accrue to special interests by the favor of existing laws.

* As direct practical evidence of the truth of the statements above made respecting the influence of the existing systems of currency and taxation, in reducing the income of the American agriculturist to the scale of paupers' earnings, we submit the following table, prepared from the columns of the Philadelphia Press, showing the price of some of the leading articles of agricultural produce in that city during the last week of July, in 1867 and 1869, respectively, with an additional column showing the prices of similar articles in New York, on the 1st of November of the latter year:

	Philadelphia, Pa., July 30, 1867.	Philadelphia, Pa., July 30, 1869.	New York, N. Y., Nov. 1, 1869.
Beef cattle:			
Common	13 *a* 14 cts.	6 *a* 7 cts.	....
Prime	14½ *a* 15½ cts.	7 *a* 8 cts.	....
Choice	16 *a* 17 cts.	9½ cts.	....
Flour and meal:			
Northwest extra	$10 00 *a* 12 75	$6 00 *a* 7 50	$6 40 *a* 6 60
Pennsylvania and Ohio extra	10 00 *a* 12 00	6 00 *a* 6 75, 8 00	6 55 *a* 6 80
Rye flour	8 75 *a* 9 00	6 12½ *a* 6 25	5 00 *a* 6 30
Grain:			
Wheat	2 20 *a* 2 75	1 49 *a* 1 68	1 38 *a* 1 55
Rye	1 55 *a* 1 60	1 35	1 07 *a* 1 07½
Corn	1 17 *a* 1 18	1 16 *a* 1 17	1 00 *a* 1 05
Oats	90 *a* 93 cts.	65 *a* 75 cts.	62 *a* 64 cts.
Potatoes	(*per bbl.*) 2 25 *a* 2 75	(*per bbl.*) 1 50 *a* 1 75	....

On this showing the editor of the Philadelphia Press comments as follows: "This is an unnatural and unhealthy condition of affairs, and the longer it continues the worse for us. High prices are not so much to be dreaded in themselves when everything advances abreast, and the man who pays high for what he consumes can also sell high what he produces. When, however, prices have come honestly down, but, through the artificial structure of society, that decline inures only to the advantage of a small class of non-producers, it is dangerous and improper. This is precisely our condition. Within two years the prices of staples which sustain life and cover the ordinary table have fallen heavily and permanently, but the people have not yet got the benefit of it. *The farmer gets one-half the price he received for his wheat two years ago, but he must pay nearly the same for what he buys.*" (Philadelphia Press, July 30, 1869.)

Let us take, first, the case of pig iron. The present annual consumption of this article in the United States (domestic and foreign) is about 1,837,000 tons. If the price of the domestic product of iron were less than the cost at which it could be imported, plus the tax (of $9 gold) now imposed upon foreign iron, we should import none. Practically, this is the exact truth, the only pig iron imported during the year 1868 being 112,000 tons mainly Scotch pig, an inferior variety, required by stove-founders for mixing, by reason of its greater fusibility—an article which is not produced in the United States, and which would doubtless continue to be imported were the duty increased from nine to eighteen dollars per ton. It therefore follows that the price of American pig iron may have been maintained at $9 per ton gold, or $11 currency, in excess of what need to have been paid by consumers but for the tax; and if thereby the sum of $20,000,000 was transferred to the comparatively few iron-masters, although it may not have been all profit to them, and may simply have warranted them in producing iron at a higher cost, yet it represents three and one-fourth per cent. of the whole annual saving of the nation, diverted or taken from those who actually earned it for the benefit of probably not over one thousand individuals, who are the proprietors of iron furnaces.

Again, let us take the case of salt, the duty on the importation of which in bulk is 18 cents per hundred pounds, or (with gold at 133) 22½ cents currency. The present consumption of salt in the United States is estimated at about 39,000,000 bushels per annum, the price of which has been enhanced from 20 @ 23 cents in 1860 to 40 @ 50 cents in 1869. Now, if we assume that the imposition of a tariff on salt of from 80 to 108 per cent. (see imports of 1868) has unnecessarily increased the general cost of this indispensable article to the extent of only 10 cents per bushel, we have thereby subjected the community to a tax of $3,900,000 per annum, or have diverted, in the consumption of this single article, from what would have been an otherwise natural distribution of the net earnings of the nation, more than half of one per cent.

Similar deductions may be made in respect to lumber, the materials which enter into the composition of boots and shoes and the manufacture of fur and felt hats, to steel, carpets, blankets, woolen goods of every description, and a great variety of other articles, the prices of all of which have been greatly and unnecessarily enhanced by special and partial legislation. The effect of these things cannot be dwarfed or made to appear of no account, as is often attempted, by showing the insignificant relation between the tax and some specific or individual expenditure—as, for example, between eighteen cents per hundred on salt and the cost of a barrel of pork; between sixty per cent. on silk and the cost of the band or lining of a common felt hat; between three cents per pound and ten per cent. ad valorem on steel and the cost of an axe; or five cents per pound on coffee and the cost of a cup of its infusion. If there were only one barrel of pork, one hat, one axe, and one cup of coffee affected, the enhancement of price would most certainly be of too little account to require notice; but when each specific and separate instance becomes multiplied by millions, the general effect cannot be otherwise than to so increase the cost of subsistence or production as to diminish the power of accumulation to all those who are not able, to a corresponding degree, to increase the aggregate of their receipts from income or wages: and that a very large proportion of the people have not been thus able is a matter of fact, which can neither be gainsayed nor disproved.

During the last few years the manifestations of discontent, on the part of the real producing classes, against what has seemed to them to be the encroachments and oppressions of capital, have rapidly increased in number and significance. To many these expressions of discontent have seemed unreasonable, inasmuch as wages have generally been greatly advanced and to some extent the hours of labor shortened. But when we consider how small, even under the most favorable circumstances, is the net saving which annually accrues to any nation as compared with the value of its annual gross product—the United States, for example, in 1860, after an existence of about three-quarters of a century as a nation, and as the result of all the labor, enterprise, and economy of its people, having been able to accumulate only what would be equivalent to about four years of current expenditures*—we can readily understand how difficult it must be, of necessity, for a producer, starting without capital, to make his first accumulation, and how slight a change in the distribution of the net annual profit of the nation may make to the masses all the difference that exists between abundance and deficiency, advancement and retrogression.

The wonder, therefore, is, not that labor, feeling itself aggrieved and not clearly seeing the cause of its sufferings, should instinctively cry out and blindly accuse capital, but rather that the outburst of remonstrance has not been more violent, and menacing.

The following letter, with its story of simple eloquence, addressed to the Commissioner by the head of a large seminary of learning in one of the middle States, in response to a circular asking for a statement of comparative expenses in 1860 and 1869, is the only additional evidence which it is proposed to present in connection with this department of the subject:

OCTOBER 12, 1869.

In reply to your circular I will answer: All my expenses have increased, and the only increase in my income which has grown out of the course of events is an advance in the price of board of those students who board with me. To make 1869 equal to 1860 I am driven to work earlier and later; to cut off my little luxuries of flowers and food; to take fewer newspapers and buy fewer books for my library; to abandon my green-house; to relinquish watering places and travel in vacation.

By the above curtailments, which came a little hard, at first, I manage to live com-

* Gross value of real and personal property of the United States in 1860, $14,183,215,000; gross product of the year, $3,804,000,000.

fortably, and experience as few of the real anxieties of life now as in 1860. I am afraid my experience will not go for much, for I cannot join with some of my friends who are afraid starvation stares them in the face. I do not know as I ought to speak of it but in confidence: the calls for charity have enormously increased, and, added to the other expenses of living, go to swell the burden.

DISCUSSION OF REMEDIES.

We come next to the consideration of the remedies which the situation of affairs in respect to trade, commerce, and industry, as above described, would seem to render necessary. Setting aside minor considerations, the chief elements of disturbance are to be found in the present condition of the currency and of the national taxation, and it is through reform in these directions that relief is mainly to be expected.

CURRENCY.

The phases of opinion in regard to the course to be taken in respect to this agency are so numerous and discordant as to render it desirable to go back to fundamental principles and endeavor to reach some general agreement as to the nature of the situation.

Original use of money.—Currency has its origin in the division of labor. No man can supply all his own wants by his own efforts; and in his recourse to others and theirs to him exchange of products begins. The original method of exchange—barter, or the direct exchange of one article against another—is only possible, to any great extent, when society is in its rudest and most primary condition. Some other method of exchange, therefore, early became a necessity of civilization and progress; and the adoption of money—that is, of some common medium for which all the products of labor should be exchanged, and which itself should in turn be freely exchanged for all or any of similar products, became a matter of original necessity and spontaneous invention, as much so as the adoption of clothing, the use of fire, or the construction of shelter.

Hence we arrive at a conclusion which is vital to any correct ideas on this subject, that money is a means to an end: that end the exchange of commodities, and not an end in itself.

It is an instrument to effect a specific purpose: that purpose exchange. In performing that office it is a labor-saving machine, as much so as a ship or a steam-engine; and, so far as the development of trade, manufactures, and commerce is concerned, is more efficacious in the saving of labor than any other machine which can be mentioned. Its utility therefore to society, like that of any other instrument or machine, is proportioned solely to the work it performs; and, as is true of any other tool or instrument, no more is wanted of this than is simply sufficient to perform the work. If two plows or two spindles are brought into existence where there is only work for one, the evident result will be that one will work all the time and the other lie idle; or that both will be employed, but only for a portion of the time in either case; and so far as the work to be performed is concerned, the two will have but the value of the one previously existing. The same law holds true of currency as an instrument, with this exception, that where an amount larger than is necessary to perform the required work is called into existence, the whole effort, conscious and unconscious, of society and industry is directed to the single end of preventing any portion of it from remaining unemployed for any appreciable length of time. But the employment of the currency thus increased can only be effected by increasing the price of the whole body of commodities already forming the subjects of trade; and this is the only way in which a greater amount of currency can be employed to perform the service for which a lesser amount formerly sufficed.

RELATION OF CURRENCY TO TRADE.

It is a common fallacy that the increase of money will of itself create trade. But what is trade? Trade is simply the exchange of commodities already existing, according to the wants of an organized society. An increase of currency neither increases the amount of commodities to be exchanged nor adds anything to the desirableness of exchange. If there is any more trade after an increase of currency, it can only be that the same commodities are being exchanged more times. But this is *not trade, but over-trading*, involving speculation and perhaps derangement of industry. In short, the only object of exchange at all is to convey the commodity from the producer to the consumer. To pass it through unnecessary hands is simply to multiply the expenses and profits with which it is charged, and to divert an undue portion of the labor and capital of the country to the work of distribution.

Now this is the exact condition of the United States at the present time. The currency has been increased in the manner we have supposed, and has found employment through the increase of prices and the multiplication of exchanges; and this increase of prices and multiplication of exchanges is one of the chief causes of the disturbance of the trade and industry of the country, for which a remedy is believed to have become imperative.

AMOUNT OF CURRENCY REQUISITE.

But it is constantly alleged, and proof in support of the assertion adduced, that there is no more currency at present in the country than is requisite to do the business of the country. This is strictly true. There is no more currency than is necessary to do the business of the country upon the present scale of prices, and with the multiplicity of exchanges which the redundancy of the currency itself has induced. And what is more, there never will be. If the present volume of the currency were to be increased in accordance with the demand of economists of a certain school, even to the extent of two-fold, the relative condition of affairs would remain the same—prices advancing and exchanges multiplying sufficiently to absorb any excess that might be authorized.

It should also be borne in mind, that irredeemable paper currency is not money in its true sense, inasmuch as it represents money to the exact extent to which it can purchase, or be exchanged for coin and no more. Now if this premise is correct, it follows that although the legislature may authorize the issue of any amount of irredeemable paper, it will not by so doing add one penny to the amount of real money in circulation. On the other hand, the natural effect of an excessive issue of irredeemable paper is to actually reduce the amount of real money in circulation by creating (through speculation) artificial and abnormal uses for capital, which under other and healthy conditions would not be presented, or at least not to the same extent; and also by creating artificial and abnormal prices which necessitate the use comparatively of a much larger amount of money to effect the exchange of an equal amount of commodities. Hence the explanation of what, to the many, seems entirely paradoxical, viz: That money should ever be scarce in the United States at the present time when the volume of the circulating medium has experienced so large an increase; or that other fact, apparent not only in the United States, but in all other countries cursed with an irredeemable paper currency, that the rates of interest are always the most advanced when there is the largest absolute amount of currency in circulation.*

EXCESS OF THE PRESENT CURRENCY.

That the present volume of currency is in excess, is proved: 1. By the indisputable fact that the general scale of the prices of domestic commodities, as measured by the common standard of international commerce, is greatly in excess of the prices of other countries, and out of all natural proportion to the prices of the same commodities in the United States before the war. The very common idea that this great advance in prices since 1861 is due in a greater or less degree to the depreciation of gold, owing to its increased production, is entirely with-

---

* In respect to this proposition, a recent American writer of the highest authority (Hon. Amasa Walker) uses the following language: "Money is scarce not in proportion to its actual quantity, but to the relative demand for it. When, therefore, in addition to the natural wants of trade, the speculative interest comes into market, the extraordinary demand is certain to create a pressure; so that, practically, it has always been true, as it is now true, that an expanded currency will be the most scarce when it is most abundant; that collections will be most unsatisfactory when the circulation is largest; and that the rates of interest will be highest when the loans of the banks are most extended.

"This important lesson the people must learn; and, if they would have money plenty and cheap, they must insist that the amount shall be reduced to its natural limit—to that point where it is at par with specie. They cannot have an easy and reliable money market until that which is called money is truly so; and we incur no risk in predicting that a satisfactory state of trade will not arrive until the currency of the nation is equivalent in value to the currency of commerce."

out foundation; as is conclusively proved by the fact that an examination of the prices of some sixty of the leading commodities dealt in on the London market since 1850 shows that, whatever advance in prices, directly or indirectly attributable to this cause, actually took place, the same occurred and reached its maximum between the periods 1857 and 1861; and that since 1861 there has been, on the average of the same articles, a steady and regular decline in prices.* (See Appendix.)

2. The excess of the present currency is also proved by the further fact, that the amount of currency in circulation has been arbitrarily increased during the past eight years considerably more than twofold, although the increase of population, production, and accumulated wealth during the same time has been by general agreement in very much smaller proportion, and although at the former date the amount of currency in circulation was not limited by any serious restrictions upon the creation of banks or the issue of paper really or nominally redeemable in specie. Furthermore, the tendency of all commercial nations is towards economy in the use of currency. The circulating medium never advances in the same ratio with the exchanges which it serves to carry on. In the State of New York, in the ten years from 1850 to 1860, the capital of banks increased one hundred and ten per cent.; loans and discounts seventy-five per cent.; deposits one hundred and thirteen per cent.; and specie one hundred and forty-one per cent.; *while the circulation increased only fifteen per cent.* The explanation of this phenomenon was, that bank deposits and other economical expedients had largely taken the place of bank notes in domestic exchanges.

It has been urged, furthermore, that by allowing the present volume of currency to remain unaltered, the increase in business and the development of the country would gradually diminish and finally remove all redundancy. To this it may be replied, that the retaining of the present amount of currency in circulation tends to increase no business but what is speculative, and to check the very development which is expected to prove remedial. In the twenty-five years which elapsed from 1835 to 1860 the paper circulation of the country, left free and untrammeled to expand itself, increased from one hundred and three millions to two hundred and seven millions, or at the rate of 4.36 per cent. per annum. Now should the future demand continue to increase in the same ratio, it would require the lapse of forty years from 1860, or until the year 1900, to bring the wants of the country up to the present

---

*The following table exhibits the relative value of gold to silver in London from 1845 to 1868–'69, inclusive. It will be observed that gold reached its *minimum* relative value in 1859, and since that date has constantly appreciated:

1845–'49 (5 years) prior to discovery of gold in California and Australia	15.892
1850–'52 (3 years) transition period	15.649
1853–'56 (4 years)	15.339
1857–'60 (4 years)	15.276
1861–'66 (6 years)	15.411
1867–'69 (2 5-12 years)	15.580

supply. In the mean time the currency would probably remain, as now, irredeemable or inconvertible.

CONTRACTION AND ITS INFLUENCE.

The simple, reasonable remedy for the evils of inflation would seem, therefore, to be *contraction, pure and simple, without artifice or indirection.* Contraction, however, is opposed on account of the immediate distress which it is supposed would follow the adoption of such a policy. But it requires no gift of prophecy to foretell that the country must soon experience all the hardships which contraction could entail, whether contraction and the ultimate benefits of contraction be secured or not. It is morally certain that prices in almost every department of industry will sooner or later be disturbed as greatly as contraction would require; the only difference being that in the one case a temporary hardship is submitted to for a permanent relief and a great good; and in the other it will be suffered to no purpose, and the causes which produced the mischief be left as entire and powerful as ever. All the incidents and all the effects of contraction, so far as it involves commercial disaster and industrial distress, are inevitably coming, and speedily. The only question which it is left us to consider is, whether we will allow this experience again and again to repeat itself.

Thus it has already been shown that the amount of our foreign indebtedness was increased during the past year to the extent of over $200,000,000 Up to this time the annual adverse balance of trade which has been experienced since the close of the war has been mainly adjusted by the transmission of national or other securities abroad. But it is evident that this process cannot be indefinitely continued; and there are clear indications that the end is not distant. When this method of settlement becomes no longer possible, one of two things must follow—either importations must be checked or the excess of importations must be paid for in some other way than as at present. That importations cannot be checked to any appreciable extent must be evident to any one who will consider what it is which we bring from abroad, and the wants and necessities which our imports supply. Thus, for example, a large proportion of the value of our imports represents the domestic consumption of tea, coffee, sugar, spices, and molasses. Now it is evident that the only cause which can seriously restrict the consumption of these articles among the masses, who are the great consumers in this country, must result from an inability to purchase, which in turn could only be the result of a degree and extent of industrial depression equal to anything which could be imagined of a period of contraction. Another large proportion of the value of imports represents the raw materials of domestic manufactures, such as drugs, dyestuffs, soda-ash, bleaching powders, hides, tin, raw silk, and other similar products. To check the importation of these would simply be to destroy a much larger value of domestic industry; while to suppose that there can be any essential curtailment in the importation of what may be regarded as luxuries, would be to ignore the fact that the tendency and effect of the present state of things is to put it in the power of the rich to indulge in such expenditures, even at the cost of the comforts and necessaries of the poorer classes. We cannot, therefore, reasonably look for any diminution in the annual volume of our foreign imports, while their continuance on the present scale, with the inevitable, speedy exhaustion of the supply of bonds or bullion available for export, involves a serious depreciation of the prices of domestic commodities, and a general convulsion of trade: the very effects on account of which contraction is opposed and deprecated.

OBJECT TO BE ATTAINED BY SPECIE PAYMENTS.

Again, there seems a general misapprehension as to the end to be accomplished by the resumption of specie payments, and an exaggerated estimate of the importance of that object. *Unless resumption implied contraction*, it could cure but a small portion of the existing evils. If it were possible to substitute seven hundred millions of gold dollars for the seven hundred millions of paper dollars in circulation, and to hold that amount in the country, there would be the same inflation of prices, the same disproportion between imports and exports, and the same inability to dispose of the products of domestic industry in foreign markets. To be sure, it would be impossible to retain such an amount of gold in the country except by laws of impossible barbarism; but wherein would the reduction of the gold currency then, through exportation, differ from the reduction of the present paper currency through a judicious and well-ordered withdrawal? After such a substitution, gold would still remain what it is now, the cheapest commodity in the country, and for that reason, as now, would continue to be taken by foreign countries in preference to our other domestic products. That this now is the case, proves that gold is relatively the cheapest commodity we have to export. That gold also is relatively cheaper than the products of our domestic manufactures, can also be shown by a more specific illustration. Thus, in 1860 a thousand dollars in gold would purchase for export 111 dozen cane-seat chairs. The same amount of gold will purchase at the present time the same number in almost any part of Europe; but in the United States it will now purchase but 102 dozen, thus proving that, as measured by this commodity, gold is cheaper with us than it was in 1860, and cheaper also with us than it is in other countries. It is therefore sent to the points where it is most highly esteemed, and where it can be used to the greatest advantage; and the chairs, in common with the cotton-cloth, furniture, tools and

* For the first four months of the fiscal year 1869-'70 (July to October inclusive) the importations of foreign goods were in excess even of the unprecedentedly large importations of 1868-'69, aggregating $149,297,278 against $137,164,952, an increase of nearly twelve millions.

implements, nails, hardware, hats, wagons, &c., of domestic manufacture, are allowed to remain at home and depress the market with an excess of competition.

It is a very common idea that it is Great Britain, of all the countries of the globe, which "floods" the United States with foreign merchandise; but so far is this from being the fact, that the British Board of Trade Reports show that, in the direct trade between the two countries for 1868, the direct exports from the United States to Great Britain exceeded the direct imports from Great Britain to the United States in the ratio of more than *two* to *one;* the value of the direct exports from the United States being £43,063,094, ($215,315,470,) while the value of the direct British imports was only £21,410,184, ($107,050,920.) But this other significant fact should also be noted in this connection, viz: that while the bulk of our importations represent raw materials purchased from countries other than Great Britain—as tea from China, sugar from Cuba, coffee from Brazil, hides from Buenos Ayres, drugs, dyestuffs, ivory, skins, raw silk, gums, and spices from India or Africa—countries all which require the very products of industry which the United States especially manfactures and desires to sell, we do not pay for such raw materials, as a rule, with such or any manufactures, but allow Great Britain to substitute herself in our place; or, in other words, not being able to sell, as formerly, any of our manufactured products to the nations producing the great raw materials of our domestic consumption, because we cannot sell cheaply, we settle the adverse balances by the purchase in the first instance of bills of exchange on England, paying a banker's profit, and probably effecting such a purchase to a greater or less extent by selling at a discount the nation's obligations of indebtedness. The debt thus transferred to Great Britain is settled by the exportation of British merchandise, paying another profit, and in British vessels, paying freights and commissions. Now the point to which the Commissioner would especially direct attention, and which, although pointed out in former reports, has received little consideration, is: that there is no such thing possible as the resumption *and continuance* of specie payments with a continuance of this abnormal system of foreign trade and exchanges; and for the simple reason that gold will not stay here, and would long ago have left us to the last dollar, had not the bonds of the national government been available for the settlement of adverse foreign balances in the place of gold. We must reduce prices, so that foreign nations will be willing, because it is for their interest, to exchange product for product. And to accomplish this, there must be contraction, for, to reduce prices *permanently and equitably*, while maintaining seven hundred millions of irredeemable paper money, is simply an impossibility.

AMOUNT OF GOLD NEEDED FOR REDEMPTION.

The question how much gold is needed to begin and sustain a system of redemption, depends wholly upon the answer to the prior question how much currency there shall be to redeem. Seven hundred millions of paper could not be kept redeemable with less than seven hundred millions of gold, because with such an amount of currency it would inevitably be depreciated, and hence gold would bear a premium which every holder of paper would be desirous to realize. With four hundred millions of paper, on the other hand, a hundred millions of gold would probably be ample, because the currency, not being in excess of the wants of commerce, would not suffer depreciation, and, gold and paper being on otherwise equal terms, paper would be preferred for its greater convenience in use, just as in 1860 the banks were fully able to redeem all of their circulation which was presented for payment, although having but eighteen cents of specie on each dollar of immediate liabilities. It is not the ratio between gold and paper that needs to be regulated, but the ratio between the amount of paper in circulation and the volume of national production and exchange, of which it is the instrument. Much criticism has been passed upon the Treasury for not adopting the policy of hoarding gold with a view to returning to specie payments; but if what has been stated above is true, such a policy could lead to no good results unless accompanied by a measure of contraction; while contraction would obviate the necessity of any such a policy, inasmuch as gold would then come to us, or be retained by us—our currency being in a healthful condition—to just that extent to which it was needed, obeying the same laws as any other commodity. Equally untenable is it to suppose that any progress can be made toward resumption by a reduction, through government purchase and cancellation, of the principal of the funded debt. If we had no national debt; if the two thousand millions of public bonds were by some process to be transformed into an equal amount of private "securities," exchanged between citizens, the premium on gold would not be appreciably affected. It is not at all the condition of the credit of the nation which causes gold to be at a premium, as is proved by the fact that in Italy, Austria, and Russia—countries maintaining large standing armies, constantly threatened with war, whose debts are larger, relatively to their resources, than our own, and are in no respect in the process of extinguishment, and whose annual expenditures, as a rule, are in excess of their ordinary revenues—in none of these three countries has the recent depreciation of the paper money been more than one-half as great as in the United States; the reason being that this paper money is not as much in excess as ours.*

* Austria abandoned specie payments in 1848. Yet by limiting the amount of legal-tender paper, she was on the eve of resuming specie payments in 1859, in spite of the disorganized condition of her political fabric which seemed to render an immediate dissolution probable. At that time, however, the Italian war broke out; new issues of paper money took place, and, as was to be expected, were at once followed by an advance in the premium on gold. Italy, with a population two-thirds as great as our own, although weighted with an enormous debt, and suffering from a permanent and almost hopeless deficit, has thus far limited the legal-tender currency of the kingdom to about ninety millions. As a consequence, the premium on gold ranges but from twelve to fourteen per cent.

But it is urged by some that no restriction should be laid upon the issue of currency, or any limitation of its amount be attempted; but that the people themselves should be left to determine the extent to which they will use it. This is sound doctrine when applied to currency subject to redemption. It is not true when applied to a currency whose sole constituent is credit, and which circulates by force of law. Credit currency is the alcohol of commerce; it alternately stimulates and depresses, but poisons all the time. It creates its own appetite. It would be as reasonable to leave the drunkard, whos system is thoroughly poisoned by alcoholic stimulants, to determine the quantity which is good for him, as it is to assume that the body of trade, debauched by currency stimulants originally forced upon it, will of its own choice absorb thereafter only so much as is conducive to its welfare. The parallel between the effects of artificial stimulants upon the human body and the effects of credit money upon the body industrial and commercial, holds good in every particular, as has been shown conspicuously by the experience of the United States since the inauguration of the present system. The first effects have been to excite to an abnormal action and to produce the false appearance of health and vigor. This in turn has been succeeded by a condition of depression, and the lassitude inevitably consequent upon undue excitement and the violation of the laws of nature. And it is precisely in this condition that the poor victim of drink cries out for "more rum," and the broken-down body of trade feels the strongest craving for fresh draughts of credit to carry it through the period of reaction and prostration.

Unpopular, therefore, as the declaration may be, the Commissioner, in view of the above considerations, is constrained to believe that contraction, direct and undisguised, is the one necessity of the situation; the only remedy for existing evils so far as the currency has relation to them, and that the nation cannot emerge from its embarrassments and difficulties until the makers and administrators of the law have the honesty and courage to take it up and carry it forward to the end.

TAXATION.

We come next to consider what remedial measures can be effected by a change in the existing system of taxation. But before attempting to reach any conclusions as to what ought to be done, it is necessary, in the first instance, to inquire what is actually feasible.

Taxation is seldom a matter of choice so much as of necessity; not the reason of the case, but the absolute exigencies of the government, deciding the question of imposition. Fortunately the United States, at the present moment, through increased efficiency in the collection of its taxes and a thorough and searching reduction of expenditures, is in a position to choose between taxes, and to decide upon pure economical considerations which should be retained and which remitted. With a surplus available for the reduction of taxation (after an ample provision for the reduction of the debt) like that which the government at present enjoys, it will be inexcusable if great advantages are not secured to industry. With the power to remit, by a single act, fifty millions of taxation, a magnificent opportunity is afforded for removing the burdens of the people, such as has never, apart from our own history, been the privilege of the legislature of any nation.

THE SURPLUS.

The excess of receipts over expenditures for the fiscal year ended June 30, 1869, was in round numbers forty-nine millions of dollars; and upon the supposition that no change is made in existing laws, we are warranted in assuming that, with an equal amount of expenditures, the same surplus will be realized during the present year, and this may safely be assumed as the basis of estimate. To this amount must be added two specific items of expenditure provided for out of the receipts of 1868–'69, which will not be carried over into the present year, and must therefore be reckoned as net gain to the treasury, namely: $13,000,000 on account of bounties, which now are substantially settled; $7,200,000 in gold, (equivalent to $9,350,000 in currency,) disbursed in payment for the Alaska purchase.

ELASTICITY OF THE REVENUE.*

The present annual elasticity of revenue, or its increase from the growth of the country, is another and most important element in determining the surplus of the future. It should be noted that, while the annual increase of capital in the United States, available for reproduction, is not probably equal to that of Great Britain, yet the more equal distribution of wealth among the people of the United States admits of a freer consumption, per capita, of most other articles, namely, sugar, coffee, spices, spirits, tobacco, and the like, which will bear the highest rates of taxation, and from which all governments find it convenient to raise the largest proportion of their revenue.

Now the average amount of national revenue which has been raised annually by the British government, through its various forms of taxation, for eight years past, namely, £70,000,000, ($350,000,000,) closely approximates to the annual amount which the revenue system of the United States, as at present constituted, is calculated to produce. The "elasticity" of the British revenue Mr. Gladstone found to average, from 1860 to 1866 inclusive, £1,780,000 ($8,900,000) per annum, or about two and a half per cent.; which increment has been annually applied, in part, for the reduction of taxes, especially the income tax, (which is always regarded as a reserve force in the British system, to be increased

*This is the term used by British financiers to describe the natural increase of revenue. It is evidently a misuse of the word. Growth is not elasticity. Elasticity is the property of a body by which it yields under pressure, but resumes its size or shape after that pressure is removed.

or diminished according to circumstances,) and in part to meet increasing expenditures.

If, then, we have the fact of a present revenue nearly of equal amount in the two countries, and a certain rate of increase in one, the question whether we may expect an equal rate of increase in the other, or that the increase would be more or less, will depend mainly upon two considerations: first, whether the present taxation presses more or less severely here than there—more or less nearly up to the strength of the people, (on the principle that, if the incidence of existing taxation in either country is really distressing and exhausting, a part at least of the otherwise naturnl increase, from the natural growth in population, might be absorbed for the relief and repair of economical interests that had suffered;) and, secondly, whether the rate of increase in population may be expected to be alike in both countries.

Both these considerations, in fact, favor the expectation of a freer and larger growth here. The present scale of taxation does not tell so heavily upon the people as in England, where the great body of wealth does, and, by the aristocratic constitution of the government, will, for a long time at least, escape its fair share of the public burdens. And at the same time it is notorious that the rate of increase in population here is greatly in excess of that of the United Kingdom. On the other hand, we have the consideration that the amount of realized and available capital, (the accumulation of past labor,) whether for the purposes of agriculture, manufactures, trade, or of luxurious consumption, is less with us; and, therefore, while our "hands" multiply faster, the tools they must use, and on which depends much of their success in production, are fewer, less adapted to their purposes, and rendered unnecessarily expensive at present by the peculiarities of our financial condition.

On the whole, after reviewing all the circumstances, the Commissioner is of the opinion *that the average annual "elasticity" of our present revenue, taking the years in groups of not less than three, will, for the present, average more than has been experienced in Great Britain, say from* $12,000,000 *to* $15,000,000 *per annum.* If the increase as thus estimated takes place, it will be in consequence of the freer circulation of society, conducing to a more rapid interchange of commodities; the more uniform distribution of wealth, allowing a larger consumption of certain taxed articles on which government obtains the largest revenue; and the higher rate of increase in population, in circumstances where no labor can, except under the most transient conditions, be in excess of the demand.

This conclusion finds support in the fact that in no year, since 1865, in which internal revenue taxes have been repealed or abated, has the revenue been found to decrease in proportion to the reductions; and this difference in favor of the revenue has apparently amounted to from twelve to twenty-four millions per annum.*

* In the foregoing discussion the Commissioner has purposely kept out of view the consideration whether the ability of the government to exact revenue, or of the people

V

GAIN FROM THE REFORM OF REVENUE ADMINISTRATION.

Taking the lowest figure we have named for the natural increase of the revenue for the current year, we shall have from this source twelve millions more added to the surplus thus far obtained. The further probable gain to the internal revenue from the more efficient administration of the laws and collection of taxes has recently been estimated by the Comissioner of Internal Revenue at fifteen millions; but as more than half of this amount was gained in the first three months of the present fiscal year, the estimate of the Commissioner may be regarded as very moderate. As the receipts from customs made a very considerable and somewhat unexpected advance during the past fiscal year, it is, perhaps, safest, in estimating the probable surplus of another year,

---

to render it, is helped or hindered, at the present time, by the abnormal monetary condition of the country; and whether, therefore, a return to a natural order of things, in this respect, would facilitate or retard the collection of taxes. It will be remembered that it was considered necessary, in order to carry through the gigantic loans which the necessities of the war demanded, to "float the bonds" by an issue of paper. Now it was not supposed, by anybody that this act added one cubit to the industrial stature of the nation, or that it increased by a single dollar the real amount of property which the people had to contribute or the government could reach by taxation. Yet, notwithstanding this plain truth, it was then fully believed by the great majority of business men, as by the majority in Congress, that the negotiation of the loans actually depended on this measure of flooding the money market with legal-tender. And, while some able financiers doubted whether the step was absolutely necessary, and thought that, in view of ultimate consequences, it should be avoided if it were possible to raise the money without it, there probably was no one who doubted that the loan negotiated would be collected far *more easily* under such conditions.

The question now is, whether the present facility of taxation is due to the continuance, in part, of the same causes, and may be expected to suffer, in any degree, by the return of specie payments; or, on the contrary, whether the present incidence of taxation be more painful and less productive, by reason of the derangement of trade and the increasing discouragement of industry, especially in those branches which look to foreign countries for a market. The present causes are unquestionably operative to a very great extent; and the question is, in which direction? The Commissioner thinks there can be no doubt at all as to the way in which they influence the substantial prosperity of the country; but the ease of taxation and the convenience of finance are not always coincident with the best condition of the people. Facility of revenue may be an evil, and not a good; and the very causes which are working permanent injury to industry may also prove for the temporary benefit of the exchequer—just as lotteries, the manufacture and sale of ardent spirits, and the licensed indulgence of vice, are notoriously more gainful to government, as well as less painful to those who pay, than the contributions exacted of honest and sober industries. All governments have found a fruitful source of revenue in the lower appetites and passions of their people; and the same unnatural excitement which stimulates over-trading and general industrial profligacy may increase the receipts of the Treasury. In a word, enhanced revenues may be one of the ways which an inflated and irredeemable currency takes to deplete and distress a people.

It seems, therefore, to the Commissioner that there can be no doubt that, other things equal—population and production remaining stationary—it will be much harder to raise $350,000,000 of revenue in 1871, should specie payments then have been restored, than it is now—if for no other reason than that those three hundred and fifty millions would then be *real dollars*. But the expenses of the government ought not,

with reference to the question of reducing taxation, to estimate the receipts from this source at the figures of the last fiscal year, 1868–'69, viz, $180,000,000. The experience of the past five months of the current fiscal year indicates, however, a decided gain in the above figures.

REDUCTION OF EXPENDITURES.

The gain from this source, including the reduction of the interest charge consequent on the reduction of the principal of the debt, is estimated by the Secretary of the Treasury at twenty-six millions of dollars.*

---

need not, to remain the same. Many of its charges, to be sure, are permanently fixed, like those on our debt. The present grade of salaries, moreover, being generally lower than the average of private employment, and not much above ante-war figures, would not probably be retrenched greatly on the first return of specie payments. But there are other and important charges of government which should decline equally with the great decline in the prices of merchandise and labor that must accompany a restoration to financial soundness. And while the amount of these charges, which would be fair subjects of such a reduction, in the event of a general fall of prices, is not, perhaps, equal to the amount of those charges which must be regarded as more fixed in their character, yet it is certain that the present enhancement of the former, by means of an inflated and suspended currency, much exceeds the premium on gold which measures the enhancement of the charge of the debt, the diplomatic service, &c., &c. It would require an immense amount of labor, with access to all the vouchers for expenditures in some past year, to make any estimate, in figures, of the degree to which the expenditures might be reduced by the mere return to specie payments; but the Commissioner has sufficient confidence in the revenue capabilities of the country to believe that the people will bear all the proper charges of government then as easily as they do their present burdens.

And even of those charges which are regarded as fixed, it is reasonably certain that a considerable portion might be retrenched in the event of a restoration of specie payments, and the reduction of the general prices of the country within healthful and natural limits. The charge of the debt most assuredly can and ought to be the first to undergo reduction by any means consistent with the public faith.

This discussion of the influence of a return to financial soundness upon the revenue capabilities of the country has assumed that population and production remain constant. What advance in those elements may fairly be predicated from the experience of the last quarter century the Commissioner has already attempted to exhibit.

* The following table exhibits the actual expenditures for the first quarter, and the expenditures for the second, third, and fourth quarters, of the present fiscal year, as estimated by the Secretary of the Treasury:

	Actual—1st qr., 1869–'70.	Estimated—2d, 3d and 4th qrs., 1869–'70.	Aggregate—Actual and estimated.	Actual—1868-'9.
Civil service	$15, 102, 202 05	$40, 000, 000 00	$55, 102, 202 05	$56, 474, 061 53
Indians and pensions	13, 547, 942 79	21, 000, 000 00	34, 547, 942 79	35, 519, 544 84
War Department	13, 595, 468 05	40, 500, 000 00	54, 095, 468 05	78, 501, 990 61
Navy Department	5, 782, 630 96	14, 000, 000 00	19, 782, 630 96	20, 000, 757 97
Interest on public debt	37, 452, 270 74	93, 750, 000 00	131, 202, 270 74	130, 694, 242 80
Premium on 7. 30 U. S. notes				300, 000 00
Total	85, 480, 514 59	209, 250, 000 00	294, 730, 514 59	321, 490, 597 75

Reduction of expenditures for 1868–'9, $26,760,023 16.

TOTAL SURPLUS.

The sum of these several items added to the surplus of last year make up the large aggregate of one hundred and twenty-four millions. Yet the most careful examination of the several elements fails to detect any degree of misstatement or overestimate. The whole calculation, however, assumes that the laws imposing taxation remain unaltered, and that the industry of the year will enjoy an average of success.

DISPOSITION OF THE SURPLUS.

The possession of a surplus so large invests with more than ordinary interest the question of its disposition. Shall the whole of this sum be applied to the reduction of the principal of the national debt, or shall a fair proportion of it be remitted to the people by the abatement or removal of their taxes? Of these two courses the Commissioner unhesitatingly declares his conviction that the latter is the more expedient—if indeed it is not absolutely imperative; demanded alike by the highest economical considerations and by the almost unanimous sentiment of the people. With this view he proposes that the sum of fifty millions be taken as the measure of the taxes to be removed or reduced; and that such reduction should be directed, first, to relieving industry as much as possible of unnecessary burdens, and allowing it to obtain its material at the minimum cost; and secondly, to the diminution of the cost of the elements of living to the great mass of the people, in their capacity as consumers, irrespective of the consideration whether they are or are not also producers of wealth.

With this object it is proposed to consider, first, what taxes can be best removed or abated under the head of Internal Revenue.

The three principal sources of receipts under the internal revenue are the taxes on distilled spirits and fermented liquors, on tobacco, and on incomes. The rate of taxation on the first two of these has been fixed at a standard which the experience of the past year has proved to be most productive. The taxes on whisky, beer, and tobacco should not, in the opinion of the Commissioner, be modified, unless it is desired to repeat the disagreeable experiences of former years and to perpetuate the power of corrupt organizations. No change can be made, either to raise or lower the rates, which will not, at least temporarily, inure to the benefit of other interests than those of the Treasury.

THE INCOME TAX.

The tax levied under this head is of a different character, and demands essential modification. The Commissioner would recommend that, beginning with the next regular assessment, the present rate of five per cent. be reduced to three per cent. upon the net income of individuals. The reason for this recommendation is that the tax of five per cent. is excessive and constitutes a real grievance, being greater than that ever imposed by any other nation, except in extraordinary national exigencies. An additional reason is that an assessment of three per cent. would probably yield to the treasury a sum very nearly equal to that at present collected; inasmuch as, while the reduction of the rate would afford a great and welcome relief to the classes who now pay, it would at the same time bring within reach of the tax great numbers who now either avoid giving in lists at all, or, while doing so, force the constituents of their income so as to escape contribution entirely. The tax as fixed at present is evidently too high for revenue purposes, and is passing through much the same experience as the whisky tax when at its maximum. It should be also borne in mind that the true measure of the *onus* or burden of any tax is the sum which it would yield if fully and honestly collected; the fact that some portions of it are not collected bringing no relief to the community, if, indeed, that fact does not work an additional injury, by placing the honest tax-payer at a disadvantage in comparison with his neighbor or business competitor who escapes.

In connection with this reduction of the general rate, the Commissioner would recommend that, while the absolute exemption to all persons should be allowed to remain as now fixed, namely, at $1,000, the exemption on account of Rent should not be left indefinite, as at present, but should be strictly limited to an amount sufficient only to relieve from taxation the rentals of the laboring classes, for instance, $200. It is evident that no claim can be made for the exemption of rent to any extent, which would not be equally valid in support of the exemption of any other expenditure; and certainly high rents are as much a luxury as any form of expenditure, and as little deserving of economical sympathy. If the recommendation of the Commissioner in regard to the exemption of rentals should be adopted, he is confident that, notwithstanding the reduction of the tax from five to three per cent., the amount that will accrue to the treasury from this source will not be impaired; and, but for the unfavorable condition of industry during the past year, there is great reason to believe that a very decided gain would be realized. But though the amount yielded would in this case be equal or greater, the change would constitute a marked relief to the community, inasmuch as a larger proportion than now would be contributed by the classes best able to afford it, and who owe most to the protection of the government.

In respect to the proposition, seriously advocated in many quarters, that this tax should be wholly removed, the Commissioner thinks that the attention of the country should be called to the fact that this tax was paid during the year 1868 by so small a number as 250,000 persons out of the entire population, yet representing an aggregate income of not less than $800,000,000, exclusive of the amounts remitted by reason of rents and the minor exemptions. Allowing, then, for the families of these 250,000 contributors, it is evident that only about a million of the population are interested in having the tax removed, while the remaining thirty-eight and a half millions of the people are interested in having it maintained.

To sum up what has been said upon the income tax, the Commissioner is of the opinion that a reduction of the rate of assessment from five to three per cent. upon individual incomes, without any other change in the law, would not reduce the receipts from this source by more than five millions of dollars at the outside; while, if the exemption of rent were to be limited as suggested, or even fixed at five hundred dollars, there would be no falling off nor abatement in the receipts.

MISCELLANEOUS TAXES.

There then remains a large body of minor and miscellaneous taxes under the internal revenue, which together yielded in 1868 less than fifty millions of dollars. Of these the Commissioner would recommend that the taxes embraced in what is known as "Schedule A," viz, the taxes assessed on watches, silver plate, pianos, billiard tables, and carriages, should be entirely remitted. They are inquisitorial in character, highly offensive in collection, petty and contemptible in the revenue yielded. If these taxes are intended to have a sumptuary bearing, they are altogether out of the sympathies of modern civilization; if their object is to secure revenue, they are absurd failures. Ten times the amount could be obtained with the same effort in some other direction, and without exciting half as much of odium and hostility.

As best calculated to carry out the two objects proposed at the outset of this inquiry, the Commissioner would further recommend the repeal of the following taxes, now levied under the internal revenue:

1st. The whole body of what is known as special taxes or licenses—those levied on banks and bankers, and upon manufacturers and dealers in spirits, beer, and tobacco, being, however, retained. The loss of revenue on this account will not be in excess of ten millions of dollars.

2d. The taxes on the gross receipts of railroads, stage coaches, insurance, telegraph, and express companies, canals, ferries, ships, barges, and steamboats. The loss of revenue from this source will not be in excess of seven millions of dollars.*

3d. The taxes on the sales of articles not otherwise specifically taxed. The receipts from this source will approximate eight millions of dollars.

Allowing, then, for the extreme possible loss under incomes, the amount of taxation above proposed to be remitted to the people in consideration of the present large and increasing surplus of receipts over expenditures, would be in the neighborhood of twenty-six millions of dollars.

*As illustrating the excessive rate and burdensome character of those taxes, it has been officially shown that in the case of the largest telegraph company in the United States, the direct taxes now levied are sufficient to absorb the entire profit on one-seventh of the entire gross receipts from all sources. If to this was to be added the increased cost of wire and chemicals, due to the influence of the tariff, the aggregate of taxation for this particular business would be represented by much larger figures.

THE TARIFF.

We come next to the consideration of the expediency of changes to be made under the tariff in view of the present condition of industry and the important fact of a large and increasing surplus. The discussion of this question, however, is attended by this peculiarity: that it has hitherto been impossible for any one to suggest any reduction or modification whatever, looking to the abatement of prices artificially maintained in the interest of special industries, without being immediately assailed with accusations of corrupt and unpatriotic motives. These cries have thus far had the effect for which alone they are raised, namely, to prevent discussion, and to divert the attention of the people from the real and true issues. These issues do not at present involve either the theory of free trade or the fact of protection. The questions arising are practical questions purely, concerning only the expediency of individual and specific taxes. The question in each case is a question of proportion between the benefit known or supposed to accrue from the maintenance of the tax to a class or section of the community, and the relief which would be afforded to the whole of that community by the removal or reduction of the tax. However doctrinaires or extremists on either side may declaim, it is unquestionably true that, in the condition of public feeling as it has been, and at any stage of political philosophy heretofore reached in this country, a tax imposed under the tariff which could be proved to be necessary to the maintenance of an industry already established; which employs large numbers of workmen and distributes fairly among them a due proportion of the profits of manufacture; more especially if such manufacture prepares an article for direct and immediate consumption in sufficient quantity to meet the demands of the country; it is not to be denied that, whether wisely or not in the largest view of the case, the past temper of the American people has approved of such a tax. But it is furthermore equally true, and will shortly be found so to the satisfaction of any skeptic, that the advance in sentiment and the diffusion of knowledge among the people on this subject within the last two years has been such that, when it can be proved that any tax thus laid upon the community *is not necessary* to maintain a protected industry in a moderate degree of prosperity; if, moreover, the industry be one which, whatever its absolute proportions, yet contributes to the general wealth and welfare less than it requires; if it be one which yields its profits mainly to the capitalist, instead of dividing the returns equitably among large classes of skilled or ordinary operatives; and especially if it be one whose product is to become in turn the raw material of other and still more extensive industries, so that the enhancement of price at the bottom is repeated through the several successive stages, and thus becomes a tax not only on the final consumer but on each intermediate producer—in such cases the people of the United States will exercise their right to think and to speak of such a tax, whoever may seek to intimidate the official or unofficial organs of public sentiment; and will exercise an independent judgment without respect to the will of highly organized and aggressive associations of capitalists, as to the amount in which that tax shall be reduced, or the time in which it shall be wholly removed. And those who deprecate such reforms, be they parties or individuals, will find, however much they may appeal "to the fathers," that "the children's teeth are set on edge."

THE TRUE PRINCIPLES OF TARIFF REFORM.

The experience of the last few years has been equivalent to a demonstration that any attempt to reconstruct the tariff as a whole, on any basis of principle, is practically impossible; the diverse interests of the different sections of industries being sufficiently powerful under almost any circumstances to ingraft upon a bill during its passage such modifications as would effectually deprive it of any pretensions to consistency or harmony. There would therefore seem to be but one available method of tariff reform; which is to adopt the same course that has been taken in respect to the reforms heretofore made in the internal revenue, and which furthermore finds a precedent in all the experience of Great Britain in legislating upon these subjects, viz: to make such modifications or removals of duties, year by year, as experience or the condition of the Treasury may indicate as practicable and desirable; and thus, by pruning, rather than by reconstruction, to gradually attain the greatest degree of simplicity and effectiveness with the least possible burden upon industry and the people. With the adoption of this method of reform as a matter of expediency, the following principle should also be insisted upon as fundamental, viz:

That the maintenance of an average duty of forty-seven per cent., as under the existing tariff, upon all dutiable imports, is excessive and unnecessary, and opposed alike to the highest interests of civilization and humanity, as well as to the proper and healthy growth of all domestic commerce and industry; and that under no circumstances, except for the supplying of certain technical omissions in existing laws, or for the sole and avowed purpose of revenue, should any increase of rate be hereafter permitted.

On such a basis, the work sought to be accomplished in the way of reform would naturally divide itself under two heads: First, reforms made purely and solely in the interest of revenue and administration; and second, reforms having in view the relief of industry from contributions, a small portion only of which accrues to the Treasury; and also a reduction to the minimum of the contributions exacted from that large portion of the community who are consumers of taxed articles without being in turn the producers of protected products.

In respect to reforms pertaining to the first head there can be no essential difference in the policy of any party, inasmuch as the only question which can arise concerning any proposition will be in regard to the accuracy and completeness of the facts alleged. A fundamental consideration, furthermore, in this connection, by universal admission, is that the number of impositions should be made as few as is consistent with the obtaining of the amount of necessary revenue. The people of the United States cannot afford to have a tax collected, for revenue purposes simply, which yields less than half a million of dollars per annum, as a smaller sum affords no compensation for the necessary disturbance to trade and the trouble and expense of collection. On the other hand, the government should particularly refrain, in the collection of its revenue, from affording any opportunity for evasion and fraud to the dishonest importer which will put his honest competitor at disadvantage. To fret and divert the course of trade by petty obstructions of the character of many now forming a part of the existing tariff, and which have no probable or possible relation to American industry or to the policy advocated by any school of economists, is both useless and mischievous. Of such a nature are the taxes on quicksilver, seaweed, coal-oil, glycerine, gum-benzoin, lard, manufactures of platinum, annato, paving-stones, and bamboo, which, during the fiscal year 1868, yielded severally to the Treasury sums varying from $10 40 to $579, and an aggregate revenue of $1,475 50. The experience of every year, moreover, affords fresh evidence that in nearly every instance where the amount of duty imposed on any article of small bulk is disproportionate to its value and excessive in rate, the business of importing passes to a greater or less degree out of the hands of the legitimate trade, and into the control of the contrabandist and illicit dealer. Most noticeable examples of the truth of this assertion are to be found in the case of segars, camel's-hair shawls, nearly all expensive chemical preparations, the costly varieties of lace, some varieties of spice, and precious stones in settings. On this last the duty collected on the importations of 1868 was $366, and from morphine and its salts the total revenue was $160. A leading house engaged in the importation of cloves thus writes to the Commissioner: "From 1857 to 1862 we imported 1,258,641 pounds of cloves from Zanzibar. Of that quantity 1,222,114 pounds were entered for consumption, the duty being from four to eight cents per pound. From 1862 to 1869 our importation of cloves from the same place was 779,091 pounds, of which 349,267 pounds were entered for consumption, and the balance sold in bond. What was done with them we know not, but have reason to suppose that, as the duty was from fifteen to twenty cents per pound, (gold,) they were smuggled back into the country. The importation of cloves, both in New York and Boston, has been large during the last few years, and, if our information is correct, sold mostly in bond. A duty of ten cents per pound on cloves and five cents on clove-stems would, I feel sure, yield a large revenue, and also protect the honest trader." The article of musk is one also in which the regular importation is reported to the Commissioner to have entirely ceased, although the domestic consumption remains mainly as before. Whatever of business remains is concentrated in the hands of a single dealer in New York City, who, by making the matter a specialty, is enabled to supply promptly all demands of the trade, and on terms so favorable as to admit of no competition.

In short, of the two thousand articles which are specifically catalogued upon the list of dutiable imports, it is probable that at least one-third might be immediately placed upon the free list without seriously diminishing the revenue, and with great benefit to the trade, industry, and morals of the country.

In the inauguration and carrying out of reforms in the tariff of the character indicated under this first head there would seem to be, as already remarked, but little occasion for difference of opinion; but when we come to propositions for reform in tariff taxation having in view a reduction of the cost of domestic production and consumption, the case is different. Against such reforms every special interest whose profits, although possibly excessive, are like to be diminished, arrays itself; and it is broadly taken for granted that whatever of legistation will prove advantageous to the few will, at least, bring nothing of detriment to the many. But it is from the effects of legislation which, intentionally or otherwise, has, since 1862, been based on just this principle, coupled with legislation based on no principle or intelligence whatever, that the country now more especially demands relief. And although the truth of this assertion has been sufficiently substantiated by a large body of evidence submitted by the Commissioner in his previous reports, yet the importance of the subject renders it desirable that such further facts as the experience of another year has afforded should also be made public. To a brief statement of these, therefore, and to the recommendations which the facts naturally suggest, the Commissioner would next ask attention.

INCIDENTAL INFLUENCE OF INCREASING THE DUTY UPON COPPER.

A striking illustration of the injurious effect of attempting to exceptionally foster one of a series of interconnected and interdependent industries is afforded by a certain curious experience that has followed the passage of the enactment of February, 1869, increasing the duties upon copper. By this bill the duty on all manufactures of which copper constituted a chief component was uniformly increased to forty-five per cent., and included in its provisions was an article known as Dutch metal, extensively used in the manufacture of paper-hangings as a substitute for gold-leaf, and on which a duty had formerly been levied of ten per cent. The result which followed such legislation is briefly told in the following extract from a statement presented to the Commissioner by leading representatives of the paper-hanging industry of the country:

"The article of 'Dutch metal,' or 'Florence leaf,' is all imported—mostly from Germany. It is composed of an alloy of copper and zinc, and is beaten out by hand like gold leaf. It cannot possibly be made in this country, even if the present duty was increased, owing to the high price of labor, inasmuch as nearly the whole cost of the article represents the labor of beating it out, the cost of the material itself being a mere nothing. Heretofore the duty on this article has been ten per cent., but under the provisions of the recent bill increasing the duties on copper the rate has been increased to forty-five per cent. When the duty was ten per cent. we did not complain; but the increase to forty-five per cent. has been too much for us, and *we have all been obliged to increase the price of our goods from five to twenty-five cents per roll, according to the quantity of leaf used on each roll. The consequence is that the trade are all complaining of a falling off in the sales of our goods, owing to the high price, and the difficulty of making the consumer understand the reason why we charge more for them.*"

Now although it may be said, and with truth, that there was no intention, in increasing the duties upon copper, to increase the duties upon Dutch metal, the fact, nevertheless, remains, that the increase in question was effected; that sufficient consideration was never given to the measure to fully understand the extent and scope of its influence, and that thereby serious detriment was inflicted upon an industry which, in 1860, employed directly more than one-fifth as many operatives as at that time were engaged in copper mining.

RELATION OF THE TARIFF TO THE MANUFACTURE OF LEATHER.

A similar but more extensive illustration of the injurious influence of taxation originally imposed and afterward maintained under the tariff, most probably through lack of information or want of consideration, is to be found in an analysis of the present cost of the manufacture of leather and its principal products.

Thus, for example, the value of the product of leather of various kinds in the United States for the year 1868 was about $124,000,000. Now it is susceptible of demonstration that the cost of this product was enhanced, by reason of the duties imposed on the materials which enter into its composition, to an average of from eight to ten per cent., or to an aggregate of nearly ten millions of dollars as a minimum; while the whole amount of revenue which passed into the Treasury during the fiscal year 1868, from the duties levied on undressed hides and skins, animal oils, and tanning material, was not in excess of two and one-half millions; or, in other words, for every two and a half dollars which the government took under the tariff for the purpose of revenue it indirectly imposed seven and a half dollars more upon consumers of an indispensable article in the first stages of its production.*

* In illustration and support of the above statement the Commissioner submits the following table, (prepared by an expert,) showing the relative cost of the manufacture

It is further to be noted of the duties which thus augment the cost of leather, that while, on account of the present surplus in the Treasury, they are not needed for revenue, they cannot pretend to claim continuance on the ground of protection. Thus, of the hides required in the first instance, the domestic production is only sufficient for about seventy per cent. of the domestic consumption. Before the war American leather was largely exported, and even to England; while the slow process of tanning abroad, the absence of hemlock bark, the necessity of relying almost exclusively upon chemicals to supply the place of tannin, coupled with the lack of mechanical appliances—all these are sufficient guarantees that the United States can never, under any circumstances, be exposed to serious competition in this department of industry. Of the oils used in currying, furthermore, we possess so great a control of the market, that in 1868 the entire imports of such oils amounted to the small sum of $3,510.

But large as is the sum by which these unnecessary duties increase the cost of leather, the whole story, in its bearing upon the consumer, has not been told. Taxes thus laid upon what may be termed the basic materials of a series of industries repeat and enlarge themselves at every stage, and thus become a burden upon every intermediate producer before accumulating upon the ultimate consumer. This is strikingly exemplified in the industry under consideration.

It has been shown in the case of leather that the cost of the annual product is increased directly, by reason of the tariff, to the extent of about ten millions. If we turn next to the manufacture of boots and shoes, the analysis of a single department presents the following exhibit:

---

of waxed upper leather under the existing tariff, or with its constituent materials free of duty:

	Existing tariff.	Duty free.
Rio Grande or Buenos Ayres hides, 100 lbs., costing 22½ cts. gold	$22 50	$20 45
Premium on gold, (135)	7 87	7 15
Commission paid by tanner for buying and credit	1 51	1 38
Cost of tanning with bark $15 per cord	12 00	....
Cost of tanning with bark free of duty, or $13 50 per cord	....	10 80
Cost of currying with oil at 90 cts. per gallon	8 70	....
Cost of currying with oil free of duty, 74 cts. per gallon	....	8 20
Interest six months, at 7 per cent	1 84	1 64
Commission, paid by tanner for selling, (5 per cent.)	2 85	2 60
Product: 180 ft. of wax leather and 15 lbs. of splits, costing	57 27	52 22
Value of the same, apportioned, viz:		
15 lbs. of splits	34 cts. per lb.	32 cts. per lb.
180 ft. waxed leather	28. 98 per ft.	26. 30 per ft.

$28\frac{98}{100}$ less $26\frac{30}{100} = 2\frac{68}{100}$ cents per foot reduction of cost by remission of duty, thus proving that an addition of about ten per cent. is now made to the cost of this variety of leather through the existence and continuance of the present duties.

The number of pairs of boots and shoes manufactured for men's and youths' wear in 1868 is estimated by the trade at 51,500,000, possessing an aggregate value, at an average of $2½ per pair, of $129,750,000. Now, an examination of the various elements which enter into the composition of these products—made for the Commissioner by experts—affords a demonstration that the aggregate cost as above given is enhanced by reason of the tariff to the extent of about 7½ per cent.,* or upwards of nine millions of dollars; a sum nearly equal to the enhanced cost which, by reason of the duties, accrues on the whole annual domestic product of leather. But boots and shoes for men and boys' wear constitute but a part of the product of the boot and shoe industry; for during the year 1868 there were also manufactured boots and shoes for women, misses, and children to an estimated number of 47,000,000 pairs, possessing an aggregate value of $98,500,000. If we suppose the cost of these products to be enhanced by reason of the tariff to the same extent as in the case of the boots and shoes manufactured for men and boys, we must further carry to the account of indirect taxation, to be paid by the consumer, the additional sum of $7,387,500; making a total unnecessary burden annually imposed upon consumers of boots and shoes in the United States of more than fifteen millions of dollars.

One further statement is necessary to complete this exhibit. As already stated, the product of women's, misses', and children's shoes is about 47,000,000 pairs per annum. Of these it is estimated that at least 15,000,000 pairs are composed in part of two fabrics of wool, technically known as "lasting" and "serge." Shoes thus fabricated are worn by all classes of women, the lasting and serge being materials well adapted to the climate of all seasons, very light, very durable, and, unlike leather, suffering but little deterioration when worn under rubbers in wet weather. The present import of lasting and serges to meet the requirements of the boot and shoe industry is estimated at about 3,000,000 yards, possessing a value of eighty-seven cents (gold) per yard, or $2,610,000, or in currency, (with gold at 133⅓,) $3,480,000.

* *Table showing the comparative cost of the manufacture of men's standard, first quality, sixteen-inch leg kip boots under the existing tariff, and with the materials directly or indirectly used in manufacture admitted free of duty.*

	Taxed.	Free.
Cost of uppers, per dozen	$20 46	$18 67
Cost of soles, per dozen	8 04	7 44
Labor	8 00	8 00
Finding, &c	2 00	1 70
Interest six months, at seven per cent	1 35	1 20
Commission for selling, at six per cent	2 53	2 36
Cost of twelve pairs of boots	42 38	39 37

$42 38 — 39 37 = $3 01 per dozen, which is equivalent to an addition of $7\frac{64}{100}$ per cent. to the cost of boots of the above description by reason of the imposition and continuance of the existing tariff taxes.

On these imports the price is enhanced by reason of the duties as follows:

Specific duty 50 cents per pound, (13 pounds per piece)......	$650,000
Ad valorem duty..	507,000
Total gold value of duties..........................	1,157,000
Total currency value of do., gold at 133⅓............	1,542,666

which sum represents the burden annually imposed, first, on one department of the largest specific branch of industry in the country; and secondly upon the whole female population, who are consumers of these products. And for what? Certainly not for revenue; and then, if for protection, for the interest of one or two small establishments in Massachusetts, employing but few hands and a limited capital. Or, to put the case differently, the government, to all intents and purposes, has in addition to all its other business become a partner in the lasting and serge business, and runs one or two small establishments at an expense to the people of $1,500,000 currency per annum—a sum greater than is at present annually required to defray the expenditures of the whole foreign intercourse of the country.

But this does not comprise all the direct taxes imposed upon this class of manufactures. Nearly one-half of the lasting and serge goods are fitted with elastic gores made of rubber webbing inserted in the sides. This material is nearly all imported, and pays from thirty-five to sixty per cent. duties ad valorem. These duties, it is represented to the Commissioner by the trade, are equivalent to a tax of *five* cents per pair on all the goods using webbing as a constituent of their composition. We conclude this analysis by an extract from a statement submitted to the Commissioner by leading representatives of this branch of the boot and shoe industry: "Before the war a cheap gaiter boot for women's wear was sold for sixty cents; now the same article commands $1 05. Before the war there was a large and increasing demand for export of our goods for South America, Central America, Mexico, and the West Indies; but now, owing to the largely increased cost of the same goods, this trade is almost entirely cut off, except a very limited demand for Cuba."

The result which might be expected to follow from a removal of the above referred-to duties is thus expressed in a recent number of the American Workman, a paper published in the interest of the "Crispin," or shoemakers' union of the United States:

"The workmen" (in this branch of industry) "have suffered, as every one admits, for several years, for lack of steady employment. The quantity of boots and shoes now required for use is not in proportion to the number of shoe workmen; consequently in New England there has been full work for them only *ten* months of the year, and so wages have been low. With the removal of the duties referred to the increase which would follow in the quantity of boots and shoes to be made would be sufficient to cause these men to be fully employed all the year, and then there would be but little difficulty in adjusting the rate of wages."

In view of these facts and considerations, the Commissioner submits the following recommendations:

First. That the importation of hides and skins of every description, and all leather except morocco, japanned and patent leather, be hereafter admitted free of duty. It has been shown above to what extent the existing duty of ten per cent. forms a burden upon the production and manufacture of boots and shoes for American consumption, and upon the production of leather to be used in that manufacture. An additional and even stronger reason for the removal of the tax is found in the fact that the present duty is, so far as the most careful canvass of the trade allows the Commissioner to determine, the only obstacle to the revival of the export of leather and its manufactures from the United States at the present time. The Commissioner must not be understood that no other cause operates to put the American producer at a disadvantage in this line of articles; but that, notwithstanding the injurious effects of an inflated and irredeemable currency upon this as upon all other branches of business, the superior endowments and facilities enjoyed by this country for the making of leather, and for the manufacture of articles from it, particularly boots and shoes, are so decided and considerable as to afford very strong assurance that, by removing the duties on hides and skins, leather could again be exported in great quantities; while, by reducing the cost of leather to the manufacturer, the export of boots and shoes to the British Provinces and to Central and South America and Australia, which formed so considerable a part of that trade before the war, will revive at an early date. It is very suggestive in this connection that hides and skins are now being imported from South America into Canada, (landed at New York and sent clear across the United States under bond for exportation) tanned there, and exported to England in large amounts; and that in consequence of the advantage enjoyed by the trade in Canada from the absence of duties upon the material, some of the most important American establishments upon the frontier have been moved across the line and are sharing in the benefit of a production which enjoys access to all the markets of the world.

It must be remembered that the cost of labor (which is the element of production on account of which protective duties are especially claimed) is comparatively inconsiderable in the manufacture of leather. At the same time, the United States, as the producer of this article, enjoys the advantage of cheaper tanning materials and more perfect and extensive apparatus and machinery than any other country in the world. Bark, which in England costs from $25 to $35 a cord, can be had here of equally good quality for $5 and upwards, according to locality, the greater portion used probably not exceeding $6. The American superiority in processes and machinery is no less marked. Splitting machines are but little used in England, leather being generally reduced to the required thickness by the old-fashioned method of shaving down, which is equally wasteful of labor and of material. So far is this true that, even since the total cessation of our export of leather, "splits" have been shipped in considerable quantities to England, for the reason that they are not made there to any extent.

The manufacture of boots and shoes has experienced the same effects from the imposition of duties as the raw material. Indeed, the duty upon hides may be taken as the measure of the duties successively laid upon manufactures from them; that is, the duty on hides is the only thing which makes a duty on leather necessary. Give the tanners and leather-dressers of the country free hides, and they will need, and will ask, no protection against imported leather. Again, give the boot and shoe manufacturers their material at such prices as could be afforded with free leather, and they will need no protection against imported boots and shoes. Indeed, they hardly require any at the present time for the purpose of commanding the domestic market, even though their material is taxed as it is. The processes of manufacture are so much better understood here than abroad, that in both quality and price the American trade article of pegged goods is superior to any of French or English manufacture; and it is only the enhancement of the cost of production by the duty under consideration which prevents the exportation of boots and shoes at the present time from the United States to a very great extent.

Second. The Commissioner would further recommend the free importation of hemlock or other barks used for tanning; of sumac, and of the fabrics of wool known as lasting and serge, when the same are woven or made in patterns of size, shape, and form, and cut in such manner as to be fit for shoes or bootees exclusively, and not combined with India-rubber.

RELATION OF THE TARIFF TO THE COST OF IRON.

The examples of tariff influence in increasing cost and restricting production and consumption, thus far cited, are of such a character that it would seem to be only necessary to present a clear statement of the facts in order to insure a prompt remedy. We now propose to cite some illustrations of a class of cases where excessive and unnecessary duties have been imposed and maintained, with a view of enhancing the cost of articles indispensable to many other branches of production; and this, too, with a full knowledge and demonstration of the fact that the detriment thereby brought to industry in general, far outweighs any measure of benefit which can possibly accrue to the special or class interest thus favored. Of such cases the article of pig iron constitutes a conspicuous example.

The average expenditure requisite to produce a ton of pig iron in the United States at the present time, including a liberal interest upon the capital invested and a fair allowance for repairs and incidentals, may be fairly estimated at from $24 to $26, currency; and as confirmatory of this estimate, the Commissioner submits the following evidence:

In a letter under date of September 2, 1869, Mr. George T. Lewis, of Clarksville, Tennessee, who is endorsed as one of the most intelligent and experienced iron manufacturers of the Southwest, says: On the line of the Nashville and Chattanooga railroad, pig iron can be made *and delivered* in Nashville at a cost of $19 per ton, currency. In the city of Nashville itself Mr. Lewis states the present cost, including interest on capital and incidentals, at $22 60, currency, per ton. At Carondelet, Missouri, Mr. S. Waterhouse, of St. Louis, in a letter under date of February 20, 1869, states the cost of making pig iron, including an allowance of $1 50 per ton for interest, taxes, and insurance, at $25, currency, per ton; and adds, this "is not an estimate, but an exhibit copied from the books of the company." The distance of Carondelet from St. Louis, a central market, is six and a quarter miles. An estimate furnished by one of the largest iron-works at Pittsburg, Pennsylvania, gives $27 98 as the cost per ton when ore of sixty-six per cent. is used, and an allowance made of eighty cents per ton for interest and twenty-five cents per ton for repairs and incidentals. In the valley of the Cumberland, and in the anthracite districts of Pennsylvania, and at Scranton, the Commissioner is informed by those conversant with the business that the average cost of manufacture in the case of furnaces favorably situated, under good management, and with coal at ordinary prices, is not in excess of from $24 to $26 per ton, and in some instances is much less than this figure. These estimates, furthermore, it should be observed, include a liberal interest on the capital invested, which is turned on an average from two to three times per annum.

The mean market price of pig iron in Great Britain for the year 1867-'68, taking Welsh pig (the best quality) as a standard, was £4 3*s.* 9*d.*, ($20 39,) or (with gold at 133) $27 12.

The average price of all the varieties of pig iron in the principal markets of the United States for the past year is estimated by the secretary of the American Iron and Steel Association at $35 25 per net ton. Other recognized authorities report a higher average to the Commissioner, viz: from $36 to $36 50 and $37 50 as a fair average in New York City. The average value at the furnaces of the Lehigh Valley during the past year has been about $38 for No. 1, $36 for No. 2, and $34 for No. 3. It is therefore obvious that, adopting the minimum market price, and allowing for the cost of one hundred miles of railroad transportation, the price of pig iron to the American consumers has been unnecessarily enhanced during the past year to an average of *from eight to ten dollars per ton;* the result of which, in short, is, that, while the average cost of producing pig iron, reckoned on a gold basis, is but little, if any, in excess of the average cost in Great Britain, and less than the average cost of production upon the continent of Europe, the price of iron to the consumer in the United States is greater than in any other civilized commercial and manufacturing nation.

Now, it is not necessary for the Commissioner to enter into any extended argument to show the disadvantage under which the United States is placed as a nation by reason of this state of things, be the cause what it may. The mere fact of an increased cost is of itself a sufficient and unanswerable argument for an immediate abatement of the same at almost any sacrifice; inasmuch as iron is the essential element of modern civilization, and whatever enhances its price restricts its consumption and use, increases the cost of all production and transportation, and checks development. A striking illustration of the truth of this is to be found in the fact that there is to-day upon all of the inland lakes and canals of the United States hardly a single boat or vessel constructed of iron engaged in the transportation of merchandise, although the introduction of such boats or vessels, by reason of their smaller displacement, would be equivalent to an enlargement of the Erie canal or the deepening of St. Clair flats, (an iron vessel of 1,200 tons drawing thirteen inches less water than a wooden vessel of the same tonnage and burden.) To this advantage must also be added the increased economy due to greater durability and reduction of insurance.

That the excessive cost of iron is now the principal reason why such vessels are not constructed admits of demonstration. In 1867 an enterprising citizen of the Northwest visited Great Britain for the purpose of contracting for an iron vessel suitable for the grain trade of the upper lakes. This vessel it was proposed to ship in sections, and with the patterns and some skilled workmen, imported, to establish an iron shipbuilding yard in the vicinity of Chicago. The project, however, was abandoned when the aggregate of the duties on the proposed imports, ranging from thirty-eight to sixty-six per cent., were calculated; and so Chicago still waits for the inception of what, at some day, must constitute one of the greatest industries of the Northwest. The Commissioner is also informed that, but for the extreme cost of iron, a line of iron boats would have been constructed during the present winter, and placed on the Erie canal during the ensuing spring.*

---

* On this point, also, a representative of one of the best-known establishments engaged in the construction of iron vessels thus writes to the Commissioner:

"WILMINGTON, DELAWARE, *October* 9, 1869.

"Since 1854 improvements in the machinery used by iron-ship builders for utilizing and economizing labor have more nearly brought together the prices at which the hulls of first-class iron and wooden ships can be built; and now any iron-ship builder having practical experience in his business, and whose works possess the modern appliances for economizing material and labor, can furnish an iron ship at the same or even less cost than a wooden one of the same size and model can be built for, if the

But the usual and almost the only argument offered in reply to such statements as that above given is, that a continuance of the present duties imposed on pig iron is necessary to insure employment to American labor. To this the Commissioner would reply, that all the facts show that a reduction or entire repeal of the duty would in no degree affect the manufacture, but only reduce its profits to a par with those realized in other branches of domestic industry; and, furthermore, that under an abatement or repeal of the duty no more pig iron would be imported than at present, for the American manufacturer would simply reduce his prices, and thus retain, as now, full command of the domestic market. It is also to be noted that, if the duty on pig iron were entirely removed, the American producer in the interior would still enjoy a protection in the cost of transportation to the extent of at least $1 50 per ton for every one hundred miles that intervene between the place of production and a port of entry, which circumstance renders the transport of a single pound of foreign pig iron to any considerable distance into the interior a matter of ordinary commercial impossibility. It is also well, when the claim to the maintenance of high duties on pig iron is preferred in behalf of labor, to consider what amount of protection and opportunity for employment is thereby taken away from other branches of industry. In the case of ship-building this point admits of determination with approximative accuracy.

---

latter be made of first-rate sea-coast oak, copper-fastened and coppered; while the iron ship will outlast the wooden one in the proportion of two to one, and always carry upon the same displacement fifteen to eighteen per cent. more cargo, with the absolute certainty of no damage being sustained from leaking.

"It is the general opinion that the English builders of iron ships have great advantages over those of our country in the matter of greatly-cheapened labor. From the personal knowledge of gentlemen well acquainted with the methods of conducting work in the best English and Scotch yards, and whose knowledge of the business enables them to decide intelligently upon this point, and whose information has been fully communicated to the writer, he is clearly of the opinion that any advantages they may have in this regard is quite counterbalanced by the superior mechanical appliances and labor-saving machinery in use at the yards of the American builders.

"A little reflection supplies a reason for this seeming anomaly. The high rates of labor which have ruled in this country for a number of years have forced our American builders to avail themselves of all the labor-saving machinery which the natural mechanical skill of our people, fostered by a generous system of patent laws, has placed at their command; and to-day we find that a given sum of money expended in labor upon an iron ship in an American ship yard of first class will produce as much and go as far toward her construction as the same sum applied in England.

"In the construction of iron ships nearly six-tenths of the whole cost is for labor alone, the remaining four-tenths representing the material consumed. Now, it is my opinion that, if Congress would repeal the law taxing imported iron, or at least that which was used for the purpose of building iron ships, then American iron-ship yards would in a single year rival in activity those on the Clyde, and American iron steam merchant ships be found in every port in the world, as English-built vessels are now, and the commerce of our country, without which no nation can rate as a first-class power, which to-day lies crushed and flattened, ('protected' to death,) would more than regain its former measure of greatness."

	Tons.
Thus the sea-going tonnage that would have been built in the year 1866, according to the average rate of increase from 1827 to 1857, would have been	500,000
Deduct the amount built in 1867	50,000
And we have	450,000

an amount equivalent to six hundred ships of seven hundred and fifty tons each. At the present ratio in England but ten per cent. of these would have been of wood. But to build these six hundred ships would have employed for the year a force of about thirty thousand men, or more than two and a half times as many as are at present *directly* engaged in the manufacture of pig iron.* To man these six hundred ships six thousand men for the year would have been necessary; and to supply them with chains, canvas, rigging, and other furniture, would have further required the labor of at least four thousand more men. So we may estimate that this protection to the manufacture of pig iron by twelve thousand five hundred men directly, or fifty-two thousand five hundred, both directly and indirectly, in 1867, so enhanced the cost of iron, as to deprive more than forty thousand other workmen of employment during that same year, in connection with the single industry of the building, equipment, and sailing of sea-going vessels; to say nothing of the construction of vessels for use upon our inland waters. Another illustration of the benefit likely to accrue to domestic industry from a reduction of the rate of duty on pig iron is to be found in the recent experience of the country in respect to imported scrap iron, which article, through a probable oversight in the first instance, is admitted at the comparatively low rate of eight dollars per ton, or one dollar per ton less than is imposed on foreign pig iron. The result has been, that nearly all the rolling mills in the country, within two hundred miles or more of tide-water, have gladly availed themselves of the opportunity to use this product; and the mere ability to so use it has, in very many instances, constituted all the difference between running the mills at a moderate profit, or running at a loss, or entire suspension. Furthermore, little rolling mills, adapted to use scrap iron exclusively, have sprung up at various points along the seaboard, affording steady employment to large numbers of laborers, and constituting the center of other little domestic industries; and all this without bringing anything of detriment to the revenue, to any other branches of industry, or to the community in general; but, on the contrary, it has increased the revenue, developed and strengthened the business of production, and benefited consumers.

* The whole number of workmen at present engaged at the blast furnaces of the United States is estimated at twelve thousand five hundred; in addition to which, however, forty-two thousand are estimated as engaged in the preparation of coal and ore for the same.

But it is frequently asked: Why, if the production of pig iron is as profitable as is represented, is not a greater amount of capital attracted to its manufacture; and why is not production stimulated to an extent sufficient to reduce prices through competition to a minimum? The answer to this is simple: capital does flow and is flowing into the manufacture of pig iron in the United States to as great an extent as could be expected in view of the present conditions of its supply and distribution, and to a greater comparative extent than is the case as respects any other specific branch of manufacturing industry. The present increase in the consumption of pig iron in the United States is at the rate of about ten per cent., or 170,000 tons per annum, to meet and supply which not only must every existing furnace be kept working to its present capacity, but twenty-eight new furnaces, of a capacity of six thousand tons each, must be annually added, involving new capital to the extent of from five to seven millions of dollars. Anything less than this would occasion a deficiency; and, in fact, so closely does consumption press upon supply, that for the last three years there never has been at any one time a considerable surplus upon the market, but, on the contrary, the price-currents have been characterized by expressions like the following: "*Prices unchanged, with scarcely enough in market to make any business;*" "*Offerings few and stock exhausted;*" "*No. 1 continues very scarce, with the demand in excess of supply; No. 2 is also hard to find.*" Nor is this all; for, in addition to the annual increase in production necessary to meet the requirements of consumption growing out of the natural increase of wealth and population, a further increase is constantly demanded to meet the new conditions of civilization in respect to engineering and the mechanic arts. How great the demand of the future is likely to prove may be inferred from the circumstance that, while the *per capita* consumption of Great Britain and Belgium, after allowing for exportation, has reached one hundred and eighty-nine pounds per annum, the present annual consumption of the United States is not in excess of one hundred pounds *per capita.* No nation, furthermore, at the present time, with the exception of Great Britain, is producing pig iron in sufficient excess of its needs to allow of a surplus for exportation; and in Great Britain the prospect of any future increase is entirely dependent upon the uncertain condition of her being able to supply coal on a scale of consumption that is already in excess of one hundred and four millions of tons per annum. The assumption, therefore, that the continuance of the present protective duty on pig iron is necessary to the maintenance and expansion of this branch of industry in the United States, or that domestic competition alone is likely soon to reduce prices, is one that has no good or sufficient foundation.

In view, therefore, of the above facts, the Commissioner would recommend a reduction of the existing duty of *nine* dollars per ton on the importation of pig iron to *three* dollars; and in this recommendation the Commissioner has good and sufficient reason to believe that he is sustained by a majority of the proprietors of rolling mills and other workers of iron, who are not at the same time interested in the production of pig metal; while members of the American Iron and Steel Association have not hesitated to express their sympathy with any movement looking to some abatement of duty in this particular.

SALT, COAL, AND LUMBER.

The Commissioner would renew the recommendations of his previous report in favor of the abatement of the duty on salt, and the entire removal of the duties on coal and on manufactured lumber, on the general ground that the benefit likely to be experienced by the few from a continuance of these taxes affords no sufficient compensation for the detriment which these continuances seem to entail upon the many.

Salt.—The specific character and influence of the duties imposed on salt were so fully discussed and illustrated in a former report, that the Commissioner will at present call attention only to the following points:

1st. Their excessive character is strikingly shown by the circumstance that if the government were to exact its duties, like tithes, in kind, it would require that each vessel arriving in the United States with a cargo of foreign salt should be accompanied by another of equal size, and a third smaller craft of from eight to fifty per cent. capacity of the former, to convey the duty.*

2d. That the existing duty is not required to sustain and develop the domestic manufacture of salt is proved by the fact that the United States annually exports upward of five hundred thousand bushels of salt to the British Possessions, and maintains such an export year after year in defiance of all competition; and further, that for the purpose of retaining full control of the domestic market, salt is always sold by the domestic producer to fishermen, who have the right to withdraw salt from bond free of duty, at rates which admit of no advantage as respects price to the use of the imported article.

3d. As regards the profits which result from the manufacture of salt in the United States under the present system, the Commissioner, in

* As illustrating the actual ad valorem duty on foreign salt, the following table, showing the amount of salt withdrawn from bond for the fisheries in the district of Gloucester, Massachusetts, for the third quarter of the calendar year 1869, with the value, amount of duty remitted, and the duty, specific and ad valorem, as officially returned, is herewith submitted:

Months.	Pounds.	Rate.	Value.	Duty.	Per cent. of value.
July	4, 184, 433	18 c.	$4, 853	$7, 532 00	155. 20
August	2, 408, 350	18 c.	2, 724	4, 335 02	159. 14
September	1, 429, 995	18 c.	1, 730	2, 573 96	148. 78
Total	8, 022, 778	......	9, 307	14, 440 98	155. 16

addition to the evidence previously presented, will ask attention only to the following table showing the cost of making salt at one of the principal furnaces on the Ohio River for the year 1868:

Number of bushels (of 56 pounds each) produced		327,000
Cost of barrels	$23,468 99 or	7.18 cents per bushel.
Cost of coal	19,902 19 or	6.09 cents per bushel.
Wages and salaries	21,075 96 or	6.44 cents per bushel.
Repairs and incidentals	10,584 50 or	3.24 cents per bushel.
Total	75,031 64 =	22.95 cents per bushel.

To this must be added the cost of transportation, interest, commissions, &c.

The cost of manufacturing 319,000 bushels of salt at the same furnace in 1860 was 13.38 cents gold per bushel, or (with gold at 133) 17.84 cents currency. The average market price of salt in 1860 was from 20 to 23 cents per bushel gold, or (with gold at 133) 26⅓ to 30⅝ cents currency. The price of salt in Cincinnati in 1868, was 48 cents currency. It thus appears that while the cost of manufacturing has advanced 5 cents per bushel, currency, since 1860, the market price for salt during the year 1868 advanced 17 to 22 cents per bushel.* The Commissioner could name the rate of dividend paid during the year 1868 by the furnace referred to, were it not communicated confidentially. The reader can, however, approximately determine it by calculation.†

The Commissioner does not assert, and never has asserted, that the manufacture of salt under all circumstances, in the United States, is always attended with large profits; but he does assert, that when this industry has been established under favorable conditions and is conducted with skill and energy, it is sufficiently remunerative to sustain itself without the assistance of duties ranging from eighty to one hundred and fifty per cent. And in proof of this he asks attention to the following extract of a communication addressed to him by the agent of one of the largest salt-producing associations in Western Virginia.

"The cost of making salt here is very variable, and dependent not only in a large degree upon the quality of the brine and size of furnace, but upon the personal energy of the proprietor and his acquaintance with the business. There are some of our furnaces which I am sure are operated with very slight or no profit, while others, by the purchase of superior property, and free investment of capital and skill, are enabled to make substantial profit. A furnace with a capacity of less than two hundred thousand bushels per annum is not a profitable investment here—I mean will not invite investment, although such furnaces are operated here, because the small profit will keep the property in repair which one year's inactivity will almost destroy. A furnace having

* In November, 1869, the market quotations of Ohio salt in Cincinnati were from forty to forty-five cents per bushel.

† It is pertinent to this discussion to here call attention to the fact that one of the first acts of the new and more liberal government of Spain, on its accession to power, was to abolish the government monopoly of salt, (heretofore an important source of revenue,) to sell the national "salines," and to permit importations.

that capacity, if it can be increased to say two hundred and fifty thousand bushels, *will find the extra quantity almost entire profit.* A larger increase in quantity would require much more capital, but still the proportionate profit is greater on all above two hundred thousand bushels."

Now if there is anything of value in the above testimony, the question in respect to the manufacture of salt in West Virginia resolves itself simply to this. Good furnaces, properly located and managed, can make large profits; furnaces improperly located and improperly managed, cannot. Shall the whole people of the United States be taxed on the consumption of one of the necessaries of life, to help maintain branches or forms of industry which, by the very conditions of their existence, never can be made remunerative, and whose continuance involves a misapplication and waste of both capital and labor?*

Lumber.—The following table shows the advance which has taken place in the price per thousand feet of mixed lumber, by the cargo, in Chicago, from 1861 to 1868, inclusive:

	Mean of daily averages.
Year ended December 31, 1861	$6 50 per M feet.
March 31, 1866	14 80 per M feet.
March 31, 1867	17 70 per M feet.
March 31, 1868	15 10 per M feet.

* In this connection the following correspondence, addressed to the Commissioner, has much of significance. Under date of August 2, 1869, Duncan Stewart, president of the Saginaw (Michigan) Salt Association, writes to the Commissioner: "Salt can now be made at Saginaw in great abundance at very low rates, where the making of it is carried on in connection with saw-mills and shingle-mills. Using exhaust steam and waste wood for effecting evaporation, I am satisfied it can *be made in that way in sufficient quantities to supply all the western States, at a price so low that no section of the country can compete with the Saginaw Valley in the markets of these States. One thing is certain—no higher tariff is needed for the protection of Saginaw salt than that now in force, and it should be cut down one-half, the present high tariff being simply an outrage on the best interests of the country.*"

"If the business has not paid much in the way of profit heretofore, want of knowledge of the business, bad management in some cases, dishonest management in others—with a reckless competition among makers—the hostility of Syracuse, and a steamboat combination for high freights, were such obstacles to success that it is a great marvel that the attempt to make salt in the Saginaw Valley did not prove an absolute failure. A determined spirit of perserverance has overcome all difficulties, and nothing now is wanting but prudent management to give Saginaw the entire control of the markets of the western States."

"SPARTA, GEORGIA, *March* 26, 1869.

"*To the Special Commissioner of the Revenue:*

"SIR: In answer to your inquiry respecting the use and necessity of salt in the cultivation of cotton, I would say I have been engaged for the last twenty-two years in planting. I find salt to be essential to success in the cultivation of cotton. In combination with guano and plaster it is an almost total preventive of rust, which is one of the worst enemies the cotton planter has to contend with. Salt makes the cotton bear longer in the season, and stand drought better.

"The price of salt varied before the war in Savannah from fifty cents to one dollar, according to supply. In January, 1861, I bought five hundred sacks (two hundred

The following table, compiled by William G. Thomas, esq., of Albany, New York, gives the relative value of pine lumber in that market from 1859 to 1868, inclusive:

	Per M feet.		Per M feet.
1859	$15 94	1864	$31 21
1860	16 23	1865	22 12
1861	14 46	1866	29 83
1862	15 02	1867	27 42
1863	23 69	1868	25 95

The statement, therefore, made by the Commissioner in his report for 1868–'69, and which has been questioned, "that the increase in the price of lumber since the commencement of the war has been far in advance of the average increase in the price of labor and of other commodities," is fully confirmed.

The above tables also clearly illustrate the effect of the imposition of the tariff on prices. Thus the existing duty of twenty per cent. on lumber became operative on lumber imported from the British Possessions (our only foreign source of supply) by the expiration of the reciprocity treaty in the spring of 1866. The subsequent advance in prices in Chicago was from $14 80 per thousand feet in 1865–'66, to $17 70 in 1866–'67; and in Albany from $22 12 per thousand feet in 1865, to $29 83 in 1866, and $27 42 in 1867. As the prices paid for lumber, furthermore, have been as a rule higher in Canada since the expiration of the reciprocity treaty and the imposition of the twenty per cent. duty, while the sales have been larger, it is evident that the duty falls wholly upon the American consumer.

Coal.—The Commissioner would also again renew his recommendation for the entire removal of all duties imposed upon the importation of coal, on the broad general principle that a tax upon coal is not justifiable except in the case of such an extreme emergency as would justify a tax upon the breadstuffs and food of a nation. Such an emergency

---

pounds) of salt for fifty cents per sack. In January last I purchased, in Savannah, two hundred sacks at $1 90 (which was the lowest point) to $2 25.

"In my opinion, all means should be taken by the government to lessen the cost of cotton, as it costs much more to produce it than formerly. All manures should come in as raw material to be grown into crops. What is the difference in growing raw manure into cotton-lint and manufacturing raw material into fabrics?

"I am yours, respectfully,

"DAVID DICKSON."

The Commissioner would add, that it is now proposed to take advantage of that provision of the existing tariff which allows of the import of fertilizers free of duty, by mixing salt with Prussian blue or unrefined petroleum, and then importing it as a manure; or, in other words, of destroying a portion of the utility of an indispensable article at some considerable cost, as a condition of enabling agriculturists to obtain it at a reduction of price. One is tempted to inquire, in view of this circumstance, whether we are really living in the last half of the nineteenth century, or have gone back to the dark ages.

of course may arise, for there are times when taxes which trench upon and absorb capital become necessary and justifiable; but such extreme occasions can be only temporary. Further than this, objections to a tax upon coal to meet the ordinary requirements for revenue may be briefly stated as follows: Coal is a necessity of life—next in importance to food; indeed, as both are in our climate absolutely indispensable, it cannot be said that either is more or less needful than the other, for life cannot be sustained without both. The universally recognized principle of taxation—that a tax should be taken from what can be spared—forbids the laying of a tax upon that which is indispensable to rich and poor alike. Coal, moreover, is not only a necessary of life, but the source of motive power. To tax coal, therefore, is to tax power; to tax the force of the steam engine, to starve the laborer on whose strength we depend for work. To do this as a part of a plan of promoting domestic industry seems the reverse of wisdom.

In 1862, when the internal revenue system was projected and the necessities for revenue required that the system of taxation should be all pervading, an internal tax was laid upon coal of three and a half cents per ton. This was raised to five, and afterward to six cents, under which rates $1,240,106 was collected for the year 1865–'66. But it is worthy of remark that this tax, trifling as it was in amount, was among the very first to be repealed; and this circumstance may fairly be looked upon as conveying the sense of the country upon the expediency of such a tax for revenue. The question of an excise upon coal may be considered, therefore, as definitely settled. But if an excise is unwise, can anything be said in favor of an import duty? In fact, an import duty as a source of revenue is still less justifiable. All taxes should be as equally borne by the community as possible. A tax which reaches only one part of the country and leaves all the rest untouched is manifestly unjust.

A law which enacted in terms that a duty of fifty per cent. upon an article should be levied at Pittsburg, Cincinnati, and St. Louis, while no duty on the same should be paid in Boston or New York, would be so manifestly monstrous that the proposition would not receive a moment's thought; yet an import duty on coal produces a precisely similar result. It can affect only a very small portion of the country, which the rest escapes from. Nature has been bountiful to the United States in many things, but in none more so than in the distribution of coal over its surface. Of the immeasurable wealth to grow out of it no one can adequately conceive. But in this provision New England, New York, and the Atlantic coast have no immediate part. The coldest, and so most dependent on fuel; the oldest, and so most bare of wood; the most densely peopled, and so the largest consumers of fuel in proportion to its area—this portion of the country happens to be the only part upon which a coal duty bears at all. It would seem as if no fair-minded person could wish to have this point urged further. But when it is considered that manufactures such as iron, in which fuel is most largely used, are carried on in New York and New England in competition, to a certain extent, with those parts of the country where coal is untaxed, because found on the spot, the gross unfairness of a tax upon the productive industry of one section that is not borne by the other seems more obvious.

When a duty is imposed on tea, coffee, or spices, it is equal all over the country. Let us suppose that the duty on coal as now fixed—$1 25 in gold, equal to, say, $1 50 in currency, per ton—were levied upon all the coal used in the country, as the duty on tea is levied upon all tea, would it be borne with equanimity? The amount of such a duty, if collected, would exceed $25,000,000 in currency. The suggestion seems monstrous, and yet the coal duty now levied does actually, to the extent of the area to which it is confined, burden the industry subject to it to that extreme degree. It is hard to enlarge upon such a proposition—a plain question of equity, of fair play, needs only a plain statement, and not an elaborate argument. But this duty is urged as a *protective* measure. The theory of protection is the encouragement of particular industries by prohibiting or obstructing the competition of foreigners who are engaged in the same industries; but when its aid is invoked to justify the obstruction of an industry in our own country, for the gain of persons engaged in another form of industry, it would seem to require some justification stronger than a mere word. The protection of coal means, then, the enhancement of its price by a duty, so that the consumer may be obliged to buy coal raised in the United States rather than that procured abroad. This duty is necessary because it is impossible that the parts of the country destitute of coal should be supplied with it as cheaply if raised in the United States as if brought from abroad. This increased cost is not a question of skill, or capital, or wages, but a mere question of the amount of labor necessary to produce a certain result.

The cost of coal in any market consists of the cost of raising the coal (an amount varying but little in different places) and the cost of transportation to the place of consumption. This latter is always the larger, and increases regularly with the distance. Every coal field has an area which it can naturally supply more cheaply, *i. e.*, with less labor per ton, than any other can. Each place, then, has its natural source of supply. If an obstacle to transportation exist between it and the nearest coal field, a more remote field is sought so long as that obstacle exists. It may be that a railway or canal has been destroyed by a flood, or a river course dried up by a drought; for the time being, the supply comes from the more remote and expensive source. This happens sometimes on our western rivers. The cities of Cincinnati and Louisville have occasionally seen winter approach when there was an insufficient supply of coal on hand, and the Ohio River, their natural highway, was too low for navigation. In this case, the railroads in Ohio are relied upon to make up the deficiency; but, of course, they do it at a great increase of cost. While the low water continues they are "*protected*" against the cheap transportation of the river. Now this obstruction to a cheap supply, deprecated justly as a public calamity, is in its results precisely analogous to the obstruction offered by a duty to the cheap supply of the northeastern States with coal from Nova Scotia.

If the enhanced price paid by the consumer for his coal, in consequence of the existence of this duty, were all pàid to the Pennsylvania miner, it would be, of course, great injustice; but the country would be none the poorer because the law took money from one man and gave it to another. But it happens that, while the consumer pays the increase, the immediate producer is not benefited, inasmuch as the whole enhanced price is expended in paying for the transportation of the coal to a greater distance—in other words, the payment is for unnecessary transportation, *i. e.*, useless labor. Now, no acquisition of skill can change this. It is fixed by the laws of nature. To the end of time it will cost more, *i. e.*, it will take more labor, to bring every ton of coal from western Pennsylvania, across the Alleghany Mountains, to the northeastern seaboard, than to bring it from Nova Scotia. So long as a duty makes it possible to bring coal from the former source, so long that unnecessary work will be done; but the price does not represent a profit, but the cost of useless labor.

The theory of *protection*, then, as applied to coal, is that, in order to promote American industry, the source of motive power must be enhanced in price, and so production to that extent discouraged and obstructed in order that unnecessary labor may be paid for. Now, considering that the ingenuity of man has been and is daily taxing itself to save labor in all forms of production, and that the United States especially has no surplus of either labor or capital, can anything be more retrograde than such a policy? But if protection be wise in this matter, all parts of the country should have the benefit of it—yet that is impossible. The field of protection is as narrow as the field of exaction; as the duty is borne by only one section, so the benefits of protection (if any) are enjoyed by only one; and so, again, the law of the equality of burdens and benefits is violated.

In Gulliver's voyage to Brobdingnag occurrs this passage: "And he gave it for his opinion, that whoever could make two ears of corn, or two blades of grass, to grow upon a spot of ground where only one grew before, would deserve better of mankind and do more essential service to his country than the whole race of politicians put together." The Commissioner leaves it to his readers to make the application.

WOOL AND WOOLENS.

In March, 1867, an act was passed by Congress increasing the duties on the importation of wool and woolens to a degree unprecedented, and far in advance of the average rate of the then existing tariff. The object aimed at was to promote alike the interests of the grower of wool and the manufacturer of fabrics. The results attained to, however, have been so remarkable and so contrary to expectation that a detailed history of the whole movement deserves to be put on record as a most important contribution to *politico-economic* science, and as affording a new and most striking illustration of the impolicy of the oft-renewed effort to unnaturally influence the course of industry and trade by a resort to legislation.

The breaking out of the war in 1861, and the curtailment of the usual supply of cotton, created both in the United States and in Europe a greatly increased demand for wool and for woolen fabrics, and prices, as was to have been expected, advanced in proportion. Domestic fleece wools in New York rose from thirty-five to forty-eight cents per pound in April, 1861, to ninety to one hundred and seventeen cents in August, 1864; and manufacturers who had stock on hand, or contracted for, during the first years of the war, or who afterwards bought progressively, realized immense profits.*

At the close of the war, (which was followed by a marked decline in the prices of wool,) a number of gentlemen claiming to represent the wool-growers of the United States, but who appear to have been more especially interested in the breeding of sheep than in the growing of wool, conceived the idea, that if all foreign wool could be shut out by legislation from competition with the domestic product, the war prices of domestic wool could be maintained, and great gain be thereby made to accrue to all concerned. Measures to accomplish this object were accordingly set on foot; and as the scheme looked especially toward the promotion of the interest of the agriculturists of the country, it gave promise of success from its very outset. Meantime, the manufacturers of wool, clearly perceiving that a restriction of supply and increase in the price of wool would place them at a disadvantage in respect to foreign competition, became alarmed, and proposed co-operation to the Wool-growers' Association. The offer was accepted, the parties entered into union, and by means of delegates entered upon their work. What was this

* In his report for 1866–'67, the Commissioner called attention to the circumstance that, although the profits which had accrued in the manufacture of cotton during the period of the war were acknowledged by one of the leading manufacturers of the country to have been "painfully large," yet such profits were the result of extreme advances in the prices of raw and manufactured material previously on hand, rather than of the operations of strictly legitimate business; and in proof of this assumption, a statement was submitted, showing that in the case of one large cotton manufacturing corporation in New England, if their mills had been burnt at the commencement of the war, their insurance lost, and their whole capital, other than that invested in cotton, sunk, but the cotton on hand sold at the highest obtainable prices, the result would have afforded to the stockholders a permanent annuity of at least twelve per cent. on their original investment. Now, what was true of cotton manufacturing at that period was equally true of the wool manufacture; and in a majority of instances the large profits realized by the woolen manufacturers of the United States from 1863 to 1866 were due rather to the rise in the price of their raw material than to any legitimate profits derived from the manufacture and sale of their productions.

work? Not to increase the revenues of the national treasury; not to promote the interests of the great mass of the people to whom woolen fabrics are almost as much a necessity as food and shelter; nor to increase the wages or comforts of the laborers who grow the wool or manufacture the cloth; but simply and exclusively to influence legislation for the promotion of their respective private gains and interests.

The basis of the agreement on which the two interests united was substantially as follows:

That the duty on raw or unwashed wools and hair, other than wools adapted for carpets, should be fixed at rates varying from ten to twelve cents per pound, and from ten to eleven per cent. ad valorem. In order, then, to compensate the manufacturer for such a prospective enhancement of the price of his raw material, it was agreed that, in consideration of the fact that *four* pounds of the cheapest imported wool, (mestiza,) paying an aggregate duty of forty-six cents, were *sometimes* employed in the fabrication of a pound of finished cloth, the duty on cloth should be fifty cents per pound, and on other fabrics of wool of varying weight a duty in like proportion. In order, next, to give the manufacturer protection against his foreign competitor, twenty-five per cent. ad valorem was added; and in order to further compensate for the payment of an internal revenue tax of six per cent., *which tax was repealed in the succeeding year, ten per cent. more was added*, thus making the aggregate duties on cloths, shawls, and woolen goods generally, fifty cents per pound* and thirty-five per cent. ad valorem. It will thus be seen that if the manufacturers, as is often alleged, did not enter into the arrangement for an increase of duties through their own seeking, they nevertheless managed to secure full compensation for all that was granted to the wool-growers; and in addition to that, through force of subsequent circumstances, an additional protection in excess of what, according to their own showing, they considered necessary.

Nearly two years have now elapsed since these measures were consummated, giving ample time for experience to test the principle. And what, to-day, is that experience?

1st. Wool to the agriculturist at a lower price in gold than has almost ever before been experienced; the average price of medium American washed wools from 1827 to 1862 having been $42\frac{8}{10}$ cents per pound, (gold,) while the average price of Ohio wools for the year 1868, reduced to gold, was only 35.21 cents; which is less than the average price of 1858, when, under the influence of the disastrous crisis of 1857, a large portion of the mills of the country were standing absolutely idle. For

* It is worthy of note, as constituting a valuable precedent for a certain class of American economists, that Charles V of Spain imposed, in 1519, a duty similar to that of the present United States tariff, viz., fifty cents per pound on all woolen cloth imported into the kingdom; and that under the influence of this and other similar measures the wool production and woolen manufacture of Spain gradually sunk into insignificance.

the year 1869, the price paid in Ohio for medium wools, according to estimates presented to the Commissioner, has been about 43 cents, currency.

2d. A decrease in the number of sheep in the United States, estimated by the Commissioner of Agriculture at *four millions* for the single year, 1868, while other authorities place the total decrease as high as twenty-five per cent. since the passage of the wool tariff.

In the whole history of the fluctuations of American industry there never has been a more discouraging and disastrous record than that presented by the Department of Agriculture in its report for March and April, 1869; some seven pages of which are occupied with a detailed statement of the condition of sheep husbandry in one hundred and seventy counties of twenty-one different States, in only one of which, Missouri, is there anything which indicates a condition of even moderate prosperity for this particular branch of industry. As illustrating the nature of these statements, we give the following quotations:

Vermont.—Orange County—The best wool-growers "hold on;" some have sold one-half, some three-fourths, and a few have sold all. *Orleans County*—All sheep and lambs (fine wool) that drovers would buy were sold for market last fall, and twenty-five per cent. of the remainder were sold to be killed for their pelts and tallow.

Massachusetts.—Berkshire County—Probably one-third of the flocks of last year have been sold or slaughtered; in some cases the prices were scarcely more than the value of the pelts.

New York.—Chautauqua County—Ten per cent. have been pelted or shipped off. *Genesee County*—Decrease of sheep thirty per cent. *Onondaga County*—Perhaps one-fourth have been sold; no such destruction has occurred for twenty years previously.

Pennsylvania.—Butler County—One-third of last year's flocks have been sold. *Lawrence County*—So great has been the destruction that mutton has sold for twenty-five cents per quarter all winter. *Mercer County*—Many slaughtered; some have sold seventy-five per cent. of their flocks.

Kentucky.—Greenup County—About four-tenths have been sold to be killed for tallow and pelts.

West Virginia.—Harrison County—Stocks are being sold off; sheep husbandry is unpopular. *Ohio County*—Reduction of sheep for pelts and tallow forty per cent.

Missouri.—Worth County—Twenty per cent. sold for mutton and tallow. *Pemiscot County*—Forty per cent. of the sheep sold out of the State for mutton.

Illinois.—Menard County—Number reduced three-tenths by slaughter and shipment. *Mercer County*—At least twenty per cent. of the sheep have left the State. *Sangamon County*—Many thousands sold at about the worth of pelt and tallow. *Lee County*—Many died from neglect, and many have been slaughtered. *Logan County*—Many killed for their pelts; the number reduced from 70,000 three years ago to 18,000 now.

Indiana.—Madison County—Fully one-fourth sent out of the State. *Randolph County*—Flocks reduced one-half. *Elkhart County*—Flocks greatly reduced by sheep being killed for pelts; carcasses fed to hogs. *Bartholomew County*—Probably one-fourth of the sheep killed for pelts and tallow.

Ohio.—Highland County—Great many sheep slaughtered for mutton. *Holmes County*—Large number sold, for pelts and tallow, at twenty-five to seventy-five cents per head; fifteen to twenty per cent. of the entire number. *Morrow County*—From one-fourth to one-third killed, or sold for pelts. *Putnam County*—One-fourth of the whole stock. *Tuscarawas County*—One-third of the stock. *Athens County*—Flocks reduced one-third in eighteen months. *Fulton County*—Twenty per cent. killed. *Jackson County*—Thirty per cent. sold for pelts and tallow.

Michigan.—St. Clair County—Large number killed for mutton. *Washtenaw County*—Great number killed for pelts, tallow, and mutton; the latter being sold as low as one cent. per pound for inferior class. *Clinton County*—One man sold four hundred at one dollar per head. *Jackson County*—Fifty per cent. sold, mostly for pelts, tallow, and hams.

Wisconsin.—Milwaukee County—Stock much reduced by slaughter, *Rock County*—Flocks reduced one-fourth. *Buffalo County*—Flocks reduced twenty-five per cent. *Ozaukee County*—Flocks reduced thirty per cent.

Minnesota.—Le Sueur County—Flocks reduced two-tenths. *Watonwan County*—A large number killed for mutton.

Iowa.—Dubuque County—Fifty per cent. sold to butchers. *Lucas County*—Flocks reduced six to seven per cent. *Jasper County*—Flocks reduced ten per cent. *Madison County*—Flocks reduced fifty per cent *Allamakee County*—Flocks reduced by sale at low prices. *Des Moines County*—Stock considerably reduced. Whole flocks sold.

3d. A condition of the woolen manufacture characterized by a greater depression than that of any other branch of industry in the country, with the exception of ship-building; small profits accruing to a few, heavy losses to the many, with numerous and constantly recurring failures. At the date of writing, November, 1869, the attention of the Commissioner is called to the sale of a woolen-mill property, which will give to the stockholders $105,000 upon a capital of $700,000, thus showing a loss of eighty-five per cent. of the whole capital in from four to five years of operations.

4th. An increase in the importation of foreign fabrics of wool; the imports for the fiscal year 1868 being returned at $32,458,884, and for 1869 at $34,620,943.

5th. Encouragement of smuggling, and its apparent reduction to a system. During the first year of the increased duties on the imports of wool and woolens into the United States, (1867,) the importation of woolen goods into Canada from Great Britain was returned at $8,012,439 as compared with $5,489,039 in 1865, or two years previously. The report of the Boston Board of Trade for January, 1869, says, significantly: "It is well known that Canadian tailors openly solicit orders for clothing to be delivered here at low prices, and are countenanced in it by men of high standing in this community."

It is also to be noted that "Cape wools," which the existing tariff will not permit American manufacturers to import, are now passing into Canada in considerable quantities, both by direct importation and by transmission in bond from American ports of entry; thus proving that certain branches of wool industry which have been crushed out in the United States are establishing themselves across the frontier. And it is further the opinion of those conversant with these imports, that they will nearly all, in the form of fabric, ultimately find their way into the United States without payment of any duty.

In his report for 1866–'67, the Commissioner predicted that one effect of increasing the duties on wool would be to still further reduce the little foreign commerce which the war had left to the United States, and to especially impair the Cape of Good Hope and Australian trade, in which a very considerable number of vessels were employed in carrying out the products of American industry and receiving in payment of the same, in great part, the wools of these respective countries, which the United States does not produce, and which are absolutely necessary for the maintenance and extension of certain departments of the woolen industry. To show how far this prediction has been verified, the Commissioner would ask attention to the following exhibit of the imports and exports of the principal American house engaged in the Cape of Good Hope and New Zealand trade, for the years 1859–'60, and 1867–'68, respectively:

Articles.	1859–'60.		1867–'68.	
	Quantities.	Value.	Quantities.	Value.
IMPORTS.				
Wool	bales, 9,226	£173,197	bales, 2,749	£34,464
Sheep-skins	4,625	44,076	577	3,841
Goat-skins	1,958	34,394	298	9,024
Hides	17,249	18,322	1,381	318
Horns	945	20		
Aloes		532		
Argols	lbs., 13,062	442		
Arrowroot	3,763	90		
Ostrich feathers		365		
Total value imports		£271,438		£47,647

Exhibit of imports and exports in the Cape of Good Hope and New Zealand trade, 1859–'60, *and* 1867–'68, *&c.*—Continued.

Articles.	1859–'60.		1867–'68.	
	Quantities.	Value.	Quantities.	Value.
EXPORTS.				
Agricultural implements and mechanics' tools	....	$66, 527	....	$75, 497
Clothing and cloth	....	56, 649	....	No exports.
Building material and furniture	....	85, 763	....	28, 553
Wooden ware	....	4, 017	....	9, 974
Manufactures of wood and iron	....	21, 993	....	7, 135
Provisions and grains	....	182, 987	....	23, 476
Naval stores	....	7, 778	....	1, 763
Tobacco	....	103, 876	....	15, 715
Miscellaneous	....	3, 848	....	1, 434
Total	....	533, 438	....	163, 547

The manner in which the present extravagant duties on the importation of foreign wools operate to prevent the prosperity and extension of the domestic woolen manufacturing industry, and to reduce the price of domestic wool, is a matter not difficult of explanation.

The wools of the United States are mainly the merino clothing wools, which can be produced in any quantity, and at prices which defy foreign competition. Wool has been raised in Texas during the last year (1868–'69) in large quantities, at an estimated cost of seven cents gold per pound; and has commanded readily in the market twenty-five cents gold per pound.* It is furthermore to be noted that German Saxon wool, which during the past year has touched the lowest price almost of the century, could not now be imported, even in the absence of all duty, and sold at so low a price as the average prices which XX Ohio wools have commanded during the past season in the New York market.

On the other hand, wools which the existing tariff excludes are mainly wools which are either not grown in the United States, or grown in very limited and insufficient quantities. The American manufacturer, therefore, being restricted in the selection of his raw material, is, of

* As evidence in part of the above statement, attention is asked to the following extract of a correspondence of the Boston Cultivator, under date of August 21, 1869:

"Permit me to say a word to the readers of the Cultivator regarding the views of Judge Colburn, given in the issue of July 24. I fully agree with him that a tariff on wools that will prevent the importation of them will be a great help to the Vermont wool-grower. A like policy regarding silk and oranges might enable the amateur hot-house growers there to turn their fancies to some account, and I have no doubt that with sufficient 'protection' cotton might be successfully produced in this little State—but on the whole, would it pay?

"What I wish to say is that Judge C. is not well informed about the wool-growing of Texas, because he says that it is a chimera, for the most part, that the southwestern States have so great an advantage over the northern States in this business. I think the reader will agree with me that it is a very substantial chimera when I say that one of our wool-growers, Chamberlin, of Bell county, has just marketed his clip of 1869 of 60,000 pounds of wool, at twenty-five cents gold a pound. The cost of production here is generally estimated at seven cents a pound. That $15,000, in good round double

necessity, restricted in the variety of his products; and the great quantity of machinery brought into existence by the demands of the war has, in consequence, been forced, in great part, into *one line* of production; overstocking the markets with certain descriptions of fabrics, unnaturally reducing prices, restricting diversity and extension of production, and bringing disaster upon the whole business of wool-manufacturing.

That this has been and will continue to be the inevitable effect of restrictions imposed by the existing tariff on importation of desirable wools is also clearly shown by the commissioners of the United States to the Paris Exposition of 1867, in their report on "Wool and Manufactures of Wool." In this report, (written by a gentleman who has no superior in general intelligence and specific acquaintance with the manufacture of wool in the United States, but who, at the same time, ostensibly supports the existing tariff restrictions,) the author on his first page and in his first lines gives the following as the result of his study and inspection of the greatest variety of wools and manufactures of wool ever brought together in one collection. He says: "*The first impression made upon an American manufacturer by an observation of the woolen manufactures of Europe, as displayed at the Exposition, is the* IMMEASURABLE ADVANTAGE *which the woolen manufacturer of Europe has in the command of an unlimited supply of wool, and other raw materials of every variety, free of duty.* The policy of the modern governments of Europe is first and foremost to develop the manufactures of their several countries. Freedom from duties on raw material and breadstuffs is one method of protection."

And again: "*The advantages which the European enjoys over the American in the command of an unlimited supply of every variety of wool cannot be overestimated. The range of fabrication of the American manufacturer in clothing and combing wools is limited to the produce of American flocks, under the almost prohibitory duty upon those wools. The European can*

eagles, would, I fancy, look like a very good sort of a chimera to almost any Vermont farmer. Chamberlin has been engaged about a dozen years in wool-growing in Texas. He started out from the foot of Mt. Ascutney, not ten miles from where Judge Colburn still pursues the solid and substantial business of wool-growing and tariff-making, and has cultivated the chimera until his herds are upwards of 10,000 head of grade and fine-wool sheep. His is not a singular case either. Numerous fortunes have been made in sheep here. The chimera, in fact, don't reside in Texas; it has moved off and gone, I think, to the valleys of the Black, the Queche, and other streams of Vermont, to stay.

"Our Texas wool-growers, though they have little to do with the government as yet, are very well satisfied to see Vermont wools protected. It is nuts to them. They would be willing to see wool go up to a dollar, and would in nowise hesitate to pocket the proceeds of their little 60,000-pound clips, at that or any other figure that may be found necessary to keep their Vermont friends in good humor.

"The idea I wish to come at, however, is this: that if Vermont wool-growers will take their flocks and bring them to our rich pastures, with their skill, good sense, and energy, they will, in a very few years, not only supply the country with wool without a tariff, but make it a leading article of export, and so an important source of wealth instead of a costly chimera to the United States."

select from the peculiar products of every climate and soil of the whole world. Hence the infinite variety of European manufactures, and hence the capacity of the European manufacturer to relieve himself from home competition by changing at pleasure the character of his fabrics."

Speaking also of the qualities of the German and Australian wools, the commissioner to the Exposition (page 8) says: "Without the command of wool of this character for filling, it is hopeless to attempt the manufacture of the best face goods. Our foreign importation of German cloths is mainly confined to black broadcloths, cassimeres, and doeskins made from these wools. There is no difficulty in commanding the skill required for this manufacture, as is evinced by the goods exhibited by Mr. Slater, of Rhode Island. All the difficulties of manufacture can be surmounted by the importation of German workmen. Several hundred sets of machinery could be occupied here in the manufacture of these goods demanded for home consumption. The warps, which could be made of such American fleece as is now grown here, would take up two-fifths of the wool required for the manufacture. This would be so much added to the demand for this character of wool. The relief afforded to the manufacturer, by being able to vary his fabrics, would diminish the competition among those compelled to manufacture only one style of goods, and, giving more profits to the manipulator of the wool, would secure better prices to the wool-grower."

Now, if these are words of truth and soberness, if the commissioner to the Exposition has not stultified himself and spoken falsely, there is no need of further argument. For if the European manufacturer has by virtue of circumstances obtained an *immeasurable advantage* over his American competitor, then one of two things is certain—either the wool-manufacturing industry of the United States must continue, as it now is, a dwarfed, sickly, and depressed industry, to support which the people must be taxed; or else some steps must be taken to do away and overcome this "immeasurable advantage," and place the American manufacturer on a fair basis of equality with his foreign competitor. And how any man can claim to be a friend of American industry, and to desire the independence, diversity, and extension of American manufactures, and yet seek to continue a state of things which places the great woolen industry of the country forever under "immeasurable disadvantage"—a state in which, of necessity, there can never be any permanent prosperity—is something which is entirely beyond the Commissioner's comprehension.

But it may be said, have not the wool-growers, who outnumber the woolen manufacturers ten to one, any claim and right to protection? The answer to this is also very simple, and is to be found: *first*, in the fact that under the existing tariff, which affords a protection entirely in accordance with the wishes of those who claimed to represent the interests of the wool-grower, domestic American wool has touched and maintains a lower price than has almost ever before been experienced;

and *secondly*, this other fact, which can neither be ignored nor controverted, that the periods when the American wool-grower has received the highest price in gold for his wool, have been coincident with the periods when imported wools have been subjected to the lowest duties—as from 1858 to 1860, when wools costing less than twenty cents per pound were admitted free of duty. This circumstance finds a ready explanation in the fact that during the periods referred to the American manufacturer was enabled to purchase cheaply and sell cheaply, and, competing advantageously with the foreign producer, to furthermore sell largely; and under the increased consumption which followed, the supply of domestic wool became inadequate to the demand.

All who are familiar with the history of Great Britain, moreover, know that when that country first abolished the duties on foreign wool, the wool-growers made earnest opposition to the measure in the expectation that their interests would be destroyed. No such result followed; but on the contrary, from that day to this, the amount of wool grown, manufactured, exported, and consumed in Great Britain has annually increased, and with great profit to all who were, either directly or indirectly, interested. That the experience of France is also to the same effect is shown in a recent report by M. Baudrillard to the Emperor of the French on this subject, in which it is proved that when the duty on wool was reduced in France from thirty-three to twenty-two per cent. ad valorem, the price of wool *increased* and was maintained at from six to eight per cent. above the former rates. As an explanation of this M. Baudrillard says: "The home product is not sufficient for the daily increasing wants of our industry. Every check thrown in the way of the latter affects its activity. As soon as manufacturers cannot procure foreign wools they decrease their production, because they cannot find at home the required qualities; and French wool, which they would have used to mix in, lies about in the markets. The statistical tables of England lead exactly to the same conclusions—high duty, low wool at home; moderate duty or free wool, prices good at home."

In his report for 1866, the Commissioner, deprecating the proposed increase of the duties on wool, used the following language: "To the extent to which we now deprive the American wool-manufacturer of advantages in the selection and cost of his raw material, to a certain if not an equal extent do we increase those of his foreign competitors. The seventy million pounds of foreign wool annually imported into the United States, to meet a demand which the production of American wool does not supply, will not cease to be produced because the American manufacturer is forbidden to take it. Diverted from its present channel of consumption it must find its way to the markets of Europe, and through the diminution of prices which always follows an excess of supply, an advantage will be given to the foreign over the American manufacturer, largely additional to what he now possesses; and this, coupled with the use of shoddy and cotton, will lead to an importation of foreign woolens into the United States which no tariff short of absolute prohibition can suppress." The Commissioner also suggested that, in consequence of the withdrawal of the American demand, the European manufacturer might be enabled to obtain his supply of certain foreign wools at a less price even than the duties alone would amount to in the United States.

Had the Commissioner been endowed with the gift of prophecy, he could not, in many respects, have spoken more truly. Wool from the date of the passage of the wool-tariff bill in March, 1867, has continually fallen in price in Europe, and European manufacturers have been enabled to obtain their supplies of raw material at such low rates as to allow them to overcome the obstacles of the tariff and to continue their importations. That this fall of prices has been due in a great degree to the exclusion of foreign wools from the United States is acknowledged by all who have examined the subject. The official report by the French commissioners of the Paris Exposition to their own government assigns it as one of the principal causes; and Mr. Helmuth Schwartze, of London, one of the largest wool brokers in the world, in a recent report on the wool market, takes the same position, and in answer to objections uses the following language:

"It is argued by some that the quantity of wool imported by the United States is so inconsiderable, compared with that consumed in Europe, that it cannot affect prices there; but such people forget that it is the last million pounds that make a scarcity or overstock."

It is also a matter of importance for those who are interested in maintaining the price of American wools to note how the prices of foreign wools, such for example as are brought from the Cape or South Africa, have varied. Thus, in the years 1859, '60, and '61, when these wools in an unwashed state were admitted free of duty, their cost at the port of export was from 18 to 19.4 cents per pound. In 1863, a duty of from three cents per pound to five per cent. ad valorem having been imposed, the price fell to 16.2 cents; in 1864, the duty having been still further increased to six cents per pound, the price fell in 1865 to 14.8 cents. In the first half of 1867 the price was 15.1 cents; but in the spring of this year the duty was increased to ten cents per pound, and eleven per cent. ad valorem, and for the last six months of the year the price was 13.4. In 1868 the price still further declined to 10.9, thus giving the European manufacturer an opportunity to purchase at a less price than the duties imposed under the United States tariff.*

* The report of the Boston Board of Trade, presented January, 1868, adds the following further evidence on this subject. It says: "By reference to the table of imports it will be seen that the importation of wools of the class Nos. 1 and 2 (*i. e.*, Buenos Ayres, Australian, and Cape of Good Hope wools) has nearly ceased.

"This is looked upon by the wool-growers as a favorable result which will lead to high prices for wool of home growth. In this they may be disappointed. For already the wools have fallen abroad to an extent which nearly balances the added duty, consequently they can be imported for about the same prices as before. But these our

But it may be said, that, granting the truth of all of the above statements; granting that wool returns less in money to the grower than ever before; that the number of sheep in the country is rapidly diminishing; that the wool-manufacturing industry is in a most depressed and unprofitable condition; that foreign imports are increasing, and smuggling becoming systematized; yet the consumer is none the worse off, inasmuch as he is enabled to purchase his cloth at a price nearly or quite as low as previous to the war. That this may be true in respect to a few varieties of fabrics is not disputed,* but at the same time, those who use

manufacturers cannot afford to give, to put into goods to compete with those made of the same wool obtained at the cheap rates now ruling in Europe.

"Take, for instance, a yard of broadcloth weighing one pound, as given in table A of the statement of the executive committee of the national association of wool-manufacturers, addressed to the United States revenue commission, May, 1866, page 36; we have shown that already, in less than a year from the passage of this tariff, the prediction of Mr. Wells has been fully verified, and that in spite of the enormously high duties a yard of broadcloth made of these competing wools can be imported cheaper than under the old tariff, and that consequently we can neither afford to import wool nor to pay as much for American wool for this manufacture as we could under the tariff of 1864, high as that was, and not nearly as much as we did under that of 1857, when all these wools came in free. We do not present these facts with any desire to effect an immediate change in the tariff, but that they may be brought to the attention of the people, particularly of the wool-growers, who, perhaps, may be induced to watch the course of trade until they shall become convinced that the world is now too intimately bound together to make any violent attempts to disturb the laws of trade successful."

* The following table, prepared at the request of the Commissioner, by the house of A. T. Stewart & Co., of New York, shows the selling price of certain leading varieties of woolen goods in 1860 and 1869, respectively:

	1860.	1869.
Cadet cloths, government standard	$2 75	$3 25
Harris cassimeres, 14 oz	1 37½ *a* 1 50	1 75 *a* 2 00
Cotton warp cloths, 14 oz	1 00 *a* 1 25	1 75
All-wool cloths, 14 oz	1 50	2 75
Middlesex sackings	1 10	1 25
Middlesex doeskins	1 05	1 15
Middlesex shawls	7 00	7 00
Middlesex beavers	3 75	4 25
Middlesex opera flannels	47½	50
Broadbrook cassimeres	1 62½ *a* 1 75	1 75
Broadbrook beavers	2 75	3 00
Spring cassimeres, 8 to 9 oz	1 12½ *a* 1 25	1 25 *a* 1 37½
Glenham repellants	1 10 *a* 1 15	1 20
Glenham sackings	1 05	1 15
Swift River fancies, 11 to 12 oz	90	1 00 *a* 1 10
Royalston cassimeres	Aver. 1 07½	1 25
Fitchburg cassimeres	Aver. 1 07½	1 25

The report accompanying the above table adds: "It is difficult to obtain reliable data in respect to the comparative cost of domestic woolens in 1860 and 1869, inasmuch as there are few goods made now that are identical in quality with those made in 1860. Of all of the above, probably the first item, viz, cadet mixed cloths, used by the institution at West Point, is the most reliable to show the difference of value at the different dates, on account of not being so much subjected to caprices of fashion or to competition of other makers."

this argument in support of the existing duties take very good care not to mention the fact that the prices of woolen goods, under the influence of wool unnaturally cheapened, and improvements in manufacturing, have fallen comparatively to an equal or greater extent in Europe,* while the wages paid to the operatives of the European woolen mills have tended during the same time to an advance. The price of woolen fabrics generally is reported to the Commissioner, by those qualified to judge, to be at least twenty per cent. less at the present time in Europe than it was in 1860; but of this decline, even granting that all American woolens are as low now as they were in 1860, (which is not the case,) the American consumer has evidently received no benefit. In short, the Commissioner feels convinced that if the great mass of the American people, especially the working men and the working women, toiling to elevate themselves, with the multitude of clerks, accountants, professional men, pensioners, and others, who deny themselves and economize their slender incomes to make the year's receipts balance the year's expenditures, could only once fully realize the extent of the addition to their resources could they be permitted to purchase clothing as cheap in the United States as in Great Britain, they would never stop to inquire according to what particular theory of economy tariffs were enacted, but would at once so direct public opinion and suffrage as to compel the abandonment of the existing policy.

In short, what is now needed to restore prosperity to the woolen industry, is a removal of all duties on the importation of foreign wools and dyestuffs, and a general reduction of the duties on manufactured woolen fabrics of every description to twenty-five per cent. ad valorem. On this basis the most experienced woolen manufacturers of the country assure the Commissioner that they can at once extend, diversify, and secure prosperity to their business. On this basis the cost of domestic woolen fabrics will be so far reduced as to give great relief to the consumer, and lead to an immediate and largely increased consumption. And on this basis only can the wool-grower expect any immediate increased demand for his staple product of merino fleece; while in respect to the combing and the finer wools it is sufficient to say, that the

* The following table, derived from another authority from that above cited, shows the extent of the recent reductions which have taken place in the importing prices of standard French woolens:

	1859.	1866.	1869.
	Francs.	*Francs.*	*Francs.*
French merinos, all worsted	2.62	2.40	1.90
	3.03	3.00	2.00
	3.22	3.15	2.40
Dyed mousseline de laines, all worsted	1.13	.98	.79
	1.22	1.06	.85
French dyed poplins, all worsted	....	1.75	1.19
	....	2.15	1.69

supply of these wools has not for the last few years increased in proportion to their consumption, and that the extension of their use in American industry, which would inevitably follow a remission of the duties upon their import, would so far increase their demand as to give to the domestic producer all the encouragement that would prove necessary.

ON THE REDUCTION OF PRICES EFFECTED THROUGH COMPETITION.

The Commissioner deems it appropriate in this connection to say a word in reference to the idea adopted and advocated by a school of American economists, that it is for the advantage of the country to endeavor to effect a reduction of prices by the creation, through legislation or otherwise, of an excessive or artificial stimulus to production.

That the creation of an artificial stimulus to domestic production—such as is almost always temporarily afforded by an increase of the tariff, or such as was afforded during the war by the necessity for extraordinary supplies—does have the effect, in the first instance, to increase and quicken production, and subsequently to reduce prices through the competition engendered, cannot be doubted. But the Commissioner, after a careful examination of the subject, is fully satisfied that it can be shown, in almost every instance where competition has thus reduced prices, that the result has been rather to the detriment than to the advantage of the country, the main exceptions to the rule being in the case of certain small articles—nickel for example—which, owing to their comparative insignificance and limited production and consumption, are capable of being entirely controlled and monopolized by two or three individuals or associations. That the result thus indicated must follow as a matter of necessity, will appear obvious upon a little reflection. Thus the first effect of cutting off or checking the competitive supply of a foreign product, or otherwise creating an extraordinary domestic demand, is to increase prices; which in turn affords large profits to those in the possession of "stocks on hand," or of the machinery of production ready for immediate and continuous service. The fact of the possibility of the realization of large profits immediately tempts others to engage in the same branch of production—in very many cases with insufficient capital, (raised often through the medium of a stock company,) and without that practical knowledge of the details of the undertaking necessary to insure success. The supply of skilled labor being at all times limited in the United States, the producers last in the field bid against the older for the control of specialties of labor; wages advance abnormally, and abnormally increase the cost of the product. As production goes on, supply gradually becomes equal and finally in excess of demand. The producers working on insufficient capital or with insufficient skill, are soon obliged, in order to meet impending obligations or to dispose of imperfect stock, to force sales through a reduction of prices; and the older, in order to retain their markets and their customers, are compelled to follow their example. This in turn is followed by new concessions alternately by both parties, which is accompanied by the usual resort of turning out articles or products of inferior quality, but with an external good appearance; slate being substituted in the place of coal; cinder in the place of iron; shoddy in the place of wool; starch and sizing in the place of cotton; pasteboard in the manufacture of boots and shoes in the place of leather; and clay and plaster in the manufacture of paper in the place of fiber. And so the work of production goes on, until gradually the whole industry becomes depressed and demoralized, and the weaker producers succumb, with a greater or less destruction of capital and waste of product.

Affairs having now reached their minimum of depression, recovery slowly commences. The increase of the country causes consumption to gradually gain upon production; and finally the community suddenly becomes aware of the fact that supply has all at once become unequal to demand. Then those of the producers who have been able to maintain their existence experience another season of remarkable prosperity; others again rush into the business, and the old experience is again and again repeated. Such has been the history of the industry of the country for the last thirty years under the influence of the frequent modifications of the tariff, and latterly under the influence of the war; and such is most noticeably its present experience. To use a familiar expression, it has always been either "high water or low water;" no middle course, and no stability. What the people gain, as consumers, at one time from low prices, they more than compensate for at another by the recurrence of extreme rates, and, as producers, by periodical suspension of industry, reduction of wages, and depression of business. Meantime the loss to the country from the destruction of capital and the waste and misapplication of labor is something which no man can estimate.

The specific illustrations of this experience are too striking to admit of being passed over in silence. That afforded by the present condition of the wool industry has already been adverted to.

A further and still more striking illustration is afforded in the recent history of the manufacture of paper. Thus, in 1863-'64-'65, it was found that the supply of paper of domestic manufacture was insufficient for the consumption of the country, and a tariff of from twenty to thirty-five per cent. restricted importations. The price of paper rose accordingly with great rapidity, nearly or quite to the extent of one hundred per cent.; and the profits of the paper manufacturers who were then in the possession of the machinery of production were so great that the Commissioner, in his report for 1866-'67, referred to them as most anomalous and extraordinary. The usual effect followed. A host of individuals rushed into the business, and during the years 1864-'65-'66, it is estimated that more paper mills were constructed and put in operation than in the twelve years previous. As a matter of course, the markets became rapidly overstocked, prices fell with great rapidity, many abandoned the business, and sold their mills for much less than the cost of construction; while in the spring of 1869, in the same section of the country where the incomes of paper manufacturers in 1865 were reported as so extraordinary, the representatives of the trade of New England met together in convention to consider the advisability of "decreasing the production of paper, in consideration of the depressed condition of the business." In fact, at the present time, the business of paper manufacturing, next to ship-building and the woolen manufacture, is probably one of the most depressed of the various industries of the country; and while wages and the price of the raw materials used have receded but little, the price of the finished product is nearly as low in currency as it was in gold anterior to the war. In October, 1869, a storm of great violence swept over the northern portion of the country, and in the flood which followed the mills engaged in the manufacture of paper especially sustained injury by the destruction of their dams and otherwise. A leading New England journal, in one of the paper manufacturing districts, in commenting on the effects of the storm, uses this language: "There seems to have been an unusual fatality among paper mills; but this disaster will work to the advantage of those who escaped the flood; and we doubt not that those that did stand will do a better business in consequence of the lessened supply." Or, in other words, the condition of this particular branch of industry had become so prostrated, that the occurrence of a great public calamity, with a vast attendant destruction of property, had come to be regarded by some in the light of a special blessing.

Now, the lesson of this experience, which might be further illustrated to almost any extent, would seem most certainly to be, that whatever advantage is temporarily gained by stimulating industries into an unnatural growth and development, is subsequently more than compensated for by a resulting waste and misapplication of both capital and labor. And of these two elements of wealth and civilization, the United States, of all industrial and commercial nations, has the least available surplus. What rather should be sought for is that mean of encouragement—call it protection if you will, or otherwise—which would give to every branch of legitimate domestic industry an equal opportunity and a condition of stability as respects supply and demand; which would insure permanence of price, incentives to the exercise of skill and economy, and such a moderate degree of profit as should effectually discourage inconsiderate and excessive competition. Did space suffice, the Commissioner could here add a chapter of the most interesting facts and incidents, showing the enormous waste which as a general rule characterizes American protected manufactures in contradistinction to European manufactures; and which is due, in his opinion, in great part to the fact that the American manufacturers have so long been accustomed to look to legislation for support, that the idea of self-dependence, through the exercise of more economic and skillful working, scarcely receives consideration.

With these specific illustrations and recommendations of the influence of certain existing duties, the Commissioner would further submit the following recommendations of modifications of the tariff.

RECOMMENDATIONS IN THE INTEREST OF DOMESTIC INDUSTRY IN GENERAL.

On pig iron, a duty of $3 *per ton.* The present duty is $9 per ton, and the amount of revenue derived from the same during the fiscal year 1867–'68, was $1,011,109 96.

On scrap iron, a duty of $3 *per ton.* Present duty, $8 per ton; amount of revenue received in 1867–'68, $640,294 60.

On salt in bulk, 9 *cents per hundred pounds; on salt in bags,* 12 *cents per hundred pounds.* Present duty, 18 and 24 cents, respectively; amount of revenue received, 1867–68, on salt in bulk, $395,955 17; in bags, $740,270 59; total, $1,136,225 76.

The extent of revenue reduction, arising from the adoption of the above modifications, will, in the opinion of the Commissioner, be as follows:

In respect to pig iron a reduction of the duty would, undoubtedly, be followed by such a reduction in the price of the domestic product as, added to freights and commissions on the foreign article, would leave the relations between the domestic and foreign producers the same substantially as at present. No material increase of imports being probable, the loss to the revenue would, therefore, be approximately $750,000. A reduction of $6 per ton in the cost of a domestic consumption of 1,800,000 tons (domestic and foreign) would, however, relieve the community of taxation, in the first instance, to the extent of $10,800,000 per annum. The reduction of the duty on scrap iron would probably be followed by an increase of imports, and so compensate, to some extent, for a loss of revenue. This loss the Commissioner estimates at $400,000. The indirect gain to the community by the consequent tendency to cheapen bar iron and promote industry, would, however, be considerable.

A reduction in the duty on salt would, probably, as in the case of pig iron, be followed by a corresponding reduction in the price of the domestic article; and this in turn would prevent any great increase in importations. The loss from this reduction would, in the opinion of the Commissioner, approximate $600,000; a reduction of the cost of the domestic consumption of salt (39,000,000 bushels per annum) to the extent of 10 cents per bushel, would relieve the community of a tax, in the first instance, of $3,900,000 per annum.

Lumber.—On all timber, round, square, or sided; on all sawed and unplaned planks, boards, and deal; on laths, clapboards, and shingles, *an entire removal of all duties.* Present duty, twenty per cent. Revenue received, 1867–'68, $1,262,020 47. In his report for 1868–'69 the Commissioner estimated that, apart from the beneficial influence of the removal of these duties in respect to the retardation of the wasteful destruction of American forests, the immediate and direct gain to the people, through a reduction of the cost of lumber, would approximate $16,000,000 per annum.

On *coal*, of every variety, an entire removal of all duties. Present duties, on anthracite, 40 cents per ton; on bituminous, $1 25 per ton. Revenue received in 1867–'68, on anthracite, $30 40; on bituminous, $492,526 56.

On *firewood*, an entire removal of all duty. Present duty, 20 per cent. Revenue received in 1867–'68, $42,605 12. The Commissioner is assured that the removal of the duty on this article of import would greatly favor the manufacture of salt in Michigan, and prove a great boon to consumers upon all the frontier States, where the consumption is rapidly increasing, while the local supply is rapidly diminishing.

On *copper ore*, an entire removal of all duty. Present duty, three cents per pound on each pound of pure copper contained therein. Import, at present, substantially prohibited.

In 1869, Congress, with a view of promoting the interests of the copper industry largely increased the duties on copper, copper ores, and all manufactures of copper. The immediate effect of this law was to prohibit the importation of foreign ores of copper, to close up and substantially destroy two great centers of smelting industry at Baltimore and Boston, and to inflict serious injury upon the manufacturers of paper-hangings, by increasing the cost of Dutch metal. The enactment of the law has been also followed by a reduction in the price of ingot copper. Thus, the market price a short time previous to the passage of the bill was 26 @ 27 cents; immediately after the passage of the bill the price fell to 24, and subsequently to 22 @ 23, at which point it remains.*

In the effort to promote the interests of domestic copper production by increasing the duties on competitive imports, two points seem to have been overlooked: First, that the United States is a copper-exporting rather than a copper-importing country, as is shown by the fact that in the ten years from 1859 to 1869, inclusive, the value of the exports exceeded the value of the imports by the sum of $487,990. During the fiscal year 1868 the exports and re-exports of copper in pigs, bars, and ingots were returned at 1,365,144 pounds, while the imports amounted to only the trifling quantity of 14,248 pounds. The attempt to regulate the domestic price of an article, of which the country produces a surplus for export, by means of an import duty, is, therefore, on its face an absurd-

---

* It is reasonable, therefore, to suppose, as the copper-mining industry of the United States is in a condition of as great depression now as at any former period, and as every argument and fact urged in February, 1869, for an increase of duties on copper is as true and as cogent now as then, that the advocates of relief by legislation, in order to maintain their consistency, will again petition Congress to still further increase the duties, which, judged from the point of efficiency, are so low as to demand immediate consideration.

ity, and has utterly failed, as might have been expected. Second, an examination of the general statistics of copper production and consumption since 1858 shows a continued tendency to the disuse of copper in the arts, and a substitution of iron or other cheaper metals in its place. This is strikingly shown by the fact that, while the actual increase in the shape of imported and produced copper in Great Britain from 1858 to 1867 was only about 11 per cent., the increase in the production and consumption of iron in the same country during the same period were about 42 per cent. It would seem manifest, therefore, from the mere presentation of this statement, that any attempt to resist, by arbitrary legislation, this cheapening of copper which is taking place through economical influences, or, what is the same thing, to resist the substitution of a cheaper for a dearer metal, must, from the very nature of things, not only be equivalent, to attempting an impossibility, but that the whole influence of such legislation, by interfering with the course of trade and of prices, must be to promote the very tendency which those interested in copper production especially deprecate; and such, the Commissioner believes, is the influence of the duties levied under the existing tariff on copper. The Commissioner would further recommend, in this connection, that the duty on copper in plates or sheets, known as braziers' copper, and on copper in the form of rods, bolts, nails, spikes, and copper bottoms, be reduced from 45 per cent. ad valorem to 25 per cent. ad valorem, on the ground that the existing duty is prohibitive and entirely destructive of revenue. During the fiscal year 1867–'68, when the duty on these articles was 35 per cent. ad valorem, the whole amount of revenue received was 35 cents. Since then the duty has been increased to 45 per cent., thus rendering it probable that not even the receipts of the previous year will be maintained Again, the Commissioner would ask attention to this statement: The price of ingot copper in Great Britain is at present 16¼ cents gold per pound; the price of rolled copper—braziers' sheets, such as is used for the manufacture of copper boilers—in Great Britain, is 17¼ cents per pound, or only one cent higher than ingot copper. Now, the price of ingot copper in New York is 22½ @ 23 cents per pound, and the price for rolled or braziers' sheets is 33 cents per pound, or 10 @ 10½ cents difference.

On *jute and sun-hemp*, an entire removal of all duty. Present duty, $15 per ton. Revenue received, 1867–'68, $57,542 75.

The object of this recommendation is the development of an industry which, although possessing gigantic proportions in Europe, can hardly be said to have as yet an existence in the United States. Indeed it is a fact in the history of our industrial experience especially worthy of notice, that while as a nation professing extreme devotion to the principle of extending domestic industry we have not only neglected but by the maintenance of a high duty persistently discouraged the introduction and development of a branch of textile industry which in Great Britain ranks next in importance to cotton and wool; the import of jute fiber into Great Britain for the year 1868 having been upwards of *two hundred and eighteen millions* of pounds, while the United States, during the same period, consumed only about *eight millions* of pounds. In view, therefore, of the enormous and rapidly increasing use of this new raw material, whose use in Europe as a textile fiber dates back but little beyond the year 1852, the Commissioner would fail of his duty did he not earnestly ask the attention of Congress to the importance of legislating in such a manner as will help to give henceforth to the United States a participation in the profits of this great branch of industry.

The articles into which jute is manufactured are mainly coarse fabrics, such as burlaps, padding, coarse canvas, carpet yarns and twines, all of which the United States annually imports in large quantities, but which might readily be manufactured at home. The free admission of jute has heretofore been opposed, mainly from the idea that it would prove a rival to domestic flax and hemp; but in the opinion of the Commissioner, it is really not analogous to, and would not compete with, any of the products of the United States. Its color is somewhat lighter than that of flax, while its fiber, varying from fifteen to twenty feet in length, is coarser, weaker, and far less flexible than the fibers of the most inferior varieties of domestic flax or hemp.

RECOMMENDATIONS IN THE INTEREST OF THE BOOT AND SHOE INDUSTRY AND OF THE MANUFACTURE OF LEATHER.

On *hides* and *undressed skins* of every description—*an entire removal of all duties.* Present duty, ten per cent. Revenue received, 1867-'68, $977,325 12.

Leather.—On leather of all descriptions, except morocco, japaned and patent leather—*an entire removal of all duties.* Present duties, twenty-five and thirty-five per cent. Revenue received, 1867-'68, $1,363,481 51.

On hemlock, oak, and all other barks used for the tanning of leather—*an entire removal of all duties.* Present duty, ten per cent.

On sumac—*an entire removal of duty.* Present duty, ten per cent. Revenue received, 1867-'68, $53,608 56.

Lastings and serge.—On fabrics of wool or hair, known as lasting and serge, when the same are woven or made into patterns of size, shape, and form, and in such manner as to be fit for shoes and bootees exclusively, and not combined with India-rubber—*an entire removal of all duties.* Present duty, fifty cents per pound, and thirty-five per cent. ad valorem. Revenue received, 1867-'68, (estimated,) $1,157,000.

The extent of revenue reduction, by the removal of the above specified duties, would, in the opinion of the Commissioner, approximate $3,500,000. The burden of taxation, in the first instance, from which the people would be relieved, however, by the removal of these duties, taking leather and all the manufactures of leather into consideration, will, as already demonstrated, approximate the sum of $18,000,000.

RECOMMENDATION IN THE INTEREST OF THE MANUFACTURE OF PAPER-HANGINGS.

On *bronze* or *Dutch metal* or *Florence leaf*, in leaf or powder—*an entire removal of the duty*. Present duty, forty-five per cent. ad valorem. Revenue received, 1868–'69, (estimated,) $20,000. The removal of this duty, as already shown, would reduce the cost of the manufacture of the better class of paper-hangings to the extent of from five cents to twenty-five cents per roll.

RECOMMENDATIONS IN THE INTEREST OF THE MANUFACTURES OF SULPHURIC ACID, SOAP, GLASS, PAPER, COAL OIL, CHEMICALS, AND OF THE BLEACHING AND DYEING INDUSTRIES.

On *crude sulphur—an entire removal of the duty*. Present duty, $6 per ton, or twenty-five per cent. Revenue received, 1867–'68, $108,903 30.

The Commissioner would recommend, in this connection, that the duties on flour-of-sulphur, at present $20 per ton, and fifteen per cent. ad valorem, be reduced to $10 per ton; and on refined brimstone, in rolls, that the present duty, $10 per ton, be reduced to $5 per ton. The reason for the recommendation of these reductions is, that the present duties are excessive and destructive of revenue; the revenue received from these two sources during the year 1867–'68 being only $1,119 20.

On *soda ash—an entire removal of the duty*. Present duty, one half cent per pound. Revenue received, 1867–'68, $545,228 83.

On *chloride of lime*, or bleaching powders—*an entire removal of the duty*. Present duty, thirty cents per hundred pounds. Revenue received, 1867–'68, $73,486 78.

On *waste paper*, or waste material of any kind fit only for the manufacture of paper—*an entire removal of the duty*. Present duty, ten per cent.

On *esparto* or *Spanish grass*, a crude material for the manufacture of paper—*an entire removal of all duty*. Present duty, twenty per cent.

RECOMMENDATIONS IN THE INTEREST OF THE BREWERS, AND OF THE INTERNAL REVENUE COLLECTED FROM THE TAXATION OF MALT LIQUORS.

On *barley—an entire removal of the duty*. Present duty, fifteen cents per bushel. Revenue received, 1867–'68, $566,547 39.

The reasons in support of this recommendation are clearly stated in the following communication, addressed to the Commissioner by the president of the Brewers' Association of the United States:

Previous to the war the average price of barley in the city of New York was about eighty cents per bushel, and the price of beers and ales about $6 per barrel, while the price per glass of ale or beer, containing fully one-third more than the glasses now in use, was six cents. Since the duty was imposed the price of barley in New York has been as high as $1 70 per bushel; that of malt liquors, say, $10 per barrel, and by the glass, say, eight cents. The cost of manufacturing by the brewers has been fully one hundred per cent. more, exclusive of the $1 tax per barrel. The price of barley in the United States has been from twenty-five to fifty cents higher relatively than those of other cereals; a fact to be attributed to the small crops of the former suitable for malting purposes; and as only northern climates are adapted to the production of barley, the main dependence of the brewers has been on the production of the Canadas for their lager and storing beers."

"The high cost of barley, and the expenses attendant upon the brewing of malt liquors, has prevented the brewers from selling their beers at such prices as would render them the popular beverage, and merely give to them an equal increase of consumption, as compared to other articles of staple manufacture which are not interfered with by foreign importations. To render beer popular it must be sold by the retailers at a low price, as is the case in Great Britain and Germany."

"Long experience has proved that the barley crops of those States from whence the brewers derive their supplies, viz., New York, Western Pennsylvania, Ohio, Illinois, Wisconsin, Iowa, and Minnesota, are very unreliable as regards the quality of the grain; but not so of the Canadas, whose soil and climate are admirably adapted for the production of the best American barley."

Under these circumstances, the representatives of the brewing interest of the United States claim that it is both impolitic and unjust for the national government to assess an annual sum of over six millions of dollars on the products of their industry, and at the same time, by imposing a duty on the importation of barley, indirectly increase the cost of their manufacture and restrict the extension of their business. They also claim that the removal of the duty in question would increase the internal revenue derived from malt liquors to an extent far more than sufficient to compensate for any loss through the customs. The Commissioner would add that the capital at present invested in the business of brewing in the United States is estimated by the Brewers' Association at $56,856,000, giving direct employment to 9,814 workmen.

RECOMMENDATIONS IN THE INTEREST OF THE SILK, FUR, AND FELT HAT INDUSTRY.

On hatter's and cut furs—an entire removal of all duties. Present duty, twenty per cent. Revenue received, 1867-'68, $282,976 40.

On silk-plush, silk linings, and silk hat-bands, cut in such a manner as to be fit for the manufacture of hats exclusively, *an entire removal of all duties.* Present duties, sixty per cent. Revenue received, 1867-'68, $600,000, (estimated.) The representatives of this most important industry, employing in the fur and felt hat department alone an estimated capital of $20,000,000, state the present condition of their business as one of extreme depression, the domestic consumption of felt and fur hats having been reduced during the last three years at least twenty-five per cent. The following are extracts from the answers returned to official inquiries made by the Commissioner respecting the latter industry:

Question. Was there a demand in 1860-'61 for your product for exportation?—Answer. Yes. There was a large demand from Canada, Cuba, the West Indies, Mexico, and South America. In the years named, about one-seventh of the sales would be shipped to points outside of the United States; or, in a house selling 700,000 hats, 100,000 could be reasonably estimated as on foreign account; to some manufacturers this would not apply, but to others the proportion would be greater.

Question. Does the foreign demand now continue?—Answer. At present there is no demand for our goods, nor has there been for several years of any moment. Of course there are still a few goods in our line sold to Canada, but no other market takes any, or at least the amount is so inconsiderable as not to enter into the calculation. The reason is that our tariff on such materials as we consume (they are all imported) enables France, England and Germany to produce the same classes of goods much cheaper; and we cannot compete with them as formerly in supplying these markets. Had the duties remained the same as in 1860 we could have competed with any country for the foreign trade to the countries above mentioned, and, as we have heretofore, successfully. The present duty of thirty-five per cent. on hats does not protect, as we pay in duties on materials and in taxes a little above that percentage. The importation of foreign hats increases, therefore, rather than diminishes. If we had a low tariff on raw materials, we could export a great many hats, not simply upon fur, but on silk bands and bindings and skivers. Silk and satin and bands and binding could be cut and put into such shape as to be only available for the purpose of trimming hats.

MISCELLANEOUS.

The Commissioner in the interest of general domestic industry would further recommend the entire remission of the duties on the following specific articles or classes of articles:

Articles.	Present duty.	Revenue received 1867–8.
Ivory unmanufactured and imported direct from countries of production.	10 per cent.	$42, 117 40
Ivory nuts, vegetable	10 per cent.	1, 217 20
Animals, living, of all kinds	20 per cent.	466, 404 01
Bristles	15 per cent.	79, 199 40
Chalk, white	$10 per ton.	105, 714 13
Annato, seed or extract	20 per cent.	188 40
Argols, or crude or partially refined tartar	6 cts. per lb.	126, 739 11
Barks, all medicinal	20 per cent.	82, 246 80
Antimony, crude or regulus of	10 per cent.	8, 382 20
Camphor, crude	30 cts. per lb.	59, 893 20
Cutch or catechu	10 per cent.	10, 623 60
Corkwood, unmanufactured	30 per cent.	48, 260 10
Feathers and downs for beds	30 per cent.	4, 373 61
Glue stock	10 per cent.	1, 266 50
Gums of all kinds, unmanufactured and unrefined, used in the manufacture of varnish.	10 cts. to 50 cts. per lb.	439, 039 30
Gutta-percha, crude	10 per cent.	2, 121 80
India-rubber, crude	10 per cent.	196, 911 40
Kryolite	20 per cent.	13, 726 40
Bamboo	10 per cent.	579 90
Willow or ozier, unmanufactured	30 per cent.	8, 661 60
Cudbear	10 per cent.	4, 324 60
Bones, crude and unmanufactured	10 per cent.	....
Horns	10 per cent.	6, 234 30
Lithographic stones	20 per cent.	2, 651 60
Total	....	1, 710, 876 56

Gunny cloth and bags.—The present duty on gunny cloth and gunny bags is three cents per pound, (gold,) or within a fraction of one hundred per cent. of their market value in bond—a rate so excessive that the importation of these articles from Calcutta has almost entirely ceased. Thus the import of gunny cloth, which was returned at 75,000 bales in 1860, was reduced to 14,000 bales in 1868, and, for the year 1869, has not exceeded 5,000 bales. The latest advices from India furthermore state, that "not a bale of gunny cloth is now loading, or to load this season, for the States." The result of the present duty is therefore manifestly detrimental to the revenue; and, also, to the shipping interest, inasmuch as the commodities in question are indispensable for light or measurement freight in the India trade, and without them no vessel can be loaded with a full cargo for the United States. A reduction of the price of gunny cloth would also result to the advantage of the agriculturists ot the country, affording a cheaper material for the enclosure and transportation of cotton, corn, and other similar products. The Commissioner would, therefore, recommend a reduction of the duty on gunny bags and gunny cloth to one cent per pound as the maximum.

RECAPITULATION.

The abatement or entire removal of the duties as above recommended would, as nearly as can be estimated, reduce the revenue derived from customs to the extent of about twelve millions. On the other hand, the direct relief experienced by the community through the abatement of prices which would follow the removal or abatement of the taxes in question would, in the opinion of the Commissioner, be not less than sixty million dollars; while the indirect gain, and the value of the stimulus afforded thereby to domestic industry, must be represented by a much larger figure.

RECOMMENDATIONS FOR MODIFICATIONS OF THE TARIFF, SUBMITTED MAINLY WITH A VIEW OF INCREASING THE REVENUE, OR OF FACILITATING OR SIMPLIFYING THE LAWS FOR THE COLLECTION OF REVENUE.

The Commissioner would further recommend the following modifications of the tariff, with a view of increasing thereby the national revenue, or of facilitating or simplifying the laws for the collection of revenue.

Wines.—On all wines, irrespective of quality, (champagne and other sparkling wines excepted,) a specific duty of fifty cents per gallon is recommended.

The experience afforded since 1867 has in every respect confirmed the assertion made by the Commissioner in his previous report, (January, 1867,) "that the ad valorem system as applied to wines, has proved detrimental to all legitimate business, destructive of revenue, and an endless source of litigation between the government and the importers." If the rate named may seem too low a duty to be imposed on an article so essentially a luxury as wine, the Commmissioner would ask attention to the following facts.

According to the official reports, there were imported for the fiscal year 1867–'68, 6,102,479 gallons of wine, as compared with 9,476,814 imported in 1865–'66. Of this quantity, 5,383,347 gallons were returned as valued at not over fifty cents per gallon, and paying a duty of twenty cents per gallon and twenty-five per cent. ad valorem, or at the rate of twenty-seven cents per gallon; 515,580 gallons valued at over fifty cents and not over one dollar per gallon, and paying a duty of fifty cents per gallon and twenty-five per cent. ad valorem, or at the rate of sixty-eight cents per gallon; and 203,552 gallons valued at over one dollar per gallon and paying a duty of one dollar per gallon and twenty-five per cent. ad valorem, or at the rate of one dollar and fifty-eight cents per gallon; making a total revenue from the duties on wines of $2,155,524, and the average rate thirty-five cents per gallon. It is, therefore, evident that the rates proposed, while they are entirely satisfactory to the importing interest, are really a large advance upon the existing tariff; and, supposing the importation to remain the same as for 1867–'68, will yield an additional revenue of about $900,000. The truth of the matter, however, is, that by reason of the almost utter impossibility of accurately determining the specific value of a wine, the imports of wines are almost always undervalued; and the constant differences which have arisen between the officers of the customs and the importers have contributed much to the interruption of the regular trade in and importation of the products in question. With a removal of these difficulties by the adoption of a specific duty, there is no reason to doubt but that the importation will resume its former average, and that the gain to the treasury will approximate two and a half millions per annum.

If, however, it should be objected that under a uniform specific duty the high-priced Johannisberger or Madeira will pay no more than the common low-priced *vin ordinaire*, the fact heretofore pointed out may again be cited, viz: that out of over six million gallons imported in 1867–'68 *only* 203,452 *gallons, or less than* 4 *per cent. of the whole importation, were entered as costing over one dollar per gallon.* The Commissioner would also call attention to the fact that both in the United States and Great Britain a uniform duty on tea has been found both by the trade and the government to be entirely unexceptionable; and yet the diversity in the prices of tea in China is much greater than the range in prices of wines at the points of exportation.

FORM OF LAW.—The following form of law, covering the importation of all wines, is recommended: *On wines of all kinds in bulk, irrespective of quality, cost of cask included, containing not more than twenty-two per centum of alcohol, Tralle's hydrometer, fifty cents per gallon:*

Provided, that upon all liquors containing more than twenty-two per cent.

of alcohol, which shall be entered under the name of wines, there shall be levied and paid the same duty as that which is imposed upon brandy. *

Mineral or medicinal waters.—The present duty on mineral waters is three cents per bottle, and twenty-five per cent. ad valorem. The Com-

---

* As illustrative of the present condition of the native wine industry of the United States the Commissioner would ask attention to the following letter addressed to him on this subject by a gentleman who is everywhere acknowledged as an authority in regard to the question under discussion:

"RAHWAY, N. J., *June* 24, 1869.

"SIR: In a recent conversation touching the effects of the high duties levied on the importation of foreign wines on the wine produced in this country, you requested me to give you the substance of my experience in this matter, which I now do with pleasure.

"The history of our native wine trade is familiar to you. I need not, therefore, refer to the various endeavors of the pioneers in grape culture until a perfect wine was produced from the pure juice of the Catawba grape by Nicholas Longworth about twenty-four or five years ago. This wine, however, in its pure state, was too acidulous to please the popular taste, but it was much relished by the German settlers of Ohio, who were accustomed to such wines in their own country. It however was a capital wine to mix with sugar and ice for cobblers, as a substitute for sherry, and it also made an excellent sparkling wine. Some of the latter I tasted in Chillicothe, Ohio, in 1850. It struck me then that it might be popularized in New York. I opened a correspondence with Mr. Longworth, and in 1852 had the pleasure of receiving a small invoice of it—the first that had ever been in the city—indeed, as Mr. Longworth said, 'the first that had ever crossed the mountains,' (the Alleghanies.) The wine speedily became popular, and continued to be until the death of Mr. Longworth, whose agent I continued to be until that time—a period of many years. The still wines did not succeed so well; except for Catawba cobblers, the sale was very limited. The truth was, our people, accustomed to the heavily brandied wines of Europe, the sherries, Madeiras, and ports, with an alcoholic percentage of 19 to 24 per cent., did not much fancy a pure wine of only 8 to 9 per cent. of fixed alcohol. It was not strong enough. But the sparkling wines with a slight addition of brandy or sugar, which by fermentation resolves itself into brandy, met with better success.

"At this time the sparkling Catawba could be laid down in New York at a cost a little exceeding that of the most popular French champagne, 'the Heidsick,' but it was sold by the case at the same price, say $14. Yet it kept its own, and sales grew larger, notwithstanding this formidable competitor. At that time the sale of champagne was immense, but its low price (at wholesale) did not tempt imitators to manufacture a spurious Heidsick and sell it for the real article. The market was full of good brands of champagne, but the native wine was steadily growing in favor without protection and in spite of so many rivals. Another formidable antagonist to the sale of native wines *was the trade!* There was more money to be made by selling imported wines, and therefore the whole of the wine trade in New York turned its back upon sparkling Catawba. Nevertheless it worked its way without recommendation into favor with the public. The heavy duties imposed upon foreign wines during the war diminished at once the greater part of the supply from that source. Native wines had the full benefit of protection, and, besides, were free from internal tax. And we must not overlook another great advantage in their favor; the improvements in the manufacture, the results of experience and enterprise, had produced sparkling wines far superior in quality to those of twenty or even ten years ago. For delicacy of flavor and fragrance of boquet, the sparkling Catawbas of the Pleasant Valley Wine Company; of the Urbana Wine Company; of Chas. Bottlers, of Cincinnati; of Weeks's Sparkling and Longworth's Golden Wedding, (all of which took diplomas of 'honorable mention' at the Paris Exposition, where they were in competition with the choicest champagnes of France,)

missioner would recommend, if it be considered desirable to retain the duty on these imports, that they be made specific with the following

FORM OF LAW: On mineral or medicinal waters, or waters from springs impregnated with minerals, seventy-five cents for each dozen bottles or jugs containing not more than one pint each, and one dollar and twenty-five cents for each dozen bottles or jugs containing more than one pint and not over one quart.

Sardines.—Sardines are imported in cases of 100 tin boxes each, with a limitation of the boxes to three sizes, viz., quarter, half, and whole boxes. The duty imposed under the present tariff is fifty per cent. ad valorem, which may be easily and with advantage changed into a specific duty by adopting as a basis the cubic-inch measure. This would give for the quarter boxes a duty of four cents gold; for the half boxes, six and one half cents; and for whole boxes, fourteen and a fourth cents per

---

are so greatly in advance of Longworth's old wines of twenty years ago, that a comparsion between them would be like (to use a homely simile) as 'cheese is to chalk' in the list of alimentary substances.

"But great as have been the improvements in the manufacture of sparkling wines, greater have been those in the production of still wines, from which our sparkling wines are made.

"The southern shore of Lake Erie now seems to be our proper vine-land, and the still Catawbas from this favored locality will compare with credit with the very best growth of the Rhine.

"We may instance those delicate light wines of Kelley's Island, which are produced under the superintendence of Messrs. Kelley and Huntington, and have acquired so marked a preference in late years. For purity and excellence they may be put in competition with the wines of any climate.

"Now under such favorable auspices one would think the native wine trade would thrive and prosper a hundred-fold. One would think that with vast improvements in the production and manufacture of the wines; with high scientific skill in the cultivation of the grape itself; with a heavy protective duty on foreign wines; and no tax at all on wines of home growth, this important branch of industry would have increased to a magnitude corresponding to its supposed advantages.

"But such is not the fact. With such an enormous amount of floating capital, seeking investment in the country at large, no measurable amount has found its way in this direction, no vast establishments have grown up as it were in a day, to supply the enormous deficiency caused by prohibitory duties upon foreign wines; the old wine establishments remain nearly as they were before the war; native wines have not become a national beverage, and except by persistent private enterprise even these establishments would be financially wrecked, like so many others, which were once flourishing and wealth-producing. With all the *protection* a very slight revenue tax would tax them out of existence. They are too weak to bear this burden.

"The main cause of it all lies in this—protection of the native wine trade means a premium on spurious wines. When real champagne is worth per dozen from $20 to $24 *in gold,* and imitation champagne can be made for $8 a dozen in paper money, the premium is in the difference between the two sums. Vast wine cellars for the manufacture of spurious wines sprung up like mushrooms all over the land.

"These poisonous compounds at low prices tempt the cupidity of the dealer. The New York label manufacturer readily furnishes the label—the 'brand'—of any known wine. The whisky distiller furnishes the stimulus; the chemist the flavor; the sugar-box. The Commissioner would recommend on this article the following:

FORM OF LAW: On Sardines packed in oil, in tin boxes, fourteen cents per whole box, measuring not more than five inches long, four inches wide, and three and one-half inches deep; seven cents for each half box measuring not more than five inches long, four inches wide, and one and one-half inches deep; and four cents for each quarter box, measuring not more than four inches and three-quarters long, three and one-half inches wide, and one and one-eighth inches deep.

Umbrella and parasol frames.—These articles are imported chiefly from England, and are at present subjected to a duty of thirty-five per cent. ad valorem. Although varying greatly in size and value, a classification sufficiently exact for the determination of a specific duty is entirely practicable, and the Commissioner would recommend the following as equivalent to the ad valorem rates now in force:

FORM OF LAW.—On umbrella and parasol frames, steel ribs and iron furniture, not exceeding twelve inches in length, fifty cents per dozen; exceeding twelve inches and not exceeding twenty-one inches in length, sixty cents per dozen. On umbrella and parasol frames made of steel and brass, or other metallic furniture, not exceeding twelve inches in length, fifty cents per dozen; exceeding twelve inches and not exceeding twenty-one inches in length, sixty cents per dozen.

On umbrella and parasol ribs and stretchers, made of iron or steel, sixty cents per dozen sets. On umbrella tubes and runners, and furniture other than ribs, made of iron or steel, fifty cents per gross pieces. On umbrella tubes and runners, and other furniture made of other material than steel or iron, one dollar and fifty cents per gross pieces.

---

house the sirup, and the gas-pump the effervescence. With these antagonists to contend with, good pure wines, both native and foreign, go to the wall—competition is out of the question.

"In the production of native wines heavy duties increase also the costs. As, for instance, transportation; the freight tariff is increased on the railroads. All materials are obliged to be imported, bottles, corks, &c., and two freights to pay on these—duties, &c.; and then the cost of labor is four-fold in this country to what it is in France.

"Another great evil is that in the manufacture of '*domestic wines*,' *i. e.*, wines made here or compounded, a class of poor native wines, or wines of half-ripened or rotten, poorly cultivated grapes, are eagerly bought up at low prices, and are then *doctored*, colored, whiskied, and sweetened, and sold under the names of Madeiras, sherries, or ports.

"This gives encouragement to the worst class of vineyardists, who, taking examples from their patrons, learn to introduce unripe blackberries, rhubarb, cider, whisky, sugar, and water, into their vile compounds. All this stuff, being *doctored*, finds its way to the abodes of our citizens, to the hospitals, and to the communion table. Shocking as all this may appear, yet it is true. It is in everybody's experience. He who runs may read.

"Respectfully,

"FRED. S. COZZENS.

China straw matting.—This article is imported exclusively from China, and in pieces of twenty and forty yards each, known as half and whole pieces. The average cost at the ports of exportation is eighteen cents per square yard. The existing duty is thirty per cent. ad valorem, the equivalent specific of which is $5\frac{45}{100}$ cents. The Commissioner would recommend a duty of three cents per square yard.

Macaroni and vermicelli.—This article is imported exclusively from Italy, and costs on the average, at port of exportation, nine cents per pound. The present duty is thirty-five per cent. ad valorem, the equivalent specific of which would be $3\frac{1}{6}$ cents per pound. The Commissioner would recommend a specific duty of three cents per pound.

Glue, unrefined.—This article is extensively manufactured in the United States, and is also imported to a certain extent from Germany, the duty at present being twenty per cent. ad valorem. The exact value of dark unrefined glue in Germany is ten cents per pound. The equivalent specific on this would be two cents, which rate the Commissioner hereby recommends. A higher duty, which has been heretofore proposed and asked, would probably prove prohibitory.

FORM OF LAW.—On dark glue and glue sizings, and on all glue unrefined, two cents per pound.

Refined glue and gelatine.—The average price of refined glue and gelatine, imported mainly from Germany, is twenty thalers ($13 80) per hundred-weight. The present duty is thirty-five per cent., the specific equivalent of which would be four and one-quarter cents per pound.

Corks.—Corks are imported chiefly from Spain and Portugal, and are at present subjected to a duty of fifty per cent. ad valorem.

Heavy frauds in the importation of this article are perpetrated in the following manner: Corks of fine and of inferior quality, thoroughly mingled together, are imported in bags containing about 15,000 each, and the whole importation is invoiced as of inferior and low-priced quality. When once admitted, the corks are carefully reassorted and placed in the market at their separate and true values. Respectable importers represent to the Commissioner that, owing to these frauds, the legitimate trade is greatly impaired, and that a specific duty is especially desirable.

An examination of numerous invoices shows that corks may, in general, be divided into two classes, viz: corks of $1\frac{1}{8}$ inch in diameter, and those in excess of that size. The average duty levied upon the former would be equivalent to about seventy cents, and on the latter $2 85 per thousand. The Commissioner would recommend that the specifics thus averaged, with a removal of the duty on cork wood, be made, respectively, sixty cents and two dollars per thousand corks. The revenue derived from the importation of the manufactures of corks during the fiscal year 1867–'68 was $84,426.

FORM OF LAW.—On corks, not exceeding $1\frac{1}{8}$ inches in diameter, sixty cents per thousand; exceeding $1\frac{1}{8}$ inches in diameter, two dollars per thousand.

Gloves.—The average price of Paris kid gloves imported into the United States is thirty-five francs per dozen pairs. If, however, we exclude certain varieties, which, on account of the reputation of a particular maker, command an extra price, the average value of gloves imported will probably fall below thirty francs (six dollars, gold) per dozen. The present duty levied on kid gloves is fifty per cent. ad valorem. The Commissioner would recommend the change of the present ad valorem into a specific duty of three dollars per dozen on gloves of leather and skin of every description. The importation of gloves of skin or leather is returned for the years 1867–'68 at 379,302 dozen, paying a revenue of $1,260,558, or an average of $3 32 per dozen.

China preserved ginger and chow-chow.—These articles are imported exclusively from China, in cases of six pots each, which form of importation is never varied. Their average cost at ports of shipment is $4 25 per box. The duty at present imposed on these articles is fifty per cent. ad valorem, the equivalent specific of which is $2 12½ per case. The Commissioner would recommend a specific duty on these articles of two dollars per box, with a proviso that the importation of the same be restricted to boxes not in excess of seventy-five pounds gross weight.

FORM OF LAW.—On ginger preserved in sugar, or preserved fruit known as chow-chow, two dollars for each case containing six pots, and weighing not over seventy-five pounds gross weight per case.

Corsets.—This article is imported chiefly from Germany, and is produced to but a limited extent in the United States. The average importing cost of corsets made of linen or cotton, as reported to the Commissioner by the appraisers in New York, is twelve guilders, or $4 80 per dozen.

The present duty is thirty-five per cent. ad valorem, the equivalent specific of which is $1 68 per dozen. The following duty and form of law are recommended:

FORM OF LAW.—On corsets, of whatever material composed, except silk, $1 50 per dozen.

Cotton suspenders.—These articles are imported from Great Britain and France, and also extensively manufactured in the United States. The average price of cotton and rubber suspenders imported, as returned to the Commissioner by the custom-house appraisers, is 16*s.* per dozen from England, and sixteen francs per dozen from France; on which a duty of thirty-five per cent. ad valorem is now levied. The equivalent specific duty of this rate would be about $1 26 per dozen.

The Commissioner would, therefore, recommend a specific duty on suspenders and braces made of cotton and India-rubber combined, of $1 25 per dozen, which would effectually prevent all under-valuation and simplify the collection of the revenue.

India-rubber, cotton, and silk webbing.—This article, used mainly in the manufacture of boots and shoes, is imported largely from England and Germany, and is produced to but a limited extent in the United States. The duty at present levied on cotton and India-rubber webbing is thirty-five per cent. ad valorem, and on silk and India-rubber webbing fifty per cent. ad valorem. With these duties it is the opinion of the appraisers that under-valuations are most extensive and difficult of detection. A change, therefore, is most desirable, and the following specific rates, prepared for the Commissioner by experts in this business, are herewith submitted:

FORM OF LAW.—On webbing or fabrics of India-rubber and other materials combined, except silk, in the piece, and not less than one-half inch wide and not over one inch wide, three cents per lineal yard; over one inch wide and not over two and a half inches wide, six cents per yard; over two and a half inches wide and not over four inches wide, twelve cents per lineal yard; over four inches wide and not over five inches and one-eighth wide, eighteen cents per lineal yard; over five and one-eighth inches wide and not over seven inches wide, twenty-five cents per lineal yard; over seven inches wide, for every additional inch, five cents per lineal yard. On India-rubber and cotton braid webbing, "sawdalling," and cord made of India-rubber and cotton, less than half an inch, one dollar for every one hundred and forty-four yards. On webbing or fabrics of India-rubber and silk, or of which silk is a component part, not less than one-half inch wide and not over one and one-half inch wide, six cents per lineal yard. Over one and one-half inch wide and not over two and one-half inches wide, twelve cents per lineal yard; over two and one-half inches wide and not over four inches wide, twenty-four cents per lineal yard; over four inches wide, and not over five inches wide, forty cents per lineal yard; over five inches wide, for every additional inch in width, eight cents per lineal yard. On India-rubber and silk cords, braid, webbing, and "sawdalling," under half an inch wide, two dollars and seventy-five cents for each one hundred and forty-four yards.

Worsted or Scotch caps.—These caps are exclusively a manufacture of the north of Scotland, and are the product of hand knitting by women and children during the long winter evenings of that country. They are sold in the first instance to manufacturers, who felt and prepare them for market.

These caps are almost entirely worn by sailors, fishermen, and the poorer classes of the northern section of the country, and the conditions of the manufacture would seem to be such as to preclude the possibility of their successful production in the United States. The imposition, therefore, of a low duty on these articles would not seem to be antagonistic to any existing manufacturing interests of the country. Under the present tariff, Scotch caps pay fifty cents per pound and thirty-five per cent. ad valorem, which is equivalent to a duty of $2 25 per dozen on an average cost of importation of 16*s.* sterling (four dollars, gold) per dozen for men's and boys' caps. The Commissioner is of the opinion that the revenues would be augmented, the poorer classes benefited, and no industrial interest in the United States injured, by a reduction of the duty on this article to one dollar and twenty-five cents per dozen.

Tin.—This metal is imported into the United States chiefly from Great Britain. The average price of block tin ranges from £90 to £100 per ton of 2,240 pounds. During the past year the average price has been about £90 per ton. The present importations are about 4,000 tons, or nearly nine million pounds per annum. The duty at present imposed is fifteen per cent. ad valorem, the corresponding specific of which would be about three cents per pound, which specific rate is hereby recommended.

A large amount of tin is exported from the Straits of Malacca, but as there is little or no direct trade with the United States the metal is mainly shipped to Holland. If brought from thence to the United States, it is subjected to the additional duty of ten per cent. imposed on the indirect importation of articles from countries east of the Cape of Good Hope. The continuance of this duty is represented to the Commissioner as a grievance, and that its repeal would essentially reduce the cost of a raw material of great importance, and at the same time encourage a direct trade with Holland.

FORM OF LAW.—On tin in pigs, bars, or blocks, irrespective of the place of importation, three cents per pound.

Tin plates.—This article is not manufactured in the United States. Some idea, however, of its extensive consumption in this country may be formed from the fact that the value of its importations for the fiscal year 1867–'68 is returned at about seven millions of dollars, gold, ($6,893,072,) affording a revenue of $1,723,200.

The duty now levied on tin plates is 25 per centum ad valorem, the nearest equivalent specific to which, taking the average of the different varieties imported, would be about 1¼ cent per pound, gross, including the boxes. An examination of the invoices of numerous importations of tin plate shows the average value of a box, 112 pounds, to be 25*s.* sterling, ($6 05, gold,) 25 per cent. on which would be $1\frac{35}{100}$ cent per pound net, or 1¼ cent gross—the box weighing about eight pounds. Such a conversion of ad valorem to specific finds a general concurrence both on the part of importers and appraisers, while at the same time it effectually prevents all possibility of under-valuation; and as bearing on this latter point, furthermore, it is interesting to note that an examination of numerous invoices entered at the custom-house shows constant diversity in the valuation of what appears to be the same article.

The Commissioner would recommend that the present practice of allowing damage on the importation of tin plates be no longer continued; inasmuch as there can be no doubt that it is constantly made the occasion of gross frauds upon the revenue. As a compensation, however, for the discontinuance of such an allowance, it is recommended the that specific duty on tin plate be fixed at one cent per pound, gross, instead of 1¼ cent, which, as above shown, is equivalent to the present ad valorem rate. That the revenue would be increased rather than diminished by such an adjustment, all the investigations made by the Commissioner tends to confirm.

FORM OF LAW.—On tinned iron, known as tin plates, one cent per pound, including packages: *Provided*, that no allowance shall be hereafter made for any sea damage sustained on the voyage of importation.

Dried fruits.—The present duty of five cents per pound on dried fruits is excessive, and bears hard upon the masses, to whom raisins, currants, prunes, and figs are not only a simple luxury, but also, to some extent, articles of nutritious food. As restricting consumption, the present duty is also injurious to the revenue.

It is also to be noted that, while this rate of duty, as will hereafter be shown, is paid by the consumers, it is not, as a general rule, paid by the importer. Thus, an examination of the custom-house returns of the city of New York shows that during the eleven months ending November 1, 1869, there were invoices of imported currants, raisins, and figs presented for entry at that port calling for an aggregate of 2,895,893 pounds. This amount was reduced by the weighers to 2,819,630 pounds, or 77,263 pounds less than what the importers paid for at the port of export. On this reduced weight there was apparently due the United States for duties the sum of $146,831 78; but this charge was liquidated by the payment of $108,336 65, or, in other words, $38,495 13 was further allowed to the importers on the ground of damage. The duty actually paid on the above imports were therefore but three and three-quarter cents per pound, in place of five cents, the rate designated by law. To further carry out this investigation, inquiry, with an ostensible view to purchase, was next made in the New York market, under the direction of the Commissioner, for fruit which, by reason of damage, might be bought at a reduction from current rates; but none such could be found, thus indicating that, although large quantities of what is claimed as damaged fruit passes the custom-house, it is subsequently nearly or quite all sold to the consumers as of first quality and at first-quality prices.

The Commissioner, regarding the continuance of a system like this, which gives all the advantage to the importer, and defrauds alike both the government and the consumer, as one not worthy to be tolerated, would recommend that hereafter the duties on dried fruits be fixed at a uniform rate of two cents per pound, and that no allowance whatever be made by the custom-house for damage accruing on the voyage of importation. For such damage as may unavoidably occur, a sufficient protection ought to be found by the importer in the insurance.

Green fruits.—The present duty levied on green fruits is twenty-five per cent. ad valorem, but, owing to large and apparently excessive allowances made on nearly every cargo imported for damage, the rate really paid is much less. The Commissioner would recommend that the duty on green fruit be reduced to ten per cent. ad valorem, and that no allowance be hereafter made for damage.

Steel.—At present the duties levied on steel are of two kinds, ad valorem and specific. The attempt to impose ad valorem duties on an article of such varying value is, however, manifestly an absurdity, and a continued temptation to fraud through undervaluation or imperfect appraisement; inasmuch as no man can tell by the eye, or by any test readily available in the custom-house, whether cast steel is worth forty, fifty, or sixty pounds per ton, or can readily distinguish, by inspection, cast steel in bars from German steel in the same form. The result has been, that during the past year the government and the importers of steel have been brought into continual disagreement; the agents and officers of the one alleging that the steel regularly imported was systematically and scandalously undervalued with a view of defrauding the revenue; while the English importers and their commission agents in the United States, including men of the highest reputation for integrity in both countries, have with equal positiveness denied this accusation. Meantime the domestic manufacturers of steel, not satisfied with the existing duties, have earnestly besought the government to decide in opposition to the importers, and so practically raise the tariff; while on the other hand the American manufacturers who use steel as a raw material have felt alarmed at what seemed to them to be an unnecessary interference with their business, and in not a few instances have declared to the Commissioner that if any higher rates were to be imposed upon this indispensable article they might as well abandon any idea of attempting to extend, perfect, and diversify their special products. The Commissioner, therefore, with a view of putting an end at once and forever to these difficulties, would propose the duties on steel be made wholly specific, and on the following basis: *On scrap steel, one-fourth cent per pound; on blister steel in bars, broken up for melting, one and one-half cent per pound; on German steel in bars, two cents per pound; on shear steel, in bars, two and one-half cents per pound; on cast-steel ingots, and on all rough and unfinished castings in steel, one cent per pound; on castings in steel, drilled, bored, or hammered cold, one and one-fourth cent per pound; on cast steel in bars, two and one-half cents per pound; on cast or German steel in plates to sixteen wire-gauge, inclusive, two cents per pound; from seventeen to twenty-four, two and one-half cents per pound; above twenty-four, three cents per pound; on cast or German steel in form of wire and sheets which are drawn or rolled cold, to sixteen wire-gauge, inclusive, three cents per pound; thinner than sixteen wire-guage, three and one-half cents per pound. On cast steel tires for rolling stock for railroads, two cents per pound; on cast-steel straight axles, shafts, piston rods, and general forgings to pattern, one cent per pound; do., do., rough-turned, one and one-half cent per pound; finished ready for use, two cents per pound; on cast-steel crank axles forged to shape, only one and one-fourth cent per pound; rough-turned, planed, and slotted, one and one-half cent per pound; finished ready for use, two and one-half cents per pound. On cast-steel rails, one and one-half cent per pound. On steel not otherwise provided for, two cents per pound.*

By a schedule of substantially this character, which can be enlarged and made more minute if desirable, the duties on steel can be readily determined by the eye and weight, and all difficulties arising from undervaluations be at once and forever done away with. If it be objected that such a schedule involves a lower scale of duties than is now imposed, the Commissioner would reply that he believes that the interests of the country and of the revenue alike demand that the existing duties should be reduced, on the ground that they are at present excessive and more than are required to sustain the domestic manufactures in a condition of firm prosperity. The whole number of persons engaged in the *direct* manufacture of steel in the United States at the present time is not in excess of three thousand five hundred. It would, however, be a low estimate to place the number of those who use steel as a raw material in the manufacture of axes, chisels, files, cutlery, spades, shovels, pistols, machinery, and other tools and implements, at less than two hundred thousand; while an addition of those indirectly interested in having cheap steel would swell this number to at least one million and a half of individuals, who are at the same time the most important and valuable of all those who by their industry add to the annual product of the country.

DRUGS AND CHEMICALS.

In respect to the following articles, included in the list of drugs and chemicals, the Commissioner would recommend an entire removal of all duties, mainly for the reason that the amount of revenue received from them specifically or in the aggregate is too small to compensate for the complications thereby occasioned in the administration of the tariff and the disturbance of legitimate trade and industry:

Asphaltum, albumen, chalk of all kinds; acids, (benzoic, carbolic, citric, gallic, muriatic, nitric, oxalic, sulphuric, tannic;) acetates of ammonia, baryta, iron, copper, magnesia, potassa, soda, and strontia; aloes; ammonia and its salts; aniline colors or dyes; arsenic; assafœtida; balsams of all kinds; Peruvian and other medicinal barks; buchu leaves; camphor, crude; cantharides; chemical preparations not specified in the existing tariff; tartar emetic; cubebs; cuttle-fish bone; dragon's blood; all other drugs and dyestuffs not specified in the existing tariff; seaweed; dulce; ergot; all medicinal flowers, leaves, and plants not specified in the existing tariff; extract of indigo; iodine, crude, sublimed or compounded; ipecacuanha; jalap; lac, seed and stick; madder extract and garancine; magnesia and its salts; manna; musk; medicinal preparations not specified in the existing tariff; nitrate of soda; nut galls; phosphorus; chlorate of potash; rhubarb; saltpeter; chloride of potash; rose leaves; safflower; santonine; sarsaparilla; strychnine and its salts; barytes and its salts; Epsom salts; sulphate of zinc; clay and Fullers' earth of all kinds; mosses, sea-weeds, and other similar vegetable substances; all volatile, essential, and illuminating oils not specifically provided for; olive, palm, and cocoa-nut oils; tar, turpentine; lime-juice; cobalt; and all seeds and roots not specifically provided for. The loss of revenue involved in these reductions would not, as near as can be estimated, exceed two millions of dollars.

The Commissioner would also call attention to certain peculiarities of the existing tariff in connection with the importation of drugs and chemicals, which are especially worthy of attention.

Thus, crude camphor pays a duty of thirty cents per pound, while "refined camphor," as it is called, is subject to a duty of forty cents per pound. Now, the fact is that all camphor of commerce is a crude product of special countries, more or less impure, which can be easily refined for about three cents per pound, and the effect of making a difference of ten cents per pound between what is called "refined" and "crude," has been to shut out all foreign competition in marketable camphor, and to give an almost exclusive control of the domestic trade within the United States to a single refiner in New York City.

Castor oil is subject to a duty of $1 per gallon, (gold,) or $1 10 if not imported direct from the East Indies; in the interior of which country, as also in Mexico and other tropical regions, the plant grows almost spontaneously. As a rule, furthermore, it costs less to express and deliver the oil at a shipping point than it does to deliver the oil in the beans. The existing tariff imposes a duty of sixty cents per bushel on castor beans, which is equivalent to thirty-five cents per gallon on the oil in the beans. This is less sensible than to so legislate as to force the export of all our wheat and other cereals with the straw attached, for, while there is some value in the straw pertaining to the cereals, castor-oil beans have no value except for the oil they contain.

The result of such a system has been that, while castor oil can be imported direct from the East Indies for about eighty-seven cents per gallon in gold, the price has ruled in the American market for the past three years at about $2 50 per gallon in currency, and the cultivation of these cathartic beans has been forced to a considerable extent in States that should grow cotton and cereals; on the other hand, the government derives less than two cents per gallon in the place of $1 per gallon on the whole amount, some 200,000 gallons, consumed yearly, and some two or three parties hold a practical monopoly in all our interior trade in this article, while the foreign commerce in the commodity has practically ceased.

In like manner the tariff duties on borax, morphine, bichromate of potash, and sugar of lead, are at present all calculated to give large and unjust profits to a few manufacturers, to the great detriment alike of the revenue and of the masses of the people.

It is hardly necessary to add that the adoption of the foregoing recommendations of the Commissioner would necessitate, in the interests of the revenue, a change in the duties now levied on many articles in a more advanced stage of manufacture; inasmuch as the reduction effected in the cost of the elementary material of certain domestic industries would render many of the provisions of the existing tariff absolutely prohibitory, and thus destroy the revenue at present derived from the import of similar articles.

WHAT CONSTITUTES A REVENUE TARIFF.

The Commissioner has thus presented a statement of some of the modifications of the tariff now in force which seem to be immediately demanded by the present condition of industry, rendered possible by the surplus revenue now accruing and in accordance with existing public sentiment.

In thus providing for a reduction of the customs revenue to an extent of about fourteen millions per annum, the Commissioner asserts, and has proved, that the relief to be experienced by the people, through the removal of indirect burdens, will be far greater than the sum of the direct taxes abated; as the result cannot fail to effect a reduction of the excessive cost of very many articles of prime necessity, the artificially enhanced price of which is now either a dead loss to the community, or a payment of taxes which are not received by the treasury. The commissioner has also considered it desirable, in view of the present general interest in the question of revenue reform, and especially in the simplification of collection, to present a schedule, showing in what manner a new tariff might be constructed, with the primary object of obtaining from the smallest number of articles, and without excessive duties, an annual revenue of one hundred and fifty millions, and which at the same time would not expose the branches of industry which have been stimulated by protection to any danger of collapse; it being assumed that the relief to be experienced by manufacturers from the abatement of taxes upon their raw materials would, to a large extent, compensate for the reduction of duties upon their product; thus enabling them, through a reduction of cost, to extend their markets, increase consumption, and resume exports.

SCHEDULE OF A TARIFF CONSTRUCTED WITH A VIEW OF OBTAINING FROM THE SMALLEST NUMBER OF IMPORTED ARTICLES AN ANNUAL REVENUE OF ONE HUNDRED AND FIFTY MILLIONS OF DOLLARS.

CLASS 1.—*Articles of food and drink.*

	Revenue estimated on the basis of receipts 1868–'69.
Beer, ale, and porter	$250,000
Chocolate and cocoa	100,000
Dried fruits at 2 cents per pound, and green fruits at 10 per cent. ad valorem, with no allowance for damage	3,000,000

	Revenue estimated on the basis of receipts 1868-'69.
Cigars, at $2 per pound	$5,000,000
Tobacco, unmanufactured, at 25 cents per pound	1,250,000
Coffee and substitutes for coffee	12,000,000
Molasses and melado	5,000,000
Sugars	33,000,000
Tea	10,000,000
Spirits, at $2 per proof gallon	4,000,000
Wines, other than sparkling, at 50 cents per gallon	4,000,000
Sparkling wines at $6 per dozen	1,000,000
Spices	2,000,000
Rice	1,150,000
Sardines, meats, preserves, &c	150,000
Nuts	450,000
Pickles, sauces, vermicelli, macaroni, sago, &c	150,000
Total	82,500,000

CLASS 2.—*Textile fabrics and wares. Duties to be in specific form as far as possible, but at the specific amount represented by the rates named in the following list.*

Silks, at 35 per cent., this being the highest rate which it is easy or possible to collect without great loss from smuggling	$10,000,000
Wool and worsted manufactures, 15 to 35 per cent., averaging 25 per cent., specific	10,000,000
Cotton manufactures, 15 to 35 per cent., averaging 25 per cent., specific	5,000,000
Flax manufactures, 15 to 35 per cent., averaging 25 per cent., specific	5,000,000
Hemp and jute manufactures, 15 to 35 per cent., averaging 25 per cent., specific	2,000,000
Gloves, hats, and bonnets	1,000,000
Paper and manufactures of paper, 10 per cent	500,000
Furs and manufactures of furs	500,000
Earthen, stone, china, and glass, 25 per cent., specific	4,000,000
Total	38,000,000

CLASS 3.—*Metals.*

Iron, steel, lead, tin, and manufactures of same, at such specific rates as shall amount to 25 per cent	$15,000,000

CLASS 4.—*Fancy goods, at such specific rates as shall be equivalent to 35 per cent. ad valorem.*

Clocks, watches, embroideries, toys, musical instruments, pipes, perfumes, ornaments, feathers, fire-crackers, &c..	$4,000,000
Laces, braids, and fancy webbing.....................	1,000,000

CLASS 5.—*Drugs and chemicals.*

Licorice, opium, oils, preparations containing spirits, and patent medicines..................................	$1,500,000

CLASS 6.—*Miscellaneous, at such specific rates as shall be equivalent to from 15 to 35 per cent. ad valorem.*

Brooms, brushes, mats, millinery, manufactures of India-rubber, marble, cork, and hair, soap, hops, &c	$2,000,000

Recapitulation.

Articles of food and drink..............................	$82,500,000
Textiles and wares..................................	38,000,000
Metals..	15,000,000
Fancy goods...	5,000,000
Drugs, chemicals, and oils..............................	1,500,000
Miscellaneous.......................................	2,000,000
	144,000,000

The above estimates present an aggregate of $144,000,000, to which may be added the sum accruing from fines, penalties, and forfeitures—say $1,000,000—making a total of $145,000,000. To this, however, must be further added the amount which represents the elasticity of the customs revenue, arising from the rapid increase of the country in wealth and population, which cannot be fairly estimated at less than $5,000,000 per annum, on an average; and this sum, it is to be remembered, would also represent the amount which, after the first year, would be annually applicable for the reduction of the rates upon tea, coffee, sugar, or such other articles as might be deemed desirable.

CONCLUSION.

The Commissioner offers no apology for the length of this report. The subject of using the national resources for the purpose of obtaining a large, but necessary, revenue, and of perfecting the existing revenue laws, enlarges the more it is investigated; and although a few simple principles serve as a key to the whole question, it has seemed expedient to the Commissioner to illustrate their application in different ways, and in respect to many different topics. As the present constitutes the last regular report of the Commissioner, (his office expiring, by limitation of law, at the close of the present fiscal year, June 30, 1870,) he has endeavored, moreover, to complete, as far as possible, the statement of the result of his investigations. And in respect to these investigations, commenced under the Revenue Commission in 1865, and continued uninterruptedly to the present, the Commissioner claims the privilege to assert that he has endeavored faithfully and conscientiously to discharge the duties of his office; has sought to know only the truth, and to speak that only which has seemed to him to be for the best interests of the whole country. He is well aware that in expressing opinions and recommendations, which have been forced upon him by conviction, he has placed himself in antagonism to many with whom he was formerly in close agreement; but he feels confident that time, experience, and free discussion will confirm the correctness of his general conclusions and vindicate his position. In confirmation of this opinion he would call attention to the circumstance that, from the very first, none of his recommendations received at the outset anything of general support from either Congress or the public. Thus in the case of distilled spirits: although the impolicy and waste of the two-dollar tax were demonstrated in 1865 by facts and examples drawn from our own and the experience of other nations, and its abatement earnestly recommended, the proposition found barely a single supporter in either branch of Congress, while the Commissioner was accused, by means of an anonymous circular laid upon the desk of each member, of having been influenced in his statements and recommendations by corrupt and unworthy motives. A like disfavor also attended nearly all the other principal recommendations by him *first* submitted; as, for example, the repeal of the tax upon raw cotton; crude petroleum; the cumulative and onerous taxes on all manufacturing industry; the proposition to collect the revenue from fermented liquors by means of stamps; and from tobacco by the joint application of the stamp and package system; the appointment of supervisors; the uniform tax upon cigars, and the like; and yet the adoption of all of these measures has been subsequently found necessary through experience, and has, by general acknowledgment, resulted in great and permanent benefit alike to the government and the people. Feeling confident, therefore, from such a retrospect, as to the issues of the future, the present report, with its recommendations, is respectfully submitted.

DAVID A. WELLS,
United States Special Commissioner of Revenue.

Hon. GEORGE S. BOUTWELL,
Secretary of the Treasury.

APPENDIX A.

Proportion and numbers of the population of the United States constantly sick and disabled.

[Communicated to the Special Commissioner of Revenue by Edward Jarvis, M. D.]

The proportion and numbers of our population, between the ages of eighteen and sixty-five, who by reason of sickness or other physical disability are constantly incapacitated for labor, cannot be accurately determined from any existing data. There is no record of any inquiry as to the physical condition and power of our people, nor is this ascertained in any country. Governments have been content with merely counting their subjects, without further inquiry as to their power or value to the body politic. In all nations each individual is presumed to be a complete integer, and all to contribute equally to the sum total of national wealth and force.

The nearest apparent approach to any analysis of the people in respect to their available power, the best approximate representation of the proportion of the people who are able to labor and who are incapacitated for so doing, is the result of the experience of the friendly societies of Europe. These associations have been in operation for several generations. They include several hundred thousand persons in Great Britain. The members contribute certain amounts of money at stated periods, quarterly, monthly, or weekly, to the communal fund, while they are able to work, on condition of receiving certain specified sums weekly or daily when they are sick or disabled, and cannot labor. The treasurer then must keep a record of all the time in which the members are in health and able to work, and in which they are sick and deprived of power to engage in their usual employments.

These records, including a vast population of working men, women and youth, and extending through many years, are of very great value as indications of the health and working power, the sickness and disabilities of the people. They have been examined and analyzed, and extensive and elaborate reports made upon them, by men of high culture and authority, especially by Mr. Alexander Finlaison, under the authority of the British government, and by Mr. Neison, actuary of the British Medical and Invalid Life Insurance Company.

The results of all these investigations do not materially differ, and have been taken as the basis for estimating the proportion of the population, at varying ages, assumed to be now living in the United States, who are constantly incapacitated for labor by reason of sickness or other physical disability; subject, however, to the following qualifications, which are peculiarly American or local:

1. The basis, the experience of the friendly societies, is not of American but of British population. To this it may be answered that it is extremely probable that the inferences are at least true, as a *minimum* if not as a *maximum* of disability. We have at least as much, if not more sickness than the people of England and Scotland. Some years ago there were many health insurance companies established in the United States, which assumed the British rates of sickness as the rule of their action, but after a few years' experience they found it a losing business, inasmuch as their assessments or payments into their treasuries were not equal to their payments out of their treasuries; or the amount of sickness was more than they had calculated or provided for.

2. These societies do not include all the people even in Great Britain.

a. They belong almost exclusively to the laboring classes, which, however, Mr. Neison considers the healthiest population of that country.

b. Although none are turned out of these societies on account of sickness or other physical infirmity, as loss of sight or hearing, yet none are admitted who suffer under disabilities or disqualifications. They admit only the sound.

c. These societies retain only those who are sufficiently industrious and thrifty to pay their periodical assessments. Thus the intemperate, the dissolute, the idle, the vagabonds, who are the least healthy and whose more frequent and protracted sickness and injuries would swell the average amount of disability, are dropped out of the societies and omitted in the calculations. As these societies exclude the lowest classes who have the most disability, and also the higher—the wealthy and fashionable—who have dangers and disabilities peculiar to themselves, there is some reason for Mr. Neison's opinion that they are the healthiest class of the people; and the results of their experience fail to show the full measure of the disabilities of England; and further, they must fail to show the full proportion of sickness and disability of the people of the United States. But it is at least safe to assume this British rate of sickness, and to admit that we have in our whole population, from eighteen to sixty-five, as large a proportion of those incapacitated for labor as are among those of the same age in England and Scotland. Especially is this true of the South, where there is more sickness and shorter life than in the northern States. With these explanations the following table is submitted:

Distribution of the population of the United States in 1869 assumed to be in 39,000,000; males, 19,951,100, ratio 51,157; females, 19,048,900, ratio 48,843.

Distribution in ages.

Age.	Males.		Females.		Persons.	
	Number.	Proportion in 10,000.	Number.	Proportion in 10,000.	Number.	Proportion in 10,000.
All	**19,951,100**	**10,000**	**19,048,900**	**10,000**	**39,000,000**	**10,000**
Under fifteen	8, 038, 305	4, 029	7, 777, 669	4, 083	15, 815, 974	4, 055
Fifteen to sixteen	442, 914	222	384, 787	202	827, 701	212
Under sixteen	8, 481, 219	4, 252	8, 162, 456	4, 285	16, 643, 675	4, 268
Fifteen to eighteen	1, 322, 757	663	1, 280, 086	672	2, 602, 843	668
Under eighteen	9, 361, 062	4, 692	9, 057, 755	4, 755	18, 418, 817	4, 723
Fifteen to twenty	2, 048, 973	1, 027	2, 120, 142	1, 113	4, 169, 115	1, 069
Eighteen to twenty	726, 216	364	840, 056	441	1, 566, 272	402
Twenty to thirty	3, 615, 139	1, 812	3, 489, 758	1, 832	7, 104, 897	1, 822
Thirty to forty	2, 643, 520	1, 325	2, 344, 919	1, 231	4, 988, 439	1, 279
Forty to fifty	1, 729, 760	867	1, 514, 387	795	3, 244, 147	832
Fifty to sixty	1, 037, 457	520	963, 874	506	2, 001, 331	513
Sixty to sixty-five	327, 198	164	293, 353	154	620, 551	159
Eighteen to sixty-five	10, 079, 290	5, 052	9, 446, 547	4, 959	19, 525, 637	5, 007
Sixty-five to seventy	237, 418	119	241, 921	127	479, 339	123
Over sixty-five	510, 748	256	544, 798	286	1, 055, 546	271

Proportion and numbers constantly sick and disabled—proportion calculated from Neison and Finlaison's tables of males and females; numbers calculated from the proportion.

Age.	Males.		Females.		Persons.	
	Constantly sick in 100,000.	Number.	Constantly sick in 100,000.	Number.	Constantly sick in 100,000.	Number.
Eighteen to twenty	1, 590	12, 780	1, 760	14, 784	1, 680	27, 564
Twenty to thirty	1, 690	61, 095	1, 100	38, 387	1, 390	99, 482
Thirty to forty	1, 929	50, 993	2, 510	58, 857	2, 200	109, 850
Forty to fifty	2, 945	50, 951	3, 180	48, 157	3, 050	99, 098
Fifty to sixty	5, 385	55, 867	4, 770	45, 976	5, 080	101, 843
Sixty to sixty-five	10, 570	34, 585	6, 410	18, 863	8, 610	53, 448
Eighteen to sixty-five	2, 420	266, 261	2, 380	225, 024	2, 500	491, 285

In this connection the statement of the proportions of recruits rejected as unfit for military service becomes a matter of interest. The proportions of these rejections differ in different nations and in different conditions of the same nation. In those countries where, as in France, Prussia, &c., all of a certain age are conscripted, many more are found unfit than in other countries, as Great Britain and the United States, where none but volunteers are examined.

There is a difference, also, in this respect in peace and war. In peace, when business is good and employment readily obtained and liberally rewarded, the candidates for the army include a large proportion of the poorest and most worthless men, among whom are many who are broken down from dissipation—the débris of society, whom all other occupations reject; the residuum after all desirable places have made their selections; then, as a last resort of the hopeless, they offer their services to the army.

On the contrary, in times of war such as our last, when appeals are made to the patriotism of the people, a much larger proportion of the best and healthiest classes offer as candidates. Yet even in such a war, if an attempt is made to enforce the enlistment or draft, the rate of rejections and acceptance is not a test of the ability or disability to labor. The army requires the highest standard of health. Common business accepts a much lower; and even some that are in full strength contrive to convince the inspectors that they are unable to sustain the fatigues consequent upon military life.

In a thousand candidates for the army who were examined, there were rejected for physical disability:

In Great Britain, 1830 to 1850	318
In France, 1831 to 1843	324
United States, 1839 to 1854	618
United States, in late war	257

Beside the objection to this experience as evidence of general disability in the fact above mentioned, it must be considered that the manifestly disabled are not included in the number of candidates. But if all were included, the proportion deemed fit for military service would be much smaller.

APPENDIX B.

Table showing the exact cost of the support of forty persons employed in the manufacture of cotton goods in the town of ——, in Massachusetts, for the twenty-seven weeks ending November 1, 1869.

	Quantity.	Value.	Total value.	Quantity per week for each person.
Provisions:				
Meat	3,464 pounds	$585 92		3 1-5 pounds.
Flour	5,920 pounds	208 70		5½ pounds.
Potatoes	63 bushels	48 92		¼ peck.
Fish	652 pounds	45 57		6-10 pound.
Lard	283½ pounds	119 36		¼ pound.
Pastry		117 61		
Butter	844½ pounds	342 99		12½ ounces.
Sugar	1,675½ pounds	229 15		1½ pound.
Eggs	269⅓ dozen	89 91		3 eggs.
Crackers	8½ barrels	37 10		1.5-4 pound.
Beans	9 quarts	1 38		
Cheese	316½ pounds	80 69		4⅔ ounces.
Rice	69½ pounds	9 96		1 ounce.
Meal	5 pounds	20		
Tea	79 pounds	90 59		1 1-6 ounce.
Coffee	15 pounds	7 35		1-5 ounce.
Apples, green	15½ bushels	24 92		
Apples, dried	55 pounds	11 35		
Pickles	17¾ gallons	21 73		
Molasses	24½ gallons	21 95		
Corn starch	14 pounds	2 28		
Raisins	54 pounds	12 50		
Spices		10 84		
Cream tartar	6¼ pounds	4 65		
Saleratus	13 pounds	1 82		
Vinegar	12 gallons	5 40		
Salt	7 pecks	3 08		
Milk, sweet	1,336 quarts	80 20		2½ pints.
Milk, sour	29 quarts	87		
Citrons		60		
Cabbages		3 70		
Squashes		3 50		
Vegetables, sundry		43 33		
Onions		3 53		
Prunes	90 pounds	21 10		
			$2,292 75	
Sundries:				
Matches, stove blacking, &c		2 66		
Stone jars		3 50		
Lamp chimneys, burners, and wicking		6 05		
Washing fluid and bluing		3 04		
			15 25	
Soap:				
Hard	116 pounds	17 40		
Soft	4 barrels	18 00		
			35 40	
Oil:				
Kerosene	51 gallons	22 15		
			22 15	
Fuel:				
Coal	8,660 pounds	38 64		
Wood	6½ cords	37 50		
			76 14	
			2,551 69	
Labor, cooking, waiting, &c.:				
Boarding mistress, 27 weeks, at $13 50		364 00		
One hand, 14 weeks at $1		14 00		
One hand, 7 weeks, at $1 50		10 40		
One hand, one-third time for 6 weeks, at $3		6 00		
			395 00	
Labor, washing, &c.:				
One hand, one-third of each week for 27 weeks, at $3		27 00		
One hand, one-third of each week for 14 weeks, at $1 50		7 00		
One hand, one-third of each week for 13 weeks, at $2 75		11 92		
			45 92	
Care of rooms:				
One hand, two-thirds of each week for 21 weeks, at $3		42 00		
One hand, two-thirds of each week for 14 weeks, at $1 50		14 00		
One hand, one-third of each week for 6 weeks, at $3		6 00		
One hand, two-thirds of each week for 13 weeks, at $2 75		23 83		
			85 33	
			2,968 44	

Number of persons boarded, including housekeeper and servants.

	Adult males.	Adult females.	Children, male.	Children, female.	Total.
May	21	18	6	5	50
June	16	22	5	2	45
July	14	14	4	2	34
August	28	12	3	3	46
September	23	13	1	2	39
October	16	17	1	2	36
Average	$19\frac{2}{3}$	16	$3\frac{1}{3}$	$2\frac{2}{3}$	$41\frac{2}{3}$
Deduct for children					$1\frac{2}{3}$
Equal to adults					40

Cost as above	$2,968 44
Rent of house, at $350	175 00
Twenty-seven weeks, at $116 42	$3,143 44

Or, for forty adults, $2 91 per week each. House and help competent for forty-five boarders, which would reduce average, say to $2 75 per week.

APPENDIX C.

Analysis of the industry of the United States engaged in the production of leather and of the manufactures of leather, as prepared for the Special Commissioner of the Revenue by representatives of the trade.

RAW HIDES AND SKINS USED FOR TANNING IN UNITED STATES IN 1868.

Foreign hides imported at New York, loose	1,777,700	pieces.
Foreign hides imported at New York, in bales	150,000	pieces.
Foreign hides imported at Boston, loose	339,626	pieces.
Foreign hides imported at Boston, in bales	321,460	pieces.
Foreign hides imported at other ports	170,000	pieces.
Domestic production of hides in United States	6,700,000	pieces.
Total number hides available	9,458,786	pieces.

Number hides exported	100,000		
Foreign hides re-exported	200,000		
		300,000	pieces.
Number tanned in United States		9,158,786	pieces.

The above are worked and valued as follows:

Into sole leather, 3,800,000 hides, valued at $7 each in currency	$26,600,000
Into upper leather, 4,458,786 hides, valued at $5½ each in currency	24,523,323
Into harness, hose, &c., 900,000 hides, valued at $8 each in currency	7,200,000
	58,323,323

There are tanned besides the above hides—

Calfskins produced in United States, 2,250,000 skins, valued at $1 75	$3, 937, 500
Goatskins imported into United States, 1,900,000 skins, valued at	1, 970, 291
Sheepskins produced in United States, 1,000,000 dozen skins, valued at $2 per dozen	2, 000, 000
Sheepskins imported in United States, 100,000 dozen skins, valued at $3 per dozen	300, 000
Total value of raw material in currency	66, 531, 114

Production of leather in United States in 1868.

No. hides tanned.	Into what.	Value per hide.	Total value hides.	Produced from hides.	Value of production.
3, 800, 000	Sole leather	$7 00	$26, 600, 000	133, 760, 000 lbs.	$44, 140, 800
4, 458, 786	Upper leather	5 50	24, 523, 323	153, 628, 111 ft.	43, 015, 871
				(split) 13, 376, 358 lbs.	4, 547, 961
900, 000	Harness, hose, belting, carriages, &c.	8 00	7, 200, 000	37, 800, 000 lbs.	18, 900, 000
2, 250, 000	Calfskins	1 75	3, 937, 500	6, 000, 000 lbs.	6, 600, 000
1, 900, 000	Goatskins		1, 970, 291	11, 821, 746 ft.	2, 965, 437
1, 100, 000	Dozen sheepskins	2 & 3 00	2, 300, 000	1, 100, 000 doz.	4, 600, 000
	Totals		66, 531, 114		124, 760, 069

A small portion of the above tanned calf, goat, and sheepskins are worked into fancy goods, bags, portemonnaies, binding for books, skirts, &c.

The remainder of the production, excepting the item of harnesses, &c., is worked into boots and shoes.

Production of leather apportioned as follows:

Due to raw material	$66, 531, 114
Due to added material	24, 328, 955
Due to labor	20, 000, 000
Due to capital	13, 900, 000
	124, 760, 069

Capital employed in the process, $55,000,000. Labor employed in the process, 30,000 persons.

Production of boots and shoes in United States in 1868.

MATERIAL USED.

Sole leather, 133,760,000 lbs., valued at	$44, 140, 800
Upper leather, 153,628,111 ft., valued at	43, 015, 871
Splits, upper leather, 13,376,358 lbs., valued at	4, 547, 961
Calfskins, (domestic,) 5,900,000 lbs, valued at	6, 490, 000
Calfskins, (imported,) 6,666,656 lbs., valued at	8, 999, 976
Goatskins, 11,500,000 ft., valued at	2, 875, 000
Sheepskins, 1,000,000 dozen, valued at	4, 400, 000
Lastings, 3,000,000 yards, valued at	3, 480, 000
Cottons, ducks, 6,000,000 yards, valued at	1, 000, 000
Other sundries	11, 220, 000
Total	130, 169, 608

PRODUCED FROM SAME.

For men's, boys', and youth's wear, 51,500,000 pairs. For women's, misses', and children's wear, 47,000,000 pairs—valued at $246,250,000.

Value apportioned as follows:

Due to original material	$130, 169, 608
Due to added material	9, 371, 959
Due to capital	24, 625, 000
Due to labor	82, 083, 433
	246, 250, 000

Capital employed, $62,000,000. Laborers employed in manufacture, 126,333 persons; add for cobblers 5,000—131,333 persons. The laborers are employed about ten months of the year on shoes, for two months at other work.

Combined production of all goods of which hides are the raw material.

Raw material, valued at $66,531,114.
Produced from same:

Commodity.	Capital used in the production.	Persons employed.	Value of product.
Boots and shoes	$62, 000, 000	131, 333	$246, 252, 000
Harness, hose, belting, &c	12, 000, 000	15, 000	55, 800, 000
Bags, portemonnaies, skirts, &c	1, 500, 000	4, 000	7, 500, 000
Leather worked into boots and shoes	55, 000, 000	30, 000	....
Total	130, 500, 000	180, 333	309, 552, 000

The above values are the manufacturers' values; the jobbers add to the above twenty per cent; the retailers add to the jobbers' values twenty per cent. additional.

APPENDIX D.

Life table of American seagoing sailing vessels, approximate.

[Calculated from original data, for the Special Commissioner of the Revenue, by E. B. Elliott.]

Age.		Proportion surviving at specified ages.	Average future duration from specified ages.
	Years.		
(New built,)	0	1000. 0	13. 8
	10	584. 4	9. 3
	20	219. 5	7. 2
	30	57. 2	6. 2
	40	11. 1	2. 7
	50	(nearly) 0. 0	(nearly) 0. 0

The values in this table were calculated from annual official records, in the United States Treasury Department, of nearly twenty-seven thousand seagoing sailing vessels, built during a long series of years, and also from the proportionate distribution of about four thousand survivors of these vessels, in the year 1866, according to the American Lloyds' Register, as collated by Mr. Joseph Nimmo, jr., chief of the division of tonnage in the Bureau of the Register of the United States Treasury Department.

According to the above table, if we may judge of the future by the past, it is probable that five hundred and eighty-four out of every one thousand newly-built American seagoing sailing vessels will survive ten years; that two hundred and twenty newly-built vessels will survive a period of twenty years; fifty-seven a period of thirty years; eleven a period of forty years; while not one in twenty thousand will survive a period of fifty years. The number of seagoing sailing vessels which are known to have attained the extraordinary age of fifty years is so limited, and the instances so exceptional, as not to be worth taking into account.

This table also indicates that the average duration or mean after life-time of American seagoing sailing vessels, when newly built, is nearly fourteen years, (13.8;) of vessels which have attained the age of ten years the mean future duration is about nine years, (9.3,) of those twenty years of age, seven years, (7.2;) of those thirty years of age, six years, (6.2;) of those forty years of age, three years, (2.7;) while the mean future lifetime of the exceptionally few which may be supposed to attain the age of fifty years is less than one-twentieth of a year, and consequently too small to occupy a place in the table.

This table is believed to be the *first* of the kind ever constructed to illustrate the law of the destruction (or mortality) of *vessels* or *vehicles* engaged in transportation, although tables have not unfrequently been calculated, of similar form, designed to exhibit the laws of *human* mortality.

APPENDIX E.

Rates of discount in Europe.

SYNOPTICAL TABLE SHOWING THE TRUE MEAN RATES OF DISCOUNT IN EACH OF THE PRINCIPAL PLACES OF EUROPE DURING THE FOURTEEN YEARS, 1855 TO 1868, INCLUSIVE.

[The values of the ten years 1855–'64 are taken from the Treatise on banks of issue and discount (*Les banques d'émission et d'escompte*) of M. Maurice Aubry. The values for the four years 1865–'68 were prepared for the Special Commissioner of the Revenue, by E. B. Elliott.]

Annual means of the rates of discount.

Places.	1855.	1856.	1857.	1858.	1859.	1860.	1861.	1862.	1863.	1864.	Average of the ten years 1855–1864.
	Per cent.	*Per cent.*	*Per cent.*	*Per cent.*	*Per cent.*	*Per cent.*	*Per cent.*	*Per cent.*	*Per cent.*	*Per cent.*	*Per cent.*
Hamburg	3. 28	6. 22	6. 30	1. 91	2. 15	1. 98	2. 44	3. 13	3. 33	4. 38	3. 41½
Frankfort	3. 44	4. 29	4. 67	3. 56	3. 48	2. 49	3. 20	3. 06	3. 35	3. 60	3. 50
Berlin	4. 08	4. 94	5. 76	4. 30	4. 20	4. 00	4. 00	4. 00	4. 08	4. 75	4. 37
London	4. 88	6. 08	6. 55	3. 23	2. 73	4. 17	5. 26	2. 56	4. 24	6. 98	4. 42
Paris	4. 43	5. 55	6. 13	3. 70	3. 46	3. 63	5. 54	3. 80	4. 63	6. 49	4. 54
Leipzig	4. 91	5. 05	6. 35	4. 62	4. 80	4. 00	4. 00	4. 00	4. 35	5. 05	4. 70
Madrid	6. 00	6. 00	5. 21	5. 00	5. 00	5. 00	6. 00	5. 72	5. 84	7. 60	5. 53
Italy	6. 00	6. 00	6. 74	5. 29	4. 50	4. 58	6. 31	5. 06	5. 66	7. 70	5. 57
Amsterdam	3. 20	4 28	4. 94	3. 75	3. 00	3. 00	3. 07	4. 73	3. 62	4. 85	3. 63
Vienna	6. 00	6. 00	5. 21	5. 00	5. 00	5. 00	6. 00	5. 72	5. 83	7. 60	5. 53

Places.	1865.		1866.		1867.		1868.		Average of the four years 1865–1868.		Average of the 14 years, 1855–1868.
	Bank rate.	Open market.	Bank rate.	Open market.	Bank rate.	Open market.	Bank rate.	Open market.	Bank rate.	Open market.	
	Per cent.	*Per cent.*	*Per cent.*	*Per cent.*	*Per cent.*	*Per cent.*	*Per cent.*	*Per cent.*	*Per cent.*	*Per cent.*	*Per cent.*
Hamburg	......	4. 25	......	5. 30	......	2. 59	......	1. 90	......	3. 51	3. 44
Frankfort	4. 60	4. 00	4. 70	5. 30	2. 75	2. 28	2. 50	1. 87	3. 64	3. 36	3. 54
Berlin	5. 40	4. 90	6. 20	6. 00	4. 00	2. 92	4. 00	2. 75	4. 90	4. 14	4. 52
London	5. 47	6. 05	6. 00	6. 50	2. 53	3. 12	5. 20	3. 05	4. 80	4. 68	4. 53
Paris	4. 00	3. 95	3. 70	3. 50	2. 44	4. 16	2. 50	1. 71	3. 16	3. 33	4. 75
Leipzig	......	......	......	......	......	......	......	......	......	......	......
Madrid	8. 80	......	8. 25	......	5. 25	......	5. 00	......	7. 82	......	6. 19
Italy	5. 20	5. 10	5. 80	5, 75	5. 25	......	3. 00	......	4. 81	5. 42	5. 35
Amsterdam	4. 40	4. 30	5. 80	5. 70	3. 25	2. 94	2. 70	2. 60	4. 04	3. 88	3. 75
Vienna	5. 20	5. 25	4. 80	5. 20	4. 00	4. 00	4. 00	4. 00	4. 50	4. 61	5. 24

Maxima and minima rates of discount in each of the principal places of Europe, during the fourteen years 1855–'68.

Places.	Annual average rates.	
	Maximum.	Minimum.
	Per cent.	*Per cent.*
Hamburg	6. 30 (1857)	1. 90 (1868.)
Frankfort	5. 30 (1866)	1. 87 (1868.)
Berlin	6. 20 (1866)	2. 75 (1868.)
London	6. 98 (1864)	2. 53 (1867.)
Paris	6. 49 (1864)	1. 71 (1868.)
Leipzig	6. 35 (1857)	4. 00 (1861–'62–'63.)
Madrid	8. 80 (1865)	5. 00 (1858–'59–'60–'68.)
Italy	7. 70 (1864)	3. 00 (1868.)
Amsterdam	5. 80 (1866)	2. 60 (1868.)
Vienna	7. 60 (1864)	4. 00 (1867–'68.)

APPENDIX F.

Relative values of gold and silver at different periods.

TABLE SHOWING THE AVERAGE PRICES OF STANDARD SILVER BARS ($\frac{111}{120}$ FINE) IN THE LONDON MARKET FOR A PERIOD OF NEARLY TWENTY-FIVE YEARS, (1845–'69;) ALSO, THE CORRESPONDING RELATIVE VALUES OF GOLD TO SILVER.

[Prepared for the Special Commissioner of the Revenue, by E. B. Elliott.]

Years.	Average prices of standard silver bars in London.	Relative values of gold to silver.	
	Pence per troy oz.		
1845	59. 255	15. 914 to 1.	
1846	59. 323	15. 896 to 1.	
1847	59. 703	15. 795 to 1.	1845–9 (5 years,) 15. 892 to 1.
1848	59. 474	15. 856 to 1.	
1849	59. 687	15. 799 to 1.	
1850	59. 995	15. 718 to 1.	
1851	60. 198	15. 665 to 1.	1850–2 (3 years,) 15. 649 to 1.
1852	60. 578	15. 567 to 1.	
1853	61. 531	15. 326 to 1.	
1854	61. 536	15. 324 to 1.	
1855	61. 370	15. 366 to 1.	1853–6 (4 years,) 15. 339 to 1.
1856	61. 474	15. 341 to 1.	
1857	61. 766	15. 267 to 1.	
1858	60. 401	15. 358 to 1.	
1859	62. 052	15. 197 to 1.	1857–60 (4 years,) 15. 276 to 1.
1860	61. 708	15. 282 to 1.	
1861	60. 833	15. 500 to 1.	
1862	61. 396	15. 359 to 1.	
1863	61. 328	15. 386 to 1.	
1864	61. 365	15. 353 to 1.	1861–6 (6 years,) 15. 411 to 1.
1865	61. 021	15. 454 to 1.	
1866	61. 177	15. 415 to 1.	
1867	60. 562	15. 571 to 1.	
1868	60. 443	15. 602 to 1.	1867–9 (2 5-12 years,) 15. 580 to 1.
1869	60. 575	15. 567 to 1.	

NOTE.—In 1845, for example, the price of standard silver in bars in the London market was 59. 255 pence sterling, and consequently gold was worth 15. 914 times silver.

The mint-price, in London, of standard gold ($\frac{11}{12}$ fine) is fixed by law at 77 shillings 10½ pence sterling per ounce troy.

The gold fields of California were discovered in 1848; those of Australia in 1850.

From the above table it will be seen that during the five years, 1845-'49, just prior to the opening of the gold fields of California and Australia, the value of pure gold in the London market was *fifteen and seven-eighths* (15.89) times that of pure silver; that subsequent to the opening of the new gold fields the relative value of gold gradually fell until it reached a minimum of 15.2 times in the year 1859, averaging for the four years, 1857-'60, *fifteen and one-fourth* (15.28) times that of silver; and that from this period the market value has steadily advanced to its present rate, averaging in the two and a half years ending with the middle of the year 1867, *fifteen and six-tenths* (15.58) times that of silver, a point at which it now seems to be nearly at a stand-still.

For the two hundred and fifty years from the middle of the fourteenth to the close of the sixteenth century, the market value of gold is believed to have averaged about *eleven and one-third* times that of silver, (varying from twelve and a half times in the middle of the fourteenth to ten times in the middle of the sixteenth century.) From the commencement of the seventeenth century this relative value gradually advanced, reaching in the middle of that century *fourteen and a half* times. In the last half of the eighteenth century, during the thirty years, 1769-'89, it averaged *fourteen and a half*, and during the twenty years, 1790-1809, embracing the commencement of the present (or nineteenth) century, it averaged nearly *fifteen* (14.9) times the value of silver; since which time it gradually advanced, averaging for the thirty years, 1820-'49, just prior to the discovery of the new gold fields, nearly *fifteen and seven-eighths* (15.82) times that of silver.

After the opening of the new gold fields, the relative value of gold to silver fell, as already stated, reaching its minimum of 15.2 in the year 1859, since which time it has advanced to 15.6, the point it now holds.

APPENDIX G.

Comparison of wholesale prices of certain commodities in the markets of London and Manchester before and subsequent to the discoveries of the new gold fields of California and Australia.

[Prepared for the Special Commissioner of the Revenue by E. B. Elliott.]

AVERAGE OF THE PRICES DURING THE SIX YEARS 1845-'50, AND THE PRICES FOR THE YEARS 1868 AND 1869 COMPARED; THE AVERAGE PRICES OF THE PERIOD 1845-'50 BEING REPRESENTED BY THE NUMBER 100.

Commodities.	1845-50, six years.	1868.	1869.
General mean	100	118¼	118¼
Coffee—Jamaica fine, ordinary to fine	100	133½	125½
Sugar—average of four sorts	100	74¾	74½
Tea—Congou, common to middling	100	82	75½
Tobacco—Virginia leaf, average two sorts	100	200	166
Wheat—Gazette price	100	122	96
Beef—average of inferior, middling, and prime large	100	118½	127
Mutton—average of middling and prime	100	107	109
Pork—large, average *two* sorts	100	109½	121
Cotton—Surat	100	149	154
Silk—raw Cassimbuzar, average of two sorts	100	169½	182½
Flax—Friesland	100	121½	121½
Hemp—St. Petersburg, clean raw	100	118	128
Wool—average of English Southdown, Port Philip lambs, South Australian lambs, and South Australian locks	100	111	96
Dies—Logwood, Jamaica	100	95	105½
Indigo, Bengal, average of two sorts	100	127½	114¾
Oils—average of seal, pale; olive, gallipoli; palm	100	133	124
Timber—average of Dantzic and Memel; Canadian yellow pine	100	96	97
Tallow—St. Petersburg	100	102	111
Leather—English butts, average of two sorts	100	137	137
Saltpeter—English, refined	100	86	104
Ashes—Canadian, pearl, (Montreal)	100	104	100
Copper—tough cake	100	87	88½
Iron—average of British bars, and Swedish	100	84	83½
Lead—English pig	100	110	109
Steel—Swedish, in kegs	100	99	97
Tin—British bars, in barrels	100	116	130
Cotton—raw, average of upland fair, upland good fair, and Pernambuco	100	164½	174
Yarn—mule, No. 40, fair 2d quality	100	143	149
Cotton cloths—average printers, and gold-end shirtings	100	127½	129½

NOTE.—The data from which the above condensed series of results have been prepared were derived from extensive tables published in a late number of the London Economist. A quantity of coffee, for example, which in 1845-'50 would cost 100 pence, cost in 1868 133½, and in 1869, 125½ pence.

From the above table it appears that the average prices of commodities in London and Manchester in 1868 and 1869, as compared with those of the six years 1845-'50, just prior to the influence of the newly-discovered gold fields, are greater by about *eighteen* per cent. This increase is believed to be mainly due to the new discoveries of precious metals.

The yield from the new gold fields of California (discovered in 1848) and of Australia (in 1850) was greatest during the four or five years, almost immediately subsequent to their discovery, (*i. e.*, in 1852–'56,) but the prices of commodities did not immediately sympathize with the increased product. These prices, however, appear, in general, to have reached their culminating points many months since, different commodities at different times, and the prices of most commodities have now for a considerable period of time been either stationary or slowly declining. The price of silver, relatively to gold, as shown in another table, reached its maximum between the years 1857 and 1860.

Appendix H.

The tariffs of the United States.

STATEMENT SHOWING THE REVENUE COLLECTED EACH YEAR FROM 1789 TO 1868, THE AMOUNT OF DUTIABLE IMPORTS AND FREE GOODS IMPORTED ANNUALLY, AND THE AVERAGE RATE OF DUTY ON IMPORTS, ANNUALLY.

	Tariffs.	Customs.	Imports.			Per cent. on dutiable.	Per cent. on aggregate.
			Free.	Dutiable.	Total.		
From Mar. 4, 1789, to Dec. 31							
1790—Aug. 10..	General						
1791—Mar. 3..	Spirits.	$4, 399, 473 09			$52, 200, 000		8½
1792—May 2..	General	3, 443, 070 85			31, 500, 000		11
1793		4, 255, 306 56			31, 100, 000		13½
1794—June 7..	General	4, 801, 065 28			34, 600, 000		14
1795—Jan. 29..	Supplementary	5, 588, 461 26			69, 756, 268		9
1796		6, 567, 987 94			81, 436, 164		8½
1797—Mar. 3..	General	7, 549, 649 65			75, 379, 406		10
1798		7, 106, 061 93			68, 551, 700		10⅓
1799		6, 610, 449 31			79, 069, 148		8½
1800—Mar. 13..	Sugar and wines	9, 080, 932 73			91, 252, 768		9¼
1801		10, 750, 778 93			111, 363, 511		9
1802		12, 458, 235 74			76, 333, 333		16
1803		10, 479, 417 61			64, 666, 666		16
1804—Mar. 26..	Mediterranean fund	11, 098, 565 33			85, 000, 000		14
1805—Mar. 27..	Light money	12, 936, 487 04			120, 600, 000		10½
1806		14, 667, 698 17			129, 410, 000		11⅓
1807		15, 845, 521 61			138, 500, 000		11½
1808		16, 363, 550 58			56, 990, 000		30
1809		7, 296, 020 58			59, 400, 000		12
1810		8, 583, 309 31			85, 400, 000		10
1811		13, 313, 222 73			53, 400, 000		25
1812—July 1..	War: double duties.	8, 958, 777 53			77, 030, 000		11½
1813—July 13..	Salt	13, 224, 623 25			22, 005, 000		60
1814		5, 998, 772 08			12, 965, 000		47
1815		7, 282, 942 22			13, 041, 274		55
1816—April 27..	Min. for protection	36, 306, 874 88			147, 103, 000		25
1817		26, 283, 348 49			99, 250, 000		27
1818—April 20..	Iron and alum	17, 176, 385 00			121, 750, 000		14
1819—Mar. 3..	Wines	20, 283, 608 76			87, 125, 000		23
1820		15, 005, 612 15			74, 450, 000		20½
1821		18, 475, 703 57	$10, 082, 313	$52, 503, 411	62, 585, 724	35. 6	29. 5
1822		24, 066, 066 43	7, 298, 708	75, 942, 833	83, 241, 541	31. 7	28. 9
1823		22, 402, 024 29	9, 048, 288	68, 530, 979	77, 579, 267	32. 7	28. 8
1824—May 22..	General rise	25, 486, 817 86	12, 563, 773	67, 985, 234	80, 549, 007	37. 5	31. 6
1825		31, 653, 871 50	10, 947, 510	85, 392, 565	96, 340, 075	37. 1	32. 8
1826		26, 083, 861 97	12, 567, 769	72, 406, 708	84, [illegible]74, 477	34. 6	30. 7
1827		27, 948, 956 57	11, 855, 104	67, 628, 964	79, 484, 068	41. 3	35. 1
1828—May 19..	Min. extended	29, 951, 251 90	12, 379, 176	76, 130, 648	88, 509, 824	39. 3	33. 8
1829		27, 688, 701 11	11, 805, 501	62, 687, 026	74, 492, 527	44. 3	37. 1
1830—May 20.	Coffee, tea, molasses	28, 389, 505 05	12, 746, 245	58, 130, 675	70, 876, 920	48. 8	40
1831		36, 596, 118 19	13, 456, 625	89, 734, 499	103, 191, 124	40. 8	35. 4
1832—July 14..	Modifications	29, 341, 175 65	14, 249, 453	86, 779, 813	101, 029, 266	33. 8	29

The tariffs of the United States, &c.—Continued.

	Tariffs.	Customs.	IMPORTS.			Per cent. on dutiable.	Per cent. on aggregate.
			Free.	Dutiable.	Total.		
1833—Mar. 2	Compromise	$24, 177, 578 52	$32, 447, 950	$75, 670, 361	$108, 118, 311	31. 9	22. 4
1834		18, 960, 705 96	68, 393, 180	58, 128, 152	126, 521, 332	32. 6	15
1835		25, 890, 726 66	77, 940, 493	71, 955, 249	149, 895, 742	36. 0	17. 2
1836		30, 818, 327 67	92, 056, 481	97, 923, 554	189, 980, 035	31. 6	16. 2
1837		18, 134, 131 01	69, 250, 031	71, 739, 186	140, 989, 217	25. 3	12. 4
1838		19, 702, 825 45	60, 860, 005	52, 857, 399	113, 717, 404	37. 8	17. 3
1839		25, 554, 533 96	76, 401, 792	85, 690, 340	162, 092, 132	29. 9	15. 8
1840		15, 104, 790 63	57, 196, 204	49, 945, 315	107, 141, 519	30. 4	14. 1
1841—Sept. 11	Free list taxed	19, 919, 492 17	66, 019, 731	61, 926, 446	127, 946, 177	32. 2	15. 6
1842—Aug. 30	General rise	16, 662, 746 84	30, 627, 486	69, 534, 601	100, 162, 087	23. 1	16. 6
1843		10, 208, 000 43	35, 574, 584	29, 179, 215	64, 753, 799	35. 7	15. 7
1844		29, 236, 357 38	24, 766, 881	83, 668, 154	108, 435, 035	35. 1	26. 9
1845		30, 952, 416 21	22, 147, 840	95, 106, 724	117, 254, 564	32. 5	26. 4
1846—Aug. 6	Revenue tariff	26, 712, 668 00	24, 767, 730	96, 924, 058	121, 691, 797	26½	21. 9
1847		23, 747, 865 00	41, 772, 636	104, 773, 002	146, 545, 638	22½	16. 2
1848		31, 757, 071 00	22, 716, 603	132, 282, 325	154, 998, 928	24	20. 4
1849		28, 346, 739 00	22, 377, 665	125, 479, 774	147, 857, 439	23	19. 2
1850		39, 668, 686 00	22, 710, 382	155, 427, 936	178, 138, 318	25. 2	22. 3
1851		49, 017, 568 00	25, 106, 587	191, 118, 345	216, 224, 932	26	22. 6
1852		47, 339, 326 00	29, 692, 934	183, 252, 508	212, 945, 442	26	22. 2
1853		58, 931, 865 00	31, 383, 534	236, 595, 113	267, 978, 647	25	22
1854		64, 224, 190 00	33, 285, 821	271, 276, 560	304, 562, 381	23. 5	21. 1
1855		53, 025, 794 00	40, 090, 336	221, 378, 184	261, 468, 520	23	20. 3
1856		64, 022, 863 00	56, 955, 706	257, 684, 236	314, 639, 942	25	20. 3
1857—Mar. 3	General	63, 875, 905 00	66, 729, 306	294, 160, 835	360, 890, 141	21. 5	17. 7
1858		41, 789, 621 00	80, 319, 275	202, 293, 875	282, 613, 150	20	14. 8
1859		49, 565, 824 00	79, 721, 116	259, 047, 014	338, 768, 130	19	14. 6
1860		53, 187, 511 00	90, 841, 749	279, 872, 327	362, 166, 254	19	14. 7
1861 { Mar. 2, Aug. 5, Dec. 24 }		39, 582, 186 00	*134,559,196	218, 180, 191	352, 739, 387	18. 1	11. 2
1862—July 14	General	49, 056, 398 00	*91, 603, 481	183, 843, 458	275, 446, 939	26. 7	17. 7
1863—Mar. 3		69, 059, 642 00	44, 826, 029	208, 093, 891	252, 919, 920	33. 2	23, 7
1864—June 30	General	102, 316, 153 00	*54, 244, 183	275, 320, 951	329, 565, 134	37. 2	31
1865—Mar. 3		84, 928, 260 00	54, 329, 588	194, 226, 064	248, 555, 652	43. 7	34. 2
1866 { Mar. 14, May 16, July 28 }		179, 046, 630 00	69, 728, 618	375, 783, 540	445, 512, 158	47. 06	40. 2
1867—Mar. 2	Wool and woolens	176, 417, 811 00	39, 105, 708	372, 627, 601	411, 733, 309	47. 34	42. 8
1868		164, 464, 599 56	29, 804, 147	343, 605, 301	373, 409, 448	47. 86	44
1869..Feb. 24	Copper increased	180, 048, 426 63	41, 179, 172	395, 847, 369	437, 026, 541	45. 48	41. 2

*In these amounts are included imports into the southern ports during the war, from which no revenue was derived, viz: In 1861, $17,089,234; in 1862, $90,789, and in 1864, $2,220.

APPENDIX J.

A STATEMENT

OF THE

PRINCIPAL ARTICLES ENTERING INTO CONSUMPTION IN THE UNITED STATES

DURING

THE FISCAL YEARS ENDED JUNE 30, 1867, 1868, AND 1869, WITH THE RATES OF DUTIES AND AMOUNTS OF DUTIES ACCRUING ON THE SAME.

PREPARED FOR THE

SPECIAL COMMISSIONER OF THE REVENUE

BY THE

BUREAU OF STATISTICS.

A statement of the principal articles entering into consumption in the United States during the fiscal years ended June 30, 1867, 1868, and 1869, with the rates of duties and amounts of duties accruing on the same. (Prepared for the Special Commissioner of the Revenue by the Bureau of Statistics.)

ARTICLES.	Rate of duty.	1867.			1868.			1869.		
		Quantity.	Value.	Amount of duty.	Quantity.	Value.	Amount of duty.	Quantity.	Value.	Amount of duty.
Animals, living, of all kinds	20 per cent		$2, 263, 743 74	$452, 748 75		$2, 332, 020 03	$466, 404 01		$3, 575, 596 31	$715, 119 26
Articles, the growth, produce, and manufacture of the United States, brought back; dutiable under act of July 28, 1866, section 12	5 per cent		225 45	11 27		69, 901 00	3, 635 05		6, 199 00	309 95
Articles of the United States brought back	2 per cent		821 00	16 42		1, 024 00	26 50			
Articles of the United States brought back	6 per cent		3, 572 00	214 32		4, 667 00	270 02			
Articles of the United States brought back	3 per cent								330 00	9 90
Articles of the United States brought back ... gallons	50 cents per gall.							5, 006½	3, 048 00	2, 503 25
Articles of the United States brought back ... gallons	$2 per gallon							1, 147½	1, 807 00	2, 295 00
Arrow-root	30 per cent		27, 585 50	8, 275 65		16, 731 00	5, 055 60		16, 926 87	5, 078 06
Asphaltum ... pounds	25 per cent		6, 268 00	1, 567 00	369, 368	5, 632 00	1, 408 00	405, 410	10, 559 00	2, 639 75
Beer, ale, and porter:										
In casks ... gallons	20 cents per gall.	103, 591	44, 486 46	20, 718 20	160, 211¼	77, 439 49	32, 042 25	211, 692½	88, 091 00	42, 338 50
In bottles ... do	35 cents per gall.	527, 096½	536, 141 71	184, 483 78	582, 540¾	543, 217 47	203, 889 26	667, 840¾	636, 464 80	233, 744 26
Blacking	30 per cent		14, 748 68	4, 424 60		49, 930 00	14, 979 00		26, 121 00	7, 836 30
Books, periodicals, pamphlets, and all printed matter	25 per cent		1, 148, 138 87	287, 034 71		1, 177, 603 24	294, 400 81		1, 480, 346 45	370, 086 61
Books, blank	25 per cent		23, 661 60	5, 915 40		16, 970 92	4, 242 73		13, 961 80	3, 490 45
Brass and manufactures of:										
Bars and pigs ... pounds	15 per cent		3, 099 00	464 85	31, 104	2, 671 00	400 65	33, 179	2, 456 80	368 52
Old and fit only for re-manufacture ... pounds	15 per cent		26, 467 95	3, 970 19	120, 913	11, 698 78	1, 754 82	131, 640	10, 838 35	1, 625 75
Manufactures not specified	35 per cent		170, 873 63	59, 805 56		181, 113 51	63, 389 73		198, 306 21	69, 407 17
Bristles ... pounds	15 cents per lb.	764, 545	677, 571 00	114, 681 75	527, 996	552, 716 00	79, 199 40	585, 646½	609, 972 00	87, 846 98
Brooms	35 per cent		2, 418 28	846 40		185 00	64 75		120 00	42 00
Brushes	40 per cent		337, 678 15	135, 071 26		239, 688 38	95, 875 35		243, 852 33	97, 540 93
Butter ... pounds	4 cents per lb.	3 340, 465	580, 454 80	133, 618 60	6, 685, 093⅜	1, 197, 672 33	267, 403 75	3, 684, 417	841, 192 07	146 68
Buttons and button-molds	30 per cent		1, 550, 133 39	465, 040 01		1, 652, 039 35	495, 611 81		1, 206, 904 94	362, 071 48
Candles and tapers:										
Adamantine ... pounds	5 cents per lb.	16, 144	2, 798 00	807 20	36, 654¼	6, 479 00	1, 832 71	4, 618	732 00	230 90
Stearine ... do	5 cents per lb.	1, 652	269 00	82 60				1, 491	268 25	74 55
Spermaceti and wax ... do	8 cents per lb.	7, 987	3, 474 00	638 96	3, 547¼	1, 680 00	283 80	5, 385½	2, 544 50	430 84
Paraffine ... do	8 cents per lb.				1, 050½	391 00	84 01	4, 031	1, 293 63	322 48
Tallow and all other not sp. do	2½ cents per lb.	1, 460	142 50	36 50	227	34 05	5 67	460½	56 72	11 52

Cards for playing:										
Value 25 cts. or less per p'k. packs.	25 cents per pack	18,743	3,273 00	4,685 75	13,858	2,277 00	3,464 50	15,696	2,492 40	3,924 00
Value over 25 cts. per pack. do....	35 cents per pack	2,221	780 00	777 35	2,676	901 00	936 60	3,538	1,022 00	1,238 30
Carpets or carpeting of flax, cotton, or other material not specified....	40 per cent	....	....	....	....	1,472 00	588 80	....	2,382 00	952 80
Carriages and parts of..............	35 per cent	....	19,482 37	6,818 83	....	29,468 18	10,313 86	....	26,147 93	9,151 77
Chalk:										
Billiard................pounds..	50 per cent	....	484 00	242 00	....	106 00	53 00	10,310	619 00	309 50
French ....do....	20 per cent	....	1,500 00	300 00	....	2,158 00	431 60	73,138	1,834 00	366 80
Red.......................do....	20 per cent	....	6,783 00	1,356 60	....	1,212 00	242 40	4,463	250 00	50 00
White ....cwt...	$10 per ton	211,956	12,435 00	105,978 00	211,428¼	12,682 00	105,714 13	302,735	27,840 00	151,367 50
All other ....pounds..	25 per cent	....	5,945 00	1,486 25	....	22,484 00	5,621 00	51,973	1,644 00	411 00
Cheese ....do....	4 cents per lb....	1,688,792	224,510 01	67,551 68	1,586,029¾	219,976 49	63,577 49	1,962,195½	283,613 19	78,487 82
Chemicals, dyes, drugs, and medicines:										
Acids—										
Acetic, acetous, and pyroligneous, specific gravity 1.040 or less..............pounds..	25 cents per lb...	1,464	185 00	366 00	965	189 00	241 25	292	66 00	73 00
Specific gravity ov'r 1.040.do....	80 cents per lb...	174	65 00	139 20	41¼	19 00	33 00	101	49 00	80 80
Benzoic	10 per cent	....	5,334 00	533 40	....	4,397 49	443 24	....	7,023 00	702 30
Boracic ....pounds..	5 cents per lb....	770,756	73,396 00	38,537 80	243,993	22,845 00	12,199 65	988,033	109,974 00	49,401 65
Citric, white or yellow...do....	10 cents per lb....	95,091	41,532 00	9,509 10	75,643	34,134 00	7,564 30	154,682	94,786 00	15,468 20
Gallic.....................do....	$1 50 per lb......	195	388 00	292 50	57¼	89 00	85 88	44	44 30	66 00
Muriatic.........................	10 per cent	....	731 00	73 10	....	650 14	65 01	....	961 00	96 10
Nitric...........................	10 per cent	....	30,070 00	3,007 00	....	366 18	36 61	....	....	....
Oxalic...................pounds..	4 cents per lb....	299,445	62,994 00	11,977 80	244,383	37,577 00	9,775 32	308,884	43,418 00	12,355 36
Sulphuric, or oil of vitriol do....	1 cent per lb.....	1,327	95 00	13 27	516	54 00	5 16	20,870	1,140 00	208 70
Tannic.....................do....	$2 per pound	41	86 00	82 00	33¾	40 00	67 50	44½	51 00	89 00
Tartaric ....do....	20 cents per lb...	243,294½	73,806 00	48,658 90	235,683	65,803 00	47,136 60	290,177	74,941 00	58,035 40
Acetates of—										
Ammonia ....do....	70 cents per lb...	....	....	....	4	8 00	2 80	....	....	....
Baryta ....do....	40 cents per lb...	....	....	....	3	3 00	1 20	....	....	....
Lead ....do....	20 cents per lb...	4,477	673 00	895 40	5,536	486 00	1,107 20	1,229	122 00	245 80
Copper, (verdigris).......do....	6 cents per lb....	172,233	38,324 08	10,333 98	97,913	20,252 00	5,874 78	147,420	32,435 00	8,845 20
Magnesia ....do....	50 cents per lb..	2	3 00	1 00	....	....	....	....	....	....
Potassa ....do....	75 cents per lb..	....	....	....	....	....	....	1,091¼	2,814 00	818 44
Soda.......................do....	50 cents per lb..	110	12 00	55 00	25	2 00	12 50	10	3 00	5 00
Aloes ....do....	6 cents per lb....	98,936¼	10,547 00	5,936 18	141,315	20,052 00	8,590 00	133,423¼	15,626 40	8,005 41
Alum, glum, substitute, aluminous cake, and sulphate of alumina, pounds......................	60 cts. per 100 lbs.	5,573,285	85,760 00	33,439 70	3,110,095	47,887 00	18,726 97	2,038,549	34,385 00	12,231 29
Ammonia, sal ammonia, and carbonate of ammonia	20 per cent	....	117,400 72	23,480 14	....	125,473 50	25,094 70	....	83,429 00	16,685 80
Ammonia, muriate of, or sal ammonia	10 per cent	....	....	....	....	13,259 00	1,325 90	....	36,453 00	3,645 30
Analine dyes or colors...pounds..	$1 per lb. and 35 per cent.......	27,079	82,986 00	56,124 10	34,156¼	85,841 00	64,200 60	50,224	157,944 00	105,504 40
Annatto, seed or extract	20 per cent	....	311 00	62 20	....	942 00	188 40	27,499	2,999 00	599 80
Antimony, crude, or regulus of, lbs.	10 per cent	....	63,919 23	6,391 92	1,033,336	83,822 00	8,382 20	....	129,918 00	12,991 80
Argols, or crude or partially refined tartar ....pounds..	6 cents per lb....	1,941,375	284,372 00	116,482 50	2,112,318½	282,744 00	126,739 11	2,424,572	338,375 00	145,474 32

A statement of the principal articles entering into consumption in the United States, &c.—Continued.

ARTICLES.	Rate of duty.	1867.			1868.			1869.		
		Quantity.	Value.	Amount of duty.	Quantity.	Value.	Amount of duty.	Quantity.	Value.	Amount of duty.
Chemicals, dyes, &c.—Continued.										
Arsenic .... pounds..	20 per cent	....	$17, 700 00	$3, 540 00	1, 442, 142	$19, 191 00	$3, 838 20	....	$29, 450 00	$5, 890 00
Asafœtida .... do....	20 per cent	....	4, 008 00	801 60	164, 696	8, 369 00	2, 002 20	44, 470	5, 215 00	1, 043 00
Balsam copaiva .... do....	20 cents per lb...	63, 481	17, 866 00	12, 696 20	68, 059	22, 615 00	13, 611 80	82, 463¼	27, 892 25	16, 492 65
Balsam, Peruvian .... do....	50 cents per lb..	859	1, 199 00	429 50	3, 314	4, 711 00	1, 657 00	2¼	1 00	1 13
Balsam, tolu .... do....	30 cents per lb..	7, 865½	5, 180 00	2, 359 65	13, 700	14, 797 00	4, 110 00	7, 111	3, 445 00	2, 133 30
Bark, Peruvian, Cinchona, Lima, and calisaya .... pounds..	20 per cent	....	435, 384 00	87, 076 80	1, 068, 656	411, 234 00	82, 246 80	....	483, 567 00	96, 713 40
Bark, quilla .... do....	20 per cent	....	1, 522 00	304 40	....	....	....	....	....	....
Bitter apples, colocynth or colo-quintida .... pounds..	10 cents per lb..	22, 299	4, 055 00	2, 229 90	18, 203½	2, 829 00	1, 820 35	31, 063	4, 494 00	3, 106 30
Borax:										
Crude or tincal .... do....	5 cents per lb....	5, 672	711 00	283 60	22, 293	2, 985 00	1, 114 65	54, 822	8, 011 33	2, 741 10
Refined .... do....	10 cents per lb..	49, 652	6, 601 50	4, 965 20	79, 183	10, 127 00	7, 918 30	89, 695	12, 799 00	8, 969 50
Buchu leaves .... do....	10 cents per lb...	35, 323	3, 913 00	3, 532 30	29, 748	3, 157 00	2, 978 80	39, 386	3, 357 00	3, 938 60
Calomel	30 per cent	....	4, 242 00	1, 272 60	....	4, 440 42	1, 332 12	....	4, 515 36	1, 354 60
Camphor:										
Crude .... pounds..	30 cents per lb..	339, 732	92, 613 00	101, 919 60	199, 644	52, 750 00	59, 893 20	518, 540	108, 969 00	155, 562 00
Refined .... do....	40 cents per lb..	9, 542	3, 893 95	3, 816 80	1, 572	620 00	648 10	1, 743	734 00	697 20
Cantharides or Spanish flies . do....	50 cents per lb..	9, 376	5, 150 00	4, 688 00	13, 465	6, 743 00	6, 732 50	9, 250	5, 061 00	4, 625 00
Cocculus indicus .... do....	10 cents per lb ..	827	58 00	82 70	6, 237	472 00	662 40	2, 933	192 00	293 30
Chemical preparations not specified	20 per cent	....	....	....	....	156, 181 39	31, 361 08	....	242, 059 10	48, 411 82
Chloroform .... pounds..	$1 per pound	330	265 00	330 00	121	81 00	121 00	47½	41 23	47 50
Chloride of lime or bleaching pow-der .... pounds..	30 cts. per 100 lbs.	27, 142, 919	798, 391 74	81, 428 75	24, 495, 594	636, 608 00	73, 486 78	33, 800, 056	819, 610 92	101, 400 17
Collodion .... do....	$1 per pound	4	2 00	4 00	3	3 00	3 00	9	4 00	9 00
Copperas, green vitriol, or sulphate of iron .... pounds..	½ cent per pound.	2, 267, 575	15, 095 58	11, 337 87	181, 354	1, 062 00	906 77	597, 418	3, 362 00	2, 987 09
Cream of tartar .... do....	10 cents per lb..	1, 594, 574	306, 214 44	159, 457 40	2, 050, 813	348, 725 00	205, 081 30	2, 323, 045½	389, 444 00	232, 304 55
Tartar emetic .... do....	15 cents per lb..	658	214 00	98 70	2, 558	762 00	383 70	2, 736	885 00	410 40
Cubebs .... do....	10 cents per lb..	28, 278	4, 275 00	2, 827 80	62, 553	8, 695 00	6, 406 30	37, 712	2, 744 50	3, 771 20
Cuttle-fish bone .... do....	5 cents per lb....	14, 329	1, 011 00	716 45	17, 250	1, 251 00	862 50	18, 404	1, 292 00	920 20
Cutch or catechu, and terra japo-nica .... pounds..	10 per cent	3, 374, 628	67, 950 00	6, 795 00	1, 046, 128	104, 419 00	10, 623 60	1, 644, 290	98, 959 00	9, 895 90
Dragon's blood .... do....	10 cents per lb..	4, 525	1, 727 00	452 50	2, 073	850 00	238 70	3, 995	1, 234 00	399 50
Drugs and dyes not specified	20 per cent	....	....	....	....	174, 261 00	35, 170 00	....	379, 930 37	75, 986 07
Dulce, (sea-weed) .... cwt...	$5 per ton and 10 per cent	....	....	....	50	121 00	24 60	491¼	3, 503 77	473 19
Ergot .... pounds..	20 cents per lb..	8, 319	4, 550 00	1, 663 80	9, 279	4, 634 00	1, 855 80	12, 168¾	6, 147 00	2, 433 75
Nitric ether .... do...	50 cents per lb..	....	....	....	31	10 00	15 50	....	....	....

Gunny cloth and gunny bags, or other manufactures, wholly or in part of hemp, jute, or like material, value less than 10 cents per square yard.......pounds..	3 cents per lb....	32, 058, 814	1, 297, 381 70	961, 764 42	27, 180, 586	1, 004, 759 74	816, 427 88	24, 356, 673⅓	871, 432 77	730, 700 20
value over 10 cents per square yard.................pounds..	4 cents per lb....	317, 659	16, 986 28	12, 706 36	18, 244	2, 161 04	729 76	16, 300	1, 495 70	652 00
Hemp or jute carpeting ...yards..	6½ cents per yd...	1, 483, 838½	291, 580 40	96, 449 50	123, 628	23, 364 00	8, 035 81			
Hemp or jute carpeting ....do....	8 cents per yd ...				1, 666, 431½	303, 444 50	133, 314 52	1, 537, 767	251, 086 00	123, 021 36
Hemp yarn ....pounds..	5 cents per lb....	131, 130	27, 352 25	6, 556 50	219, 128	51, 955 00	10, 956 40	222, 853	48 829 00	11, 142 65
Hemp yarn..................do....	5 cents per lb., and 30 per cent.				7, 667	2, 236 00	1, 054 15			
Jute butts, tons, 1867; cwt., 1868 and 1869..........................	$6 per ton.......	2, 153 1-10	53, 859 00	12, 918 60	29, 892	33, 157 00	8, 967 60	114, 240½	161, 160 00	34, 272 15
Jute and sun hemp, tons, 1867; cwt. 1868 and 1869	$15 per ton	4, 596 7-20	359, 623 00	68, 945 25	76, 657	260, 118 00	57, 542 75	111, 257	363, 036 00	83, 442 75
Jute yarn ....pounds..	25 per cent		119, 240 00	29, 810 00		108, 551 00	28, 160 75		145, 500 00	36, 375 00
Manilla, tons, 1867; cwt., 1868 and 1869..........................	$25 per ton	17, 567 11-24	2, 195, 092 00	439, 186 46	306, 837¼	2, 214, 554 00	373, 546 56	350, 958½	2, 684, 776 00	438, 698 12
Russian, tons, 1867; cwt. 1868 and 1869	$40 per ton	2, 915¼	503, 699 00	116, 620 00	41, 047¼	360, 602 00	82, 094 50	30, 884	286, 897 00	61, 768 00
All other not specified ....cwt..	$40 per ton				220	2, 419 00	440 00			
Sail duck...................yards..	30 per cent		226, 601 63	67, 980 49		85, 698 00	25, 709 40	93, 475	24, 667 00	7, 400 10
Seines of hemp ....pounds..	6½ cents per lb...	43, 334	20, 815 37	2, 816 71	7, 501	2, 208 00	487 62	1, 594	661 00	103 61
Sheetings of hemp, (Russia,) brown or white ....yards..	35 per cent		114, 555 00	40, 094 25		70, 406 44	24, 642 25	162, 346	29, 727 44	10, 404 60
Sisal grass and like cordage material, tons, 1867; cwt., 1868 and 1869..........................	$15 per ton	791	102, 366 00	11, 865 00	30, 185	232, 091 00	23, 887 45	43, 884	338, 935 00	32, 913 00
All other vegetable and fibrous substances used for cordage, tons, 1867; cwt., 1868 and 1869..	$5 per ton, and 10 per cent......	31 11-28	4, 499 00	606 86	1, 267	3, 025 00	675 25	3, 473	7, 366 06	1, 604 86
All other manufactures of hemp, jute, &c	30 per cent		771, 241 14	231, 372 34		2, 638, 038 43	791, 411 53		354, 625 40	106, 387 62
Hides and skins........................	10 per cent		9, 626, 242 81	962, 624 28		9, 770, 354 22	977, 325 12		11, 165, 408 07	1, 116, 540 81
Honey..................gallons..	20 cents per gall .	104, 437	59, 017 11	20, 887 40	130, 609	71, 899 90	26, 121 80	140, 596	78, 639 85	28, 119 20
Hops ....pounds..	5 cents per lb....	725 508½	213, 388 25	36, 275 42	3, 270, 997½	859, 316 39	163, 668 98	280, 111	55, 154 00	14, 005 55
India-rubber:										
Unmanufactured..................	10 per cent		2, 025, 677 00	202, 567 70		1, 969, 114 00	196, 911 40		2, 672, 569 00	267, 256 90
Shoes, boots, webbing, and other manufactures of................	35 per cent		477, 274 06	167, 045 92		456, 857 58	159, 900 15		525, 224 77	183, 828 67
Manufactures of India-rubber and silk..........................	50 per cent		332, 028 50	166, 014 25		395, 844 00	197, 922 00		428, 951 99	214, 477 49
Ink and ink powders	35 per cent		66, 574 00	23, 300 90		68, 148 29	23, 851 90		71, 701 30	25, 095 45

A statement of the principal articles entering into consumption in the United States, &c.—Continued.

ARTICLES.	Rate of duty.	1867.			1868.			1869.		
		Quantity.	Value.	Amount of duty.	Quantity.	Value.	Amount of duty.	Quantity.	Value.	Amount of duty.
Chemicals, dyes, &c.—Continued.										
Soda and salts of:										
Carbonate of..........pounds..	½ cent per pound.	135, 422	$3, 491 00	$677 11	11, 236	$158 29	$56 17	485, 695	$7, 637 80	$2, 428 47
Caustic ....do....	1½ cent per pound	12, 942, 017	548, 858 00	194, 130 25	12, 101, 490	460, 609 93	181, 522 35	13, 705, 254	448, 661 00	205, 578 81
Glauber salts, (sulphate of soda,) pounds....................	½ cent per pound.	79, 351	1, 228 00	396 75	167, 039	2, 011 00	835 20	346, 003	3, 786 00	1, 730 01
Nitrate of soda........pounds..	1 cent per pound.	29, 429, 469	563, 624 20	294, 294 69	18, 433, 173	282, 785 00	184, 331 73	28, 866, 364	600, 691 00	288, 663 64
Rochelle salts, (tartrate of soda,) pounds....................	15 cents per lb..	874	221 00	131 10	256	47 00	38 40	750	149 00	112 50
Soda, ash................pounds..	½ cent per pound.	111, 410, 794	2, 481, 106 00	557, 053 97	109, 045, 765	2, 227, 826 00	545, 228 83	131, 348, 209	2, 356, 640 00	656, 741 05
Soda, sal..................do....	½ cent per pound.	16, 947, 382	251, 640 00	84, 736 91	23, 823, 740	319, 875 72	119, 118 70	19, 215, 883	228, 229 00	96, 079 42
Strychnine and its salts..ounces..	$1 50 per ounce..	8	21 00	12 00	122½	146 00	183 75	2	6 00	3 00
Sulphate of barytes .....pounds..	½ cent per pound.	14, 968, 181	141, 273 00	74, 840 90	2, 755, 547	26, 739 00	13, 777 74	1, 117, 335	8, 565 00	5, 586 67
Sulphate of copper, (blue vitriol,) pounds....................	25 per cent	1, 971, 902	118, 166 00	29, 541 50	726, 452	44, 469 00	11, 117 25	....	47, 325 00	11, 831 25
Sulphate of copper, (blue vit.) lbs..	5 cents per lb....	....	....	....	....	....	....	19, 841	1, 052 00	992 05
Sulphate of magnesia, (Epsom salts) ....pounds..	1 cent per pound.	9, 717	205 00	97 17	28, 362	563 00	283 62	55, 421	980 00	554 21
Sulphate of quinine .....ounces..	45 per cent	79, 478	89, 195 00	40, 137 75	40, 675	50, 979 00	22, 940 55	....	111, 886 00	50, 348 70
Sulphate of zinc, (white vitr'l).lbs	20 per cent	....	2, 422 00	484 40	....	94 00	18 80	....	5, 460 00	1, 092 00
Sulphur or brimstone, rolls, crude, cwt	$6 per ton......	490, 882	629, 373 00	147, 264 60	363, 011	446, 547 00	108, 903 30	471, 793¾	678, 642 00	141, 538 13
Sulphur, flour of. cwt (lbs., 1869)..	$20 per ton and 15 per cent	2, 201	5, 509 00	3, 027 35	329½	948 00	471 70	216, 359	4, 576 00	2, 618 16
Sulphur or brimstone, rolls, refined .... cwt...	$10 per ton	4, 611	10, 915 00	2, 305 50	1, 295	2, 721 00	647 50	12, 900¾	27, 149 00	6, 450 38
Sumac ....pounds..	10 per cent	10, 634, 342	494, 251 00	49, 425 10	....	536, 085 00	53, 608 50	....	572, 578 00	57, 257 80
Chiccory:										
Ground or prepared ....do....	5 cents per lb....	2, 907, 375	94, 942 00	145, 368 75	2, 656, 003	89, 075 00	132, 895 45	3, 334, 864	126, 794 31	166, 743 20
Root.......................cwt...	4 cents per lb....	....	....	....	1	3 00	04	36, 346	1, 195 00	1, 453 84
Chocolate ....pounds..	7 cents per lb....	7, 459	2, 409 75	522 13	9, 661	3, 134 98	676 27	14, 179	4, 550 00	992 53
Cocoa:										
Ground ....do....	9 cents per lb....	7, 139	1, 936 00	642 51	6, 879	1, 601 00	619 11	5, 775	1, 308 00	519 75
Not ground ....do....	3 cents per lb....	2, 319, 690	313, 122 60	69, 590 70	1, 999, 974	242, 334 00	59, 999 22	2, 313, 476	209, 631 81	69, 404 28
Shells and leaves..........do....	2 cents per lb....	....	....	....	2, 090	76 00	41 80	....	....	....
Clay, unwrought pipe clay, fire-clay, and kaoline ....tons...	$5 per ton	6, 383¾	72, 204, 00	31, 918 75	8, 384½	66, 958 00	41, 923 00	12, 963¾	84, 645 00	64, 818 75
Fullers' earth..............do....	$3 per ton	280¼	3, 113 00	840 75	211	2, 522 00	633 00	324 1-10	3, 587 00	972 30
Clocks and watches:										
Chronometers, box and ships', and parts of	10 per cent	....	381 00	38 10	....	4, 571 00	457 10	....	2, 155 00	215 50

Clocks and parts of	35 per cent	....	210, 929 45	73, 825 30	....	212, 387 21	74, 583 72	....	247, 339 90	86, 568 96
Watches of gold or silver	25 per cent	....	1, 313, 893 00	328, 473 25	....	723, 332 58	180, 833 14	....	355, 192 00	88, 798 00
Watches, all other, and watch materials	20 per cent	....	1, 027, 071 00	205, 414 20	....	1, 432, 257 00	286, 451 40	....	2, 273, 668 00	454, 733 60
Coal, bituminous ... tons	$1 25 per ton	509, 802 9-40	1, 412, 596 52	637, 252 78	394, 021¼	1, 259, 513 17	492, 526 56	437, 228⅓	1, 222, 118 58	546, 535 43
All other ... do	40 cents per ton	117½	646 25	47 00	76	428 00	30 40	6	97 50	2 40
Coffee ... pounds	5 cents per lb	172, 741, 783	19, 250, 604 15	8, 637, 089 15	212, 379, 267	22, 315, 316 15	10, 637, 845 35	230, 814, 376¾	22, 779, 574 46	11, 540, 718 83
Coffee, acorn, and all other substitutes for ... pounds	3 cents per lb	890	38 00	26 70	471	89 00	14 13	1, 438	71 00	43 14
Copper and manufactures of copper:										
Manufactures not specified	35 per cent	....	15, 985 68	5, 594 99	....	21, 491 91	7, 522 17	....	18, 835 40	6, 592 39
Old copper ... pounds	1½ cent per lb	569, 732½	81, 930 02	8, 545 99	318, 705	42, 651 74	4, 789 57	225, 279	27, 308 55	3, 379 18
Ore ... cwt	5 per cent	....	936, 271 12	46, 813 55	30, 675	199, 267 75	9, 513 38	....	436, 295 00	21, 814 75
Pigs, bars, or ingots, and including other in forms not manufactured and not otherwise specified ... pounds	2½ cents per lb	1, 635, 953	287, 831 00	40, 898 82	61, 394	6, 935 00	1, 534 85	6, 024	778 00	150 60
Rolled plates, called braziers' copper, sheets, pipes, eyelets, copper bottoms, and rods	35 per cent	....	1, 100 75	385 26	7	1 00	35	114¾	39 00	23 65
Sheathing copper ... pounds	3½ cents per lb	437, 796½	85, 516 97	15, 322 87	87, 463	15, 822 00	3, 061 21	114, 524¼	19, 702 00	4, 008 35
Yellow metal ... do	3 cents per lb	220, 889	37, 717 00	6, 626 67	101, 488	18, 852 25	3, 323 30	43, 669	6, 592 00	1, 310 67
All manufactures not otherwise specified	45 per cent	....	....	....	....	....	....	....	24, 377 00	10, 969 65
Old copper ... do	4 cents per lb	....	....	....	....	....	....	65, 591	7, 511 21	2, 620 04
Ore ... do	3 cents per lb	....	....	....	....	....	....	176, 348	12, 192 00	5, 290 44
Pigs, bars, or ingots, &c ... do	5 cents per lb	....	....	....	....	....	....	7, 188	1, 365 00	359 40
Cork, Manufactures of	50 per cent	....	254, 909 97	127, 454 98	....	167, 811 00	84, 426 60	....	195, 627 73	97, 813 87
Unmanufactured	30 per cent	....	137, 659 00	41, 297 70	....	160, 867 00	48, 260 10	....	186, 635 07	55, 990 52
Cotton, and manufactures of cotton:										
Cotton, unmanufactured, under act of March 3, 1865 ... pounds	5 cents per lb	63, 434	11, 943 00	3, 171 70	....	....	....	....	....	....
Under act of July 28, 1866 ... do	3 cents per lb	120, 177	37, 509 00	3, 605 31	275, 077	54, 651 20	8, 252 31	121, 886	26, 999 00	3, 656 58
Cottons, plain, brown, or not bleached, value 16 cents or less per square yard ... sq. yards	5 cents per sq. yd	1, 981, 153¼	155, 050 22	99, 057 66	151, 874	13, 178 10	7, 628 05	820, 164	44, 976 04	41, 008 20
Value over 16 cents per square yard ... sq. yards	35 per cent	....	152, 327 04	53, 314 46	222, 824	89, 931 00	31, 475 85	251, 484	43, 636 00	15, 272 60
Plain bleached, value 20 cents or less per square yard . sq. yards	5¼ cts. per sq. yd	17, 793, 305¾	3, 574, 263 15	978, 631 81	14, 431, 544½	1, 902, 610 17	893, 842 55	17, 619, 748½	2, 345, 738 48	969, 086 17
Value over 20 cents per square yard	35 per cent	....	785, 429 23	274, 900 23	2, 945, 217	649, 885 00	227, 459 75	3, 915, 583	861, 653 00	301, 578 55
Cottons, bleached ... yards	3 cents per yard	....	....	....	20, 634	1, 342 00	619 62	1, 453, 112	102, 789 00	43, 593 36
Cottons, printed or colored . sq. yds	3½ cents per yard	....	....	....	....	....	....	73, 450	5, 041 00	2, 570 75
Cotton book cloth ... do	2½ cents per yard	....	....	....	680	23 00	17 00	17, 199	699 00	529 97
Printed or colored, value 25 cents or less per square yard, not over 100 threads per square inch, including warp and filling, and weighing over 5 ounces per square yard ... sq. yards	5½ cents per sq. yd. & 10 per cent	127, 053	19, 481 98	8, 936 11	212, 454½	26, 755 08	14, 360 51	12[illegible], 894	16, 852 37	8, 334 41

A statement of the principal articles entering into consumption in the United States, &c.—Continued.

ARTICLES.	Rate of duty.	1867. Quantity.	1867. Value.	1867. Amount of duty.	1868. Quantity.	1868. Value.	1868. Amount of duty.	1869. Quantity.	1869. Value.	1869. Amount of duty.
Cotton, and manufactures of cotton—Continued.										
Over 100 and not over 200 threads to the square inch, including warp and filling.....sq. yards..	5½ cts. per sq. yd. and 20 per cent..	24, 778, 269¼	$4, 023, 142 89	$2, 167, 433 38	13, 033, 440	$1, 853, 001 63	$1, 087, 439 53	15, 192, 487¾	$2, 033, 943 02	$1, 242, 375 42
Value over 25 cents per sq. yard ..	35 per cent	....	747, 028 12	261, 459 84	1, 619, 531¼	466, 992 74	163, 447 46	1, 763, 568	473, 026 35	165, 559 22
Jeans, denims, drillings, bed-ticking, ginghams, &c., not exceeding 20 cents per square yard, not bleached or colored, not over 200 threads per square inch, counting warp and filling ....sq. yards..	6 cents per sq. yd.	2, 728	532 94	163 68	6, 228	1, 140 03	373 68	8, 323	1, 501 67	499 38
Over 200 threads per square inch, count'g warp and filling.sq. yds..	7 cents per sq. yd.	19	4 60	1 33	....	....	....	....	....	....
Bleached, not over 200 threads per square inch, counting warp and filling................sq. yards..	6½ cents per sq. yd.	15, 168¼	4, 219 55	1, 985 93	12, 885	2, 279 00	837 53	5, 301	848 00	344 57
Over 200 threads per square inch, count'g warp and filling.sq. yds..	7½ cts. per sq. yd..	5, 905	1, 368 00	442 88	451	52 05	33 83	....	....	....
Colored, painted, or printed.do....	3½ cts. per sq. yd. and 10 per cent ..	....	....	....	....	....	....	1, 317, 252	101, 199 00	56, 222 72
Colored, painted, or printed.do....	3½ cts. per sq. yd. and 20 per cent ..	....	....	....	7, 386	579 00	316 41	1, 834	190 00	102 19
Printed, painted, or colored, not over 100 threads per square inch, counting warp and filling...... ....sq. yards..	6½ cts. per sq. yd. and 10 per cent ..	44, 485	10, 172 88	3, 908 81	49, 651	9, 251 89	4, 152 49	18, 489	2, 830 27	1, 484 80
Over 100 threads and not over 200 threads per square inch, count'g warp and filling.sq. yds..	6½ cts. per sq. yd. and 15 per cent..	9, 546, 779½	1, 672, 624 85	871, 434 36	6, 566, 237½	945, 975 30	568, 701 78	7, 346, 427	1, 054, 261 00	635, 656 90
Over 200 threads per square inch, count'g warp and filling.sq. yds..	7½ cts. per sq. yd. and 15 per cent..	54	17 04	6 60	2, 972¾	353 60	276 00	92	23 25	10 29
Jeans, denims, &c., over 20 cents per square yard, not bleached, bleached, or printed..sq. yards..	35 per cent	....	3, 424 00	1, 198 40	2, 779	598 09	209 33	813	355 00	124 25
Cotton velvet......................	35 per cent	....	290, 307 13	101, 607 49	1, 072, 215	323, 687 54	113, 290 64	....	627, 816 00	219, 735 60

Cotton thread on spools:										
Of 100 yds. each, or less..dozens..	6 cts. per doz. and 30 per cent....	3, 419, 873 and 5-12ths.	666, 434 35	405, 122 71	3, 927, 175½	705, 298 50	447, 220 08	4, 315, 295	724, 227 89	476, 186 06
Excess of 100 yards each...do....	6 cts. per doz. and 35 per cent....	3, 762, 395 and 10-12ths.	729, 992 65	481, 241 17	4, 267, 292¼	776, 720 72	527, 889 80	4, 473, 932	765, 784 04	536, 460 33
Cotton thread not on spools, per skein or hank of 840 yds. skeins..	4 cents per skein and 30 per cent.	51	53 00	17 94	9	2 00	96	....	....	....
Other cotton thread, not on spools..	40 per cent	....	235, 148 25	94, 059 30	....	242, 063 34	96, 825 33	....	347, 382 00	138, 952 80
Shirts and drawers, wov'n or made in frames, wholly of cotton	35 per cent	....	18, 543 73	6, 490 30	....	859, 507 75	300, 827 71	....	41, 620 13	14, 567 05
Cotton hosiery..................	35 per cent	....	5, 404, 915 00	1, 891, 720 25	....	2, 727, 917 22	954, 771 03	....	3, 942, 575 92	1, 379, 901 57
Laces, braids, trimmings, gimps, cords, and galloons	35 per cent	....	2, 054, 522 02	719, 082 70	....	1, 764, 696 05	617, 643 62	....	2, 135, 290 05	747, 351 52
Manufactures, all other, wholly or in part of cotton, not otherwise provided for..............	35 per cent	....	2, 066, 772 18	723, 370 26	....	2, 013, 206 41	704, 622 24	....	2, 086, 693 40	730, 342 69
Ready-made clothing..............	35 per cent	....	1, 207, 158 01	422, 505 30	....	1, 256, 683 27	439, 839 14	....	1, 300, 302 03	455, 105 71
Diam'ds and gems, real and imitat'n:										
Not set	10 per cent	....	1, 317, 420 00	131, 742 00	....	1, 060, 544 00	106, 054 40	....	1, 997, 282 00	199, 728 20
Set...............................	25 per cent	....	291 00	72 75	....	1, 465 00	366 25	....	23 00	5 75
Glaziers'.........................	10 per cent	....	906 00	90 60	....	484 00	48 40	....	445 00	44 50
Earthenware and china:										
Brown earthen and common stoneware	25 per cent	....	48, 617 68	12, 154 42	....	47, 207 62	11, 801 90	....	34, 260 40	8, 565 10
China, porcelain, and parian ware, plain white	45 per cent	....	418, 492 51	188, 321 62	....	309, 960 00	139, 485 90	....	400, 894 21	180, 402 39
China, porcelain, and parian ware, gilded or ornamented...........	50 per cent	....	439, 823 74	219, 911 87	....	403, 554 63	201, 777 32	....	555, 425 32	277, 712 66
All other earthen, stone or crockery-ware	40 per cent	....	4, 280, 924 24	1, 712, 369 69	....	3, 244, 988 84	1, 297, 995 54	....	3, 468, 970 22	1, 387, 588 09
Embroideries of cotton, silk, or wool, not otherwise specified.........	35 per cent	....	1, 983, 924 00	694, 373 40	....	1, 349, 414 00	472, 294 90	....	1, 439, 294 00	503, 752 90
Emery:										
Ore or rock.................tons..	$6 per ton	428	14, 373 00	2, 568 00	85¼	4, 531 00	513 00	964⅛	35, 205 00	5, 786 00
Pulverized...............pounds..	1 cent per lb.....	924, 431	38, 831 00	9, 244 31	834, 286	33, 549 00	8, 342 86	924, 161	42, 711 00	9, 241 61
Fancy articles:										
Alabaster and manufactures of, and spar ornaments............	30 per cent	....	26, 129 00	7, 838 70	....	27, 891 00	8, 367 30	....	21, 564 00	6, 469 20
Beads and bead ornaments........	50 per cent	....	975, 366 42	487, 683 21	....	842, 556 31	421, 278 15	....	198, 433 00	99, 216 50
Canes and walking sticks.........	35 per cent	....	28, 814 00	10, 084 90	....	27, 511 05	9, 628 86	....	37, 388 00	13, 085 80
Combs and manufactures of shell, bone, horn, ivory, and vegetable ivory, not specified.........	35 per cent	....	215, 808 20	75, 532 87	....	156, 524 65	54, 783 63	....	162, 555 90	56, 894 56
Coral, cut or manufactured.......	30 per cent	....	....	....	....	....	....	....	22, 295 00	6, 688 50
Fans, palm leaf...........number..	1 cent each	1, 980, 173	41, 628 00	19, 801 73	1, 194, 342	21, 129 00	11, 943 42	493, 485	14, 858 00	4, 934 85
all other.........................	35 per cent	....	289, 554 13	101, 343 95	....	163, 832 40	57, 341 34	....	205, 201 00	71, 820 35
Feath'rs, ornamt'l, and artific'l flow'rs:										
Crude............................	25 per cent	....	200, 609 00	50, 152 25	....	155, 462 00	38, 865 50	....	198, 286 00	49, 571 50
Dressed..........................	50 per cent	....	552, 644 86	276, 322 43	....	558, 532 50	279, 266 25	....	792, 774 00	396, 387 00

A statement of the principal articles entering into consumption in the United States, &c.—Continued.

ARTICLES.	Rate of duty.	1867. Quantity.	1867. Value.	1867. Amount of duty.	1868. Quantity.	1868. Value.	1868. Amount of duty.	1869. Quantity.	1869. Value.	1869. Amount of duty.
Ivory or bone dice, chessmen or balls.	50 per cent	....	$10,424 00	$5,212 00	....	$7,292 00	$3,646 00	....	$6,159 00	$3,079 50
Perfumeries and cosmetics, cologne water and other alcoholic perfumery ....gallons..	$3 per gal. and 50 per cent	7,956 7-40	101,515 30	74,626 18	11,153¼	162,610 50	114,765 00	10,614 1-5	181,105 30	122,395 25
All kinds not specified	50 per cent	....	208,234 56	104,117 28	....	151,615 26	75,807 63	....	131,893 01	65,946 50
Pipes of clay, common or white	35 per cent	....	118,891 00	41,611 85	....	90,117 74	31,541 21	....	102,291 00	35,801 85
Pipes and bowls, meerschaum for smoking, not otherwise provid'd for ....gross..	$1 50 per gross and 75 per cent.	18,811 1-6	262,680 00	225,226 75	14,113¾	245,167 25	205,046 07	12,850 11-12	178,411 70	153,085 15
Pipes, cases, stems, and mountings, and all parts of pipes and pipe fixtures, and all smokers' articles..	75 per cent	....	65,172 50	48,879 38	....	70,429 00	52,821 75	....	52,179 06	39,134 30
Toys	50 per cent	....	350,132 93	175,066 46	....	301,481 39	150,740 69	....	300,488 00	150,244 00
Dolls	35 per cent	....	230,802 00	80,780 70	....	153,467 00	53,713 45	....	176,393 00	61,737 55
Feather beds	20 per cent	....	1,093 61	218 72	....	3,647 00	729 40	....	5,189 58	1,037 92
Feathers and downs for beds	30 per cent	....	108,797 33	32,612 20	....	14,578 71	4,373 61	....	12,171 29	3,651 38
Fire-crackers ....boxes..	$1 per box	144,517	125,348 50	144,517 75	73,671¾	94,861 12	73,671 75	81,914¼	86,914 00	81,914 25
Fish:										
Mackerel ....barrels..	$2 per barrel	66,838	612,073 41	133,676 00	30,686	289,175 93	61,376 30	27,468⅞	306,695 57	54,937 75
Herring ....do..	$1 per barrel	86,908	292,209 86	86,908 00	61,451¼	288,223 20	61,451 25	91,567½	425,212 90	91,567 50
Salmon ....do..	$3 per barrel	5,431	115,633 64	16,293 00	6,173½	88,016 18	18,520 50	8,454¾	110,591 00	25,364 25
All other, in barrels ....do..	$1 50 per barrel	11,561¼	95,495 80	17,342 25	4,215½	31,834 00	6,323 25	9,732	65,538 95	14,598 00
All not in barrels, sold by weight ....pounds..	50 cts. per 100 lbs.	6,955,665	210,551 66	34,778 32	6,333,808	189,660 95	31,669 04	8,943,318	287,934 45	44,716 59
Sardines and anchovies, preserved in oil or otherwise	50 per cent	....	559,413 14	279,706 57	....	516,309 38	258,154 69	....	640,159 40	320,079 70
Flax and manufactures of flax:										
Not manuf ..tons, 1867; cwt. 1868 and 1869	$15 per ton	1,163 13-30	452,668 54	17,451 50	30,400	543,588 18	22,800 00	33,136½	581,723 00	24,852 37
Tow of flax ....do....do..	$5 per ton	1,686 3-20	111,315 00	8,430 75	4,705	24,552 00	1,176 25	15,991	72,583 00	3,997 75
Linen, brown or bleached:										
Value 30 cts. or less p. s. y. sq. yds..	30 per cent	....	10,428,542 46	3,649,989 86	....	171,832 00	51,549 60	....	1,540,622 00	462,186 60
Value 30 cts. or less p. sq. yd. do..	35 per cent	....	....	....	....	2,397,213 60	839,024 76	....	5,420,302 05	1,897,105 71
Value over 30 cts. per sq. yard	40 per cent	....	3,790,017 60	1,516,007 04	....	1,796,168 60	718,467 44	....	1,750,858 58	700,343 43
Other, value ov'r 30 cts. pr. sq. yd..	35 per cent	....	....	....	....	3,255,039 46	1,139,263 81	....	205,675 00	71,986 25
Brown hollan's, burlaps, canvas coatings, crash, diaper, duck, handkerchiefs, huckabacks, lawns, paddings, and all like manufac-										

tures, of which flax or hemp shall be the material of chief value.										
Value 30 cents or less pr. sq. yard	35 per cent		2,132,260 50	746,291 17		1,670,919 00	584,821 65		2,375,560 80	831,446 28
Other, value 30 cts. or less pr. sq. yd.	30 per cent					704,963 00	211,488 90		2,150,023 00	645,006 90
Value over 30 cents per sq. yard	40 per cent		165,469 68	66,187 87		276,019 00	110,407 60		960,674 60	384,269 60
Other, value over 30 cts. pr. sq. yd.	35 per cent					557,939 59	195,278 85		111,615 82	39,065 59
Flax or linen yarns for carpets:										
Value 24 cents or less per pound	30 per cent		131,738 75	39,521 62		97,995 00	29,398 50	227,773	44,389 00	13,316 70
Value over 24 cents per pound	35 per cent		26,387 00	9,235 45		17,875 00	6,256 25		6,945 00	2,430 75
Thread, pack thread and twine	40 per cent		1,099,935 17	439,974 07		922,325 49	368,930 20		1,110,898 22	444,359 29
Thread lace and insertings	30 per cent		309,216 00	92,764 80		231,915 00	69,574 50		244,317 00	73,295 10
All other manufactures of flax	40 per cent		674,036 33	269,614 53		741,512 97	296,605 19		194,609 41	77,843 76
Fruits:										
Oranges, lemons, and limes	25 per cent		1,812,180 54	453,045 13		1,567,511 06	391,887 86		2,080,983 63	520,245 41
Bananas and limes	20 per cent					133,002 26	26,609 55		175,883 57	35,176 71
Pineapples plantains and bananas	25 per cent		195,465 07	48,866 27		111,008 81	27,782 30		167,832 77	41,958 19
Fruits in juice, and fruit juice	25 per cent		32,923 00	8,230 75		33,664 20	8,416 05		56,057 27	14,014 82
Fruits preserved in bottles or jars in brandy, sugar, &c	35 per cent		165,521 43	57,932 50		242,967 10	85,038 49		199,331 34	69,765 97
Green, dry, and ripe fruits, not otherwise provided	10 per cent		49,835 69	4,983 56		75,093 71	7,509 37		150,475 70	15,047 57
Prunes and plums.......pounds	5 cents per lb.	5,656,812	372,203 00	282,840 60	7,963,561	463,806 00	398,178 05	13,678,827	713,810 80	683,941 35
Dates.......do	2 cents per lb.	1,488,847	52,689 00	29,776 94	2,686,577	70,291 00	53,731 54	1,937,916	50,001 00	38,758 32
Currants, Zante and all oth'r. do	5 cents per lb.	6,685,109	295,606 52	334,255 45	6,736,229	253,302 43	336,811 45	7,920,376	257,248 00	396,018 80
Figs.......do	5 cents per lb.	5,842,516	240,688 51	292,125 80	4,114,303	242,455 50	205,715 15	3,880,456	226,064 84	194,022 80
Raisins.......do	5 cents per lb.	19,868,856	1,380,173 24	993,442 80	21,043,560	1,543,830 30	1,052,178 00	25,204,705	1,732,641 48	1,260,235 25
Furs:										
Undressed, on the skin	10 per cent		680,157 60	68,015 76		582,578 80	58,257 88		671,478 56	67,147 86
Dressed, on the skin	20 per cent		832,983 19	166,596 63		725,657 01	145,131 40		771,834 33	154,366 86
Dressed, not on the skin	20 per cent								9,243 00	1,848 60
Hatters' furs	20 per cent		1,326,929 89	265,385 97		1,414,882 00	282,976 40		1,566,602 00	313,320 40
Fur caps, hats, and all manufactures of fur	35 per cent		76,605 94	26,812 08		38,659 61	13,700 76		60,307 55	21,107 64
Ginger:										
Root.......pounds	5 cents per lb.	1,329,078	88,209 00	66,453 90	1,268,900	77,003 36	64,313 80	1,401,144	77,651 25	70,057 20
Ground.......do	8 cents per lb.	209	35 00	16 72	2,042½	136 00	163 40	3,580½	282 62	286 44
Preserved or pickled	50 per cent		30,695 00	15,347 50		20,691 60	10,345 50		22,206 23	11,103 12
Glass and manufactures of glass:										
Cylinder, crown, or common window glass, not above 10 by 15 inches.......pounds	1¼ cent per lb.	16,418,434	442,148 44	246,276 51	11,347,564	348,587 61	170,213 46	12,446,968	375,365 68	186,704 52
Above 10 by 15 and not above 16 by 24 inches.......pounds	2 cents per lb.	11,788,160	386,521 23	235,763 20	8,328,778½	277,826 79	166,575 57	9,034,815½	339,440 42	180,696 31
Above 16 by 24 inches and not 24 by 30.......pounds	2½ cents per lb.	6,013,298	270,379 27	150,332 45	5,083,603¼	250,837 65	127,425 48	6,976,840¼	326,607 63	174,421 01
Above 24 by 30 inches.......do	3 cents per lb	4,772,621	298,786 13	143,178 63	4,043,023	283,497 50	121,290 69	4,623,511	339,449 13	138,705 33
Cylinder and crown glass, polish'd, not above 10 by 15 in. sq. feet	2½ cts. pr. sq. foot	685,418	37,785 10	17,135 45	188,949	10,828 00	4,723 73	292,771	16,354 00	7,319 27
Above 10 by 15 and not above 16 by 24 inches.......sq. feet	4 cts. per sq. foot	162,702	23,042 00	6,508 08	80,973	15,418 00	3,238 92	21,547	4,705 00	861 88
Above 16 by 24 and not above 24 by 30 inches.......sq. feet	6 cts. per sq. foot	363,812	[illegible]	21,828 72	63,698	16,820 00	3,821 88	40,687¼	12,658 00	2,441 25

A statement of the principal articles entering into consumption in the United States, &c.—Continued.

ARTICLES.	Rate of duty.	1867.			1868.			1869.		
		Quantity.	Value.	Amount of duty.	Quantity.	Value.	Amount of duty.	Quantity.	Value.	Amount of duty.
Glass and manuf. of glass—Cont'd.										
Above 24 by 30 and not above 24 by 60 inches ....sq. feet..	20 cts. pr. sq. foot.	5, 294½	$2, 038 23	$1, 058 90	11, 533	$4, 761 00	$2, 306 60	13, 108⅓	$6, 092 00	$2, 621 67
Above 24 by 60 inches.... ..do...	40 cts. pr. sq. foot.	2, 411	2, 408 00	964 40	2, 300	1, 657 00	920 00	330	295 00	132 00
Fluted, rolled, or rough plate, excess one pound per square foot, in proportion, not above 10 by 15 inches........sq. feet..	¾ cent pr. sq. foot.	35, 966	1, 434 00	269 74	9, 260	950 00	69 45	30, 459	1, 555 00	228 44
Above 10 by 15 and not above 16 by 24 inches............sq. feet..	1 cent pr. sq. foot.	48, 250	1, 460 00	482 50	62, 973	2, 394 00	629 73	34, 173	3, 323 00	341 73
Above 16 by 24 and not above 24 by 30 inches...........sq. feet..	1½ cts. pr. sq. foot	1, 785, 647	59, 546 00	26, 784 70	346, 602	13, 117 00	5, 199 03	492, 216	18, 103 00	7, 383 24
Above 24 by 30 inches.......do....	2 cts. pr. sq. foot .	1, 064, 759	57, 862 00	21, 295 18	221, 123	15, 299 00	4, 422 46	778, 631½	28, 362 00	15, 572 63
Cast, polished, plate glass, not silvered, not above 10 by 15 inches....................sq. feet..	3 cts. pr. sq. foot .	561, 957	40, 723 00	16, 858 71	94, 201	8, 938 00	2, 826 03	314, 390	24, 867 00	9, 431 70
Above 10 by 15 and not above 16 by 24 inches...........sq. feet..	5 cts. pr. sq. foot .	17, 262 5-6	6, 447 00	863 14	13, 466	5, 412 00	673 30	19, 622	8, 982 00	981 10
Above 16 by 24 and not above 24 by 30 inches ....sq. feet..	8 cts. pr. sq. foot	81, 365¾	40, 224 00	6, 509 26	41, 705¼	21, 116 00	3, 336 42	89, 745¾	38, 591 00	7, 179 66
Cast, polished, plate glass, not silvered, above 24 by 30 and not above 24 by 60 inches ...sq. feet..	25 cents per sq. ft.	281,183 1-6	138, 560 75	70, 295 79	169, 847½	88, 941 25	42, 461 88	275, 950	141, 173 00	68, 987 50
Above 24 by 60 inches.....do....	50 cents per sq. ft.	640, 156¼	364, 265 00	320, 078 12	590,041 5-6	331, 440 75	295, 020 91	846, 410½	503, 063 00	423, 205 25
Cast, polished, plate glass, silvered, not above 10 by 15 inches .sq. ft..	4 cents per sq. ft .	234, 125	47, 628 00	9, 365 00	191, 657	38, 360 00	7, 666 28	363, 434¾	61, 826 00	14, 537 39
Above 10 by 15 and not above 16 by 24 inches ....sq. feet..	6 cents per sq. ft .	544, 567	125, 277 00	32, 674 02	644, 887	172, 303 00	38, 693 22	961, 162	202, 258 00	57, 669 72
Above 16 by 24 and not above 24 by 30 inches ....sq. feet..	10 cents per sq. ft.	619, 630	221, 375 00	61, 963 00	625, 197	185, 319 00	62, 519 70	806, 850	255, 434 00	80, 685 00
Above 24 by 30 inches and not above 24 by 60 inches..sq. feet..	35 cents per sq. ft.	125, 088⅓	71, 738 99	43, 780 91	84, 563	41, 864 00	29, 597 05	148, 278¾	77, 970 00	51, 897 57
Above 24 by 60 inches .....do....	60 cents per sq. ft.	31, 945⅛	26, 299 73	19, 167 20	35, 585⅓	23, 566 00	21, 351 30	35, 454¼	28, 815 60	21, 272 55
Glass bottles.....................	35 per cent......	....	47, 378 14	16, 582 35	....	17, 111 10	5, 988 88	....	48, 838 45	17, 093 46
Glass bottles containing liquors. doz. 1867, number, 1868–'69	2 cents each	470,206 10 12	....	112, 849 64	4, 088, 117	148, 728 72	81, 762 34	4, 911, 375	181, 551 84	98, 227 50
Crystals for watches...............	40 per cent	....	9, 077 00	3, 630 80	....	40, 972 00	16, 388 80	....	28, 457 00	11, 382 80
Glassware:										
Plain	35 per cent	....	169, 085 81	59, 180 03	....	118, 281 00	41, 398 35	....	135, 435 14	47, 402 29
Cut	40 per cent	....	296, 216 35	118, 486 45	....	160, 790 00	64, 316 00	....	207, 569 14	83, 027 66

Bohemian, porcelain, ornamented glassware	40 per cent		156, 148 75	62, 459 50		139, 794 30	55, 917 72		171, 426 00	68, 570 40
Glass manufactures not specified	40 per cent		319, 853 42	127, 941 37		316, 301 14	126, 520 45		396, 369 63	158, 517 85
Gold and silver manufactures:										
Gold leaf ... packs	$1 50 per pack	465	2, 142 00	697 50	262	1, 076 00	393 00	272	1, 392 00	408 00
Silver leaf ... do	75 cents per pack	9, 707	8, 503 00	7, 280 25	6, 574	6, 366 00	4, 930 50	2, 986	2, 834 00	2, 239 50
Gold and silver, and manufact's of	25 per cent					26 00	6 50			
Epaulettes, galloons, laces, knots, stars, tassels, embroideries, and rings of gold or silver	35 per cent		80, 880 00	28, 308 00		87, 452 00	30, 608 20		69, 565 00	24, 347 75
Silver-plates, metal and plated wares	35 per cent		102, 545 23	35, 890 83		73, 736 28	25, 807 70		77, 738 75	27, 208 56
All other manufactures of gold and silver	40 per cent		47, 687 85	19, 075 14		38, 976 31	15, 590 52		29, 863 00	11, 945 20
Gums:										
Arabic, Jedda, myrrh, Senegal, and all other ... pounds	20 per cent		540, 206 06	108, 041 21	2, 619, 471	594, 549 92	118, 951 98	3, 021, 753	550, 246 50	110, 049 30
Copal, Kourie, Sandarac, damar, and other varnish gums ... lbs	10 cents per lb	3, 753, 219	468, 786 68	375, 321 90	4, 078, 026	508, 339 00	439, 039 30	4, 458, 509	545, 356 00	445, 850 90
Mastic ... do	50 cents per lb	816	1, 451 00	408 00	588	829 00	294 00	3, 257½	2, 615 00	1, 628 75
Shellac ... do	10 cents per lb	729, 354½	107, 916 00	72, 935 45	640, 844	95, 340 30	64, 530 00	1, 086, 207	167, 575 00	108, 620 70
Benzoin or benjamin ... do	10 cents per lb	3, 573	1, 316 00	357 30	227	69 00	28 90			
Gunpowder:										
Value 20c. or less per pound ... do	6c. per lb. & 20 p. c.	194	32 31	18 10	627¼	87 00	55 04	50	7 00	4 40
Value over 20c. per pound ... do	10c. pr. lb. & 20 p. c.	348½	75 23	49 90	10, 243	5, 831 00	2, 190 50	13, 637½	7, 270 59	2, 817 87
Gutta percha:										
Crude	10 per cent		13, 074 00	1, 307 40	49, 042	17, 078 00	2, 121 80	35, 089	15, 587 00	1, 558 70
Manufactures	40 per cent		828 03	331 21		3, 118 31	1, 247 32		7, 636 33	3, 054 53
Grindstones, rough or unfinished	10 per cent								99, 715 03	9, 971 50
Do ... finished	20 per cent								15, 878 00	3, 175 60
Gypsum, or plaster of Paris, ground or calcined	20 per cent		29, 894 52	5, 978 90		33, 988 00	6, 797 60		51, 874 98	10, 374 99
Hair of the Alpaca goat, and other like animals, and m'f's of class 2:										
Value 32 cents or less per pound	10c. pr. lb. & 11 p. c.							200	24 00	22 64
Value over 32c. per pound ... lbs	12c. pr. lb. & 10 p. c.	1, 249	2, 013 00	351 18	394	709 00	118 18	9, 604	3, 656 00	1, 518 08
Dress goods, wholly or in part of mohair, alpaca, &c., gray or uncolored, value 30 cents or less per sq. yard ... sq. yards	4c. per sq. yd. and 25 per cent	3, 077¾	862 33	338 69						
Gray or uncolored, value over 30 cents per sq. yard ... sq. yards	6c. per sq. yd. and 30 per cent	36½	17 96	7 58						
Colored or printed, value 30 cents or less per sq. yard ... sq. yard	4c. per sq. yd. and 30 per cent	510, 177	113, 787 87	54, 543 44						
Colored or printed, value over 30 cents per sq. yard ... sq. yard	6c. per sq. yd. and 35 per cent	219, 865	87, 508 87	43, 820 00				9, 931	2, 316 00	1, 092 04
Angora goat-skins with the wool on, washed or unwashed	30 per cent					664 00	199 20			

A statement of the principal articles entering into consumption in the United States, &c.—Continued.

Articles.	Rate of duty.	1867.			1868.			1869.		
		Quantity.	Value.	Amount of duty.	Quantity.	Value.	Amount of duty.	Quantity.	Value.	Amount of duty.
Manufactures of hair of the alpaca goat, and other like animals, not exceeding 20 cents per sq. yard .... yards..	6c. pr. yd. & 35 p.c.	....	....	....	5, 854	$1, 087 00	$731 69	41, 787	$7, 184 00	$5, 021 62
Value exceeding 20 cents per sq. yard .... yards..	8c. pr. yd. & 40 p.c.	....	....	....	3, 520	994 00	679 20	15, 234½	4, 317 00	2, 945 56
Weighing 4 ounces and over per sq. yard .... yards..	50c. p. yd. & 35 p.c.	....	....	....	702	774 00	621 90	2, 105	3, 633 00	2, 324 05
Hair and manufactures of hair:										
Manufactures of mohair and goat's hair, not specified	50 per cent	....	$202, 655 22	$101, 327 61	....	5, 777 00	2, 888 50	....	18 00	9 00
Hair, and its manufacture (lastings)	10 per cent	....	181, 984 00	18, 198 40	....	68, 520 09	6, 864 30	....	....	....
Hair pencils	35 per cent	....	12, 646 00	4, 426 10	....	12, 346 00	4, 340 00	....	13, 053 00	4, 568 55
Hair, curled, for beds or mattresses	20 per cent	....	2, 662 00	532 40	....	500 00	118 00	....	1, 157 00	231 40
Hair cloth and hair seatings, and other hair manufactures	30 per cent	....	388, 872 05	116, 661 61	....	211, 591 70	63, 477 51	....	278, 779 70	83, 633 91
Human hair, not cleaned	20 per cent	....	19, 619 86	3, 923 97	....	26, 577 61	5, 315 52	....	59, 250 00	11, 850 00
Human hair, cleaned or drawn	30 per cent	....	102, 609 00	30, 782 70	....	182, 573 00	54, 771 90	....	389, 434 00	116, 830 20
Human hair, manufactured	40 per cent	....	35, 875 20	14, 350 08	....	31, 448 00	12, 579 20	....	31, 677 00	12, 670 80
Hair bracelets, braids, curls, and ringlets	35 per cent	....	4, 461 00	1, 561 35	....	4, 174 00	1, 460 90	....	5, 994 00	2, 097 90
Hair nets .... pounds..	60 cts pr. lb. and 35 per cent	....	....	....	425	172 00	315 20	....	....	....
Hair of hogs .... pounds..	1 cent per lb	48, 781	2, 705 00	487 81	4, 007	709 00	40 07	2, 558	1, 185 67	25 58
Hats and bonnets of hair or whalebone	40 per cent	....	106, 849 34	42, 739 73	....	202, 041 22	80, 816 48	....	11, 516 00	4, 606 40
Hats and bonnets of straw, chip, or palm leaf, or any vegetable substance .... pounds..	40 per cent	....	203, 397 71	81, 359 08	....	159, 540 67	63, 816 27	....	387, 576 36	155, 030 54
Hemp, and manufactures of hemp:										
Cables and cordage, all other. lbs...	3½ cents per lb ...	97, 831	9, 340 96	3, 424 10	89, 869	10, 687 00	3, 145 42	411, 208	20, 759 63	14, 392 28
Manilla, untarred .... pounds..	2½ cents per lb ...	228, 536	21, 466 86	5, 713 40	134, 112	13, 638 52	3, 352 80	120, 017	12, 798 00	3, 000 42
tarred .... do ...	3 cents per lb ...	1, 312, 505	139, 987 74	39, 375 15	489, 736	78, 948 14	14, 692 08	588, 080	61, 690 51	17, 642 40
Codilla or tow of hemp. tons, 1867.. cwt., 1868 and 1869..	$10 per ton	244½	32, 439 00	2, 445 00	2, 125	12, 854 00	1, 062 50	371	3, 012 00	185 50
Coir yarn .... pounds..	1½ cent per lb ...	938, 632	62, 132 00	14, 079 48	1, 019, 681	85, 700 00	17, 692 61	916, 980	67, 639 00	13, 754 70
Grass cloth	30 per cent	....	2, 564 00	769 20	....	3, 935 00	1, 180 50	....	18, 399 00	5, 519 70

All other ethers not specified .do...	$1 per pound	590	704 00	590 00	416¼	342 00	416 25	1,601 1-16	894 43	1,601 06
Flowers, leaves, and plants (medicinal) not specified	20 per cent	....	62,785 85	12,557 17	....	74,686 00	15,489 00	....	87,287 35	17,457 47
Glycerine	30 per cent	....	....	....	....	57 00	17 10	....	36,272 00	10,881 60
Glue	20 per cent	....	....	....	....	11,888 00	2,377 60	....	337,867 00	67,561 40
Hoffman's anodyne .....pounds..	50 cents per lb...	134	218 00	67 00	....			....		
Indigo, extract of	10 per cent	....	17,547 23	1,754 72	....	88,010 00	8,810 00	....	55,220 00	5,522 00
Iodine:										
Crude ....pounds..	50 cents per lb..	12,347	28,013 00	6,173 50	18,994½	55,869 00	9,497 25	17,241	50,625 00	8,620 50
Re-sublimed ....do....	75 cents per lb..	3,199	6,764 00	2,399 25	5,527	16,178 25	4,145 25	5,882	18,356 00	4,411 50
Iodate, hydriodate, and acetate of potash, and iodide of potassium, pounds	75 cents per lb..	25,213	61,952 00	18,909 75	23,766	63,474 00	17,824 50	33,483	87,111 00	25,112 25
Ipecac ....pounds..	50 cents per lb..	16,116	23,781 00	8,058 00	11,144	19,304 00	5,572 00	11,071	19,132 00	5,535 50
Jalap ....do....	50 cents per lb..	11,357	8,295 00	5,678 50	20,690	14,936 00	10,345 00	17,462	8,939 00	8,731 00
Lac, seed lac, and stick lac.do....	10 cents per lb..	11,285	2,137 00	1,128 50	37,996	4,378 00	3,871 10	39,836	5,973 00	3,983 60
Juniper berries..........do....	10 cents per lb..	112	3 00	11 20	....	....	....	....	....	....
Licorice:										
Paste ....do....	10 cents per lb..	3,695,976¾	450,910 29	369,597 65	3,865,257	469,045 75	386,525 70	2,936,999	379,012 80	293,699 90
Root ....do....	2 cents per lb....	2,790,615	95,207 00	55,812 90	2,824,747	81,113 00	56,494 94	1,992,663	55,705 00	39,853 26
Logwood and other dyewood ext's.	10 per cent	....	10,143 00	1,014 30	....	12,400 00	1,240 00	....	666 00	66 60
Madder extract and garancine....	10 per cent	....	709,205 00	70,920 50	....	901,837 00	90,183 70	....	1,408,652 00	140,865 20
Magnesia:										
Calcined ....pounds..	12 cents per lb..	22,066½	8,140 36	2,647 98	21,900½	7,889 39	2,628 06	18,306¼	6,062 42	2,196 75
Carbonate..........do....	6 cents per lb....	111,082	11,278 00	6,664 92	98,610	12,426 00	5,916 60	114,654	13,546 00	6,879 24
Manna ....do....	25 cents per lb..	20,830	8,366 00	5,207 50	20,133½	8,062 00	5,033 38	7,897½	4,115 00	1,974 38
Medical preparations or patent medicines	50 per cent	....	....	....	....	33,672 65	16,836 33	....	38,042 73	19,021 36
Medicinal preparations not spec'd.	40 per cent	....	....	....	....	70,700 64	28,280 26	....	123,592 78	49,437 11
Morphine and its salts...ounces..	$2 50 per ounce..	687½	1,738 00	1,718 75	64	144 00	160 00	1,439¾	9,192 00	3,599 37
Opium ....pounds..	$2 50 per pound.	94,188 1-10	331,144 00	235,470 25	91,726	348,930 00	229,315 00	90,996¾	525,802 25	227,491 88
Opium prepared for smoking.do..	100 per cent......	32,971	290,623 00	290,623 00	....	323,751 50	323,751 50	....	168,718 75	168,718 75
Opium, extract of..........	100 per cent......	....	29 00	29 00	....	24 00	24 00	....	34 00	34 00
Phosphorus..........	20 per cent	....	30,081 00	6,016 20	....	29,990 19	5,998 04	....	46,531 00	9,306 20
Potash and salts of potash:										
Bicarbonate of potash or saleratus ....pounds..	1½ cent per lb....	2,005,034	114,865 99	30,075 51	1,613,324	90,866 21	24,199 86	362,237	20,649 00	5,433 55
Chlorate of potash.......do....	6 cents per lb....	170,915	45,054 00	10,254 90	229,707	55,040 00	13,782 42	270,006	64,262 00	16,200 36
Chromate and bichromate of potash..........pounds..	3 cents per lb....	875,205	88,787 27	26,256 15	777,855	68,634 00	23,335 65	877,432	78,288 00	26,322 96
Prussiate of potash, red......do..	10 cents per lb..	43,530	17,507 00	4,353 00	45,525	18,410 00	4,552 50	25,560	10,576 00	2,556 00
Prussiate of potash, yellow...do..	5 cents per lb....	193,350	48,703 00	9,667 50	94,976	23,904 00	4,748 80	146,219	35,703 00	7,310 95
Salt petre, or nitrate of potash:										
Crude ....pounds..	2½ cents per lb..	8,544,912	295,250 00	213,622 80	6,137,155	197,286 00	153,428 88	8,878,996	313,114 16	221,974 90
Refined ....do....	3 cents per lb....	273,916	14,681 96	8,217 48	43,379	2,265 00	1,301 37	106,007	4,435 00	3,180 21
Rhubarb ....do....	50 cents per lb..	50,363	60,831 25	25,181 50	51,808¾	39,813 00	27,712 23	66,457½	47,515 02	33,228 75
Rose leaves ....do....	50 cents per lb..	1,016	551 00	508 00	2,596	1,448 00	1,298 00	2,198	941 00	1,099 00
Safflower..........	10 per cent	....	23,409 00	2,340 90	....	21,737 00	3,491 90	....	53,061 00	5,306 10
Santonine ....pounds..	$5 per pound ...	1,748	12,586 00	8,740 00	338	2,312 00	1,690 00	1,870¼	14,669 00	9,351 25
Sarsaparilla ....do....	20 per cent	....	18,735 00	3,747 00	47,151	11,071 82	2,214 36	187,019	20,870 00	4,174 00
Soda and salts of:										
Bicarbonate of ....do....	1½ cent per pound	20,902,050	805,348 05	313,530 75	23,544,057	607,771 56	353,160 85	18,092,250	540,263 00	271,383 75

A statement of the principal articles entering into consumption in the United States, &c.—Continued.

ARTICLES.	Rate of duty.	1867.			1868.			1869.		
		Quantity.	Value.	Amount of duty.	Quantity.	Value.	Amount of duty.	Quantity.	Value.	Amount of duty.
Iron and steel, and manufactures of:										
Pig iron, tons, '67; cwt., '68 and '69..	$9 per ton	116,519 19-20	$2, 620, 079 59	$1, 048, 679 55	2, 246, 911	$1, 837, 911 64	$1, 011, 109 96	2, 666, 139	$2, 072, 288 34	$1, 199, 762 55
Bar-iron, rolled or hammered: flats, not less than 1 inch nor more than 6 inches wide, nor less than ⅝ nor more than 2 inches thick; rounds, not under ¾ and more than 2 in. in diameter; squares, not less than ¾ inch and more than 2 inches square, pounds..	1 cent per lb.....	124, 456, 645	2, 567, 687 88	1, 244, 566 45	107, 194, 445	2, 192, 770 84	1, 071, 944 45	157, 778, 137	2, 868, 612 53	1, 577, 781 37
Bar-iron, in flats, less than ⅝ inch and more than two inches thick, or less than 1 inch and more than 6 inches wide; rounds, less than ¾ and more than 2 inches in diameter; squares, less than ¾ inch and more than 2 inches square..................pounds..	1½ cent per lb....	26, 251, 288	615, 177 38	393, 769 32	17, 562, 202	376, 481 56	263, 433 04	15, 298, 871	345, 724 86	229, 483 06
Bar-iron	35 per cent	....	....	....	....	66, 947 00	23, 431 45	32, 721	1, 439 77	503 92
Railroad iron, made to pattern, and fitted to be laid down..pounds..	70 cts. per 100 lbs.	236, 012, 911	3, 299, 024 19	1, 652, 090 37	313, 734, 584	4, 056, 830 16	2, 196, 142 09	501, 951, 213	6, 777, 406 00	3, 513, 658 49
Boiler and other plate, not less than 3-16 inch in thickness..pounds..	1¼ cent per lb....	131, 252	5, 658 00	1, 968 78	472, 214	14, 539 93	7, 083 31	722, 943	24, 412 26	10, 844 15
Iron wire, bright, coppered or tinned, drawn and finished, not over ¼-inch in diameter, and not less than No. 16, wire gauge ......pounds..	2 cts. per lb. and 15 per cent.....	1, 436, 982	60, 458 94	37, 808 48	2, 644, 876	99, 130 93	67, 767 16	3, 435, 183	131, 204 19	88, 384 28
Iron wire, above No. 16 and not above No. 25 ....pounds..	3½ cts. per lb. and 15 per cent.....	20, 292	1, 297 30	904 82	22, 173	1, 449 00	993 31	40, 192	2, 243 00	1, 743 17
Above No. 25...	4 cts. per lb. and 15 per cent.....	560	96 00	36 80	606	122 00	42 54	65½	20 00	5 61
Iron wire covered with cotton, silk, and other material:										
Not less than No. 16.....pounds..	7 cts. per lb. and 15 per cent.	....	....	....	109	51 00	15 28	800	113 00	72 95
No. 16 to No. 25............do....	8½ cts. per lb. and 15 per cent. ...	1, 741	564 60	232 58	1, 636	665 00	238 81	344½	194 00	58 36

XI

Above No. 25..............do....	9 cts. per lb. and 15 per cent	435	196 00	68 55	130	87 00	24 75	527	177 00	73 98
Spiral springs for furniture, made of iron wire ....pounds..	2 cts. per lb. and 15 per cent	....	....	....	12, 036	483 00	313 17	29, 420	1, 135 00	758 65
Sheet-iron, common or black, not thinner than No. 20....pounds..	1¼ cent per lb	17, 473, 853	394, 626 30	218, 423 16	11, 705, 179	258, 878 74	146, 314 75	11, 081, 918	235, 644 97	138, 523 98
Sheet-iron, common, No. 20 to No. 25..............pounds..	1½ cent per lb	9, 545, 681½	258, 246 70	143, 185 22	8, 414, 551	212, 762 55	126, 218 27	7, 278, 484	172, 359 37	109, 177 26
Thinner than No. 25 ....do....	1¾ cent per lb	2, 764, 836	101, 265 54	48, 384 63	1, 678, 379¼	50, 080 01	29, 371 63	1, 373, 700	39, 810 23	24, 039 75
Sheet-iron, smoothed or polished ....pounds..	3 cents per lb....	5, 839, 071	425, 212 00	175, 172 13	4, 639, 673	360, 121 00	139, 190 19	5, 399, 756	489, 112 00	161, 992 68
Band, hoop, and scroll iron, from ⅛ to 6 inches wide:										
Not thinner than ⅛ inch, pounds..	1¼ cent per lb....	9, 725, 075	213, 286 90	121, 563 44	7, 546, 392	144, 313 96	94, 329 90	6, 051, 617	114, 540 79	75, 645 21
Under ⅛ inch to No. 20 ...do....	1½ cent per lb....	14, 974, 871	345, 725 57	224, 623 06	12, 769, 246½	268, 055 69	191, 538 69	9, 680, 980	195, 917 20	145, 214 70
Thinner than No. 20 ......do....	1¾ cent per lb....	2, 369, 270	69, 210 47	41, 462 22	2, 170, 205	65, 581 60	37, 978 59	2, 359, 278	61, 911 84	41, 287 36
Slit rods ....do....	1½ cent per lb....	1, 847, 476	50, 342 25	27, 712 14	6, 871, 374	161, 000 00	103, 070 62	16, 827, 626	372, 009 60	252, 414 39
All other roll'd or hammer'd, not otherwise provided for..p'ds..	1¼ cent per lb....	659, 323	14, 019 50	8, 241 54	897, 951	16, 909 20	11, 224 39	2, 071, 287	37, 149 00	25, 891 09
Locomotive tires..........do....	3 cents per lb....	1, 138, 429	73, 772 00	34, 152 87	348, 828	20, 516 00	10, 464 84	21, 306	1, 399 00	639 18
Mill irons, and wrought iron for ships and engines, in pieces of 25 pounds or more......pounds..	2 cents per lb....	373, 720	27, 896 96	7, 474 40	110, 152	5, 788 50	2, 203 04	72, 755	1, 127 96	1, 455 10
Anchors, and parts of ....do....	2¼ cents per lb...	466, 193	21, 677 19	10, 489 34	313, 736	13, 272 90	7, 059 06	151, 555	5, 696 67	3, 409 99
Anvils ....do....	2½ cents per lb...	4, 219, 286¼	164, 191 05	105, 482 15	772, 016½	43, 632 83	19, 300 41	1, 504, 162	81, 910 93	37, 604 05
Cables and cable chains ....do....	2½ cents per lb...	6, 843, 967	260, 810 94	171, 099 17	3, 492, 169¼	106, 952 44	87, 304 23	2, 658, 093½	88, 242 47	66, 452 33
Hammers, sledges, axles, and other, wrought........pounds..	2½ cents per lb...	259, 772	14, 438 60	6, 494 30	194, 716¾	9, 045 30	4, 898 28	269, 327	15, 003 17	6, 733 17
Halter, fence, and trace chains:										
Not less than ¼ inch ...pounds..	2½ cents per lb...	3, 505, 134	128, 766 91	87, 628 35	4, 767, 105	178, 103 11	119, 177 63	6, 585, 540	238, 043 94	164, 638 50
Less than ¼ inch and not under No. 9 ....pounds..	3 cents per lb....	1, 056, 917½	66, 406 53	31, 707 52	793, 060	35, 004 37	23, 721 80	1, 014, 250	55, 398 86	30, 427 50
Under No. 9, wire gauge	35 per cent	....	18, 707 00	6, 547 45	93, 016	10, 006 20	3, 502 17	166, 339	17, 107 00	5, 987 45
Horse-shoe nails..........pounds..	5 cents per lb....	181, 655¼	27, 330 08	9, 082 77	95, 604¾	14, 542 83	4, 780 24	61, 833	8, 260 87	3, 091 65
Malleable iron in castings ..do....	2½ cents per lb...	963	75 70	24 07	13, 778	514 00	344 45	924, 888	64, 796 00	23, 122 20
Wrought-iron railro'd chains, nuts, and washers, punched .pounds..	2 cents per lb....	445, 901½	9, 659 79	8, 918 03	432, 097½	23, 983 19	8, 641 95	598, 811	16, 860 42	11, 976 22
Wrought hinges, bed screws, board nails, spikes, rivets, and bolts ....pounds..	2½ cents per lb ...	459, 273	23, 122 74	11, 481 82	535, 366	25, 500 13	13, 384 15	1, 192, 602½	69, 060 89	29, 815 06
Cut nails and spikes ....do..	1½ cent per lb....	238, 028	7, 774 50	3, 570 42	16, 159	866 95	242 39	15, 730	602 30	235 95
Cut tacks, brads, and sprigs:										
Not over 16 ounces per M...M..	2½ cents per M...	2, 905	149 00	72 62	385	63 83	9 62	15½	10 94	1 26
Over 16 ounces per M..pounds..	3 cents per lb....	2, 123	149 00	63 69	58	4 00	1 74	1, 404	171 00	42 12
Screws, for wood:										
2 inches or more in length ..do..	8 cents per lb....	212, 280	30, 684 66	16, 982 40	69, 867	9, 186 11	5, 589 36	32, 076	4, 930 58	2, 566 08
Less than 2 inches in length do..	11 cents per lb ...	1, 240, 388	182, 503 70	136, 442 68	336, 802	52, 060 17	37, 048 22	94, 585	17, 232 10	10, 404 35
Wrought steam, gas, and water tubes and flues........pounds..	3½ cents per lb ...	1, 700, 148½	103, 302 76	59, 505 19	1, 122, 810	72, 060 48	39, 298 35	1, 953, 753	126, 844 43	68, 381 36
Cast-iron pipe, vessels, stoves, and stove plates...........pounds..	1½ cent per lb	1, 434, 621	29, 413 57	21, 519 31	1, 529, 060	21, 029 81	22, 935 90	373, 113	9, 273 47	5, 596 69

A statement of the principal articles entering into consumption in the United States, &c.—Continued.

ARTICLES.	Rate of duty.	1867. Quantity.	1867. Value.	1867. Amount of duty.	1868. Quantity.	1868. Value.	1868. Amount of duty.	1869. Quantity.	1869. Value.	1869. Amount of duty.
Iron and steel, &c.—Continued.										
Andirons, sadirons, tailors and hatters' irons .... pounds..	1½ cent per lb....	41, 023	$932 00	$615 31	61, 842	$1, 530 01	$927 63	597	$42 00	$8 96
Cast butts and hinges .... do..	2½ cents per lb...	22, 585	1, 195 51	564 62	82, 635	5, 079 26	2, 065 87	84, 012	5, 103 30	2, 100 30
Hollow-ware, glazed or tinned. do..	3½ cents per lb ...	271, 791	19, 822 22	9, 512 68	108, 908	9, 475 03	3, 811 78	78, 910	3, 790 24	2, 761 85
Squares, marked on one side . do..	3 cts. per lb. and 30 per cent	617	57 00	35 61	373	22 00	17 79	330	27 00	18 00
Squares, all other .... do..	6 cts. per lb. and 30 per cent	3, 252	284 97	280 61	1, 516	175 00	145 26	1, 483	163 09	137 90
Taggers' iron, and castings of iron not specified	30 per cent	....	61, 644 33	18, 493 30	....	43, 495 18	13, 048 55	....	56, 948 09	17, 084 43
All other manufactures of iron	35 per cent	....	2, 649, 235 06	927, 232 27	....	1, 952, 728 70	683, 455 04	....	2, 105, 565 29	736, 947 85
Old scrap iron, tons, 1867; cwt., 1868 and 1869	$8 per ton	30, 962 9-20	585, 145 52	247, 699 60	1, 600, 736½	1, 567, 156 29	640, 294 60	2, 788, 984¼	2, 559, 823 06	1, 115, 593 70
Iron, galvanized or coated with any metal by electric battery . pounds-	2½ cents per lb ...	508, 646	28, 641 54	12, 716 15	1, 193, 031	69, 235 00	29, 851 47	1, 955, 593	97, 036 19	48, 889 82
Steel, in ingots, bars, sheets, or wire not less than one-quarter of an inch in diameter, valued at 7 cents per pound, or less . pounds..	2¼ cents per lb...	27, 363, 328	1, 285, 806 47	615, 674 88	19, 478, 322	907, 618 56	438, 262 25	25, 626, 988	1, 200, 921 05	640, 674 70
Value 7 and not above 11 cents per pound .... pounds..	3 cents per lb....	12, 655, 514	1, 227, 633 57	379, 665 42	9, 527, 637	917, 836 48	285, 829 11	12, 907, 492	1, 277, 521 00	387, 224 76
Value above 11 cents per pound, pounds	3½ cts. per lb. and 10 per cent	2, 023, 103	264, 642 20	97, 272 82	1, 071, 066½	136, 369 60	51, 124 29	864, 878	117, 571 36	42, 027 87
Steel, above 11 cts. pr. p'nd . p'nds..	3½ cents per lb...	12, 594	1, 833 00	437 64	....	....	....	....	....	....
Steel-wire, less than one-quarter inch in diameter, and not less than No. 16 wire gauge . pounds..	2½ cts. per lb. and 20 per cent	143, 558	23, 887 00	8, 366 35	115, 161	19, 326 00	6, 744 23	88, 826	17, 563 60	5, 733 25
Finer than No. 16 .... do....	3 cts. per lb. and 20 per cent	107, 885	37, 831 00	10, 802 75	79, 761	32, 572 00	8, 907 23	66, 843	33, 651 00	8, 735 49
Steel in forms not otherwise provided for .... pounds..	30 per cent	....	458, 931 00	137, 679 30	4, 487, 921	273, 659 00	82, 097 70	....	39, 793 50	101, 938 05
Cross-cut saws .... lineal feet..	10 cts. per lineal foot	6, 913	3, 118 75	691 30	15, 690½	3, 634 00	1, 569 05	2, 909	1, 107 00	290 90
Mill, pit, and drag saws, not over 9 inches wide .... lineal feet .	12½ cts. per lineal foot	2, 193½	1, 157 00	274 19	340½	411 35	42 56	691	331 00	86 37
Over 9 inches wide .... do.....	20 cts. per lineal foot	81	49 00	16 20	206	257 00	41 20	....	....	....

Hand-saws, not over 24 inches in length........dozens..	75 cents per doz. and 30 per cent.	3,457⅓	20,765 16	8,822 55	2,663	18,472 00	7,538 86	2,247	16,000 00	6,485 25
Over 24 inches in length....do....	$1 per doz. and 30 per cent.....	13,135	103,360 58	44,143 17	8,646	68,236 77	29,117 03	4,705 10-12	42,267 00	17,385 93
Back-saws, not over 10 inches in length........dozens.	75 cts. per doz. and 30 per cent.	1,095	6,193 00	2,679 15	760	5,789 00	2,306 51	666¼	4,523 00	1,856 59
Over 10 inches in length....do....	$1 per dozen and 30 per cent.....	2,799	20,140 00	8,841 00	1,161	12,066 00	4,780 80	638¾	6,717 00	2,653 35
Files, rasps, and floats, not over 10 inches in length....pounds..	10 cts. per lb. and 30 per cent.....	633,366½	285,583 00	149,011 55	722,695¼	327,768 53	170,600 09	690,485	314,583 82	163,423 65
Over 10 inches in length....do....	6 cts. per lb. and 30 per cent.....	1,332,112	296,214 20	168,790 98	1,555,316	359,535 87	201,179 72	1,377,739¾	322,167 22	179,314 55
Skates, costing 20 cents or less per pair........pairs..	8 cts. per pair ...	15,458	2,193 00	1,236 64	13,525	3,058 00	1,082 00	10,508	1,664 00	840 64
Costing over 20 cents per pair.do..	35 per cent	14,840	6,096 50	2,133 77	21,517	5,566 16	1,948 16	....	4,296 00	1,503 60
Pen knives, jack knives, and pocket knives..............	50 per cent	....	1,163,660 71	581,830 35	....	849,400 35	424,700 17	....	895,549 82	447,774 91
All other cutlery..............	35 per cent	....	1,204,088 27	421,430 89	....	748,069 23	261,824 23	....	726,062 39	254,121 84
Needles....................M..	$1 per M and 35 per cent.	647 5-6	4,273 27	2,143 48	718	3,362 00	1,894 70	965¾	5,751 00	2,978 60
All other needles..............	25 per cent	....	360,852 00	90,213 00	....	316,346 68	79,086 67	....	333,872 58	83,468 14
Side arms......................	35 per cent	....	9,000 00	3,150 00	....	146 00	51 10	....	3,099 00	1,084 65
Fire-arms, muskets, rifles, and other..................	35 per cent	....	487,599 30	170,659 76	....	326,270 40	114,194 64	....	266,523 47	93,283 21
All other manufactures of, wholly or in part of steel	45 per cent	....	2,741,410 40	1,233,634 68	....	2,718,219 42	1,223,198 73	....	3,580,939 15	1,579,022 62
Istle, or Tampico fibre ....pounds..	1 cent per lb.....	475,569	39,124 00	4,755 69	687,668	34,473 00	6,876 68	833,666	54,884 00	8,336 66
Ivory, not manufactured..........	10 per cent	....	411,477 00	41,147 70	351,914	404,531 00	42,117 40	....	503,470 00	50,347 00
Ivory manufactures, all other.......	35 per cent	....	19,137 00	6,697 95	....	17,383 35	6,084 17	....	19,311 00	6,758 85
Ivory nuts, vegetable	10 per cent	....	68,664 00	6,866 40	....	12,172 00	1,217 20	....	45,776 00	4,577 60
Japanned wares, all kinds, not otherwise provided for	40 per cent	....	50,871 88	20,348 75	....	30,740 02	12,296 01	....	22,640 00	9,056 00
Jellies, of all kinds..............	50 per cent	....	16,501 06	8,250 53	....	10,385 47	5,192 73	....	10,158 95	5,079 48
Jet, and manufactures of jet........	35 per cent	....	58,482 00	20,468 70	....	62,536 00	21,887 60	....	44,684 00	15,639 40
Jewelry, real, or imitations of, wholly or in part of gold and silver, or precious stones...........	25 per cent	....	520,641 52	130,160 38	....	596,224 20	149,056 05	....	688,441 25	172,110 31
Kryolite..........................	20 per cent	....	32,876 00	6,575 20	....	68,632 00	13,726 40	....	108,303 00	21,660 60
Lead, and manufactures of lead:										
In pigs and bars.........pounds..	2 cents per lb....	65,322,923	2,812,668 00	1,306,458 46	63,254,677	2,668,915 47	1,265,093 54	87,865,471	3,653,481 13	1,757,309 42
In sheets, pipe and shot....do....	2¾ cents per lb...	185,825¼	9,560 25	5,110 20	142,137	7,229 24	3,908 77	307,424	15,530 67	8,454 16
Old and scrap...............do....	1½ cent per lb....	1,255,233	53,202 04	18,828 49	2,465,575	101,586 26	36,983 62	2,983,272	123,068 14	44,749 08
Lead ore ....do....	1½ cent per lb....	611	25 00	9 16	6,945	239 00	104 18	....	....	....
Manufactures of lead not specified.	35 per cent	....	6,222 00	2,177 70	....	6,603 70	2,311 30	....	18,884 90	6,609 71
Leather, and manuf. of leather:										
Bend and sole...........pounds..	35 per cent	....	1,575 88	551 56	408	241 92	84 67	11,654½	2,303 00	806 05
Tanned calfskins.................	30 per cent	....	3,580,638 57	1,074,191 57	....	3,888,564 17	1,167,011 01	....	3,747,526 08	1,124,257 82
Skins tanned and dressed, and all other upper leather....dozens..	25 per cent	....	920,433 12	230,108 28	53,795¾	785,335 34	196,385 83	....	1,141,319 62	285,329 90

A statement of the principal articles entering into consumption in the United States, &c.—Continued.

ARTICLES.	Rate of duty.	1867.			1868.			1869.		
		Quantity.	Value.	Amount of duty.	Quantity.	Value.	Amount of duty.	Quantity.	Value.	Amount of duty.
Leather, &c.—Continued.										
Japanned, polished, or patent...	35 per cent	....	$76, 371 00	$26, 729 85	....	$45, 153 00	$15, 803 55	....	$38, 937 59	$13, 628 16
Gloves of skin or leather..dozens..	50 per cent	....	2, 633, 233 42	1, 316, 616 71	379, 302½	2, 521, 118 46	1, 260, 795 63	....	2, 549, 799 81	1, 274, 899 90
All other manufactures of leather.	35 per cent	....	818, 496 27	286, 473 69	....	498, 757 75	174, 565 21	....	502, 394 01	175, 837 90
Macaroni and vermicelli..........	35 per cent	....	52, 602 25	18, 410 79	....	61, 561 50	21, 546 52	....	72, 158 00	25, 255 30
Marble, white or statuary, in bl'ks, rough or square....cubic feet..	$1 per cubic foot and 25 per cent.	1, 018	2, 540 00	1, 653 00	1, 413	4, 403 00	2, 513 75	1, 453	3, 898 00	2, 427 50
Marble, veined, and all other rough ....cubic feet..	50 cts. per cubic ft. and 20 p. c..	294, 682	192, 514 00	185, 843 80	262, 725	309, 750 00	243, 312 50	378, 497⅛	359, 881 00	261, 224 87
Marble, manuf. not specified......	50 per cent	....	51, 978 00	25, 989 00	....	85, 783 50	43, 568 35	....	101, 309 00	50, 654 50
Mats of cocoa-nut, China, and all other floor mattings............	30 per cent	....	490, 907 40	147, 272 22	....	494, 286 82	148, 308 84	....	407, 188 76	122, 156 62
Cocoa mats.....................	25 per cent	....	....	....	....	48, 842 20	12, 210 55	....	78, 647 00	19, 661 75
Meats:										
Beef and pork ....pounds..	1 cent per lb.....	745, 496	46, 923 79	7, 454 96	539, 512	36, 990 66	5, 395 12	426, 659	29, 896 72	4, 266 59
Bacon and hams............do....	2 cents per lb....	116, 520	15, 045 67	2, 330 40	142, 884½	20, 692 16	2, 857 69	151, 281	23, 369 09	3, 025 62
Meats, preserved in cans or otherwise, and sausages.............	35 per cent	....	51, 732 59	18, 106 41	....	29, 471 25	10, 314 94	....	42, 153 00	14, 753 55
Metals not elsewhere specified:										
Platina manufacture, not specified	40 per cent	....	456 00	182 40	....	290 00	116 00	....	184 20	73 68
Britannia, and all manuf. of, and pewter......................	35 per cent	....	257, 242 00	90, 034 70	....	165, 121 00	57, 792 35	....	148, 235 00	51, 882 25
Bronze or Dutch metal, in leaf....	10 per cent.......	....	129, 873 00	12, 987 30	....	79, 715 00	7, 971 50	....	87, 471 00	8, 747 10
Powders.......................	20 per cent	....	54, 773 00	10, 954 60	....	63, 387 00	12, 677 40	....	48, 022 40	9, 604 48
Manufactures not specified	35 per cent	....	....	....	....	208, 357 88	72, 925 26	....	298, 695 00	104, 543 25
Pewter, old............pounds..	2 cents per lb....	7, 912	881 00	158 24	10, 064	1, 309 50	201 28	7, 972	1, 056 00	159 44
All other metals, and metal composition, old and other, not otherwise provided................	20 per cent	....	32, 746 00	6, 549 20	....	32, 658 91	6, 531 78	....	42, 451 69	8, 490 34
Mineral waters:										
Per bottle of 1 quart or less..doz..	3 cents per bottle and 25 per cent.	30, 884 1-6	24, 913 27	17, 346 62	241, 702	18, 437 60	11, 860 46	344, 691	25, 635 30	16, 749 55
Excess over 1 quart......quarts..	3 cents per quart and 25 per cent.	3, 792	360 30	203 83	22, 819	2, 052 44	1, 197 68	9, 739	802 00	492 67
Not in bottles ....gallons..	30 per cent	....	136 73	41 02	554	104 00	31 20	....	127 61	38 28
Mosses, sea-weed, and other vegetable substances used as mattresses.......................	20 per cent	....	15, 804 00	3, 160 80	....	18, 056 00	3, 611 20	....	44, 131 00	8, 826 20
Music, printed, bound or unbound ..	20 per cent	....	34, 514 51	6, 902 90	....	47, 466 00	9, 493 20	....	48, 851 00	9, 770 20

Musical instruments	30 per cent	....	552, 555 30	165, 766 59	....	543, 054 84	162, 951 25	....	591, 246 79	177, 374 04
Music strings of anim'l fiber, gut stri'gs	30 per cent	....	52, 410 00	15, 723 00	....	34, 376 75	10, 313 03	....	39, 863 95	11, 959 18
Music strings of metal	35 per cent	....	13, 490 00	4, 721 50	....	9, 528 00	3, 334 80	....	9, 540 42	3, 339 15
Nuts:										
Almonds, not shelled ....pounds..	6 cents per lb	2, 368, 855	258, 657 00	142, 131 30	1, 969, 064	237, 638 00	118, 143 84	2, 315, 376	306, 527 00	138, 922 56
Almonds, shelled ....do..	10 cents per lb	729, 789	118, 858 00	72, 978 90	456, 486	85, 077 00	45, 648 60	1, 046, 218	162, 371 00	104, 621 80
Cocoanuts	25 per cent	....	163, 940 44	40, 985 11	....	104, 562 37	26, 141 59	....	132, 044 39	33, 011 10
Filberts and walnuts ....pounds..	3 cents per lb	3, 025, 823	154, 865 85	90, 774 69	2, 899, 098	132, 947 00	87, 287 94	3, 463, 555	161, 560 40	103, 906 65
Peanuts, and other ground nuts, not shelled ....pounds..	1 cent per lb	7, 208, 608	203, 294 50	72, 086 08	12, 812, 659	322, 173 74	128, 126 59	6, 159, 437	184, 071 05	61, 594 37
Shelled ....do..	1¼ cent per lb	291, 336	16, 491 00	4, 370 04	297, 891	8, 030 00	4, 468 36	855, 818	30, 832 00	12, 837 27
All other nuts not specified.do..	2 cents per lb	1, 557, 850	75, 022 12	31, 157 00	1, 739, 334½	57, 143 79	34, 786 69	1, 949, 435	84, 207 07	38, 988 70
Oil-cloths, for floors:										
Value 50 cents or less, per square yard ....sq. yds..	35 per cent	....	....	....	....	....	....	32, 624	14, 743 15	5, 160 10
Do.	30 per cent	....	1, 186 00	355 80	4, 384	2, 079 00	727 65	....	....	....
Do.	40 per cent	....	59, 442 52	23, 777 01	....	14, 484 00	6, 517 80	....	....	....
Value over 50 cents per square yard ....sq. yds..	45 per cent	....	....	....	....	....	....	....	4, 186 35	1, 883 86
All other oil-cloths, not otherwise specified	45 per cent	....	4, 115 00	1, 851 75	....	33, 448 40	15, 051 78	....	26, 667 00	12, 000 15
Oil-cloths, all other, except silk, (tariff June 30, 1864)	40 per cent	....	....	....	2, 890	2, 056 00	822 40	....	....	....
Oil-silk, cloth	60 per cent	....	....	....	....	29 00	17 40	....	66 00	39 60
Oils, fixed or expressed:										
Almond ....pounds..	10 cents per lb	16, 557	7, 493 00	1, 655 70	26, 237	9, 656 00	2, 623 70	20, 567	7, 260 00	2, 056 70
Bay or laurel ....do..	20 cents per lb	1, 593	342 00	318 60	1, 575	324 00	315 00	2, 496	370 00	499 20
Castor ....gallons..	$1 per gallon	35, 367½	20, 866 00	35, 367 50	2, 790¼	2, 750 80	2, 828 65	29, 626	21, 891 26	29, 626 00
Coal oil, crude ....do..	15 cents per gall	....	....	....	....	....	....	78	6 00	11 70
Coal oil, refined ....do..	40 cents per gall	55	23 00	22 00	40	23 00	16 00	21	17 00	8 40
Croton oil ....pounds..	$1 per pound	2, 695¾	8, 356 00	2, 695 75	2, 618	4, 297 00	2, 618 00	4, 545¼	5, 618 00	4, 545 25
Flaxseed, or linseed ....gallons..	23 cents per gall	3, 326, 449 1-6	2, 204, 817 25	765, 083 31	829, 189	546, 486 80	190, 920 57	123, 015	70, 648 00	28, 293 45
Hempseed, or rapeseed ....do..	23 cents per gall	56, 963	38, 017 00	13, 101 49	3, 534	3, 247 00	812 82	9, 536½	6, 492 00	2, 193 40
Illuminating oils, from coal, shale, asphaltum, peat, &c ....gallons..	40 cents per gall	9	13 00	3 60	15	6, 500 00	6 00	10	10 00	4 00
Mace ....pounds..	50 cents per lb	264	299 00	132 00	51	70 00	27 50	10	23 00	5 00
Mustard ....gallon..	25 cents per gall	....	....	....	....	....	....	5	5 00	1 25
Neatsfoot and other animal ....gall..	20 per cent	18, 848	9, 312 00	1, 862 40	....	3, 514 08	702 81	....	3, 685 00	737 00
Nut ....gallons..	23 cents per gall	....	....	....	....	....	....	138, 635	53, 641 00	31, 886 05
Olive in casks ....gallons..	25 cents per gall	161, 843	142, 844 00	40, 460 75	46, 146¼	53, 484 00	11, 553 43	264, 110¾	227, 245 00	66, 027 69
In bottles ....gallons..	$1 per gallon	116, 675¼	195, 435 75	116, 675 25	99, 256½	192, 372 76	99, 460 60	169, 265⅛	296, 872 50	169, 265 13
Palm and cocoanut ....do..	10 per cent	682, 116	287, 978 00	28, 797 80	717, 572	296, 207 00	29, 620 70	....	232, 354 00	23, 235 40
Petroleum, crude ....do..	20 cents per gall	3, 391	1, 582 87	678 20	28	6 40	5 60	320	44 00	64 00
Refined ....do..	40 cents per gall	809	714 00	323 60	312	282 00	124 80	30	28 80	12 00
Salad ....do..	$1 per gallon	30, 174	49, 399 00	30, 174 00	50, 066¾	89, 884 00	50, 066 75	7, 475	15, 886 00	7, 475 00
Seal ....do..	10 per cent	....	188, 236 83	18, 823 68	134, 986	63, 224 07	6, 322 40	429, 432	242, 937 00	24, 293 70
Whale ....do..	20 per cent	....	35, 568 92	7, 113 78	39, 088	18, 406 00	3, 681 20	....	182, 702 64	36, 540 53
Oils, volatile or essential:										
Almond ....pounds..	$1 50 per pound	1, 408	10, 630 00	2, 112 00	1, 094¼	9, 108 00	1, 641 75	1, 098¾	10, 359 00	1, 648 13
Amber, crude ....do..	10 cents per lb	663	171 00	66 30	1, 048	180 00	104 80	856	190 00	85 60
Amber, refined ....do..	20 cents per lb	1, 273	567 00	254 60	1, 277	472 00	255 40	866	315 00	173 20
Anise ....do..	50 cents per lb	2, 608	4, 485 00	1, 304 00	5, 382¼	10, 600 00	2, 747 35	8, 013¼	13, 930 00	4, 006 75

A statement of the principal articles entering into consumption in the United States, &c.—Continued.

ARTICLES.	Rate of duty.	1867.			1868.			1869.		
		Quantity.	Value.	Amount of duty.	Quantity.	Value.	Amount of duty.	Quantity.	Value.	Amount of duty.
Oils, volatile or essential:										
Bergamot .... pounds..	$1 per pound	25, 619¼	$92, 513 00	$25, 619 25	17, 102	$74, 842 12	$17, 102 00	31, 988	$130, 386 00	$31, 988 00
Cajeput .... do....	25 cents per lb...	1, 071½	888 00	267 87	1, 186	850 09	311 30	1, 716	1, 207 00	429 00
Caraway .... do....	50 cents per lb...	3, 402	4, 325 00	1, 701 00	3, 323½	4, 358 00	1, 661 75	6, 123½	8, 766 00	3, 061 75
Cassia .... do....	$1 per pound.....	9, 604	13, 524 00	9, 604 00	14, 489	18, 635 00	14, 763 00	14, 947	17, 318 00	14, 947 00
Cinnamon .... do....	$2 per pound	50½	242 00	101 00	48¼	512 00	96 50	132½	588 00	265 00
Citronella .... do....	50 cents per lb...	15, 632½	20, 198 00	7, 816 25	14, 788¾	16, 319 00	8, 342 98	21, 994¼	22, 564 00	10, 997 13
Cloves .... do....	$2 per pound	507¼	375 00	1, 014 50	130	123 00	260 00	57¾	78 00	115 50
Cognac, or œnanthic ether ... oz..	$4 per ounce.....	184½	148 00	738 00	26	18 00	104 00	32½	25 00	130 00
Cubebs .... pounds..	$1 per pound	460	890 00	460 00	359	504 00	359 00	491¼	638 00	491 25
Fennel .... do....	50 cents per lb...	451	373 00	225 50	83	102 00	41 50	372½	284 00	186 25
Fruit ethers, essences, or oils, or imitations of .... pounds..	$2 50 per pound..	242	386 00	605 00	275	341 00	687 50	65½	120 00	163 75
Fusil oil, or amylic alcohol .. gal..	$2 per gallon	46	716 00	92 00	2, 187	2, 106 00	4, 374 00	5, 155	4, 273 50	10, 310 00
Juniper .... pounds..	25 cents per lb...	12, 230	8, 448 00	3, 057 50	4, 281½	2, 219 00	1, 070 38	4, 598¼	3, 116 00	1, 149 56
Orange and lemon .... do....	50 cents per lb...	45, 270	93, 217 00	22, 635 00	37, 843	75, 102 72	18, 945 00	68, 123½	135, 687 00	34, 061 75
Roses, otto of .... ounces..	$1 50 per ounce..	7, 087½	35, 023 00	10, 631 25	7, 670¾	37, 010 00	11, 560 83	4, 688¾	19, 605 00	7, 033 12
Rum and bay rum essences or oil .... ounces..	$2 per ounce.....	48	11 00	96 00	....	....	....	8	1 00	16 00
Thyme, red, or origanum . pounds..	25 cents per lb...	9, 652	5, 217 00	2, 413 00	17, 665	9, 427 00	4, 436 55	23, 937	13, 696 00	5, 984 25
Thyme, white .... do....	30 cents per lb...	684	630 00	205 20	1, 334	821 00	400 20	1, 194½	1, 105 00	358 35
Valerian .... do....	$1 50 per pound..	121	872 00	181 50	88	574 00	132 00	50½	408 00	75 75
All other essential oils, not specified	50 per cent	....	38, 455 69	19, 227 84	....	117, 012 60	58, 583 70	....	50, 365 51	25, 182 75
Paintings in oil and otherwise, not by American artists, and statuary.	10 per cent	....	509, 193 53	50, 919 35	....	628, 032 31	62, 803 23	....	541, 604 00	54, 160 40
Photographs	20 per cent	....	....	....	....	52, 173 00	10, 434 60	....	50, 509 00	10, 101 80
Paints and colors:										
White lead .... pounds..	3 cents per lb....	6, 636, 508	430, 805 42	199, 095 24	7, 533, 225	455, 698 38	225, 996 75	8, 948, 642	515, 783 00	268, 459 26
Red lead .... do....	3 cents per lb....	926, 843	53, 087 00	27, 805 29	1, 291, 144	76, 773 00	38, 734 32	808, 686	46, 481 00	24, 260 58
Litharge .... do....	3 cents per lb....	230, 382	8, 941 00	6, 911 46	250, 615	12, 225 00	7, 518 45	187, 333	7, 767 00	5, 619 99
Nitrate of lead .... do....	3 cents per lb....	174, 388	12, 443 50	5, 231 64	193, 706	13, 538 00	5, 811 18	241, 229	16, 758 00	7, 236 87
Sugar of lead .... do....	20 cents per lb...	467, 273	44, 647 00	93, 454 60	45, 986	6, 064 00	9, 197 20	5, 999	565 13	1, 199 80
Whiting and Paris white, dry. do. ..	1 cent per lb.....	8, 168, 123	40, 879 00	81, 681 23	5, 530, 042	19, 390 00	55, 300 42	3, 438, 396	17, 289 00	34, 383 96
Whiting and Paris white, ground in oil	....	....	....	....	....	....	....	....	....	....
Putty .... pounds..	1½ cent per lb....	92, 602	2, 039 67	1, 389 03	117, 291	3, 679 00	1, 759 37	37, 512	697 00	562 68
Ochres:										
Umber .... do....	⅛ cent per lb.....	2, 147, 342	15, 946 00	10, 736 71	345, 173	2, 750 00	1, 725 86	570, 771	6, 159 00	2, 853 85
Indian red and Spanish brown..	25 per cent	....	35, 374 00	8, 843 50	....	11, 164 91	2, 791 23	....	31, 624 00	7. 906 00

Mineral green, French and Paris green	30 per cent		2,083 20	624 90		499 69	149 90		2,495 00	748 50
Ultramarine	25 per cent		78,490 00	19,622 50		69,638 00	24,373 30		72,101 00	18,025 25
All other ochres, dry, not specified ....pounds	50 cts per 100 lbs.	1,430,118	9,923 00	7,150 59	3,670,093	32,102 00	18,350 47	5,379,478	39,546 00	26,897 39
All other ochres, ground in oil. do	$1 50 per 100 lbs.	11,373	385 00	170 59	6,949	333 00	104 23	65,344	2,496 00	980 16
Prussian blue	30 per cent		10,662 00	3,198 60	12,363	4,945 00	1,532 40		4,743 00	1,422 90
Vermilion	25 per cent		123,506 00	30,876 50		90,648 00	22,662 00	247,382	145,665 17	36,416 29
Blanc fixe, satin white, enameled white, &c., of barytes. pounds	3 cents per lb.	445,310	12,615 00	13,359 30	177,995	5,876 00	5,339 85	182,984	6,292 00	5,489 52
Nitrate of barytes	20 per cent		383 00	76 60		852 00	170 40		1,454 00	290 80
Oxide of zinc ....pounds	1¾ cent per lb	1,569,322	91,330 00	27,463 13	1,954,485	95,518 59	34,203 49	1,819 208	105,844 00	31,836 14
Water colors, dry or liquid	35 per cent		45,368 23	15,878 88		31,216 29	10,925 70		36,655 00	12,829 25
All other paints and painters' colors.	25 per cent		142,307 11	35,576 78		172,876 93	43,219 23		218 441 00	54,610 25
Paper and manufactures of paper:										
Printing paper	20 per cent					206,955 90	41,391 18		97,960 05	19,592 01
Writing paper	35 per cent		999,489 54	349,821 34		464,634 77	162,622 17		282,937 87	99,028 25
Paper hangings	35 per cent		198,647 49	69,526 62		107,713 00	37,699 55		80,267 00	28,093 45
Paper boxes	35 per cent		49,894 77	17,463 17		46,418 00	16,246 30		64,017 00	22,405 95
Manufactures of, not specified	35 per cent		408,267 83	142,893 74		369,918 54	129,542 40		441,449 62	154,507 36
Parchment	30 per cent		10,229 00	3,068 70		9,472 00	2,841 60		13,344 00	4,003 20
Papier-maché and manufactures of, not specified	35 per cent		10,125 00	3,543 75		26,368 00	9,228 80		40,197 28	14,069 04
Paraffine										
Pens, metallic ....gross	10 cents per gross and 25 per cent	236,030½	85,455 89	44,967 02	173,751	59,688 51	32,297 23	208,033½	75,071 88	39,571 32
Penholders and pen tips	35 per cent		10,315 00	3,610 25		6,103 00	2,136 05		10,457 00	3,659 95
Pencils, black lead, including all of wood with lead or other filling. gross	50 cents per gross and 30 per cent	127,827½	212,888 00	127,780 15	74,588	127,505 03	75,545 50	50,187¾	89,314 14	51,888 12
Percussion caps and fulminates	40 per cent		159,806 28	63,922 51		133,263 16	53,305 26		98,673 13	39,469 25
Pickles, sauces, and capers	35 per cent		154,864 45	54,202 56		172,912 84	60,519 49		229,059 44	80,170 80
Pins, all metallic	35 per cent		76,008 00	26,602 80		53,515 00	18,730 25		72,881 55	25,508 54
Plumbago, or black lead ......tons	$10 per ton	1,385 13-20	54,131 07	13,856 50	*68,620	149,083 00	40,783 60	*74,846	351,004 00	37,423 00
Potatoes ....bushels	25 cents per bush.	199,341½	88,822 50	49,835 37	190,179¼	121,671 24	47,544 81	131,141	80,396 46	32,785 25
Quicksilver ....pounds	15 per cent		15,248 00	2,287 20	152	68 00	10 20		11 00	1 65
Rags, woolen	10 per cent		33,251 63	3,225 16						
Ratans and reeds, manufactured or partly manufactured	25 per cent		2,907 00	726 75		1,359 00	373 45		1,729 00	432 25
Rice:										
Cleaned ....pounds	2½ cents per lb.	43,136,975	1,560,029 31	1,078,424 37	36,256,132	1,101,823 86	906,403 30	31,668,143	865,867 33	791,703 58
Uncleaned ....do	2 cents per lb.	4,869,319	97,519 25	97,386 38	5,996,847	72,554 00	180,279 64	4,301,003	89,586 00	86,020 06
Paddy ....do	1½ cent per lb.	2,517,068	37,279 00	37,756 02	3,973,539	36,389 00	59,603 08	1,259,133	25,720 00	18,886 99
Rosin	20 per cent		390 60	78 00		1,144 00	228 80		357 20	71 44
Saddlery wares, not otherwise provided for	35 per cent		111,262 60	38,941 91		72,240 65	25,284 23		67,642 00	23,674 70
Sago and sago flour ....pounds	1½ cent per lb.	1,092,516	32,976 50	16,387 74	1,300,615	38,907 00	20,237 52	1,078,503	32,993 94	16,177 55
Salt:										
In bulk ....pounds	18 cts. per 100 lbs.	229,304,323	336,301 46	412,747 78	219,975,096	365,457 66	395,955 17	256,765,240	351,167 72	462,177 43
In bags ....do	24 cts. per 100 lbs.	254,470,862	696,570 15	610,730 67	308,446,080	915,546 51	740,270 59	297,382,750	895,272 13	713,718 60

* Cwt.

A statement of the principal articles entering into consumption in the United States, &c.—Continued.

ARTICLES.	Rate of duty.	1867.			1868.			1869.		
		Quantity.	Value.	Amount of duty.	Quantity.	Value.	Amount of duty.	Quantity.	Value.	Amount of duty.
Seeds:										
Anise ....pounds..	5 cents per lb....	111,097	$9,181 00	$5,554 85	84,631	$7,583 00	$4,246 85	88,885	$6,142 00	$4,444 25
Anise, star ....do....	10 cents per lb...	3,316	578 00	331 60	2,642	430 00	264 20	2,360	427 00	236 00
Canary....................bushels..	$1 per bushel....	23,159¼	40,557 00	23,159 25	23,435	46,939 00	23,435 00	31,436 6-10	63,038 00	31,436 60
Caraway ....pounds..	3 cents per lb....	222,411	16,278 00	6,672 33	300,603	26,185 00	9,018 09	279,663½	24,889 00	8,389 91
Cardamom ....do....	50 cents per lb...	20,757	26,253 00	10,378 50	12,199	18,532 00	7,818 40	13,730	23,998 00	6 865 00
Castor seeds or beans....bushels..	60 cents per bush.	60,588	67,687 00	36,352 80	14,760	17,325 00	8,856 00	11,397	14,099 00	6,838 20
Coriander ....pounds..	3 cents per lb....	55,965	2,521 00	1,678 95	116,765	4,814 00	3,502 95	96,751	3,768 00	2,902 53
Cummin ....do....	5 cents per lb....	165	9 00	8 25	500	21 00	25 00	6,587	553 00	329 35
Fennel....................do....	2 cents per lb....	47,248	1,847 00	944 00	59,027	2,437 00	1,180 54	87,864	4,236 00	1,757 28
Fenugreek ....do....	2 cents per lb....	69,125	2,524 84	1,382 50	53,692	2,023 00	1,073 84	79,672½	3,089 00	1,593 45
Flaxseed or linseed .....bushels..	16 cents per bush.	1,744,270¾	2,660,883 61	279,083 32	2,191,663½	3,125,130 25	350.666 16	2,954,731	4,224,137 50	472,756 96
Hemp ....pounds..	½ cent per lb.....	156,339	5,390 00	781 69	462,902	14,633 00	2,314 51	214,480	6,035 00	1,072 40
Mustard....................do....	3 cents per lb....	1,059,419	59,336 00	31,782 57	1,125,716	56.356 00	33,771 48	678,911	36,366 00	20,367 33
Rape ....do....	1 cent per lb.....	96,314	4,318 00	963 14	73,162	4,138 00	731 62	49,120	2,194 00	491 20
Garden and agricultural seeds and seeds of flowering plants and bulbous roots	30 per cent	....	308,117 36	92,435 20	....	232,556 73	69,767 02	....	289,428 14	86,828 44
Silk and manufactures of silk, (raw silk, free:)										
Silk in the gum, not more advanced than singles, train, organzine................pounds..	35 per cent	....	378,173 00	132,360 55	50,669	378,870 00	132,604 50	9,907	73,988 00	25,895 80
Spun silks for filling, in skeins or caps ....pounds..	35 per cent	....	22,871 00	8,004 85	....	26,385 00	9,234 75	6,326	31,984 00	11,194 40
Silk floss	35 per cent	....	9,590 77	3,356 77	....	1,006 00	352 10	....	6,297 00	2,203 95
Sewing silk in the gum, and purified	40 per cent	....	96,691 29	38,676 52	5,526	30,356 00	12,142 40	....	38,877 20	15,550 88
Velvets..................	60 per cent	....	1,604,199 81	962,519 89	....	1,123,749 00	674,249 40	....	1,040,353 85	624,212 31
Ribbons	60 per cent	....	3,450,633 16	2,070,379 90	....	4,105,608 69	2,463,365 21	....	3,749,665 97	2,249,799 58
Dress and piece goods............	60 per cent	....	8,803,046 94	5,281,828 16	....	7,544,510 07	4,526,706 04	....	9,919,989 34	5,951,993 60
Pongees and vestings	60 per cent	....	8,619 00	5,171 40	....	11,645 00	6,987 00	....	11,286 00	6,771 60
Shawls..................	60 per cent	....	1,965,102 00	1,179,061 20	....	431,617 28	258,970 37	....	49,819 00	29,891 40
Hosiery	60 per cent	....	8,179 00	4,907 40	....	92,906 67	55,744 00	....	41,649 00	24,989 40
Hats, caps, and bonnets..........	60 per cent	....	124,291 94	74,575 16	....	4,062 54	2,437 52	....	15,463 01	9,277 81
Laces, braids, fringes, galloons, &c.	60 per cent	....	79,834 10	47,900 46	....	1,358,994 00	815,396 40	....	1,615,896 09	969,537 65
Ready-made clothing............	60 per cent	....	191,555 53	114,933 32	....	363,832 92	218,299 75	....	392,845 39	235,707 23
Umbrellas, parasols, sunshades...	60 per cent	....	....	....	....	34,189 81	20,513 88	....	32,161 66	19,297 00
Umbrellas, &c., not otherwise provided for......	35 per cent	....	....	....	....	19,021 00	6,657 35	....	11,496 00	4,023 60

Silk buttons	40 per cent	....	....	....	....	61, 908 00	24, 763 20	....	394, 248 00	157, 699 20
Silk manufactures, wholly of silk, not specified	50 per cent	....	285, 004 65	142, 502 32	....	108, 993 00	54, 496 50	....	353, 000 60	176, 500 30
Silk manufactures, wholly or in part, not otherwise provided for	50 per cent	....	2, 172, 719 99	1, 086, 359 99	....	2, 554, 927 53	1, 177, 463 76	....	4, 442, 621 00	2, 221, 310 50
Slates, roofing	35 per cent	....	85, 204 00	29, 821 40	....	118, 776 00	41, 571 60	....	85, 364 00	29, 877 40
Slates, slate pencils, mantels, slabs for tables, and all other manufactures of slate	40 per cent	....	37, 509 84	15, 003 94	....	16, 045 47	6, 418 19	....	19, 553 00	7, 821 20
Soap:										
Common, Castile, and all like .lbs	1 cent per lb. and 30 per cent	2, 146, 208	153, 706 15	67, 573 92	2, 809, 429	189, 336 00	84, 895 09	3, 404, 516	239, 642 33	105, 937 85
Toilet or shaving, and all perfumed ......pounds	10 cents per lb. and 25 per cent.	328, 095¼	99, 781 14	57, 754 84	257, 302½	77, 297 79	45, 054 70	260, 044	82, 266 09	46, 570 92
Spices:										
Cassia ......pounds	20 cents per lb	1, 364, 320	218, 075 00	272, 864 00	1, 015, 858	128, 933 00	203, 851 10	1, 212, 675	173, 546 00	242, 535 00
Cassia, ground ......do	25 cents per lb	201	116 00	50 25	94, 452	11, 444 00	23, 613 00	....	....	....
Cassia buds ......do	25 cents per lb	8, 810	3, 150 00	2, 202 50	26, 184	5, 680 00	6, 546 00	18, 819	5, 336 00	4, 704 75
Cinnamon ......do	30 cents per lb	4, 241	1, 965 00	1, 272 30	5, 256	2, 628 40	1, 775 80	5, 397¼	1, 821 40	1, 619 25
Cloves ......do	20 cents per lb	527, 430	28, 145 50	105, 486 00	853, 220½	48, 143 60	170, 727 90	735, 517	42, 093 10	147, 103 40
Clove stems ......do	10 cents per lb	29, 520	440 00	2, 952 00	161, 160	4, 177 00	16, 116 00	88, 750	1, 092 00	8, 875 00
Mace ......do	40 cents per lb	44, 657	15, 729 00	17, 862 80	53, 745	19, 891 00	22, 258 90	66, 651	27, 554 50	26, 660 40
Mustard, in bulk ......do	12 cents per lb	60, 207	9, 758 68	7, 224 84	43, 456	6, 442 00	5, 214 72	59, 188	8, 457 00	7, 102 56
Mustard, in glass or tin ......do	16 cents per lb	218, 470	44, 511 00	34, 955 20	190, 959¼	39, 455 64	30, 553 52	254, 440	55, 274 25	40, 710 40
Nutmegs ......do	50 cents per lb	550, 396¼	163, 223 81	275, 198 13	574, 573½	152, 492 92	291, 145 15	683, 714	205, 128 85	341, 857 00
Pepper:										
Black and white ......do	15 cents per lb	4, 411, 815	322, 404 50	661, 772 25	5, 264, 849	265, 897 85	792, 490 45	5, 328, 649½	299, 564 15	799, 297 43
Black and white, ground ......do	18 cents per lb	61	22 23	10 98	1, 522	241 00	273 96	493	249 00	88 74
Cayenne ......do	15 cents per lb	191, 051	8, 069 00	28, 657 65	36, 527	1, 810 00	5, 479 05	128, 639	6, 791 00	19, 295 85
Cayenne, ground ......do	18 cents per lb	248	228 60	44 64	531½	330 40	95 67	1, 850¼	727 83	333 05
Pimento ......do	15 cents per lb	930, 394½	72, 084 88	139, 559 17	953, 210	37, 991 00	112, 981 50	1, 057, 695	54, 527 25	158, 654 25
Pimento, ground ......do	18 cents per lb	....	....	....	21	525 00	3 78	....	....	....
Vanilla beans ......do	$3 per lb	5, 608	15, 169 00	16, 824 00	12, 442 5-6	45, 276 00	37, 328 50	10, 235¾	42, 505 00	30, 707 25
Spirits and wines:										
Brandy, 1st proof ......gallons	$3 per gallon	601,578 23-30	793, 009 58	1, 804, 736 30	487, 235 1-6	710, 097 94	1, 461, 712 70	530, 395 1-6	752, 938 05	1, 591, 185 50
Brandy ......do	50 per cent	....	....	....	90	994 00	497 00	....	....	....
Brandy, act of June, 1864 ..do	$2 50 per gallon	1, 231	1, 719 00	3, 077 50	....	....	....	....	....	....
Spirits from grain, 1st proof .do	$2 50 per gallon	218,732 13-80	119, 425 01	546, 830 40	341, 113½	186, 897 35	853, 214 15	568, 061¼	321, 371 21	1, 420, 153 13
Spirits from other materials, 1st proof ......gallons	$2 50 per gallon	407,683 25-40	179, 204 09	1, 019, 209 06	356, 810½	163, 388 87	892, 026 25	201, 718½	109, 343 64	504, 296 25
Cordials, liqueurs, arrack, and all like spirituous beverages. galls	$2 50 per gallon	62, 941 5-6	74, 392 00	157, 354 58	42, 279	50, 350 50	105, 792 25	41, 775¼	60, 098 30	104, 438 12
Spirituous liquors, 1867, and wine-bitters, 1869 ......gallons	50 cts. per gallon and 100 per cent.	433	883 00	1, 099 50	....	....	....	1, 111	2, 802 00	3, 357 50
Bay water, or rum ......do	$1 50 per gallon	28, 108 5-6	16, 918 18	42, 163 25	7, 792¼	3, 235 00	11, 688 38	3, 542¼	1, 905 25	5, 313 38
Whisky; act of June, 1864 ..do	$2 per gallon	45	24 00	90 00	....	....	....	....	....	....
Wines, value 50 cts. per gal .do	20 cts. per gallon and 25 per cent.	6, 499, 817¼	1, 954, 226 32	1, 788, 520 08	5, 383, 347 5-6	1, 662, 318 37	1, 492, 249 16	6, 323, 129¼	2, 024, 910 39	1, 770, 853 49

A statement of the principal articles entering into consumption in the United States, &c.—Continued.

ARTICLES.	Rate of duty.	1867.			1868.			1869.		
		Quantity.	Value.	Amount of duty.	Quantity.	Value.	Amount of duty.	Quantity.	Value.	Amount of duty.
Spirits and wines—Continued.										
Wines, value over 50 cts. and not over $1 per gallon....gallons...	50 cts. per gallon and 25 per cent.	715,968¼	$493,909 11	$481,459 15	515,583¾	$375,129 53	$351,703 88	474,872	$345,894 86	$323,909 71
Wines, value over $1 per gall. do...	$1 per gallon and 25 per cent	217,627	463,538 39	333,511 60	203,552¾	428,603 41	310,753 20	192,639	424,844 39	298,850 10
Wines, sparkling, in bottles:										
Containing over 1 pint and not over 1 quart.........dozens..	$6 per dozen.....	126,050⅔	1,240,243 84	756,304 00	120,154⅜	1,222,525 88	721,262 90	163,939¼	1,602,810 45	983,635 50
Containing 1 pint, or less..do....	$3 per dozen.....	20,500	110,653 28	61,500 00	35,416½	181,821 37	106,249 50	47,799¾	237,903 04	143,398 50
Spirituous comp'ds or preparations, component part of chief value:										
Spirituous liquors not otherwise provided for....................	100 per cent	....	....	....	....	....	....	....	12,808 00	12,808 00
Brandy spirits, 1st proof..gallons..	$3 per gallon	....	....	....	2¾	5 00	8 25	....	....	....
Spirits from grain, 1st proof. do....	$2 50 per gallon..	4,069	4,414 00	10,172 50	1,082½	582 00	2,706 25	6,079	3,079 00	15,197 50
Spirits from other materials, 1st proof...................gallons..	$2 50 per gallon..	5	6 00	12 50	62½	55 00	156 25	2,025	1,735 00	5,062 50
Bitters.......................do....	50 cts. per gallon and 100 per cent.	....	....	....	845	1,668 00	2,090 50	....	....	....
Spirits of turpentine ....do....	30 cts. per gallon.	231	110 00	69 30	1,089¼	763 22	326 78	½	1 00	15
Sponges............................	20 per cent	....	99,156 69	19,831 34	....	100,885 22	20,177 04	....	74,731 43	14,946 29
Starch, of rice ....pounds..	3 cts. per lb. and 20 per cent......	135	13 00	6 65	1,496	60 00	58 88	2,788½	136 34	110 92
Starch, of potatoes or corn...do....	1 cent per lb. and 20 per cent......	1,370,400	43,430 00	22,390 00	288,758	9,270 00	4,741 53	871,833	27,646 00	14,247 53
Straw laces, braids, and chip and palm-leaf ornaments	30 per cent	....	1,421,846 58	426,553 97	....	934,363 00	280,345 00	....	895,877 00	268,763 10
Sugar:										
All not above No. 12, Dutch standard in color.....pounds..	3 cts. per lb......	868,415,665	34,896,937 77	26,052,469 95	927,123,351¼	39,422,164 61	27,814,182 74	938,831,762	43,647,275 89	28,164,952 86
Above No. 12, and not above No. 15 ....pounds..	3½ cts. per lb.....	58,736,535½	2,903,725 89	2,055,778 74	52,588,832	2,868,700 59	1,840,609 11	55,131,964	3,392,448 26	1,929,618 74
Above No. 15, and not above No. 20, not stove-dried.....pounds..	4 cts. per lb......	9,195,261	550,760 61	367,810 44	17,421,655½	1,005,848 53	696,866 22	13,243,776	779,862 62	529,751 04
Loaf and other, refined and stove-dried, above No. 20....pounds..	5 cts. per lb......	438,778	38,905 45	21,938 90	164,492	11,055 27	8,224 60	418,255	42,109 20	20,912 75
Sugar candy and confectionery:										
Not colored...........pounds..	10 cts. per lb.....	22,219	1,759 00	2,221 90	12,410	1,195 00	1,241 00	13,294	1,299 00	1,329 40
Colored, valued at 30 cents or less per pound ......pounds..	15 cts. per lb.....	4,945	1,122 05	741 75	....	....	....	1,097	132 00	164 55

Colored, value over 30 cents per pound.........pounds..	50 per cent	....	32,650 00	16,325 00	....	11,496 00	5,748 00	....	7,871 00	3,935 50
Sirup of cane juice or melado..do....	2¼ cts. per lb	2,899,768	87,193 50	72,494 20	3,542,817	113,629 50	88,570 42	11,146,867	387,662 20	278,671 67
Molasses from sugar cane..gallons..	8 cts. per gallon	50,116,517¼	8,916,311 49	4,009,321 38	55,006,060	11,884,702 31	4,402,624 10	52,111,252	11,847,827 06	4,168,900 16
Tallow..........pounds..	1 cent per lb	17,040	972 64	170 40	29,006	923 00	290 06	27,597	1,310 00	275 07
Lard..........do....	2 cts. per lb	9,799½	1,162 76	195 99	2,808	294 22	56 16	6,018	1,029 75	120 36
Tapioca..........	20 per cent	....	31,083 00	6,216 60	....	49,591 00	9,918 20	1,247,612	55,831 00	11,166 20
Tar..........	20 per cent	....	3,278 50	655 70	....	831 52	166 30	....	1,480 00	296 00
Tea..........pounds..	25 cts. per lb	34,135,214¾	10,839,326 61	8,533,803 69	37,545,733½	11,948,111 86	9,414,664 29	39,141,755½	12,889,383 30	9,785,438 88
Tin and manufactures of tin:										
In blocks, pigs, or bars.....cwt..	15 per cent	....	1,210,354 02	181,553 10	....	1,454,327 36	230,674 50	80,811⅓	1,709,385 00	256,407 75
In plates, sheets, and terne tin..do..	25 per cent	....	6,276,136 78	1,569,034 19	....	6,893,072 07	1,723,268 02	....	8,565,432 56	2,141,358 14
Plates, galvanized or coated by battery..........pounds..	2½ cts. per lb	4,060	664 00	101 50	38,137	3,565 00	953 42	5,690	400 00	142 25
Foil..........	30 per cent	....	27,367 00	8,210 10	....	15,044 00	4,513 20	....	19,892 00	5,967 60
Manufactures not specified..........	35 per cent	....	11,904 35	4,166 52	....	18,768 27	6,568 90	....	12,648 37	4,426 93
Tobacco and manufact's of tobacco:										
Leaf, unmanufactured and not stemmed..........pounds..	35 cts. per lb	2,849,239½	747,354 80	997,233 82	3,564,515½	1,181,096 45	1,247,580 43	4,645,314	1,603,997 56	1,625,859 90
Stemmed, and all manufactures not specified..........pounds..	50 cts. per lb	134,200½	22,729 54	67,100 25	123,179	23,310 50	61,686 60	123,532½	34,994 75	61,766 25
Stems..........	15 cts. per lb	....	....	....	....	....	....	52	19 00	7 80
Tobacco brought back...pounds..	40 cts. per lb	....	....	....	499	248 00	199 60	....	....	....
Snuff..........do....	50 cts. per lb	8,246½	2,681 00	4,123 25	12,755½	4,641 00	6,377 75	20,506	6,111 00	10,253 00
Cigars, imported under act prior to act July 28, 1866, and act of July 20, 1868......pounds..	$2 50 per pound and 25 per cent.	....	....	....	....	....	....	334,601¼	1,099,298 35	1,111,327 72
Cigars, valued at $15, or less, per thousand..........pounds..	75 cts. per lb., and 20 per cent	115,558¾	113,691 00	109,407 26	1,277	1,107 00	1,118 17	....	....	....
Cigars, valued over $15, and not over $30 per thousand..pounds..	$1 25 per pound and 30 per cent.	149,285¼	305,585 00	278,282 06	968	1,734 00	1,730 20	200	300 00	340 00
Cigars, valued over $30, and not over $45 per thousand..pounds..	$2 per pound and 50 per cent	21,081½	62,606 00	73,466 00	559	1,966 00	2,101 00	103	302 00	357 00
Cigars, valued over $45 per thousand..........pounds..	$3 per pound and 60 per cent	7,634¾	27,494 00	39,400 65	188	583 00	913 80	....	....	....
Cigars, imported under act of July 28, 1866..........pounds..	$3 per pound and 50 per cent	155,746 17-20	447,894 75	691,187 92	248,116⅜	734,756 02	1,111,727 14	28,053¼	82,745 00	125,532 25
Cigars, imported and returned...	$5 per M	....	....	....	10	492 00	50 00	....	....	....
Types, type-metal, and stereotype plates..........	25 per cent	....	11,467 87	2,866 97	....	17,783 45	4,445 86	....	16,173 00	4,043 25
Umbrellas and parasols..........	35 per cent	....	250,293 01	87,602 55	....	....	....	....	....	....
Umbrellas and parasols, not otherwise specified..........	50 per cent	....	....	....	....	15,073 00	7,536 50	....	23,335 00	11,667 50

A statement of the principal articles entering into consumption in the United States, &c.—Continued.

ARTICLES.	Rate of duty.	1867. Quantity.	1867. Value.	1867. Amount of duty.	1868. Quantity.	1868. Value.	1868. Amount of duty.	1869. Quantity.	1869. Value.	1869. Amount of duty.
Varnish:										
Valued at $1 50 per gall....galls..	50 cts. per gallon, and 20 per cent.	11, 723	$20, 326 35	$9, 926 77	7, 344	$8, 703 00	$5, 412 60	1, 341	$1, 584 00	$987 30
Valued at over $1 50 per gall..do...	50 cts. per gallon, and 25 per cent.	18, 180 1-6	52, 477 71	22, 209 51	20, 403	60, 134 53	25, 235 13	20, 030	62, 116 75	25, 544 19
Vegetables, yams, and all other edibles, crude, not specified.........	10 per cent......	....	253, 245 27	25, 824 53	....	390, 376 56	39, 234 65	....	459, 367 11	45, 936 71
Vegetables, prepared or preserved, of all kinds, not otherwise provided for......................	35 per cent	....	112, 537 00	39, 387 95	....	96, 114 00	33, 639 90	....	122, 386 00	42, 835 10
Vinegar...... ....gallons..	10 cts. per gallon	223, 075½	43, 779 14	22, 307 55	232, 227½	46, 394 65	23, 222 75	257, 211	52, 844 07	25, 721 10
Wax manufactures, not otherwise provided for....................	35 per cent	....	3, 288 70	1, 151 04	....	2, 281 90	798 66	....	6, 098 00	2, 134 30
Beeswax ....pounds..	20 per cent	9, 824	2, 510 16	512 03	....	5, 512 04	1, 460 71	25, 303	4, 841 30	968 26
Whalebone.........................	20 per cent	561	242 00	48 40	....	422 00	84 40	3, 030	962 00	192 40
Wheat, grain, flour, and meal:										
Wheat ....pounds..	20 cts. per bush..	2, 302, 599	3, 836, 594 96	460, 519 80	1, 144, 619½	1, 941, 928 01	228, 923 90	983, 656¾	1, 270, 588 85	196, 731 35
Wheat flour ....barrels..	20 per cent	....	1, 485, 740 89	297, 148 18	61, 623¼	455, 072 39	91, 014 48	78, 956¾	406, 817 85	81, 363 57
Rye.....................bushels..	15 cts. per bush..	285, 846	176, 535 02	42, 876 90	58, 269½	60, 288 62	8, 740 43	107, 636½	97, 080 10	16, 145 45
Rye flour ....cwt..	10 per cent	....	1, 875 00	187 50	....	77 00	7 70	448	824 00	82 40
Barley ....bushels..	15 cts. per bush ..	4, 206, 085¼	2, 623, 454 57	630, 912 79	3, 776, 982½	3, 093, 718 13	566, 547 39	5, 161, 804½	5, 873, 139 61	774, 270 68
Oats ....do....	10 cts. per bush ..	816, 586½	303, 368 14	81, 658 65	393, 450	353, 270 21	39, 345 00	262, 913 7-12	119, 631 27	26, 291 36
Oat meal ....cwt..	10 per cent	....	75, 329 25	7, 532 93	....	111, 849 57	11, 184 95	....	83, 817 09	8, 381 71
Indian corn.............bushels..	10 cts. per bush ..	52, 004	28, 895 99	5, 200 40	50, 459½	37, 968 96	5, 045 95	88, 298½	72, 254 00	8, 829 85
Indian meal.............barrels..	10 per cent	161½	698 12	69 81	87¼	224 74	22 47	160¼	448 11	44 81
Pearl or hulled barley...pounds..	1 cent per pound.	13, 976	859 00	139 76	33, 119	2, 541 00	331 19	257, 011	14, 378 96	2, 570 11
Grain of all kinds, not specified...	20 per cent	....	....	....	....	17, 265 00	3, 453 00	....	155, 775 00	31, 155 00
Willow or ozier, prepared for use...	30 per cent	....	36, 302 00	10, 890 60	....	28, 872 00	8, 661 60	....	37, 512 00	11, 253 60
Willow or ozier wares, baskets, and all manufactures of like materials.	35 per cent	....	202, 956 50	71, 034 78	....	155, 304 00	54, 356 40	....	178, 689 10	62, 541 19
Wood, and manufactures of wood:										
Cabinet ware, house furniture, and all manufactures, not specified..	35 per cent	....	727, 123 30	254, 493 15	....	723, 214 86	253, 125 20	....	872, 435 54	305, 352 44
Boards, plank, and scantling	20 per cent	....	3, 334, 258 04	666, 851 60	....	2, 069, 572 94	413, [illegible]14 59	....	3, 241, 497 84	648, 299 57
Hewn timber.....................	20 per cent	....	176, 840 05	35, 368 01	....	107, 635 76	21, 527 15	....	477, 757 70	95, 551 54
Rough timber and unmanufactured wood.....................	20 per cent	....	535, 157 09	107, 031 42	....	445, 698 23	89, 170 95	....	979, 267 01	195, 853 40
Other lumber.....................	20 per cent	....	1, 924, 963 54	384, 992 71	....	3, 613, 327 05	722, 665 41	....	1, 681, 078 19	336, 215 63
Laths..........................	20 per cent	....	56, 567 49	11, 313 50	....	78, 711 85	15, 742 37	....	134, 641 71	26, 928 34
Staves for pipes, hogsheads, casks, &c............................	10 per cent	....	127, 368 35	12, 736 84	....	119, 682 33	11, 968 23	....	66, 053 00	6, 605 30

Firewood	20 per cent	....	234, 890 25	46, 978 03	....	213, 025 58	42, 605 12	....	177, 917 75	35, 583 55
Wool, and manufactures of wool:										
Wool on the skin, or wool skins	20 per cent	....	324, 967 56	64, 993 51	....	....	....	....	....	....
Under act of March 3, 1865, wool, value 12 cents, or less, per pound......pounds	3 cts. per pound	13, 986, 817	1, 440, 745 92	419, 604 51	9, 020, 818	966, 594 00	270, 624 54	19, 003, 481	2, 038, 131 05	570, 104 43
Under act of July 28, 1866, wool, value 12 cents per pound, or less, cost increased by adding charges to over 12 cents per pound......pounds	4 cts. per pound	128	38 00	5 12	4, 000	400 00	160 00	....	....	....
Value over 12 cents, and not over 24 cents per pound....pounds	6 cts. per pound	22, 276, 072	3, 891, 290 43	1, 336, 564 32	9, 000, 893	1, 728, 526 60	540, 053 58	8, 646, 890	1, 614, 951 00	518, 813 40
Value over 24 cents, and not over 32 cents per pound....pounds	10 cts. per lb., and 10 per cent	150, 302	31, 827 10	18, 212 91	....	....	....	....	....	....
Value 32 cts., or less, per lb..p'nd	10 cts. per lb., and 11 per cent	567, 010	149, 663 74	73, 164 01	6, 262, 870	1, 165, 045 49	754, 442 00	6, 391, 251	1, 370, 380 47	789, 866 95
Value over 32 cts. per lb..pounds	12 cts. per lb., and 10 per cent	702, 097	263, 932 67	110, 644 91	219, 916	85, 363 74	37, 252 62	654, 317	227, 631 28	101, 281 17
Sheep-skins and goat skins, raw or unmanufactured, with the wool on, washed or unwashed	30 per cent	....	....	....	....	129, 982 45	38, 994 74	....	561, 936 43	168, 580 93
Woolen rags, waste, shoddy, mungo, and flocks....pounds	3 cts. per pound	5, 313, 786	482, 526 00	159, 413 58	....	....	....	....	....	....
Rags, woolen......do	10 per cent	....	....	....	110, 650	9, 823 00	982 30	....	....	....
Woolen rags, waste, &c., under act of March 2, 1867....pounds	12 cts. per pound	248, 003	19, 628 00	29, 760 36	619, 916	89, 767 00	74, 389 92	574, 579	63, 334 00	68, 949 48
Washed wool......do	12 cts. per lb., and 22 per cent	....	....	....	2, 914	353 00	427 34	....	....	....
Wool, scoured......do	36 cts. per lb., and 30 per cent	....	....	....	251	141 00	132 66	....	....	....
Carpet wools......do	4 cts. per pound	....	....	....	62, 880	8, 372 00	2, 515 20	....	....	....
Manufactures of wool and worsted:										
Woolen cloths, wholly or in part of wool......pounds	50 cents per lb. and 45 per ct	....	....	....	7½	25 40	15 18	....	....	....
Value less than $2 per sq. yd. do	24 cents per lb. and 40 per ct	8, 040, 505½	9, 185, 084 09	5, 603, 754 96	339, 849	400, 490 00	241, 759 76	59, 692	50, 990 95	34, 722 46
Value over $2 per sq. yd...do	24 cents per lb. and 45 per ct	26, 882 3-5	58, 145 44	32, 617 27	1, 849	4, 213 00	2, 339 61	....	....	....
Under act March 2, 1867...do	50 cents per lb. and 35 per ct	816,138 17-40	1, 301, 866 18	863, 722 38	4, 181, 678½	6, 479, 254 14	4, 358, 578 20	4, 275, 679½	6, 171, 933 17	4, 298, 016 36
Under act March 2, 1867...do	50 cents per lb. and 40 per ct	611⅛	1, 198 01	784 77	....	....	....	....	....	....
Woolen rags, waste, &c., under act March 2, 1867	....	....	....	....	....	....	....	....	....	....
Shawls, wholly or in part of wool, value 32 cents or less per pound, act March 2, 1867......pounds	24 cents per lb. and 40 per ct	43, 097½	61, 311 40	34, 867 90	....	....	....	....	....	....

A statement of the principal articles entering into consumption in the United States, &c.—Continued.

ARTICLES.	Rate of duty.	1867.			1868.			1869.		
		Quantity.	Value.	Amount of duty.	Quantity.	Value.	Amount of duty.	Quantity.	Value.	Amount of duty.
Manufactures of wool, &c.—Cont'd. Value over $2 per sq. yd. pounds..	24 cents per lb. and 45 per ct. ..	6,486	$17,765 90	$9,551 29	....	....	....	....	....	....
Under act March 2, 1867 ...do....	50 cents per lb. and 40 per ct. ..	46,383	155,914 35	85,557 24	161,630	$646,101 00	$346,213 30	....	....	....
Shawls ....do....	50 cents per lb. and 35 per ct. ..	....	....	....	104,081½	305,873 17	159,096 36	41,857½	$139,904 47	$69,895 31
All manufactures, wholly or in part of wool, not otherwise provided for ....pounds..	50 cents per lb. and 35 per ct. ..	....	....	....	1,079,431½	1,212,725 85	964,169 80	235,364¾	329,909 97	233,150 86
Woolen manufactures not otherwise provided for .....pounds..	40 cents per lb. and 50 per ct. ..	....	....	....	382¼	1,669 00	987 40	....	....	....
Flannels composed wholly or in part of worsted, the hair of the alpaca goat, or other like animals, value not over 40 cents per pound ....pounds..	20 cents per lb. and 35 per ct. ..	1,820	610 00	577 50	11,745½	4,692 40	3,991 44	1,371	412 00	418 40
Not colored, value 30 cents or less per square yard ......pounds..	24 cents per lb. and 30 per ct. ..	16,656⅛	16,026 65	8,805 46	....	....	....	....	....	....
Colored and white, value over 30 cents per square yard .pounds..	24 cents per lb. and 35 per ct. ..	73,411¾	104,838 18	54,312 18	4,276	6,686 00	3,366 34	264	338 00	181 66
Value over 40 and not over 60 cts. per pound ....pounds..	30 cents per lb. and 35 per ct. ..	10,002	5,797 00	5,029 55	4,427½	4,427 50	2,877 88	74	45 05	37 96
Flannels composed in part of silk	50 per cent	....	186,067 00	93,033 50	....	....	....	....	....	....
Flannels, value over 60 cents and not over 80 cents per lb. pounds	40 cents per lb. and 35 per ct ..	322	237 00	211 75	3,523	2,739 08	2,367 88	948½	660 00	610 40
Under act March 2, 1867 ...do...	50 cents per lb. and 35 per ct. ..	2,181½	2,697 47	2,034 86	751	1,154 00	779 40	7,970¼	17,603 45	10,146 34
Blankets composed wholly or in part of wool, the hair of the alpaca goat, or other like animals, under act March 2, 1867, pounds......................	50 cents per lb. and 35 per ct. ..	2,043½	2,846 40	2,017 99	7,372¼	6,089 00	5,817 28	3,231½	3,466 00	2,828 85

Value not over 28 cents per lb., pounds	12 cents per lb. and 20 per ct.	740,727	156,320 78	120,151 40	316	167 00	71 32	....	....	....
Value over 28 and not over 40 cents per pound.......pounds	24 cents per lb. and 25 per ct.	58,562	21,272 00	19,372 88	1,473	551 00	491 27	....	....	....
Value over 40 cents per lb..do	24 cents per lb. and 30 per ct.	136,912¼	85,451 02	58,494 25	2,663	1,333 00	1,039 02	....	....	....
Value over 40 and not over 60 cts. per pound..........pounds	30 cents per lb. and 35 per ct.	1,170	616 25	566 69	12,752½	6,412 00	6,069 95	11,157	5,730 55	5,352 79
Under act March 2, 1867 ...do	40 cents per lb. and 35 per ct.	8,934½	13,792 38	8,401 13	2,530	1,841 75	1,656 61	3,704	2,661 45	2,413 11
Value not over 40 cents per lb., pounds	20 cents per lb. and 35 per ct.	....	....	....	27,899	12,866 25	10,082 99	1,135½	316 34	338 82
Hats, wool............pounds	24 cents per lb. and 35 per ct.	15,022	12,773 15	8,075 88	....	....	....	....	....	....
Hats, wool, value over 40 and not over 60 cents per lb...pounds	30 cents per lb. and 35 per ct	....	....	....	1,778	1,523 00	1,066 45	142	69 30	66 82
Value over 60 and not over 80 cents per pound.......pounds	40 cents per lb. and 35 per ct.	....	....	....	1,569	1,112 00	1,016 80	433	308 00	281 00
Value over 80 cents per lb..do	50 cents per lb. and 35 per ct.	31,955	38,035 00	29,289 75	60,414	125,565 24	74,154 83	55,515½	97,651 77	61,935 87
Knit goods...............do	20 cents per lb. and 35 per ct.	....	....	....	....	....	....	24	15 00	10 05
Hosiery, (1869)...........do	30 cents per lb. and 35 per ct.	....	....	....	....	....	....	11,015	5,636 00	5,277 10
Shirts, and other knit goods of wool or mixed.....pounds	20 cents per lb. and 30 per ct.	370,504¾	841,423 50	326,528 00	19,341	46,182 00	17,722 80	....	....	....
Hosiery, shirts, drawers, and other knit goods......pounds	40 cents per lb. and 35 per ct.	....	....	....	....	....	....	4,307	3,129 00	2,817 95
Act March 2, 1867.........do	50 cents per lb. and 35 per ct.	24,239	60,568 00	33,318 30	224,416¼	575,586 61	313,663 44	223,685½	515,559 95	292,288 73
Worsted shirts, &c., act March 2, 1867..................pounds	35 per cent	....	896 00	313 60	....	....	....	....	....	....
Shirts and drawers........do	20 cents per lb. and 30 per ct.	....	....	....	....	....	....	272	1,058 00	371 80
Shirts and drawers........do	30 cents per lb. and 35 per ct.	....	....	....	....	....	....	33,325	17,184 00	16,011 90
Shirts and drawers........do	40 cents per lb. and 35 per ct.	....	....	....	....	....	....	10,160	6,647 00	6,390 45
Shirts and drawers........do	50 cents per lb. and 35 per ct.	....	....	....	....	....	....	12,304½	19,271 15	12,897 03
All other knit goods.......do	30 cents per lb. and 35 per ct.	....	....	....	2,081	1,133 00	1,020 85	....	....	....

A statement of the principal articles entering into consumption in the United States, &c.—Continued.

ARTICLES.	Rate of duty.	1867.			1868.			1869.		
		Quantity.	Value.	Amount of duty.	Quantity.	Value.	Amount of duty.	Quantity.	Value.	Amount of duty.
Manufactures of wool, &c.—Cont'd. Clothing, ready-made, and wearing apparel of every description; and balmoral skirts and skirting, and goods of similiar description, composed wholly or in part of wool or worsted, made up, manufactured wholly or in part by the tailor, seamstress, or manufacturer:										
Articles of wear	50 cents per lb. and 40 per ct	....	....	....	....	....	....	894, 874¾	$1, 549 295 50	$1, 067, 155 58
Ready-made .... pounds	50 cents per lb. and 40 per ct	32, 550	$91, 977 68	$53, 066 07	253, 553¾	$889, 126 10	$482, 427 32	69, 399½	313, 831 93	160, 232 52
Ready-made clothing .... pounds	24 cents per lb. and 40 per ct	69, 560	113, 803 90	62, 215 96	2, 517	4, 170 00	2, 272 08	530	1, 050 00	547 20
Balmorals, composed wholly or in part of worsted, the hair of the alpaca goat, or other like animals, value not over 40 cents per pound .... pounds	20 cents per lb. and 35 per ct	....	....	....	39	59 00	28 45	10	4 00	3 40
Value over 40 and not over 60 cents per pound .... pounds	30 cents per lb. and 35 per ct	....	....	....	5, 516	3, 214 00	2, 779 70	5	3 00	2 55
Value over 60 and not over 80 cents per pound .... pounds	40 cents per lb. and 35 per ct	....	....	....	13, 867	10, 415 05	9, 192 05	11, 838	8, 368 00	7, 664 00
Value over 80 cents per lb. . do	50 cents per lb. and 35 per ct	....	....	....	27, 721½	41, 210 48	28, 284 41	152, 351	195, 686 00	144, 665 60
Balmorals and all skirti'gs of wool, worsted, or other material . . lbs	24 cents per lb. and 35 per ct	322, 985	308, 407 00	185, 458 85	28, 592	23, 659 00	15, 142 73	....	....	....
Balmorals, under act of March 2, 1867 .... pounds	5 cts. per lb. and 35 per cent	467	476 00	189 95	....	....	....	....	....	....
Dress goods for women and children, composed wholly or in part of wool, alpaca goat, or other like animals:										

XII

Woolen dress goods, value not over 20 cts. per sq. y'd. sq. y'ds..	6 cts. per y'd and 35 per cent.....	....	....	....	24, 575, 749½	4, 381, 543 91	3, 008, 085 34	31, 479, 908½	5, 566, 827 62	3, 816, 184 17
Woolen dress goods, value over 20 cents per sq. yard...sq. yards..	8 cts. per y'd and 40 per cent.....	5, 539, 183½	1, 737, 707 68	1, 138, 217 75	37, 151, 682¼	10, 641, 765 05	7, 228, 840 62	33, 054, 470⅝	10, 538, 625 52	6, 859, 807 86
Dress goods of wool or worsted, wholly or in part gray or uncolored, value not over 30 cents per square yard..square yards..	4 cts. per sq. yard and 25 per cent.	508, 146	104, 889 63	46, 548 25	57, 342	8, 895 00	4, 517 43	....	....	....
Over 30 cts. per sq. yard...do....	6 cts. per sq. yard and 30 per cent	155, 914	70, 197 79	30, 414 18	2	1 00	42	....	....	....
Dress goods of wool or worsted, wholly or in part printed or colored, value not over 30 cts. per square yard..square yards..	4 cts. per sq. yard and 30 per cent.	42, 392, 628	10, 094, 737 79	4, 724, 126 46	1, 138, 231	218, 723 57	111, 181 71	9, 931	2, 316 00	1, 092 04
Value over 30 cts. per sq. yd. do....	6 cts. per sq. yard and 35 per cent.	19, 122, 502½	8, 008, 549 41	3, 950, 342 44	....	....	....	....	....	....
Dress goods weighing 4 ozs. and over per square yard..pounds..	50 cts. per lb. and 35 per cent.....	110, 873	138, 376 00	103, 868 10	863, 450¾	1, 608, 068 52	994, 549 36	1, 218, 405½	2, 217, 430 53	1, 385, 303 43
Yarns, woolen and worsted. do....	24 cts. per lb. and 30 per cent.....	....	....	....	9, 242	4, 156 00	3, 464 88	....	....	....
Value less than 50 cts. per pound and not above No. 14..pounds..	16 cts. per lb. and 25 per cent.....	1, 508	1, 766 85	682 99	....	....	....	....	....	....
Value over 50 cents, and not above $1 per pound..........pounds..	20 cts. per lb. and 25 per cent.....	37, 176¼	31, 403 12	15, 286 03	....	....	....	....	....	....
Value over $1 per pound....do....	24 cts. per lb. and 30 per cent.....	325, 238 7-12	409, 731 29	200, 976 65	....	....	....	....	....	....
Value not over 40 cts. per lb. do....	20 cts. per lb. and 35 per cent.....	7, 503⅝	3, 549 77	2, 743 57	2, 646½	1, 935 00	1, 206 55	1, 335½	449 00	424 25
Value over 40, and not over 60 cents per pound.......pounds..	30 cts. per lb. and 35 per cent.....	407	231 02	202 96	4, 951¼	2, 839 65	2, 479 26	14, 202	7, 376 00	6, 842 20
Value over 60, and not over 80 cents per pound.......pounds..	40 cts. per lb. and 35 per cent.....	49	40 00	33 69	12, 557¾	9, 142 00	8, 222 80	6, 458¾	4, 527 00	4, 167 95
Value over 80 cts. per pound. do....	50 cts. per lb. and 35 per cent,....	60, 515	80, 844 00	58, 566 90	499, 423¾	636, 930 89	472, 637 69	450, 441¼	531, 016 22	411, 076 31
Worsted, all manufactures of, composed wholly or in part of worsted, the hair of the alpaca goat, or other like animals, value not over 40 cts. per lb. pounds..	20 cts. per lb. and 35 per cent.....	....	....	....	5, 525	2, 749 00	2, 067 15	15, 401	5, 491 05	5, 002 07
Value over 40 and not over 60 cts. per pound ....pounds..	30 cts. per lb. and 35 per cent.....	....	....	....	33, 398	16, 141 00	15, 668 75	3, 444	1, 793 00	1, 660 75

A statement of the principal articles entering into consumption in the United States, &c.—Continued.

ARTICLES.	Rate of duty.	1867.			1868.			1869.		
		Quantity.	Value.	Amount of duty.	Quantity.	Value.	Amount of duty.	Quantity.	Value.	Amount of duty.
Wool and manuf. of wool—Cont'd: Value over 60 and not over 80 cts. per pound ....pounds..	40 cts. per lb. and 35 per cent.....	....	....	....	101, 992¼	$76, 584 76	$67, 601 67	5, 409½	$4, 153 00	$3, 617 35
Wool and worst'd manufac's do....	35 cts. per lb. and 50 per cent.....	....	....	....	4, 679	6, 083 00	4, 679 15	....	....	....
Wool and worsted manufactures..	50 per cent	....	....	....	....	43, 628 00	21, 814 00	....	....	....
All manufactures of wool not specified, value less than $2 per square yard...........pounds..	24 cts. per lb. and 40 per cent.....	13, 859	$21, 010 08	$11, 730 19	....	....	....	....	....	....
Value over $2 per sq. yard..do....	24 cts. per lb. and 45 per cent.....	38, 672	66, 454 00	39, 185 58	....	....	....	....	....	....
Manufactures of wool not otherwise provided for: Act March 2, 1867....pounds..	20 cts. per lb. and 35 per cent.....	14, 865	6, 183 00	5, 137 05	3	3 69	1 89	....	....	....
Act March 2, 1867......do....	40 cts. per lb. and 30 per cent.....	60	147 00	68 10	....	....	....	....	....	....
Manufactures of wool not otherwise provided for: Act March 2, 1867......do....	40 cts. per lb. and 35 per cent.....	884	715 00	603 85	....	....	....	....	....	....
Act March 2, 1867......do....	50 cts. per lb. and 35 per cent.....	228, 639¼	287, 864 72	215, 072 28	....	....	....	1, 559, 117¼	1, 896, 948 00	1, 443, 490 42
Act March 2, 1867......do....	50 cts. per lb. and 40 per cent.....	319	1, 026 00	569 90	....	....	....	....	....	....
Act March 2, 1867......do....	50 cts. per lb. and 45 per cent.....	200	2, 558 00	1, 701 10	....	....	....	....	....	....
Bunting, and all other manufactures of worsted, mohair, alpaca, or goats' hair, or of which worsted, mohair, &c., shall be a material, not otherwise provided for	50 per cent	....	6, 841, 104 03	3, 420, 552 01	....	189, 239 00	94, 619 50	....	8, 960 00	4, 480 00
Bunting ....sq. yards..	20 cts. per sq. yd. and 35 per cent.	....	....	....	31, 049	9, 555 00	9, 554, 05	43, 038	9, 429 00	11, 907 75
Bunting....................do....	6 cts. per sq. yard and 30 per cent.	....	....	....	7, 809	3, 010 00	1, 371 54	....	....	....

Webbings, beltings, bindings, braids, galloons, &c., of wool, worsted, or mohair, or of which either is a component material.................pounds..	50 cts. per lb. and 50 per cent	92, 892	166, 616 00	129, 754 00	376, 003¾	742, 113 00	559, 058 38	182, 714¼	356, 918 00	269, 816 13
Endless belts or felts for paper or printing machines.....pounds..	20 cts. per lb. and 35 per cent	130, 755	140, 368 00	75, 279 80	91, 882	92, 465 37	50, 739 28	102, 593	97, 221 09	54, 545 95
Wool on skins, act March 2, 1867.	30 per cent	....	16, 964 27	5, 089 28	....	....	....	....	....	....
Carpets and carpeting; Wilton, Saxony, Aubusson, velvet, and all Jacquard woven, value $1 25 or less per sq. yard..sq. yards..	70 cts. per sq. yd.	62, 531 5-7	73, 990 33	43, 772 20	....	....	....	....	....	....
Value over $1 25 per sq. yd. do....	80 cts. per sq. yd.	376, 260⅛	555, 959 00	301, 008 10	12, 743½	19, 298 00	10, 194 80	1, 819¼	2, 781 00	1, 455 40
Brussels or tapestry, printed on the warp............sq. yards..	50 cts. per sq. yd.	1, 552, 567¼	1, 571, 135 25	779, 283 62	13, 819	16, 287 00	6, 909 50	....	....	....
Treble-ingrain, three-ply, and worsted chain Venetian sq. y'ds	40 cts. per sq. yd.	54, 055¾	41, 428 50	21, 622 30	2, 808	717 00	1, 123 20	....	....	....
Two-ply, ingrain, and yarn, Venetian ....sq. yards..	35 cts. per sq. yd.	158, 377¾	111, 754 00	55, 432 21	....	....	....	....	....	....
Carpets of wool, flax, or whatever material, not otherwise provided for	40 per cent	....	132, 525 98	53, 010 39	....	....	....	....	132, 956 00	53, 182 40
Yarn, Venetian, and two-ply ingrain, under act March 2, 1867 ....sq. yds..	12 cents per yard and 35 per cent.	25, 191	18, 095 82	9, 356 46	75, 895½	51, 936 38	27, 285 19	56, 761	38, 404 75	20, 252 98
Treble-ingrain, three-ply, and worsted chain Venetian carpet, under act March 2, 1867.sq. yds..	17 cents per yard and 35 per cent.	14, 346	13, 951 00	7, 321 67	29, 158½	28, 010 31	14, 760 56	21, 950½	19, 717 54	10, 632 72
Tapestry Brussels, under act March 2, 1867..........sq. yds..	28 cents per yard and 35 per cent.	568, 334⅞	551, 927 77	352, 308 27	1, 839, 487¾	1, 601, 039 15	1, 075, 420 27	2, 056, 737	1, 687, 002 37	1, 166, 337 19
Patent velvet and tapestry velvet, under act March 2, 1867.sq. yds..	40 cents per yard and 35 per cent.	52, 399	86, 841 00	51, 353, 95	245, 248¼	380, 782 00	231, 373 10	285, 217	462, 600 00	275, 996 80
Brussels carpet, wrought by Jacquard machines, under act March 2, 1867 ....sq. yds..	44 cents per yard and 35 per cent.	158, 664½	240, 966 00	154, 150 48	547, 976¾	735, 764 97	498, 627 51	887, 820¾	1, 160, 453 00	796, 799 68
Saxony, Wilton, and Tournay velvet, wrought by the Jacquard machines, under act March 2, 1867 ....sq. yds..	70 cents per yard and 35 per cent.	13, 355	31, 986 00	20, 543 60	61, 080½	126, 039 00	86, 869 83	99, 339¼	197, 127 00	138, 532 10
Aubusson and Axminster, and carpets woven whole for rooms, under act March 2, 1867........	50 per cent	....	39, 272 00	19, 636 00	....	313, 863 18	156, 931 59	....	289, 364 00	144, 682 00
Carpets, under act March 2, 1867 .	30 cts. per sq. yd.	207	....	62 10	....	....	....	....	....	....

A statement of the principal articles entering into consumption in the United States, &c.—Continued.

ARTICLES.	Rate of duty.	1867.			1868.			1869.		
		Quantity.	Value.	Amount of duty.	Quantity.	Value.	Amount of duty.	Quantity.	Value.	Amount of duty.
Wool and manuf. of wool—Cont'd.										
Hemp carpets, under act March 2, 1867	8 cts. per sq. yd.	422, 806	$80, 038 00	$33, 824 48						
Carpets and carpeting, druggets and bocking, printed, colored, or otherwise, under act March 2, 1867 ..... sq. yds.	25 cts per sq. yd. and 35 per cent.	9, 447	4, 945 00	4, 092 50	65, 772¾	$29, 298 00	$26, 697 48	43, 294	$19, 700 61	$17, 718 71
Druggets, bockings, and felt carpets ..... sq. yds.	25 cts. per sq. yd.	265, 934¼	129, 297 00	66, 483 63	1, 506	493 00	376 50			
Carpets, druggets, &c., not otherwise provided for ..... sq. yds.	40 per cent					154, 137 00	61, 654 80			
Mats, screens, rugs, covers, &c., all carpets of like material, and all other mats of wool	50 per cent								2, 008 00	1, 004 00
Other material	45 per cent		139, 050 00	62, 572 50		55, 972 00	25, 187 40		70, 386 40	31, 673 88
Rugs ..... sq. yds.	50 cents per yard and 35 per cent.				203	212 00	175 70			
Carpets ..... do.	50 cents per yard and 50 per cent.				279	930 00	604 50			
Do ..... do.	25 cents per yard.				351½	203 00	87 88			
Do ..... do.	80 per cent					227 00	181 60			
Fur waste ..... do.	3 cts. per pound				500	94 00	15 00			
Ready-made clothing ..... do.	50 cts. per lb. and 35 per cent				3, 231	6, 910 00	4, 034 00			
Do ..... do.	6 cts. per lb. and 35 per cent				30, 925	6, 510 00	4, 134 00			
Wool, sheepskins, &c ..... do.	20 per cent					677 00	135 40			
Cloths ..... do.	20 cts. per lb. and 35 per cent				113	134 00	69 50			
Lastings ..... do.	40 cts. per lb. and 35 per cent				3, 856	3, 979 00	2, 935 05			
Wool on the skins ..... do.	20 per cent					100 00	20 00			
Do ..... do.	4 cts. per lb				8, 009	875 00	320 36			
Woolen yarns ..... do.	24 cts. per lb. and 40 per cent				633	803 00	473 12			
Do ..... do.	20 cts. per lb. and 25 per cent				2½	1 00	75			
Shawls ..... do.	24 cts. per lb. and 35 per cent				34	38 00	21 46			

Zinc, spelter, or teutenegue:										
In blocks or pigs ....do....	1½ ct. per lb	5, 752, 611	256, 366 00	86, 289 17	9, 327, 968	417, 273 00	139, 919 52	13, 211, 575¼	590, 332 00	198, 173 63
In sheets ....do....	2¼ cts. per lb	5, 142, 417	311, 767 29	115, 704 38	3, 557, 448	203, 883 00	80, 042 58	8, 306, 723½	478, 646 00	186, 901 28
Zinc nails, and all other manufactures of zinc..................	35 per cent	....	1, 835 00	642 25	....	1, 623 00	568 05	....	2, 083 00	729 05
Dress goods, act June 30, 1864, square yards	5¼ cts. per sq. yd. and 35 per cent.	....	....	....	....	....	....	696	156 00	92 88
Articles worn by men, women, or children, of whatever materials composed, made up in whole or in part by hand, not otherwise provided..	35 per cent	....	....	....	....	....	....	....	177, 509 00	62, 128 15
Acetate of lime	25 per cent	....	....	....	....	....	....	....	67, 044 00	16, 761 00
Albumen	25 per cent	....	....	....	....	....	....	....	83, 732 00	20, 933 00
Paper stock, waste, &c	10 per cent	....	....	....	....	....	....	....	441, 288 57	44, 128 86
Jugs..........................No..	3 cents each	....	....	....	....	....	....	50	1 50	1 50
Lastings, woven or made in patterns, or cut in such manner as to be fit for shoes, &c..................	10 per cent	....	....	....	....	....	....	....	208, 179 00	20, 817 90
Philosophical apparatus for schools.	15 per cent	....	....	....	....	....	....	....	22, 538 00	3, 380 70
Philosophical instruments, &c	40 per cent	....	....	....	....	....	....	....	35, 745 00	14, 298 00
Merchandise paying *ad valorem* duties	5 per cent	....	9, 829 00	491 45	....	1, 541 00	77 05	....	....	....
Do...............do..........	10 per cent	....	1, 594, 641 20	159, 464 12	....	1, 101, 262 60	110, 167 70	....	749, 117 95	74, 911 79
Do...............do..........	15 per cent	....	183, 848 65	27, 577 30	....	130, 443 37	19, 566 50	....	137, 919 00	20, 687 85
Do...............do..........	20 per cent	....	1, 351, 948 41	270, 389 68	....	1, 089, 234 55	217, 846 91	....	467, 323 00	93, 464 60
Do...............do..........	25 per cent	....	260, 317 70	65, 079 42	....	158, 164 61	39, 541 16	....	4, 668 68	1, 167 17
Do...............do..........	30 per cent	....	178, 946 25	53, 683 88	....	199, 322 91	62, 832 27	....	141, 269 61	42, 380 88
Do...............do..........	35 per cent	....	2, 490, 533 04	871, 686 56	....	310, 667 32	108, 733 56	....	108, 128 79	37, 845 07
Do...............do..........	40 per cent	....	236, 047 72	94, 419 09	....	169, 288 38	67, 715 35	....	6, 356 79	2, 542 72
Do...............do..........	45 per cent	....	865 00	389 25	....	33, 353 00	15, 008 85	....	303 00	136 35
Do...............do..........	50 per cent	....	877, 604 59	438, 802 29	....	15, 963 92	7, 981 96	....	2, 274 75	1, 137 38
Do...............do..........	60 per cent	....	59 08	35 45	....	....	....	....	....	....
Do...............do..........	100 per cent	....	31, 556 72	31, 556 72	....	7, 766 75	7, 766 75	....	....	....
Total dutiable		....	361,125,412 54	168,504,650 44	....	329,661,272 30	160,511,679 38	....	372,756,641 51	176, 114, 904 03
Total free of duty..................	....	....	39,103,605 00	....	....	29,071,796 00	*21,099 40	....	41,499,601 78	....
Total dutiable and free of duty..	....	....	400,229,017 54	....	....	358,733,068 30	160,532,778 78	....	414,256,243 29	....

* Additional and discriminating duties.

K.

Letter of the Secretary of the Treasury communicating, in compliance with a resolution of the Senate of the 14th instant, a statement from the Special Commissioner of Revenue, relative to the cost of American pig iron.

TREASURY DEPARTMENT,
January 26, 1870.

SIR: In response to a resolution of the Senate, dated January 14, 1870, requesting the Secretary of the Treasury to communicate certain information relative to the cost of American pig-iron, I have the honor to transmit the following statement from the Special Commissioner of Revenue.

I am yours, respectfully,

GEO. S. BOUTWELL,
Secretary of the Treasury.

Hon. SCHUYLER COLFAX,
Vice-President of the United States and President of the Senate.

TREASURY DEPARTMENT,
Office Special Commissioner of Revenue, January 27, 1870.

SIR: I have the honor to acknowledge the receipt of a copy of the following resolution of the Senate of the United States, referred by the Secretary of the Treasury to the Special Commissioner of the Revenue:

IN THE SENATE OF THE UNITED STATES,
January 14, 1870.

Resolved, That the Secretary of the Treasury be requested to communicate to the Senate the information and data which may be on file in the Bureau of Statistics, and under control of the Special Commissioner of the Revenue, upon which is based the statement in the report of said Commissioner for the year 1869, relating to the cost of American pig-iron, that "in the valley of the Cumberland, and in the anthracite districts of Pennsylvania, and at Scranton, the Commissioner is informed by those conversant with the business that the average cost of manufacture in the case of furnaces favorably situated, under good management, and with coal at ordinary prices, is not in excess of from $24 to $26 per ton; and in some instances is much less than these figures. These estimates, it is furthermore to be observed, include a liberal interest on the capital invested, which is turned, on an average, from two to three times per annum."

Attest:

GEO. C. GORHAM, *Secretary.*

In reference to this resolution, the Special Commissioner has the honor to submit the following sources of information:

I. WHAT IS KNOWN RESPECTING THE COST OF MANUFACTURING PIG-IRON IN SECTIONS OF THE COUNTRY OTHER THAN THE ANTHRACITE REGIONS OF PENNSYLVANIA.

Attention is asked to data of this character, in the first instance, because from the greater cheapness of labor in the eastern States, and from the economical advantages generally claimed and recognized as belonging to the anthracite regions of Pennsylvania, it is fair to assume, that whatever can be proved of this manufacture in other localities, applies with equal and greater force to the district concerning which information is particularly sought, but where the disinclination to assist official investigation on the part of the Commissioner has been most noticeable.

In a letter published in the Pottsville (Pennsylvania) Mining Journal, dated September 2, 1869, and written by Mr. George T. Lewis, of Clarksville, Tennessee, (whom the editor indorses "as one of the most reliable men in Tennessee, and a thoroughly experienced iron manufacturer, formerly of the firm of Woods, Lewis & Co., Cumberland Iron Works, Tennessee,") the following statements are made:

Referring to the cost of manufacturing iron in Tennessee, "in localities lying directly upon railroads completed or being built," Mr. Lewis says:

Herewith I submit an estimate of the actual cost of one ton of pig metal, supposing the capacity of the furnace to be 6,000 tons per annum, located near the beds of ore, coal, and limestone, and to cost $100,000.

Mining, loading, and transportation of two tons of ore	$4 00
Mining, loading, and transportation of eighty bushels of coal	6 40
Quarrying, loading, and transportation of one thousand pounds of limestone	50
Superintendence, labor, &c., per ton *	4 00
Wear and tear, per ton	50
Interest on investment, per ton	1 00
Incidentals, per ton	50
	16 90

Mr. Lewis further continues:

Now, sir, I will give you the cost of one ton of pig metal in Nashville:

Mining, loading, and transportation of two tons of ore	$6 00
Mining, loading, and transportation of eighty bushels of coal	9 60
Quarrying, loading, and transportation of one thousand pounds of limestone	1 00
Superintendence, labor, &c., per ton	4 00
Interest on investment, per ton	1 00
Wear and tear, per ton	50
Incidentals	50
Total	22 60

"But Nashville," continues Mr. Lewis, "is not the cheapest place to make pig metal. It can be made on the Nashville and Chattanooga railroad, and delivered in Nashville, at a cost of $19 per ton."

Again, the Commissioner would call attention to a pamphlet "on the natural adaptation of St. Louis to iron manufactures," published during the past year by Professor Sylvester Waterhouse, of St. Louis, under the auspices of the State Board of Immigration, and fully indorsed as accurate by the governor of the State, the St. Louis Board of Trade, and the Union Merchants' Exchange of St. Louis. In this pamphlet we find the following statements as to the cost of manufacturing pig-iron in different sections of the country:

The following statement of the cost of making one ton of pig-iron at Carondelet is not an estimate but an exhibit, copied from the books of the company, of the actual working expenses of the furnace during one week:

1.50 ton of Iron Mountain ore, at net cost of $5 50 per ton	$8 25
1.22 ton of coal, at net cost of $5 25 per ton	6 40

* This item of $4 per ton embraces all the employés, viz:

	Per annum.		Per annum.
1 superintendent	$3,000	4 keepers	$2,400
1 furnace manager	1,200	2 guttermen	1,000
1 book-keeper	1,500	2 cindermen	1,000
1 engineer	1,200	2 weighers	1,000
1 assistant engineer	800	6 yardmen	3,000
1 blacksmith	1,200	Extra labor	2,500
1 assistant blacksmith	600		
1 founder	1,200		24,000
4 fillers	2,400	or $4 per ton.	

0.30 ton of Connellsville coke, at net cost of $9 per ton	$2 70
0.37 ton of limestone, at 90 cents per ton	33
0.08 ton of mill-cinder, at $2 50 per ton	20
Clay and sand	12
Labor	5 50
Interest, taxes, and insurance	1 50
Total cost of one ton of pig-iron	25 00

The first and poorest product of the furnace brought $33 per ton; the latter yield has commanded from $34 to $42 per ton.

To supply the means of determining the relative cost of making iron, the following data, obtained from a leading manufactory in Johnstown, Pennsylvania, is submitted:

Cost per ton of coal	$1 30
Cost per ton of calcined ore	5 00
Labor	4 90

"The other elements of cost," says Mr. Waterhouse, "are not given."

But the Commissioner would ask attention to the difference thus shown to exist in favor of Pennsylvania, where coal, according to the Johnstown manufacturer, is obtainable at $1 30 per ton, against $5 50 per ton at Carondelet, and where the labor amounts to only $4 90 per ton against $5 50 at Carondelet, the whole showing a striking difference in favor of Johnstown, Pennsylvania, over Carondelet in all the essential items of the first cost of manufacture.

The authority above referred to continues:

The subjoined table is furnished by one of the largest iron works in Pittsburg, Pennsylvania:

Per cent. of iron in ore 0.66.

One and a half ton of ore, at $11 per ton	$16 50
Eighty bushels of coke, at 7 cents per bushel	5 60
One-third ton of limestone, at $2 50 per ton	83
Labor	4 00
Interest and taxes on $200,000 invested, for annual product of 20,000 tons of iron	80
Five thousand dollars per year for repairs and incidentals	25
Total cost of one ton of pig-iron	27 98

And again the same report adds:

Of the cost at Youngstown, Ohio, the courtesy of the proprietors of the Mahoning works enables us to speak with certainty. We quote from a letter of Messrs. Brown, Bonnel & Co.:

"In our manufacture of pig metal, we use three-fourths of Lake Superior and one-fourth of native ore to the ton of pig. The lake ore costs, delivered at our furnaces, about $9, and the native ore $3 per ton. Blackband ore, yielding about 50 per cent. of iron, costs $5 per ton. The coal costs about $2 or $2 50 per ton. It takes two and one-fourth or two and one-half tons of coal to reduce one ton of metal. The limestone used as a flux we get delivered to us at $1 12½ per ton; and the whole cost of making one ton of pig metal is about $25."

But the Commissioner has found in his investigations that it often makes a great and essential difference whether these estimates of the cost of production are made by individual manufacturers *before* or *after* consultation with each other, or with committees of manufacturing associations, and it is not unfrequently necessary to analyze such statements carefully as to the elements of cost, and to compare them with statements submitted by other parties manufacturing in the same section and under precisely similar conditions, or with statements of the same parties given at different times and under different circumstances. As an illustration of this the Commissioner would ask attention to the following letter and inclosure, received by him from General Garfield, representative in Congress from the district in Ohio in which Youngstown is situated:

HOUSE OF REPRESENTATIVES,
January 14, 1870.

MY DEAR SIR: I herewith inclose to you a letter just received from the Himrod Furnace Company, of Youngstown, Ohio, which seems to me to seriously conflict with some of the statements embraced in your recent report on the subject of the cost of manufacturing pig-iron. I have no hesitation in laying this letter before you without further discussion of its contents, since the high character of the writer enables me to indorse the trustworthiness of its statements with the utmost confidence.

I am, yours, &c.,

JAMES A. GARFIELD.

Hon. DAVID A. WELLS,
Special Commissioner, &c.

The letter referred to by General Garfield reads as follows:

OFFICE OF HIMROD FURNACE COMPANY, MANUFACTURERS OF PIG-IRON,
Youngstown, Ohio, December 20, 1869.

DEAR SIR: We learn that the Ways and Means Committee, under the pressure of the advocates of "free trade," re-enforced perhaps to some extent by consumers of pig-iron, are disposed to reduce the tariff upon pig-iron to $7 per ton. As there has been a systematic effort for months past to misrepresent the facts in regard to this manufacture, and to make it appear that enormous profits were made in the business, it is high time that these statements were confronted with the facts, and the effort made to avert the very serious damage which must result to the business from such reduction. While it was a matter of mere talk and sentiment, it was hardly worth while to contradict the falsehoods, or attempt to correct the errors in statements which have been made public; but if our legislators are to accept those statements as conclusive against us, without investigation, it will be an unwelcome proof of the fact that noise and bluster accomplish more *in some directions* than quiet attention to business.

I furnish you herewith a statement of the cost of making pig-iron, which I have made in some haste, but which *in no one particular is overstated*, as compared with our actual expenses, shown by our accounts from January 1, 1869, to December 1, 1869. Some of the items of expense vary slightly at different furnaces in this region, but I think it a fair average of the cost of making pig-iron in this valley. I append also statement of cost of getting our iron to Pittsburg and sale through commission house there, comparing the total expense with the ascertained average price of sales in Pittsburg of bituminous coal smelted Lake Superior iron for three weeks past, as reported in Pittsburg Commercial. In obtaining this average, I have reduced the prices as given to a four-months' rate, (which is the usual time given,) by adding or subtracting interest, and have excluded foundery iron, which we hardly make at all, and which varies greatly in price. It should be understood that this Pittsburg price is the standard for all this region, and the product of our furnaces has always found its principal market there. These figures show a balance of $1 54 per ton in favor of the manufacturer, which will certainly do no more than barely cover a moderate interest on the capital necessarily employed, leaving nothing whatever for risks and contingencies. Three years ago the price was about ten dollars above the present price, while the cost of manufacture was no greater than now. The recent decline in gold has seriously affected the stability of the market, and the further decline, which seems inevitable, must of necessity (without any reduction in nominal tariff rates) give us lower prices. It is true that the expense of production must *eventually* decline in the same ratio, but that expense is almost entirely dependent, more or less directly, upon the cost of labor, and experience has shown that labor is about the last thing to be affected by change in prices, especially in that direction. I argue from these figures and facts that the next year will, at the best, be one of great depression and difficulty in our business, and we are therefore very earnest in the petition that no legislation be had which tends to increase the burdens which we have to carry. While these are considerations which are private and personal to us, as manufacturers, you will understand that they affect, in a slightly modified degree, this whole manufacturing region, and in many relations affect the interests of the State and the whole country.

It is proper for me to say that this statement does not represent the total profits of our company, inasmuch as we mine a portion of our coal, upon which we make a profit, and as we also save commission upon a portion of our iron by selling it ourselves; but it does show the actual condition of that portion of our business *legitimately* belonging to manufacturing iron.

Commending the matter to your careful attention and wise action, I am, very respectfully and truly yours,

A. B. CORNELL,
Treasurer Himrod Furnace Company.

COST OF MANUFACTURE OF ONE TON PIG-IRON, EXCLUDING INTEREST ON CAPITAL EMPLOYED.

Three and one-fourth tons of coal delivered at furnace, including fuel for boilers, hot blast, drying furnace, "blowing in," screenings, &c., at $3		$9 75
One and a half ton Lake Superior ore, delivered, at $10 18		15 27
Half ton limestone, delivered, at $1 30		65
Labor		3 47
Repair		1 39
Total cost at furnace		30 53
Freight to Pittsburg	$2 00	
Weighing by railroad company, 15 cents per 2,000 pounds	17	
Commission on sales, 2 per cent., on $36 24	91	
Interest on $36 24 for 4 months, at 9 per cent., this being a 4 months' price	1 09	
		4 17
Total expense when sold		34 70
Average Pittsburg price for three weeks past, as reported in Pittsburg Commercial sales		36 24
Amount left to pay interest, risk, and contingencies		1 54

This result should be further diminished by deducting internal revenue tax on sales, $2 per $1,000, making it seven cents less.

A. B. C.

Two separate and different statements relative to the cost of making pig-iron in Youngstown, Ohio, being thus brought before the public, viz: the first given by Brown, Bonnell & Co., in a letter to Mr. Waterhouse above quoted, and the second prepared for Hon. James A. Garfield by the Himrod Furnace Company, it is important to analyze the data thus submitted, "in order that the truth may be made public, and error, however strongly indorsed, be effectually confuted."

The Commissioner would first ask attention to the following statement from the treasurer of the Himrod Company:

Three years ago the price (*i. e.*, of pig-iron) was about ten dollars above the present price, while the cost of manufacture was no greater than now.

This, then, is a direct, positive, and unmistakable confirmation of the truth of the following statement made by the Commissioner in his report for 1867-'8, page 47, but which has ever since been constantly represented by members of the manufacturing interest as wholly untrue and without foundation. This statement was as follows:

Under these circumstances the manufacturers of pig-iron have, to the detriment of the rolling-mill interest, and to the expense of every consumer of iron, from a rail to a ploughshare, and from a boiler-plate to a ten-penny nail, realized continued profits which have hardly any parallel in the history of legitimate industry; the returns of one set of furnaces in one of the Middle States, communicated to the Commissioner, showing a yearly product of 35,000 tons on a capital of $450,000, sold at a profit of from $10 to $13 per ton, (or at the rate of 77$\frac{7}{9}$ to 100 per cent. of annual profit on capital invested.)

Again, in order to exhibit more clearly the nature of the discrepancies in the statements of Messrs. Brown, Bonnell & Co., as furnished to Mr. Waterhouse, and the statements of the Himrod Company, as furnished to General Garfield, the respective data, with those of the Carondelet and Pittsburg furnaces, as also given by Mr. Waterhouse, are here thrown together in the form of a table.

NOTE.—In the statement of Messrs. Brown, Bonnell & Co., the maximum prices given by them are taken, and the use of the same quantities of ore and limestone is assumed as is given in the statement of the Himrod Company.

Brown, Bonnell & Co.—Coal, 2½ tons, at \$2 50, \$6 25; ore, 1⅛ Lake Superior, at \$9, \$10 13; ⅜ native ore, at \$3, \$1 12; limestone, ½ ton, at \$1 12½, 56 cents—total, \$18 06.

Himrod—Coal, 3¼ tons, at \$3, \$9 75; 1½ ton Lake Superior ore, at \$10 18 per ton, \$15 27; ½ ton limestone, at \$1 30, 65 cents—total, \$25 67.

Carondelet—1 2/10 coal, 3/10 coke, \$9 10; 1½ ton ore, at \$5 50, \$8 25; 37/100 limestone, at 90 cents per ton, 33 cents—total, \$17 68.

Pittsburg—Coke, \$5 60; 1½ ton ore, at \$11, \$16 50; ⅓ ton limestone, at \$2 50, 83 cents—total, \$22 93.

By a comparison of the respective statements of Messrs. Brown, Bonnell & Co., and the Himrod Iron Company, three separate items of difference become manifest.

1. *In respect to the amount and cost of coal used in smelting one ton pig metal.*—The amounts, as given by Messrs. Brown, Bonnell & Co. to Mr. Waterhouse, were from two and one-fourth to two and one-half tons, at a cost of from \$2 to \$2 50 per ton. The statement of the Himrod Company, on the other hand, gives three and one-fourth tons of coal, at a cost of \$3 per ton.

Taking the maximum of Messrs. Brown, Bonnell & Co., the discrepancy between the two statements represents an amount equal to \$3 50 in the cost of manufacture per ton.

2. *In respect to amount and cost of ore used.*—The letter of Messrs. Brown, Bonnell & Co. to Mr. Waterhouse states the price of Lake Superior ore at \$9 per ton; that of the Himrod Furnace Company at \$10 18 per ton. Messrs. Brown, Bonnell & Co. state that they use a proportion of three-quarters Lake Superior ore and one-quarter of native ore, (the latter costing \$6 per ton less than the Lake Superior,) a proportion which the Commissioner is informed constitutes the usual mixture used in the Mahoning Valley. The Himrod Company claims, on the other hand, to use in the manufacture of iron Lake Superior ore exclusively. The discrepancy of statement in this respect makes a difference amounting to \$4 03 in the cost of manufacturing one ton of ore by the respective parties.

3. *In respect to the cost of limestone.*—Messrs. Brown, Bonnell & Co., in their letter to Mr. Waterhouse, state the cost of the limestone delivered to be \$1 12½ per ton. The Himrod Company, on the other hand, fix the price at \$1 30 per ton; making a difference in this item of nine cents on the cost of every ton manufactured by the respective parties.

The aggregate of these several items of difference amounts to \$7 62, which, deducted from \$30 53, the aggregate of cost given by the Himrod Company gives \$22 91, an amount very nearly corresponding with the aggregate as presented by Messrs. Brown, Bonnell & Co. in their letter to Mr. Waterhouse.

It may seem strange that two highly respectable firms, both equally well indorsed as intelligent and trustworthy, and doing business in the same locality, and apparently under equally favorable circumstances, should come before the country with two statements of the quantities of materials used by them in the well known processes of iron manufacture so widely differing one from the other. Nor is the Commissioner at all able to explain so remarkable a discrepancy. It is, however, otherwise with another particular in which these two statements differ equally widely, *i. e.*, the cost of the different materials used. The Commissioner confesses that he would be unable to offer any explanation whatever of this point also, had not the explanation been furnished by a passage in the very letter of the Himrod Furnace Company quoted above. It says:

> It is proper for us to say that this statement does not represent the *total profits* of our company, inasmuch as we mine a portion of our coal, upon which we make a profit, and as we also save commission upon a portion of our iron by selling it ourselves.

It would seem evident, therefore, that, when Messrs. Brown, Bonnell & Co., made their statement to Mr. Waterhouse, they intended simply to show the profits on their entire business of making pig-iron, in which their capital is invested. In doing so they calculated each separate ingredient at its cost to them. They said the coal costs us so much, the ore so much, the limestone so much, and the total of these gives the cost of all the ingredients together.

But when the Himrod Furnace Company made their statement, they divided their business into all its separate branches. They were not only iron-makers, but also miners and iron merchants, and expected to make a separate profit on each of these different processes of their business, and then to make an additional profit on the whole put together. Something after the fashion of a boot-maker who should claim to be first a leather dealer and next a last-maker, and then a boot-cutter and a boot-sewer, and finally a boot-seller, and who should then expect to make a separate profit on each of these processes before he could calculate his legitimate profit on his real business of manufacturing boots.

As iron-makers, Messrs. Brown, Bonnell & Co. say that their coal costs them about $2 50 per ton. The Himrod Furnace Company say that their coal also costs them about $2 50, but that it costs them that price as coal-miners, not as iron-makers. As coal-miners, they are entitled to a separate profit on their business of not less than fifty cents per ton, thus making the coal cost to them $3 per ton as iron-makers, which as coal-miners cost them only $2 50 per ton.

As simple iron-makers, Brown, Bonnell & Co. buy their limestone at $1 12 per ton. But the Himrod Furnace Company assert theirs to cost $1 30 per ton. May not the difference constitute the profit which they make by buying limestone as limestone dealers, and selling it to themselves as iron-makers, precisely as they do with the coal?

It cannot be pretended that the difference in these items is due to any change arising in the market price of these articles between the different dates of the two communications, for the Himrod Furnace Company distinctly state that the cost of the raw materials of their manufacture are no higher now than they were a year ago.

It would seem, therefore, undeniable, that from the direct admission of the Himrod Furnace Company, and from the fair and legitimate deduction from their admissions, at least $3 48 of the difference between the cost of the raw material in the two statements is solely and exclusively due to outside profits which the Himrod Furnace Company claim to make on the separate processes of the business in which they are really engaged, and which cannot by any reasoning be admitted to enter into the legitimate cost of the article itself. The still larger difference arising from the different quantities of raw material used by the two parties, the Commissioner must leave to themselves to explain, as also the reason why the one can make good iron out of a mixture of high-priced Lake Superior ore and a low-priced native ore, while the other requires that the whole should consist of the high-priced Lake Superior ore, making in the latter case an increased cost of $2 26 per ton without adequate reason or explanation.

The Commissioner would further ask attention to the proceedings of a meeting of the citizens of Albany, held January 18, 1870, for the purpose of forming an association to engage in the manufacture of pig-iron in that city, the same being reported in the Albany Argus, of January 19. At this meeting, which was presided over by Hon. Erastus Corning, Mr. Charles E. Sackett presented the following statements of the estimated cost of the manufacture of pig-iron in the above referred to location, and also of the dividends paid by pig-iron furnaces in the immediate vicinity during the last three years. He says:

The ores required to make it will cost on an average, delivered here, $5 75 per ton, and it will take two tons of them to make a ton of iron. Limestone will cost about $2 per ton, and it will require two-thirds of a ton to the ton of iron. The whole cost of a day's running expenses, including everything from the superintendent down, allowing liberally, will be $3 50 or $5 per ton.

We will estimate office expenses liberally at $10,000 per annum, and fifty cents per ton.

Interest on capital stock, including ordinary wear, tear, and loss, 10 per cent., or $40,000 per annum.

The great contingency to which furnaces are subject is a stoppage for repairs. It is my opinion that furnaces can be so built and operated by using care, as not to blow out for repairs oftener than once in five years.

In England and Scotland it is customary to run ten and fifteen years. But let us suppose that we will have to repair once every three years. The cost of so doing will be about $20,000, but we will set aside $10,000 per annum for this purpose.

To sum up, a ton of iron costs:

For two tons of ore, at $5 75	$11 50
For one and one-quarter ton of coal, at $6 50	8 13
For two-thirds ton limestone, at $2	1 33
Labor, per ton	5 00
Total	25 96

Let us say $25 96 per ton is the primary cost with large allowances.

On a make of 20,000 tons per annum, which, as we have seen, is a moderate estimate, we have the whole cost of our production per annum	$520,000
Add for office expenses	10,000
Ten per cent. interest and ordinary repair and loss	40,000
Set aside for extraordinary repairs	10,000
Making a total of	580,000

Or $29 per ton.

This makes the value of a year's production	$720,000
Deducting cost of production	580,000
Leaves net earnings	140,000

We can pay a dividend of thirty-five per cent. on a capital stock of $400,000.

I have not arrived at this conclusion without liberal allowances in all directions. It is not for one year, but for three or five; and it is verified by the fact that the Hudson Iron Company's works, built in 1851, and which may reasonably be supposed not up to the standard of modern excellence, have paid dividends of forty per cent. for the last three years, and twenty per cent. previously.

The value of pig-iron stocked here this winter is from $36 to $40 per ton. I think none of the consumers here have got a first-class No. 1 iron delivered at less than the average of this, or $38 per ton. But, in view of a falling market, let us call it $36 per ton.

Before you is a sample of iron made under my personal supervision a few weeks ago at Charlotte Furnace, near Rochester, to test the quality of ores available to us here in any quantity. I can safely say that it is better iron than is often seen in Albany, and would meet all the wants of its consumers.

The furnace at which this sample of iron was made was started in January of last year. They declared last year a dividend of seventeen per cent., and it was submitted at the directors' meeting that there was stock enough on hand and paid for to pay off the company's debt of about $100,000. The manager told me that this furnace cleared $50,000 in the first six months of her running.

Mr. Sackett further continued:

There is a strenuous effort now being made on the part of those favoring free trade to have the tariff on pig-iron reduced, and a reduction of two dollars a ton has been recommended. From this and other causes it is apprehended there will be a reduction in the price of pig-iron. But this is to be hoped for rather than feared; twenty per cent., or about one-half of our present calculated profits, would be an ample return.

At the conclusion of the meeting Mr. Sackett further stated that "he had received an offer from an iron-ore company in Lake Champlain to supply the proposed Albany association with magnetic iron ore delivered at their furnaces, for $4 62 per ton; and in addition, to subscribe liberally to their stock." Supposing this contract to be accepted, the reduction in the cost of ore would seem to render it certain that pig-iron can be manufactured in the city of Albany—a place removed a hundred miles and upward from the natural deposits of ore and coal—for $26 74 per ton, including ten per cent. interest on the capital invested, and a very liberal allowance for office expenses, repairs, and incidentals.

And yet, notwithstanding this statement, thus publicly made on the 18th of January, 1870, the manufacturers of pig-iron in the anthracite regions of Pennsylvania, who are possessed of the cheapest and best coal in the United States,* and who also have supplies of iron ore in close proximity to their furnaces, inform the Congress of the United States and the country that the cost of their product averaged, during the year 1868, $29 16 per ton, without any allowance for interest on capital; and that in the first six months of 1869 the average cost was further increased to $29 63 per ton.

II. What can be found out in regard to the manufacture of pig-iron in the anthracite regions of Pennsylvania.

The Commissioner has encountered peculiar difficulties during the past year in obtaining such data as would admit of the formation of an independent opinion in respect to the cost of the manufacture of pig-iron in the United States; of nearly two hundred circulars and blanks sent out, asking for rates of wages, cost of coal, ore, freights, &c., only one reply in a total of four responses having been received from the district in question; the whole experience constituting a marked exception to that attending the investigation of other branches of industry by similar methods. In one case, and that one of the largest iron works in Pennsylvania, the Commissioner was informed that he had no right to expect answers to questions which, if made, would disclose the exact condition of the iron manufacturer's business.

Notwithstanding the difficulties thus experienced, sufficient information is believed to be available in regard to the production of pig-iron in the anthracite regions of Pennsylvania to fully justify the Commissioner in expressing the opinion in question, without reference to what is known of other sections of the country, which do not lay claim to special economic advantages. Thus the Commissioner would first ask attention, under this head, to the testimony of Abram S. Hewitt, esq., the best recognized authority on the subject of the manufacture of iron in the United States, late commissioner of the United States to the Paris Exposition, a practical iron-master of many years experience, and at present engaged in the manufacture of iron in the section of country referred to.

In an official report, page 48, published by the State Department, Washington, 1868, Mr. Hewitt, after reviewing the cost of the manufacture of pig-iron in Europe, says:

In the United States the cheapest region for the manufacture of pig-iron, as yet

---

* In 1858 the Philadelphia and Reading Railroad Company mined and delivered anthracite coal on cars, per contract, in the anthracite districts of Pennsylvania, for 87½ cents per ton. In 1867 the price of anthracite coal at the pit's mouth, in this same district, ranged from $1 50 to $1 75 currency per ton, (including royalty.)

extensively developed, is on the Lehigh River, in the State of Pennsylvania, where, taking coal and ore at their actual cost of mining, pig-iron is produced at an average cost of $24 per ton.

Mr. Hewitt does not explicitly say that the above estimate covers interest and taxes, but it is reasonable to suppose that it does, inasmuch as interest on capital and taxes are as much elements of the cost of manufacture as digging the ore or mining the coal. But, supposing that these elements are excluded from his estimate, we fortunately are not without the means of determining how much their inclusion would add to the above estimate of average cost.

By referring to the above data, furnished by Mr. Lewis and Professor Waterhouse, we shall see that the former states $1 per ton as sufficient to cover interest on capital, in Tennessee, and $1 additional for repairs and incidentals. Mr. Waterhouse shows that at Carondelet $1 50 per ton is sufficient to cover interest, taxes, and insurance; and that in the data furnished him from Pittsburg $1 05 per ton was all that was taken to represent interest, repairs, taxes, and incidentals. Two dollars per ton, therefore, added to Mr. Hewitt's estimate, would make the average cost not in excess of that estimated by the Commissioner, viz., $26 per ton.

It is not for the Commissioner to explain the discrepancy between the estimates of Mr. Hewitt, in 1867-'68, of the cost of making iron in the anthracite regions of Pennsylvania, and the statement of the cost for the past year, as given in the petition of the iron manufacturers; or why it is that pig-iron, in what is claimed to be the most advantageous locality in the country, costs more to produce than at Pittsburg, or other points further west, where labor and coal are of higher cost; or in other locations east of the Alleghanies, where the Commissioner has positive information that the average cost during the past year has not been in excess of $24 to $25 per ton. It is sufficient for him to have collected and presented what is publicly known upon the subject; and if he should be content to rest his case here, he claims that he has shown good and sufficient reasons for the opinion expressed in his report, that the cost of pig-iron in the anthracite regions of Pennsylvania is not in excess of $26 per ton.

But the Commissioner, in making the estimate referred to in regard to the cost of pig-iron production, was further influenced by facts communicated to him in confidence by four separate and distinct parties, all of the highest character. Of these, two claimed to speak from positive knowledge as officers or stockholders in iron manufacturing companies; while in the case of the remaining two, the information seemed equally positive, but came to the Commissioner less directly. In one of the latter cases the information came in the form of a letter addressed to a third party, and by him communicated to the Commissioner. This letter reads as follows:

On the general subject of the manufacture of iron, I would remark that the footing of English iron in the American is wholly dependent upon the short manufacture of pigs by American furnaces. The profit on pig-making in any place *where a furnace ought to have been built*, is, at least, 150 per cent. Pigs can be made from $22 to $23 per ton, and pay a profit equal to any reasonable business; all above that is extortion. Again, even this price is too large when competition is fairly opened, as the price of coal is enhanced most unfairly by excessive royalties; the price of coal in Eastern Pennsylvania being greater in the bed than it is mined in Staffordshire, England. It is certain to me, that no matter how sanguine the New York traders may be, the English supply of iron to America is nearly ended.

Furthermore, the Commissioner would say, that within twenty-four hours after the passage of the resolution in question by the Senate, a gentleman, occupying high public office in the city of Washington, called upon him and submitted the following statement, offering to verify the same, if required, under oath, viz:

That during the past year (1869) he visited the anthracite district of Pennsylvania and the furnaces of some of the parties signing the petition presented to the Senate; that, in response to questions put by him relative to the then present cost of making pig-iron, he was freely informed that the average was from $24 to $25 per ton; the following statement of items being also furnished:

Labor and incidentals	$7 00
Flux	1 00
Two tons of coal	8 50
Two and one-fourth tons of ore, not including freight	6 90
	23 40

The Commissioner was further assured that the information thus given was carefully noted at the time and place and in the presence of the persons communicating the same, and as evidence thereof the note-book containing the above record has been shown to and is now in the possession of the Commissioner.

The information thus referred to as furnished by private parties was communicated in each case with the stipulation that, while the facts might be used, the source of the information should not be made public. Having due regard to this pledge, which has been given in the case of similar information relative to other industries, especially as regards salt, lumber, coal, copper, wool, &c., the Commissioner is not at liberty to be more explicit in respect to his authorities, unless the persons concerned should hereafter permit him to make their names public, inasmuch as to do otherwise would ungenerously transfer the existing controversy from the Commissioner to third parties, and thereby possibly disturb their business or social relations.

The Commissioner is, however, authorized by Messrs. John Roach & Sons, of the Morgan Iron works, of New York City, to say, that in the course of some business negotiations carried on during the past season between them and the agent of the Reading Furnace, in Pennsylvania, the latter stated as evidence of ability to fulfill certain conditions of contract, that the cost of pig-iron manufactured by the Reading Furnace, as borne on the books of the company, did not exceed twenty-five dollars per ton.

The Commissioner would also submit the following extract of a letter addressed to him by a gentleman who, during the years 1866-'67-'68, was in part proprietor and manager of a well-known pig-metal furnace located in Bucks County, Pennsylvania:

JANUARY 21, 1870.

SIR: I have looked over my old memorandum books with a view of writing you, because I am satisfied that the estimate you make of the cost of iron is fully high enough.

I find we made in March, 1867, 985 tons, the cost of which per ton is noted as follows:

Ore	$7 11
Coal	10 01
General charges	5 27
Total	22 39

In April of the same year there were produced 825 tons, as follows:

Ore	$8 18
Coal	8 05
General charges	5 83
Total	22 06

The interest on investment does not form any part of these expenses. My estimate for the iron delivered in New York used to be $26 per ton. You will notice a difference in the cost of the items at different times. We had sometimes very poor coal. Then if the furnace worked badly the cost would be necessarily increased.

Trusting that the information thus submitted may prove satisfactory, I have the honor to be, yours, most respectfully,

DAVID A. WELLS,
Special Commissioner of Revenue.

Hon. GEORGE S. BOUTWELL,
Secretary of the Treasury.

APPENDIX L.

TABLE

SHOWING THE

COMPARATIVE RATES OF DUTY ON IMPORTS

LEVIED AND COLLECTED UNDER THE RESPECTIVE

TARIFFS OF THE UNITED STATES, GREAT BRITAIN, THE GERMAN ZOLL-VEREIN, SWITZERLAND, FRANCE, RUSSIA, THE NETHERLANDS, SPAIN, PORTUGAL, BELGIUM, AUSTRIA, DENMARK, SWEDEN, AND NORWAY, DURING THE YEAR 1869;

WITH A SUPPLEMENT

SHOWING THE MINIMUM AND MAXIMUM RATES OF DUTY ON VARIOUS CLASSES OF COMMODITIES, EXPRESSED IN UNITED STATES MEASURES AND VALUES.

PREPARED FOR

THE SPECIAL COMMISSIONER OF THE REVENUE,

BY THE BUREAU OF STATISTICS.

Comparative table of import duties in the United States and European

	ARTICLES.	UNITED STATES.	GREAT BRITAIN. (1£=$4.86⅔.)	GERMAN ZOLL-VEREIN. (1 thaler=$0.72.)	SWITZERLAND. (1 franc=$0.19⅓.)
1	Absynthe	Proof gal. $2.50	Imp. pf. gal. $2.53	Centner... $4.32	Centner... $0.68
2	Oil of, or wormwood	50 per cent	Free	Centner... 2.40	Centner... 0.097
3	Accordeons, (see Mus. Instr.)	30 per cent	Free	Centner... 2.38	Centner... 1.56
4	Acetate or pyrolignate of ammonia.	Pound.... 0.70	Free	Centner... 0.72	All acids, oxyds, and other chemical preparations not enumerated, centner. 0.68
5	potassa	Pound.... 0.75	Free	Centner... 2.40	
6	quicksilver	10 per cent	Free	Centner... 2.40	
7	iron, strontia, zinc.	Pound.... 0.50	Free	Centner... 2.40	
8	{ magnesia and soda	Pound.... 0.50	Free	Centner... 2.40	
	{ lead, white lead	Pound.... 0.20	Free	Centner... 2.40	
9	baryta	Pound.... 0.40	Free	Centner... 2.40	
10	lime	25 per cent	Free	Free	
11	Acids, acetic and pyroligneous exceeding the specific gravity of 1.040.	Pound.... 0.80	Free	Centner... 0.72	Centner... 0.68
12	as above, not over 1.040, called No. 8.	Pound.... 0.25	Free	Centner... 0.72	Centner... 0.68
13	benzoic	10 per cent	Free	Free	Centner... 0.145
14	boracic	Pound.... 0.05	Free	Free	Centner... 0.145
15	citric, white or yellow.	Pound.... 0.10	Free	Centner... 2.40	Centner... 0.68
16	muriatic	10 per cent	Free	Centner... 0.06	Centner... 0.145
17	nitric or nitricfort	10 per cent	Free	Centner... 2.40	Centner... 0.68
18	oxalic	Pound.... 0.04	Free	Centner... 0.96	Centner... 0.68
19	chromic	15 per cent	Free	Centner... 2.40	Centner... 0.68
20	tannic	Pound.... 2.00	Free	Centner... 2.40	Centner... 0.145
21	tartaric, crystals and powder.	Pound.... 0.20	Free	Centner... 2.40	Centner... 0.68
22	sulphuric, (oil of vitriol)	Pound.... 0.01	Free	Free	Centner... 0.058
23	gallic	Pound.... 1.50	Free	Centner... 2.40	Centner... 0.68
24	all for chemical or manuf'ing purposes.	Free	Free	Centner... 2.40	Centner... 0.68
25	for medicinal purposes.	10 per cent	Free	Centner... 2.40	Centner... 0.68
26	Acorns	10 per cent	Free	Free	
27	Acorn coffee, and all substitutes for coffee.	Pound.... 0.03	Free	Centner... 3.60	Centner... 0.28
28	Adhesive felt, for ships' bottoms.	Free	Free	Free	Free
29	Adhesive plaster and salve	40 per cent	Free	Centner... 3.60	Centner... 0.68
30	Adzes	45 per cent	Free	Centner... 1.92	Centner... 0.68
31	Agates	10 per cent	Free	Centner... 0.36	Centner... 0.03
32	bookbinders'	20 per cent	Free	Centner.. 0.36	Centner... 0.03
33	Alabaster	30 per cent	Free	Free	Centner... 0.03
34	Alba canella	20 per cent	Free	Centner... 4.68	Centner... 0.48
35	Albata, in sheets or otherwise.	35 per cent	Free	Centner... 0.36	Centner... 0.29
36	Albumen	25 per cent	Free	Free	Centner... 0.68
37	Alconorque	Free	Free	Free	Centner... 0.29
38	Ale in bottles	Gallon.... 0.35	{ Barrel... 4.87	{ Centner.. 0.48	Centner... 0.68
39	otherwise	Gallon.... 0.20		{ Centner.. 0.48	Centner... 0.68
40	Alkanet root	20 per cent	Free	Free	Centner... 0.68
41	Alkermes	20 per cent	Free	Free	Centner... 0.68
42	Almonds	Pound.... 0.06	Free	Pound.... 0.025	Centner... 0.68
43	shelled	Pound.... 0.10	Free	Centner... 2.82	Centner... 0.68
44	paste, and oil of	50 per cent	Pound.... 0.02	Centner... 2.40	Centner... 0.68
45	Aloes	Pound.... 0.06	Free	Free	Centner... 0.68
46	Alum, all	100 pounds 0.60	Free	Centner... 0.24	Centner... 0.06
47	Aluminum, (metal unmanufactured.)	20 per cent	Free	Free	10 per cent., and centner.. 0.68
48	Amber	20 per cent	Free	Free	
49	beads of	50 per cent	Free	Centner... 2.88	Centner... 1.56
50	oil of	Pound.... 0.10	Free	Centner... 2.50	Centner... 0.68
51	Ambergris	Free	Free	Free	Centner... 0.03
52	Amethyst	10 per cent	Free	Centner... 0.36	Centner... 0.03
53	Amylic alcohol and fusil oil.	Gallon.... 2.00	Imp. gallon. 2.53	Centner... 2.40	Centner... 0.68

countries. (Duties expressed in gold dollars of the United States.)

	FRANCE. (1 franc = $0.19⅓.)				RUSSIA. (1 ruble = $0.78.)	NETHERLANDS. (1 florin = $0.41.)	
	General tariff.		In treaty with Great Britain, &c.				
	In French vessels.	In other vessels.	In vesssels of treaty powers.	In other vessels.			
Hectoliter	$29.25	$29.25	$2.92	$2.92	Pood $0.77	Liter $0.22	1
100 kilogs	1.17	1.86	1.17	1.28	Pood 1.39	Liter 0.22	2
Each	3.51	3.51	10 per	cent.	Each 7.80	5 per cent	3
100 kilogs	13.65	14.82	0.78	0.86	All acids, &c., not specially enumerated, per pood 0.85	See Chemic'ls not enumerated.	4
100 kilogs	13.65	14.82	0.78	0.86			5
Of iron, liquid	Free	Free	Free	Free			6
Of iron, concentrated, 100 kilogs.	7.80	8.58					7
Of copper, raw, dry, 100 kilogs.	2.53	2.78					8
Of copper, crystalized, 100 kilogs.	8.00	8.79					9
							10
See Chemicals not enumerated					Pood 1.72		11
See Chemicals not enumerated					Pood 1.72		12
100 kilogs	Free	0.48	Free	0.048	Pood 1.72		13
100 kilogs	0.048	0.048	Free	0.048	Pood 0.85		14
Crystalized	0.29	0.31	Free	0.048	Pood 0.85		15
100 kilogs	0.058	0.058	0.058	0.058	Pood 0.30		16
100 kilogs	17.67	19.23	Free	0.048	Pood 0.30		17
100 kilogs	13.65	14.82	1.95	2.14	Pood 0.85		18
	Free	Free	Free	Free	Pood 0.85		19
	Free	Free	Free	Free	Pood 0.85		20
100 kilogs	13.65	14.82	Free	0.048	Pood 0.85		21
100 kilogs	8.00	9.00	Free	0.048	Pood 0.85		22
100 kilogs	Free	Free	Free	0.048	Pood 0.85		23
}							24
}	Free	Free	Free	Free	Pood 0.85		25
	Free	Free	Free	Free	Free	Free	26
See Chiccory					Pood 0.20	Free	27
100 kilogs	Free	0.48	Free	0.048	Free	Free	28
					Pood 2.31	Free	29
See Tools of steel					Pood 0.77	Free	30
Raw	Free	Free	Free	Free	Free	Free	31
Manufactures of	10 per	cent.	10 per	cent.	Free	5 per cent	32
Raw, 100 kilogs	0.19	0.48	Free	0.048	Free	Free	33
Sawn, 16 centimeters thick or more.	0.19	0.48	Free	0.048	Manufactures of—pood 0.85	Manufactures of—5 per cent.	
Less than 16 centimeters, 100 kilogs.	0.29	0.48	0.29	0.34			
100 kilogs	5.85	8.77			Pood 1.83	Free	34
100 kilogs	2.92	3.40	1.95	2.14	Free	Free	35
100 kilogs			Free	0.048	Pood 0.24	Free	36
	Free	Free	Free	Free		Free	37
Hectoliter					Pood 0.77	100 liters 1.21	38
All	1.17	1.17	0.86	0.86	Bottle 0.12	100 liters 1.21	39
		Free		Free	Free	Free	40
		Free		Free		Free	41
100 kilogs	0.21	0.21	Free	0.25	Pood 1.27	100 kilogs 1.64	42
					Pood 1.27		43
					Pood 1.49		44
100 kilogs	0.97	3.90			Free		45
Burned or calcined					Pood 0.15	Free	46
100 kilogs	17.43	18.95					
Other, 100 kilogs	4.87	5.45					
			10 per	cent.	Free	5 per cent	47
			Free	Free	Free	Free	48
100 kilogs	Prohi	bited.	10 per	cent.	Pood 1.27	5 per cent	49
See Oils					Pood 1.49	1 per cent	50
100 kilogs	0.39	0.43	0.39	0.43	Free	Free	51
	Free	Free	Free	Free	Free	Free	52
See Spirits					Pood 2.34	Liter 0.51	53

Comparative table of import duties in the United States and European

	ARTICLES.	ITALY. (1 franc = $0.19⅓.)			SPAIN. (1 escudo = $0.50.)	PORTUGAL. (1 milreis = $1.08.)
			General tariff.	Tariff in treaty with France, &c.		
1	Absynthe	Hectoliter	$11.70	$2.98	20 per cent	Hectoliter ... $1.62
2	Oil of, or wormwood	100 kilogs.	1.95	0.58	See Oils	See Oils
3	Accordeons, (see Mus. Instr.)	Each	0,39	0.39	10 per cent	20 per cent
4	Acetate of lead, (white lead)	100 kilogs	0.39	0.195		See Chemicals n. e.
5	potasse					Kilogramme . 0.27
6	quicksilver					Copper, kilog. 0.054
7	iron, strontian zinc.					Iron .... Free.
8	magnesia and soda.					See Chemicals not enumerated.
9	baryta					
10	lime					Free
11	Acids, acetic and pyroligneous, exceeding the specific gravity of 1.040.	See Chemical products not enumerated, 100 kilogs.	1.75	0.78	As chemicals not enumerated, kilogramme. $0.02	Free
12	as above, not over 1.040, called No. 8.					Free
13	benzoic	100 kilogs.	0.39	Free.		Kilogramme. 0.216
14	boracic	100 kilogs.	0.29	Free.		Free
15	citric, white or yellow	100 kilogs.	1.56	1.56		Kilogramme . 0.135
16	muriatic	100 kilogs.	0.39	0.39	100 kilogs ... $0.30	Kilogramme . 0.216
17	nitric or nitricfort	100 kilogs.	0.78	0.195	100 kilogs. .. 1.00	Kilogramme . 0.216
18	oxalic	100 kilogs.	1.56	1.56		Kilogramme . 0.216
19	pyroligneous	100 kilogs.	1.75	0.78	As chemicals not enumerated.	Kilogramme . 0.216
20	tannic	100 kilogs.	1.75	0.78		Kilogramme . 0.216
21	tartaric, crystals and powder.	100 kilogs.	1.56	1.56		Kilogramme . 0.135
22	sulphuric, (oil of vitriol)	100 kilogs.	0.195	0.195	100 kilogs.... 0.45	Kilogramme . 0.005
23	gallic	100 kilogs.	1.75	0.78	As chemicals n. e.	Kilogramme . 0.216
24	all for chemical or manuf'ing purposes.	100 kilogs.	1.75	0.78	Kilogramme . 0.02	Acids, all not spec'd. Kilogramme . 0.216
25	for medicinal purposes	100 kilogs.	1.75	0.78	Kilogramme . 0.02	....
26	Acorns	....	Free.	......	.... Free.	Free
27	Acorn coffee, and all substitutes for coffee.	....	Free.	......	....	....
28	Adhesive felt, for ships' bottoms.	Tarred, 100 kilogs	0.975	1.12	100 kilogs.... 0.15	Felt varnished, kilogramme. . 0.27
29	Adhesive plaster and salve	....	......	......	....	5 per cent.
30	Adzes	100 kilogs.	1.56	1.80	Kilogramme 0.20	Kilogramme . 0.162
31	Agates				100 kilogs .. 0.075	Free
32	bookbinders'	1 per cent	......	......	....	Free
33	Alabaster	Raw or pulverlz'd Sculptured, modelled, polished, 5 per cent.	Free.	Free. Free.	Raw or in polished pieces, per 100 kilogs. .... 0.075 In squares, plates, stairs, polished or not, per 100 kilogs. ...... 0.75 Statues and ornaments, per 100 kilogs. 1.50	Free
34	Alba canella	Kilogramme	0.23	......	....	Kilogramme . 0.108
35	Albata, in sheets or otherwise.	100 kilogs.	5.85	1.95	100 kilogs.... 0.30	Raw, free; manf'd, same as copper.
36	Albumen	100 kilogs	1.95	0.78	100 kilogs.... 0.65	Free
37	Alconorque	Free	......	......	....	Free
38	Ale in bottles	Bottle	0.019	......	....	Decaliter.... 0.734
39	otherwise	Hectoliter	1.40	0.39	Hectoliter. .. 2.50	Decaliter.... 0.734
40	Alkanet root	100 kilogs.	1.95	0.39	100 kilogs.... 2.00	Free
41	Alkermes	100 kilogs.	1.95	0.39	100 kilogs.... 2.00	Free
42	Almonds	100 kilogs.	0.97	Free.	100 kilogs.... 0.50	Kilogramme. 0.0162
43	shelled	100 kilogs.	1.95	Free.	100 kilogs.... 0.50	Kilogramme. 0.0162
44	paste, and oil of	100 kilogs.	......	......	100 kilogs.... 5.00	Kilogramme. 0.108
45	Aloes	100 kilogs.	2.93	......	....	Free
46	Alum, all	100 kilogs.	0.39	......	100 kilogs.... 0.30	10 per cent
47	Aluminum	100 kilogs.	0.39	......	100 kilogs.... 0.30	Free
48	Amber	100 kilogs.	0.097	......	Kilogramme . 0.01	Free
49	beads of	10 per cent	......	......	Manuf's, kilog 2.50	20 per cent
50	oil of	See Oils	......	......	100 kilogs.... 5.00	Kilogramme. 0.0108
51	Ambergris	100 kilogs.	0.39	......	100 kilogs.... 0.30	Free
52	Amethyst	....	Free.	Free.	100 kilogs.... 0.01	Free
53	Amylic alcohol and fusil oil	Hectoliter	1.95	0.78	Hectoliter. .. 3.75	Decaliter.... 1.188

countries. (*Duties expressed in gold dollars of the United States*)—Continued.

BELGIUM. (1 franc = $0.19½.)	AUSTRIA. (1 gulden = $0.48.)			DENMARK. (1 rigsdaler = $0.5463.)	SWEDEN. (1 Riksdaler = $0.2756.)	NORWAY. (1 speciedaler = $1.0929.)	
		General tariff.	Tariff in treaty.				
Hectoliter. $16.575	Centner	$3.88		Pot $0.09	Kande $0.55	Pot $0.218	1
Free	Centner	0.65	$0.36	Pound 0.017	Free	Free	2
6 per cent				10 per cent	5 per cent	Each 0.273	3
Free	See Chemicals not enumerated.			All chemical preparations not enumerated: Pound $0.0113	See chemical preparations.	See Chemicals not enumerated.	4
Free							5
Free							6
Free							7
Free							8
Free							9
Free							10
						Free	11
Free						Free	12
Free						Free	13
Free	Free					Free	14
Free	Chemic's n. s.			Acids, liquid: Pound $0.0028 Acids, solid: Pound 0.0113		Free	15
Free	Centner	0.20	0.19			Free	16
Free	Centner	0.20	0.19			Free	17
Free	Centner	1.20	0.96			Free	18
Free	Chemic's not enumerated.					Free	19
Free						Free	20
Free	Centner	0.72	0.72			Free	21
Free	Centner	0.20	0.192			Free	22
Free	See Chemicals not enumerated.					Free	23
Free						Free	24
Free						Free	25
Free	Free			Free	Free	Free	26
Free	Centner	3.84		Pound 0.0056	Pound 0.041	Prohibited	27
10 per cent	Centner	3.88		Pound 0.0027	Pound 0.082	Free	28
Free	Centner	7.20		Pound 0.0113	Free	Free	29
100 kilogs	Centner	7.20	5.76	Pound 0.017	See Manf. of steel.	Free	30
Free	Free			Free	Free	Free	31
Free	Centner	0.388	0.36	Free	Free	Free	32
Raw, free	Centner	0.388	0.36	Free	Free	Free	33
Manufactured— 10 per cent	Statues, &c., centner	0.48	Free				
	Ornamental articles, centner	2.16	1.20				
15 per cent	Centner	7.56		Free	Free	Free	35
Free	Free			Free	Free	Free	35
Free	Free			Free	Free	Free	36
Free	Free			Free	Free	Free	37
Hectoliter .. 1.36	Centner	2.40		Pot 0.091	Kande 0.055	Pot 0.0546	38
Hectoliter .. 1.17	Centner	0.72		Pound 0.0028	Kande 0.055	Pound 0.0228	39
Free	Free			Free	Free	Free	40
Free	Free			Free	Free	Free	41
100 kilogs .. 3.90	Centner	2.52		Pound 0.017	Pound 0.033	Pound 0.054	42
100 kilogs .. 3.90	Centner	2.52		Pound 0.017	Pound 0.033	Pound 0.054	43
Free	Centner	2.52	1.44	Pound 0.0683	Pound 0.0689	Free	44
Free	Centner	3.60	2.40	Free	Free	Free	45
Free	Centner	0.72	0.36	Free	Free	Free	46
Free	Free			Free	Free	Free	47
Free	Centner	0.388		Free	Free	Free	48
10 per cent	Centner	24.00	14.40	10 per cent	10 per cent	Free	49
Free	Centner	2.52	1.44	Pound 0.0683	Pound 0.0689	Free	50
Free	Centner	2.52	1.44	Free	Free	Free	51
Free	Free			Free	Free	Free	52
Hectoliter .. 8.36	Centner	7.20	5.76	See Spirits	See Spirits	See Spirits	53

Comparative table of import duties in the United States and European countries.

	ARTICLES.	UNITED STATES.	GREAT BRITAIN.	GERMAN ZOLL-VEREIN.	SWITZERLAND.
54	Ammonia	20 per cent	Free	Centner ... $2.40	Centner ... $0.68
55	sulphate of	20 per cent	Free	Centner ... 2.40	Centner ... 0.68
56	carb. and refined.	20 per cent	Free	Centner ... 2.40	Centner ... 0.68
57	muriate	10 per cent	Free	Centner ... 2.40	Centner ... 0.68
58	Analine dyes	35 per cent., and per pound $1.00	Free	Centner ... 2.40	Centner ... 0.68
59	Analine	20 per cent	Free	Centner ... 2.40	Centner ... 0.68
60	Ammunition	30 per cent	Free	Centner ... 1.44	....
61	Gunpowder	Pound 0.06	Free	All, centner 1.44	Prohibited
62	Gunpowder above 20 cts. value.	Pound 0.06, and 20 per cent.	Free	....	....
63	Musket balls	35 per cent	Free	Centner ... 0.72	....
64	Anchovies, in oil	50 per cent	Free	Centner ... 5.04	Centner ... 1.56
65	in salt	50 per cent	Free	Centner ... 0.36	Centner ... 1.56
66	Angelica root	20 per cent	Free	Centner ... 0.36	Centner ... 0.145
67	Angora gloves and mits	35 per cent	Free	Centner ... 14.40	Centner ... 2.93
68	Animals, for breeding	20 per cent	Free	Free	Calf, sheep, lamb, each ...... 0.019 Ass, filly, cattle, each ...... 0.095 Mule, horse, each ..... 0.57 Elephant, camel, bear, each 1.12
69	Animal oil, not otherwise enumerated.	20 per cent	Free	Centner ... 0.36	See Oils
70	Animal carbon	Free	Free	Free	Centner ... 0.03
71	Anise-seed	Pound 0.05	Free	Centner ... 0.72	Centner ... 0.03
72	star	Pound 0.10	Free	Centner ... 0.72	Centner ... 0.39
73	Annatto	Free	Free	Free	Centner ... 0.03
74	extract	20 per cent	Free	Free	Centner ... 0.03
75	Antimony, crude	10 per cent	Free	Free	Centner ... 0.03
76	sulphurate of	....	....	....	....
77	metallic	....	....	....	....
78	Antiquities, (see Cabinets)	Free	Free	Free	Centner ... 0.097
79	Apparel, in personal use	Free	Free	Free	Centner ... 0.58
80					
81	Apples	10 per cent	Free	Centner ... 0.36	Per 15 cent'r 0.12
82	Apple butter	35 per cent	Free	Centner ... 0.36	Per 15 cent'r 0.12
83	Aqua ammonia	40 per cent	Free	Centner ... 2.40	Centner ... 0.68
84	Aqua fortis	10 per cent	Free	Free	Centner ... 0.68
85	Aqua mellis	50 per cent	Free	Free	Centner ... 0.68
86	Archelia	10 per cent	Free	Free	Centner ... 0.058
87	if a vegetable dye	10 per cent	Free	Free	Centner ... 0.058
88	Argentine, (flowers of antimony.)	20 per cent	Free	Crude, free	Centner ... 0.28
89	Argol	Pound 0.06	Free	Free	Centner ... 0.03
90	Armenian stone, (dentifrice).	50 per cent	Free	Free	Centner ... 0.03
91	Arms	....	Free	....	....
92	fire	35 per cent	Free	Centner ... 7.20	Centner ... 1.56
93	side	35 per cent	Free	Centner ... 1.92	Centner ... 1.56
94	Arrack, over $5 per gallon	50 per cent	See spirits	Centner ... 4.34	Centner ... 1.56
95	first proof	Gallon 2.50	Free	Centner ... 4.34	Centner ... 1.56
96	Arrowroot	30 per cent	Free	Centner ... 1.44	Centner ... 0.68
97	Arsenic	20 per cent	Free	Free	Centner ... 0.28

(*Duties expressed in gold dollars of the United States*)—Continued.

FRANCE.					RUSSIA.	NETHERLANDS.	
	General tariff.		In treaty with Great Britain, &c.				
	In French vessels.	In other vessels.	In vessels of treaty powers.	In other vessels.			
					Pood $0.195	Free	54
100 kilogs..............	$0.097	$0.097	{ 5 per cent.		Pood 0.195	Free	55
100 kilogs..............	0.195	0.21	{ 0.58	0.64	Pood 0.195	Free	56
					Pood 0.195	Free	57
	Free...	Free...	Free...	Free...	Pood 3.43	Free	58
					Pood 3.43	Free	59
						5 per cent	60
	Prohibited.		Prohibited.		Prohibited	100 kilogs....$2.05	61
							62
						5 per cent..........	63
100 kilogs..............	1.95	2.14			Pood 3.04	100 kilogs....10.25	64
					Pood 3.04	Free	65
100 kilogs..............	Free...	0.97	Free...	0.048	Free..................	Free	66
	Prohibited.		5 per cent.		Pound......... 1.75	5 per cent..........	67
Horses, each	4.87	4.87					
Mules, each............	2.92	2.92	1.95	1.95			
Oxen, bulls, each.......	0.58	0.58	0.70	0.70			
Cows, heifers, lambs, little pigs, each.	0.019	0.019			Free	Free	68
Calves, sheep, pigs, each..	0.048	0.048	0.58	0.58			
Goats, kids, asses.......	Free...	Free...					
Dogs, all...............	Free...	Free...					
All others not enum'ed..	Free...	Free...	Free...	Free...			
See oils................					Pood 1.40	1 per cent..........	69
	Free...	Free...	Free...	Free...	Free	Free	70
100 kilogs..............	0.78	0.78	0.39	0.43	Free	Hectoliter ... 0.04	71
						Hectoliter ... 0.04	72
100 kilogs..............	Free...	0.78			Free	Free	73
	Prohibited.		Prohibited.		Free	Hectoliter ... 0.04	74
	Free...	Free...	Free...	Free...	Pood 0.16	Free	75
100 kilogs..............	0.195	0.58	Free...	0.048			76
100 kilogs..............	5.07	5.58	1.17	1.29			77
	Free...	Free...	Free...	Free...	Free..............	Free	78
100 kilogs, new.........	30 per cent.		30 per cent.		Free	5 per cent..........	79
100 kilogs, old..........	10.04	11.01					80
100 kilogs..............	Free...	0.39	Free...	0.47	Pood 0.39	Free	81
					Pood 0.39	Free	82
	Prohibited.		Prohibited.		Pood 0.195	See Chemicals ..	83
100 kilogs..............	17.67	19.23	Free...	0.048		See Chemicals ..	84
Aqua regale, 100 kilogs.	12.09	13.18				See Chemicals ..	85
100 kilogs..............	Free...	0.58	Free...	0.048	Free	Free	86
					Free	Free	87
100 kilogs..............	Free...	0.048	Free...	Free...	Free	Free	88
100 kilogs..............	Free...	0.195	Free...	Free...	Free	Free	89
100 kilogs..............	Free...	0.195	Free...	Free...	Free	Free	90
For war	Prohibited.		Prohibited.				91
For comm'ce, 100 kilogs.	39.00	41.43	46.80	49.62	Pood 14.04	5 per cent..........	92
100 kilogs.	78.00	81.40	7.80	8.58	Pood 14.04	5 per cent..........	93
Hecoliter	29.25	29.25	2.92	2.92	Pood 6.55	Hectoliter ... 1.43	94
Hecoliter	29.25	29.25	2.92	2.92	Pood 6.55		95
100 kilogs..............	0.097	0.097			Pood 0.77	Free	96
White, 100 kilogs.......	0.191	0.21	Free...	0.048	Pood 0.39	Free	97

Comparative table of import duties in the United States and European countries.

No.	ARTICLES.	ITALY.			SPAIN.	PORTUGAL.
			General tariff.	Tariff in treaty with France, &c.		
54	Ammonia				100 kilogs....$0.30	Free
55	sulphate of	20 per cent			100 kilogs.... 0.75	Free
56	carb. and refined.	20 per cent			100 kilogs.... 0.75	Kilogramme.$0.0216
57	muriate	10 per cent			100 kilogs.... 0.01	Carbonate of ammonia, kilog.. 0.054
58	Analine dyes	100 kilogs	$1.95	$0.78	100 kilogs.... 5.00	5 per cent
59	Analine	100 kilogs	1.95	0.39	100 kilogs.... 0.30	Free
60	Ammunition					
61	Gunpowder	Kilog	1.17		Prohibited, except by special permit.	Prohibited
62	Gunpowder above 20 per cent. value.	Requires special permit.			Cartridges, blank, 100 kilogs .. 5.00 Others.......12.00 Small shot, free	
63	Musket balls	100 kilogs	3.90			Free
64	Anchovies, in oil	100 kilogs	1.56	0.59	Kilogramme . 0.20	Kilogramme. 0.135
65	in salt	100 kilogs	1.56	0.59	Kilogramme . 0.20	Kilogramme. 0.0378
66	Angelica root	100 kilogs	1.95	0.39	Kilogramme . 2.00	Free
67	Angora gloves and mits	Kilog	0.39	0.39	20 per cent	Pair........ 0.108
68	Animals for breed	Horses, each	3.90	3.90	Horses, each .20.00	Horses, each. 2.484
		Mules, each	1.17	0.975	Mares, each.. 3.00	
		Oxen, each	2.93	2.93	Mules, each.. 3.00	Mules, each. 1.188
		Cows, each	1.56	1.56	Asses, each .. 0.50	Asses, each . 0.62
		Heifers, each	0.975	0.975	Cattle, each.. 1.00	Cows, each.. 0.37
		Sheep, each	0.048	0.048	Sheep, goats. 0.10	Goats and sheep free
		Bovines, under 1 year.	0.39		Swine 0.50	Swine, each. 0.12
		Goats	0.048			All not enum'd, free.
		Pigs—				
		Over 20 kilogs.	0.39	0.097		
		Below 20 kilogs	0.09	0.097		
69	Animal oil, not otherwise enumerated.	100 kilogs	0.97	1.12	100 kilogs.... 5.00	Free
70	Animal carbon	100 kilogs	0.97	0.78	Free	Free
71	Anise-seed	100 kilogs	1.95	0.39	100 kilogs.... 2.00	Kilogramme. 0.0135
72	star	100 kilogs	1.95	0.39	100 kilogs.... 2.00	Kilogramme. 0.0135
73	Annatto	100 kilogs	1.95	0.39	100 kilogs.... 0.05	Free
74	extract	100 kilogs	1.95	0.39	100 kilogs.... 0.50	Kilogramme. 0.0135
75	Antimony, crude	100 kilogs	1.95	Free.	100 kilogs.... 0.30	Free
76	sulphurate of				Kilogramme . 0.02	Kilogramme. 0.001
77	metallic				100 kilogs.... 0.30	Manf., kilog. 0.043
78	Antiquities	For collections	Free	Free.	Free	Free
79	Apparel, in personal use	New, same duty as material.			Free	Free
80		Old, one-half duty as material.			Additional 20 per cent. to duties on material.	
81	Apples	100 kilogs	0.195		100 kilogs.... 0.50	Kilogramme. 0.0108
82	Apple butter	100 kilogs	0.195		100 kilogs.... 0.50	Kilogramme. 0.0108
83	Aqua ammonia	100 kilogs	0.975		Kilogramme . 0.02	5 per cent
84	Aquafortis	100 kilogs	0.975		Kilogramme . 0.02	5 per cent
85	Aqua mellis	100 kilogs	0.975		Kilogramme . 0.02	5 per cent
86	Archelia	100 kilogs	1.95	0.39	100 kilogs.... 2.00	Free
87	of a vegetable dye	100 kilogs	1.95	0.39	100 kilogs.... 3.00	Free
88	Argentine, (flowers of antimony.)	100 kilogs	1.17	0.58	100 kilogs.... 0.30	Free
89	Argol	100 kilogs	1.95	Free.	100 kilogs.... 0.30	Free
90	Armenian stone, (dentifrice)		Free.	Free.	100 kilogs.... 0.30	Free
91	Arms				Arms of war prohibited.	Artillery 1 per cent.
92	fire	War rifles, each	0.39	0.45	Kilogramme 1.00	30 per cent
		Hunter rifles, bbl.	0.58	0.67		
93	side	Common, 100 kilog	4.68	5.40	100 kilogs .. 0.40	15 per cent
		Ornamented, each	0.44	0.51		
		Gilded, each	1.75	2.03		
94	Arrack, over $5 per gallon	See Spirits			Hectoliter ... 3.75	Decaliter.... 1.62
95	first proof					
96	Arrowroot		Free.	Free.	100 kilogs.... 0.60	Kilogramme
97	Arsenic	100 kilogs	1.95	Free.	100 kilogs.... 2 00	Free

(*Duties expressed in gold dollars of the United States*)—Continued.

BELGIUM.	AUSTRIA.			DENMARK.	SWEDEN.	NORWAY.	
		General tariff.	Tariff in treaty.				
Free	Centner	$0.72	$0.36	Free	Free		54
Free		Free.		Pound....$0.0113	Free	Free	55
Free	Centner	2,72	1.44	Pound.... 0.0113	Free	Free	56
Free				Pound.... 0.0113	Free	Free	57
See Paints	Centner	0.72		Pound.... 0.0056	Pound....$0.096	Pound ...$0.027	58
Free		Free.		Free	Free	Free	59
							60
100 kilogs ..$2.93	See Gunpowder			Pound.... 0.022	Pound.... 0.0138	Free	61
							62
	Centner	1.68	1.20	Pound.... 0.0056	Pound.... 0.005	Free	63
100 kilogs .. 1.95				Pound.... 0.04	Pound.... 0.0689	Pound ... 0.082	64
100 kilogs .. 1.95	Centner	0.388	Free.	Free	Pound.... 0.0689	Pound ... 0.0045	65
Free		Free.		Free	Free	Free	66
10 per cent	Centner	27.88	21.60	Pound.... 0.409	Pound.... 0.275	Pound ... 0.327	67
Horses, each. 2.51 Fillies ..... 1.17 Oxen, cows, heifers, calves, 100 kilogs, gross weight.... 0.195 Sheep, swine, each .... 0.078 Others, n. e., free..	Horses, each. Oxen, bulls, each Cows, each.. Calves Sheep, goats, each Lambs, kids, each Swine, each.. Game, each..	1.008 2.016 1.008 0.202 0.13 0.056 0.504 0.758	 1.80 0.72 Free. Free. Free. Free. Free.	Free	All free	Horses, each 5.46 All others Free	68
Free	Centner	0.254		Pound.... 0.017	Pound.... 0.0027	Pound ... 0.0089	69
Free	Centner	0.388	Free.	Free	Free	Free	70
Free	Centner	0.388	Free	Free	Pound.... 0.019	Free	71
Free	Centner	0.388	Free	Free	Pound.... 0.019	Free	72
Free			Free.	Free	Free	Free	73
Free	Centner	7.20		Free	Free	Free	74
Free		Free.	Free	Free	Free	Free	75
							76
							77
Free		Free.	Free.	Free	Free	Free	78
Free	See Clothing			Free	Free	Free	79
					Free		80
10 per cent		Free.	Free.	Free	Free	Free	81
Free		Free.	Free.	Free	Free	Free	82
Free	See Chemicals n. e.			Pound.... 0.0113	See Chemicals.	Free	83
Free	See Chemicals n. e.			Pound.... 0.0113	See Chemicals.	Free	84
Free	See Chemicals n. e.			Pound.... 0.0113	See Chemicals.	Free	85
Free		Free.	Free	Free	Free	Free	86
		Free.	Free.	Free	Free	Pound ... 0.002	87
Free		Free.	Free.	Pound.... 0.017	Free	Free	58
Free		Free.	Free.	Free	Free	Free	89
Free		Free.	Free.	Free	Free	Free	90
All arms, side and fire, also detached pieces, free.					Free	Free	91
Hectoliter. 11.70	Centner	7.20	7.20	Pound.... 0.017	Pound.... 0.055	Free	92
Hectoliter. 11.70	Centner	7.20	5.76	Pound.... 0.017	See Manf. of steel.	Free	93
Hectoliter. 11.70	Centner	3.88		Pot. .... 0.091 Quarter. 0.5903	Kande .. 0.303	Pound.... 0.16	94
							95
100 kilogs .. 0.23	Centner	2.52		Free	Pound.... 0.03	Free	96
Free		Free.	Free.	Pound..... 0.043	Free	Free	97

Comparative table of import duties in the United States and European countries.

	ARTICLES.	UNITED STATES.	GREAT BRITAIN.	GERMAN ZOLL-VEREIN.	SWITZERLAND.
98	Articles wholly or chiefly composed of gold, silver, pearl, and precious stones, not otherwise enumerated.	40 per cent	Free	Centner ..$36.00	Centner ...$2.93
99	Articles, not in crude state, used for dyeing and tann'g.	20 per cent	Free	Centner ... 2.40	Centner ... 0.145
100	Artific'l feathers and flowers.	50 per cent	Free	Centner ...21.60	Centner ... 2.93
101	Asbestos	25 per cent	Free	Free	Centner ... 0.03
102	Asphaltum	25 per cent	Free	Free	Centner ... 0.058
103	Assafœtida	20 per cent	Free	Free	Centner ... 0.68
104	Asses skin, (parchment)	30 per cent	Free	Centner ... 1.44	Centner ... 0.68
105	imitation	30 per cent	Free	Centner ... 0.36	Centner ... 0.68
106	Augers	45 per cent	Free	Centner ... 1.92	Centner ... 1.56
107	Auripigmentum	20 per cent	Free	Free	Centner ... 0.03
108	Ava root	20 per cent	Free	Free	Centner ... 0.68
109	Awl-hafts	35 per cent	Free	Free	Centner ... 1.56
110	Awls	45 per cent	Free	Centner ... 1.92	Centner ... 1.56
111	Axes	45 per cent	Free	Centner ... 0.96 to 1.144	Centner ... 1.56
112	Axletrees, iron	Pound $0.025	Free	Centner ... 0.96	Centner ... 0.68
113	Ayr stones	10 per cent	Free	Free	Centner ... 0.03
114	Bacon	Pound 0.02	Free	Centner ... 0.36	Centner ... 0.38
115	Bags, bead	50 per cent	Free	Centner ... 2.88	Centner ... 2.145
116	grass	30 per cent	Free	Centner ... 0.12	Centner ... 0.145
117	gunny, 10 cents	Pound 0.03	Free	Centner ... 0.48	Centner ... 0.145
118	gunny, over 10 cents.	Pound 0.04	Free	Centner ... 0.48	Centner ... 0.145
119	woolen	35 per cent., and per pound. 0.50	Free	Centner ... 7.20	Centner ... 0.145
120	worsted	50 per cent	Free	Centner ... 7.20	Centner ... 0.145
121	flax and hemp	Hemp, 30 per ct.; flax, 40 per ct.	Free	Centner ... 0.48	Centner ... 0.145
122	carpet and woolen ...	50 per cent	Free	Centner ... 7.20	Centner ... 0.145
123	silk	50 per cent	Free	Centner ...21.60	Centner ... 0.145
124	Baizes	35 per cent., and per sq. yd. 0.25	Free	Centner ...21.60	Centner ... 1.56
125	Balls, billiard	35 per cent	Free	Centner ... 2.68	Centner ... 1.56
126	cannon	30 per cent	Free	See Iron	Centner ... 0.195
127	musket	35 per cent	Free	See Lead	Centner ... 0.145
128	Balm of Gilead	40 per cent	Free	Centner ... 2.40	Centner ... 0.68
129	Balmorals, value not over 40 cents per pound. (Rates from 20 to 50 cents per pound, and 35 per cent.)	35 per cent., and per pound. 0.29	Free	See Cottons	Centner ... 1.56
130	Balsam copaiva	Pound 0.20	Free	Centner ... 0.18	Centner ... 0.68
131	of Tolu	Pound 0.30	Free	Free	Centner ... 0.68
132	medicinal	30 per cent	Free	Centner ... 0.18	Centner ... 0.68
133	Peruvian	Pound 0.50	Free	Free	Centner ... 0.68
134	all kinds of cosmetic.	50 per cent	Free	Centner ... 2.40	Centner ... 2 93
135	Bamboos, unmanufactured .	10 per cent	Free	Centner ... 0.72	Centner ... 0.058
136	Bananas	25 per cent	Free	Centner ... 1.44	Centner ... 6.68
137	Barege, wool, colored	50 per cent ..... (137–139)	Free	....	Centner ... 1.56
138	wool, gray			Centner ..18.00	Centner ... 1.56
139	worsted, or silk and cotton.			See Silk and cotton.	Centner ... 1.55
140	Bark, cork-tree, unmanuf'd.	30 per cent	Free	All for medicinal use— Centner .. 0.36 All other, free. (140–143)	Centner .. 0.145
141	Peruvian	20 per cent	Free		Centner .. 0.68
142	all not specially enumerated.	10 per cent	Free		Centner .. 0.145
143	medicinal	20 per cent	Free		....
144	Barley	Bushel 0.15	Free	Free	Centner ... 0.028
145	pearl or hulled	Pound 0.01	Free	Centner ... 0.36	Centner ... 0.39
146	Barytes, sulphate of	Pound 0.005	Free	Free	Centner ... 0.68
147	Barytes and acid combined.	Pound 0.03	Free	Centner ... 0.36	Centner ... 0.68
148	Bar-wood	Free	Free	Free	Centner ... 0.057

(*Duties expressed in gold dollars of the United States*)—Continued.

	FRANCE.				RUSSIA.	NETHERLANDS.	
	General tariff.		In treaty with Great Britain, &c.				
	In French vessels.	In other vessels.	In vessels of treaty powers.	In other vessels.			
100 kilogs..............	$97.50	$100.90	$97.50	$100.90	Pound........$25.74	5 per cent..........	98
....	Free...	Free...	Free...	Free...	Pood.......... 0.04	Free	99
100 kilogs..............	12 per cent.		Free...	0.048	Pound......... 4.62	5 per cent..........	100
100 kilogs..............	Free...	0.195	Free...	Free...	Free	Free	101
100 kilogs..............	Free...	0.195	Free...	Free...	Free	Free..............	102
100 kilogs..............	Prohibited.		5 per cent.		Pood..........23.40	Free..............	103
....	Free...	Free...	Free...	Free...	Pood.......... 3.43	2 per cent..........	104
....	Free...	Free...	Free...	Free...	....	2 per cent..........	105
....	See Manufac're of iron and steel.				Pood.......... 3.39	5 per cent.	106
....	Free...	Free...	Free...	Free...	Free	Free	107
....	Free...	Free...	Free...	Free...	Free................	Free	108
....	15 per cent.		10 per cent.		Pood.......... 0.85	5 per cent..........	109
See Tools of iron or steel	....	....	....	....	Pood.......... 0.195	5 per cent..........	110
See Tools of iron or steel	....	....	....	....	Pood.......... 0.62	5 per cent..........	111
See Manufactures of iron	....	....	....	....	Pood.......... 0.62	5 per cent..........	112
....	Free...	Free...	Free...	Free...	Free	Free..............	113
....	Free...	Free...	Free...	Free...	Pood.......... 0.51	Salted, per 100 kilogs....... 0.41 Otherwise preserv'd, 100 kilogs... 0.51	114
See Materials of which composed.	....	....	....	....	Pood.......... 0.26	5 per cent..........	115
					See Materials manufactured.	5 per cent..........	116
						5 per cent..........	117
						5 per cent..........	118
						5 per cent..........	119
						5 per cent..........	120
						5 per cent..........	121
					Pood.......... 0.23		
					See Manuf. of wool...	5 per cent..........	122
					Pood.......... 0.77	5 per cent..........	123
See Silks..............	....	....	....	....	Pood.......... 0.77	5 per cent..........	124
Kilogramme	0.78	0.86	11.70	12.76	Pood.......... 0.86	5 per cent..........	125
....	Prohibited.		Prohibited.		Prohibited..........	100 kilogs.... 0.30	126
....	Prohibited.		Prohibited.		Prohibited..........	5 per cent..........	127
100 kilogs..............	2.92	5.85	....	....	Pood.......... 0.23	Free	128
See Manufactures of cotton....		....	....	....	See Cottons..........	5 per cent..........	129
100 kilogs..............	2.92	5.85	....	....	Pood.......... 0.23	Free	130
Benzoin, 100 kilogs.....	Free...	0.48	....	....	Pood.......... 3.02	Free	131
Storax, 100 kilogs......	Free...	0.48	0.39	0.39	Pood.......... 0.23	Free	132
Styrux fluid, 100 kilogs..	0.39	0.43	0.39	0.43	Pood.......... 3.02	Free	133
Not enumr'ed, 100 kilogs.	2.92	5.85	....	....	Pood.......... 0.23	Free	134
100 kilogs..............	Free...	0.39	0.39	0.39	....	Free	135
100 kilogs..............	Free...	0.78	Free...	0.48	....	Free	136
See Manufactures of wool, cotton, and silk.	....	....	....	....	See Manufactures of wool, cotton, &c.	5 per cent	137
						5 per cent	138
						5 per cent	139
100 kilogs............	Free...	0.97	Free...	0.048	Free	Free	140
100 kilogs............	Free...	0.97	Free...	0.048	Free................	Free	141
All for tanning.......	Free...	Free...	Free...	Free...	Free................	Free	142
100 kilogs............	Free...	0.97	Free...	0.048	....	Free	143
....	Free...	Free...	Free...	Free...	Free	Hectoliter ... 0.61	144
....	Free...	Freo...	Free...	Frea...	Pood.......... 0.03	Hectoliter. .. 0.61	145
100 kilogs..............	Free...	0.195	....	....	Pood.......... 0.39	Free	146
....	Free...	Free...	Free...	Free...	Pood.......... 0.39	See Chemicals......	147
....	Free...	Free...	Free...	Freo...	Free	Free	148

Comparative table of import duties in the United States and European countries.

	ARTICLES.	ITALY.			SPAIN.	PORTUGAL.
			General tariff.	Tariff in treaty with France, &c.		
98	Articles wholly or chiefly composed of gold, silver, pearl, and precious stones, not otherwise enumerated.	Of gold, per hectogramme. Silver, per kilog. Jewelry 5 per	$1.95 3.90 cent..	5 per cent	Gold— Hectog ....$5.00 Silver— Hectog 0.70	Jewelry not specified— Kilogramme.54.00 Gems, extra, 1 per ct.
99	Articles, not in a crude state, used for dyeing and tann'g.	100 kilogs	0.39	Free.	100 kilogs.... 2.00	20 per cent.........
100	Artific'l feathers and flowers.	Kilogramme..... (See Flowers.)	0.195	......	20 per cent.........	Kilogramme.12.96
101	Asbestos	100 kilogs	1.95	Free.	100 kilogs.... 0.30	Free ....
102	Asphaltum	100 kilogs	1.95	Free.	100 kilogs.... 0.05	Free...............
103	Asafœtida	100 kilogs	1.95	$0.39	100 kilogs.... 2.00	5 per cent..........
104	Asses' skin, (parchment)....	100 kilogs	2.56	......	100 kilogs.... 8.00	Free ....
105	imitation.......	100 kilogs	2.56	......	100 kilogs.... 8.00	Free ....
106	Augers....................	100 kilogs	1.56	1.80	100 kilogs.... 5.50	Kilogramme..0.054
107	Auripigmentum, sulph. ars'c.	100 kilogs.	1.95	0.78	100 kilogs.... 0.30	Free ....
108	Ava root	100 kilogs	1.95	0.39	100 kilogs.... 2.00	Free ....
109	Awl-hafts	100 kilogs.	1.17	10 p c.	100 kilogs.... 3.50	35 per cent..........
110	Awls......................	100 kilogs.	1.56	1.80	100 kilogs.... 5.50	Kilogramme . 0.081
111	Axes......................	100 kilogs.	1,56	1.80	100 kilogs.... 1.50	Kilogramme . 0.081
112	Axletrees, iron............	100 kilogs.	1.17	1.35	100 kilogs.... 1.50	Kilogramme . 0.081
113	Ayr stones................	....	Free.	Free.	Ton......... 0.05	Free ....
114	Bacon....................	100 kilogs.	3.90	......	100 kilogs.... 1.00	Kilogramme . 0.08
115	Bags, bead					
116	grass					
117	gunny, 10 cents					
118	gunny, over 10 cents..					
119	woolen..					
		Bags, all 10 per	cent.	......	20 per cent.........	As manufactures not specified: Double duties on tissues of which they are made.
120	worsted					
121	flax and hemp.					
122	carpet and woolen. ..					
123	silk..................					
124	Baizes....................	See Silks	......	......	20 per cent.........	See Silks..........
125	Balls, billiard	100 kilogs.	9.75	9.75	Ivory, kilog.. 2.50	Kilogramme . 0.40
126	cannon	....	......	......	100 kilogs.... 1.50	Free ....
127	musket..............	100 kilogs.	3.90	......	100 kilogs.... 0.39	Free ....
128	Balm of Gilead	100 kilogs.	2.39	0.39	....	5 per cent..........
129	Balmorals, value not over 40 cents per pound. (Rates from 20 to 50 cents per pound, and 25 per cent.)	....	10 per	cent.	50 per cent. above duties on materials.	Double duties on materials.
130	Balsam copaiva............	Balsam of benzoin, and other resinous— 100 kilogs....	2.39	0.39	20 per cent.........	Balsams, natural— 5 per cent........ Medicinal— 5 per cent........
131	of Tolu...........					
132	medicinal..........					
133	Peruvian					
134	all kinds of cosmetic.					
135	Bamboos, unmanufactured.	Free............	......	......	100 kilogs.... 0.10	Each 0.108
136	Bananas	100 kilogs.	0.195	......	100 kilogs.... 0.50	Kilogramme.. 0.027
137	Barege, wool, colored......	Kilogramme ...	0.58	0.66	Kilogramme. 1.00	Kilogramme . 1.62
138	wool, gray..				Kilogramme. 1.00	Kilogramme . 1.62
139	worsted, or silk and cotton.	Kilogramme.....	1.95	0.58	Kilogramme . 1.80	See note end of table.
140	Bark, cork-tree, unmanuf'd.	For tanning, if gr	ound,	free ..	100 kilogs.... 2.00	Bark, raw, free ....
141	Peruvian	100 kilogs.	0.39	Free	100 kilogs.... 2.00	Prep'd, kilog. 0.0324
142	all not specially enumerated.	Free	......	......	100 kilogs.... 0.05	Peruvian, kilogramme.. 0.0108
143	medicinal............	100 kilogs.	1.95	0.39	100 kilogs.... 2.00	Kilogramme. 0.0108
144	Barley....................	100 kilogs	0.145	0.145	100 kilogs.... 0.45	10 kilogs.... 0.043
145	pearl or hulled......	100 kilogs.	0.145	1.145	100 kilogs.... 0.45	10 kilogs.... 0.043
146	Barytes, sulphate of........	See Chemicals not enum'ed.	......	......	SeeChemic'ls not enumerated.	Kilogramme. 0.0027
147	Barytes and acid combined.					Kilogramme. 0.216
148	Bar-wood	100 kilogs.	0.58	Free.	100 kilogs..... 0.05	See Wood ....

(*Duties expressed in gold dollars of the United States*)—Continued.

BELGIUM.	AUSTRIA.			DENMARK.	SWEDEN.	NORWAY.	
		General tariff.	Tariff in treaty.				
5 per cent	Centner	126.00	......	Pound....$0.273	Gold, ort. $0.0082 Silver, ort. 0.0082	Free	98
Free	....	Free.	Free.	Pound.... 0.005	Free.............	Free	99
10 per cent	Same as cloth	ing, m	illin'y.	Pound.... 1.092	Pound.... 0.827	Pound....$0.49	100
Free	....	Free.	Free.	Free.............	Free.............	Free	101
Free	....	Free.	Free.	Free.............	Free.............	Free	102
Free	Centner	2.52	1.44	Pound.... 0.0113	Free.............	Free	103
Free	Centner	6.24	4.80	Pound.... 0.068	Pound.... 0.055	Pound.... 0.062	104
Free	Centner	2.64	1.92	Pound.... 0.068	10 per cent.......	Pound.... 0.062	105
100 kilogs ..$0.39	Centner	2.88	2.16	Pound.... 0.017	5 per cent........	Pound.... 0.027	106
Free.	....	Free.	......	Free	Free	Free	107
Free	....	Free.	......	Free	Free	Free	108
10 per cent.	See Manufact'	s of w	ood ..	Pound..... 0.017	Pound.... 0.0027	Pound. .. 0.027	109
100 kilogs .. 0.39	Centner	2.88	2.16	Pound..... 0.017	5 per cent........	Free	110
100 kilogs .. 0.39.	Centner	2.88	2.16	Pound..... 0.017	5 per cent........	Free	111
100 kilogs .. 0.39	Centner	0.48	0.36	Pound..... 0.017	Pound.... 0.0082	Free	112
Free	....	Free.	Free.	Free	Free	Free............	113
100 kilogs .. 0.23	Centner	1.26	......	Free	Free	Pound. .. 0.009	114
					10 per cent......		115
					10 per cent......		116
							117
							118
As tissues, according to description.	See Material manufact'd.	....	......	As manufactures not enumerat'd, 10 per cent.	As tissues	As material ..	119
							120
							121
							122
							123
10 per cent	See Silks	......	......	Pound.... 0.41	10 per cent.......	See Silks........	124
10 per cent	Centner.	7.20	......	Pound.... 0.091	10 per cent.......	Pound. .. 0.158	125
100 kilogs .. 0.39	See Material .	......	......	Pound.... 0.0014	Free	Free............	126
10 per cent	Lead, centner.	1.68	1.20	Pound.... 0.0056	Free	Free	127
Free	Centner	7.20	......	Pound.... 0.027	Free	Free	128
10 per cent	See Clothing .	......	......	Double duties on material.	10 per cent.......	Above duty on material, 10 per cent.	129
Free	Centner.	2.52	1.44	All natural balsams— Pound .. 0.027	Free	Free	130
	Centner.	2.40	......		Free.	Free	131
See Drugs—	Centner.	2.40	......		Free	Free	132
Free.	Centner.	2.40	......		Free.	Free	133
10 per cent.......	Centner.	2.40	......		Free	Free	134
Free	....	Free.	......	Free	Free	Free	135
10 per cent	Centner.	2.52	......	Pound.... 0.0045	Free	Free	136
10 per cent.	See Silk and and cotton tissues.	....	....	Wool, lb.. 0.184	See Manufactures of wool, cotton, or silk.	See Manufactures of wool, cotton, or silk.	137
10 per cent.				Silk, lb... 0.41			138
10 per cent.							139
Free	....	......	Free.	Free	Free	Free	140
Free	Centner.	2.40	......	Pound.... 0.0013	Free	Free	141
Free	....	......	Free.	Free	Free	Free............	142
Free	Centner.	2.40	......	Pound.... 0.0013	Free	Free	143
100 kilogs .. 0.117	Centner.	0.086	Free.	Free	Free	Ton 0.054	144
100 kilogs .. 0.23	Centner.	0.388	Free.	Free	Free	Ton 0.054	145
Free	See Chemic's not enum'ed.	....	......	See Chemicals. ..	See Chemicals ...	See Chemicals .	146
Free							147
Free	....	Free.	......	Free	Free	Free	148

Comparative table of import duties in the United States and European countries.

	ARTICLES.	UNITED STATES.	GREAT BRITAIN.	GERMAN ZOLL-VEREIN.	SWITZERLAND.
149	Baskets, wood, osier, palm-leaf, straw, grass, or whalebone.	35 per cent	Free	Coarse, free. Fancy baskets, centner.$2.88	Wood— Centner..$0.145 Palm— Centner.. 1.56 Whalebone— Centner.. 1.56
150	Bass	20 per cent	Free	Undyed— Centner.....12 Dyed— Centner... 2.16	Centner... 0.057
151	Bast ropes	Pound $0.035	Free	Centner... 9.48	Centner... 0.29
152	Battledores	35 per cent	Free	Centner... 0.72	Centner... 1.56
153	Bay water, or bay rum, distilled from the leaf.	Gallon 1.50	Free	Centner... 2.40	Centner... 2.93
154	wax, or myrtle wax	20 per cent	Free	Centner... 2.40	Centner... 0.14
155	Bdellium, crude	20 per cent	Free	Free	Centner... 0.14
156	refined	20 per cent	Free	Free	Centner... 0.68
157	Beads, all	50 per cent	Free	Centner... 2.88	Centner... 2.93
158	Beam knives	45 per cent	Free	See Cutlery	Centner... 1.56
159	scales	35 per cent	Free	See Iron, &c	Centner... 1.56
160	Beans, tonqua	20 per cent	Free	Centner ... 0.36	Centner... 0.057
161	vanilla	Pound 3.00	Free	Centner... 4.68	Centner... 0.68
162	all other not specially enumerated.	10 per cent	Free	Medicinal— Centner... 0.36 All others, free.	Centner... 0.057
163	Bed feathers	30 per cent	Free	Centner... 0.36	Centner... 0.68
164	Beds of feathers	20 per cent	Free	Centner... 2.88	Centner... 1.56
165	Bed ticking, linen	See Flax	Free	Centner ... 2.88	Centner... 1.56
166	ticking, cotton	See Cotton	Free	Centner ... 2.88	Centner... 1.56
167	caps	35 per cent	Free	Centner... 2.88	Centner... 1.56
168	screws	Pound 0.02½	Free	Centner... 1.92	Centner... 1.56
169	sides, as carpeting	See Mats	Free	See Mats	Centner... 1.56
170	Beef	Pound 0.01	Free	Centner... 0.36	Centner... 0.095
171	Beer, in bottles	Gallon 0.35	Barrel ...$4.87	Centner ... 0.48	Centner.. 0.66
172	otherwise	Gallon 0.20			Centner.. 0.145
173	Beeswax	20 per cent	Free	Centner... 0.36	Centner... 0.145
174	Bell cranks	35 per cent	Free	See Material manufactured.	Centner.. 1.56
175	levers	35 per cent	Free		Centner.. 1.56
176	pulls	35 per cent	Free		Centner.. 1.56
177	metal, manufactured	35 per cent	Free	Centner... 1.26	Centner... 1.56
178	Bellows	35 per cent	Free	Centner... 2.88	Centner... 1.56
179	Bellows pipes	35 per cent	Free	Centner... 0.86	Centner... 1.56
180	Bells, of metal, fit only for remanufacture.	Free	Free	Free	Centner... 0.145
181	Bells, gold	40 per cent	Free	Centner ...36.00	Centner... 2.93
182	silver	40 per cent	Free	Centner ...36.00	Centner... 2.93
183	Belts, sword, leather	35 per cent	Free	Centner... 7.20	Centner... 2.93
184	endless, for pipes	35 per cent	Free	Centner... 7.20	Centner... 1.56
185	Benzoates	30 per cent	Free	Free	Centner... 0.68
186	Berries, for dyeing, all, exclusive in a crude state.	Free	Free	Free	Centner... 0.145
187	Berries, not otherwise provided for.	10 per cent	Free	Free	Centner... 0.145
188	Berlin blue	25 per cent	Free	Free	Centner... 1.045
189	Bezoar stones	10 per cent	Free	Centner... 0.18	Centner... 0.03
190	Bichromate of potash	Pound 0.03	Free	Centner... 0.36	Centner... 0.68
191	Bick irons	35 per cent	Free	Centner... 1.92	Centner... 1.56

(*Duties expressed in gold dollars of the United States.*)—Continued.

	FRANCE.				RUSSIA.	NETHERLANDS.	
	General tariff.		In treaty with Great Britain, &c.				
	In French vessels.	In other vessels.	In vessels of treaty powers.	In other vessels.			
Basket work, raw— 100 kilogs.	$1.17	$1.36	10 per	cent.	Simple baskets, free.. Fancy baskets— Pood $0.25	5 per cent	149
Cleaned— 100 kilogs.	2.34	2.73	10 per	cent.			
Split, cut— 100 kilogs.	3.70	4.68	10 per	cent.			
	Free...	Free...	Free...	Free...	Pood 0.04	Free	150
100 kilogs.	4.87	5.36	$2.92	$3.20	Pood 0.31	100 kilogs...$0.205	151
Kilogramme.	0.78	0.86	10 per	cent.		1 per cent	152
					Pood 7.80	Free	153
100 kilogs.	0.195	0.58	0.195	0.24	Pood 7.80	Free	154
	Free...	Free...	Free...	Free...	Free	Free	155
100 kilogs.	Free...	0.48	Free...	0.048	Free	Free	156
Of steel, 100 kilogs.			3.90		On strings, pood 0.50 Set, pound 0.25	5 per cent	157
See Manufactures of iron,	steel, an	d cutler	y			5 per cent	158
See Manufactures of iron,	steel, an	d cutler	y			5 per cent	159
					Carrot, pood 0.37	Beans, hectoliter 0.61	160
100 kilogs.	39.00	41.73					161
					Free	Free	162
100 kilogs.	9.75	10.72	0.67	0.74	Prohibited, unless property of travellers, pood... 0.84	Free.	163
							164
100 kilogs.	41.34	41.34	16 per	cent.	See Manufactures of	5 per cent	165
	Prohi	bited.	15 per	cent.	Linen, cotton, &c.	5 per cent	166
	See ma	nufactur	es of me	tals.		5 per cent	167
	See ma	nufactur	es of me	tals.		5 per cent	168
						5 per cent	169
Fresh, 100 kilogs	Free ..	Free ..	Free ..	0.047	Pood 0.51	100 kilogs.... 2.46	170
Hectoliter	1.17	1.17	0.86	0.86	Bottle 0.12	100 liters 1.23	171
					Pood 0.78	100 liters 1.23	172
Yellow, brown or white, 100 kilogs.	0.58	0.58	0.195	0.24	Free	Free	173
Manufactures of copper, pure or mixed, ordinary, 100 kilogs.	19.50	20.29	3.90	4.29	All articles part or wholly of brass. Pood 2.34	5 per cent	174
						5 per cent	175
						5 per cent	176
						5 per cent	177
					Pood 0.31	5 per cent	178
100 kilogs.			0.58	0.63	Pood 0.62	5 per cent	179
100 kilogs.	Free ..	0.048	Free ..	0.048	Pood 0.47	5 per cent	180
100 kilogs.	97.50	100.90			Pound 25.74	5 per cent	181
100 kilogs.	97.50	100.90			Pound 1 72	5 per cent	182
	Prohi	bited.	10 per	cent.	Pound 0.31	5 per cent	183
	Prohi	bited.	10 per	cent.	Pound 0.31	5 per cent	184
	Free ..	Free ..	Free ..	Free ..	Free	Free	185
	Free ..	Free ..	Free ..	Free ..	All berries free ..... Baccæ cocculi Indici, prohibited.	Free	186
	Free ..	Free ..	Free ..	Free ..	Free	Free	187
	Free ..	Free ..	Free ..	Free ..		Free	188
	Free ..	Free ..	Free ..	Free ..	Free	Free	189
Chromate of potassium, 100 kilogs.	29.25	31.20	10 per	cent.	Pound 0.78	Free	190
100 kilogs. See manu	facture	of iron.	3.12	3.43	See Manufac's of iron.	5 per cent	191

Comparative table of import duties in the United States and European countries.

	Articles.	Italy.			Spain.	Portugal.
			General tariff.	Tariff in treaty with France, &c.		
149	Baskets, wood, osier, palm-leaf, straw, grass, or whalebone.	Com'n, 100 kilogs. Fine, 100 kilogs.. Mats, 100 kilogs..	$0.975 3.90 0.39	$0.975 3.90 0.39	20 per cent......	Kilogramme. $0.108 Kilogramme. 0.001 Kilogramme. 0.648
150	Bass..........................	Free.............	......	......	100 kilogs....$2.00	Free..............
151	Bast ropes.................	Free.............	......	......	100 kilogs.... 4.00	Kilogramme. 0.108
152	Battledores.................	10 per cent......	......	......	20 per cent.........	See Manuf. of wood.
153	Bay water, or bay rum, distilled from the leaf.	100 kilogs.	0.195	Free.	See Spirits.........	5 per cent..........
154	wax, or myrtle wax...	100 kilogs.......	3.90	......	Kilogramme . 0.02	Kilogramme. 0.0324
155	Bdellium, crude............	100 kilogs.......	2.93	0.39	100 kilogs.... 0.30	Free..............
156	refined...........	100 kilogs.	2.93	0.39	....	5 per cent..........
157	Beads, all.	10 per cent.......	......	......	20 per cent.........	Kilogramme . 0.40
158	Beam knives..............	100 kilogs.	1.56	1.80	See Manufact'es of steel.	Kilogramme . 0.108
159	scales................	100 kilogs.	1.56	1.80		Kilogramme . 0.162
160	Beans, tonqua.............					Kilogra'me.. 0.005
161	vanilla..............					Free. ....
162	all other not specially enumerated.	Beans— 100 kilogs.	0.297	......	Beans— 100 kilogs.. 0.60	Kilogram'e.. 0.005
163	Bed feathers...............	100 kilogs.	1.95	2.25	20 per cent.........	Kilogramme . 0.054
164	Beds of feathers.	100 kilogs	1.95	2.25	20 per cent.........	Kilogramme . 0.054
165	Bed ticking, linen..........	See Linen.......	......	......	See Manuf. of flax .	Kilogramme . 1.08
166	cotton.................	See Cotton	......	......	See Manuf. of cotton	See Cotton.........
167	caps...................	....	......	......	20 per cent.........	Kilogramme . 0.27
168	screws................	100 kilogs	2.93	2.38	20 per cent.........	Kilogramme . 0.054
169	sides, as carpeting....	....	......	......	See Mats	Kilogramme . 0.002
170	Beef......................	100 kilogs	0.47	Free.	Corned, 100 kgs 0.50 Other 1.00	Kilogramme . 0.081
171	Beer, in bottles............	Bottle...........	0.019	......	Hectoliter.... 2.50	Decaliter 0.734
172	otherwise	Hectoliter.......	0.39	0.39	Hectoliter.... 2.50	Decaliter 0.734
173	Beeswax..................	See wax	......	......	Kilogramme . 0.02	Yellow, kilog. 0.0108 White, kilog. 0.0324
174	Bell cranks................	100 kilogs	9.75	9.75	All metals manufactured, containing copper or tin.	Kilogramme . 0.27
175	levers................	100 kilogs	9.75	9.75		Kilogramme . 0.27
176	pulls.................	100 kilogs	9.75	9.75		Kilogramme . 0.27
177	metal, manufactured..	100 kilogs	2.93	3.38	100 kilogs....25.00 Other 7.50	Kilogramme .0.0216
178	Bellows...................	10 per cent......	......	......	20 per cent	Kilogramme . 0.002
179	Bellows pipes	10 per cent......	......	......	20 per cent	Kilogramme . 0.054
180	Bells, of metal, fit only for remanufacture.	100 kilogs	0.78	0.78	100 kilogs.... 2.00	Kilogramme . 0.024
181	Bells, gold.................	Hectogramme...	1.95	5 pr. cent	See Gold	Kilogramme .54.00
182	silver...............	Kilogramme.....	2.34		See Silver.........	Kilogramme .32.80
183	Belts, sword, leather.......	100 kilogs	9.75	9.75	20 per cent.........	Kilogramme . 0.40
184	endless, for pipes	100 kilogs	9.75	9.75	20 per cent.........	Free..............
185	Benzoates.................	100 kilogs	1.95	0.39	100 kilogs.... 0.30	10 per cent.........
186	Berries, for dyeing, all, exclusive in a crude state.	100 kilogs	0.39	Free	100 kilogs.... 2.00	Free..............
187	Berries, not otherwise provided for.	100 kilogs	Free.	Free.	100 kilogs.... 2.00	Free..............
188	Berlin blue................	100 kilogs	1.95	1.95	100 kilogs.... 1.50	20 per cent.........
189	Bezoar stones	Free............	Free.	Free.	100 kilogs.... 0.30	Free..............
190	Bichromate of potash......	100 kilogs	1.95	0.78	See Chemicals, n. e.	Kilogramme .0.0108
191	Bick irons.................	See Iron	......	......	100 kilogs.... 1.50	Kilogramme . 0.054

(*Duties expressed in gold dollars of the United States.*)—Continued.

Belgium.	Austria.	General tariff.	Tariff in treaty.	Denmark.	Sweden.	Norway.	
10 per cent	Baskets of straws, cane,						
10 per cent	&c., centner.	$1.20	$0.72	Pound. ..$0.091	Baskets of willow, lb. ..$0.011 Others, lb. 0.0689	Pound ..$0.013 Of unpeeled willow, free.	149
10 per cent	Centner.	7.20	......				
Free	Free	......	......	Free	Free	Free	150
Free	Centner.	0.12	......	Pound.... 0.005	Free	Pound... 0.009	151
10 per cent	See Manufact's of wood ..			Pound.... 0.017	Pound.... 0.0027	Free	152
Hectoliter ..$8.36	See Perfumeries....			Pound.... 0.091	See Spirits.......	Spirits	153
Free	Centner	1.44	1.20	Pound.... 1.017	Free	Pound. .. 0.009	154
Free	......	......	Free.	Free	Free	Free	155
Free	Centner.	2.40		Free	Free	Free	156
10 per cent	According to material....			10 per cent.......	10 per cent.......	10 per cent	157
100 kilogs .. 0.78	See Cutlery..	......	......	Pound.... 0.017	Pound.... 0.0065	Pound. .. 0.027	158
100 kilogs .. 0.78	See Iron or steel manuf'ed.			Pound.... 0.017	Pound.... 0.0065	Pound. .. 0.027	159
10 per cent	Centner....	7.56	......	Free............	Free	Free............	160
10 per cent	Centner....	0.086	Free	Pound .. 0.273	Pound.... 1.515	Pound. .. 1.748	161
100 kilogs .. 0.117				Free	Free	Ton 0.109	162
Free	Centner.	0.384	Free.	Pound.... 0.028	Free	Free	163
10 per cent	Same as the tick ...	......	......	Pound.... 0.028	As the tick.......	As the tick......	164
See Tissues of flax.	See Tissues of flax.	......	......	See Tissues of flax	See Linen.........	See Tissues.	165
See Tissues of cotton.	See Tissues of cotton.	......	......	See Tissues of cotton.	See Cotton.......		166
See Material manufactured.	See Material manufact'd.	......	......	Pound.... 0.045	10 per cent.......	10 per cent	167
		......	......	Pound.... 0.045	Pound.....0.0165	(Copper) lb. 0.011	168
See Mats	See Mats.....	......	......	Pound.... 0.0042	See Mats.........	See Mats	169
100 kilogs .. 0.23	Fresh, centner	0.388	......	Free	Free	Fresh, free ...... Salted, lb...0.009	170
Hectoliter.. 1.36	Centner	2.40	......	Pot........ 0.091	Kande..... 0.055	Pot 0.054	171
Hectoliter .. 1.17	Centner	0.72	......	Pound.... 0.0028	Kande..... 0.055	Pound 0.0228	172
Free	Centner	1.42	1.20	Pound.... 0.017	Free	Pound 0.009	173
See Copper, worked.	See Copper manufactured.	......	......	Pound.... 0.045	See Manuf. of copper or brass	Pound 0.047	174
		......	......	Pound.... 0.045		Pound 0.047	175
		......	......	Pound.... 0.045	Pound..... 0.041	Pound 0.047	176
		......	......	Free	Pound..... 0.041	Pound 0.047	177
10 per cent	Centner	5.76	3.60	10 per cent.......	10 per cent.......	10 per cent	178
10 per cent	See Manufac's of iron.	......	......	Pound.....0.0056	Of India-rubber, free.	Free	179
Free	Free	......	......	Free	Free	Free	180
5 per cent	See Gold	......	......	Pound.... 0.091	See Gold.........	Loth 0.03	181
5 per cent	See Silver....	......	......	Pound.... 0.091	See Silver	Loth 0.03	182
10 per cent	Centner	12.00	7.20	10 per cent.......	10 per cent.......	Pound 0.08	183
10 per cent	Centner	5.76	3.60	Pound.... 0.028	10 per cent.......	Above material, 10 per cent.	184
Free	Centner	2.40	......	Free	Free	Free	185
Free	Free	......	......	Free	Free	Free	186
Free	Free	......	......	Free	Free	Free	187
Free	Centner	0.388	Free.	Pound.... 0.0056	Free	Free	188
Free............	Free	......	......	Free	Free	Free	189
Free............	See Chemicals not enum'd.	......	......	Pound.... 0.0113	Free	See Chemicals.	190
See Iron and steel	See Iron manufactured.	......	......	Pound.... 0.017	See iron	Pound 0.027	191

Comparative table of import duties in the United States and European countries.

	ARTICLES.	UNITED STATES.	GREAT BRITAIN.	GERMAN ZOLL-VEREIN.	SWITZERLAND.
192	Binding, carpet, if worsted	50 per cent	Free	Centner...$7.20	Centner...$1.56
193	cotton	35 per cent	Free	Centner... 7.20	Centner... 1.56
194	silk	60 per cent	Free	Centner...28.80	Centner... 1.56
195	leather	35 per cent	Free	Centner... 2.88	Centner... 1.56
196	linen	40 per cent	Free	Centner...14.40	Centner... 1.56
197	quality	50 per cent	Free	Centner...14.40	Centner... 1.56
198	Bird's-eye stuff, linen	See Flax	Free	Free	See Linen
199	Birds	20 per cent	Free	Free	....
200	Bismuth	Free	Free	Free	Centner... 0.145
201	oxide of	20 per cent	Free	Centner... 2.40	Centner... 0.68
202	Bitter apple	Pound $0.10	Free	Free	Centner... 0.145
203	Bits, carpenter's	45 per cent	Free	Centner... 1.92	Centner... 1.56
204	Bitumen	20 per cent	Free	Free	Centner... 0.145
205	Blacking	30 per cent	Free	Centner... 2.40	Centner... 0.68
206	Black, lamp	20 per cent	Free	Free	Centner... 0.68
207	lead, pots	35 per cent	Free	Centner... 2.40	Centner... 0.68
208	lead, powder	20 per cent	Free	Free	Centner... 0.29
209	Blacksmith's hammers	Pound 0.02¼	Free	Centner... 1.88	Centner... 0.68
210	sledges	Pound 0.02¼	Free	Centner... 1.88	Centner... 0.68
211	Bladders	20 per cent	Free	Centner... 0.36	Centner... 0.68
212	manufactures of	30 per cent	Free	Centner... 7.20	Centner... 1.56
213	Blankets, value not over 40 cents per pound.	35 per cent., and per pound. 0.20	Free	Blankets	Cotton, per centner 0.39
214	Blankets, value 40 to 60 cts. per pound.	35 per cent., and per pound. 0.30	Free	All......	All other........
215	Blankets, value 60 to 80 cts. per pound.	35 per cent., and per pound. 0.40	Free	Centner... 7.20	Centner... 1.56
216	Blankets, value over 80 cts. per pound.	35 per cent., and per pound. 0.50	Free	....	....
217	Bleaching powders	100 pounds. 0.30	Free	Centner... 0.36	Centner... 0.68
218	Blue, Prussian	30 per cent	Free	....	....
219	vitriol	Pound 0.05	Free	....	....
220	Blue gall	Free	Free	Free	Centner... 0.097
221	Blooms, iron	See Iron in bars	Free	Free	Centner... 0.058
222	Boards, planed	20 per cent	Free	Free	15 centner, 0.12
223	rough	20 per cent	Free	Free	15 centner. 0.12
224	Bobbin	35 per cent	Free	Centner .. 0.60	Centner .. 0.39
225	wire-covered cotton	Same as Wire...	Free	Same as Wire...	Centner .. 0.19
226	Bocking, all	35 per cent., and per sq. yd. 0.25	Free	Centner .. 2.88	Centner .. 1.56
227	Bodkins, gold	40 per cent	Free	Centner ..36.00	Centner .. 2.93
228	silver	40 per cent	Free	Centner ..36.00	Centner .. 2.93
229	steel	45 per cent	Free	Centner .. 1.92	Centner .. 2.93
230	other	35 per cent	Free	Centner .. 1.92	Centner .. 2.93
231	Boiler plates	Pound $0.01½	Free	Centner .. 0.29	Centner .. 0.68
232	Bologna sausages	30 per cent......	Free	Centner .. 0.36	Centner .. 0.39
233	Bolting cloths	Free	Free	Free	Centner .. 0.68
234	Bolts, composition	35 per cent......	Free	Centner .. 1.92	Centner .. 1.56
235	Boltrope, as cordage, tarred	Pound 0.03	Free	Free	Centner .. 0.29
236	not manilla	Pound 0.03½	Free	Free	Centner .. 0.29
237	Bone, black	25 per cent......	Free	Bone, raw or in plates, free. Coarse manufactures, per centn'r, $0.72. Fancy articl's, per centner, $2.88.	Centner .. 0.29
238	alphabets	35 per cent......	Free		All manufac's. per centner, $1.56.
239	chessmen	50 per cent......	Free		
240	whale, rosettes	35 per cent......	Free		
241	tip and bones	10 per cent......	Free		
242	whale	35 per cent......	Free		
243	manuf. of whalebone, not Amer. fisheries.	10 per cent......	Free		
244	all other manuf	50 per cent......	Free		
245	Bonnets, Leghorn	40 per cent......	Free	Each...... 0.05	Centner .. 2.93
246	chip, grass, straw	40 per cent......	Free	Each.. ... 0.05	Centner .. 2.93
247	silk	60 per cent......	Free	....	....

(*Duties expressed in gold dollars of the United States.*)—Continued.

FRANCE.					RUSSIA.	NETHERLANDS.	
	General tariff.		In treaty with Great Britain, &c.				
	In French vessels.	In other vessels.	In vessels of treaty powers.	In other vessels.			
			10 per cent.		See Materials manufactured.	5 per cent	192
			15 per cent.			5 per cent	193
			10 per cent.			5 per cent	194
						5 per cent	195
			15 per cent.			5 per cent	196
			15 per cent.			5 per cent	197
			15 per cent.			5 per cent	198
	Free	Free	Free	Free	Free	Free	199
	Free	Free	Free	Free	Free	Free	200
See Chemicals not enumerated.			10 per cent.		Pood $0.85	Free	201
			10 per cent.		Free	Free	202
Articles of steel not denominated, 100 kgs.			$3.90	$4.29	See Manufac's of steel.	5 per cent	203
	Free	Free	Free	Free	Free	Free	204
100 kilogs	$23.98	$25.66	0.78	0.78	Pood 0.85	Free	205
100 kilogs	0.195	0.58			Free	Free	206
100 kilogs	19.50	20.95	0.58	0.63	Pood 0.62	Free	207
100 kilogs	Free	0.048	Free	0.048	Pood 0.31	Free	208
100 kilogs	24.37	26.27	2.92	3.20	Pood 0.62	5 per cent	209
100 kilogs	24.37	26.27	2.92	3.20	Pood 0.62	5 per cent	210
						Free	211
	10 per cent.		10 per cent.			5 per cent	212
Blankets, all	Prohibited.		10 per cent.		Blankets, all	5 per cent	213
					Pound 0.31	5 per cent	214
						5 per cent	215
							216
					Pood 0.85	Free	217
	Free	Free	Free	Free		Free	218
	Prohibited.		10 per cent.			Free	219
	Free	Free	Free	Free	Free	Free	220
	See Iron.				See Iron.	Free	221
Sawn, over 2 decimeters thick, 100 kilogs.	Free	0.195			Free	1 per cent	222
Sawn, less than 2 decim. thick, 100 kilogs.	0.19	1.36			Free	1 per cent	223
See Machinery, pieces of steel					Pood 0.156	1 per cent	224
100 kilogs	5.85	6.43	1.95	2.14	See Wire	5 per cent	225
See Manufactures of wool or flax					30 per cent	5 per cent	226
100 kilogs	97.50	100.90	10 per cent.		Pound 25.74	5 per cent	227
100 kilogs	97.50	100.90	10 per cent.		Pound 1.72	5 per cent	228
100 kilogs	34.12	36.20	3.90	4.29	Pood 3.51	5 per cent	229
100 kilogs	24.37	26.27	2.92	3.20	Pood 3.51	5 per cent	230
100 kilogs	5.85	6.43	See Machines.		Pood 0.34	5 per cent	231
	Free	Free	Free	Free	Pood 0.51	100 kilogs 2.46	232
						5 per cent	233
100 kilogs	19.50	20.95	3.90	4.29	Pood 2.34	5 per cent	234
See Cordage					Pood 0.31	100 kilogs 0.21	235
					Pood 0.31	100 kilogs 0.21	236
					Raw	Raw, free	237
					Pood 0.16	All manufactures of, 5 per cent.	238
Raw or white calcined, per 100 kilogs.	Free	0.39			All Manufac's, per pound 0.26		239
							240
Fancy articles of bone, &c., per kilogs.	0.78	0.86	10 per cent.				241
							242
Toys, per 100 kilogs	15.60	16.86	10 per cent.				243
							244
			10 per cent.		Pound 1.01	5 per cent	245
			10 per cent.		Pound 1.01	5 per cent	246
			10 per cent.			5 per cent	247

Comparative table of import duties in the United States and European countries.

	ARTICLES.	ITALY.			SPAIN.	PORTUGAL.
			General tariff.	Tariff in treaty with France, &c.		
192	Binding, carpet, if worsted..	See Manufactures of materials.	......	......	See Manufactures of materials.	Kilogramme .$0. 486
193	cotton		......	......		Kilogramme . 0. 459
194	silk		......	......		See Silk ....
195	leather		......	......		See Leather........
196	linen		......	......		Kilogramme . 0. 54
197	quality		......	......		Kilogramme . 0. 54
198	Bird's eye stuff, linen		......	......		See Manuf's of flax.
199	Birds	Free	......	......	Free	Free ....
200	Bismuth	100 kilogs	$1. 95	Free.	100 kilogs....$0. 30	Free ....
201	oxide of	100 kilogs	1. 95	$0. 78	See Chemicals, n. e.	Kilogramme . 0. 756
202	Bitter apple	100 kilogs	1. 95	Free.	100 kilogs.... 0. 30	20 per cent.........
203	Bits, carpenter's	100 kilogs	1. 56	1. 80	See Steel manuf's ..	Kilogramme . 0. 162
204	Bitumen	Free	......	......	100 kilogs.... 0. 05	Free ....
205	Blacking	100 kilogs	0. 97	0. 39	100 kilogs.... 1. 50	Kilogramme . 0. 081
206	Black, lamp	100 kilogs	0. 97	0. 78	100 kilogs.... 1. 50	20 per cent.........
207	lead, pots	100 kilogs	0. 97	0. 78	100 kilogs.... 1. 50	Kilogramme . 0. 054
208	lead, powder.......	100 kilogs	0. 97	0. 39	100 kilogs.... 1. 50	Kilogramme .0. 0027
209	Blacksmith's hammers	100 kilogs	1. 56	1. 80	See Iron and steel manufactures.	Kilogramme . 0. 081
210	sledges	100 kilogs	1. 56	1. 80	See Iron and steel manufactures.	Kilogramme . 0. 081
211	Bladders	Free	......	......	100 kilogs.... 1. 50	5 per cent..........
212	manufactures of ..	10 per cent	......	......	20 per cent.........	Kilogramme . 0. 40
213	Blankets, value not over 40 cents per pound.	Kilogramme.....	0. 27	......	Blankets .... Cashmere, kilog 0.81	Covers, cashmere or other hair, kilog, 0. 81.
214	Blankets, value 40 to 60 cts. per pound.	See Woolen manufactures.	......	......	Wool...............	
215	Blankets, value 60 to 80 cts. per pound.		......	......	Kilogramme . 0. 45	
216	Blankets, value over 80 cts. per pound.	....			....	
217	Bleaching powders	Free	......	......	100 kilogs.... 1. 50	20 per cent.........
218	Blue, Prussian	100 kilogs	1. 95	Free.	100 kilogs.... 5. 00	Free ....
219	vitriol	100 kilogs	0. 39	0. 39	100 kilogs.... 5. 00	Kilogramme . 0. 054
220	Blue gall	Free	......	......	100 kilogs.... 0. 30	Free ....
221	Blooms, iron	See Iron	......	......	Iron...............	See Iron in bars....
222	Boards, planed	Free	......	......	100 kilogs.... 0. 50	See Wood ....
223	rough	Free			100 kilogs.... 0. 50	See wood..........
224	Bobbin	....	......	......	See Machinery	Kilog......... 0. 002
225	wire-covered cotton.	100 kilogs	3. 90	4. 50	See Machinery	Kilog......... 0. 324
226	Bocking, all	See Manufac's of flax.	......	......	See Manufactures of flax.	See Manufactures of flax.
227	Bodkins, gold	Hectog	1. 95	5 p'r cent	See Gold manuf ...	Kilogramme 54. 00
228	silver	Kilog	2. 34		See Silver manuf...	Kilogramme 32. 80
229	steel	100 kilogs	3. 90	4. 50	100 kilogs.... 5. 50	Kilogramme 0. 162
230	other	....	......	......	100 kilogs.... 4. 50	Kilogramme. 0. 081
231	Boiler plates	See Iron in plates	......	......	100 kilogs.... 1. 80	Kilogramme. 0. 003
232	Bologna sausages	See Meat	......	......	100 kilogs.... 1. 00	Kilogramme. 0. 081
233	Bolting cloths	See Linen	......	......	See Linen	Free ....
234	Bolts, composition	100 kilogs	2. 93	3. 38	100 kilogs.... 4. 00	Kilogramme. 0. 27
235	Boltrope, as cordage, tarred.		0. 58	0. 58	100 kilogs.... 4. 00	Kilogramme. 0. 054
236	not manilla		0. 58	0. 58	20 per cent.......	Kilogramme. 0. 072
237	Bone, black		0. 97	0. 39		Bone, raw, dust, or burnt white, free. Manufac's of, per kilog, $3. 24. Bone, black, per kilog, $0. 01.
238	alphabets		9. 75	9. 75		
239	chessmen		9. 75	9. 75		
240	whale, rosettes		9. 75	9. 75		
241	tip and bones........		9. 75	9. 75		
242	whale		Free .	Free .		
243	manuf. of whalebone, not Amer. fisheries.		11. 70	......		
244	all other manuf......		9. 75	9. 75		
245	Bonnets, Leghorn..........	Bonnetry of cotton ...		......	Bonnets, straw, per kilog., $3. 00.	See under hats...
246	chip, grass, straw .	....	......	......		
247	silk	100 kilogs	As tissues.		Others, each..$0.20	

(*Duties expressed in gold dollars of the United States.*)—Continued.

BELGIUM.	AUSTRIA.			DENMARK.	SWEDEN.	NORWAY.	
		General tariff.	Tariff in treaty.				
10 per cent	See Manufactures of wool, cotton, &c., &c.	......	......	Pound.....$0.068	See Manuf. of wool, cotton, silks, leather, linen, &c.	See Manufactures of wool, cotton, silk, leather, &c.	192
10 per cent		......	......	Pound..... 0.068			193
10 per cent		......	......	Pound..... 0.41			194
10 per cent		......	......	Pound..... 0.091			195
10 per cent		......	......	Pound..... 0.068			196
5 per cent		......	......	Pound..... 0.068			197
10 per cent	See Manfac's of flax.	......	......	Pound..... 0.068	See Manufactures of flax.	See Manufactures of flax.	198
Free	Free		......	Free	Free	Free	199
Free	Free	......	......	Free	Free	Free	200
Free	Centner	$2.40	......	Pound.....0.0113	Free	See Chemicals	201
Free	Centner	2.52	$1.44	Free	Free	Free	202
100 kilogs ..$0.78	See Manuf. of steel.	......	......	Pound..... 0.017	See Manufactures of iron and steel.	Pound $0.048	203
Free	Free	......	......	Free	Free	Free	204
Free	Centner	0.36	......	Free	Free	Free	205
Free	Centner	0.36	......	Free	Pound.....$0.008	Free	206
Free	Centner	0.36	......	Pound..... 0.005	Free	Free	207
Free	Centner	0.36	......	Free	Centner .. 0.2067	Free	208
100 kilogs .. 0.78	See Hammers	......	......	Pound.....0.0014	Centner .. 0.2067	Free	209
100 kilogs .. 0.78	See Hammers	......	......	Pound..... 0.005	Free	Free	210
Free	Free	......	......	Free	10 per cent	10 per cent	211
10 per cent	Centner	2.04	1.44	10 per cent	......	......	212
10 per cent	See Manufactures of wool.	......	......	Pound..... 0.182	See Manufac's of wool.	See Manufac's of wool.	213
10 per cent		......	......	Pound..... 0.182			214
10 per cent		......	......	Pound..... 0.182			215
......		......	......	Pound..... 0.182			216
Free	.. ..	......	......	Free	Free	Free	217
Free	Centner	0.36	Free.	Pound.....0.0113	Free	Free	218
Free	Centner	0.388	......	Free	Free	Free	219
Free	Free	......	......	Free	Free	Free	220
Free	See Iron	......	......	Free	Free	Free	221
5 per cent	Free	......	......	Cubic foot . 0.034	Free	Free	222
5 per cent	Free	......	......	Cubic foot . 0.034	Free	Free	223
100 kilogs .. 0.78	See Machin'y.	......	......	Pound.... 0.017	See Machinery	See Machinery	224
100 kilogs .. 0.195	See Wire	......	......	Pound.... 0.0014	Copper, lb. 0.27	Copper wire, free.	225
See Manufactures of flax.	See Manuf. of flax & wool.	......	......	Pound.... 0.182	See Manufactures of flax.	Wire-w'k, lb. 0.047 See Man. of flax.	226
10 per cent	See Gold	......	......	Pound.... 0.091	Ort....... 0.0138	Loth 0.03	227
	See Silver	......	......	Pound.... 0.091	Ort....... 0.0082	Loth 0.03	228
	See Steel	......	......	Pound.... 0.017	See Man. of steel.	Pound ... 0.048	229
	See Copper	......	......	Pound.... 0.091	See Man. of steel.	Pound ... 0.048	230
100 kilogs .. 0.78	See Iron	......	......	Pound.... 0.0014	Free	Free	231
100 kilogs .. 0.23	Centner	3.88	......	Free	Pound.... 0.0275	Pound ... 0.009	232
See Tissues of flax.	See Tissues	......	......	See Tissues	See Tissues of flax.	See Tissues of flax	233
10 per cent	Centner	3.60	2.16	Pound.... 0.091	As copper	Pound ... 0.047	234
Cordage, diameter 2 mill. or more, free.	Centner	0.48	0.36	Pound.... 0.0056	Pound.... 0.0082	Free	235
Other as thread	Centner	0.48	0.36	Pound.... 0.0056	Pound.... 0.0082	Pound ... 0.039	236
Free	Manufac. of bone, centner	0.36	......	Free	Centner .. 0.2067	Free	237
10 per cent				Pound.... 0.091	10 per cent	10 per cent	238
10 per cent				Pound.... 0.091	10 per cent	10 per cent	239
10 per cent				Pound.... 0.091	10 per cent	10 per cent	240
Free				Free	Free	Free	241
Free		7.20	5.76	Free	Free	Free	242
10 per cent							243
				Pound.... 0.091	Pound.... 0.0689	10 per cent	244
10 per cent	Centner	7.20	5.76	Pound.... 0.091	Pound.... 0.0689	Pound ... 0.05	245
10 per cent	Untrimmed, centner			Each 0.364	Each 0.41	Each..... 0.409	246
10 per cent		4.80	......	Each 0.226	Each 0.41	Each..... 0.409	247

Comparative table of import duties in the United States and European countries.

	ARTICLES.	UNITED STATES.	GREAT BRITAIN.	GERMAN ZOLL-VEREIN.	SWITZERLAND.
248	Bonnets, fur, leather	35 per cent	Free		
249	Bonnet wire, covered with silk or cotton.	As Wire			
250	Bookbinders' agates, ferrule.	20 per cent	Free	Centner . . $5.76	Centner . . $0.68
251	Books, blank, bound or unbound.	25 per cent	Free	Centner . . 0.96	Centner . . 0.68
252	Books, periodicals, &c., in course of printing in the United States.	25 per cent	Prohibited—all printed books whereof the copyright subsists in the United Kingdom.	All books unbound, free. Bound, per centn'r, $0.96.	All, per centner, $0.097.
253	Books, printed magazines, pamphlets, periodicals, and illustrated newspapers, not otherwise enumerated.	25 per cent		Free	
254	Books of engravings	25 per cent		Free	
255	Books, instruments, professional, of persons arriving in the United States.	Free			
256	Books specially imported for the use of schools or Congressional Library.	Free			
257	Boots, laced, silk or satin, for children.	35 per cent	Free	Centner . . 7.20	Centner . . 1.56
258	Boots and bootees of leather.	35 per cent	Free	Centner . . 7.20	Centner . . 1.56
259	rubber	35 per cent	Free	Centner . . 7.20	Centner . . 1.56
260	Bootees for women, silk	35 per cent	Free	Centner . . 7.20	Centner . . 1.56
261	Boot web linen	35 per cent	Free	See Linen	Centner . . 1.56
262	Borate of lime	Pound $0.05	Free	Free	Centner . . 0.68
263	Borax, or tincal, crude	Pound 0.05	Free	Free	Centner . . 0.68
264	refined	Pound 0.10	Free	Free	Centner . . 0.68
265	Botany, specimens in	Free	Free	Free	Free
266	Bottles, apothecaries'	35 per cent	Free	Free	Centner . . 0.68
267	black glass	35 per cent	Free	Free	Centner . . 0.68
268	perfum'y and fancy.	40 per cent	Free	Free	Centner . . 0.68
269	containing wine, &c.	Each 0.02	Free	Free	Free
270	Boucho leaves	Pound 0.10	Free	Centner . . 0.18	Centner . . 0.68
271	Bougies	35 per cent	Free	Centner . . 1.44	Centner . . 0.68
272	Boxes, gold	40 per cent	Free	Centner . . 36.00	Centner . . 2.93
273	silver	40 per cent	Free	Centner . . 36.00	Centner . . 2.93
274	musical	30 per cent	Free	Centner. 10.80	Centner . . 1.56
275	japanned dressing	40 per cent	Free		Centner . . 2.93
276	cedar, granadilla		Free		
277	ebony, rose, and satin.	35 per cent	Free		Centner . . 1.56
278	all other wood	35 per cent	Free	Centner . . . 10.80	Centner . . 1.56
279	sand, of tin	35 per cent	Free	Centner . . . 2.88	Centner . . 1.56
280	shell, not otherwise enumerated.	35 per cent	Free	Centner . . 10.80	Centner . . 2.93
281	paper only, not japanned.	35 per cent	Free	Centner . . 2.88	Centner . . 1.56
282	snuff, paper, fancy	35 per cent	Free	Centner . . 10.80	Centner . . 2.93
283	Brace bits	45 per cent	Free	Centner . . 1.92	Centner . . 0.68
284	Bracelets, gold or set	25 per cent	Free	Centner . . 36.00	Centner . . 2.93
285	gilt	25 per cent	Free	Centner . . 10.80	Centner . . 2.93
286	hair	35 per cent	Free	Centner . . 10.80	Centner . . 1.56
287	Braces, carpenters, without bits.	35 per cent	Free	Centner . . 1.92	Centner . . 0.68
288	with bits	40 per cent	Free		
289	or suspenders, all	35 per cent	Free	Ordinary—Centner . 2.88 Fancy leather—Centner . 7.20	Centner . . 0.68

(*Duties expressed in gold dollars of the United States.*)—Continued.

	FRANCE.				RUSSIA.	NETHERLANDS.	
	General tariff.		In treaty with Great Britain, &c				
	In French vessels.	In other vessels.	In vessels of treaty powers.	In other vessels.			
....	....	....	10 per	cent.	....	5 per cent	248
See Wire	....	....	....	....	Pood........$1.16	5 per cent	249
....	Free ..	Free ..	Free ..	Free ..	....	Free	250
					Blank, per pood. 8.50		251
Books, per 100 kilogs, in dead or foreign languages:					Printed, bound or unbound, free.	Free	252
Almanacs .... Other .... In French, printed in Canada.	Free .	$0.048	Free ..	$0.048			253
In Fr'nch, scientific memoirs.	9.75	10.72	Free ..	0.048			
In French, others, publish'd in for'gn countries.	19.50	20.95	Free ..	0.048			254 255
Reprint'd from French edition.	29.25	31.20	Free ..	0.048			
Printed in France	Free ..	Free ..	Free ..	Free ..			256
Counterfeits........	Prohi	bited.					
....	Prohi	bited.	10 per	cent.	Pound 0.85	5 per cent	257
....					Pound 0.85	5 per cent	258
....					Pood........ 2.57	5 per cent	259
....					Pood........ 2.57	5 per cent	260
See Linen	....	....	....	....	See Linen	5 per cent	261
....	5 per	cent.	5 per	cent.	Free	Free	262
Raw, native, per 100 kilogs.	Free ..	0.97	Free ..	0.048	Pood........ 0.85	Free	263
Raw, artificial, per 100 kilogs.	9.70	10.17	....	....	Pood........ 0.85	Free	264
Part refined, per 100 kilogs.	12.67	13.65	....	....	....	....	
Refined, per 100 kilogs.	35.10	37.25	....	....	....	....	
....	Free ..	Free ..	Free ..	Free ..	Free	Free	265
Liter they contain........	Prohi	bited.	0.25	0.29	Pood........ 0.39	5 per cent	266
....	Prohi	bited.	10 per	cent.	Pood........ 0.39	5 per cent	267
....	....	....	....	....	Pood........ 0.39	5 per cent	268
Liter they contain........	0.029	0.029	....	....	Free	5 per cent	269
....	Free ..	Free ..	Free ..	Free ..	Free	Free	270
....	5 per	cent.	5 per	cent.	Pood........ 0.85	5 per cent	271
					Pound 25.74		272
Fancy articles, not of wood, horn, bone, ivory, &c.	Prohi	bited.	10 per	cent.	Pound 1.72		273
					Pound 0.85		274
							275
							276
							277
....	....	....	10 per	cent.	Pound 0.85	5 per cent	278
....	....	....	10 per	cent.	Pood........ 1.95	5 per cent	279
....	....	....	10 per	cent.	Pound 0.85	5 per cent	280
....	....	....	10 per	cent.	....	5 per cent	281
....	....	....	10 per	cent.	Pound 0.85	5 per cent	282
Articles of steel n. e....	Prohi	bited.	3.90	4.29	See Manuf. of steel.	5 per cent	283
100 kilogs........	97.50	100.90	97.50	100.90	Pound 25.74	5 per cent	284
Fancy articles........	....	....	....	....	Pound 0.85	5 per cent	285
100 kilogs........	Prohi	bited.	10 per	cent.	Pound 0.85	5 per cent	286
100 kilogs........	34.12	36.30	3.90	4.29	See Manuf. iron and steel.	5 per cent	287
....					....	....	288
Articles of clothing.....	30 per	cent.			Pound 0.31	5 per cent	289

Notes on the layout: on the printed page, a brace links the 5 per cent in the Netherlands column for rows 271–277. Row 273 holds the 5 per cent. Another brace groups the Free entries in the Netherlands column for rows 252–256.

Comparative table of import duties in the United States and European countries.

No.	ARTICLES.	ITALY.	ITALY. General tariff.	ITALY. Tariff in treaty with France, &c.	SPAIN.	PORTUGAL.
248	Bonnets, fur, leather.......	Trimmed, each ..	$0.78	......	Fin. by hand, ea 1.50	See under hats ....
249	Bonnet wire, covered with silk or cotton.	100 kilogs	3.90	$4.50	See Wire	Kilog $0.324
250	Bookbinders' agates, ferrule.	Free	......	......	100 kilogs....$0.30	....
251	Books, blank, bound or unbound.					Books, blank, per kilog, $0.162. Books in Portuguese, by authors living in P'rtug'l, per kilog, $0.108. Repr'ed from Portuguese editions, and in Portug'se language, if not 20 y'rs since last edition, per kil., $0.108. Bound, p'r. k. $0.054 In for'gn lan., free. In Portuguese, by authors in for'gn countries, free.
252	Books, periodicals, &c., in course of printing in the United States.					
253	Books, printed magazines, pamphlets, periodicals, and illustrated newspapers, not otherwise enumerated.	Books, Italian and other, per 100 kilogs .... Bound in leath. Bound in silk.	2.93 2.93	Free. 0.195	Books in Spanish, bound or not, 100 kilogs.....$8.00 Books in foreign languages, per 100 kilogs, $2.00. Prints, maps, designs, per kilog, $0.25.	
254	Books of engravings.......	Gilded, per kil.	0.19	0.195		
255	Books, instruments, professional, of persons arriving in the United States.					
256	Books specially imported for the use of schools or Congressional Library.					
257	Boots, laced, silk or satin, for children.	Pair	0.097	Per 100 k., $9.75.	Boots and shoes, per kilog, $1.75.	Pair......... 0.864
258	Boots and bootees of leather.	Pair	0.097			Pair......... 0.864
259	rubber	Pair	0.097			Kilog........ 0.027
260	Bootees for women. silk....	Pair	0.097			Pair......... 0.864
261	Boot web linen	See Linen	......	......	See Manuf. of Flax.	See Manuf. of flax.
262	Borate of lime.............	100 kilogs	1.95	Free.	See Chemicals n. e..	See Chemicals n. e..
263	Borax, or tineal, crude.....	100 kilogs........	1.95	Free.	100 kilogs.... 0.30	Free ....
264	refined ...	....	......	......	100 kilogs.... 0.30	Free ....
265	Botany, specimens in	....	Free.	Free.	Free	....
266	Bottles, apothecaries'.......	....	......	......	See Glass manuf..	Kilog........ 0.005
267	black glass	100	0.29	0.39		Kilog........ 0.005
268	perfum'y and fancy.	100 kilogs	1.56	0.39		Kilog........ 0.172
269	containing wine, &c.	....	......	......		Kilog........ 0.005
270	Buchu leaves	100 kilogs	0.97	0.39	100 kilogs.... 2.00	Per cent ....
271	Bougies	100 kilogs	0.97	0.97	20 per cent.........	Kilog........ 0.054
272	Boxes, gold................	Hectogramme ...	1.95	5 per c't.	Jewelry of gold and silver, per kilog, $11.00.	See Gold and silver, each, $0.248.
273	silver	Kilog	2.34		Other jewelry, per kilog, $2.00.	
274	musical	Each............	0.39	0.67		
275	japanned, dressing..	100 kilogs	19.50	19.50		Kilog........ 0.40
276	cedar, granadilla ...	100 kilogs	19.50	19.50		
277	ebony, rose, and satin.	....	......	......		35 per cent ....
278	all other wood......	100 kilogs	6.75	9.75	20 per cent	Kilog...... 0.0216
279	sand, of tin.........	100 kilogs	9.75	9.75	20 per cent	Kilog...... 0.0756
280	shell, not otherwise enumerated.	100 kilogs	9.75	9.75	20 per cent	35 per cent.........
281	paper only, not japanned.	....	......	......	20 per cent	Kilog........ 0.40
282	snuff, paper, fancy..	100 kilogs	9.75	9.75	20 per cent	Kilog........ 0.40
283	Brace bits	100 kilogs	1.56	1.80	100 kilogs.... 5.50	Kilog........ 0.162
284	Bracelets, gold or set.......	Hectolitre	1.95	5 per cent	Kilog 4.00	See Gold ....
285	gilt	Kilog	4.68		Kilog 4.00	See Jewelry ....
286	hair	100 kilogs	7.80		Kilog 2.00	Kilogs 5.40
287	Braces, carpenters, without bits.	100 kilogs	1.56	1.00	100 kilogs.... 5.50	Kilogs 0.162
288	with bits.	....	......	......	....	....
289	Braces, or suspenders, all ..	100 kilogs	10 per	cent.	20 per cent.........	Kilogs 0.40

(*Duties expressed in gold dollars of the United States.*)—Continued.

BELGIUM.	AUSTRIA.			DENMARK.	SWEDEN.	NORWAY.	
		General tariff.	Tariff in treaty.				
10 per cent	Fancy, centn .	$12600	......	Pound....$0.091	Each $0.41	Each.....$0.409	248
100 kilogs .. 0.195	See Wire....	......	......	Pound.... 0.0014	As Wire.........	See Wire........	249
Free	Free	Free .	......	Free	Free	Free	250
Typographical products, free.	Books, scientific charts, and music, centner ... Pictures on paper, from lithographs in copper, wood, or stone, photographs, c. Paintings on wood, metal or canvas; orig'l drawings; plates for printing pictures, c.	1.512 3.88 0.388	Free . Free . Free .	All books, free.	Books in foreign languages and in Swedish, present'd to the Swedish Bible Society; books printed in London and reimported, free. Books in Swedish, printed in foreign countries, not presents to Bible Soc'ty, pound, $0.041. Bound, lb. $0.049 Albums, lb $0.049	Books & Bibles in Norwegian or Danish, not imp'ted for the Bible Society; authorized hymn-books; religious text-books; laws of Norway and collections of laws publish'd for account of Norw'g'n publishers, pound, $0.045. All others, free.	251 252 253 254 255 256
10 per cent	Centner	12.00	7.20	Pound.... 0.273	Pound.... 0.2756	Pound ... 0.318	257
10 per cent	Centner	5.76	3.60	Pound.... 0.182	Pound.... 0.165	Pound ... 0.196	258
10 per cent	Centner	12.00	......	Pound.... 0.091	Pound.... 0.11	Pound ... 0.127	259
10 per cent	Centner	12.00	7.20	Pound.... 0.273	Pound.... 0.2756	Pound ... 0.218	260
See Manuf. of flax.	See Manuf. of	Flax .	......	Pound.... 0.034	See Manf. of Flax.	See Man. of Flax.	261
Free	See Chemicals	n. e...	......	Pound.... 0.0113	Free	Free	262
Free	Free	Free .	Free .	Free	Free	Free	263
Free	Centner	0.72	0.72	Free	Free	Free	264
Free	Free	Free .	Free .	Free	Free	Free	265
100 kilogs .. 0.195	Centner	0.36	0.36	Pound.... 0.008	Centner .. 0.21	Free	266
100 kilogs .. 0.195	Centner	0.36	0.36	Pound.... 0.008	Centner .. 0.21	Free	267
100 kilogs .. 0.195	White, cent'r.	1.08	0.72	Pound.... 0.008	Free	Free	268
100 kilogs .. 0.195	....	......	......	Pound.... 0.008	Free	Free	269
Free	Free	Free .	Free .	Free	Free	Free	270
10 per cent	Centner	3.84	......	Pound.... 0.034	Pound.... 0.01	Pound .. 0.018	271
	See gold.....	......	......	See Gold........	See Gold	See Gold........	272
	See silver....	......	......	See Silver	See Silver	See Silver.......	
	Centner	4.80	3.60	10 per cent	Pound.... 0.138	Pound ... 0.095	
10 per cent				Pound.... 0.091	10 per cent	10 per cent	273
							274
							275
	Jewelry, not gold, centner	48.00	......	Pound.... 0.091	10 per cent	10 per cent	276
							277
	Fancy, centn'r	5.76	......	Common, free....	Pound ... 0.0138	Pound 0.03	278
	Fancy, centn'r	7.20	5.76	Centner... 0.045	See Tines manuf.	Pound 0.047	279
	Fancy, centn'r	2.88	......	10 per cent.......	10 per cent	10 per cent	280
	Fancy, centn'r	6.00	5.76	....	Pound.... 0.0689	Pound 0.82	281
	Centner	6.00	5.76	Pound..... 0.091	10 per cent	10 per cent	282
100 kilogs.. 0.78	See Articles of steel.			Pound..... 0.017	See Steel and Iron	Pound 0.048	283
	See Gold manufactured.			See Gold	See Gold	See Gold	284
10 per cent	Centner	48.00	......	See Silver........	Pound.... 0.0964	Pound 0.109	285
	See Jewelry .	......	......	Pound..... 1.09	Pound.... 0.0964	Pound 0.109	286
100 kilogs.. 0.78	See Articles of steel.	......	......	Pound..... 0.017	See Iron and Steel	Pound 0.027	287
....	....	......	......	Pound..... 0.017	Pound.... 0.017	Pound 0.027	288
10 per cent.......	See Articles of steel.	......	......	10 per cent.......	10 per cent.......	10 per cent	289

Comparative table of import duties in the United States and European countries.

	ARTICLES.	UNITED STATES.	GREAT BRITAIN.	GERMAN ZOLL-VEREIN.	SWITZERLAND.
290	Brackets	35 per cent	Free	Centner . $11. 60	Centner . . $1. 56
291	Brads, cut, not over 16 oz. per M.	Mille $0. 02½	Free	Centner . . 1. 92	Centner . . 0. 68
292	cut, exceeding 16 oz. to the M.	Pound 0. 03	Free	Centner . . 1. 92	Centner . . 0. 68
293	Braids, cotton	35 per cent	Free	Centner . . 10. 80	Centner . . 1. 56
294	in ornaments, for head dresses.	35 per cent	Free	Centner . . 10 80	Centner . . 1. 56
295	hair, made up, for head dresses.	35 per cent	Free	Centner . . 10 80	Centner . . 2. 93
296	straw, for making bonnets	30 per cent	Free	....	Centner . . 1. 56
297	Brandy	Gal. proof . 3. 00	Imp. proof gallon $2. 53	Centner . . 4. 32	Centner . . 1. 56
298	all imitations of, under 50°.	As brandy 4. 20		....	....
299	value over $6 per gallon.	50 per cent	Imp. proof gallon 2. 53	Centner . . 4. 32	Centner . . 1. 56
300	Brass, manufactures of, not otherwise enumerated.	35 per cent	Free	Centner . . 1. 92	All manuf's of— Centner . 1. 56
301	in plates or sheets	35 per cent	Free	Centner . . 1. 26	Centner . . 0. 145
302	in bars, bigs, old, for remanufacture.	15 per cent	Free	Free	Centner . . 0.145
303	wire, rolled, battery, studs.	35 per cent	Free	Centner . . 1. 26	Centner . . 0. 29
	(If copper chief value 45 p. c.)				
304	screws	35 per cent	....	Centner . . 1. 26	Centner . . 1. 56
305	Brazier's rods, of 3-16 to 10-16-inch diameter.	35 per cent	Free	Centner . . 1. 26	Centner . . 1. 56
306	Brazil paste, (pasta de Brazil.)	10 per cent	Free	Free	Centner . . 0. 68
307	pebble	5 per cent	Free	Free	Centner . . 0. 145
308	pebbles prepared for spectacles.	40 per cent	Free	Free	Centner . . 0. 68
309	Breccia	Free	Free	Free	Centner . . 0. 145
310	Bricks, fire or roofing	20 per cent	Free	Free	15 centner. 0. 12
311	Bridles	35 per cent	Free	Centner . . 2. 88	Centner . . 1. 56
312	Brimstone, crude	Ton 6. 00	Free	Free	Centner . . 0. 145
313	rolled	Ton 10. 00	Free	Free	Centner . . 0. 145
314	Brime	Free	Free	Free	Centner . . 0. 145
315	Bristles	Pound 0. 15	Free	Centner . . 0. 36	Centner . . 0. 58
316	Bristol stones	10 per cent	Free	Free	Centner . . 0. 097
317	boards	35 per cent	Free	Free	Centner . . 0. 058
318	perforated	35 per cent	Free	Free	Centner . . 0. 058
319	Britannia ware	35 per cent	Free	Centner . . 2. 88	Centner . . 1. 56
320	Brodequins, woolen and leather.	35 per cent	Free	Centner . . 7. 20	Centner . . 1. 56
321	Bronze, casts	35 per cent	Free	Centner . . 1. 92	Centner . . 1. 56
322	all manufactures of.	35 per cent	Free	Centner . . 1. 92	Centner . . 1. 56
323	metal in leaf	10 per cent	Free	Centner . . 1. 26	Centner . . 1. 56
324	powder	20 per cent	Free	Centner . . 0. 72	Centner . . 0. 145
325	pale, yellow, white, and red.	20 per cent	Free	Centner . . 2. 40	Centner . . 0. 68
326	liquid, gold and bronze color	10 per cent	Free	Centner . . 2. 40	Centner . . 0. 145
327	Brooms, all kinds	35 per cent	Free	Wood, free ...... Others— Centner . 0. 36	15 centner. 0. 12 ....
328	Brown, rolls linen	See Linen	Free	Centner . . 0. 36	Centner . . 1. 56
329	Spanish, dry	25 per cent	Free	Centner . . 2. 40	Centner . . 0. 66
330	in oil	25 per cent	Free	Centner . . 2. 40	Centner . . 0. 68
331	smalts	20 per cent	Free	Centner . . 2. 40	Centner . . 0. 68
332	Brucine	40 per cent	Free	....	Centner . . 0. 68
333	Brushes, of all kinds	40 per cent	Free	Ordinary— Centner . . 1. 44 Fancy— Centner . . 2. 88	Centner . . 1. 56 ....

(*Duties expressed in gold dollars of the United States.*)—Continued.

FRANCE.					RUSSIA.	NETHERLANDS.	
	General tariff.		In treaty with Great Britain, &c.				
	In French vessels.	In other vessels.	In vessels of treaty powers.	In other vessels.			
100 kilogs..............	Prohi	bited.	$3.90	$4.29	Pood..........$0.234	5 per cent.........	290
100 kilogs..............	Prohi	bited.	3.90	4.29	Pood.......... 0.78	5 per cent.........	291
100 kilogs..............	Prohi	bited.	3.90	4.29	Pood.......... 0.78	5 per cent.........	292
....	Prohi	bited.	15 per	cent.	Pound 0.27	5 per cent.........	293
....	Prohi	bited.	15 per	cent.	Pound 0.27	5 per cent.........	294
....	Prohi	bited.	15 per	cent.	Pound 0.27	5 per cent.........	295
....	Prohi	bited.	15 per	cent.	Pound 0.27	5 per cent.........	296
....	....	....	....	....	Bottle......... 0.51	Hectolitre ... 1.43	297
} All	....	....	....	....	Liquors of grain in casks are prohibited.	50 per cent. 15 deg.	298
} Hectolitre	$4.87	$4.87	2.92	2.92	....	....	299
100 kilogs..............	19.50	20.95	3.90	4.29	Pood.......... 2.34	5 per cent.........	300
100 kilogs..............	2.92	3.40	....	....	Pood.......... 0.48	100 kilogs ... 0.41	301
100 kilogs..............	Free ..	0.048	....	....	Pood.......... 0.48	100 kilogs ... 0.41	302
Wire for instruments, 100 kilogs. (Other prohibited.)	19.50	20.95	....	....	Wire, pood.... 2.34	100 kilogs ... 0.41	303
100 kilogs..............	....	....	3.90	4.29	Pood.......... 2.34	5 per cent.........	304
100 kilogs..............	19.50	20.95	3.90	4.29	Pood.......... 2.34	100 kilogs ... 0.41	305
....	....	....	....	....	Free	Free	306
100 kilogs..............	Free ..	0.195	....	....	Free	Free	307
....	....	....	....	....	Free	Free	308
....	....	....	....	....	Free	Free	309
Mille	0.78	0.78	Free ..	0.048	Free	Free	310
....	Prohi	bited.	10 per	cent.	Pound 0.31	5 per cent.........	311
100 kilogs..............	Free ..	0.195	Free ..	Free ..	Free	Free	312
100 kilogs..............	Free ..	0.195	Free ..	Free ..	Free	Free	313
100 kilogs..............	Free ..	0.195	Free ..	Free ..	Free	Free	314
....	Free ..	Free ..	Free ..	Free ..	Pood.......... 1.56	Free	315
100 kilogs..............	....	....	Free ..	0.048	Free	Free	316
100 kilogs..............	29.25	31.20	1.56	1.72	Pood.......... 0.16	Free	317
100 kilogs..............	29.25	31.20	1.56	1.72	Pood.......... 0.16	Free	318
100 kilogs..............	Prohi	bited.	3.90	4.29	Pood.......... 2.34	5 per cent.........	319
....	See wo	ol and	leather.		Leather, pound 0.31	5 per cent.........	320
Bronze manufactures...	....	....	....	....	Pood.......... 9.25	5 per cent.........	321
100 kilogs..............	39.00	41.43	3.90	4.29	Pood.......... 9.25	5 per cent.........	322
100 kilogs..............	2.92	3.40	....	....	Pood.......... 0.47	100 kilogs ... 0.41	323
100 kilogs..............	Free ..	0.048	Free ..	0.048	Free	Free	324
....	Free ..	Free ..	Free ..	Free ..	Pood.......... 0.85	Free	325
....	Free ..	Free ..	Free ..	Free ..	....	Free	326
....	....	....	10 per	cent.	Pood.......... 0.19	Free	327
....	See Ma	nufactu	res of Fl	ax.	See Linen....... ...	5 per cent.........	328
....	Free ..	Free ..	Free ..	Free ..	Pood.......... 0.85	Free	329
....	Free ..	Free ..	Free ..	Free ..	Pood.......... 0.85	Free	330
....	....	....	....	....	....	Free	331
100 kilogs..............	Free ..	0.048	Free ..	0.048	Pood.......... 0.85	Free	332
....	....	....	10 per	cent.	Pood.......... 1.56	5 per cent.........	333
....	....	....	....	....	....	....	

Comparative table of import duties in the United States and European countries.

No.	ARTICLES.	ITALY.			SPAIN.	PORTUGAL.
			General tariff.	Tariff in treaty with France, &c.		
290	Brackets	100 kilogs	$1.56	$1.80	20 per cent	Kilogs ... $0.162
291	Brads, cut, not over 16 oz. per M.	100 kilogs	3.90	4.50	100 kilogs . $25.00	Kilogs ... 0.081
292	cut, exceeding 16 oz. to the M.	100 kilogs	3.90	4.50	...	Kilogs ... 0.081
293	Braids, cotton	See cotton	...	...	Kilog ... 0.90	
294	in ornaments, for head dresses.	See cotton	...	...	Kilog ... 0.90	See Cotton ...
295	hair, made up for head dresses.	100 kilogs	7.80	7.80	20 per cent	Double duties of material, kil. 5.40
296	straw, for making bonnets.	100 kilogs	2.93	0.975	20 per cent	Kilog ... 0.216
297	Brandy	Of 22°, or less, per hectolitre.	9.97	1.07	Hectoliter .. 3.75	33 degrees decaliter ... 1.188 Over 33 degrees decaliter . 1.62
298	all imitations of, under 50°.	Over 22°, per hectolitre.	1.95	1.95		
299	value over $6 per gallon.	Compound	11.70	2.93		
300	Brass, manufactures of, not otherwise enumerated.	See Manufactures of copper. As copper.	...	...		Brass, in balls, free. Cast, per kil. 0.032 For manufacture, in basins, per kilog ... 0.027 Laminated, per kilog ... 0.027 Wire, per kil 0.054 Manufactures: See Copper.
301	in plates or sheets				In bars and plates, per 100 kil. 0.25 Wire, per 100 kilogs ... 5.00 All manufactures, per 100 kil. 25.00	
302	in bars, pigs, old, for remanufacture.					
303	wire, rolled, battery, studs.	100 kilogs	2.34	2.34		
304	screws	See Copper	...	...		
305	Brazier's rods, of 3-16 to 10-16-inch diameter.		...	...	...	...
306	Brazil paste, (pasta de Brazil.)	100 kilogs	0.39	0.39	20 per cent	5 per cent
307	pebble	...	Free	Free	100 kilogs ... 0.01	Free
308	pebbles, prepared for spectacles.	100 kilogs	9.75	9.75	100 kilogs ... 16.00	...
309	Breccia	...	Free	Free	Free	Free
310	Bricks, fire or roofing	Per 1,000	0.39	Free	100 kilogs ... 0.30	Kilog ... 0.01
311	Bridles	100 kilogs	9.75	9.75	20 per cent	Kilog ... 1.08
312	Brimstone, crude	...	Free	Free	100 kilogs ... 0.25	Free
313	rolled	...	Free	Free	100 kilogs ... 0.25	Free
314	Brime	100 kilogs	1.95	Free	100 kilogs ... 0.01	Free
315	Bristles	100 kilogs	0.195	0.195	100 kilogs ... 0.01	Raw or prepared, per kil ... 0.022
316	Bristol stones	...	Free	Free	100 kilogs ... 0.01	Free
317	boards	100 kilogs	1.56	1.56	100 kilogs ... 8.00	...
318	perforated	100 kilogs	1.56	1.56	100 kilogs ... 8.00	...
319	Britannia ware	100 kilogs	19.50	19.50	100 kilogs ... 7.50	Kilogs ... 0.27
320	Brodequins, woolen and leather.	See Manufactures wool and leather.	...	...	20 per cent	...
321	Bronze, casts	Bronze, in pieces or bars, per 100 kilogs.	0.78	0.78	Bronze, unmanufactured, per 100 kilogs ... 2.00 Manufacturers of, per 100 kil. 25.00	
322	all manufactures of.					
323	metal in leaf					
324	powder	Bronze statues, per 100 kil.	9.75	Free		See Copper and its manufactures.
325	pale, yellow, white, and red.					
326	liquid, gold, and bronze color.	Manufactures, per 100 kilogs.	9.75	9.75		Free
327	Brooms, all kinds	100 kilogs	0.195	Free	100 kilogs ... 3.50	Common, free ... Others, 10 per cent.
328	Brown, rolls linen	See Linen	...	...	See Manuf. of flax	See Manuf. of flax
329	Spanish, dry	100 kilogs	1.95	0.78	100 kilogs ... 1.50	5 per cent
330	in oil	100 kilogs	1.95	0.78	100 kilogs ... 5.00	5 per cent
331	smalts	100 kilogs	0.195	0.195	100 kilogs ... 0.30	Kilogs ... 0.059
332	Brucine	100 kilogs	1.95	0.39	100 kilogs ... 2.00	5 per cent
333	Brushes, of all kinds	100 kilogs	9.75	9.75	Kilogs ... 0.40	Kilogs ... 1.08

(*Duties expressed in gold dollars of the United States.*)—Continued.

BELGIUM.	AUSTRIA.			DENMARK.	SWEDEN.	NORWAY.	
		General tariff.	Tariff in treaty.				
10 per cent.				Pound.....$0.017	10 per cent.	10 per cent	290
100 kilogs.. 0.78				Pound..... 0.017	See Iron man. not enumerated.	Free	291
100 kilogs.. 0.78				Pound..... 0.017	....	Free	292
	See Material	manuf	act'd.				
10 per cent				Pound..... 0.091	See Cotton	See Cotton	293
				10 per cent.	10 per cent.	10 per cent	294
				Pound..... 1.09	10 per cent.	10 per cent	295
	Centner	$1.20	$0.72	Pound..... 0.136	Pound.....$0.11	Pound $0.127	296
50° or less, per hec., 8.29, and for every deg. over 50°, 0.17. See also Spirituous liquors.	Centner	3.88	......	In bottles— Pot 0.091	Of 50 per cent. alcohol, at 15° C. Kande ... 0.303	In bottles— Pot 0.218	297
	Centner	3.88	......	Other—		Other—	298
	Centner	3.88	......	Quarter .. 0.466		Pound ... 0.153	299
10 per cent.	Centner	3.60	2.16	Pound..... 0.091	Pound..... 0.041	Pound 0.047	300
100 kilogs.. 1.95	Centner	2.88	1.92	Pound..... 0.017	Free	Free	301
Free	Free	......	......	Free	Free	Free	302
100 kilogs.. 1.95	Centner	2.88	1.92	Pound..... 0.017	Pound.... 0.2756	Free	303
10 per cent.	Centner	3.60	2.16	Pound..... 0.091	Pound..... 0.041	Pound 0.047	
....	....	......	......	....	....	....	304
10 per cent.	Centner	2.88	1.92	Pound..... 0.091	Pound..... 0.041	Pound 0.47	305
Free	Centner	0.36	......	Free	Free	Free	306
Free	Free	......	......	Free	Free	Free	307
10 per cent	See Stone manufactured.	......	......	10 per cent.	Free	Free	308
Free	Free	......	......	Free	Free	Free	309
Free	Free	......	......	Free	Free	Free	310
Free	Centner	5.76	3.60	Pound..... 0.091	Pound.....0.055	Pound 0.082	311
Free	Free	......	......	Free	Free	Free	312
Free	Free	......	......	Free	Free	Free	313
Free	Free	......	......	Free	Free	Free	314
Free	Free	......	......	Free	Free	Free	315
Free	See Stone	......	......	Free	Free	Free	316
10 per cent.	See Paper	......	......	Pound.... 0.0028	Per c., free	Free	317
10 per cent.	See Paper	......	......	Pound.... 0.0028	Pound..... 0.02	Pound .... 0.(25	318
10 per cent.	Centner	3.60	2.16	Pound..... 0.091	Pound..... 0.082	Pound ... 0.095	319
10 per cent.	See Manuf. leather.	of wo	ol and	Pound..... 0.182	See Wool or leather.	See Material manufactured.	3.0
							321
							322
See Copper and its manufactures.	See Copper	......	......	As copper	Pound..... 0.041	Pound 0.047	323
	Powder	7.20	7.56	Pound..... 0.017	Pound..... 0.041	Pound 0.047	324
				Free	Free	Free	325
				Pound..... 0.003	Free	Free	
Free	....	......	......		Free	Free	326
					Free	Free	
Common, free.... Others, 10 per ct.	Centner	0.12	......	Pound..... 0.017	Common, free....	Free	327
See Man. of flax .	See Manufact	ures o	f flax.	Pound..... 0.034	See Man. of flax.	See Man. of flax.	328
Free	Centner	0.72	......	Pound.....0.0056	Free	Free	329
Free	Centner	0.72	......	Pound..... 0.028	Free	Free	330
Free	Free	......	......	Free	Free	Free	331
Free	Centner	2.52	1.44	Free	Free	Free	332
10 per cent.	Common—			Common—	Common—		333
	Centner ...	2.04	1.44	Pound .. 0.0228	Pound .. 0.0137	Pound 0.018	
	Fine—			Other—	Polished—		
	Centner .. .	7.20	5.76	Pound ... 0.11	Pound .. 0.0275	Pound 0.031	
					Fancy—		
					Pound . . 0.055	Pound ... 0.0636	

Comparative table of import duties in the United States and European countries.

	ARTICLES.	UNITED STATES.	GREAT BRITAIN.	GERMAN ZOLL-VEREIN.	SWITZERLAND.
334	Buckles, all	35 per cent	Free	Of steel—Centner. $1. 92; Other material—Centner. 2. 88; Gold or silver—Centner. 36. 00	Centner .$1. 56
335	of gold, or silver	40 per cent	Free		Centner . 2. 93
336	Bugles, glass, cut	40 per cent	Free	Centner . . 2 88	Centner . . 1. 56
337	not cut	35 per cent	Free	Centner . . 0. 48	Centner . . 0. 68
338	Building stones, not provided for.	20 per cent	Free	Free	15 centner . . 0. 027
339	Bulrushes	10 per cent	Free	Free	15 centner . . 0. 027
340	Bulbs or bulbous roots	30 per cent	Free	Free, or per centner 0 18	Centner....0. 145
341	Bullets	35 per cent	Free	Free	Centner....0. 145
342	Bullion	Free	Free	Free	Free
343	Bunting	35 per cent. and per sq. y'd. $0. 20	Free	Centner....0. 48	Centner....1. 56
344	Burgundy pitch	20 per cent	Free	Free	Centner 0. 145
345	Burlaps	See Linens, (Flax)	Free	See Man. of flax.	Centner....1. 56
346	Burr stones, unbound	Free	Free	Free	Centner....0. 03
347	bound up	20 per cent	Free	Free	Centner....0. 03
348	Burning fluid	Gallon.....0. 50	Free	Free	Centner....0. 097
349	Busts, lead	35 per cent	Free	See Manufactures of lead.	Centner....1, 56
350	Butchers' knives	35 per cent	Free	Centner....1. 92	Centner....1. 56
351	Butter	Pound.....0. 04	Free	Centner....2. 54	Centner....0. 097
352	Butt hinges, cast-iron	Pound.....0. 02½	Free	Centner....0. 96	Centner....0. 68
353	Button moulds, of whatever material.	30 per cent	Free	Centner....2. 88	Centner....0. 68
354	Buttons, metal, all kinds of.	30 per cent	Free	Gold and silver p'r centn'r 36.00	Centner....1. 56
355	all other (except silk.)	30 per cent	Free	Fancy, with gold or silver, per centner . 18. 00	Centner....1. 56
356	with links	30 per cent	Free	All others..2. 88	Centner....1. 56
357	Cabinet wares	35 per cent	Free	Centner....0. 72; Carved furniture p'r centn'r. 2. 88	Centner....1. 52
358	Cables, tarred	Pound.....0. 03	Free	Centner 0. 36	Centner....0. 28
359	untarred	Pound.....0. 03½	Free	Centner....0. 36	Centner....0. 28
360	manilla, untarred	Pound.....0. 02½	Free	Centner....0. 36	Centner....0. 28
361	iron or chain or parts of.	Pound.....0. 02½	Free	Centner....0. 84	Centner....0. 68
362	Cadmium	Free	Free	Free	Centner....0 68
363	Cajeput, oil of	Pound.....0. 25	Free	Centner....0. 18	Centner....0. 68
364	Calamine	Free	Free	Free	Centner....0. 03
365	Calcined magnesia	Pound.....0. 12	Free	Centner....1. 44	Centner....0. 68
366	Calisaya bark	20 per cent	Free	Centner....0. 18	Centner....0. 68
367	Caliminars capis	30 per cent	Free	Centner....0. 18	Centner....0. 68
368	Calomel and other mercurial preparations.	30 per cent	Free	Centner....2. 40	Centner....0. 68
369	Calx, (lime)	10 per cent	Free	Free	Centner....0. 145
370	Camblets, of mohair or goat.	35 per cent	Free	Centner....2. 40	Centner....1. 56
371	Camel's hair	Free	Free	Free	Centner....0. 058
372	pencils, in quills	35 per cent	Free	Centner....2. 40	Centner....1. 56
373	pencils, other	35 per cent	Free	Centner....2. 40	Centner....1. 56
374	Cameos, real	10 per cent	Free	Free	Centner....0. 39
375	imitation	40 per cent	Free	Centner...18. 00	Centner....0. 39
376	set, real	25 per cent	Free	Centner...18. 00	Centner....2. 93
377	imitation	30 per cent	Free	Centner...18. 00	Centner....2. 93
378	Camomile flowers	20 per cent	Free	Centner....0. 18	Centner....0. 68
379	Camphor, refined	Pound.....0. 40	Free	Centner....2. 40	Centner....0. 68

(Duties expressed in gold dollars of the United States)—Continued.

	FRANCE.				RUSSIA.	NETHERLANDS.	
	General tariff.		In treaty with Great Britain, &c.				
	In French vessels.	In other vessels.	In vessels of treaty powers.	In other vessels.			
....	....	....	....	....	Steel, pood....$3.51	5 per cent	334
....	Prohibited.		10 per cent.		Gold, pound... 25.74 Silver, pound.. 1.72	....	335
....	Prohibited.		10 per cent.		Pood.......... 3.12	5 per cent	336
....	....	....	....	....	Pood.......... 1.56	5 per cent	337
100 kilogs..............	$0.19	0.48	Free ..	$0.048	Free	Free	338
....	Free ..	Free ..	Free ..	Free ..	Free	Free	339
....	Free ..	Free ..	Free ..	Free ..	Free	Free	340
....	Prohibited.		Prohibited.		Prohibited...........	5 per cent..........	341
....	Free ..	Free ..	Free ..	Free ..	Free	Free	342
See Manuf. of flax......	....	....	....	....	Pound 0.17	5 per cent	343
....	Free ..	....	Free ..	....	Free	Free	344
See Manuf. of flax......	....	....	....	....	See Tissues of flax...	5 per cent	345
....	Free ..	0.048	Free ..	0.048	Free	Free	346
....	Free ..	0.148	Free ..	0.048	Free	Free	347
100 kilogs..............	0.145	0.156	0.175	0.188	Pood 0.43	1 per cent	348
See Lead	....	....	....	....	See Manuf. of lead...	Free	349
See Cutlery............	....	....	....	....	See Cutlery	5 per cent	350
Fresh..................	Free ..	Free ..	Free ..	Free ..	Free	Free	351
Salted, 100 kilogs	0.48	0.52	0.48	0.52			
Hinges, 100 kilogs......	Prohibited.		0.87	0.95	See Man. of iron, &c.	5 per cent	352
Moulds, 100 kilogs......	2.53	2.78	2.53	2.78	According to material.	5 per cent	353
						5 per cent	
Buttons, of tissues— Cotton, pure or mixed, except with wool or silk, simple 100 kilogs.... Figured .... Not of tissues— common, 100 kilogs. fine.................	 19.00 39.00 19.50 39.00	 20.95 41.43 20.90 41.43	10 per cent.		Buttons, metal, except gold, silver, or platina, per pound........0.39 All of linen, cotton, wool, silk, per pound........0.23 Of glass, porcelain, mother of pearl, &c., per pound....0.08	5 per cent........	354 355 356
....	15 per cent.		10 per cent.		See Furniture.......	5 per cent	357
Carved, 100 kilogs......	....	....	1.36	1.50			
....	10 per cent.		....	....	Pood...........0.31	100 kilogs ...$0.20	358
....	....	....	....	....	Pood...........0.31	100 kilogs 0.20	359
....	10 per cent.		....	....	Pood...........0.31	100 kilogs 0.20	360
100 kilogs..............	7.30	8.03	1.56	1.72	....	1 per cent..........	361
100 kilogs..............	0.39	0.43	Free ..	0.048	Free	Free	362
....	1.17	1.36	1.17	1.28	Pood 0.43	1 per cent	363
100 kilogs..............	0.39	0.43	Free ..	0.048	Free	Free	364
....	....	....	5 per cent.		Pood...........0.85	Free	365
....	Free ..	Free ..	Free ..	Free ..	Free	Free	366
....	Free ..	Free ..	Free ..	Free ..	Free	Free	367
....	Prohibited.		5 per cent.		Pood...........0.85	Free	368
....	Free ..	Free ..	Free ..	Free ..	Free	Free	369
....	Prohibited.		10 per cent.		See Manufactures of wool, hair.	5 per cent	370
....	Free ..	Free ..	Free ..	Free ..	Free	Free	371
....	15 per cent.		10 per cent.		Pound 0.23	5 per cent	372
....	....	....	....	....	Pound..........0.23	5 per cent	373
....	Free ..	Free ..	Free ..	Free ..	Free	Free	374
....	10 per cent.		10 per cent.		Free	Free	375
....					Pound.........0.85	Free	376
....					Pound 0.85	Free	377
....	Free ..	Free ..	Free ..	Free ..	Free.................	Free	378
100 kilogs..............	0.39	0.43	0.39	0.43	Pood...........0.23	Free	379

Comparative table of import duties in the United States and European countries.

	ARTICLES.	ITALY.			SPAIN.	PORTUGAL.
			General tariff.	Tariff in treaty with France, &c.		
334	Buckles, all	See Manufactures	of mat	als.	20 per cent.	Fancy, kilog$2. 14
335	of gold or silver.				See Gold and silver	See Gold and silver.
336	Bugles, glass, cut	100 kilogs	$1. 56	$0. 975	100 kilogs....$3. 50	Kilog........0. 1728
337	not cut......	....	......	......	100 kilogs.... 1. 60	Kilog........0. 1728
338	Building stones, not provided for.	100 kilogs...... Marble, 5 pr. ct.	.0. 48	Free.	100 kilogs 0. 01	100 kilogs ...0. 01
339	Bulrushes	....	Free.	Free.	Free	Free ....
340	Bulbs or bulbous roots	100 kilogs	1. 95	0. 39	100 kilogs 2. 00	5 per cent..........
341	Bullets	100 kilogs.......	3. 90	......	100 kilogs 0. 30	Free ....
342	Bullion....................	....	Free.	Free.	Free	Free ....
343	Bunting	See Linen.......	......	......	See Manuf. of flax..	Kilogs.......0. 54
344	Burgundy pitch............	....	Free.	Free.	100 kilogs 0. 30	Free ....
345	Burlaps	See Linen	......	......	See Manuf. of flax..	Kilogs.......0. 54
346	Burr stones, unbound	100 kilogs.......	0. 48	Free.	100 kilogs 0. 01	Free ....
347	bound.........	100 kilogs.......	0. 48	Free.	100 kilogs 0. 01	Free ....
348	Burning fluid......	100 kilogs.......	1. 95	1. 17	100 kilogs 1. 60	Kilogs.......0. 0108
349	Busts, lead	100 kilogs.......	1. 17	0. 58	100 kilogs 1. 60	Kilogs.......0. 054
350	Butchers' knives...........	100 kilogs.......	1. 56	1. 80	100 kilogs 5. 50	Kilogs.......0. 27
351	Butter......	100 kilogs.......	0. 39	Free.	100 kilogs 8. 00	Kilogs.......0. 149
352	Butt hinges, cast-iron	....	1. 56	1. 80	100 kilogs 1. 50	Kilogs...... 0. 081
353	Button moulds, of whatever material.	According to	mater	ial.	Accord'g to materi'l.	Accord'g to materi'l
354	Buttons, metal, all kinds of.	Buttons, cotton, as tissues.			Buttons of shell, ivory, mother of pearl; also, engraved, per kilogs 0. 40	According to material.
355	all other, (except silk.)	Buttons, gold and silver thread, per kilogs	1. 95	2. 14	All other, except lace buttons, per kilogs 0. 20	
356	with links.........	of silk, pure, kilogs	1. 17			
		of silk, mixed, kilogs........	0. 39			
357	Cabinet wares	See Household	furnit	ure.	See Household furniture.	See household furniture.
358	Cables, tarred	100 kilogs.......	0. 58	0. 58	100 kilogs ...4. 00	Kilogs......0. 054
359	untarred	100 kilogs.......	0. 58	0. 58		Kilogs 0. 072
360	manilla, untarred ...	100 kilogs.......	0. 58	0. 58	100 kilogs 4. 00	Kilogs.......0. 072
361	iron or chain or parts of.	100 kilogs.......	1. 17	1. 36	100 kilogs 1. 50	Kilogs.......0. 0108
362	Cadmium..................	100 kilogs.......	1. 95	Free.	Kilogs.........0. 02	Free ....
363	Cajeput, oil of	100 kilogs.......	0. 97	1. 12	100 kilogs 1. 60	Kilogs.......0. 0108
364	Calamine..................	100 kilogs.......	1. 75	Free.	100 kilogs 0. 75	Free ....
365	Calcined magnesia	100 kilogs.......	1. 95	0. 78	Kilogs 0. 02	5 per cent...........
366	Calisaya bark	100 kilogs.......	1. 95	0. 39	100 kilogs 2. 00	Kilogs.......0. 0013
367	Caliminaris capis...........	100 kilogs.......	1. 95	0. 78	100 kilogs 2. 00	5 per cent ....
368	Calomel and other mercurial preparations.	100 kilogs.......	1. 95	0. 39	20 per cent	5 per cent ....
369	Calix, (lime)...............	100 kilogs.......	1. 95	Free.	100 kilogs 0. 02	Free ....
370	Camblets, of mohair or goat.	5 per cent.......	......	......	Kilogs.........0. 30	See Manuf. of wool
371	Camel's hair...............	100 kilogs.......	0. 95	......	100 kilogs 0. 40	Free ....
372	pencils, in quill	5 per cent.......	......	......	20 per cent	Kilogs.......1. 08
373	pencils, other	5 per cent.......	......	......	20 per cent	Kilogs.......1. 08
374	Cameos, real..............	1 per cent.......	......	......	100 kilogs 0. 075	½ per cent ....
375	imitation	1 per cent.......	......	......	100 kilogs.....0. 075	Kilogs.......0. 54
376	set, real............	5 per cent.......	......	......	Kilogramme.. 4. 00	1 per cent ....
377	imitation.......	5 per cent.......	......	......	Kilogramme .. 2. 00	1 per cent ....
378	Camomile flowers..........	100 kilogs.......	0. 97	Free.	100 kilogs 0. 30	Free ....
379	Camphor, refined	100 kilogs.......	1. 95	0. 39	20 per cent	Kilogs.......0. 054

(*Duties expressed in gold dollars of the United States.*)—Continued.

BELGIUM.	AUSTRIA.			DENMARK.	SWEDEN.	NORWAY.	
		General tariff.	Tariff in treaty.				
10 per cent	Centner	$3.60	$2.16	Pound $0.091	....	See Material manufactured.	334
10 per cent	See Gold and Silver.	......	......	Pound 0.091	See Manuf. of Gold or other metal.	See Gold or Silver.	335
10 per cent	Centner	3.48	1.92	Pound 0.04	See Glass	Pound 0.009	336
100 kilogs .. 0.195	Centner	0.36	0.36	Pound 0.008	....	....	337
Free	See Stone	......	......	Free	Free	Free	338
Free	Free	......	......	Free	Free	Free	339
Free	Free	......	......	Free	Free	Free	340
See Manufactures iron and lead.	Centner	1.60	1.20	Pound 0.0056	Free	Free	341
Free	Free	......	......	Free	Free	Free	342
See Manuf. of flax.	See Manuf. of flax		......	Pound 0.034	See Manuf. of flax	See Manuf. flax	343
Free	Free	......	......	Free	Free	Free	344
See Manuf. of flax.	See Manuf. of flax		......	See Manuf. of flax.	See Manuf. of flax	See Manuf. flax	345
Free	See Stones	......	......	Free	Free	Free	346
Free	See Stones	......	......	Free	Free	Free	347
Free	Centner	0.648	0.36	Pound 0.017	Pound ... $0.0082	Pound 0.0089	348
10 per cent	See Lead	......	......	Pound 0.091	See Lead	Pound 0.011	349
100 kilogs ... 0.78	See Cutlery	....	......	Pound 0.017	Pound 0.016	Free	350
100 kilogs 0.975	Centner	1.26	0.96	Free	Free	Pound 0.0045	351
100 kilogs 0.78	See Manuf. of wool		......	Pound 0.0056	Pound 0.0165	Pound 0.0045	352
As material manufactures.	....	......	......	Pound 0.0056	As material	See Material Manufactures.	353
Buttons, 10 per cent, except of silk, &c., as tissues.	According to material manufact'd.	......	......	Pound 0.091	Pound 0.082	See Material manuf.	354 355 356
10 per cent	See Househ'd furniture		..	See Household furniture.	See Manuf. of Wood.	See Household furniture.	357
See Cordage	See Cordage	......	......	Pound 0.0056	Pound 0.0082	Free	358
See Cordage	See Cordage	......	......	....	Pound 0.0082	Pound 0.013	359
See Cordage	See Cordage	......	......	....	Centner .. 0.2067	Iron, ½-in. thick, free; less than ½ in., lb., $0.0045	360
100 kilogs 0.78	See Cordage	1.68	1.20	....	Free		361
Free	Free	......	......	Free	Free	Free	362
Free	See Oils	......	......	See Oils	Free	Free	363
Free	Free	......	......	Free	Free	Free	364
Free	See Chemicals	not enum'td.		Pound 0.0113	Free	Free	365
Free	Free	......	......	Free	Free	Free	366
Free	Medic'ns prepar'd, centn'r.	7.20	......	Free	Free	Free	367
Free	......do	......	......	Pound 0.0113	Free	Free	368
Free	Free	......	......	Free	Free	Free	369
10 per cent	See Manuf. of wool.	......	......	Pound 0.182	Pound 0.0689	Pound 0.073	370
Free	Free	......	......	Free	Free	Free	371
10 per cent	Centner	7.20	5.76	10 per cent	10 per cent	10 per cent	372
10 per cent	Centner	7.20	5.76	10 per cent	10 per cent	10 per cent	373
Free	Centner	5.04	2.88	Free	Free	Free	374
Free	See Glass	......	......	10 per cent	Free	Free	375
5 percent	See Jewelry	......	......	See Jewelry	See Gold manuf.	See gold	376
5 per cent	See Jewelry	......	......	See Jewelry	Pound 0.0964	Pound 0.109	377
Free	Free	......	......	Free	Free	Free	378
Free	Centner	2.52	1.44	Pound 0.0113	Pound 0.0689	Free	379

Comparative table of import duties in the United States and European countries,

	ARTICLES.	UNITED STATES.	GREAT BRITAIN.	GERMAN ZOLL-VEREIN.	SWITZERLAND.
380	Camphor, crude	Pound $0.30	Free	Centner...$0.18	Centner...$0.68
381	Canary seed	Bushel.....1.00	Free	Free	Centner....0.39
382	Cancrorum oculi, crab's eye	20 per cent	Free	Centner....0.18	Centner....0.68
383	Candles, tallow	Pound 0.02½	Free	Centner....0.90	Centner....0.39
384	Candles, wax or sperm	Pound 0.08	Free	Centner....1.44	Centner....1.56
385	other	Pound 0.05	Free	Centner....1.44	Centner....1.56
386	Candlesticks, alabaster, spar	30 per cent	Free	As Fancy goods, more or less costly, p'r centner......10.80	Centner....1.56
387	glass cut, gold and silver, Japan.	40 per cent	Free		Gold centner 2.93
388	marble	50 per cent	Free		Centner....1.56
389	glass not cut, all others.	35 per cent	Free		Centner....1.56
390	common stoneware	25 per cent	Free		Centner....0.39
391	Candy, colored, value over 30 cents per pound.	50 per cent	Per cwt..$2.92	Centner....2.10	Centner....0.68
392	colored, value over 30 cents per pound or less.	Pound 0.15			
393					
394	sugar, not colored	Pound 0.10			
395	Canella, alba	20 per cent	Free	Centner....4.70	Centner....0.68
396	Canes, walking, finished or not.	35 per cent	Free	Centner....0.72	Centner....1.56
397	Canetile, a wire ribbon	See Iron wire	Free	Centner...10.80	Centner... 0.68
398	Cannon, brass or iron	35 per cent	Free	Iron, cent. 0.29 Brass, cent 2.88	Centner... 0.39
399					....
400	Cantharides	Pound 0.50	Free	Centner... 0.36	Centner... 0.68
401	Canton crapes	See Silk	Free	Centner...28.80	Centner... 2.93
402	Canvas, for floor cloth or wearing apparel, linen.	See Flax	Free	See Linen	Centner... 1.56
403	Caoutchouc gums	10 per cent	Free	Free	Centner... 0.145
404	Capers	35 per cent	Free	Centner... 1.44	Centner... 1.56
405					
406	Cap wire, covered with silk or cotton thread.	As Wire, and 5 per cent. in addition.	Free	Centner... 0.84	Centner... 0.29
407	Caps, of lace, leather, cotton, linen, &c.	35 per cent	Free	Centner..28.80	Centner... 2.93
	of chip	40 per cent	....		
408	of silk, pure	60 per cent	Free		
409	Caps, gloves, leggins, mits, socks, stockings, wove shirts and drawers, and all similar articles made in frames and worn by women or children, not otherwise provided for.	35 per cent	Free	See Manufactu's of Cotton, Wool, Silk, &c.	Centner... 2.93
410	Caps, lace, sewed or not	35 per cent	Free	Centner...28.80	Centner... 2.93
411	Cap pieces, for stills	35 per cent	Free	Centner... 2.88	Centner... 1.56
412	Capsules	40 per cent	Free	Centner... 2.88	Centner... 1.56
413	Carbines or carabines	35 per cent	Free	Centner... 7.20	Centner... 0.39
414	Carbonate of magnesia	Pound 0.06	Free	Free	Centner... 0.68
415	sal, or brinal soda.	Pound 0.035	Free	Free	....
416	ammonia	20 per cent	Free	Centner... 2.40	Centner... 0.68
417	iron	20 per cent	Free	Centner... 2.40	Centner... 0.68
418					
419	Carboys	35 per cent	Free	Centner... 0.12	Centner... 0.68
420	Carbuncles	10 per cent	Free	Free	Centner... 0.097
421	Cardamom seed	Pound 0.50	Free	Centner... 0.36 Free, exept for medical use.	Centner... 0.68

(*Duties expressed in gold dollars of the United States.*)—Continued.

	FRANCE.				RUSSIA.	NETHERLANDS.	
	General tariff.		In treaty with Great Britain, &c.				
	In French vessels.	In other vessels.	In vessels of treaty powers.	In other vessels.			
100 kilogs	Free	$0.39	$0.39	$0.43	Pood $0.23	Free	380
100 kilogs	Free	0.097	....	....	Free	Hectolitre $0.04	381
100 kilogs	Free	0.048	Free	0.048	Free	Free	382
							383
Candles, all	5 per cent.		5 per cent.				384
					Candles, all, per pood 0.85	100 kilogs 1.23	385
						5 per cent	386
Mercery, common, 100 kilogs.	19.50	20.95	10 per cent.		As fancy goods, per pound 0.85	5 per cent	387
fancy, 100 kilogs.	39.00	41.43					388
							389
100 kilogs	2.92	3.20	Free	0.048	....	....	390
							391
See Sugar	....	....	....	....	Pood 3.51	100 kilogs 14.30	392
							393
							394
100 kilogs	5.85	8.77	....	....	Pood 1.17	5 per cent	295
100 kilogs	1.95	2.92	5 per cent.		Pood 0.19	Free	396
See Wire	....	....	....	....	Pood 2.34	5 per cent	397
....	Prohibited.		....	....	Prohibited	Iron, 100 ki'ls 0.51	398
....	....	....	....	....	....	Metal 3.06	399
Dried, 100 kilogs	0.39	0.43	0.39	0.43	Free	Free	400
See Tissues of silk	....	....	....	....	See Silks	5 per cent	401
Of at least 8 threads per 5 square millimeters, 100 kilogs.	14.63	14.63	15 per cent.		See Linen	5 per cent	402
100 kilogs	Free	0.58	....	....	Pood 0.23	Free	403
100 kilogs	11.70	12.77	1.56	1.72	Pood 0.78	Free	404
					In sealed vessels, pood 2.34	....	405
See Wire	....	....	....	....	As wire	5 per cent	406
....	15 per cent.		10 per cent.		Caps, woolen fezes, or Turkish caps, embroider'd or not, dozen 1.40	5 per cent	407
See Manufact's of Silk	....	....	....	....	....	5 per cent	408
....	Prohibited.		10 per cent.		35 per cent	5 per cent	409
....	Prohibited.		10 per cent.		35 per cent	5 per cent	410
See Copper	....	....	....	....	Pood 2·34	5 per cent	411
....	Prohibited.		Prohibited.		Prohibited	5 per cent	412
....	Prohibited.		Prohibited.		Prohibited	5 per cent	413
100 kilogs	39.00	41.44	Free	0.048	Free	Free	414
Carb. potash, 100 kilogs.	Free	0.78	Free	0.048	Pood 0.078	Free	415
Carbonate (salt) baryte, 100 kilogs.	Free	0.39	....	....	Pood 0.04	Free	416
Carbonate of lead	Free	Free	Free	Free	Pood 0.04	Free	417
							418
See Glass manufactures.	....	....	....	....	Pood 0.30	5 per cent	419
....	Free	Free	Free	Free	Free	5 per cent	420
....	Free	Free	Free	Free	Pood 1.95	Hectoliter 0.04	421

Comparative table of import duties in the United States and European countries.

	ARTICLES.	ITALY.			SPAIN.	PORTUGAL.
			General tariff.	Tariff in treaty with France, &c.		
380	Camphor, crude	100 kilogs	$1.95	$0.39	20 per cent	Kilogs $0.027
381	Canary seed	Free			100 kilogs 0.60	Kilogs 0.013
382	Cancrorum oculi, crab's eye	100 kilogs	1.95	0.39	100 kilogs 0.30	Free
383	Candles, tallow	100 kilogs	0.97	0.97		Kilogs 0.032
384	wax or sperm	100 kilogs	7.80	3 p.c.	Kilogs 0.15	Kilogs 0.054
385	other	100 kilogs	1.95	1.95		Kilogs 0.054
386	Candlesticks, alabaster, spa.		5 p. ct.	Free.	20 per cent	Kilogs 0.0108
387	glass cut, gold and silver, Japan.	See Gold, silver, &c.			20 per cent	Kilogs 0.1728
388	marble		5 p. ct.	Free.	20 per cent	Kilogs 0.0108
389	glass not cut, all others.	100 kilogs	1.56	0.97	20 per cent	Kilogs 0.054
390	common stoneware	100 kilogs	1.56	1.56	100 kilogs 1.50	Kilogs 0.001
391	Candy, colored, value over 30 cents per pound.					
392	colored, value over 30 cents per pound or less.	100 kilogs	4.87	5.63	100 kilogs 5.40	See Sugar
393						
394	sugar, not colored					
395	Canella alba	Fine, per kilogr other, per 100 kilogs raw	0.23 9,75 Free.	 Free	100 kilogs 0.30	Kilogs 0.108 Crude, each 0.108
396	Canes, walking, finished or not	Finished, per 100 kilogs	0.195	0.195	100 kilogs 5.00	Finished 0.206
397	Canetile, a wire ribbon	100 kilogs	1.36	1.58	See Wire	Kilogramme 0.054
398	Cannon, brass or iron	Iron	1.17	1.56	100 kilogs 1.00	1 per cent
399		Brass	2.93	3.38		
400	Cantharides	100 kilogs	1.95	Free.	100 kilogs 1.10	Free
401	Canton crapes	See Silk			See Silk	See Silk
402	Canvas, for floor cloth or wearing apparel, linen.	See Linen			See Manufactures of flax.	See Manufactures of flax.
403	Caoutchouc gums	100 kilogs	0.48		100 kilogs 1.00	Free
404	Capers	Capers, prese'd, 4,100 kilogs.	1.56	1.56	Kilogs 0.20	5 per cent
405						
406	Cap wire, covered with silk or cotton thread.	100 kilogs	3.90	4.50	See Wire	Kilogramme 0.324
407	Caps, of lace, leather, cotton, linen, &c. of chip	Caps, each	0.097		20 per cent	See Hats
408	of silk, pure	Mil. keppy, each	0.195		20 per cent	Each 0.432
409	Caps, gloves, leggins, mits, socks, stockings, wove shirts and drawers, and all similar articles made in frames and worn by women, or children, not otherwise provided for.				20 per cent	Double duties of tissues.
410	Caps, lace, sewed or not	Each	0.097		20 per cent	Each 0.432
411	Cap-pieces, for stills	See Copper, with Iron			100 kilogs 5.50	Kilogramme 0.27
412	Capsules	100 kilogs	1.95	0.39	100 kilogs 35.00	Kilogramme 0.27
413	Carbines or carabines	See Arms			See Arms	30 per cent
414	Carbonate of magnesia	100 kilogs	1.56		100 kilogs 0.75	
415	sal, or brinal soda.	Of baryte (100 kilogs.)	0.39	0.39	100 kilogs 0.75	Carb. of potassium, raw, kilogs 0.005
416	ammonia	Of lead (100 kilogs.)	1.95	0.73	100 kilogs 0.75	Potass'm, refi'd 0.004
417	iron	Of potassium (100 kilogs.)	0,097	Free.	100 kilogs 0.75	Of soda, raw, free.
418		Of iron (100 kilogs.)				
419	Carboys	100 kilogs	1.56	0.39	20 per cent	Kilogramme 0.1728
420	Carbuncles		Free.	Free.	100 kilogs 0.30	½ per cent
421	Cardamom seed	100 kilogs	1.17	Free.	100 kilogs 1.60	Kilogramme 0.027

(*Duties expressed in gold dollars of the United States.*)—Continued.

BELGIUM.	AUSTRIA.			DENMARK.	SWEDEN.	NORWAY.	
		General tariff.	Tariff in treaty.				
Free	Centner	2.52	1.44	Pound 0.0113	Pound 0.0689	Free	380
Free	Centner	0.388	Free.	Free	Pound 0.011	Free	381
......	Free	......	......	Free	Free	Free	382
Candles, all 10 per cent	Tallow, c'tner	1.512	......	Pound 0.017	Pound 0.0082	Pound ...0.018	383
	Wax, centner	3.84	......	Pound 0.034	Pound 0.0138		384
	Stain, &c., c'nr	2.52	......	Pound 0.034	Pound 0.0138		385
Free	Centner	5.76	5.76	Pound 0.091	10 per cent	10 per cent	386
10 per cent	Centner	3.48	1.92	Pound 0.091	Pound 0.0138	See Glass, gold, &c.	387
Free	Centner	5.76	5.76	Pound 0.091	10 per cent	10 per cent	388
10 per cent	Centner	3.48	1.92	Pound 0.04	Pound 0.0138	See Glass	389
10 per cent	Centner	2.16	1.20	Pound 0.0056	Free	Pound.....0.018	390
							391
See Sugar refined.	See Sugar	......	......	Pound 0.0314	See Sugar	See Sugar	392
							393
							394
Free	Centner.	3.84	......	Free	Free	Free	395
10 per cent	See Wood	......	......	Pound 0.0042	Pound 0.32	Pound 0.014	396
100 kilogs .. 0.78	Centner	7.20	5.76	Pound 0.017	See Wire	Pound 0.031	397
Free	Special perm	it	......	Pound 0.0056	Free	Free	398
......	......	......	......	......	......	......	399
Free	Centner	2.52	1.44	Free	Free	Free	400
See Silk	See Silks	......	......	See Silks	See Silk	See Silk	401
See Manufactures of flax.	See Manufact	uresof	flax.	See Manufactur's of flax.	See Manufactur's of flax.	See Manufactu's of flax.	402
Free	Free	......	......	Free	Free	Free	403
100 kilogs .. 1.95	Centner	3.88	......	Free	Pound .. 0.0689	Pound 0.218	404
							405
5 per cent	See Wire	......	......	Pound 0.017	See Wire	See Wire	406
10 per cent	Trimmed—Centner.	126.00	......	Each......0.364	See Hats	See Hats	407
......	......	......	......	......	......	See Hats	
10 per cent	Trimmed—Centner.	126.00	......	Each...... 0.226	See Hats	Each 0.409	408
10 per cent	Trimmed—Centner.	37.80	......	Double duties on material manufactured,	Additio'l to duty on material, 20 per cent,	Additional to material, 10 per cent.	409
10 per cent	See Clothing	......	......	Each......0.364	Addition'l to material, 20 per ct.	Each 0.409	410
10 per cent	See Article of	copp	er....	Pound 0.045	Pound.... 0·041	Pound 0.047	411
10 per cent	......	7.68	5.76	Pound 0.0227	Pound.... 0.138	Pound 0.082	412
Free	......	7.20	7.20	Pound 0.091	Pound.... 0.055	Pound 0.182	413
Free	See Chemic'ls	n. e ..	......	Pound 0.0113	Free	Pound 0.073	414
Free	Centner	0.72	0.72	Pound 0.0113	Free	Free	415
Free	See Chemic'ls	......	......	Pound 0.0113	Free	Free	416
Free	See Chemic'ls	......	......	Pound 0.0113	Free	Free	417 418
10 per cent	Centner	0.36	......	Free	Pound.... 0.041	Free	419
Free	Free	......	......	Free	Free	Pound 0.047	420
15 per cent	Centner	3.84	......	Pound 0.0113	Pound.... 0.0689	......	421

Comparative table of import duties in the United States and European countries.

	ARTICLES.	UNITED STATES.	GREAT BRITAIN.	GERMAN ZOLL-VEREIN.	SWITZERLAND.
422	Card cases, of whatever composed.	35 per cent......	Free............	Centner..$21.60	Centner...$2.93
423	Cards, playing, value 25 cts.	25 cts. per pack.	Doz. packs$0.91	Centner... 7.20	Centner... 2 93
424	over 25 cts..	35 cts. per pack.	....	....	....
425	visiting	35 per cent......	Free............	Free............	Centner... 1.56
426	Cards, wool, if iron pins....	35 per cent......	Free............	Free............	Centner... 0.058
427	wool, cotton, if steel pins.	45 per cent......	Free............	Free............	Centner... 0.058
428	Carmine, water color.......	35 per cent......	Free............	Free............	Centner... 0.68
429	dry...............	25 per cent......	Free............	Free............	Centner... 0.60
430	liquid dye.........	20 per cent......	Free............	Free............	Centner... 0.68
431	Carpeting.—Aubusson and Axminster.	50 per cent......	Free............	All carpets, or carpet'g, centner 7.20	Carpets of jute or wool, centner....0..18
432	when woven for rooms..	50 per cent......	Free.		
433	Saxony, Wilton, and Tournay velvet, wro't by the Jacquard machine.	Sq. yard .$0.70 and 35 per cent.	Free.		Brussels & finished carpets, centner 2.93
434	Brussels, wroug't by the Jacquard machine.	Sq. yard. 0.44 and 35 per cent.			
435	patent velvet and tapestry velvet, printed on the warp or otherwise.	Sq. yard . 0.40 and 35 per cent.			
436	tapestry, Brussels, printed on the warp, or otherwise.	Sq. yard . 0.28 and 35 per cent.			
437	treble ingrain, three-ply, and worsted chain Venetian.	Sq. yard . 0.17 and 35 per cent.			
438	yarn, Venetian, and two-ply ingrain.	Sq. yard . 0.12 and 35 per cent.			
439	hemp or jute............	Sq. yard . 0.08			
440	of wool, flax, or cotton, or parts of either, or other material, not otherwise enumerat'd, provided that mats, rugs, screens, covers, hassocks, bedsides, and other portions of carpets or carpeting, shall be subject to the rate of duty therein imposed.	40 per cent......	Free.		
441	Carriages of all descriptions and parts thereof.	35 per cent......	Free............	Free except iron work, taxed as such.	Carriages, 10 per cent; railroad cars, 1½ p. cent; wagons, 5 per cent.
442	Carriage springs...........	35 per cent......	Free............	Centner ... 1.92	Not polished, centner. 0.68 Pol'd, cen'r 1.56
443	Carvers....................	35 per cent......	Free............	Centner ... 2.88	Centner... 1.56
444	Caraway seed.............	Pound..... 0.03	Free............	Free............	Centner... 0.097
445	Cascarilla bark............	20 per cent......	Free............	Centner ... 0.36	Centner... 0.68
446	Casement rods, iron for....	See Iron........	Free............	See Iron........	Centner... 0.39
447	Cassimere, woolen.........	See Woolens....	Free............	Centner ... 7.20	Centner ... 1.56

(Duties expressed in gold dollars of the United States.)—Continued.

	FRANCE.				RUSSIA.	NETHERLANDS.	
	General tariff.		In treaty with Great Britain, &c.				
	In French vessels.	In other vessels.	In vessels of treaty powers.	In other vessels.			
100 kilogs	Prohibited.		$11.70	$12.76	Pound $0.25	5 per cent	422
Pack	Prohibited.		0.09 and 15 per cent.	0.09	Prohibited	5 per cent	423
....	....	......					424
100 kilogs..............	....	....	Free...	0.48	Free	5 per cent	425
100 kilogs..............	$5.85	$6.43	1.17	1.29	Carding thistles, free.	5 per cent	426
100 kilogs..............	5.85	6.43	1.17	1.29	Cards, pood ... 0.62	5 per cent	427
....	Free...	Free...	Free...	Free...	Free	Free	428
....	....	....	....	....	....	....	429
....	....	....	....	....	....	Free	430
							431
							432
Carpets, all imported direct from the Orient	15 per cent.		10 per cent.		Carpets, all, per pound...... 0.23	All, 5 per cent..	433
From all other countries, single, chain of linen, thread, or flax, wrong side presenting canvas, velvety, by Dunkirk, 100 kilogs.....	48.75	48.75					434, 435, 436
By other ports	58.50	61.90					437
Others, by all ports...							438
Other carpets, pure or mixed, not having canvas on wrong side, 100 kilogs	97.50	100.90					439, 440
Worsted, chain, other than linen or flax, 100 kilogs	97.50	100.90					
Chain, linen, or flax, 100 kilogs..........	58.50	61.20					
Carriages, on springs, painted and furnished	Prohibited.		10 per cent.		Carriages, large, with springs, each . 78.00 Light, with springs, each .... 54.40 Spring wagons, each ....23.40 All without springs, pood ....7.80 Railway cars, each, 58.50 Covered freight cars, each ....78.00 Passenger cars, 3d class, each...136.50 Pass'r cars, 1st and 2d class, each.. 234.00	Carriages, all..... 5 per cent.	441
Others	15 per cent.		10 per cent.				
....	15 per cent.		10 per cent.		Pood 3.12	5 per cent	442
....	See Cutlery....		....	....	Pood.......... 9.36	5 per cent	443
....	Free...	Free...	Free...	Free..	Free	Hectoliter ...$0.04	444
....	Free...	Free...	Free...	Free...	Free	Free...............	445
....	See Iron	....	....	....	Pood.......... 0.273	5 per cent..........	446
....	See Wool		....	....	Pound..........2.23	5 per cent..........	447

Comparative table of import duties in the United States and European countries.

	ARTICLES.	ITALY.			SPAIN.	PORTUGAL.
			General tariff.	Tariff in treaty with France, &c.		
422	Card cases, of whatever composed.	10 per cent......	......	......	20 per cent	20 per cent ....
423	Cards, playing, value 25 cts.	Pack	$0.04	$0.04	See Paper, Prints..	Kilogramme .$0.108
424	over 25 cts...	....	......	......	....	....
425	visiting	100 kilogs.......	11.70	Free.	Kilogs.......$0.25	Kilogramme. 0.108
426	Cards, wool, if iron pins ...	100 kilogs.......	0.975	......	10 per cent	Kilogramme. 0.081
427	wool, cotton, if steel pins.	....	0.95	......	10 per cent	Kilogramme. 0.162
428	Carmine, water color	100 kilogs.......	11.70	2.25	100 kilogs ... 5.00	Free ....
429	dry	....	......	......	....	....
430	liquid eye	....	11.70	2.25	100 kilogs ... 5.00	Free ....
431	Carpeting.—Aubusson and Auxminster.					
432	when woven for rooms..					
433	Saxony, Wilton, and Tournay velvet, wro't by the jacquard mamachine.					
434	Brussels, wought by the jacquard machine.	Carpets of hair, kilogr.	0.097	......		
435	patent velvet and tapestry velvet, printed on the warp or otherwise.	Carpets of hair, 100 kilogs.	......	11.26		
436	tapestry, Brussels, printed on the warp, or otherwise.	Carpets, wool, or rags, kilogs.	0.097	0.05	Carpets, cotton, kilogs.... 0.05	Carpet, of wool, one or more colors, kilogr. 0.378
437	treble ingrain, three-ply, and worsted chain Venetian.	Other, not wool.	0.195	0.06	Of wool, 100 kilogrammes . 35.00	Cotton, kil'r. 0.216
438	yarn, Venetian, and two-ply ingrain.	Other, wool, kilogs.	0.39	0.45		Flax, kilogr. 0.27
439	hemp or jute					
440	of wool, flax, or cotton, or parts of either, or other material not otherwise enumerat'd, provided that mats, rugs, screens, covers, hassocks, bedsides, and other portions of carpets or carpeting, shall be subject to the rate of duty therein imposed.	Foot rags, linen, kilogs.	0.39	0.078		
441	Carriages of all descriptions and parts thereof..........	Carriages, by travelers.... or each....... by merchants, each........ or per cent....	5 per 1.95 0.975 5	cent. 1.95 0.975 5	Coaches of four seats, new or old, each ..... 200.00 Buggies of two seats, omnibuses, new or old, each .... 150.00 Carriages, two or four wheels, new or old, each .... 62.50 Railroad and all n. o. e., p. cent. 25	Carriages. Wagons, for carrying goods, each 12.42 Carts, hand, each ...... 2.12 Carts, others, each ...... 75.60 Carriages, each .... 248.40 Sedans, and litters, each.. 5.94
442	Carriage springs	100 kilogs	2.93	2.93	100 kilogs.... 5.50	Kilogramme . 0.027
443	Carvers	100 kilogs	1.56	1.80	100 kilogs.... 5.50	See Cutlery.........
444	Caraway seed	100 kilogs	1.95	0.39	100 kilogs.... 1.60	5 per cent.........
445	Cascarilla bark.............	100 kilogs	1.95	6.39	100 kilogs.... 0.30	5 per cent..........
446	Casement rods, iron for....	See Iron	......	......	100 kilogs.... 4.50	Kilogramme . 0.081
447	Cassimere, woolen	See Wool	......	......	Kilogramme . 1.60	Kilogramme . 0.81

(*Duties expressed in gold dollars of the United States.*)—Continued.

BELGIUM.	AUSTRIA.			DENMARK.	SWEDEN.	NORWAY.	
		General tariff.	Tariff in treaty.				
10 per cent ...	As fancy articles, cent'r.	$12. 00	$7. 20	10 per cent	Pound... $0. 0689	Pound...$0. 182	422
							423
	Centner	15. 12	......	Pack.....$0. 0113	Gross..... 4. 96	Pound....0. 082	424
				....	....	....	
	Centner	6. 00	5. 76	Sta'p duty. 0. 045	Pound.... 0. 022	Prohibited	425
100 kilogs ..$2. 34	Centner	7. 20	5. 76	Visiti'g, lb. 0. 0028	....	....	426
100 kilogs .. 2. 34	Centner	7. 20	5. 76	Pound 0. 017	Free	Pound....0. 025	427
				Pound 0. 017	Free	Free............	
Free	Centner	7. 20	5. 76	Pound 0. 08	Pound.... 0. 0964	Free............	428
....	....	......	......	Pound 0. 08	....	Free............	429
Free	Centner	0. 72	......	Pound 0. 08	Pound.... 0. 0964	Pound....0. 073	430
							431
							432
							433
							434
							435
							436
Carpets, as tissues, according to description.	Carpets, cotton, centner.	17. 28	12. 00	Carpet, wool, pound..0. 068	Carpets of wool, pound 0. 082 Cotton, lb 0. 0496	Carpets, cotton, per lb....0. 0364	437
	Wool	17 28	12. 00	Other tissues according to description.	Linen, lb. 0. 0496	Wool, lb 0. 073	438
							439
							440
10 per cent	Wagons and sleighs, for freight, each Carriages & sleighs, for passengers, with't leather work or upholstery, each ...... Do. finished, each... Railroad cars, each.	1. 26 7. 56 50. 40 144. 00	....	Carriages, covered, each 16. 38 others, each 6. 55 Children's carriages, sleighs, &c. pound 0. 017	Carriages, single horse, two wheels, and sleighs, each .... 5. 512 oth's, each 27. 56	Carriages, for children, each .... 0. 327 Omnibuses, each.... 21. 85 Four-wheel carriages, covered, each..... 10. 92 Do. not covered, each.... 4. 27 Two-wheel carriages, each 2. 19	441
100 kilogs.. 0. 78	See Manuf of s	teel ..	......	Pound..... 0. 017	Pound.....0. 0275	Pound.... 0. 27	442
100 kilogs.. 0. 78	See Cutlery..	......	......	Pound..... 0. 017	Pound.....0. 0275	Free	443
Free............	Centner	0. 1296	Free.	Pound..... 0. 017	Centner ... 0. 41	Pound 0. 009	444
Free............	....	Free.	......	Free	.... Free.	Free	445
100 kilogs.. 0. 78	See Iron.....	......	......	Pound..... 0. 017	See Iron.........	See Iron	446
See Manuf. of wool	See Wool (ma	nufact	ured).	See Wool'n tissues	See Woolens.....	See Wool manuf.	447

Comparative table of import duties in the United States and European countries.

	ARTICLES.	UNITED STATES.	GREAT BRITAIN.	GERMAN ZOLL-VEREIN.	SWITZERLAND.
448	Casks, empty	35 per cent	Free	Free	Iron hoops, per centner..$0. 39
449	Cassada, or meal of	20 per cent	Free	Centner .. $1. 44	Centner ... 0. 68
450	Cassia, Chinese, Calcutta, Sumatra.	Pound $0. 20	Free	Centner ... 4. 68	Centner ... 0. 68
451	Cassia, ground buds	Pound 0. 25	Free	Centner ... 4. 68	Centner ... 0. 68
452	Cassia, fistula	20 per cent	Free	Centner ... 4. 68	Centner ... 0. 68
453	Castanas, (a nut)	Pound 0. 02	Free	Free	Centner ... 0. 39
454	Castings of plaster	40 per cent	Free	Centner ... 2. 88	Centner ... 0. 68
455	Castor beans	Bushel 0. 60	Free	Centner ... 0. 36	Centner ... 0. 68
456	oil	Gallon 1. 00	Free	Centner ... 2. 40	Centner ... 0. 68
457	Castors, brass or iron	35 per cent	Free	Centner ... 2. 88	Centner ... 1. 56
458	wood	35 per cent	Free	Centner ... 2. 88	Centner ... 1. 56
459	silver, with't glasses	40 per cent	Free	Centner ... 2. 88	Centner ... 2. 93
460	plated	35 per cent	Free	Centner ... 2. 88	Centner ... 2. 93
461	Castor glasses, not in frames or cruits, cut.	40 per cent	Free	Centner ... 2. 88	Centner ... 0. 68
462	not cut	35 per cent	Eree		
463	Castoreum, (crude drug)	20 per cent	Free	Centner ... 0. 36	Centner ... 0. 68
464	Cast iron vessels	See Iron			
465	Catches, brass, copper, iron.	35 per cent	Free	See Manufac. of brass, copper, iron.	Centner ... 1. 56
466	Catechu	10 per cent	Free	Free	Centner ... 0. 68
467	Catgut	30 per cent	Free	Free	Centner ... 0. 68
468	Catsup	40 per cent	Free	Centner ... 2. 40	Centner ... 0. 68
469	Caulking mallets	35 per cent	Free	Centner ... 0. 72	Centner ... 1. 56
470	Caustic soda	Pound 0. 01½	Free	Free	Centner ... 0. 145
471	Cayenne pepper	Pound 0. 15	Free	Centner ... 4. 68	Centner ... 0. 68
472	ground	Pound 0. 18	Free	Centner ... 4. 68	Centner ... 0. 68
473	Celtz water	30 per cent	Free	Free	Centner ... 0. 145
474	Cement, Roman	20 per cent	Free	Free	Centner ... 0. 145
475	Chafing dishes, copper	35 per cent	Free	Centner ... 2. 88	Centner ... 1. 56
476	iron or tin	35 per cent	Free	Centner ... 1. 92	Centner ... 1. 56
477	Chain cables	Pound 0. 02½	Free	See Iron manufac.	See Iron
478	Chain curbs, gilt	35 per cent	Free	Centner ... 2. 88	Centner ... 1. 56
479	Chains, hair	35 per cent	Free	Centner .. 16. 60	Centner ... 2. 03
480	Chains, gold or silver, not jewelry.	40 per cent	Free	Centner .. 36. 00	Centner ... 2. 93
481	Chains, gold or silver, jewelry.	25 per cent	Free	Centner .. 36. 00	Centner ... 2. 03
482	Chairs, sitting	35 per cent	Free	See Furniture	See Furniture
483	Chalk, billiard	50 per cent	Free	Free	Centner ... 0. 028
484	red	20 per cent	Free	Free	All other, per centner 0. 028
485	French	20 per cent	Free	Free	
486	white	Ton 10. 00	Free	Free	
487	all other n. e	25 per cent	Free	Free	
488	Camomile flowers	20 per cent	Free	Centner ... 0. 36	Centner ... 0. 68
489	Chandeliers, brass	35 per cent	Free	Centner ... 1. 92	Centner ... 1. 56
490	Chandeliers, glass, cut	40 per cent	Free	Centner ... 2. 88	Centner .. 1. 56
491	Chapapote, (asphaltum)	25 per cent	Free	Free	Centner .. 0. 095
492	Charts	25 per cent	Free	Free	Centner .. 0. 095
493	books	25 per cent	Free	Free	Centner .. 0. 095
496	Cheese	Pound 0. 04	Free	Centner ... 2. 40	Centner .. 0. 39
497	Chemical preparations, not otherwise enumerated.	20 per cent	Free	Centner .. 2. 40	Centner .. 0. 68
498	Chenille, cord or trimmings, cotton.	35 per cent	Free	Centner .. 21. 60	Centner .. 2. 93
499	Cheroots, (India cigars)	See Cigars			
500	Cherry rum—a cordial	Gallon $2. 50	Cherries, dried, per lb $0. 02	Centner .. 4. 52	Centner .. 1. 56

(*Duties expressed in gold dollars of the United States.*)—Continued.

	FRANCE.				RUSSIA.	NETHERLANDS.	
	General tariff.		In treaty with Great Britain, &c.				
	In French vessels.	In other vessels.	In vessels of treaty powers.	In other vessels.			
	Free	Free	Free	Free	Free	Free	448
	Free	Free	Free	Free	Pood $0.85	Free	449
100 kilogs	$5.85	$8.77			Free	Free	450
100 kilogs	Free	3.90			Free	Free	451
As comfits, 100 kilogs	8.19	8.58			Free	Free	452
100 kilogs	Free	0.048	Free	$0.048	Free	Free	453
100 kilogs	Free	Free				Free	454
100 kilogs	Free	3.29	Free	0.048	Free	Hectoliter $0.61	455
100 kilogs	0.39	0.43	$0.39	0.43	Pood 1.40	100 killogs 0.51	456
					Pood 2.34	5 per cent	457
100 kilogs as fancy articles.						5 per cent	458
	Prohibited.		11.70	12.76	Pood 0.85	5 per cent	459
						5 per cent	460
	See Glassware				Pound 1.72	5 per cent	461
					Pood 9.36	Free	462
	Free		Free		Pood 3.12	5 per cent	463
Ton	0.39	0.39	0.39	0.39	All sea and river vessels, free.	5 per cent	464
	See Manuf. of brass, iron, &c.				See Manufactures of brass, iron, &c.	5 per cent	465
	Free	Free	Free	Free	Free	Free	466
	15 per cent.		10 per cent.		Free	Free	467
100 kilogs	4.87	5.35	5.87	5.35	Pood 0.78	Free	468
			10 per cent.		Pood 1.95	5 per cent	469
100 kilogs			1.25	1.36	Pood 0.23	Free	470
100 kilogs	9.75	11.89			Pood 1.17	100 kilogs 0.61	471
100 kilogs	9.75	11.89				100 kilogs 0.61	472
	Free	Free	Free	Free	Bottle 0.016	100 bottles 0.20	473
100 kilogs	Free	0.048	Free	0.048	Free	1,000 kilogs 0.30	474
	See Copper manuf.				Food 2.34	5 per cent	475
Tin, 100 kilogs	Prohibited		5.85	6.43	Pood 0.78	5 per cent	476
100 kilogs	7.30	8.03	1.56	1.72	Pood 0.312	1 per cent	477
100 kilogs	39.00	41.43	3.90	4.29	Pood 3.12	5 per cent	478
100 kilogs	Prohibited.		10 per cent.		Pound 0.461	5 per cent	479
100 kilogs	Prohibited.		11.70	12.76	As Jewelry	5 per cent	480
100 kilogs	97.50	100.00	97.50	100.90		5 per cent	481
	15 per cent.		10 per cent.		See Furniture	5 per cent	482
100 kilogs	Free	0.195	Free	Free	Free	Free	483
100 kilogs	Free	0.195	Free	Free	Free	Free	484
100 kilogs	Free	0.195	Free	Free	Free	Free	485
100 kilogs	Free	0.195	Free	Free	Free	Free	486
						Free	487
	Free	Free	Free	Free	Free	Free	488
100 kilogs as fancy goods	Prohibited.		3.90 10 per cent.	4.29	Pood 2.34	5 per cent	489
	Prohibited.		10 per cent.		Pood 3.12	5 per cent	490
	Free	Free	Free	Free	Free	Free	491
100 kilogs	58.50	61.90	Free	0.048	Free	Free	492
					Free	Free	493
100 kilogs	2.92	3.22	0.78	0.86	Pood 0.34	100 kilogs 2.05	496
	Prohibited.		5 per cent.		Pood 0.85	Chemical and all preparations containing alcohol, p'r liter 0.37; all others, not enumerated, free.	497
See Cotton					See Cotton	5 per cent	498
						See Cigars	499
Hectoliter	29.25	29.25	2.92	2.92	Pood 6.63	Hectoliter 1.43	500

Comparative table of import duties in the United States and European countries.

	ARTICLES.	ITALY.			SPAIN.	PORTUGAL.
			General tariff.	Tariff in treaty with France, &c.		
448	Casks, empty	100 kilogs	$1.17	$5 p. c.	In return .... Free.	Kilogramme .$0.02
449	Cassada, or meal of	100 kilogs	0.24	......	In return .... Free.	Kilogramme . 0.008
450	Cassia, Chinese Calcutta, Sumatra.	100 kilogs	1.17	Free	100 kilogs....$2.00	5 per cent
451	Cassia, ground buds	100 kilogs	1.17	Free.	100 kilogs.... 2.00	5 per cent
452	Cassia, fistula	(Ligna) 100 kilogs	9.75	......	100 kilogs.... 2.00	5 per cent
453	Castanas, (a nut)	100 kilogs	0.58	Free	100 kilogs.... 2.00	Kilogramme .0.0108
454	Castings of plaster		5 per	cent.	100 kilogs.... 1.50	Kilogramme . 0.01
455	Castor beans	100 kilogs	1.95	0.78	100 kilogs.... 2.00	Kilogramme .0.0016
456	oil	100 kilogs	0.97	1.12	100 kilogs.... 1.60	Decaliter 0.54
457	Castors, brass or iron	See Manufac. of brass, iron, silver, &c.			20 per cent	Brass, kilogr. 0.27
458	wood				20 per cent	See Wood manufac.
459	silver, with't glasses				Kilogramme 2.00	See Silver manufac.
460	plated					Kilogramme . 0.54
461	Castor glasses, not in frames or cruits, cut.	100 kilogs	2.93	1.36	20 per cent	Kilogramme . 0.1728
462	not cut.		......	......		
463	Castoreum, (crude drug)	100 kilogs	1.95	0.39	100 kilogs.... 2.00	5 per cent
464	Cast iron vessels	See Iron	......	......	100 kilogs.... 1.50	Kilogramme . 0.081
465	Catches, brass, copper, iron	See Manuf. of brass or copper			See Brass, copper, and iron.	Kilogramme 0.27 Kilogramme 0.162
466	Catechu	100 kilogs	0.48	......	100 kilogs.... 1.00	Kilogramme . 0.027
467	Catgut	100 kilogs	0.48	......	100 kilogs.... 0.30	Kilogramme . 0.027
468	Catsup	100 kilogs	5.85	4.88	Kilogramme . 0.20	
469	Caulking mallets	Per cent	10	10	20 per cent	
470	Caustic soda	100 kilogs	0.97	......	100 kilogs.... 0.76	See Chemicals n. e.
471	Cayenne pepper	100 kilogs	7.80	......	Kilogramme . 0.05	Guinea, kilogr 0.027
472	ground	100 kilogs	7.80	......	Kilogramme . 0.05	Other, kilogr. 0.081
473	Celtz water	100 kilogs	0.195	Free	.... Free.	Kilogramme . 0.01
474	Cement, Roman		Free	Free.	100 kilogs.... 0.01	Kilogramme .0.0001
475	Chafing dishes, copper	100 kilogs	3.90	3.90	See Manuf. of copper	Kilogramme . 0.27
476	iron or tin	100 kilogs	2.93	2.93	See Man. of iron, tin	Tin, kilogr... 0.054
477	Chain cables	100 kilogs	1.17	1.56	100 kilogs.... 1.50	Kilogramme .0.0108
478	Chain curbs, gilt	100 kilogs	19.50	19.50	100 kilogs.... 4.50	See Manuf. of mat'l.
479	Chains, hair	Per cent	5	5	20 per cent	Kilogramme . 5.40
480	Chains, gold or silver, not jewelry.	See Gold and silver		......	See Gold and silver.	See Gold and silver.
481	Chains, gold or silver, jewelry.	See Jewelry	......	......	See Jewelry	See Jewelry
482	Chairs, sitting	100 kilogs	1.95	10p. c.	100 kilogs.... 3.50	35 per cent
483	Chalk, billiard	100 kilogs	0.48	Free.	100 kilogs.... 0.01	Kilogramme .0.0027
484	red	100 kilogs	0.48	Free.	100 kilogs.... 0.01	Kilogramme .0.0027
485	French	100 kilogs	0.48	Free.	100 kilogs.... 0.01	Kilogramme .0.0027
486	white	100 kilogs	0.48	Free.	100 kilogs.... 0.01	Kilogramme .0.0027
487	all other, n. e	100 kilogs	0.48	Free.	100 kilogs.... 0.01	Crude, kilogr. 0.0027
488	Camomile flowers	100 kilogs	0.97	0.39	100 kilogs.... 0.30	.... Free.
489	Chandeliers, brass	100 kilogs	3.90	3.90	100 kilogs.... 2.00	Pound....... 0.27
490	Chandeliers, glass, cut	100 kilogs	2.93	1.36	20 per cent	Kilogramme .0.1728
491	Chapapote, (asphaltum)	Free	......	......	100 kilogs.... 0.01	Free
492	Charts	100 kilogs	5.85	Free.	Kilogramme . 0.25	Kilogramme . 0.27
493	books	100 kilogs	5.85	Free.	Kilogramme . 0.25	Kilogramme . 0.27
496	Cheese	100 kilogs	2.73	0.78	Kilogramme. 0.05	Ordinary, kil. 0.081 Fine, kilogs . 0.162
497	Chemical preparations, not otherwise enumerated.	100 kilogs	1.95	0.78	20 per cent. or kilogramme 0.02	10 per cent
498	Chenille, cord or trimmings, cotton.	See Cotton	......	......	See Cottons	See Manufactures of cotton.
499	Cheroots, (India cigars)	See Cigars	......	......	See Cigars	Kilogramme . 0.432
500	Cherry rum—a cordial	Hectoliter	1.95	......	Hectoliter ... 3.75	Decaliter 1.62

(*Duties expressed in gold dollars of the United States.*)—Continued

Belgium.	Austria.			Denmark.	Sweden.	Norway.	
		General tariff.	Tariff in treaty.				
10 per cent	Centner	$0.12	Free.	Free	Free	Free	448
100 kilogs .. 0.23	See Flour			Free	Free	Free	449
15 per cent	Centner	7.56		Pound $0.04	Free	Free	450
15 per cent	Centner	7.56		Pound 0.04	Free	Free	451
Free	Centner	0.12	Free.	Free	Free	Free	452
Free	Centner	0.388	Free	Pound 0.005	Free	Free	453
10 per cent		Free.		Free	Free	Free	454
100 kilogs .. 0.117	Centner	2.52	$1.44	Free	Free	Free	455
Free	See Oils			Pound 0.017	Free	Free	456
5 per cent	Centner	7.20	5.76	10 per cent	10 per cent	10 per cent	457
5 per cent	Centner	5.76		Pound 0.091	10 per cent	10 per cent	458
5 per cent	See Silver			Pound 0.091	See Silver	See Silver	459
5 per cent	Centner	7.20	5.76	Pound 0.091	10 per cent	10 per cent	460
100 kilogs .. 0.19	Centner	3.48	1.92	Pound 0.04	Pound $0.165	Pound ... $0.008	461
							462
Free	Centner	2.52	1.44	Free	Free	Free	463
100 kilogs .. 0.78	Ton, capacity	2.52		Pound 0.0056	See Iron	See Iron	464
10 per cent	See Manuf. of	these	metals	See these metals manufactured.	See Copper	See Copper	465
Free		Free.	Free.	Free	Free	Free	466
Free	Strings, centn	14.40	14.40	Free	Free	Free	467
15 per cent				Free	Pound 0.044	Free	468
10 per cent	See Wood ma	nufac.		Free	Free	Free	469
Free	Centner	1.20	0.96	Pound 0.0115	Free	Free	470
Free	Centner	3.84		Pound 0.017	Pound 0.03	Pound ... 0.325	471
Free	Centner	3.84		Pound 0.017	Pound 0.03	Pound ... 0.325	472
Free		Free.		Free	Free	Free	473
10 per cent		Free.		Free	Free	Free	474
100 kilogs .. 0.078	See Manuf. of copper & tin			Pound 0.045	See Copper manuf.	See Copper	475
Tin, 10 per cent				Pound 0.017	See Tinware	See Tin, manuf.	476
Free	Centner	1.68	1.20	Pound 0.005	Centner 0.2067	Free	477
10 per cent	See Manuf. of	iron		Pound 0.091	Pound 0.082	Pound ... 0.095	478
10 per cent	See Manuf. of	hair		Pound 1.09	Pound 0.096	Pound ... 0.146	479
5 per cent	See Gold and	silver.		Pound 0.091	See Gold and silver	See Jewelry	480
5 per cent	See Jewelry			See Jewelry	See Jewelry	See Jewelry	481
10 per cent	See Manuf. of	wood		Pound 0.017	See Household furniture.	See Household furniture.	482
Prep'ed for draw'g	Centner	0.388	0.36	Free	Free	Free	483
10 per cent	Centner	0.388	0.36	Free	Free	Free	484
Otherwise, free	Centner	0.388	0.36	Free	Free	Free	485
	Centner	0.388	0.36	Free	Free	Free	486
	Centner	0.388	0.36	Free	Free	Free	487
Free		Free.		Free	Free	Free	488
10 per cent	Centner	3.60	2.16	Pound 0.045	Pound 0.03	Pound ... 0.047	489
10 per cent	Centner	3.48	1.92	Pound 0.04	Pound 0.0138	Pound ... 0.047	490
Free	Free			Free	Free	Free	491
Free	See Books			Free	Free	Free	492
Free	See Books			Free	Free	Free	493
100 kilogs. 1.90	Centner	2.16	1.20	Pound ... 0.028	Free	Pound ... 0.013	496
Free	Centner	2.40		Pound ... 0.0113	5 per cent	Free	497
See Yarns	See Cotton			Pound ... 0.091	See Cotton manuf.	See Cottons	498
100 kilogs .. 50.31	Centner	12.60		Pound ... 0.182	See Cigars	See Cigar	499
Hectoliter .. 11.70	Centner	3.88		Pot 0.091	Kande 0.303	Pound ... 0.16	500

Comparative table of import duties in the United States and European countries.

	ARTICLES.	UNITED STATES.	GREAT BRITAIN.	GERNAN ZOLL-VEREIN.	SWITZERLAND.
501	Chessmen, bone, ivory	50 per cent	Free	Centner . . $2.88	Centner . . $2.93
502	wood	35 per cent	Free	Centner . . 2.88	Centner . . 2.93
503	Chest handles	35 per cent	Free	Centner . . 2.88	Centner . . 1.56
504	Chiccory root	Pound $0.04	Cwt $6.45	Centner . . 0.48	Centner . . 0.058
505	ground, prepared	Pound 0.05	Pound 0.08	Centner . . 0.48	Centner . . 0.058
506	Children's shoes and slippers.	35 per cent	Free	Centner . . 2.88	Centner . . 2.93
507	Chili pepper	Pound 0.15	Free	Centner . . 4.68	Centner . . 0.68
508	China ware	45 per cent	Free	Centner . . 1.26	Centner . . 1.56
509	ornamented	50 per cent	Free	Centner . . 2.88	Centner . . 1.56
510	root	20 per cent	Free	Centner . . 0.26	Centner . . 0.68
511	Chincona bark	20 per cent	Free	Free	Centner . . 0.68
512	root	20 per cent	Free	Centner . . 0.36	Centner . . 0.68
513	Chinese blue	25 per cent	Free	Centner . . 2.40	Centner . . 0.68
514	Chip hats or bonnets	40 per cent	Free	Price 0.05	Centner . . 1.56
515	Chisels, all	45 per cent	Free	Centner . . 1.92	Centner . . 1.56
516	Chloride of lime	100 pounds 0.20	Free	Free	Centner . . 0.058
517	Chlorometers, glass	40 per cent	Free	Free	Centner . . 0.39
518	Chloroform	Pound 1.00	Pound 0.73	Centner . . 2.40	Centner . . 0.18
519	Chocolate	Pound 0.07	Pound 0.04	Centner . . 7.92	Centner . . 1.51
520	Choppa, romals, and bandana handkerchiefs.	See Silk	Free		
521	Chromate of potash	Pound 0.03	Free	Centner . . 2.40	Centner . . 0.68
522	lead	25 per cent	Free	Centner . . 2.40	Centner . . 0.68
523	Chromic, yellow	25 per cent	Free	Centner . . 2.40	Centner . . 0.68
524	acid	15 per cent	Free	Centner . . 2.40	Centner . . 0.68
525	Chronometers and parts	10 per cent	Free	Free	Centner . . 0.39
526	Chrysolites	20 per cent	Free	Free	Centner . . 0.39
527	Cicuta, (crude drug)	20 per cent	Free	Centner . . 9.36	Centner . . 0.68
528	Cider	20 per cent	Free	Centner . . 2.88	Centner . . 0.145
529	Cinchona bark	20 per cent	Free	Centner . . 0.36	Centner . . 0.68
530	Cinchonine bark	20 per cent	Free	Centner . . 0.36	Centner . . 0.68
531	Cinnabar	20 per cent	Free	Red . . . . 2.40 green, free.	Centner . . 0.68
532	Cinnamon	Pound 0.30	Free	Centner . . 4.68	Centner . . 0.29
533	oil of	Pound 2.00	Free	See Oils	See Oils
534	Citrate of lime	20 per cent	Free	Free	Centner . . 0.68
535	Citrons in natural state	10 per cent	Free	Centner . . 1.44	Centner . . 0.68
536	preserved	35 per cent	Free	Centner . . 2.88	Centner . . 1.56
537	Citron, oil of	50 per cent	Free	Centner . . 2.40	Centner . . 2.93
538	Civet, oil of	30 per cent	Free	Centner . . 2.40	Centner . . 2.93
539	Clasps, brass	35 per cent	Free	Centner . . 2.88	Centner . . 1.56
540	gold	40 per cent	Free	Centner . . 36.00	Centner . . 2.93
541	silver	40 per cent	Free	Centner . . 36.00	Centner . . 2.93
542	gilt or plated	35 per cent	Free	Centner . . 2.88	Centner . . 2.93
543	steel	45 per cent	Free	Centner . . 2.88	Centner . . 1.56
544	iron	35 per cent	Free	Centner . . 1.92	Centner . . 0.39
545	Clay, ground or prepared	Ton 5.00	Free	Free }	Potter's clay, 15
546	pipe or fire, unground	Ton 5.00	Free	Free }	centner . . 0.280
547	Cliff stone	Ton 10.00	Free	Free	Centner . . 0.028
548	Cloaks, if wool or silk	35 per cent	Free	Centner . . 21.60	Centner . . 2.93
549	Cloak pins, gilt or plated	35 per cent	Free	Centner . . 2.88	Centner . . 1.56
550	steel	45 per cent	Free	Centner . . 2.88	Centner . . 1.56
551	Clocks and parts of	35 per cent	Free	Centner . . 2.88	Centner . . 1.56
552	Cloth, India-rubber	35 per cent	Free	Centner . . 18.00	Centner . . 1.56
553	water-proof	45 per cent	Free		
554	woolen	See Woolens	Free	Centner . . 7.20	Centner . . 1.56
555	oil, 50 cents or less	30 per cent	Free	Centner . . 0.48	Centner . . 1.56
556	oil, over 50 cents	40 per cent	Free	Centner . . 0.48	Centner . . 1.56
557	hemp	35 per cent	Free	Centner . . 7.20	Centner . . 1.56

(*Duties expressed in gold dollars of the United States.*)—Continued.

FRANCE.					RUSSIA.	NETHERLANDS.	
	General tariff.		In treaty with Great Britain, &c.				
	In French vessels.	In other vessels.	In vessels of treaty powers.	In other vessels.			
As fancy articles	......	......	......	......	Pound $0.26	5 per cent..........	501
100 kilogs	Prohi	bited.	$11.70	$12.76	Pound 0.26	5 per cent..........	502
....	15 per	cent.	10 per	cent.	Pood 0.85	5 per cent..........	503
Dry, 100 kilogs.........	$0.19	$0.21	0.19	0.21	Free	Free	504
100 kilogs	Prohi	bited.	0.97	1.06	Pood........ 0.195	Free	505
100 kilogs	Prohi	bited.	10 per	cent.	Pound 0.85	5 per cent..........	506
100 kilogs	9.75	11.89	......	......	Pood 0.85	100 pounds ..$0.61	507
....	10 per	cent.	10 per	cent.	Pood 3.12	Porcelain, 5 per ct.	508
....	10 per	cent.	10 per	cent.	Pood 6.24	5 per cent..........	509
....	Free...	Free...	Free...	Free...	Free	Free	500
....	Free...	Free...	Free...	Free...	Free	Free	511
....	Free...	Free...	Free...	Free...	Free	Free	512
....	Free...	Free...	Free...	Free...	....	Free	513
....	......	......	10 per	cent.	See Hats	5 per cent..........	514
Tools, iron and steel, 100 kilogs.	24.37	26.27	2.92	3.20	See Manufs. of steel..	5 per cent..........	515
Chlorure of lime, 100 kilos	Prohi	bited.	0.67	0.76	Pood........ 0.31	Free	516
100 kilogs	10 per	cent.	Free...	0.098	Free	5 per cent..........	617
....	Prohi	bited.	Prohi	bited.	Pood 3.43	Liter 0.51	518
100 kilogs	29.25	31.20	6.82	7.49	Pood 3.90	100 kilogs.... 0.23	519
See Manufactures of Silk	......	......	......	......	See Silk manufactures	5 per cent..........	520
100 kilogs	29.25	31.20	10 per	cent.	Pood 1.56	Free	521
100 kilogs	14.62	15.83	10 per	cent.	Pood 0.85	Free	522
....	......	......	......	......	Pood 1.56	Free	523
....	Free...	Free...	Free...	Free...	Pood 1.56	Free	524
100 kilogs	10 per	cent.	Free...	0.048	Free	5 per cent..........	525
100 kilogs	10 per	cent.	Free...	0.048	Free	5 per cent..........	526
....	Free...	Free...	Free...	Free...	Pood 0.31	Free	527
Hectoliter	0.39	0.39	0.048	0.048	Pood 0.35	100 liters 1.23	528
....	Free...	Free...	Free...	Free...	Free	Free	529
....	Free...	Free...	Free...	Free...	Free	Free	530
....	Free...	Free...	......	......	Free	5 per cent..........	531
....	......	......	......	......	Pood 1.95	5 per cent..........	532
....	......	......	......	......	See Oils..............	See Oils	533
See Chemicals not enum	erated..	......	......	......	Pood 0.85	Free	534
100 kilogs	1.95	2.14	0.39	0.43	Pood 0.19	Free	535
{In sugar or honey, 100 kilogs.	4.29	4.29	4.29	4.29	} Pood 0.38	100 kilogs....10.25	536
{Not in sugar or honey, 100 kilogs.	1.95	2.14	1.56	1.72			
Kilogramme	0.78	0.86	......	......	Pood 1.40	1 per cent..........	537
Kilogramme	0.145	0.156	0.175	0.188	Pood 1.40	1 per cent..........	538
As Fancy articles	Prohi	bited.	10 per	cent.	Pood 2.34	5 per cent..........	539
....	Prohi	bited.	10 per	cent.	Pound 25.74	5 per cent..........	540
....	Prohi	bited.	10 per	cent.	Pound 1.72	5 per cent..........	541
....	Prohi	bited.	10 per	cent.	Pound 1.72	5 per cent..........	542
....	Prohi	bited.	10 per	cent.	Pood 3.51	5 per cent..........	543
....	Prohi	bited.	10 per	cent.	Pood........ 0.85	5 per cent..........	544
{100 kilogs	Free...	0.195	Free...	0.195	Free	Free	545
{100 kilogs	Free...	0.195	Free...	0.195	Free	Free	546
....	Free...	Free ..	Free...	Free...	Free	Free	547
Clothes, new	30 per	cent.	10 per	cent.	35 per cent	5 per cent..........	548
....	Prohi	bited.	10 per	cent.	....	5 per cent..........	549
....	......	......	......	......	Pood 0.39	5 per cent..........	550
Wooden, metal movement, each.	0.39	0.39	5 per	cent.	Tower clocks, each ..	5 per cent..........	551
Other, each	0.195	0.195	or each.	..0.97	Oth's: see Time-pieces	....	
See Manufactures of In	dia-rubb	er......	......	......	Pood 17.16	5 per cent..........	552
....	......	......	......	......	....	....	553
See Manufactures of w	ool.....	......	......	......	See Manufac's of wool	5 per cent..........	554
100 kilogs	......	......	2.92	3.12	Pound......... 0.08	5 per cent..........	555
....	......	......	......	......	Pound......... 0.08	5 per cent..........	556
See Manufactures of lin	en	......	......	......	Pound......... 0.12	5 per cent..........	557

Comparative table of import duties in the United States and European countries.

	ARTICLES.	ITALY.			SPAIN.	PORTUGAL.
			General tariff.	Tariff in treaty with France, &c.		
501	Chessmen, bone, ivory	100 kilogs	$9.75	5 p.ct.	Kilogramme .$0.30	Ivory, kilog .$5.40
502	wood	5 per cent	......	......	100 kilogs.... 7.00	35 per cent.........
503	Chest handles..............	100 kilogs	9.75	$9.75	100 kilogs.... 3.50	35 per cent if wood.
504	Chiccory root..............	100 kilogs	0.58	0.19	100 kilogs.... 2.00	....
505	ground, prepared .	100 kilogs	3.90	0.97	100 kilogs.... 2.00	5 per cent..........
506	Children's shoes and slippers.	Pair	0.097	0.097	Kilogramme . 1.75	Kilogramme . 1.08
507	Chili pepper	100 kilogs	7.80	......	Kilogramme . 0.05	Kilogramme . 0.081
508	China ware.................	100 kilogs	3.12	2.34	100 kilogs....10.50	Kilogramme . 0.324
509	ornamented	100 kilogs	4.87	4.87	100 kilogs....10.50	Kilogramme . 0.324
510	root	100 kilogs	1.95	0.39	100 kilogs.... 2.00	5 per cent..........
511	Chincona bark..............	100 kilogs	1.95	0.39	100 kilogs.... 2.00	Kilog......... 0.01
512	root	100 kilogs	1.95	0.39	100 kilogs.... 2.00	5 per cent..........
513	Chinese blue...............	100 kilogs	1.95	0.78	100 kilogs.... 1.50	Free ....
514	Chip hats or bonnets.......	10 per cent	......	......	20 per cent	Each 0.972
515	Chisels, all...............	100 kilogs	1.56	1.80	100 kilogs.... 5.50	Kilogramme . 0.081
516	Chloride of lime...........	100 kilogs	0.39	0.39	100 kilogs.... 0.50	Free...............
517	Chlorometers, glass........	100 kilogs	3.90	1.95	10 per cent.........	5 per cent..........
518	Chloroform	100 kilogs	1.95	0.78	20 per cent.........	Free...............
519	Chocolate..................	100 kilogs	9.75	6.83	Kilogramme . 0.20	Kilogramme . 0.108
520	Choppa, romals, and bandana handkerchiefs.	Kilogramme.....	1.39	0.58	See Silks	Kilogramme . 5.40
521	Chromate of potash.........	100 kilogs	1.95	0.78	Kilogramme . 0.02	Kilogramme . 0.01
522	lead	100 kilogs	1.95	0.78	Kilogramme . 0.02	10 per cent.........
523	Chromic, yellow	100 kilogs	1.95	0.78	100 kilogs.... 1.50	Kilogramme . 0.054
524	acid..............	100 kilogs	1.95	Free.	Kilogramme . 0.02	10 per cent.........
525	Chronometers and parts	100 kilogs	1.75	0.78	10 per cent.........	5 per cent..........
526	Chrysolites	100 kilogs	3.90	1.95	10 per cent.........	5 per cent..........
527	Cicuta, (crude drug).......	Free	......	......	100 kilogs.... 2.00	5 per cent..........
528	Cider	Hectoliter	1.56	0.64	Hectoliter ... 2.50	Decaliter 0.734
529	Cinchona bark..............	100 kilogs	1.95	0.39	100 kilogs.... 2.00	Kilogramme . 0.01
530	Cinchonine bark	100 kilogs.......	1.95	0.39	100 kilogs.... 2.00	Kilogramme . 0.01
531	Cinnabar	100 kilogs	1.95	......	100 kilogs.... 1.50 100 kilogs.... 1.69	20 per cent.........
532	Cinnamon	100 kilogs	19.50	......	Kilogramme, 0.12; of Ceylon, kilogramme 0.25	5 per cent..........
533	oil of	Kilogramme.....	0.58	......	See Oils	Kilogramme . 0.54
534	Citrate of lime............	100 kilogs	1.95	0.78	Kilogramme . 0.02	10 per cent.........
535	Citrons in natural state...	100 kilogs	0.019	Free.	100 kilogs.... 0.50	Kilogramme . 0.016
536	preserved	100 kilogs	2.93	1.56	Kilogramme . 0.20	Kilogramme . 0.037
537	Citron, oil of.............	Kilogramme.....	0.58	......	100 kilogs.... 1.60	Kilogramme . 0.54
538	Civet, oil of..............	Kilogramme....	0.58	......	100 kilogs.... 1.60	Kilogramme . 0.54
539	Clasps, brass..............	100 kilogs	3.90	3.90	100 kilogs....25.00	Kilogramme . 0.27
540	gold................	Hectoliter.......	1.95	5 p.ct.	See Gold...........	See Gold ....
541	silver	Kilogramme.....	2.34	5 p.ct.	See Silver	See Silver ....
542	gilt or plated........	Kilogramme.....	4.68	5 p.ct.	See Silver	Kilogramme . 0.54
543	steel	100 kilogs	3.90	4.50	100 kilogs.... 5.50	Kilogramme . 0.162
544	iron	100 kilogs	2.93	2.93	100 kilogs.... 4.50	Kilogramme . 0.162
545	Clay, ground or prepared...	100 kilogs	0.487	Free	100 kilogs.... 0.01	Free ....
546	pipe or fire, unground.	100 kilogs	0.487	Free.	100 kilogs.... 0.01	Free ....
547	Cliff stone	100 kilogs	0.487	Free.	100 kilogs.... 0.01	Free ....
548	Cloaks, of wool or silk....	See Wool and silk.	......	......	One-half duties of cloth.	Double duties as tissues.
549	Cloak pins, gilt or plated...	5 per cent	......	......	20 per cent	Kilog........ 0.54
550	steel..........	100 kilogs	9.75	9.75	Kilog........ 0.60	Kilog........ 0.135
551	Clocks and parts of	100 kilogs	9.75	11.26	20 per cent	20 per cent.........
552	Cloth, India rubber	100 kilogs	4.57	5.63	Kilog........ 0.37	Kilog........ 1.08
553	water-proof	....	......	......	....	....
554	woolen.............	Metallic	......	......	See Tissues of wool	Kilog........ 1.62
555	oil, 50 cents or less...	Iron or steel, per 100 kilogs.	9.75	1.95	Kilog........ 0.20	Floor, per kil. 0.54
556	oil, over 50 cents	Copper and cotton, per 100 kil.	9.75	2.70	Kilog........ 0.20	Other, per kil. 0.81
557	hemp				See Tissues of flax..	Other, per kil. 0.81

(*Duties expressed in gold dollars of the United States.*)—Continued.

Belgium.	Austria.			Denmark.	Sweden.	Norway.	
		General tariff.	Tariff in treaty.				
10 per cent	Centner	$5.76	......	Pound ...$0.091	Bone, lb..$0.0689	Bone, lb. $0.05	501
10 per cent	Centner	5.76	......	Pound ... 0.091	Ivory, lb.. 0.138	Ivory, lb. 0.157	502
10 per cent	According to material . . .			Wood, lb. 0.039	Pound.... 0.0037	Free	503
Free	Free	......	......	Pound ... 0.005	Pound.... 0.041	Pound ... 0.009	504
Free	Centner	3.84	......	Pound ... 0.023	Pound.... 0.041	Prohibited, (See Coffee.)	505
10 per cent	Centner	5.76	$3.60	Pound ... 0.182	Pound.... 0.11	Pound ... 0.196	506
15 per cent	Centner	3.84	......	Pound ... 0.017	Pound.... 0.03	Pound ... 0.036	507
10 per cent	Centner	2.88	2.16	Pound ... 0.04	Pound.... 0.027	Pound ... 0.031	508
10 per cent	Centner	7.20	5.76	Pound ... 0.091	Pound.... 0.055	Pound ... 0.062	509
Free	Centner	2.40	......	Free	Free	Free	510
Free	Centner	2.40	......	Free	Free	Free	511
Free	Centner	2.40	......	Free	Free	Free	512
Free	Centner	0.72	......	Pound ... 0.028	Pound.... 0.064	Pound ... 0.073	513
100 kilogs ..$1.95	See Hats	......	......	Pound ... 0.364	Each 0.21	Pound ... 0.109	514
100 kilogs .. 0.78	Centner	2.88	2.16	Pound ... 0.017	5 per cent	Free	515
Free	Centner	0.72	0.72	Free	See Chemic'ls, n. e.	Free	516
Free	Centner	2.16	2.16	Pound ... 0.04	Pound.... 0.041	Free	517
Free	Centner	2.40	......	Pound ... 0.0113	See Chemicals	Free	518
100 kilogs .. 5.85	Centner	7.56	4.80	Pound ... 0.04	Pound.... 0.082	Pound ... 0.073	519
10 per cent	See Silk manufactures. . .			Pound ... 0.41	See Silk tissues	See Silks	520
Free	Centner	0.72	0.72	Pound ... 0.0113	See Chemicals	Free	521
Free	See Chemic'ls	......	......	Pound ... 0.0113	See Chemicals	Free	522
Free	Centner	0.72	0.72	Pound ... 0.0113	See Chemicals	Free	523
Free	Of lead, cent'r	1.20	0.72	Pound ... 0.0113	See Chemicals	Free	524
Free	Centner	2.16	2.16	10 per cent	Pound.... 0.041	Free	525
Free	Centner	2.16	2.16	10 per cent	Pound.... 0.041	Free	526
Free	Free	......	......	Free	Free	Free	527
Hectoliter .. 1.17	Centner	5.04	......	Pot 0.091	Same as wine	Pound ... 0.009	528
Free	Free	......	......	Free	Free	Free	529
Free	Free	......	......	Free	Free	Free	530
Free	Centner	2.40	......	Free	Free	Free	531
Free	Centner	7.56	......	Pound ... 0.04	Free	Free	532
Free	Centner	3.60	2.60	Pound ... 0.017	Free	Free	533
Free	See Chemic'ls	......	......	Pound ... 0.0113	See Chemicals	Free	534
100 kilogs .. 1.17	Centner	1.262	......	Free	Free	Free	535
100 kilogs. 1.95 In brandy, 100 kilogs .. 11.70	See Comfits	......	......	Pound ... 0.04	Pound.... 0.082	Pound ... 0.054	536
Free	See Oils	......	......	Pound ... 0.068	Free	Free	537
Free	See Oils	......	......	Pound ... 0.068	Free	Free	538
10 per cent	See Manufacture of Copper or Brass.			Pound ... 0.091	Pound.... 0.041	Pound ... 0.047	539
5 per cent	See Manuf. of Gold		......	Pound ... 0.091	See Gold	See Gold	540
5 per cent	See Manuf. of Silver		......	Pound ... 0.091	See Silver	See Silver	541
10 per cent	See Jewelry	......	......	Pound ... 0.091	Pound.... 0.0964	See Jewelry	541
100 kilogs .. 0.78	See Iron	......	......	Pound ... 0.017	Pound.... 0.0689	Pound ... 0.048	543
100 kilogs .. 0.78	See Iron	......	......	Pound ... 0.017	Pound.... 0.041	Pound ... 0.048	544
Free	Free	......	......	Free	Free	Free	545
Free	Free	......	......	Free	Free	Free	546
Free	See Stone	......	......	Free	Free	Free	547
10 per cent	See Clothing	......	......	Double duties of material.	See Clothing	Additional to material, 10 per ct.	548
10 per cent	Centner	7.20	5.76	Pound ... 0.091	Pound.... 0.0689	See Jewelry	540
10 per cent	Centner	7.20	5.76	Pound ... 0.017	Pound.... 0.0689	Pound ... 0.048	551
5 per cent.	Centner	24.00	14.40	Pound ... 0.091	Clocks, wooden frame, lb. 0.055 Parts of, lb. 0.21	Met'l case or porcelain, each. 2.18 Other, each. 1.365	559
10 per cent	Centner	5.76	4.80	Pound ... 0.091	Pound.... 0.21	Pound.... 0.127	552
......	......	......	......	......	......	......	553
See Man. of wool.	See Manuf. of wool		......	Pound ... 0.1823	See Tissu's of wool	See Wool	554
10 per cent	Centner	5.76	4.80	Pound ... 0.091	Pound.... 0.0275	Pound ... 0.0364	555
10 per cent	Centner	5.76	4.80	Silk, lb .. 0.273	Pound.... 0.0275	Pound ... 0.0364	556
10 per cent	See Manuf. of flax		......	Pound ... 0.034	Pound.... 0.137	Pound ... 0.0364	557

	ARTICLES.	UNITED STATES.	GREAT BRITAIN.	GERMAN ZOLL-VEREIN.	SWITZERLAND.
558	Clothing, ready made	35 per cent	Free	Centner . $21. 60	Centner . . $2. 93
559	of wool	40 per cent. and $0.50 per lb.	Free	Centner . . 21. 60	Centner . . 2. 93
560	other	35 per cent	Free		
561	Cloves	Pound $0. 20	Free	Centner . . 4. 68	Centner . . 0. 68
562	Clove stems	Pound 0. 10	Free	Centner . . 4. 68	Centner . . 0. 68
563	oil of	Pound 2. 00	Free	Centner . . 0. 60	Centner . . 0. 68
564	Coaches, or part thereof	35 per cent	Free	Centner . . 0. 72	Centner . . 1. 56
565	Coach furniture of all descriptions.	35 per cent	Free	Centner.. 0. 72 (Iron parts extra.)	Centner . . 1. 56
566	Coal, bituminous	Ton....... 1. 25	Free	Free	15 centners. 0. 028
567	other	Ton....... 0. 40	Free	Free	15 centners. 0. 028
568	Coal hods, copper	45 per cent	Free	Centner . . 1. 92	Centner . . 1. 56
569	iron	35 per cent	Free	Centner . . 0. 96	Centner . . 0. 68
570	Cobalt, oxide of	20 per cent	Free	Free	Centner . . 0. 68
571	ore	10 per cent	Free	Free	Centner . . 0. 058
572	Cochineal	Free	Free	Free	Centner . . 0. 068
573	Cocculus indicus	Pound 0. 10	Free	Free	Centner . . 0. 68
574	Cocks	35 per cent	Free	Free	
575	Cocoa	Pound 0. 03	Pound $0. 02	Centner . . 4. 68	Centner . . 0. 68
576	shells	Pound 0. 02	Cwt....... 0. 49	Centner . . 4. 68	Centner . . 0. 39
577	prepared	Pound 0. 09	Pound 0. 04	Centner . . 7. 92	Centner . . 0. 68
578	Cocoanuts	25 per cent	Free	Centner . . 4. 68	Centner . . 0. 68
579	Codilla, or tow of hemp or flax.	Ton....... 10. 00	Free	Centner . . 2. 88	Centner . . 0. 29
580	Coir, unmanufactured	Ton....... 15. 00	Free	Free	As flax
581	Codfish, dry	Pound 0. 00½	Free	Centner . . 0. 36	Centner . . 0. 39
582	Coffee, when imported in American vessels from the place of its growth.	Pound 0. 05	Coffee, kiln-dried, roasted, or ground, per pound, $0. 08. All other, per pound, $0. 06.	Coffee, all, per centner, $3. 60.	Coffee, all, per centner, $0.29.
583	The growth or production of the Netherlands, imported from the Netherlands in foreign vessels entitled so to do by treaty.	Pound 0. 05			
584	All other	Pound 0. 65			
585	Coffee-mills	35 per cent	Free	Centner . . 1. 92	Centner . . 1. 56
586	Coins, gold or silver	Free	Free	Free	Free
587	cabinets of	Free	Free	Free	Free
588	copper	45 per cent	Free	Free	Free
589	Coke	25 per cent	Free	Centner . . 0. 01	Centner . . 0. 028
590	Colcodium, and ether of all kinds, not otherwise provided for.	Pound 1. 00	Ether, per gallon, $6. 08. Collodion, per gallon, $5. 84.	Centner . . 2. 40	Centner . . 0. 68
591	Colcother, dry, (oxide of iron.)	20 per cent	Free	Centner . . 2. 40	Centner . . 0. 68
592	Cold cream, (cosmetic)	50 per cent	Free	Centner . . 2. 40	Centner . . 2. 93
593	Colocynth	Pound 0. 10	Free	Centner . . 0. 36	Centner . . 0. 68
594	Cologne water and other perfumery of which alcohol is the principal ingredient.	50 per cent .... Gallon .. 3. 00	See Spirits	Centner . . 2. 40	Centner . . 2. 93
595	Colombo root	20 per cent	Free	Centner . . 0. 36	Centner . . 0. 68
596	Coloquintida	Pound 0. 10	Free	Centner . . 0. 36	Centner . . 0. 68

(*Duties expressed in gold dollars of the United States.*)—Continued.

FRANCE.					RUSSIA.	NETHERLANDS.	
	General tariff.		In treaty with Great Britain, &c.				
	In French vessels.	In other vessels.	In vessels of treaty powers.	In other vessels.			
…	…	…	…	…	35 per cent…	5 per cent…	558
…	…	…	10 per cent.		35 per cent…	5 per cent…	559
…	…	…	…	…	…	…	560
100 kilogs…	$19. 50	$21. 64	…	…	Pood… $1. 17	5 per cent…	561
…	…	…	…	…	Pood… 1. 17	5 per cent…	562
See Oil…	…	…	…	…	Pood… 1. 40	1 per cent…	563
See Carriages…	…	…	…	…	See Carriages…	5 per cent…	564
…	15 per cent.		10 per cent.		Pood… 3. 43	5 per cent…	565
100 kilogs…	0. 022	0. 14	$0. 022	$0. 072	Free…	Free…	566
…	…	…	…	…	Free…	Free…	567
100 kilogs…	19. 50	20. 95	3. 90	4. 29	Pood… 2. 34	5 per cent…	568
100 kilogs…	…	…	3. 12	3. 43	Pood… 0. 78	5 per cent…	569
Vitrified, per 100 kilogs, (powder.)	5. 85	6. 44	Free…	0. 048	See Chemicals…	See Chemicals…	570
Ore…	Free…	Free…	Free…	Free…	Free…	Free…	571
100 kilogs…	Free…	2. 92	Free…	Free…	Pood… 2. 03 Extract, per pood. 3. 43	Free… …	572
…	Free…	Free…	Free…	Free…	Prohibited…	Free…	573
…	Free…	Free…	Free…	Free…	Free…	Free…	574
100 kilogs…	6. 92	7. 80	…	…	Pood… 1. 16	Free…	575
100 kilogs…	Free…	0. 58	…	…	Pood… 1. 16	Free…	576
100 kilogs…	29. 25	31. 20	6. 82	7. 49	Pood… 3. 87	Free…	577
See Fruit…	…	…	…	…	Pood… 1. 16	Free…	578
100 kilogs…	4. 87	5. 36	2. 92	3. 20	Pood… 0. 31	100 kilogs… $0. 20	579
Like flax…	…	…	…	…	Free…	Free…	580
100 kilogs…	7. 80	8. 58	…	…	Pood… 0. 85	Free…	581
Coffee, all, per 100 kilogs…	9. 83	11. 80	11. 80	11. 80	Coffee, all, per pood, $1. 17.	Free…	582 583 584
As mercery, common, per 100 kilogs.	19. 50	20. 95	10 per cent.		Pood… 1. 95	5 per cent…	585
Coin, gold, silver, per kilog.	0. 0019	0. 0019	…	…	Coins, silver or copper, if Russian, and base coins, prohibited. All others, free.	Free…	586
…	…	…	…	…			587
Copper, of legal course in France, per 100 kilogs.	0. 038	0. 038	…	…			588
Base coin, if legal, per 100 kilogs.	0. 195	0. 21	…	…			
All not legal…	Prohibited.		…	…			
100 kilogs…	0. 022	0. 14	0. 022	0. 072	Free…	Free…	589
See Chemicals not enumerated.	…	…	…	…	Pood… 0. 85	Liter… 0. 51	590
See Chemicals not enumerated.		…	…	…	Pood… 0. 85	See Chemicals…	591
See Perfumery…	…	…	…	…	Pood… 4. 29	5 per cent…	592
See Chemicals not enumerated		…	…	…	Free…	Free…	593
100 kilogs…	29. 25	31. 20	2. 92	2. 92	Pood… 7. 80	5 per cent…	594
…	Free…	Free…	Free…	Free…	Free…	Free…	595
…	Free…	Free…	Free…	Free…	Free…	Free…	596

Comparative table of import duties in the United States and European countries.

No.	ARTICLES.	ITALY.			SPAIN.	PORTUGAL.
			General tariff.	Tariff in treaty with France, &c.		
558	Clothing, ready made	New, as material.	......	......	1½ duties of material.	Double duties of material.
559	of wool..........	Old, one-half above	...	......	1½ duties of material.	
560	other	....	......	......	....	....
561	Cloves	100 kilogs	$2. 93	......	Kilog........$0. 10	Kilog........$0. 108
562	Clove stems	100 kilogs	2. 93	......	....	Kilog........ 0. 108
563	oil of................	Kilog	0. 58	......	100 kilogs.... 1. 60	Decaliter.... 0. 54
564	Coaches, or part thereof....	5 per cent	......	......	See Carriages	See Carriages. . ...
565	Coach furniture of all descriptions.	5 per cent	......	......	See Carriages	As material manufactured.
566	Coal, bituminous...........	Free	......	......	Ton 0. 25	Free...............
567	other	Free	......	......	Ton 0. 25	Free...............
568	Coal hods, upper	100 kilogs	3. 90	$3. 90	100 kilogs.....14. 00	Kilog........ 0. 27
569	iron	100 kilogs	2. 93	2. 93	100 kilogs.... 4. 50	Kilog........ 0. 081
570	Cobalt, oxide of............	100 kilogs	1. 95	0. 78	Kilog........ 0. 02	Chemicals not enumerated.
571	ore	100 kilogs	0. 195	0. 195	Ton 0. 05	Free...............
572	Cochineal	100 kilogs	1. 56	......	100 kilogs.... 9. 00	Kilog........ 0. 027
573	Cocculus indicus	100 kilogs	1. 95	0. 39	100 kilogs.... 2. 00	5 per cent ....
574	Cocks	Free	......	......	Free...............	Free...............
575	Cocoa	100 kilogs	9. 75	5. 85	100 kilogs....16. 20	Kilog........ 0. 021
576	shells	100 kilogs	1. 95	......	Of Guadalquil	Kilog........ 0. 021
577	prepared	100 kilogs	9. 75	5. 85	100 kilogs....11. 25	Kilog........ 0. 108
578	Cocoanuts	100 kilogs	0. 195	Free.	....	Kilog........ 0. 021
579	Codilla, or tow of hemp or flax.	Tow, every kind, free.	......	......	100 kilogs.... 2. 00	Kilog........ 0. 072
580	Coir, unmanufactured......	Free	......	......	100 kilogs.... 0. 20	Kilog........ 0. 004
581	Codfish, dry	100 kilogs	0. 78	0. 90	100 kilogs.... 3. 50	Kilog........ 0. 036
582	Coffee, when imported in American vessels from the place of its growth.					Coffee, raw, from Portuguese possessions, per kil., $0. 015. Other, p'r kil. $0. 06
583	The growth or production of the Netherlands, imported from the Netherlands in foreign vessels entitled so to do by treaty.	All, 100 kilogs .	9. 75	......	Coffee from Spanish colonies, per 100 kilogs, $3. 70. Other, per 100 kil., $0. 50.	Shelled, from Portuguese poss'ns, per kilog. $0. 018. Other, per kilog, $0. 075.
584	All other					
585	Coffee-mills................	5 per cent	......	......	20 per cent........	20 per cent.........
586	Coins, gold or silver........	Free	......	......	Free...............	Free...............
587	cabinets of	Free	......	......	Free...............	Free...............
588	copper...............	If legal, free	......	......	Free...............	....
589	Coke	Free	......	......	Ton 0. 25	Free...............
590	Colcodium, and ether of all kinds, not otherwise provided for.	100 kilogs	1. 95	0. 78	See Chemicals not enumerated.	Kilog........ 0. 027
591	Colcother, dry, (oxide of iron.)	100 kilogs	0. 39	0. 39	See Chemicals not enumerated.	Chemicals not enumerated.
592	Cold cream, (cosmetic)	100 kilogs	1. 95	0. 39	See Perfumery	20 per cent ....
593	Colocynth	100 kilogs	1. 95	0. 39	See Chemicals n. e.	5 per cent ....
594	Cologne water and other perfumery of which alcohol is the principal ingredient.	100 kilogs	11. 70	10 p. c.	See Perfumery	Aromatic spirits, p'r kilog, $0. 27. Cologne water, per kilog, $0. 324.
595	Colombo root..............	100 kilogs	1. 95	0. 39	100 kilogs.... 2. 00	5 per cent..........
596	Coloquintida................	100 kilogs	1. 95	0. 39	100 kilogs.... 2. 00	5 per cent..........

(*Duties expressed in gold dollars of the United States.*)—Continued.

BELGIUM.	AUSTRIA.			DENMARK.	SWEDEN.	NORWAY.	
		General tariff.	Tariff in treaty.				
10 per cent	Common, ct'r.	$37.80	......	Double duties as material.	Additional 20 per cent. to duties on material.	Additional 10 per cent. to duties on material.	558
10 per cent	Fine, centner.	75.60	......				559
	Fancy, cent'r.	126.00		Mixed, 1½ duties.			
15 per cent	Centner	7.56	......	Pound.... 0.017	Pound.... 0.0496	Pound ... 0.061	560
15 per cent	....			....	....	....	561
Free	Centner	0.648	$0.36	Pound.... 0.068	Free	Free	562
10 per cent	....	......	......	Pound.... 0.017	....	....	563
....	See Carriages	......	......	....	Each .....27.56 (1 horse ea. 5.5[illegible].)	See Carriages....	564
10 per cent	As material manufactur'd.			Pound.... 0.017	As material manufactured.	See Material manufactured.	565
Free	Free	......	......	Free	Free	Free	556
Free	Free	......	......	Free	Free	Free	567
10 per cent	See Articles of copper.....		......	Pound.... 0.0113	Pound.... 0.041	Pound ... 0.047	568
100 kilogs	See Articles of iron .		......	Pound.... 0.017	Pound.... 0.016	Pound ... 0.027	569
Free	See Chemicals	......	......	Pound.... 0.043	See Chemic'ls not enumerated.	Free	570
Free	Free	......	......	Free	Free	Free	571
Free	Centner	0.388	......	Pound.... 0.0796	Pound.... 0.0964	Free	572
....	....	......	......	....	....	....	
Free	Centner	2.40	......	Free	Free	Free	573
Free	Free	......	......	Free	Free	Free	574
100 kilogs ..$2.93	Centner	3.84	......	Pound.... 0.0227	As chocolate	See Chocolate...	575
100 kilogs .. 2.93	Free	......	......	Pound.... 0.0227	Free	Free	576
100 kilogs .. 5.87	Centner	5.04	......	Pound.... 0.04	See Chocolate....	See Chocolate...	577
10 per cent	Centner	0.388	......	Pound.... 0.0056	Each..... 0.0138	Each..... 0.018	578
Free	Free	......	......	Free	Free	Free	579
Free	Free	......	......	Free	Free	Free	580
100 kilogs .. 0.195	See Fish.....	......	......	Pound.... 0.0317	Centner .. 0.34	Free	581
							582
100 kilogs. $2.57 Roasted, per 100 kilogs, $3.41.	Centner— green	3.84	......	Pound .. 0.0227 Roast'd, lb. 0.023	Pound .. 0.0275 Roast'd, lb. 0.041	Coffee, per lb., $0.045. Roasted & substitutes, prohibited. Extract, 40 per cent.	583
	roasted ...	5.04	......				
	all substitutes.	3.84	......				
							584
10 per cent	Centner	2.40	2.16	Pound.... 0.017	10 per cent.......	Each..... 0.109	585
Free	Free.........	......	......	Free	Free	Free	586
Free	Free.........	......	......	Free	Free	Free	587
Foreign, per 100 kilogs, $11.70.	Free.........	......	......	Free	Free	Free	588
Free	Free.........	......	......	Free	Free	Free	589
Free	Centner	2.40	......	Pound.... 0.091	Kande.... 0.352	Free	590
Free	See Chemicals	......	......	Pound.... 0.0113	See Chemic'ls not enumerated.	Free	591
10 per cent	Centner	7.20	5.76	Pound.... 0.091	10 per cent.......	Pound ... 0.047	592
Free..............	See Chemicals	......	......	Pound.... 0.0113	See Chemic'ls not enumerated.	Free	593
10 per cent	Centner	7.20	5.76	....			594
10 per cent.......	....	......	......	....	....	....	
				Pound.... 0.091	Pound.... 0.11	Pound ... 0.10	
Free	Free	......	......	Free	Free	Free	595
Free	Centner	2.52	1.44	Pound.... 0.0113	Free	Free	596

Comparative table of import duties in the United States and European countries.

	ARTICLES.	UNITED STATES.	GREAT BRITAIN.	GERMAN ZOLL-VEREIN.	SWITZERLAND.
597	Coloring for brandy	50 per cent	Free	Centner . . $2.40	Centner . . $0.68
598	Colors, water	35 per cent	Free	Centner . . 2.40	Centner . . 0.68
599	Colt's foot, (crude drug)	20 per cent	Free	Centner . . 0.36	Centner . . 0.68
600	Combs, curry	35 per cent	Free	Free, cen'r. 1.92	Centner . . 0.68
601	all, for the hair	35 per cent	Free	India-rubber, centner, 2.88 to 7.20.	Centner . . 1.56
602	Comfits, preserved in sugar, brandy, or molasses.	35 per cent	Pound $0.02	Centner . . 5.04	Centner . . 1.56
603	Commode handles	35 per cent	Free	Centner . . 2.88	Centner . . 1.56
604	knobs	35 per cent	Free	Centner . . 2.88	Centner . . 1.56
605	Compasses, brass, iron	35 per cent	Free	Free	Centner . . 0.39
606	copper	45 per cent	Free	Free	Centner . . 0.39
607	steel	45 per cent	Free	Free	Centner . . 0.39
608	mariners'	35 per cent	Free	Free	Centner . . 0.39
609	wood	35 per cent	Free	Free	Centner . . 0.39
610	Composition, of glass or paste, set.	35 per cent	Free	Centner . . 5.76	Centner . . 2.93
611	for jewelers, not set.	40 per cent	Free	Centner . . 0.36	Centner . . 0.39
612	Confectionery, not otherwise enumerated, valued over 30 cents per pound, and sold by box or package.	50 per cent	Pound 0.02	Centner . . 4.64	Centner . . 1.56
613	valued at 30 cents per pound or less.	Pound ..$0.15			
614	Contrayerra root	20 per cent	Free	Centner . . 0.36	Centner . . 0.68
615	Copperas	Pound 0.005	Free	Centner . . 0.36	Centner . . 0.68
616	Copper bottoms	45 per cent	Free	Centner . . 1.26	...
617	braziers or sheets	45 per cent	Free	Centner . . 1.26	...
618	plates, engraved	45 per cent	Free	Centner . . 2.88	...
619	for use of mint	Pound 0.05	Free	...	Copper, raw, in blocks or plates, centner .. 0.145
620	in pigs, bars	Pound 0.05	Free	Centner . . 1.26	
621	old, fit only for remanufacture.	Pound 0.04	Free	Free	
622	ore, of fine copper therein.	Pound 0.03	Free	Free	Centner . . 0.029
623	rods, bolts, spikes, nails.	45 per cent	Free	Centner . . 1.26	...
624	all regulus, black or coarse.	Pound 0.04	Free	All manufactures not varnished, centner .. 1.92	...
625	all manufactures of.	45 per cent	Free	All manufactures varnished, centner 2.88	Centner . . 1.56
626	sulphate of	Pound 0.05	Free	Free	Centner . . 0.68
627	Coral	Free	Free	Centner . . 0.36	Centner . . 2.93
628	cut or manufactured	30 per cent	Free	Centner . . 36.00	Centner . . 2.93

(*Duties expressed in gold dollars of the United States.*)—Continued.

FRANCE.					RUSSIA.	NETHERLANDS.	
	General tariff.		In treaty with Great Britain, &c.				
	In French vessels.	In other vessels.	In vessels of treaty powers.	In other vessels.			
....	Free...	Free...	Free...	Free...	Pood $0.85	Free................	597
Colors, paste or liquid ..	Free...	Free...	Free...	Free...	Pood 3.43	Free................	598
....	Free...	Free...	Free ...	Free...	Free..................	Free	599
100 kilogs..............	$1.56	$1.80	....	....	Pood 0.62	5 per cent	600
100 kilogs..............	19.50	20.95	10 per	cent.	Pood 2.57	5 per cent	601
100 kilogs..............	8.19	8.58	....	....	Pood 3.90	5 per cent	602
....	15 per	cent.	10 per	cent.	Pood 0.85	5 per cent	603
....	15 per	cent.	10 per	cent.	Pood 0.85	5 per cent	604
100 kilogs..............	30 per	cent.	Free ..	$0.048	Mathematical instruments, pood .. 4.68	5 per cent	605
....	30 per	cent.	Free ..	0.048	....	5 per cent	606
....	30 per	cent.	Free ..	0.048	....	5 per cent	607
....	30 per	cent.	Free ..	0.048	....	5 per cent	608
....	30 per	cent.	Free ..	0.048	....	5 per cent	609
....	15 per	cent.	10 per	cent.	Pound 0.85	5 per cent	610
....	15 per	cent.	10 per	cent.	Pood 3.12	Free	611
							612
100 kilogs..............	4.09	4.28	....	....	Pood 3.90	100 kilogs...$10.25	
							613
100 kilogs..............	Free ..	0.97	$0.39	0.43	Free	Free	614
....	....	....	....	....	Free	Free	615
Copper, ore	Free ..	Free ..	Free ..	Free ..	Free	100 kilogs.... 1.64	616
Pure, in bars, 100 kil.	Free ..	0.048	Free ..	0.048	Copper, in sheets, plates, bars, pigs, or other form: Pood 0.48	100 kilogs.... 0.41	617
Beaten, plate, 100 kil.	2.92	3.49	1.95	2.14		100 kilogs.... 1.64	618
Spun, (wire,) painted, 100 kilogs.	19.50	20.95	1.95	2.14		Free .... Free	619 620
Spun, (wire,) not painted, 100 kilogs.	19.50	20.95	....	....	All manufactures of copper: Pood 2.34	Free .... Free	621
Alloyed with zinc, 100 kilogs.	Free ..	0.048	....	....		100 kilogs.... 0.41 100 kilogs.... 0.41	622
Alloyed, stretched, 100 kilogs.	3.92	3.40	....	....		100 kilogs.... 0.41 100 kilogs.... 0.41	623
Wire, polished, for instruments, 100 kil.	19.50	20.95	....	....		5 per cent	624
Other wire, polished..	Prohib	ited.	....	....			
Wire, not polished, 100 kilogs.	19.50	20.95	....	....			625
Filings, old pieces....	Free ..	0.048	Free ..	0.048			
Copper, gilded or silvered, in plates or ware, 100 kilogs.	19.50	20.95	19.50	20.95			
Manufactures of copper, pure or alloyed,	19.50	20.95		....			
Simply turned, 100 k.	39.00	41.43	3.90	4.29			
Fancy, 100 kilogs							
Others, 100 kilogs	Prohib	ited.		....			
See Chemicals..........	....	....	....	....	Pood 0.85	See Chemicals	626
....	Free ..	Free ..	Free ..	Free ..	Free	Free	627
100 kilogs	39.00	41.43	10 per	cent.	Pound......... 0.85	Free	628

Comparative table of import duties in the United States and European countries.

	ARTICLES.	ITALY.			SPAIN.	PORTUGAL.
			General tariff.	Tariff in treaty with France, &c.		
597	Coloring for brandy........	100 kilogs	$11.70	$2.25	See Chemicals......	Colors for writing, per kilog, $0.054.
598	Colors, water	100 kilogs	11.70	2.25	Colors, in powder, lumps, per 100 kil., $1.50. Prepar'd, 100 kilogs, $5.00. Others, 5 per cent ..	Colors for printing and lithography, free.
599	Colt's foot, (crude drug)....	Free	......	......	100 kilogs....$2.00	Free...............
600	Combs, curry..............	100 kilogs	1.56	1.80	20 per cent	Kilogs $0.081
601	all, for the hair.....	100 kilogs	9.75	9.75	20 per cent	Kilogs 0.40
602	Comfits, preserved in sugar, brandy, or molasses.	100 kilogs	7.80	......	Kilog........ 0.20	Kilogs 0.0756
603	Commode handles	As comm'n mercery, 100 kilogs.	9.75	9.75	20 per cent.........	35 per cent. if wood.
604	knobs...........					
605	Compasses, brass or iron...	100 kilogs	3.90	1.95	10 per cent.........	....
606	copper	100 kilogs.	3.90	1.95	10 per cent.........	5 per cent ....
607	steel	....	......	......	10 per cent.........	
608	mariner's	100 kilogs	3.90	1.95	10 per cent.........	
609	wood	100 kilogs	3.90	1.95	10 per cent.........	
610	Composition, of glass or paste, set.	10 per cent	......	......	100 kilogs.... 9.00	Kilogs 0.054
611	for jewelers, not set.	100 kilogs	9.75	......	100 kilogs.... 9.00	Kilogs 0.054
612	Confectionery, not otherwise enumerated, valued over 30 cents per pound, and sold by box or package.	100 kilogs	7.80	......	kilogs 0.20	Kilogs 0.135
613	valued at 30 cents per pound or less.					
614	Contrayerra root...........	100 kilogs	1.95	0.39	100 kilogs.... 2.00	5 per cent ....
615	Copperas	....	......	......	Kilog........ 0.02	10 per cent ....
616	Copper bottoms............	Copper, mineral, in pieces.	Free.	......	Copper, mineral, free.	Copper, crude and ball ..... free.
617	braziers and sheets.					
618	plates, engraved ...	Loaves, per 100 kilogs.	0.78	0.78	In brass and plates, per 100 kil.. 0.05	Pure, cast, per kilog....... 0.02
619	for use of mint.....					
620	in pigs, bars........	Laminated, 100 kilogs.	1.56	1.80	In bars, per 100 kil... 0.05 4.50	Beaten and laminated, in basins, for manufacture, kilog..... 0.021
621	old, fit only for remanufacture.	Wire or sheet, 100 kilogs.	2.34	2.34	Plates, nails, and wire, 100 k. 10.00	
622	ore, of fine copper therein.	Manufactures, not done with iron, 100 kil.	3.90	3.90	Tubes, boiler bottoms, and large pieces, per 100 kilogs 14.00	Not specified, kilog ... 0.0021
623	rods, bolts, spikes, nails.............					Wire, kilog. 0.054
624	all regulars, black or coarse.	With iron, per 100 kilogs.	2.93	3.90	Manufactures of copper, pure or mixed, per 100 kilogs 25.00	Alloyed with zinc. See Brass.
625	all manufactures of.	Gilded & silv'rd ingots, 100 kilogs.	5.85	6.76		Alloyed with pewter. See Bronze.
		laminated, 100 kilogs.	9.75	11.22		Manufactures, pure or alloyed: Fancy articles, kilog 2.16
		wire, 100 kil.	16.57	19.44		Buttons, plain, kilog..... 0.54
		manuf'ct'rs, 100 kilogs.	19.50	19.50		Buttons, fancy, kilog. ... 0.81
						Nails, per k. 0.216
						Articles gilded, kilog 0.54
						All not specified, kilog ....: 0.27
626	sulphate of.........	100 kilogs	1.95	0.78	Kilog........ 0.02	10 per cent.........
627	Coral.....................	Free	......	......	100 kilogs.... 0.10	Raw, cut, or in pieces, free.
628	cut or manufactured .	Per cent	1	10	Kilog........ 2.50	Polished or manuf., kilog....... 0.216

(Duties expressed in gold dollars of the United States.)—Continued.

BELGIUM.	AUSTRIA.			DENMARK.	SWEDEN.	NORWAY.	
		General tariff.	Tariff in treaty.				
Free	Centner	$0.72	$0.72	Pound....$0.028	Free	Free	597
Free	Centner	7.20	5.76	Pound.... 0.028	Free	Free	598
Free	Centner	0.38	......	Free	Free	Free	599
100 kilogs ..$0.78	Centner	2.40	2.16	Pound..... 0.017	10 per cent	Free	600
10 per cent.......	Centner	5.76	......	Pound..... 0.091	10 per cent	Horn, p'd .$0.061	601
100 kilogs ..11.70	Centner	7.56	4.80	Pound..... 0.04	Pound.... $0.055	Pound 0.082	602
10 per cent.......	According to material.			Pound ... 0.091	10 per cent	According to material, 10 p.c.	603
				Wood, p'd 0.017	10 per cent		604
Free............	Centner	4.80	3.60	Pound..... 0.091	Pound..... 0.041	Free	605
Free	See Instruments.			Pound..... 0.017	Pound..... 0.041	Free	606
Free............				Pound..... 0.091	Pound..... 0.041	Free	607
Free				Pound..... 0.017	Free	Free	608
							609
10 per cent	Centner	7.20	5.76	Pound..... 0.091	See Jewelry	See Jewelry.....	610
10 per cent	Centner	5.04	2.88	Pound..... 0.091	Pound..... 0.165	Pound 0.109	611
Free	Centner	7.56	4.80	Pound..... 0.04	Pound..... 0.055	Pound . . 0.061	612 613
Free	Free	......	......	Free	Free	Free	614
Free	See Chemicals	......	......	Free	Free	Free	615
Copper, crude, in blocks, sheets, and old copper, free. Beaten, drawn, or laminated, gilded or silvered, spun on thread or silk, 100 kilogs 1.95 Nails, also, if gilded, worked, bronzed, 10 per cent. Foreign coin, 100 kil...11.70 Nails, sheets for ships, free. Tissues of copper thread, for machinery, 100 kilogs ... 2.34	Copper, crude or broken pieces .... Drawn, laminated, and in coarse castings, such as bells, tubes, each piece of over 100 lbs., centner ..... Copper cylinders, for printing, centner.. Articles, not gilded, silvered, ornamented, centner.. Gilded, &c., centner ..... Plated, wire, and sheets, centner	Free. 2.88 0.36 3.60 7.20 7.20	Free. 1.92 ...... 2.16 5.76 5.76	Ore, free .... Plates, sheets, nails, wire, pound, 0.017 Bolts, plates for vessels, and other articles of yellow metal, p'd . 0.057 Manufactured articles, bronzed, varnished, gilded, silvered, or plated; other compositions, pound ..... 0.091 All other articles, plain, p'd. .0.0455	Copper, ore, sheets, blocks, &c., free. Manufactures, not polished, pound... 0.041 Polished, pound... 0.082	Copper, pure and alloyed, in plates, sheets, bars, tubes, wire, strings, and busts, not over 50 pounds, free. Nails pd'...0.021 Shts. pl'd, p'd0.095 buttons, in connection wi h glass, mother-of-pearl, pound .... 0.109 Wire-work, pound .... 0.047 Bells, candlesticks, rings, thimbles, watch-keys, pound .... 0.047 The same, gilded, &c., pound. 0.095 The same, polished, &c., pound 0.047	616 617 618 619 620 621 622 623 624 625
Free	See Chemicals	......	......	Pound.....0.0113	Free	Free	626
Free	Free	......	......	Pound..... 0.091	Free	Free	627
Free	Free....	......	......	Pound..... 0.91	Not set, free	Free............	628

Comparative table of import duties in the United States and European countries.

	ARTICLES.	UNITED STATES.	GREAT BRITAIN.	GERMAN ZOLL-VEREIN.	SWITZERLAND.
629	Cordage, tarred	Pound $0.03	Free	All, cen'r. $0.36	All, cent'r. $0.39
630	untarred	Pound 0.03½	Free		
631	manilla, untarred	Pound 0.02½	Free		
632	all other	Pound 0.03½	Free		
633	Cordials, all	Gallon 2.50	Gallon $2.53	Centner .. 4.32	Centner .. 1.56
634	Coriander seed	Pound 0.03	Free	Centner .. 0.72	Centner .. 0.028
635	Corks, and manufactures of	50 per cent	Free	Centner .. 0.36	Centner .. 0.39
636	Cork tree, bark of, unmanufactured.	30 per cent	Free	Free	Centner .. 0.029
637	Cornelian stone	10 per cent	Free	Free	Centner .. 0.029
638	rings	20 per cent	Free	Centner .. 5.76	Centner .. 2.93
639	Corn, Indian or maize	Bushel 0.10	Free	Free	Centner .. 0.029
640	meal	10 per cent	Free	Centner .. 0.36	Centner .. 0.39
641	Corrosive sublimate	20 per cent	Free	Centner .. 2.40	Centner .. 0.68
642	Corsets	35 per cent	Free	Centner .. 7.20	Centner .. 2.93
643	Cosmetics	50 per cent	Free	Centner .. 2.40	Centner .. 2.93
644	Corn fans	35 per cent	Free	Centner ..10.80	Centner .. 1.56
645	Cotton, raw	Free	Free All manufactures of, free.	Free Cotton wadding, center ... 0.98	Centner .. 0.058 Cotton wadding, centner .. 0.39

FRANCE.—Duties on cotton yarns and tissues under the

Cotton yarns measuring half kilogramme.	100 kilogramme.											
	Single.						Twisted, (double.)					
	Unbleached.		Bleached.		Dyed.		Unbleached.		Bleached.		Dyed.	
	In vessels of treaty powers.	In other vessels.	In vessels of treaty powers.	In other vessels.	In vessels of treaty powers.	In other vessels.	In vessels of treaty powers.	In other vessels.	In vessels of treaty powers.	In other vessels.	In vessels of treaty powers.	In other vessels.
20,500 meters or less	$2.92	$3.20	$3.36	$3.68	$7.80	$8.58	$3.80	$4.17	$4.37	$4.80	$8.68	$9.53
20,500 to 30,500 meters	3.90	4.29	4.48	4.93	8.77	9.66	5.07	5.57	5.83	6.40	9.94	10.91
30,500 to 40,500 meters	5.85	6.43	6.72	7.38	10.72	11.73	7.60	8.27	8.74	9.61	12.48	13.59
40,500 to 50,500 meters	7.80	8.58	8.97	8.87	12.67	13.78	10.14	11.13	11.66	12.72	15.01	16.24
50,500 to 60,500 meters	9.75	10.72	11.21	12.24	14.62	15.83	12.67	13.78	14.57	15.77	17.55	18.91
60,500 to 70,500 meters	11.70	12.76	13.45	14.60	16.57	17.88	15.21	16.46	17.49	18.84	20.07	21.57
70,500 to 80,500 meters	13.65	14.82	15.69	16.96	18.52	19.93	17.74	19.11	20.41	21.90	22.62	24.34
80,500 to 90,500 meters	17.55	18.91	20.17	21.66	22.42	24.02	21.58	24.45	26.24	28.02	27.69	29.56
90,500 to 100,500 meters	19.90	20.95	22.42	24.01	24.37	26.06	25.35	27.10	29.15	31.08	30.22	32.21
100,500 to 110,500 meters	23.40	25.06	26.91	28.74	28.37	30.16	30.42	32.43	34.98	37.20	35.29	37.54
110,500 to 120,500 meters	27.30	29.14	31.39	33.43	32.17	34.26	35.49	37.75	40.81	43.33	40.36	42.86
120,500 to 130,500 meters	31.20	33.24	35.88	38.16	36.07	38.35	40.56	43.07	46.64	49.45	45.43	48.18
130,500 to 140,500 meters	39.00	41.43	44.55	47.58	43.87	46.54	50.70	53.71	58.31	61.70	55.57	58.83
140,500 to 170,500 meters	48.75	51.67	56.06	59.34	53.62	56.74	63.37	66.78	72.88	76.28	64.45	71.66
Over 170,500 meters	58.50	61.90	67.27	70.68	63.37	66.78	76.05	79.45	87.46	90.87	80.94	84.34

(Cotton yarn in all vessels:)

Pure, twisted, single torsion, meter of length $0.0117
Triple or more, bleached or dyed, several torsions or cabled, meter of length 0.0234

Cotton yarn warped in chain, unbleached, bleached, or dyed, same as twisted double.
Cotton yarn mixed, cotton predominating, same as pure cotton yarn.

(*Duties expressed in gold dollars of the United States.*)—Continued.

	FRANCE.				RUSSIA.	NETHERLANDS.	
	General tariff.		In treaty with Great Britain, &c.				
	In French vessels.	In other vessels.	In vessels of treaty powers.	In other vessels.			
Cordage, of hemp, jute, abaca, 100 kilogs.	$4.87	$5.36	$2.92	$3.20		100 kilogs....$0.21	629
							630
Of cocoa fiber, 100 k..	0.97	1.06	1.17	1.29	All, per pood ..$0.31	100 kilogs.... 0.21	631
Of cane or reed, 100 k.	0.39	0.43	0.47	0.52		100 kilogs.... 0.21	632
Other, 100 kilogs.....	4.87	5.36	2.92	3.20		100 kilogs.... 0.21	
Hectoliter..............	29.25	29.25	2.92	2.92	Bottle 0.50	Hectoliter ... 1.43	633
Free................	....	....	....	....	Free	Free	634
....	10 per cent.		10 per cent.		Pood 0.16	100 kilogs.... 4.10	635
Raw and in leaves, 100 kilogs.	0.195	0.195	....	....	Free	Free	636
....	Free...	Free ..	Free ..	Free ..	Free	Free	637
100 kilogs..............	Prohibited.		Free ..	0.048	Pound.......... 0.85	5 per cent	638
....	Free...	....	Free ..	....	Free	Free	639
....	Free...	....	Free ..	....	Pood 0.03	Free	640
....	See Chemicals not enumerated.				Pood 0.85	See Chemicals	641
35 per cent.............	....	....	....	....	35 per cent...........	5 per cent	642
....	See Perfumeries			....	Pood 4.29	5 per cent	643
As fancy articles, 100 k.	Prohibited.		11.70	12.76	Pound 0.26	5 per cent..........	644
100 kilogs	Free ..	0.58	Free ..	0.58	Free	Free	645
With seed, 100 kilogs...	Free ..	0.145	Free ..	0.145	Cotton wadding, per pood 0.85	....	
Carded and gummed, 100 kilogs.	1.95	1.32	1.95	2.14			

tariff in treaty with Great Britain and other countries.

Cotton tissues having in chain and woof in the space of 5 square millimeters, weighing—	Unbleached.		Bleached.		Dyed.	
	In vessels of treaty powers.	In other vessels.	In vessels of treaty powers.	In other vessels.	In vessels of treaty powers.	In other vessels.
11 kilogs. or more per 100 square meters:						
35 threads or less, 100 kilogs	$9.75	$10.72	$11.21	$12.25	$14.62	$15.83
36 threads or more, 100 kilogs	15.60	16.86	17.94	19.32	20.47	21.96
1 to 11 kilogs. per 100 square meters:						
35 threads or less, 100 kilogs	11.70	12.76	13.45	14.60	16.57	17.87
36 to 43 threads, 100 kilogs	19.50	20.95	22.42	24.02	24.37	26.06
44 threads or more, 100 kilogs	39.10	41.38	44.85	47.58	43.87	46.54
3 to 7 kilogs. per 100 square meters:						
27 threads or less, 100 kilogs	15.60	16.86	17.94	19.32	20.47	21.96
28 to 35 threads, 100 kilogs	23.40	25.05	26.91	28.74	28.27	30.16
36 to 43 threads, 100 kilogs	37.05	39.39	42.60	45.22	41.92	44.50
44 threads or more, 100 kilogs	58.50	60.58	67.27	70.69	63.37	66.78

Tissues weighing less than 3 kilogs., per 100 square meters, 15 per cent, ad valorem.
Printed cotton, 15 per cent. ad valorem.

	French vessels of treaty powers.	Other vessels.
Cotton velvet, silk:		
Unbleached, 100 kilogs	$16.57	$17.88
Dyed or printed, 100 kilogs	21.45	23.01
Other cotton velvet:		
Unbleached, 100 kilogs	11.70	12.76
Dyed or printed, 100 kilogs	17.57	17.88

Cotton tissues: embroidered by hand, 10 per cent.; lace and blond, 5 per cent.; piquet, fashioned, damasked, or brilliant, also covers, 15 per cent.; gauzes, muslins, embroidered for furniture or dress, 10 per cent.

Comparative table of import duties in the United States and European countries.

	ARTICLES.	ITALY.			SPAIN.	PORTUGAL.
			General tariff.	Tariff in treaty with France, &c.		
629	Cordage, tarred	Cordage, natural or tarred, 100 kilogs.	$0.58	$0.58	Cordage, hemp or flax, per 100 kilogs $4.00	Cordage, of hemp, tarred or not, new or old, kil. $0.07. Fit to be untwisted only, free.
630	untarred					
631	manilla, untarred					
632	all other					
633	Cordials, all	Hectoliter	11.70	2.93	Liter 0.20	Decaliter 1.62
634	Coriander seed	Free	......	......	100 kilogs 0.32	Kilogs 0.054
635	Corks, and manufactures of	100 kilogs	1.95	1.95	20 per cent	Kilogs 0.027
636	Cork tree, bark of, unmanufactured.	100 kilogs	0.02	Free.	100 kilogs 0.10	Free
637	Cornelian stone	100 kilogs	0.48	Free.	Free	Free
638	rings	....	......	......	20 per cent	Kilogs 0.0108
639	Corn, Indian or maize	100 kilogs	0.145	0.145	100 kilogs 0.45	Kilogs 0.008
640	meal	100 kilogs	9.24	......	100 kilogs	Fixed by spec'l laws.
641	Corrosive sublimate	100 kilogs	1.95	0.39	Kilog 0.20	5 per cent
642	Corsets	Per cent	10	10	20 per cent	Double duties mate'l.
643	Cosmetics	100 kilogs	11.70	10 p.c.	Kilog 0.30	20 per cent
644	Corn fans	100 kilogs	9.75	9.75	20 per cent	Kilogs 0.40
645	Cotton, raw	Cotton, in wool or mass, carded or gummed, per 100 kilogs.	0.975	1.12	Cotton, raw, per 100 kil...... 0.30. In seed, per 100 kilogs 0.15	Cotton, seed, free.. Raw, per k. 0.00054. Wadding, kil. 0.216

NOTE.—Tariff regulations in regard to mixed tissues:

I. SPAIN.—An extra duty of $0.50 per 100 kilogs. on raw cotton imported by foreign vessels is levied till January 1, 1872. Cotton containing reed pays, per 100 kilogs, $0.15. A tare of 40 per cent. is allowed on cotton on spools.

Textures of linen, wool, and silk, interwoven with cotton, will pay the same duty as pure and unmixed linen, wool, and silk, respectively; textures of wool and silk, or waste of silk, the warp of which is composed of one of those two materials, will pay duty upon one-fifth of their weight like silk, and four-fifths like wool; textures of linen and silk, the warp of which is composed of one of those two materials, and textures of cotton and silk, whose warp is entirely of cotton, will pay duty on four-fifths of the weight as tissues of linen or cotton, as the case may be, and one-fifth as silk stuff, excepting plush and satin, which will pay three-fifths as cotton and two-fifths as silk; textures of linen and wool with a warp composed of one of those two materials, will pay duty on three-fifths of their weight as woolen, and on two-fifths as linen stuffs; textures of linen and cotton, with a warp entirely of cotton, will pay duty on half their weight as cotton textures, and on the other half as linen; textures having a warp of linen, wool, silk, or cotton, and containing on the other

(*Duties expressed in gold dollars of the United States.*)—Continued.

BELGIUM.	AUSTRIA.			DENMARK.	SWEDEN.	NORWAY.	
		General tariff.	Tariff in treaty.				
Cordage, of 2 millimiters or more diameter, free.	Ceutner	$0. 36	Free.	Pound.....$0. 056	Pound.....$0. 082	Free	629
	Centner	0. 36	Free.	Pound..... 0. 56	Pound..... 0. 082	Over ½ inch diameter, p'd $0.0045	630
	Centner	0. 36	Free.	Pound..... 0. 056	Pound..... 0. 082		631
As thread, free.	Centner	0. 48	$0. 36	Pound..... 0. 056	Pound..... 0. 082	All other p'd 0.018	632
Hectoliter .$16. 58	Centner	6. 312	......	Pott 0. 091	Kando 0. 55	Pot 0. 218	633
100 kilogs .. 0. 117	Centner	0. 36	Free.	Free	Free	Free	634
10 per cent	Centner	1. 20	0. 72	10 per cent	Pound..... 0. 41	Pound 0. 009	635
10 per cent	Free	......	......	Free	Free	Free	636
Free	See Stone ...	......	......	Free	Free	Free	637
10 per cent	See Stone....	......	......	Pound..... 0. 091	Free	Free	638
100 kilogs .. 0. 117	Centner	0. 1296	Free.	Free	Free	Free	639
100 kilogs .. 0. 23	Requires special permit.			Free	Free	Pound 0. 009	640
Free	Centner	2. 40	......	Pound 0. 0113	See Chemicals, free	Free	642
10 per cent	See Clothing.	......	......	Double duties mat'l	10 per cent	10 per cent	642
10 per cent	Centner	7. 20	5. 76	Pound..... 0. 091	10 per cent	Pound 0. 047	643
10 per cent	Centner	21. 00	14. 40	10 per cent.......	10 per cent	10 per cent	644
Free	Cotton, raw or waste	Free.	Free.	Free	Free	Free	645
....	Cotton, combed, centner .	0. 254	Free.	....	....	....	

side of the tissue one, two, or more of these materials, will be subject to the duties previously stated, and will be considered as being composed of linen, wool, silk, or cotton—that is to say, of the material of its mixture which pays the highest duty.

II. PORTUGAL.—The duties to which tissues of silk, mixed with other materials, are subject, are as follows:

1. Mixed tissues, in which the warp or filling are entirely silk, pay duty as silk.

2. Mixed tissues, in which the warp or the filling is half or more than half silk, and the other of different material, are charged with a mixed duty; half of the duty as if they were of silk entirely, and half the duty as if they were of the other material entirely.

3. Mixed tissues, in which the warp or filling is composed less than half of silk, pay one-quarter of the duty of same silk tissues, and three-quarters of the duty on the other material.

4. Tissues mixed with gold or silver pay twenty-five per cent. above the duties fixed for the material of which they are made.

Comparative table of import duties in the United States and European countries.

UNITED STATES.	GREAT BRITAIN.	GERMAN ZOLLVEREIN.	SWITZERLAND.	FRANCE.	General tariff. French vessels.	General tariff. Other vessels.
Cotton yarns: Spool containing, each, not over 100 yards, 6 cents per doz. and 30 p. ct. Spool over 100 yards, in addition for every 100 yards or fractional part thereof, 6 cts. per doz. and 35 p. ct. Thread or yard when advanced beyond single yarn, by twisting two or more strands together, if not on spools, 4 cents per skein or hank of 840 yards and 30 per cent.	Free.	Yarns: Single and double, raw, centner .....$1. 44 Bleached, dyed, centner . 2. 88 Triple & other bleached or dyed, centner 4. 32	Yarns: Raw, unbleached, cent'r. $0.39 Bleached, dyed, centner .. 0. 68	Yarns: The produce of Tunis, and directly imported, 100 kilogs.; like tariff of treaty powers.		
				All other cotton yarn unbleached: single, 100 kilogs	136. 50	150. 15
Thread, other, 40 per cent.				Twisted, 100 kil	156. 00	172. 60
Tissues.—Braids, 30 per cent. Cord, gimps, and galloons, 35 p. ct. Braces or suspenders, 35 per cent.				All other, without distinction of class or number	Prohi	bited.
(Except jeans, denims, drillings, bed-tickings, ginghams, plaids, cottonades, pantaloon stuff, and goods of like description,) not bleached, colored, stained, painted, or printed, and not exceeding 100 threads to the sq. inch, counting the warp and filling, and exceeding in weight 5 ounces per sq. yd., 5 cts. p. sq. yd.				Waste of cotton, 100 kilogs.	Free.	$0. 58
As above, if bleached, 5½ cents per square yard.		Tissues: Of raw yarn, bleached, centner $7. 20	Tissues: Unbleached, centner. $0. 39 Bleached, printed, dyed, &c., centner . 1. 56	Tissues: Nankins, produce of India, 100 kilogs.....	$19. 00	$92. 00
As above if colored, stained, painted, or printed, 5½ cents per square yard and 10 per cent.		Fringe and tissues mixed with metallic thread, centner..... 11. 50		Nankins, all other	Prohi	bited.
Unbleached, weight less than 5 ozs. per square yard, not exceeding 100 threads to the square inch, warp and filling, square yard, $0. 025.				Lace, by hand or otherwise, 100 kilogs.....	5 per	cent.
As above, bleached, sq. yard, $0. 03.		Muslins, gauze, lace, embroideries, centner 21. 60		Tulle, with lace work, 100 kil..	5 per	cent.
As above, colored, stained, painted, or printed, 10 per cent. and per square yard, $. 035.				All other tulle and all other cotton tissues..	Prohi	bited.
Finer or lighter, unbleached, not over 200 threads to the sq. inch, counting the warp and filling, 5 cents per square yard. As above, bleached, 5½ per sq. yard. As above, colored, stained, painted, or printed, 5 cents per sq. yd. and and 20 per cent. Unbleached, over 200 threads to the sq. inch, counting the warp and filling, 5 cents per square yard. As above, if bleached, 5½ cents per square yard. As above, if colored, stained, painted, or printed, 5 cents per square yard and 20 per cent. Jeans, denims, drillings, bed-tickings, ginghams, plaids, cottonades, pantaloon stuffs, and goods of like description, or for similar use, not over 100 threads to the sq. inch, counting the warp and filling, and exceeding five ounces to the sq. yard, if bleached, 6 cts. p. sq. yd. As above, if bleached, 6½ cts. p. sq. yd. As above, if colored, stained, painted, or printed, 6½ cents per square yard and 10 per cent.				For duties under the treaty tariff see pages 58 and 59, marked France.		

(Duties expressed in gold dollars of the Unieed States.)— Continued.

RUSSIA.	NETHERLANDS.
All yarns unbleached and bleached, pood........ $2.51 Dyed, pood .... 3.28 Tissues: Raw, bleached, or printed, containing more than 8 square arshines in 1 pound weight, pound 0.22 As above, of 8 to 12 sq. arshines in 1 lb. weight, pound 0.30 As above, of 12 to 16 sq. arshines in 1 lb. weight, pound 0.39 Over 16 sq. arshines in 1 pound weight, pound .... 0.85 Printed and dyed of 8 square arshines in 1 pound weight, pound .... 0.39 As above, of 8 to 12 square arshines in 1 lb. weight, lb. 0.48 As above, of 12 to 16 square arshines in 1 pound weight, pound .... 0.58 Over 16 sq. arshines in 1 pound weight, pound 1.03	All yarns 3 per cent. except yarns for disks, 100 kilogrammes . $0.205 All tissues 5 per ct.

ITALY.	General tariff.	Tariff in treaty.
Yarns: raw, single, of not more than 20,000 meters, per ½ kilogramme, 100kilogs ...	$2.93	} 5.63
20,000 to 30,000 meters..	3.90	
Over 30,000 meters.....	4.87	
Twisted, all, 100 kilogs.	4.87	$5.63
Bleached or dyed, all, 100 kilogs............	5.85	6.75
Tissues: unbleached, weighing 7 to 10 kil. or more per 100 square meters, and having 35 threads or less per 5 sq. millimeters, 100 kilogs.	9.75	......
Bleached, as above, 100 kilogs	11.12	......
Other raw, 100 kilogs...	12.68	......
Other bleached, 100 kil ..	14.43	......
Other printed or dyed, 100 kilogs	17.55	......
Other pressed, 100 kilogs	19.50	22.52
Embroidered in linen, cotton, or wool, 100 kilogs	39.00	55.24
Waxed, painted, or varnished, 100 kilogs.....	9.75	......
Cotton velvet, kilog....	0.145	0.164
Cotton ribbon, kilog....	0.117	......

SPAIN.
Yarns: All kinds, No. 1 to 35, kilog. $0.25
No. 36 and above, kilogramme....... 0.35
For sewing and embroidery, triple or more, all kinds, kilogramme 0.50
Tissues: pressed, unbleached, white, or colored, 25 threads in 6 millimeters square, kilogramme ... 0.60
Above 26 threads, kilogramme 0.537
Printed, worked transversely, 25 threads per square of 6 millimeters, warp and loom, kilog.... 0.80
As above, 26 threads, kilogramme .. 0.737
Muslins, batiste, gauzes, &c., kilog..... 0.60
Quilting and piquet, kilogramme ... 0.90
Velvetry and other of double texture, kilogramme....... 0.70
Illusions, (tulle,) kilogramme....... 1.00
Crochets in all forms, exclusive borders, kilogramme ... 0.60
Edgings, kilog... 0.25
Knitted goods, undershirts, drawers, kilogramme....... 0.525
Socks, stockings, gloves, &c., kilog..... 1.05

See note on mixed tissues, page 60.

Comparative table of import duties in the United States and European countries.

UNITED STATES.

Tissues—Continued.

Finer or lighter, not over 200 threads to the square inch, counting the warp and filling, if unbleached, 6 cents per square yard.

As above, if bleached, 6½ cents per square yard.

As above, if colored, stained, painted, or printed, 6½ cents per square and 15 per cent.

As above, over 200 threads to the sq. inch, counting the warp and filling, unbleached 7 cts. p. sq. yd.

As above, if bleached, 7½ cents per square yard.

As above, if colored, stained, painted, or printed, 7½ cents per square and 15 per cent.

Provided that no cotton goods having more than 200 threads to the square inch, counting the warp and filling, shall be admitted to a less rate of duty than is provided for goods which are of that number of threads.

Provided on plain woven cotton goods, not included in the foregoing schedules, over 16 cents per sq. yard, unbleached, shall pay 35 per cent.

As above, if bleached, and valued over 20 cents per square yard, 35 per cent.

As above, if colored, valued over 25 cents per square yard, 35 per cent.

Or cotton jeans, denims, and drillings, valued over 20 cents per sq. yard, unbleached, 35 per cent.

On all other cotton goods, valued over 25 cents per square yard, 35 per cent.

Shirts, woven, or made on frames, 35 per cent.

Drawers, woven, or made on frames, 35 per cent.

Velvet, 35 per cent.

Bagging or other manufactures not otherwise provided for, suitable for the uses to which cotton bagging is applied, composed in whole or in part of hemp, jute, flax, gunny bags, gunny cloth, or other material, and valued less than 10 cents per sq. yard, 35 cts. per lb.

As above, valued over 10 cents per square yard, 4 cents per pound.

Caps, gloves, leggings, mits, socks, stockings made on frames, bleached or colored, 35 per cent.

Hose, unbleached, 35 per cent.

Mits, bleached or colored, 35 per ct.

Gloves, bleached or colored, 35 p. ct.

Inserting, 35 per cent.

Lace, known as trimmings, or bobbinet, 35 per cent.

Lace, colored, 35 per cent.

Stockings, 35 per cent.

PORTUGAL.

Yarns:

Single, raw, kilogramme $0.1458

Single, white, kilog...... 0.216

Single, dyed, kilogramme. 0.243

Twisted, kilogramme.... 0.324

Tissues, loose and transparent:

Lace, kilogramme....... 2.70

Lace of ordinary thread, kilogramme 0.595

Muslin and gauze webbing, kilogramme 0.162

Barege, kilogramme..... 0.648

Cambrics, not finished, kil. 0.216

Others not enumerated, kil 0.756

Closely woven: sailing cloth, kilogramme 0.108

Dutch, kilogramme...... 0.162

Muslin, white, kilog...... 0.297

Muslin, printed, kilog.... 0.594

Not specified: unbleached of 11 threads warp in 5 millimeters, kilogramme 0.108

Unbleached of 12 threads or more in 5 millimeters, kilog. 0.162

Bleached of 11 threads warp in 5 millimeters, kilog. .. 0.135

Bleached of 12 threads or more in 5 millimeters, kilogs. 0.189

Printed or stamped, kilog. 0.594

Mixed with wool: linsey, one color, kilogramme 0.594

More than one color, kil. 0.81

Covers: mole skins dyed, kilogramme 0.243

Mole skins pressed, kilog. 0.459

Velvets: Shag, kilog 0.594

Velveteen and corded velveteen, kilogramme 0.243

Cotton velvets, kilog 0.486

Damasked, kilogramme.. 0.432

Braided, ribbed, or smooth:

Quiltings, kilogramme... 0.864

Flurt silk and caps, kilog. 1.188

Serge, raw, kilogramme. 0.216

Counterpanes, kilog..... 0.594

Not specified: bleached or unbleached, kilogramme. 0.459

Painted or stamped, kilog. 0.594

Ribbons, kilogramme.... 0.486

Shawls and laces of tissues, printed or pressed, kilog. 0.756

Other not specified, as tissues of which made: cotton wicks, kilogramme 0.54

Cotton carpets, kilog 0.216

Other manufactures of cotton:

Mesh work, Scotch, kilog 1.404

Mesh work not specified, kilogramme 1.188

Figured, not specified, kil. 1.188

Other manufactures not enumerated: double duty as tissues of which made.

BELGIUM.

Yarns—Unbleached & bleached, measuring per ½ kilogramme:

20,000 meters or less, 100 kil. $0.93

20,000 to 30,000 meters, 100 kilogs 3.90

30,000 to 40,000 meters, 100 kilogs 5.85

40,000 to 65,000 meters, 100 kilogs 7.80

Over 65,000 meters, 100 kilogs. 1.95

Dyed or warped, measuring per ½ kilogramme:

20,000 meters or less, 100 kil. 4.87

20,000 to 30,000 meters, 100 kilogs 5.85

30,000 to 40,000 meters, 100 kilogs 7.80

40,000 to 65,000 meters, 100 kilogs 9.95

Over 65,000 meters, 100 kilogs 1.95

Tissues of cotton, unbleached:

1st class, weighing 11 kilogs. or more per 100 square meters of 35 threads or less, 100 kilogs. $9.75

Of 36 threads or more, 100 kil. 15.60

2d class weighing 7 to 11 (exclusive) kilogs. per 100 sq. meters of 35 threads or less, 100 kilogs. 11.70

Of 36 to 43 threads, 100 kil.. 19.50

Of 44 threads or more, 100 kil. 39.00

3d class weighing 3 to 7 (exclusive) kilogs. per 100 sq. meters of 27 threads or less, 100 kilogs. 15.60

Of 28 to 35 threads, 100 kil.. 23.40

Of 36 to 43 threads, 100 kil.. 37.05

Of 44 threads or more, 100 kil. 58.50

Bleached:

1st class weighing 11 kilogs. or more per 100 square meters of 35 threads or less, 100 kilogs. 11.20

Of 35 threads of more, 100 kil. 17.94

2d class weighing 7 to 11 (exclusive) kilogs. per 100 sq. meters of 35 threads or less, 100 kilogs. 13.46

Of 35 to 43 threads, 100 kil.. 22.43

Of 44 threads or more, 100 kil. 44.86

3d class weighing 3 to 7 (exclusive) kilogs. per 100 sq. meters of 27 threads or less, 100 kilogs. 17.94

Of 28 to 35 threads, 100 kil.. 26.91

Of 36 to 43 threads, 100 kil.. 42.46

Of 44 threads or more, 100 kil. 67.27

Dyed:

1st class, weighing 11 kilogs. or more per 100 square meters, of 35 threads or less, 100 kilogs. 14.63

Of 36 threads or more, 100 kil. 20.48

2d class weighing 7 to 11 (exclusive) kilogs. per 100 sq. meters of 35 threads or less, 100 kilog. 16.58

Of 36 to 43 threads, 100 kil.. 24.38

Of 44 threads or more, 100 kil. 43.88

3d class weighing 3 to 7 (exclusive) kilogs. per 100 sq. meters of 27 threads or less, 100 kilogs. 20.48

Of 28 to 35 threads, 100 kil.. 28.08

Of 36 to 43 threads, 100 kil.. 41.93

Of 44 threads or more, 100 kil. 63.38

See note on mixed tissues, page 61.

(*Duties expressed in gold dollars of the United States.*)—Continued.

AUSTRIA.			DENMARK.	SWEDEN.	NORWAY.
Cotton yarns, tissues, &c.	General tariff.	Tariff in treaty.			
Yarns: pure or mixed with wool, not bleached, not dyed, single or double, centner........	$2.52	$1.92	Yarn of one line thick, lb ..$0.17	Yarns, single or double, also spools, not dyed, pound $0.022	Yarns: not twisted or dyed, pound ...$0.016
Bleached, triple or more, not dyed, centner.....	5.04	2.88	Dyed and all other, pound 0.045	All dyed, lb... 0.038	All other, pound.. 0.045
Dyed, all, centner.......	6.312	......	Tissues: not dyed or figured, pound.... 0.068	Tissues: bookbinders' cloth, pound. 0.045	Tissues: sail cloth, and others not dyed, weighing 18 loth per square ell, pound...... 0.018
Tissues: pure or mixed with linen or India-rubber thread—			Various colors not printed, lb. 0.136	Plush, shag, felt, pound 0.11	Wadding, pound . 0.036
Common, unbleached, closely woven, not dyed or printed, not velvetry; also nets, marly, wick, centner..	17.28	12.00	Tricots and velvets, also printed tissues, lb ... 0.182	Gauze, muslins, batiste, pound... 0.21	Tissues bleached, printed, dyed, of 10 loth or more per square ell; also fishing nets, pound 0.073
Medium, finished, bleached, dyed, one or more colored, printed, velvetry, fringe, button goods, ribbons, stockings, centner.	29.76	21.60	Lace, loose tissues, mixed with gold, velvet, or glass thread, lb. 0.273	Sail cloth, lb... 0.016	Wicks, ribbons, tissues mixed with India-rubber, &c., pound. 0.159
Fine, all loose tissues, centner................	43.20	33.60	Oil cloth, lb. 0.091	Tulle, pound... 0.34	Drill, damask, handkerchiefs, pound... 0.146
Fancy, bobbinet, tulle, lace, embroideries, mixed with gold or silver thread, fine or imitated, or with glass thread, centner	126.00	......		Others unbleached, not dyed.... 0.0068	Stockings made by hand; crochet work, dyed, or not, pound..... 0.159
				Bleached or dyed, pound 0.138	Lace, tulle, bobbinet, ...and.......... otner loose tissues, pound 0.241
				Printed or pressed, pound 0.21	Other close tissues painted, pound...... 0.182
				Mixed with linen, same as pure cotton sheeting, lb.. 0.11	As above, several colors or bleached, lb. 0.073
				Damask, pound. 0.138	As above, unbleached, pound 0.036
				Drill, pound ... 0.18	
				Carpets, pound. 0.049	

Comparative table of import duties in the United States and European countries.

	ARTICLES.	UNITED STATES.	GREAT BRITAIN.	GERMAN ZOLL-VEREIN.	SWITZERLAND.
1	Counters, bone, ivory, rice ..	35 per cent......	Free............	Centner...$2.88	Centner...$1.56
2	gold or silver.....	40 per cent......	Free............	Centner...36.00	Centner... 2.93
3	pearl, (shell).....	35 per cent......	Free............	Centner...36.00	Centner... 2.93
4	Counting-house boxes, paper	35 per cent......	Free............	Centner... 0.72	Centner... 0.38
5	with brass rings.	35 per cent......	Free............	Centner... 2.88	Centnero.. 1.56
6	Court plaster	35 per cent......	Free............	Centner... 2.40	Centner... 0.68
7	Cowhides, raw	10 per cent......	....	Free............	See Hides.......
8	tanned	35 per cent......	....	Centner .. 1.44	See Leather.....
9	Cowage or cowitch	20 per cent......	Free............	Free............	Centner... 0.29
10	Cowries (shells)...........	Free............	Free............	Free............	Centner... 0.29
11	Cravats, silk...............	60 per cent......	Free............	Centner..21.60	Centner... 2.93
12	wool or other......	35 per cent......	Free............		
13	Crayons....................	30 per cent......	Free............	Centner... 2.40	Centner... 1.56
14	Cream of tartar............	Pound $0.10	Free............	Free............	Centner... 0.145
15	Cremnitz, white	As white lead ...	Free............	Free............	Centner .. 0.68
16	Crocus (polishing) powder..	25 per cent......	Free............	Free............	Centner .. 0.29
17	Crome yellow..............	25 per cent......	Free............	Free............	Centner .. 0.68
18	Crowns, Leghorn hat	40 per cent......	Free............	Centner... 2.88	Centner... 2.93
19	Crucibles, black lead.......	20 per cent......	Free............	Free............	Centner... 0.39
20	sand	25 per cent......	Free............	Free............	Centner... 0.39
21	Crystals, watch............	40 per cent......	Free............	Centner... 1.92	Centner... 1.56
22	Cubebs....................	Pound......0.10	Free............	Centner... 4.68	Centner... 0.68
23	Cudbear	10 per cent......	Free............	Free............	Centner... 0.195
24	Cummin seed..............	Pound.....0.05	Free............	Centner... 0.72	Centner... 0.029
25	Cupboard turns............	35 per cent......	Free............	Centner... 2.88	Centner... 1.56
26	Curls, hair................	35 per cent......	Free............	Free............	Centner... 2.93
27	Currier's knives...........	45 per cent......	Free............	See Cutlery.....	Centner... 0.68
28	Currants	Pound.....0.05	Cwt 1.71	Centner... 2.88	Centner... 0.68
29	Cutch	10 per cent......	Free............	Free............	Centner... 0.145
30	Cutlasses	35 per cent......	Free............	Centner... 0.96	Centner... 1.56
31	Cutlery, of all kinds, not enumerated. pocket, pen, and jack-knives.	50 per cent......	Free............	Centner... 0.96	Centner..1.56 If not tools.
32	Daggers	35 per cent......	Free............	Centner... 0.96	Centner... 1.56
33	Daguerrotype plates.......	35 per cent......	Free............	Centner... 2.88	Centner... 0.39
34	Dates, green, ripe, or dried	Pound 0.02	Free............	Centner... 2.88	Centner... 0.68
35	preserved in mo-lasses or sugar.	35 per cent....			
36	Decanters, cut glass........	40 per cent......	Free............	Centner... 2.88	Centner... 1.56
37	plain	35 per cent......	Free............	Centner... 0.48	Centner... 0.68
38	Demijohns	40 per cent	Free............	Centner... 0.12	Centner... 0.68
39	Dentrifice	50 per cent......	Free	Centner... 2.88	Centner... 2.93
40	Dextrine, (artificial gum)...	20 per cent	Free............	Centner .. 2.40	Centner .. 0.68
41	Diamonds	10 per cent......	Free............	Centner... 0.36	Centner... 0.39
42	set	25 per cent......	Free............	Centner... 2.88	Centner... 2.93
43	glazier's......	10 per cent	Free............	Centner... 0.36	Centner... 0.68
44	Dice, ivory or bone	50 per cent	Pair 5.11	Centner... 2.88	Centner... 1.56
45	Direct'ns for pat'nt medicines	25 per cent	Free............	Free............	Centner... 0.68
46	Distilled vinegar, medicinal.	See Acetic acid..	Free............	Centner... 0.96	Centner.. 1.56 In bottles, centner 0.68
47	Dishes, chafing, copper.....	45 per cent....	Free............	Centner... 1.92	Centner... 1.56
48	iron or tin..........	35 per cent....			
49	Diuretic sal...............	20 per cent......	Free............	Centner... 2.40	Centner... 0.68
50	Dividivi, crude	Free............	Free............	Free............	Centner... 0.68

(*Duties expressed in gold dollars of the United States.*)—Continued.

FRANCE.					RUSSIA.	NETHERLANDS.	
	General tariff.		In treaty with Great Britain, &c.				
	In French vessels.	In other vessels.	In vessels of treaty powers.	In other vessels.			
	15 per	cent.	10 per	cent.	Pound $0.85	5 per cent	1
100 kilogs	$97.50	$100.90	$97.50	$100.90	See Gold and silver manufactures.	5 per cent	2
As jewelry					Pound 0.85	5 per cent	3
Fancy goods, 100 kilogs.	19.50	20.95	10 per	cent.	Pood 0.85	5 per cent	4
					Pood 2.34	5 per cent	5
					Pood 2.34	Free	6
See Hides					Free	2 per cent	7
See Hides					Pood 3.43	2 per cent	8
	Free	Free	Free	Free	Free	Free	9
	Free	Free	Free	Free	Free	Free	10
See Manuf. of silk					35 per cent	5 per cent	11 12
100 kilogs	1.95	2.14	0.195	0.22	Pood 0.04	5 per cent	13
100 kilogs	5.85	6.43	Free	0.048	Pood 0.16	Free	14
	Free	Free	Free	Free	Pood 0.39	Free	15
	Free	Free	Free	Free	Pood 0.195	Free	16
	Free	Free	Free	Free	Pood 1.56	Free	17
See Hats					Pood 0.624	5 per cent	18
	Free	Free	Free	Free	Free	1 per cent	19
	Free	Free	Free	Free	Free	1 per cent	20
Raw, 100 kilogs Cut, 100 kilogs	1.95 39.00	2.14 41.44	10 per	cent.	Pound 0.062	5 per cent	21
	Prohib	ited	10 per	cent.	Pood 2.34	Free	22
100 kilogs	Free	0.97	0.39	0.43	Free	Free	23
	Free	Free	Free	Free	Free	Free	24
See Manuf. of wood					Pood 0.195	5 per cent	25
100 kilogs	1.95	2.14	2.34	2.87	Pound 0.47	5 per cent	26
See Cutlery					See Cutlery	5 per cent	27
Dry, 100 kilogs	3.12	3.42	1.56	1.72	Pood 0.78	100 kilogs....$0.61	28
	Free	Free	Free	Free	Free	Free	29
			15 per	cent.	See Side-arms	5 per cent	30
	Prohi	bited.	15 per	cent.	Cutlery, mounted with common material, pood .... 9.36 Mounted with silver plate, metal, ivory, &c., pood .....18.72 Farmers' pock't knives, pood 4.68	5 per cent	31
See Cutlery					Ordinary, pood. 8.60 Silver-mounted, pood 17.20	5 per cent	32
						5 per cent	33
Fresh, 100 kilogs	Free	0.78	Free	0.47	Pood 0.78	5 per cent	34
Dry, 100 kilogs	3.12	3.43	1.56	1.72		5 per cent	35
Preserved	4.09	4.29	4.29	4.29		100 kilogs....10.25	
See Manuf. of glass					Pood 3.12	5 per cent	36
See Manuf. of glass					Pood 0.85	5 per cent	37
See Manuf. of glass					Pood 0.85	5 per cent	38
100 kilogs	35.88	38.16	1.95	2.14	Pood 2.34	5 per cent	39
			10 per	cent.	Pood 0.85	Free	40
	Free	Free	Free	Free	Free	Free	41
					Pound 0.85	5 per cent	42
					Free	Free	43
100 kilogs As fancy articles, kilogs	 0.78	 0.86	11.40 or 10	12.76 per ct.	Pood 4.68	5 per cent	44
	Free	Free	Free	Free	Free	Free	45
See Vinegar					In bbls., pood. 0.78 In bottles, each 0.08	100 liters 1.21	46
See Manf. of these metals					Pood 2.34	5 per cent	47 48
See Chemicals not enumerated.					Pood 0.85	5 per cent	49
	Free	Free	Free	Free	Free	Free	50

Comparative table of import duties in the United States and European countries.

	ARTICLES.	ITALY.			SPAIN.	PORTUGAL.
			General tariff.	Tariff in treaty with France, &c.		
1	Counters, bone, ivory, rice..	100 kilogs	$9.75	$9.75	20 per cent	Bone, kilog ..$3.42
2	gold or silver	See Gold and Silver.	......	......	Hectogramme $5.00	Gold, kilogs..54.09
3	pearl, (shell)	100 kilogs	19.50	19.50	Silv'r, hectog. 0.70	Shell, kilogs. 5.40
4	Counting-house boxes, paper	100 kilogs	9.75	9.75	20 per cent	As fancy goods, n. e., kilogs 0.40
5	with brass rings.	100 kilogs	9.75	9.75	20 per cent	
6	Court-plaster	Free	......	......	20 per cent	Free
7	Cowhides, raw	100 kilogs	7.80	2.93	100 kilogs.... 1.50	Kilogramme. 0.005
8	tanned				Kilogramme. 0.25	Kilogramme. 0.054
9	Cowage or cowitch	Free	......	......	100 kilogs.... 0.20	Kilogramme. 0.004
10	Cowries, (shells)	Free	......	......	100 kilogs.... 2.00	Free
11	Cravats, silk	As tissues of material.			1½ duties on mater'l,	Silk, three-fold duties of material.
12	wool or other					
13	Crayons	100 kilogs	1.95	......	20 per cent	Kilogramme. 0.054
14	Cream of tartar	Free	......	......	20 per cent	5 per cent
15	Cremnitz, white	100 kilogs	1.95	0.78	20 per cent	5 per cent
16	Crocus, (polishing,) powder.	100 kilogs	1.95	0.78	20 per cent	Free
17	Crome yellow	100 kilogs	1.95	0.78	100 kilogs.... 5.00	5 per cent
18	Crowns, Leghorn, hat	Each	0.097	0.097	20 per cent	Kilogramme. 0.54
19	Crucibles, black lead	100 kilogs	1.97	0.58	100 kilogs.... 1.60	Kilogramme. 0.001
20	sand	100 kilogs	1.56	1.56	100 kilogs.... 0.30	Kilogramme. 0.001
21	Crystals, watch	100 kilogs	9.75	9.75	100 kilogs....16.00	20 per cent
22	Cubebs	100 kilogs	1.95	0.39	20 per cent	5 per cent
23	Cudbear	100 kilogs	0.39	0.39	100 kilogs.... 2.00	5 per cent
24	Cummin seed	100 kilogs	0.195	Free.	100 kilogs.... 0.32	5 per cent
25	Cupboard turns	100 kilogs	9.75	9.75	20 per cent	35 per cent
26	Curls, hair	100 kilogs	0.195	......	20 per cent	Kilogramme. 5.40
27	Currier's knives	100 kilogs	1.56	1.80	See Cutlery.	Kilogramme. 0.108
28	Currants	100 kilogs	1.56	1.56	100 kilogs.... 0.30	Kilogramme. 0.016
29	Cutch	100 kilogs	0.195	0.195	100 kilogs.... 2.00	Free
30	Cutlasses	100 kilogs	1.56	1.80	See Cutlery.	Kilogramme. 0.27
31	Cutlery, of all kinds, not enumerated. pocket, pen, and jack-knives.	100 kilogs	1.56	1.80	Kilogramme. 0.20	With handles of ivory, shell, &c., kilogs .... 0.378 Handles of whalebone and other hard material, kilogs .... 0.324 Wood or metal, kilogs .... 0.27 Inlaid gold, &c., kilogs .... 0.54 Clasp kn'ves. wd'n handl's, kilog 0.108
32	Daggers	100 kilogs	4.68	5.40	Kilogramme. 0.40	See Cutlery
33	Daguerrotype plates	As manuf. of metal.		......	100 kilogs.... 0.30	Free
34	Dates, green, ripe, or dried	Fresh, 100 kilogs.	0.19	Free.	100 kilogs... 0.50	Kilogra'me. 0.0027
35	preserved in sugar	Dry, 100 kilogs..	2.34	1.56	Kilogramme 0.20	In spirits, kil. 0.075
	or molasses.	Pres'vd, 100 kil..	2.93	1.56		In vineg'r, kil. 0.037
36	Decanters, cut glass	100 kilogs	2.93	1.36	100 kilogs.... 3.50	Kilogramme. 0.172
37	plain	100 kilogs	1.56	0.975	100 kilogs.... 3.50	Kilogramme. 0.054
38	Demijohns	100 kilogs	1.56	0.39	100 kilogs.... 1.60	Kilogramme. 0.054
39	Dentrifice	Per cent	10	10	100 kilogs.... 0.30	20 per cent
40	Dextrine, (artificial gum)	100 kilogs	......	0.76	100 kilogs.... 2.00	5 per cent
41	Diamonds	Per cent	1	10	Free	½ per cent
42	set	Per cent	1	10	Kilogramme. 4.00	1 per cent
43	glaziers'	Per cent	1	Free.	Free	½ per cent
44	Dice, ivory or bone	100 kilogs	9.75	9.75	20 per cent	Ivory, kilogs. 5.40
45	Direct'ns for pat'nt medicines	Free	......	......	Kilogramme. 0.25	Free
46	Distilled vinegar, medicinal.	Hectoliters	0.64	......	20 per cent	Decaliter.... 0.377
47	Dishes, chaffing, copper	100 kilogs	3.90	3.90	100 kilogs.... 7.50	See manuf. of Copper, Iron, or Tin.
48	iron or tin	100 kilogs	1.56	1.80	100 kilogs.... 4.50	
49	Diuretic sal	100 kilogs	0.39	0.39	100 kilogs.... 0.75	5 per cent
50	Divi divi, crude	100 kilogs	0.39	Free.	100 kilogs.... 2.00	5 per cent

(*Duties expressed in gold dollars of the United States.*)—Continued.

BELGIUM.	AUSTRIA.			DENMARK.	SWEDEN.	NORWAY.	
		General tariff.	Tariff in treaty.				
10 per cent	Centner	$7.20	$5.76	Pound $0.091	10 per cent	Bone, pound 0.05	1
5 per cent.	See Gold and	silver.		Pound 0.091	See Gold or Silv'r	See Gold & silver.	2
10 per cent	Centner	7.20	5.76	Pound 0.091	See Jewelry	See Jewelry.	3
10 per cent	Centner	6.00	5.76	See Paper	10 per cent	Pound ... 0.082	4
				Pound ... 0.091	10 per cent	10 per cent	5
Free	Centner	2.64	1.92	Free	Free	Free	6
Free	......	Free.	Free.	Free	Free	Free	7
100 kilogs... 0.975	Centner	1.26	......	Pound 0.034	Pound $0.027	Pound 0.062	8
Free	Centner	0.36	Free.	Free	Free	Free	9
Free	......	Free.	......	Free	Free	Free	10
10 per cent	See Clothing	......	......	10 per cent	10 per cent	10 per cent	11
							12
10 per cent	Centner	0.12	0.36	Pound 0.028	Pound 0.041	Pound 0.047	13
Free	Centner	2.40	......	Pound.... 0.0113	Free	Free	14
Free	Centner	0.72	Free.	Pound.... 0.0056	Free	Free	15
Free	......	Free.	......	Free	Free	Free	16
Free	Centner	0.72	Free.	Pound 0.028	Free	Free	17
10 per cent	See Hats	......	......	Pound 0.364	See Hats	See Hats	18
Free	Centner	5.76	2.16	Free	Free	Free	19
Free	......	Free.	......	Free	Free	Free	20
10 per cent	Centner	3.48	1.92	Pound 0.04	Pound 0.027	Pound 0.047	21
Free	Centner	3.84	......	Pound.... 0.0113	Free	Free	22
Free	......	Free.	......	Free	Free	Free	23
100 kilogs .. 0.117	Centner	0.388	Free.	Free	Free	Free	24
100 kilogs.. 0.29	Manuf. of	Woo	d.	Pound 0.017	See Manf. of Wood	Free	25
10 per cent	See Hair	......	......	Pound 1.09	Pound 0.096	Free	26
100 kilogs .. 0.78	See Cutlery	......	......	Pound 0.017	Pound 0.0165	See Tools, &c., free	27
10 per cent	Centner	2.52	......	Pound 0.034	Free	Free	28
Free	......	Free.	......	Free	Free	Free	29
100 kilogs .. 0.78	See Cutlery	......	......	Pound 0.017	Pound 0.0165	Pound 0.073	30
100 kilogs. 0.78	Com'n kn'vs, centner... Other knives and scissors, c'tnr.	2.88 7.20	2.16 5.76	Handles, ivory, mother of pearl, &c., lb.. 0.091 All others of steel or iron, pound... 0.017	Pen-knives, pound... 0.138 Common knives, pound...0.0165 Table knives & forks, with iv'ry h'dls, lb.. 0.138 do. other handles...... 0.0275 Other articles, not polished, pound...0.0275 do. pol'd lb 0.0689	Table knives & forks, fancy handles, pen-knives, razors, pound ...0.109	31
100 kilogs... 0.78	Centner	7.20	5.76	Pound 0.017	Pound.... 0.0689	Pound 0.073	32
10 per cent	Centner	1.44	1.20	Free	Free	Free	33
10 per cent	Centner	2.52	......	Pound 0.004	Pound 0.041	Free	34
100 kilogs...11.70	See Comfits	......	......	Pound 0.04	Pound 0.082	Pound 0.082	35
10 per cent	Centner	3.48	1.92	Pound 0.04	Pound 0.041	Pound 0.047	36
100 kilogs... 0.195	Centner	1.08	0.72	Pound 0.04	Pound 0.041	Pound 0.047	37
100 kilogs... 0.195	Centner	7.20	5.76	Pound 0.04	Pound 0.041	Pound 0.047	38
10 per cent	Centner	7.20	......	Pound 0.091	Free	Free	39
Free	Centner	2.52	1.44	Pound 0.0113	Free	Free	40
Free	Diam'ds, w'kd cut, centn'r.	5.76	5.76	Pound 0.091	Free	Free	41
5 per cent				Pound 0.091	See Gold & J'wly	See Gold & J'wly.	42
Free	......	......	......	Pound 0.091	Free	Free	43
10 per cent	Centner	7.20	5.76	Pound 0.091	Iv'ry, pound 0.138	Iv'ry pound 0.158	44
Free	......	Free.	Free.	Free	Free	Free	45
Free	Centner	7.20	......	Pound.... 0.0113	Free	Free	46
See manuf. of each metal.	See Manuf. of iron, or tin.	copp	er,	Tin, pound 0.04	See manuf. of each metal.	See Manuf. of each metal.	47 48
Free	Centner	2.52	1.44	Pound....0.0113	Free	Free	49
Free	......	Free.	Free.	Free	Free	Free	50

Comparative table of import duties in the United States and European countries

	ARTICLES.	UNITED STATES.	GREAT BRITAIN.	GERMAN ZOLL-VEREIN.	SWITZERLAND.
1	Dividers, silver	40 per cent	Free	Free	Centner...$0.68
2	others	35 per cent	Free	Free	Centner... 0.68
3	Dolls, of every description	35 per cent	Free	Centner...$7.20	Centner... 1.56
4	Dominoes, bone or ivory	35 per cent	Free	Centner... 2.88	Centner... 1.56
5	metal	35 per cent	Free	Centner... 2.88	Centner... 1.56
6	of toys	50 per cent	Free	Centner...10.80	Centner... 1.56
7	Down, all kinds	30 per cent	Free	Centner... 0.36	Centner... 0.36
8	Dragon's blood	Pound....$0.10	Free	Free	Centner... 0.48
9	Drawing pencils	30 per cent	Free	Centner... 2.88	Centner... 1.56
10	Drawings	20 per cent	Free	Free	Centner... 1.56
11	Draw knobs of brass and glass. }	} 40 per cent	} Free	} Centner... 2.88	} Centner... 1.56
12	of cut glass entirely. }				
13	of plain glass, ivory, bone, gilt plated, &c.	35 per cent			
14	Drawers, silk, wove	60 per cent	Free	Centner...28.80	Centner... 1.56
15	cotton wove, blacked or colored.	35 per cent	Free	See Co(tons	Centner... 1.56
16	Dried pulp	20 per cent	Free	Free	Centner... 0.097
17	Drugs, dyeing, not otherwise enumerated, }	} 20 per cent	Free	Free	Centner... 0.68
18	not crude.				
19	Drugs, dyeing and tanning, crude.	Free	Free	Free	Centner... 0.68
20	Drugs, medicinal, not otherwise enume- }	} 20 per cent	Free	Centner... 0.36	Centner... 0.145
21	rated, crude.				
22	Duck, sail, all	30 per cent	Free	Centner... 0.48	Centner... 1.56
23	Dulce (sea-weed)	10 per cent. per ton 5.00	Free	Free	Centner... 0.029
24	Dutch metal, in leaf	10 per cent }	} Free	Free	Centner... 0.29
25	copper, chief value.	45 per cent }			
26	Dust pans	35 per cent	Free	Centner... 2.88	Centner... 1.56
27	Dye-woods	Free	Free	Free	Centner... 0.058
28	Dyeing, drugs, and materials, not otherwise enumerated.	Free	Free	Free	Centner... 0.68
29	Earth, in oil	100 pounds 1.50	Free	Free	Centner... 0.68
30	brown, red, blue, yellow, dry, as ochre.	100 pounds 0.50	Free	Free	15 centners 0.29
31	Earthenware, common	25 per cent	Free	Free	} Glazed or not, centner. 0.145 Ornament'd, per centner. 1.56
32	stone or crockery	....	....	White, per centner..... 1.25	
33	all other, dyed, printed, painted.	40 per cent	Free	Print'd, per centner...... 1.44	

(*Duties expressed in gold dollars of the United States.*)—Continued.

FRANCE.					RUSSIA.	NETHERLANDS.	
	General tariff.		In treaty with Great Britain, &c.				
	In French vessels.	In other vessels.	In vessels of treaty powers.	In other vessels.			
See Instruments	....	....	....	....	Free	Free	1
See Instruments	....	....	....	....	Free	5 per cent	2
100 kilogs	$15.60	$16.86	10 per cent.		Pound $0.27	5 per cent	3
Kilogramme	0.78	0.86	$0.117	$0.127	Pood 4.68	5 per cent	4
As manuf. of metal or					Pood 2.34	5 per cent	5
as toys, 100 kilogs	15.60	16.86	10 per cent.		Pound 0.27	5 per cent	6
See Bed feathers	....	....	....	....	Free	Free	7
100 kilogs	Free	0.97	0.39	0.43	Free	Free	8
110 kilogs	1.95	2.14	0.195	0.22	Pood 0.04	5 per cent	9
....	Free	Free	....	....	Free	Free	10
							11
See Manuf. of glass	....	....	....	....	Pood 3.12 Pood 4.68	5 per cent	12 13
....	....	....	Free	Free	Pound 2.34	5 per cent	14
See Cottons	....	....	....	....	See Cottons	5 per cent	15
....	Free	Free	Free	Free	Free	Free	16
							17
....	Free	Free	Free	Free	Free	Free	18
100 kilogs	Free	0.195	Free	Free	Free	Free	19
							20
....	Free	0.97	Free	0.048	Free	Free	21
See Manuf. of flax	....	....	....	....	Pound 0.35	Bolt 0.12	22
....	Free	Free	Free	Free	Free	Free	23
							24
See Copper, alloyed	....	....	....	....	Pound 0.47	Free	25
100 kilogs	Prohibited.		2.73	2.99	Pood 2.34	4 per cent	26
....	Free	Free	Free	Free	In logs, pood 0.039 In chips, pood 0.195	Free	27
....	Free	Free	Free	Free	Pood 0.85 Dye ext's, pood 1.15	Free	28
Earthen clay, raw, per 100 kilogs.	0.19	0.48	Free	C.C48	Free	Free	29
....	....	....	....	....	....	Free	30
Of common earth. Earthenware, per 100 kilogrammes:	1.17	1.29	Free	0.048	Earthen vessels, per pood 0.16	5 per cent	31
Retorts for gas, and others of graphite, as plumbago, draining tubes, and others.					Ornamented, per pood 0.78		32
					White, not ornamented, pood 0.59	5 per cent	33
Clay pipes, and other articles of pipe-clay not varnished; varnished articles without ornament.	....	....	Free	0.048	White, ornamented, pood 0.78 White, painted, or gilded, pood 1.95		34
In sandstone. Earthenware, ornamented.	....	....	0.97	1.06			
Utensils, apparatus, in chemistry.	1.95	2.14	Free	0.048			
Jars, &c., for kitchen.	2.92	3.20	0.78	0.86	....	....	35
Finer articles	prohibited.		15 per cent.				
Ordinary fayence	9.55	10.52	Free	0.048			
Fancy fayence, glazed, painted, &c.	prohibited.		15 per cent.				

Comparative table of import duties in the United States and European countries.

No.	ARTICLES.	ITALY.			SPAIN.	PORTUGAL.
			General tariff.	Tariff in treaty with France, &c.		
1	Dividers, silver	Kilogramme	$2.34	$2.34	Hectogramme $0.70	5 per cent
2	others	According to material.			100 kilogs.... 5.50	5 per cent
3	Dolls, of every description	100 kilogs	7.80	7.80	20 per cent	Kilogramme .$0.27
4	Dominoes, bone or ivory	100 kilogs	9.75	9.75	20 per cent	See Bone, ivory, or metal, manuf.
5	metal	100 kilogs	9.75	9.75		Kilogramme . 0.27
6	if toys	100 kilogs	9.75	9.75		Kilogramme . 0.054
7	Down, all kinds	100 kilogs	1.95	2.25		
8	Dragon's blood	100 kilogs	0.39	Free.	100 kilogs.... 2.00	5 per cent
9	Drawing pencils	100 kilogs	1.95	......	20 per cent	Kilogramme. 0.054
10	Drawings	Free	......	......	Kilogramme . 0.25	Kilogramme. 0.054
11	Draw knobs of brass and glass.					
12	Draw knobs, of cut glass entirely.	100 kilogs	9.75	9.75	20 per cent	Kilogramme 0.172 See Manuf. of glass, ivory, copper, gilded.
13	Draw knobs, of plain glass, ivory, bone, gilt plated, &c.					
14	Drawers, silk, wove	As silk tissues.	......	......	See Silks	3-fold dut's on mat'l.
15	cotton wove, blacked or colored.	As cotton tissues.	......	......	See Cotton	Double duties on material.
16	Dried pulp	Free	......	......	100 kilogs.... 0.30	Free
17	Drugs, dyeing, not otherwise enumerated.	100 kilogs	1.95	0.39	100 kilogs.... 2.00	20 per cent
18	not crude.					
19	Drugs, dyeing and tanning, crude.	100 kilogs	0.39	Free	100 kilogs.... 0.30	5 per cent
20	Drugs, medicinal, not otherwise enumerated.	100 kilogs	1.95	0.39	100 kilogs.... 0.30	5 per cent
21	crude.					
22	Duck, sail, all	See Linen	......	......	See Manuf. of flax	See Manuf. of flax cotton.
23	Dulce, (sea weed)	Free	......	......	100 kilogs.... 2.00	Free
24	Dutch metal, in leaf	As copper	......	......	100 kilogs.... 0.30	Kilogramme . 0.0027
25	copper, chief value.					
26	Dust pans	100 kilogs	1.56	1.80	100 kilogs.... 4.50	Kilogramme. 0.27
27	Dye-woods	100 kilogs	0.39	Free.	100 kilogs.... 0.05	Kilogramme . 0.001
28	Dyeing, drugs, and material, not otherwise enumerated.	100 kilogs	0.39	Free.	100 kilogs.. 0.30	Drugs, 20 per cent.
29	Earth, in oil	Earth, crude, 100 kilogs.	0.48	Free.		5 per cent
30	brown, red, blue, yellow, dry, as ochre.	Earthen squa's, for paving, 100 kilogs.	0.39	0.39	100 kilogs ... 0.01	5 per cent
31	Earthenware, common	Vessels, white, 100 kilogs.	1.56	1.56	Tiles, bricks, tubes, 100 kilogs.. 0.30 Crockery, of flint or fine clay, 100 kilogs 7.50	Earthenware, common, per kilogramme ... 0.021 Fine, kilog . 0.108 Stone, ordinary, kilog .....0.0027 Stone, fine, kilogramme ... 0.080
32	stone or crockery	Vessels, gilded, 100 kilogs.	2.34	2.34		
33	all other, dyed, printed, painted.					

(*Duties expressed in gold dollars of the United States.*)—Continued.

BELGIUM.	AUSTRIA.			DENMARK.	SWEDEN.	NORWAY.	
		General tariff.	Tariff in treaty.				
Free	See Instruments.			Pound $0.091	Pound $0.041	Free	1
Free	See Instruments.		Free.	Pound 0.091	Pound 0.041	Free	2
10 per cent	Centner	$7.20	......	Pound 0.091	Pound 0.068	Pound $0.082	3
10 per cent	Centner	7.20	$5.76	Pound 0.091	Iv'y, pound 0.138	Iv'ry, pound 0.158	4
10 per cent	As metal manufactures.			Pound 0.045	Bone, pound 0.068	Bone, pound 0.05	5
10 per cent	Centner	7.20	5.76	Acc'dng to mat'rl.	Toys, pound 0.068	Toys, pound 0.082	6
Free	Centner	0.384	Free.	Pound 0.028	Free	Pound 0.047	7
Free	Centner	2.52	1.44	Pound 0.0113	Free	Free	8
10 per cent		Free.		Pound 0.028	10 per cent	Pound 0.047	9
Free		Free.		Free	Free	Free	10
							11
10 per cent	Centner	7.20	5.76	Pound 0.091	As copp'r manuf. As manuf. of glass or jewel'y, (not of gold.)	As mat'rl manuf. do.	12
						do.	13
As cloth'g, 10 perct.	See Silk tissues.			Pound 0.546	See Clothing	See Clothing	14
10 per cent	See Cotton tissues.			Pound 0.068	See Clothing	do	15
Free			Free.	Free	Free	Free	16
Free		Free.	Free.	Pound 0.043	Free	Free	17
					All drugs, medicines, & apothecary's ingredients or preparations, free.	Free	18
Free		Free.	Free.	Free			19
							20
Free		Free.	Free.	Free			21
See Tissues of flax.	See Tissues of flax ..			Pound 0.034	See Manf. of flax..	Pound 0.018	22
Free		Free.	Free.	Free	Free	Free	23
Free	Centner	1.44	1.20	Free	Free	Free	24
							25
10 per cent	Manuf. of iron	......	......	Tin, pound 0.045	See Manf. of tin.	Free	26
Free	In sticks.... Ground, cent.	Free. 0.254	Free.	Free	Free	Free	27
Free		Free.	Free.	Pound... 0.0113	Free	Free	28
Free	Free	......	......	Pound 0.0056	Free	Free	29
Free	Free	......	......	Pound 0.0113	Free	Free	30
100 kilogs. 0.29	Very com'on, crucibles, glazed pottery, cent'r.	0.12	Free.	Retorts, tubes, tiles, lb..0.0014	Pottery, per pound...0.0082	Glazed, painted, pound ..0.0045	31
10 per cent	Common, one colo'd, jars, with tin cov's, centner.	2.16	1.20	Other pottery, pound...0.0056	Stone, plates, pound...0.0082	Fancy, lb. 0.018	32
					Other articles, pound...0.0138		33
	Medium, gilded, silver'd, many col'd, centner.	2.88	2.16				34
	Fancy, per centner.	7.20	5.76				
							35

Comparative table of import duties in the United States and European countries.

	ARTICLES.	UNITED STATES.	GREAT BRITAIN.	GERMAN ZOLL-VEREIN.	SWITZERLAND.
1	Ebony, unmanufactured ...	Free............	Free............	Free............	Centner...$0. 058
2	manufactures of....	35 per cent......	Free............	Furniture, per centner .$0. 72	....
3				Fancy goods, per centner . 2. 88	....
4	Eggs.....................	10 per cent......	Free............	Free............	15 centner. 0. 12
5	Elastic garters, (wire and leather.)	35 per cent......	Free............	Centner...10. 80	Centner... 1. 56
6	Elephants' teeth	10 per cent......	Free............	Free............	Centner... 0. 39
7	Elecampane, (crude drug)..	20 per cent......	Free............	Centner .. 0. 36	Centner... 0. 68
8	Embroideries, all in gold or silver, fine or half fine, as other metal.	35 per cent......	Free............	Embroideries: made by machine or hand, per centner: 1. Cotton .26. 60 2. Linen. .14. 40 3. Silk....28. 80 4. Silk and cotton ...26. 60 5. Wool ..26. 60 6. Leather 10. 80	Centner... 2. 93
9	Emeralds..................	10 per cent......	Free............	Centner... 0. 26	Centner... 0. 058
10	Emery ore....	Ton $6. 00	Free............	Free............	15 centner 0. 29
11	pulverized.........	Pound.... 0. 01	Free............	Free............	Centner... 0. 058
12	Emetic, tartar, medicinal...	Pound.... 0. 15	Free............	Centner... 0. 36	Centner... 0. 68
13	Engraved plates of steel, copper, &c.	25 per cent......	Free............	Centner... 2. 88	Centner... 0. 39
14	Encaustic tiles.............	35 per cent......	Free............	Free	....
15	Engravers' copper, prepared or polished.	35 per cent......	Free............	Centner... 2. 88	Centner... 0. 39
16	Engravers' scrapers and burnishers.	45 per cent......	Free............	Free............	Centner... 0. 097
17	Engravings, books of	25 per cent......	Free............	Free............	Centner... 0. 097
18	Epaulets, worsted	50 per cent......	Free............	Centner...14. 40	Centner... 2. 93
19	all others	35 per cent......	Free............	Centner...10. 80	Centner... 2. 93
20	Ergot......................	Pound.... 0. 20	Free............	Scheffel... 0. 01	Centner... 0. 145
21	Escutcheons, silver	40 per cent......	Free............	Centner ..36. 00 gilt, cent'r 10. 60	Centner... 2. 93
22	brass, iron, gilt, plated..	35 per cent......	Free............	Brass, " 7. 20	Centner... 1. 56
23	Essence of rum and bay-rum.	Ounce 2. 00	....	Essences, per centner . 2. 40	All not perfumed, per centner 0. 68
	For other essences see oils, essential, or essences.	25 per cent.			
24	Essence of fruit	Pound.... 2. 50	....	....	All perfumed, centner . 2. 93
25	Etchings or engravings....	25 per cent......	Free............	See Engravings .	See Engravings .
26	Ethers, all not provided for	Pound 1. 00	Gallon $6. 08	Centner... 2. 40	Centner... 0. 69
27	Etoiles, or stars for ornaments.	35 per cent......	Free............	Gold and silver p. centner 36. 00 others... 10. 60	Centner... 2. 93
28	Extracts of belladonna, cicutae, colocynth, claterium, gentian, hyoscyamus, nux vomica, rhatania, rhubarb, stramonium.	40 per cent	Free............	Centner... 2. 40	Centner... 0. 68
29	Extracts of opium..........	100 per cent	Free............	Centner... 2. 40	Centner... 0. 68
30	Extracts of Campeachy wood, indigo, logwood, madder.	10 per cent	Free............	Of logwood and indigo free, of madder .. 0. 36	Centner... 0. 68
31	Extracts and decoctions of dyewoods, n. o. s.	10 per cent	Free............	Free............	Centner... 0. 68

(Duties expressed in gold dollars of the United States.)—Continued.

	FRANCE.				RUSSIA.	NETHERLANDS.	
	General tariff.		In treaty with Great Britain, &c.				
	In French vessels.	In other vessels.	In vessels of treaty powers.	In other vessels.			
See Wood.	....	....	....	....	Free	Free	1
....	15 per	cent.	10 per	cent.	Furniture, 25 per ct. and per pood. $0. 85	5 per cent	2
....	....	....	....	....	Other, pood ... 0. 85	....	3
All, includ'g silk-worm eggs.	Free ..	Free ..	Free ..	Free ..	Free	Free	4
....	....	....	....	....	Pood........ 4. 68	5 per cent	5
100 kilogs........	Free ..	$0. 58	Free ..	$0. 048	Free	Free	6
100 kilogs........	Free ..	0. 47	Free ..	0. 048	Free	Free	7
Silk tissues, embroidered with gold, fine, kilogs.	$6. 04	6. 64	$2. 34	2. 37	....	....	8
Imitation, kilogs........	Prohi	bited.	0. 68	0. 71	Pound 0. 85	5 per cent.	
100 kilogs........	Free ..	0. 48	Free ..	0. 048	Pood........ 0. 195	Free	9
....	Free ..	Free ..	Free ..	Free ..	Pood........ 0. 195	Free	10
....	Free ..	Free ..	Free ..	Free ..	Pood........ 0. 195	Free	11
100 kilogs........	5. 85	6. 43	Free ..	0. 048	Pood........ 0. 85	Free	12
See Steel and Copper...	....	....	....	....	Pood........ 0. 47	5 per cent	13
See Tiles	....	....	....	....	Pood........ 0. 156	Free	14
See Copper	....	....	....	....	Pood........ 0. 47	5 per cent	15
See Copper	....	....	....	....	Pood........ 0. 47	5 per cent	16
100 kilogs........	58. 50	61. 90	Free ..	0. 048	Free	Free	17
See Wool........	....	....	....	....	35 per cent	5 per cent	18
....	....	....	....	....	35 per cent	5 per cent	19
100 kilogs........	Free ..	0. 048	Free ..	0. 048	Free	Free	20
See Silver	....	....	....	....	Pound 1. 72	5 per cent	21
See Manufactures of these metals.	....	....	....	....	Gilt, less than 1 lb-wgt. pood, 31.20; more than 1 lb., pood ......15. 60 Brass, pood..... 3. 51	5 per cent	22
See Chemicals not enumerated, or perfumed water containing alcohol, 100 kilogs.	29. 25	31. 20	2. 92	2. 92	Classify as chemicals and perfumeries.	See Chemicals and Perfumeries.	23
Not alcoholic........	19. 50	20. 95	1. 95	2. 14	Pood........ 0. 35	Free	24
100 kilogs........	58. 50	61. 90	Free...	0. 045	Free........	Free	25
....	....	....	....	....	Pood 3. 43	Liter $0. 51 to $0. 82	26
According to material or as fancy goods.	....	....	....	....	Gold and silver 1. 95 per pound. others p.pound 0. 25	5 per cent	27
See Chemicals n. e.	....	....	....	....	Pood........ 0. 85	Free	28
See Chemicals n. e	....	....	....	....	Pood........ 0, 85	Free	29
See Chemicals n. e.....	....	....	....	....	Pood........ 0. 85	Free	30
Black, violet p.100 kilogs	prohibit	ed	3. 90	4. 29	Pood 0. 85	Free	31
Red, yellow p.100 kilogs	prohibit	ed.	5. 85	6. 43	Pood........ 0. 85	Free.	

Comparative table of import duties in the United States and European countries.

	ARTICLES.	ITALY.			SPAIN.	PORTUGAL.
			General tariff.	Tariff in treaty with France, &c.		
1	Ebony, unmanufactured ...	See Wood.......	......	......	100 kilogs ...$0. 10	See Wood.........
2	manufactures of....	100 kilogs.......	$9. 75	10 p.c.	100 kilogs ... 7. 00	35 per cent........
3						
4	Eggs......................	....	Free.	Free.	100 kilogs ... 0. 75	Free ....
5	Elastic garters, (wire and leather.)	100 kilogs.......	9. 75	$9. 75	20 per cent........	Kilogramme. $2. 70
6	Elephants' teeth	100 kilogs.......	1. 95	Free.	100 kilogs ... 0. 10	Free ....
7	Elecampane, (crude drug)..	100 kilogs.......	0. 39	Free.	100 kilogs ... 2. 00	5 per cent ....
8	Embroideries, all in gold or silver, fine or half fine, as other metal.	Embroideries in linen, cotton, wool, 100 kilogrammes.	39. 00	55. 24	20 per cent........	Gold lace work, kilogs .....21. 60 Silver.......10. 80
		Hair, kilogs.....	0. 58	0. 66	....	....
9	Emeralds..................	....	Free.	......	Free	Free ....
10	Emery, ore................	....	Free.	......	Ton......... 0. 05	Free ....
11	pulverized.........	100 kilogs.......	0. 48	Free.	Kilogs 0. 40	Kilogramme. 0. 001
12	Emetic tartar, medicinal ...	....	Free.	......	20 per cent	5 per cent ....
13	Engraved plates of steel, copper, &c.	As manufactures of steel or copper.			Steel, 100 kilogramme... 5. 50	Copper plates, free.
14	Encaustic tiles	Per thousand....	0. 58	Free.	100 kilogs ... 0. 30	Kilogramme. 0. 054
15	Engravers' copper, prepared or polished.	As copper manufact's.		......	100 kilogs ...10. 00	Copper plates, free.
16	Engravers' scrapers and burnishers.	100 kilogs.......	0. 78	0. 78	100 kilogs ...14. 00	Free ....
17	Engravings, books of	....	Free.	Free.	Kilogramme. 0. 25	Kilogramme. 0. 054
18	Epaulets, worsted	As material manufactured.			20 per cent	Double duties as material.
19	all others........	....	......	......	20 per eent	Double duties as material.
20	Ergot	100 kilogs.......	0. 48	Free.	100 kilogs ... 0. 30	Free ....
21	Escutcheons, silver	See Silver and other maters.			20 per cent	5 per cent ....
22	brass, iron, gilt, plated..	....	......	......	20 per cent........	10 per cent ....
23	Essence of rum and bay-rum. For other essences see oils essential or essences.	Essences, if perfumery, 100 kilogs.	11. 70	10 p.c.	Essences, per kilogramme... 0. 30	Essences, medicinal, 5 per cent. Perfumery, 20 per cent.
24	Essence of fruit	If medical or chemical preparations, 100 kilogs.	1. 95	0. 78		
25	Etchings or engravings.....	....	Free.	Free.	Kilogramme . 0. 25	Free...............
26	Ethers, all not provided for.	100 kilogs	1. 95	0. 78	....	Kilogramme . 0. 27
27	Etoiles, or stars for ornaments.	As manufactured material.	......	......	Kilogramme . 0. 02 and 20 per cent.	According to material manuf.
28	Extracts of belladonna, cicutae, colocynth, claterium, gentian, hyoscyamus, nux vomica, rhatania, rhubarb, stramonium.	100 kilogs	1. 95	0. 78	Kilogramme . 0. 02	Extracts of saffron per kilogramme 0. 032; liquids, or in mass of roots, barks, &c., per kilogramme 0. 001, others free.
29	Extracts of opium..........	100 kilogs	1. 95	0. 75	Kilogramme . 0. 02	5 per cent..........
30	Extracts of Campeachy wood, indigo, logwood, madder.	100 kilogs	0. 39	0. 29	Kilogramme . 0. 02	Free................
31	Extracts and decoctions of dyewoods, n. o. s.	100 kilogs	0. 39	Free.	100 kilogs.... 1. 50	Free...............

(*Duties expressed in gold dollars of the United States.*)—Continued.

BELGIUM.	AUSTRIA.			DENMARK.	SWEDEN.	NORWAY.	
		General tariff.	Tariff in treaty.				
Free	See Wood			Free	Free	Free	1
10 per cent	See Manufac	tu's of	wood	See Wood	Pound ...$0. 0138	Pound ...$0. 018	2
							3
Free	Free			Free	Free	Free	4
10 per cent	Centner	$5. 76	$3. 60	10 per cent	10 per cent	10 per cent	5
Free	Free			Free	Free	Free	6
Free	Free			Free	Free	Free	7
10 per cent	Centner	126. 00		10 per cent., or pound..$0. 091	Additional, 20 per cent. on material of which manufactu'd, or of silk, per pound ... 0. 41	Additional to duty on material embroide'd, 20 per cent.	8
Free	Free			Free	Free	Free	9
Free	Free			Free	Free	Free	10
Free	Free			Free	Free	Free	11
Free	Centner	2. 40		Pound ... 0. 0113	Free	Free	12
10 per cent	Centner	0. 388	Free.	Free	Pound 0. 027	Free	13
Free	Free			Free	Free	Free	14
10 per cent	Centner	2. 88	1. 92	Free	Free	Free	15
10 per cent	Centner	2. 88	1. 92	Free	Free	Free	16
Free	Free			Free	Free	Free	17
10 per cent	See Clothing.			Pound 0. 091	10 per cent	10 per cent	18
10 per cent	See Clothing.			10 per cent	10 per cent	10 per cent	19
Free	Free			Free	Free	Free	20
5 per cent	See Articles	of sil	ver...	10 per cent	See Manufactu's of silver.	See Silver	21
10 per cent	See Manufact metals.	ures o	f the	10 per cent	See Manufactu's of these materials.	See Manufactu'd metals.	22
All vegetable essences, not alcoholic, for use in perfumery, 10 per cent.	Perfu'd vinegars, oils, balsams, &c., centner.	3. 60	2. 40	Perfumeries, essences, per pound...0. 091	Essences, same as volatile oils, pound...0. 0689	Essences, (see Perfumed oils and waters.) Pound.... 0. 10	23
Others, not alcoholic, free.				Medicinal, per pound...0. 0113			24
Free	Free			Free	Free	Free	25
Free	Chemicals, etc			Pound..... 0. 091	Kande..... 0. 352	Free	26
10 per cent	According to material.			10 per cent	Same as material of which made.	10 per cent	27
Extracts, alcoholic, as spirits: others, free.	Medicines, prepared per centner.	7. 20			Free	Free	28
					Free	Free	29
Free	Centner	0. 72		Extracts, 0. 091 medicinal pound	Free		30
Free	Centner	0. 72		Dyeing, lb. 0. 028	Free	Free	31

Comparative table of import duties in the United States and European countries.

	ARTICLES.	UNITED STATES.	GREAT BRITAIN.	GERMAN ZOLL-VEREIN.	SWITZERLAND.
1	Extracts, all other medicinal	40 per cent	Free	Centner...$2.40	Centner...$0.69
2	Eyes and rods for stairs....	35 per cent	Free	Centner... 1.92	Centner... 1.56
3	Eyes, bull's, a bean	10 per cent	Free	Free	Centner... 0.029
4	glass	35 per cent	Free	Centner... 2.88	Centner... 1.56
5	False collars..............	35 per cent	Free	Centner ... 2.88	Centner... 1.56
6	Fans, palm leaf............	Each.......$0.01	Free	....	Centner... 1.56
7	all others............	35 per cent	Free	Centner...10.80	Centner... 2.93
8	Fancy or perfumed soap....	Pound 0.10 and 25 per cent.	Free	Centner... 1.44	Centner... 0.145
9	Fastenings, shutter or other, of copper, brass, iron, gilt, plated.	35 per cent	Free	}	}
10	Fastenings of steel and copper.	45 per cent......	Free	} Centner.. 1.92	Centner.. 1.56 {
11	Fastenings of steel and copper, japanned.	40 per cent......	Free	}	}
12	Feathers, ornamental, crude	25 per cent......	Free	Centner... 0.36	Centner... 1.56
13	for beds	30 per cent......	Free	Centner... 0.36	....
14	manufactured.....	50 per cent	Free	Centner... 2.88	Centner... 1.56
15	Feather beds..............	20 per cent......	Free	Centner... 2.88	....
16	Feldspar..................	20 per cent	Free	Free	Centner... 0.029
17	Felts or hat bodies, made in whole or part of wool.	See Woolens	Free	See Woolens	Centner... 0.68
18	Felt roofing	20 per cent......	Free	Free	....
19	Fiddles....................	30 per cent......	Free	Centner... 2.88	Centner... 1.56
20	Fifes, bone, ivory, wood...	30 per cent......	Free	Centner... 2.88	Centner... 1.56
21	Figs	Pound 0.05	Cwt.......$1.71	Centner... 1.44	Centner... 0.39
22	Figures, alabaster..........	10 per cent......	Free	Fancy goods of alabaster per centner. 10.60	Centner... 1.56
23	other..............	10 per cent	Free	....	....
24	plaster	40 per cent.......	Free	Free	....
25	Figures, gold or silver	40 per cent......	Free............	Centner...36.00	Centner... 2.93
26	of bronze metal..	45 per cent......	Free............	Busts of, free....	Centner... 0.39
27	marble............	10 per cent......	Free............	Sculpture, free ..	Centner... 0.097
28	Fig blue..................	25 per cent......	Free............	Free............	Centner... 0.68
29	Filberts	Pound ... 0.03	Free............	Free............	Centner... 0.29
30	Files and file blanks, not over 10 inches long.	30 per cent. and $0.10 per lb.	Free............	Centner .. 1.92	Centner... 0.68
31	Files and file blanks, over 10 inches long.	30 per cent. and $0.06 per lb.	Free............	Centner .. 1.92	Centner... 0.68
32	Filtering stones............	20 per cent......	Free............	Free............	Centner... 0.029
33	Filtering stones, unmanufactured.	10 per cent......	Free............	Free............	Centner... 0.029
34	Finishing powders.........	25 per cent......	Free............	....	....
35	Firearms, other than muskets and rifles.	35 per cent......	Free............	Centner .. 2.88	Centner... 0.39
36	Fire-crackers	Box 1.00	Free............	Centner .. 0.36	Prohibited ......
37	Fire-irons and screens......	35 per cent......	Free............	Centner .. 1.92	Centner... 1.56
38	Flasks or bottles that come in gin cases.	35 per cent......	Free............	Centner .. 0.12	Centner... 0.39
39	Flasks, powder, brass, copper.	35 per cent......	Free............	Centner .. 2.88	Centner... 1.56
40	Flasks, horn...............	35 per cent......	Free............	Centner .. 2.88	Centner... 1.56
41	Flat irons	Pound.... 0.01½	Free............	Centner .. 0.96	Centner... 0.68

(*Duties expressed in gold dollars of the United States.*)—Continued.

	FRANCE. General tariff. In French vessels.	FRANCE. General tariff. In other vessels.	FRANCE. In treaty with Great Britain, &c. In vessels of treaty powers.	FRANCE. In treaty with Great Britain, &c. In other vessels.	RUSSIA.	NETHERLANDS.	
See Chemicals n. e.					Pood $0.85	Free	1
See Manuf. of brass					Pood 9.36	5 per cent	2
	Free	Free	Free	Free	Free	Free	3
See Manuf. of glass					Pood 6.24	5 per cent	4
	15 per	cent	10 per	cent	Pood 4.68	5 per cent	5
	15 per	cent	10 per	cent	Pound 0.62	5 per cent	6
	15 per	cent	10 per	cent	Pound 0.85	5 per cent	7
100 kilogs	$31.98	$34.07	$1.17	$1.29	Pood 4.29	100 kilogs $2.46	8
See Manuf. of these materials.					Articles of brass, pood 2.34	5 per cent	9
Articles of steel n. e.					Mfs. of alloy, weighing less than 1 lb., not gild'd, pd. 9.36	5 per cent	10
100 kilogs	prohibit	ed	3.90	4.29	Same, gild., pd. 31.20 Over 1 lb., gilded, pood 15.60	5 per cent	11
	Free	Free	Free	Free	Pood 4.68	Free	12
100 kilogs	9.75	10.72	0.67	0.74	Free	Free	13
					Pound 4.68	Free	14
					Pood 0.78 if brought in by travellers, otherwise prohibited.	Free	15
100 kilogs	Free	0.97	Free	0.048	Free	Free	16
Each	0.29	0.29	10 per	cent	Pound 0.078	1 per cent	17
felt sheath'g 100 kilogs	19.50	20.95	10 per	cent.			
other manuf. 100 kilogs	78.00	81.40	10 per	cent.			
See above					Pood 0.156	1 per cent	18
Each	0.58	0.58	10 per	cent	Pound 0.11	5 per cent	19
Each	0.145	0.145	10 per	cent	Pound 0.11	5 per cent	20
Dry, 100 kilogs	3.12	3.43	1.65	1.72	Pood 0.85	100 kilogs 0.41	21
100 kilogs	15 per	cent	Free	0.048	Pood 0.85	5 per cent	22
See Marble and stone						5 per cent	23
							24
					See Gold or silver	5 per cent	25
100 kilogs			Free	0.048	See Copper	5 per cent	26
100 kilogs			Free	0.048	Pood 0.35	5 per cent	27
Free					Free	Free	28
Free					Pood 0.39	Free	29
Ordinary, 100 kilogs	14.62	15.83	3.90	4.29	Pood 0.62	5 per cent	30
Polished, 17 centimeters or more.	35.10	37.53	3.90	4.29		5 per cent	31
Polished, less than 17 centimeters.	43.37	46.58	3.90	4.29		5 per cent	
Free	Free	Free	Free	Free	Free	Free	32
Free	Free	Free	Free	Free	Free	Free	33
					Pood 0.195	Free	34
See Arms					Pood 14.04	5 per cent	35
					Prohibited	5 per cent	36
					See Manuf. of iron	5 per cent	37
Liter of contents	0.029	0.029	0.25	0.29	Free	5 per cent	38
100 kilogs	29.00	41.43	3.90	4.29	Pood 6.24	5 per cent	39
100 kilogs	19.50	20.95	10 per	cent.	Pood 6.24	5 per cent	40
See Iron					Pood 3.51	5 per cent	41

Comparative table of import duties in the United States and European countries.

	ARTICLES.	ITALY.			SPAIN.	PORTUGAL.
			General tariff.	Tariff in treaty with France, &c.		
1	Extracts, all other medicinal	100 kilogs	$1.95	$0.39	20 per cent	5 per cent ....
2	Eyes and rods for stairs	100 kilogs	3.90	3.90	Copper manufact'd.	Kilogramme .$0.27
3	Eyes, bull's, a bean	100 kilogs	0.297	Free.	100 kilogs....$0.60	Free................
4	glass	100 kilogs	1.95	Free.	See Glass...........	Kilogramme . 0.172
5	False collars	10 per cent.......	......	......	20 per cent	....
6	Fans, palm leaf............	5 per cent.......	......	......	20 per cent.........	Fans ....
7	all others	5 per cent.......	......	......	20 per cent.........	Kilogramme . 1.08
8	Fancy or perfumed soap....	100 kilogs	11.70	1.17	100 kilogs.... 3.75	20 per cent.........
9	Fastenings, shutter or other, of copper, brass, iron, gilt, plated.	See Manufactures of these materials.	......	......	See Manufactures of these materials.	See Manufactures.. Gilded, kilog. 0.54
10	Fastenings of steel and copper.	See Manufac. of these materials.	......	......	100 kilogs.... 5.50	Kilogramme . 0.162
11	Fastenings of steel and copper, japanned.	See Manufac. of these materials.	......	......	100 kilogs.... 5.50	Kilogramme . 0.162
12	Feathers, ornamental, crude	100 kilogs	0.195	......	Feath's and manuf.	Ornamental feathers manuf. p. kilogramme . 2.70 others for writing, kilog.. 0.054
13	for beds	100 kilogs	1.95	2.25		
14	manufactured.....	Ornamental, prepared, 100 kilogs.	5.85	......	20 per cent	
15	Feather beds	100 kilogs	1.95	2.25	20 per cent	Kilogramme . 0.054
16	Feldspar	100 kilogs.......	0.48	......	100 kilogs.... 0.30	Free................
17	Felts or hat bodies, made in whole or part of wool.	Felts, tarred or for soles, 100 kilogs for hats per 100 kilogs.	0.97 2.93	1.12 3.37	100 kilogs.... 0.15	Felts, simple, p. kilogramme ... 0.432 Felts, varnished, per kilogramme. 0.27 Felt for hats, each 0.324.
18	Felt roofing.................	100 kilogs	0.97	1.12	100 kilogs.... 0.15	Pasteboard of hair and tar, per kilogramme .. 0.0054
19	Fiddles	Fiddles 5 per cent	......	......	10 per cent.........	25 per cent.........
20	Fifes, bone, ivory, wood....	Fifes 5 per cent..	......	......	10 per cent.........	25 per cent.........
21	Figs.......................	100 kilogs	0.195	......	100 kilogs.... 0.50	Kilogramme . 0.016
22	Figures, alabaster..........	5 per cent.......	......	Free.	100 kilogs.... 1.50	Kilogramme. 0.01
23	other	5 per cent.......	......	Free.	100 kilogs.... 1.50	Kilogramme . 0.001
24	plaster............	....	......	......	....	....
25	Figures, gold or silver	See Manufact's of	gold,	&c.	20 per cent	See Gold or silver..
26	of bronze metal...	100 kilogs	2.93	Free.	20 per cent	Articles for museums and collections, free.
27	marble............	5 per cent.......	......	Free.	100 kilogs.... 1.50	
28	Fig blue	100 kilogs	0.39	Free.	100 kilogs.... 1.50	5 per cent..........
29	Filberts	100 kilogs	0.195	Free.	100 kilogs.... 0.59	Kilog........ 0.016
30	Files and file blanks, not over 10 inches long.	As tools, 100 kilogs.	1.56	1.80	100 kilogs.... 1.59	Kilog........ 0.081
31	Files and file blanks, over 10 inches long.	5 per cent.......	......	Free.	100 kilogs.... 1.50	Kilog........ 0.081
32	Filtering stones............	5 per cent.......	......	Free.	100 kilogs.... 0.75	Kilog........ 0.001
33	Filtering stones, unmanufactured.	Free	......	......	100 kilogs.... 0.075	Free ....
34	Finishing powders.........	Free	......	......	100 kilogs.... 0.30	5 per cent..........
35	Firearms, other than muskets and rifles.	Barrel	0.19	0.22	Prohibited	30 per cent.........
36	Fire-crackers..............	100 kilogs	2.05	2.05	20 per cent.........	Free ....
37	Fire-irons and screens......	100 kilogs	1.56	1.80	100 kilogs.... 1.50	....
38	Flasks or bottles that come in gin cases.	100 kilogs	1.56	0.39	100 kilogs.... 1.60	Kilog........ 0.005
39	Flasks, powder, brass, copper.	100 kilogs	3.90	3.90	20 per cent.........	Kilog........ 0.27
40	Flasks, horn...............	100 kilogs	9.75	0.58	20 per cent	Kilog........ 3.24
41	Flat-irons	100 kilogs	1.56	1.80	See Iron............	Kilog........ 0.003

(*Duties expressed in gold dollars of the United States.*)—Continued.

BELGIUM.	AUSTRIA.			DENMARK.	SWEDEN.	NORWAY.	
		General tariff.	Tariff in treaty.				
Free	Centner	$7.20	......	Pound.....$0.028	Free	Free	1
10 per cent	See Copper	......	......	Pound..... 0.045	See Mat'ial manuf	See Metal manuf.	2
100 kilogs ..$0.117	Free	......	......	Free	Free	Free	3
100 kilogs .. 0.195	Centner	0.36	$0.36	Pound..... 0.04	See Glassware	See Glass	4
10 per cent	Centner	2.64	1.92	100 per cent	10 per cent	10 per cent	5
10 per cent	Centner	7.20	5.76	Pound..... 0.056	10 per cent	10 per cent	6
10 per cent	Centner	7.20	5.76	10 per cent	10 per cent	10 per cent	7
100 kilogs .. 1.17	Centner	7.56	......	Pound..... 0.091	Pound.....$0.033	Pound....$0.013	8
10 per cent	See Manuf. of these mat'ls.	......	......	Copper, lb. 0.045 Gilt, pound 0.091	See Material manufactured.	See Material manufactured.	9
100 kilogs .. 0.78	See Steel manufactures.	......	......	Pound..... 0.017	Pound.... 0.0275	Pound.... 0.027	10
10 per cent	See Steel manufactures.	......	......	Pound..... 0.017	Pound.... 0.0689	Pound.... 0.048	11
10 per cent	Centner	0.388	Free.	Pound..... 1.092	(See, also, Ornamental feathers) Free	Pound.... 0.496	12
Free	Centner	Free.	......	Pound..... 0.028	Free	Pound.... 0.047	13
10 per cent	Fancy goods, per centner.	5.76	......	Pound..... 0.028	Pound..... 0.041	Pound.... 0.047	14
10 per cent	As ticks	......	......	As material of cover.	Pay duty for cover.	Duty for cover..	15
Free	Free	......	......	Free	Free	Free	16
10 per cent	See Wool	......	......	Pound..... 0.068	Pound.... 0.082	Pound.... 0.109	17
10 per cent	Centner	3.88	......	Pound.....0.0027	Free	Free	18
6 per cent	Centner	4.80	3.60	10 per cent	Each 0.275	Each	19
6 per cent	Centner	4.80	3.60	10 per cent	Each 0.138	Each	20
100 kilogs .. 1.17	Centner	1.262	......	Pound.....0.0045	Pound..... 0.017	Pound.... 0.927	21
10 per cent	See Stone...	......	......	Pound..... 0.091	Free	Free	22
10 per cent	See Stone	......	......	Pound..... 0.091	Free	Free	23
....	....	......	......	....	....	....	24
5 per cent	See Gold and silver.		......	Pound..... 0.091	See Gold & silver.	See Gold & silver.	25
10 per cent	Centner	3.60	2.16	Pound..... 0.091	Pound..... 0.041	Pound 0.047	26
10 per cent	See Manuf. of stone.	......	......	Pound..... 0.091	Free	Free	27
Free	Centner	0.388	Free.	Pound..... 0.028	Pound..... 0.01	Pound 0.027	28
Free	Centner	0.388	Free.	Pound..... 0.017	Free	Free	29
100 kilogs .. 0.76	Centner	2.88	2.16	Pound..... 0.017	As tools	As tools	30
100 kilogs .. 0.76	Centner	2.88	2.16	Pound..... 0.017	5 per cent	Free	31
10 per cent	Centner	0.48	0.36	Free	Free	Free	32
Free	Free	Free.	......	Free	Free	Free	33
Free	Centner	0.388	Free.	Free	Free	Free	34
Free	Centner	7.20	5.76	Pound..... 0.091	Pound..... 0.055	Pound 0.073	35
100 kilogs .. 2.93	Centner	2.40	......	Pound..... 0.017	10 per cent	Free	36
100 kilogs .. 0.78	See Manuf. of iron		......	Pound..... 0.017	Pound..... 0.016	Pound 0.027	37
100 kilogs .. 0.195	Centner	0.36	0.36	Free	Free	Free	38
10 per cent	Centner	7.20	5.76	Pound..... 0.045	Pound..... 0.041	Pound 0.047	39
10 per cent	Centner	7.20	5.76	Pound..... 0.091	Pound 0.138	Pound 0.061	40
100 kilogs .. 0.78	Centner	2.88	2.16	Pound..... 0.017	Pound 0.0165	Pound 0.027	41

Comparative table of import duties in the United States and European countries.

	ARTICLES.	UNITED STATES.	GREAT BRITAIN.	GERMAN ZOLL-VEREIN.	SWITZERLAND.
1	Flannels, of worsted, alpaca, goat, or like hair, not over 40 cents per pound in value.	35 per cent. and $0.20 per lb.	Free............	Centner. $14.40	Centner.. $1.56
2	Flannels, of 40 to 60 cents value.	35 per cent. and $0.30 per lb.	Free............	Centner ..14.40	Centner... 1.56
3	Flannels, of 60 to 80 cents value.	35 per cent. and $0.50 per lb.	Free............	Centner ..14.40	Centner... 1.56
4	Flannels composed of wool.	35 per cent. and $0.50 per lb.	Free............	Centner ..14.40	Centner... 1.56
5	Flax, unmanufactured	Ton $15.00	Free............	Free............	Centner... 0.058
	linen thread, twine, packthread.	40 per cent......	Free............	Yarn, unbl'ched by machine, per centner, $1.44. By hand, per centner, $0.12. Bleached, per centner, $2.16. Sewing thread, per centner, $2.88. Lin. tissu's, raw, (unbleached,) per centner, $2.88. Same, bleach'd, printed; table cloth, linen, batiste, &c., per centner, $7.20. Same, gauze, ribbons, hosiery, and tissu's mix'd with metal thread, per centner, $14.40. Linen lace, per centn'r, $28.80.	Yarn, unbl'ch'd, per centner, $0.39. Bl'ch'd or dyed, per centner, $0.68. Lin. tissu's, raw, partly bl'ched, per centner, $0.39. Bleached, printed, dyed, per centner, $1.56. Tulle, lace, embroideries, per centner, $2.93.
	manufactures of, valued not over 30 cts. per square yard.	35 per cent......	Free............		
	manufactures of, valued over 30 cents per square yard.	40 per cent......	Free............		
	manufactures of, all others.	40 per cent......	Free............		
	manufact's of thread, packthread, and twine.	40 per cent......	Free............		
	tow of...............	Ton 5.00	Free............		
	all manufactures not specified, bags, canvas for shoes or bootees.	40 per cent......	Free............		
	as above, for buttons only.	10 per cent......	Free............		
	linen mits, wove on frames.	35 per cent......	Free............		
	linen tape............	40 per cent......	Free............		
	linens, brown Hollands, blay, coatings, drills, damasks, value not above 30 cents per square yard.	30 per cent......	Free............		
	the same, value over 30 cents per square yard.	35 per cent......	Free............		

(Duties expressed in gold dollars of the United States.)—Continued.

	FRANCE.				RUSSIA.	NETHERLANDS.	
	General tariff.		In treaty with Great Britain, &c.				
	In French vessels.	In other vessels.	In vessels of treaty powers.	In other vessels.			
See Wool	Prohibited.		10 per cent.		Pound...... $0.31	5 per cent	1
	Prohibited.		10 per cent.				2
	Prohibited.		10 per cent.				3
	Prohibited.		10 per cent.				4
Free					Free	Free	5
Linen tissues, for mattresses, p'r 100 kilogs.	$41.34	$41.34					
Waxed linen, having, per 5 millimeters, less than 8 threads, per 100 kilogs.	13.65	13.65					
Same, 8 to 13 threads, per 100 kilogs.	23.40	23.40				Yarns, 3 per cent.	
Same, 13 to 20 threads, per 100 kilogs.	33.15	33.15					
Same, 20 threads or more, per 100 kilogs.	42.29	42.29					
Imitation of stucco for tapestry.	35.88	38.06					
Wax'd linen, for packing, per 100 kilogs.	0.97	1.06					
Same, for furniture, per 100 kilogs.	2.92	3.12					
Pressed linen, coarse, unbleached, per 100 kilogs.	11.70	11.70					
Pressed linen, other, per 100 kilogs.	17.55	17.55					
Ticking, bedding, per 100 kilogs.	41.34	41.34			Yarn, linen, and hemp, of every kind, per pood, $3.12.		
For dress, unbleach'd, per 100 kilogs.	62.79	62.79					
For dress, other, per 100 kilogs.	70.98	70.98			Tissues of flax, not dyed, 30 per cent.		
Table linen, having in chain per space of 5 centim's, 16 threads or less, per 100 kilogs.	(Figured, unbleached.) 51.76	(Figured, bleached.) 80.31			Table linen, batiste, printed linen, per pound, $0.507.	All manufactures of, 5 per cent.	
Same, 17 threads, per 100 kilogs.	55.96	89.11			Drill, per lb., $0.35.		
Same, 18 to 19 threads, per 100 kilogs.	57.91	93.01			Tulle, per lb., $0.31.		
Same, 20 threads, per 100 kilogs.	66.69	110.56			Lace, per lb., $2.34.		
Same, over 20 threads, per 100 kilogs.	91.06	159.31					
Same, 16 threads or less, per 100 kilogs.	(Damask, unbl'ch'd.) 62.47	(Damask, bleached.) 97.57					
Same, 17 threads, per 100 kilogs.	67.16	106.94					
Same, 18 to 19 threads, per 100 kilogs.	69.50	111.62					
Same, 20 threads, per 100 kilogs.	80.03	132.68					
Same, over 20 threads, per 100 kilogs.	109.28	191.18					
(For additional duties, see Tissues and yarns of flax, and pages 86 to 89, note.)							

Comparative table of import duties in the United States and European countries.

	ARTICLES.	ITALY.			SPAIN.	PORTUGAL.
			General tariff.	Tariff in treaty with France, &c.		
1	Flannels, of worsted, alpaca, goat, or like hair, not over 40 cents per pound in value.					
2	Flannels, of 40 to 60 cents value.	See Manufactures of wool.	......	......	See Manufactures of wool.	See Manufactures of wool.
3	Flannels, of 60 to 80 cents value.					
4	Flannels composed of wool.					
5	Flax, unmanufactured	Free	......	......	100 kilogs....$0. 50	....
	linen thread, twine, packthread.	Yarns of hemp or flax, single, bleached or unbleached, 100 kilogs.	$1. 95	$2. 24	Yarn, single, per 100 kilogs, $5. 50. Yarn, twisted, per 100 kilogs, $24.50. Tissues, all, per 100 kilogs, $0. 25. Simple, 10 threads, per square of six milimeters, per kilog, $0. 25. Same, 11 to 24 threads, per kilog, $0. 50. Same, above 25 threads, per kilog, $0. 85. Transversely worked, per kil., $0. 40. Lace, per kilog, $2. 50. Carpets, per kilog, $0. 05.	Flax, raw, p'r kil., $0.0043. White, per kilog, $0.129. Combed, per kilog, $0.648. Yarns, single, unbl'ch'd kil., $0. 27. Same, white, kil., $0. 39. Same, dyed, kilogs, $0. 54. Twist'd, unbl'chd, kilogs, $1. 08. Same, white, kilogs, $1. 62. Same, dyed, kilogs, $2. 16. Glazed thread, kilogs, $0. 864. Tissues: Loose or transparent lace, network, per kilog, $2.70. Gauze webbing, per kilog, $0.216. Not specified, per kilog, $1.62. Closely woven: Hessian, glossed, per kilog, $0.075. Sail-cloth, raw, per kilog, $0.162. Sail-cloth, dyed, per kilog, $0.27. Dutch, per kilog, $0.27. Canvas, raw, per kilog, $0.484. Canvas, half bl'ch., per kilog, $0.27. Canvas, bleached, per kilog, $0.594. Sack-cloth, raw, per kilog, $0.484. Sack-cl'th, bl'ch'd, per kilog, $0.594. Others, per kilog, $1.08. Damasked, p'r kil., $0.81. (Articles manufactured pay double duties as tissues.)
	manufactures of, valued not over 40 cts. per square yard.	Dyed, 100 kilogs	3. 90	4. 58		
	manufactures of, valued over 30 cents per square yard.	Twist'd, bleach'd or not, 100 kil.	3. 90	4. 58		
	manufactures of, all others.	Dyed, 100 kilogs	5. 85	6. 75		
	manufact's of thread, packthread, and twine.					
	tow of					
	all manufactures not specified, bags, canvas for shoes or bootees.	Tissues of flax; also if mixed with cotton or wool; unbl'chd or bleached, six threads warp in five millimeters, per 100 kilogs.	......	4. 58		
	as above, for buttons only.	Per kilog	0. 039	......		
	linen mits, wove on frames.	Of more than six threads, and other, raw or bleached, per 100 kilogs.	......	11. 25		
	linen tape	Per kilog	0. 097	......		
	linens, brown Hollands, blay, coatings, drills, damasks, value not over 30 cents per square yard.	Dyed, per 100 kilogs.	......	7. 41		
	the same, value over 30 cents per square yard.	Per kilog	0. 195	......		
		Pressed, per kil.	0. 195	0. 22		
		Print'd in colors and all others, per 100 kilogs.	......	17. 55		
		Per kilog	0. 145	......		

(*Duties expressed in gold dollars of the United States.*)—Continued.

BELGIUM.	AUSTRIA.			DENMARK.	SWEDEN.	NORWAY.	
		General tariff.	Tariff in treaty.				
							1
See Tissues of wool.	See Tissues of wool.	....	......	Pound ..$0. 182	See Tissues of wool.	See Manufact's of wool.	2
							3
							4
Free	Centner	0. 0288	Free.	Free	Free	Free	5
Yarns, measuring, per kilog, 20,000 meters or less, not twist'd or dyed, per 100 kilogs, $1.95. Same, twisted and dyed, per 100 kil., $2.93. Measuring, per kil., over 20,000 meters, not twist'd or dyed, per 100 kilogs, $5.85. Tissues of flax, 10 per cent. Linen lace, 5 per cent.	Linen y'rns: Raw, not bleach'd, dyed or twisted, per centner ...	$0. 36	Free.	Yarns, including thread, not dyed, per lb., $0.017. Dyed, p'r pound, $0.045. Tissues, unbl'ched, weighing, per square yard, 44 quints or more, or having, per half in. sq., less than 24 threads, per pound, $0. 0114. Of other weight, per lb., $0.034. Sail-cl'th, weighing, per square yard, 44 quints or more; also carpets, per lb., $0.034. Lace, fringe, per lb., $0.273. Damask, drill, plain, per lb., $0.068. Dyed, figured, per lb., $0.1363.	Yarn: single or double; also on spools, not dy'd, per lb., $0.022. Same, dyed, per lb., $0.0385. Tissues: canvas, per lb., $0.041. Sheetings, per lb., $0.11. Batiste, damask and other, per lb., $0.21. Carpet, per lb., $0.0496. Sail-cloth, per lb., $0.022. Drill, per lb., $0.18.	Yarn, not dyed, per lb., $0.019. Dyed, not twisted, per pound, $0.061. Dyed and twisted, per pound, $0. 091. Tissues: drill, damask, p'r lb., $0.15. Lace, tulle, per lb., $0.236. Tricot, st'ckings, per lb., $0.159. Others, loosely woven, per lb., $0.237. Others, closely woven, weighing $5\frac{1}{2}$ oz. per sq. ell, bleach'd or not, per lb., $0.018. Same, weighing $3\frac{1}{2}$ to $5\frac{1}{2}$ oz. or more, bleach'd, per lb., $0.054. Same, printed, per lb., $0.182. Same, of several colors, not printed, p'r lb., $0.109. S'me, uncolor'd, as bleached, (unless of less than $3\frac{1}{2}$ oz. per square ell.) Same, not bl., of less than $3\frac{1}{2}$ oz. per square ell, per pound, $0.036.	
	Mach. thr'd, raw, not twisted, bleached, or dyed, p'r c.	1. 26	$1. 44				
	Bl'ch'd, dy'd, not tw., per centner ...	2. 88	2. 16				
	Tw., per c't.	6. 312	......				
	Lin'n tissu's: *a.* cordage or rope-m'k'rs work, nets, &c., not bl., p'r centner.	0. 48	0. 36				
	b. Same, bl., (packth'd,) per centn'r.	0. 72	0. 36				
	c. common tissu's, raw, unbleach'd, not figur'd, per centner	4. 80	2. 88				
	d. bleached, dyed one or more col'rs, close, printed, figured, p'r centn'r.	17. 28	12. 00				
	e. medium: butt'n cl'th, ribbons, stockings, and all tissues of over 100 threads, (loom,) per Vienna in., per centn'r.	33. 60	21. 60				
	f. fine: batiste, gauze, linen, and other loose tissues, per centner ...	33. 00	33. 60				
	g. fancy: lace, braid, embroideries, & oth'rs mixed with gold, silver, or glass thread, per centner ...	126. 00	......				

Comparative table of import duties in the United States and European countries.

	ARTICLES.	UNITED STATES.	GREAT BRITAIN.	GERMAN ZOLL-VEREIN.	SWITZERLAND.
1	Fish: mackerel............	Barrel....$2. 00	Free............	Centner ..$0. 36	Centner...$0. 39
2	herring, pickled or salted.	Barrel.... 1. 00	Free............	Centner .. 0. 36	Centner... 0. 39
3	salmon...............	Barrel.... 3. 00	Free............	Centner .. 0. 36	Centner... 0. 39
4	all other, pickled, in barrels.	Barrel.... 1. 50	Free............	Centner .. 0. 36	....
5	all other, not in barrels.	Pound.... 0. 005	Free............	Centner .. 0. 36	....
6	fresh, foreign........	Free............	Free............	....	....
7	all in oil, not otherwise provided for.	30 per cent......	Free............	Centner .. 3. 60	Centner... 1. 56
8	glue, (isinglass)......	30 per cent......	Free............	Centner .. 0. 36	....
9	hooks..............	45 per cent......	Free............	Centner .. 2. 88	Centner... 1. 56
10	sauce..............	35 per cent......	Free............	Centner .. 5. 04	....
11	skins, raw...........	20 per cent......	Free............	Free............	....
12	Fishing nets...............	35 per cent......	Free............	Linen, bleached, per centner, $0.36 to $2.88.	Centner... 1. 56
13	lines, silk..........	50 per cent......	Free............	Centner ..21. 60	Centner... 1. 56
14	Flageolets, wood	30 per cent......	Free............	Centner .. 1. 44	Centner... 1. 56
15	bone or ivory...	30 per cent......	Free............	Centner .. 1. 44	Centner... 1. 56
16	Flats, for making hats or bonnets.	30 per cent......	Free............	Centner .. 0. 96	Centner... 0. 68

NOTE. FRANCE.—*Duties on*

General tariff.

Manuf. of flax or linen.	Unbleached, per 100 kilogs.	Bleached, per 100 kilogs.	Dyed, per 100 kilogs.	Printed, per 100 kilogs.
Smooth linen, having in the chain, per space of 5 millimeters, less than 5 threads.	$11. 70	$17. 55	$17. 55	$17. 55
Same, 8 threads..........	15. 60	22. 62	22. 62	22. 62
Same, 9 to 12 threads, exclusive.	24. 57	37. 24	28. 47	37. 24
Same, 12 threads.........	28. 08	41. 12	32. 56	41. 12
Same, 13 to 16 threads, exclusive.	39. 19	59. 67	42. 12	59. 67
Same, 16 threads.........	52. 06	80. 08	56. 35	80. 08
Same, 17 threads.........	55. 96	89. 11	61. 81	89. 11
Same, 18 to 19 threads....	57. 91	93. 01	64. 15	93. 06
Same, 20 threads.........	66. 19	110. 56	73. 60	110. 56
Same, above 20 threads...	91. 06	159. 31	104. 71	159. 31

Tariff in treaty with Great Britain, &c.

Manuf. of flax or linen.	Unbleached. In vessels of treaty powers.	Unbleached. In other vessels.	Bleached, dyed, or printed. In vessels of treaty powers.	Bleached, dyed, or printed. In other vessels.
Unique or colored, having in the chain, per space of 5 millimeters, 5 threads or less, per 100 kilogs.	......	......	$0. 97	$1. 06
Same, 5 to 8 threads, per 100 kilogs.	$5. 46	$7. 41	5. 46	7. 41
Same, 9 to 11 threads, per 100 kilogs.	10. 72	11. 73	13. 65	14. 82
Same, 12 threads, per 100 kilogs.	12. 47	15. 01	18. 52	19. 93
Same, 13 to 14 threads, per 100 kilogs.	17. 55	18. 90	23. 40	25. 06
Same, 15 to 17 threads, per 100 kilogs.	22. 42	24. 02	30. 22	32. 21
Same, 18 to 20 threads, per 100 kilogs.	33. 15	35. 29	44. 85	47. 58
Same, 21 to 23 threads, per 100 kilogs.	50. 70	53. 71	68. 25	71. 65
Same, 24 threads or more, per 100 kilogs.	58. 50	61. 90	78. 00	81. 40

(Duties expressed in gold dollars of the United States.)—Continued.

	FRANCE.				RUSSIA.	NETHERLANDS.	
	General tariff.		In treaty with Great Britain, &c.				
	In French vessels.	In other vessels.	In vessels of treaty powers.	In other vessels.			
Fish, fresh, free	Free ..	Free ..	Free ..	Free ..	Free	Free	1
							2
							3
Prepared, 100 kilogs	$0.97	$1.06	$0.97	$1.06			4
Codfish, 100 kilogs	7.80	8.58	....	....		In air-tight boxes, per 100 kilogs, $10.25.	
All sea fish, except cod, dry, fresh, 100 kilogs.	0.97	1.06	0.97	1.06	All, pickled, per pood, $0.85.		5
Same, salt'd or smok'd, 100 kilogs.	7.89	8.58	0.97	1.06	In oil or in hermetically sealed vessels, p'r pood, $2.34.	In oil, per 100 kilogs, free.	6
In oil, 100 kilogs	4.87	5.36	1.95	2.14		Hooks, 5 per cent.	7
Hooks, 100 kilogs	39.00	41.43	9.75	10.72		Stockfish, per 100 kilogs, $10.25.	
Stockfish, 100 kilogs	1.95	2.14	0.97	1.06			
							8
							9
							10
Free	....	....	....	....	....	Free	11
100 kilogs	4.87	5.32	3.90	4.29	Pood 0.31	5 per cent	12
Fish glue, 100 kilogs	7.81	8.77	7.81	8.77	Pound 3.90	5 per cent	13
Each	0.12	0.12	10 per	cent.	Pound 0.11	5 per cent	14
Each	0.12	0.12	10 per	cent.	Pound 0.11	5 per cent	15
See Hats	....	....	....	....	Pood 1.15	5 per cent	16

tissues and yarns of flax—Continued.

General tariff.

Manufactures of flax, (linen.)	Vessels.	
	French.	Other.
Handkerchiefs, (like linen tissues)	......	......
Batiste and lawn, per kilog	$4.87	$5.35
Lace, 5 per cent	......	......
Tulle, prohibited	......	......
Hosiery, per 100 kilogs	39.00	41.43
Thread lace, unbleached, brown, per 100 kilogs.	15.60	16.86
Thread lace, mixed with white, per 100 kilogs.	23.40	25.05
Thread lace, dyed, whole or in part, per 100 kilogs.	29.25	31.20
Ribbons, per 100 kilogs	97.50	100.90
Close tissues, for floor carpet, of linen thread, of at least 8 threads to 5 millimeters, per 100 kilogs.	14.63	14.63

Tariff in treaty with Great Britain, &c.

Manufactures of flax, (linen.)	Vessels of—	
	Treaty powers.	Other nations.
Ticking, unique or fashion'd, unbleach'd, bleached, dyed, or printed, per cent.	16	16
Damask linen, per cent	16	16
Handkerchiefs, not embroidered, per c't.	10	10
Handkerchiefs, embroidered, per cent	16	16
Batiste and lawn, per cent	16	16
Lace, per cent	5	5
Tulle, hosiery, ribbons, per cent	15	15
Articles of dress, ready made in part or whole, per cent.	16	16
Articles not denominated, per cent	15	15

Comparative table of import duties in the United States and European countries.

	Articles.	Italy.			Spain.	Portugal.
			General tariff.	Tariff in treaty with France, &c.		
1	Fish: mackerel	Fresh, sweet water, per 100 kilogs.	$0.78	$0.90	Fresh or salted, per 100 kilogs, $0.20. Pickled, per 100 kilogs, $1.60. Shell-fish, per 100 kilogs, $0.50.	Fresh or prepared, sweet water, per kilog, $0.037. Sea fish: sardines, per kilog, $0.0048. Not enumerated, $0.036. Preserv'd in oil, p'r kilog, $0.075. Shell-fish, per kil., $0.0027.
2	herring, pickled or salted.					
3	salmon					
4	all other, pickled, in barrels.	S'lt-water fr'sh, per 100 kilogs.	0.78	0.90		
5	all other, not in barrels.	Dried and salt'd or smoked, per 100 kilogs.	0.78	0.90		
6	fresh, foreign					
7	all in oil, not otherwise provided for.	100 kilogs	1.95	1.95		
8	glue, (isinglass)	100 kilogs	1.95	2.23	100 kilogs 1.10	5 per cent
9	hooks	100 kilogs	3.90	4.50	100 kilogs 5.50	Kilog 0.162
10	sauce	100 kilogs	5.85	4.88	Kilog 0.20	....
11	skins, raw	Free	......	......	100 kilogs 1.50	5 per cent
12	Fishing nets	100 kilogs	2.34	2.80	20 per cent	Silk, kilog ... 6.80 Linen, kilog .. 1.08
13	lines, silk	Kilog	0.58	Free.	20 per cent	Kilog 2.70
14	Flageolets, wood	Each	0.39	0.39	10 per cent	25 per cent
15	bone or ivory	Each	0.39	0.39	10 per cent	25 per cent
16	Flats, for making hats or bonnets.	100 kilogs	1.56	1.80	20 per cent	Kilog 0.081

NOTE. FRANCE.—*Duties on*

Yarns of flax.	General tariff.											
	Unbleached.				Bleached.				Dyed.			
	Single.		Twisted.		Single.		Twisted.		Single.		Twisted.	
	In French vessels.	In other vessels.	In French vessels.	In other vessels.	In French vessels.	In other vessels.	In French vessels.	In other vessels.	In French vessels.	In other vessels.	In French vessels.	In other vessels.
Linen, measuring, per kilogramme, 6,000 meters or less, per 100 kilogs.	$7.41	$8.15	$8.58	$9.44	$10.53	$11.54	$11.89	$12.95	$11.31	$12.36	$13.65	$14.82
Same, 6,001 to 12,000 met's, per 100 kilogs.	9.36	10.30	11.70	12.76	12.87	14.00	15.79	17.05	13.65	14.82	16.77	18.09
Same, 12,001 to 24,000 met's, per 100 kilogs.	15.60	16.86	20.28	21.78	20.67	22.00	26.52	28.33	20.67	22.72	26.13	27.92
Same, 24,001 to 36,000 met's, per 100 kilogs.	24.37	26.07	32.56	34.67	31.78	33.85	32.92	44.50	31.20	33.24	39.97	42.44
Same, over 36,000 meters, per 100 kilogs.	32.17	34.26	43.87	46.44	41.34	43.89	55.76	59.24	39.00	41.43	50.70	53.71

(*Duties expressed in gold dollars of the United States.*)—Continued.

BELGIUM.	AUSTRIA.			DENMARK.	SWEDEN.	NORWAY.	
		General tariff.	Tariff in treaty.				
Fresh, smoked or dry, salt, per 100 kil., $0.195. Preserved, per 100 kil., $1.95.	Fresh, per centner . . . Dried, sm'k-ed, salted, p'r centn'r. Preserv'd in oil, p'r cent-ner	$0.36 0.72 7.56	Free. $0.72 4.80	Fresh, free. Dried, pickled, smoked, per pound, $0.0017.	Fresh, salted or preserved, free. Anchovies, sardines, per lb., $0.0689. Salmon, p'r cent-ner, $0.303. Others, per cent-ner, $0.2067. Dried or smok'd, p'r c'tn'r, $0.689. Same, eel and sal-mon, per cent-ner, $1.65. Herring, per cu. foot, $0.033.	Fresh, free. Preserved, smoked, or in oil, lb., $0.027.	1 2 3 4 5 6 7
10 per cent	Free	Free.	. . . . . .	Free	Free	Free	8
100 kilogs . . 0.78	See Manuf. of steel .		. . . . . .	Pound $0.017	Pound $0.041	Free	9
15 per cent	Centner	7.56	4.80	Pound 0.04	Pound 0.068	Pot $0.109	10
Free	Free	Free.	. . . . . .	Free	Free	Free	11
Free	Centner	0.48	0.36	Pound 0.091	Addition'l to duty on yarn.	Addition'l to duty on yarn.	12
As yarn or thread.	Centner	3.88	. . . . . .	Pound 0.41	10 per cent	10 per cent	13
6 per cent	Centner	4.80	3.60	10 per cent	Each 0.138	. . . .	14
6 per cent	Centner	4.80	3.60	10 per cent	Each 0.138	Each 0.137	15
100 kilogs . . 0.78	Centner	2.88	2.16	Pound 0.017	Pound 0.0165	Pound . . . 0.027	16

tissues and yarns of flax—Continued.

Tariff in treaty with Great Britain, &c.

Yarns of flax.*	Unbleached.				Bleached or dyed.			
	Single.		Twisted.		Single.		Twisted.	
	In vessels of treaty powers.	In other vessels.	In vessels of treaty powers.	In other vessels.	In vessels of treaty powers.	In other vessels.	In vessels of treaty powers.	In other vessels.
Linen, measuring, per kilogramme, 6,000 meters or less, per 100 kilogs.	$2.92	$3.20	$3.80	$4.17	$3.90	$4.29	$5.07	$5.77
Same, 6,001 to 12,000 meters, per 100 kilogs.	3.90	4.29	5.07	5.77	5.26	5.79	6.84	7.51
Same, 12,001 to 24,000 meters, per 100 kilogs.	5.85	6.43	7.60	8.36	7.80	8.58	10.14	11.13
Same, 24,001 to 36,000 meters, per 100 kilogs.	7.02	7.72	8.97	9.87	9.36	10.30	12.16	13.26
Same, 36,001 to 72,000 meters, per 100 kilogs.	11.70	12.76	15.21	16.46	15.60	16.86	20.28	21.78
Same, over 72,000 meters, per 100 kilogs.	19.50	20.95	25.35	27.10	25.93	27.70	33.71	35.88

* All yarns, mixed, flax predominating, as pure linen yarns.

Comparative table of import duties in the United States and European countries.

	ARTICLES.	UNITED STATES.	GREAT BRITAIN.	GERMAN ZOLL-VEREIN.	SWITZERLAND.
1	Flaxseed, (52 lbs. per bush).	Bushel .. .$0. 16	Free	Free	Centner . .$0. 028
2	Fleams	35 per cent	Free	Free	Centner . . 1. 56
3	Fleshers, (knives)	45 per cent	Free	Centner . .$2. 88	Centner . . 0. 68
4	Flies, Spanish, (cantharides)	Pound 0. 50	Free	Centner . . 0. 36	Centner . . 0. 68
5	Flints, flint stones	10 per cent	Free	Free	Centner . . 0. 028
6	Float files, not over 10 inches long.	30 per cent., and per pound, 0. 10.	Free	Centner . . 1. 92	Centner . . 0. 68
7	over 10 inches long.	30 per cent., and per pound, 0. 06	Free	Centner . . 1. 92	Centner . . 0. 68
8	Flocks, wool	Pound 0. 12	Free	Free	Centner . . 0. 058
9	other	20 per cent	Free	Free	Centner... 0. 058
10	Flor benzoin, (benzoic acid)	10 per cent	Free	Free	Centner . . 0. 145
11	Floss, silk, and other similar silk purified from gum.	35 per cent	Free	Raw or spun, free; if dyed, cen. 2. 88	Centner . . 0. 058
12	Flour, of wheat	20 per cent	Free	Free	Centner . . 0. 097
13	rye	10 per cent	Free	Free	Centner . . 0. 097
14	sago	Pound 0. 01½	Free	Free	Centner . . 0. 097
15	Flower water, orange	See Cologne water	Free	Free	Centner . . 2. 93
16	Flour, sulphur	15 per cent., and per ton, 20. 00	Free	Free	Centner . . 0. 68
17	Flowers, artificial	50 per cent	Free	Centner . .21. 60	Centner . . 2. 93
18	medicinal	20 per cent	Free	Centner ... 0. 36	Centner... 0. 68
19	all, not otherwise provided.	10 per cent	Free	Free	Free
20	crude, for dyeing.	Free	Free	Free	Centner . . 0. 39
21	Flutes, of wood	30 per cent	Free	Centner . . 2. 88	Centner . . 1. 56
22	of ivory or bone entirely.	30 per cent	Free	Centner . . 2. 88	Centner . . 1. 56
23	Foils, fencing, steel	45 per cent	Free	Centner . . 1. 92	Centner . . 0. 39
24	Foil, copper	45 per cent	Free	Centner . . 1. 92	Centner . . 1. 56
25	silver	40 per cent	Free	Centner . .36. 00	Centner . . 2. 93
26	tin	30 per cent	Free	Centner . . 1. 92	Centner . . 0. 29
27	Fol digitalis, (crude drug) ..	20 per cent	Free	Free For medical use, per cent., 0. 36	Centner . . 0. 029
28	Forks, of gold or silver	40 per cent	Free	Centner . .36. 00	Centner . . 2. 93
29	all other	35 per cent	Free	Centner . . 2. 88	Centner . . 1. 56
30	Forge hammers	Pound ... 0. 025	Free	Centner . . 1. 92	Centner . . 0. 68
31	Fossils	10 per cent	Free	Free	....
32	Fox glove, (crude drug)	20 per cent	Free	Free	Centner . . 0. 029
33	Frames or sticks, for umbrellas, parasols.	35 per cent	Free	Centner . . 0. 72	Centner . . 1. 56
34	Frames, plated, cruet	35 per cent	Free	Centner . . 2. 88	Centner . . 1. 56
35	quadrant	35 per cent	Free	Centner . . 2. 88	Centner . . 1. 56
36	silver, cruet	40 per cent	Free	Centner . .10. 60	Centner . . 1. 56
37	Frankincense, (a gum)	20 per cent	Free	Free	Centner . . 0. 145
38	Fringes, cotton	35 per cent	Free	Centner . .21. 60	Centner . . 1. 56
39	wool	50 per cent., per pound, 0. 50	Free	Centner . .21. 60	Centner . . 1. 56
40	Frizettes, hair	35 per cent	Free	Centner . . 5. 76	Centner . . 2. 93
41	silk, with wool	60 per cent	Free	Centner . .21. 60	Centner . . 2. 93
42	Frosts, glass	20 per cent	Free	Centner . . 2. 88	Centner . . 1. 56
43	Fruit, ethers	Pound 2. 50	Free	Centner . . 2. 40	Centner . . 0. 68
44	juice	25 per cent	Free	Centner . . 0. 36	Centner . . 0. 68
45	Fruits, preserved in brandy.	....	....	....	....
46	or sugar.	35 per cent	Centner...$0. 02	Centner ... 5. 04	Centner... 1. 56
47	pickled	35 per cent	Free	Centner... 0. 36	Centner... 1. 56
48	preserved in their own juice.	25 per cent	Free	Centner... 0. 36	Centner... 1. 56

(*Duties expressed in gold dollars of the United States*)—Continued.

FRANCE.					RUSSIA.	NETHERLANDS.	
	General tariff.		In treaty with Great Britain, &c.				
	In French vessels.	In other vessels.	In vessels of treaty powers.	In other vessels.			
100 kilogs	Free	$0.39	Free	$0.048	Free	Hectoliter ...$0.04	1
100 kilogs	30 per	cent.	Free	0.048	Free	5 per cent	2
See Cutlery	Prohib	ited.	15 per	cent.	Pood ...$9.36	5 per cent	3
Free						Free	4
100 kilogs	Free	0.195	Free		Free	Free	5
Ordinary, 100 kilogs	$14.62	15.83	Tools of iron: 1.95	2.14	Pood 0.62	5 per cent	6
Polished, 100 kilogs			Iron and steel: 2.92	3.20	Pood 0.62	5 per cent	7
length of 17 centimeters, or more;	35.10	37.33	Steel, pure: 3.90	4.29			
length less than 17 centimeters.	43.87	46.58					
Flock wool, free					Free	Free	8
					Free	Free	9
100 kilogs	Free	0.48	Free	0.048	Pood 0.85	Free	10
Free					Pood 0.39	3 per cent	11
100 kilogs	0.097	0.097			Pood 0.05	100 kilogs 0.16	12
Free					Pood 0.03	100 kilogs 0.16	13
Free					Pood 0.03	100 kilogs 0.16	14
100 kilogs	19.50	20.95	1.05	2.14	Free	5 per cent	15
Free					Free	Free	16
100 kilogs	12 per	cent.	Free	0.048	Pound 4.68	5 per cent	17
							18
					Free	Free	19
Free							20
Each	0.145	0.145	Free	0.048	Pound 0.11	5 per cent	21
Each	0.145	0.145	Free	0.048	Pound 0.11	5 per cent	22
See Arms					Pood 14.04	5 per cent	23
See Manuf. of copper					Pound 0.09	5 per cent	24
See Manuf. of silver					Pound 1.72	5 per cent	25
See Manuf. of tin					Pood 1.75	5 per cent	26
Free					Free	Free	27
					Forks of gold, per pound 25.74	Free	
100 kilogs	97.50	100.90	97.50	100.90	Forks, silver, p'd 1.72	5 per cent	28
100 kilogs	19.50	20.95	10 per	cent.	Pood 9.36	5 per cent	29
See Iron					Pood 1.10	5 per cent	30
Free					Free	Free	31
Free					Free	Free	32
					Each frame 0.23	5 per cent	33
	15 per	cent.	10 per	cent.	Pood 0.85	5 per cent	34
					Pood 0.85	5 per cent	35
					Pound 0.26	5 per cedt	36
100 kilogs	Free	0.58	Free		Free	Free	37
	Prohib	ited.	5 per	cent.	Pound 0.27	5 per cent	38
	Prohib	ited.	10 per	cent.	Pound 0.39	5 per cent	39
Free					Pound 0.47	5 per cent	40
						5 per cent.	41
	Prohib	ited.	10 per	cent.	See Glass	5 per cent	42
					Pood 0.85	See Chemicals	43
Free						See Lemon juice	44
100 kilogs	19.11	22.55				Brandy, 10 per cent.	45
100 kilogs	4.09	4.29	4.28	4.29	Pood 2.34	Sugar, 100 klgs 7.30	46
					Pood 0.39	10 per cent.	47
Preserved without sugar or honey, 100 kilogs.	1.95	2.14	1.56	1.72	Pood 0.39	In air-tight boxes, 100 kilogs.. 10.28	48

Comparative table of import duties in the United States and European countries.

	ARTICLES.	ITALY.			SPAIN.	PORTUGAL.
			General tariff.	Tariff in treaty with France, &c.		
1	Flaxseed, (25 lbs. per bush).	100 kilogs	$0.195	Free.	100 kilogs....$0.20	Kilogs $0.0016
2	Fleams	100 kilogs	9.75	9.75	See Steel	See Instrum'ts surg'l
3	Fleshers, (knives)	100 kilogs	1.56	1.80	Kilog 0.20	Kilogs 0.27
4	Flies, Spanish, (cantharides)	100 kilogs	1.95	0.78	100 kilogs.... 2.00	5 per cent
5	Flints, flint stones	Free	......	......	100 kilogs.... 0.01	Free
6	Float files, not over 10 inches long.	100 kilogs	1.56	1.89	100 kilogs.... 5.50	Kilogs 0.081
7	over 10 inches long.	100 kilogs	1.56	1.80	100 kilogs.... 5.50	Kilogs 0.081
8	Flocks, wool	Natural wool, free	......	......	100 kilogs.... 2.50	Kilogs 0.0005
9	other	......	......	......	......	......
10	Flor benzoin, (benzoic acid)	100 kilogs	0.39	Free.	Kilog......... 0.02	Kilogs 0.216
11	Floss, silk, and other similar silk purified from gum.	Free	......	......	See Silk	Kilogs 0.081
12	Flour, of wheat	Flour, all, per 100 kilogs.	0.24	......	100 kilogs.... 0.90	Lisbon, 10 k. 0.059
13	rye		......	......	100 kilogs.... 0.675	Lisbon, 10 k. 0.054
14	sago	......	......	......	100 kilogs.... 2.40	Kilogs....... 0.008
15	Flower water, orange	See Perfumeries.	......	......	Perfumery	Kilogs....... 0.324
16	Flour, sulphur	100 kilogs	1.17	Free.	100 kilogs.... 0.30	Kilogs, free
17	Flowers, (artificial)	Kilog.	2.34	0.975	20 per cent	Kilogs 12.96
18	medicinal	Free	......	......	100 kilogs.... 2.00	Free (18–20)
19	all, not otherwise provided.	Free	......	......	100 kilogs.... 2.00	
20	crude, for dyeing.	100 kilogs	0.39	Free.	100 kilogs.... 0.30	
21	Flutes, of wood	Each	0.39	0.39	10 per cent	25 per cent
22	of ivory or bone entirely.	Each	0.39	0.39	10 per cent	25 per cent
23	Foils, fencing, steel	100 kilogs	3.90	4.50	See Steel	Kilogs 0.162
24	Foil, copper	100 kilogs	2.34	2.34	See Copper	Kilogs 0.27
25	silver	100 kilogs	0.78	0.90	See Silver	See Silver
26	tin	100 kilogs	1.56	1.17	See Tin	As copper
27	Fol digitalis, (crude drug)	100 kilogs	0.39	Free.	100 kilogs.... 0.30	5 per cent
28	Forks, of gold or silver	See Gold and silver..		......	See Gold and silver.	See Gold and silver.
29	all other	100 kilogs	1.56	1.80	20 per cent.	See Cutlery
30	Forge hammers	100 kilogs	1.56	1.80	100 kilogs.... 1.50	Kilogs 0.081
31	Fossils	For collections	Free.	......	Free	Free
32	Fox glove, (crude drug)	100 kilogs	0.39	Free.	100 kilogs.... 0.30	5 per cent
33	Frames or sticks, for umbrellas, parasols.	100 kilogs	3.90	3.90	20 per cent	Each frame .. 0.864
34	Frames, plated, cruet	10 per cent	......	......	20 per cent	Kilogs 0.54
35	quadrant	10 per cent	......	......	10 per cent	5 per cent
36	silver, cruet	10 per cent	......	......	20 per bent	5 per cent
37	Frankincense, (a gum)	100 kilogs	0.39	Free	100 kilogs.... 2.00	5 per cent
38	Fringes, cotton	See Cotton	......	......	See Cotton	Kilogs 1.188
39	wool	See Wool	......	......	See Wool	Kilogs 1.76
40	Frizettes, hair	Kilog	0.39	......	20 per cent	Kilogs 5.40
41	silk, with wool	Kilog	0.58	......	20 per cent	Each head-dress 2.16
42	Frosts, glass	100 kilogs	1.56	0.975	100 kilogs.... 1.60	Kilog 0.172
43	Fruit, ethers	Hectoliter	1.56	Free.	See Ether	5 per cent
44	juice	Hectoliter	1.56	Free.	100 kilogs.... 0.50	5 per cent
45	Fruits, preserved in brandy.	......	......	......	......	......
46	or sugar..	Fruit, green, per 100 kilogs.	0.195	Free	Kilogramme . 0.20	Fruit, fresh, from Europe, kilgr 0.01
47	pickled	Dry, 100 kilogs..	1.56	1.56	Kilogramme . 0.20	Exotic, kilgr 0.0027
48	preserved in their own juice.	Preserved in oil, 100 kilogs.	2.93	1.56	Kilogramme . 0.20	Preserv'd in brandy, 0.074; dry, Europe, kilogramme. 0.075

(*Duties expressed in gold dollars of the United States.*)—Continued.

BELGIUM.	AUSTRIA.			DENMARK.	SWEDEN.	NORWAY.	
		General tariff.	Tariff in treaty.				
100 kilogs ..$0.117	Centner	$0.028	Free.	Free	Free	Free	1
100 kilogs .. 0.78	Centner	2.88	2.16	Pound.....$0.017	Pound.....$0.041	See Surg. inst's..	2
100 kilogs .. 0.78	See Cutlery..	......	......	Pound..... 0.017	Pound.....0.0165	Pound $0.048	3
Free	Centner	2.52	1.44	Pound.....0.0113	Free	Free	4
Free	Centner	0.388	Free.	Free	Free	Free	5
100 kilogs .. 0.78	Centner	2.88	2.16	Pound..... 0.017	5 per cent......	Pound 0.027	6
100 kilogs .. 0.78	Centner	2.88	2.16	Pound..... 0.017	5 per cent......	Pound 0.027	7
Free	Free	......	......	Free	Free	Free	8
......	......	......	......	......	......	......	9
Free	See Chemicals	......	......	Pound.....0.0113	See Medicinal and chem'l prepar'ns.	Free	10
Free	Free	......	......	Pound..... 0.273	Silk, dy'd, p'd 0.11 Silk, raw, free.	Pound .... 0.127 Free	11
100 kilogs .. 0.23	Flour and other products of the mill:			Free	Free	Lis.pound. 0.054	12
100 kilogs .. 0.23				Free	Free	Lis. pound 0.0054	13
100 kilogs .. 0.23	Centner	0.288	Free.	Free	Free	Pound 0.018	14
10 per cent	Centner	7.20	5.76	Pound..... 0.091	Pound..... 0.11	Pound 0.10	15
Free	Centner	0.388	Free.	Free	Free	Free	16
10 per cent	Centner	5.76	5.76	Pound.... 1.092	Pound..... 1.378	Pound 0.49	17
Free	Free	......	......	Pound .. 0.0113	Free		18
				Of wax, rice, shells: pound.. 0.091		Free	19
							20
6 per cent	Centner	4.80	3.60	10 per cent......	Each 0.138	Each 0.137	21
6 per cent	Centner	4.89	3.60	10 per cent......	Each 0.138	Each 0.137	22
100 kilogs .. 0.78	See Manuf. of steel	......	......	Pound..... 0.017	As manuf. of steel	Pound 0.078	23
100 kilogs .. 1.95	See Manuf. of copper	......	......	Pound..... 0.045	As man. of copper	Pound 0.047	24
Free	See Manuf. of silver.	......	......	Pound..... 0.091	As man. of silver.	Loth 0.03	25
Free	See Manuf. of tin ...	......	......	Pound..... 0.045	As manuf. of tin.	Pound 0.047	26
Free	Free	......	......	Pound.....0.0113	Free	Free	27
5 per cent	See Gold and silver.	......	......	Pound..... 0.091	See Gold and silver	Loth 0.03	28
100 kilogs .. 0.78	See Cutlery..	......	......	See Cutlery......	See Cutlery......	See Cutlery	29
100 kilogs .. 0.78	Centner	2.40	2.16	Pound..... 0.005	Centner ...0.2067	Pound 0.004	30
Free	Free	......	......	Free	Free	Free	31
Free	Free	......	......	Free	Free	Free	32
10 per cent	Centner	5.76	......	Pound..... 0.091	Pound..... 0.051	Pound 0.047	33
10 per cent	Centner	7.20	5.76	Pound..... 0.091			34
Free	Centner	2.16	2.16	10 per cent......	As material of manufacture.	Pound .. 0.095	35
Free	See Silver ...	......	......	Pound..... 0.091			36
Free	Centner	2.52	1.44	Pound.....0.0113	Free	Free	37
See Cotton	See Manuf. of of cotton and of wool.	......	......	Pound..... 0.273	See Cotton......	Pound 0.407	38
See Wool		......	......	Pound..... 0.273	See Wool	Pound 0.236	39
10 per cent	See Hair	......	......	Pound..... 1.092	Pound..... 0.096	See Wool manuf.	40
10 per cent	See Silk	......	......	Pound..... 1.092	Pound..... 0.275	Pound 0.241	41
10 per cent	Centner	0.36	0.36	Pound..... 0.091	Pound..... 0.165	Pound 0.109	42
See Ether.	Fruit, comm'n	Free.	Free	Pound..... 0.091	Kande..... 0.352	Pot 0.218	43
Free	Dried, centner	0.388	Free.	Pott....... 0.018	Free	See Cider	44
......	......	......	......	......	......	......	45
100 kilogs ..11.70	Fruit, tropic, centner.	2.52	......	See Apples, 0.04 oranges, &c., lb.	Fruits, pre- 0.082 served, pound.	Pound 0.082	46
10 per cent	Dried. cent'r	0.1008	......	Pound.... 0.0056	Dried, lb... 0.016	Pound 0.054	47
10 per cent	Preserved in sugar, centn.	7.56	4.89	Pound.... 0.0056	......	Pound 0.055	48

Comparative table of import duties in the United States and European countries.

	ARTICLES.	UNITED STATES.	GREAT BRITAIN.	GERMAN ZOLL-VEREIN.	SWITZERLAND.
1	Fruit, green, ripe, or dried..	10 per cent	Free	Free	Centner ...$0. 29
2	Frying pans...............	35 per cent	Free	Centner...$0. 96	Centner... 0. 68
3	Fuller's boards	35 per cent	Free	Free	Centner... 0. 39
4	earth..............	Ton $3. 00	Free	Free	Centner... 0. 029
5	Fulminates, fulminating powder.	30 per cent	Free	Centner ... 0. 36	Centner... 0. 68
6	Furniture, coach and harness.	35 per cent	Free	Centner ... 1. 92	Centner... 1. 56
7	Furniture, household, n. o. p. for.	35 per cent	Free	Centner ... 0. 72	Centner... 1. 56
8	Furs, dressed, all on the skin.	20 per cent	Free	Centner ... 4. 32	Centner... 1. 56
9	Fur, hats or caps of	35 per cent	Free	Centner...15. 84	Centner... 2. 93
10	hat bodies or felt......	35 per cent	Free	Centner ... 7. 20	Centner... 0. 68
11	muffs or tippets, and other manufactures n. o. p. for.	35 per cent	Free	Centner...15. 84	Centner... 2. 93
12	Fusil oil, or amylic alcohol.	Gallon 2. 00	Free	Centner... 2. 40	Centner ... 1. 56
13	Fustic......................	Free	Free	Free	....
14	Galanga, (crude drug,).....	20 per cent	Free	Centner ... 0. 36	Centner... 0. 68
15	Gallengal or gall-root	20 per cent	Free	Centner ... 0. 36	Centner... 0. 68
16	Galloons, gold or silver, fine or half-fine.	35 per cent......	Free	Centner ...36. 00	Centner ... 2. 93
17	Galls, nut	Free	Free	Free	Centner... 0. 058
18	Gambia, (Terra Japonica,).	10 per cent	Free	Free	Centner ... 0. 058
19	Gamboge, crude or refined	10 per cent	Free	Free	Centner ... 0. 68
20	Game bags, leather or twine.	35 per cent	Free	Centner ... 7. 20	Centner... 1. 56
21	Garancene, extract of madder, prepared.	10 per cent	Free	Free	Centner... 0. 68
22	Garden seeds, n. o. e.......	30 per cent	Free	Free	Centner ... 0. 029
23	Garnets, a precious stone...	10 per cent	Free	Free	Centner... 0. 39
24	imitation of......	40 per cent	Free	Centner ... 2. 88	Centner... 1. 56
25	hardware	35 per cent	Free	Centner ... 1. 92	Centner... 1. 56
26	Garters, elastic, made of wire, covered with leather.	35 per cent	Free	Centner ... 7. 20	Centner... 1. 56
27	Gas-retorts, common earthen or stone-ware, not ornamented.	25 per cent	Free	Free	15 Centner 0. 12
28	Gelatine..................	35 per cent......	Free	Centner... 0. 36	Centner... 0. 68
29	Gems	10 per cent......	Free	Centner... 0. 36	Centner... 0. 39
30	set	25 per cent......	Free	Centner... 5. 76	Centner... 2. 93
31	Gentian root..............	20 per cent......	Free	Centner ... 0. 36	Centner... 0. 058
32	German silver, manufact'd.	40 per cent......	Free	Centner... 2. 88	Centner... 1. 56
33	unmanuf'd.	40 per cent......	Free	Free	Centner... 0. 39
34	Gig harness, (saddlery,)....	35 per cent......	Free	Centner... 2. 88	Centner... 1. 56
35	springs...............	35 per cent......	Free	Centner... 1. 92	Centner... 1. 56

(*Duties expressed in gold dollars of the United States.*)—Continued.

	FRANCE.				RUSSIA.	NETHERLANDS.	
	General tariff.		In treaty with Great Britain, &c.				
	In French vessels.	In other vessels.	In vessels of treaty powers.	In other vessels.			
100 kilogs	Free	$0.39	Free	$0.47	Green ... Free Dried ... $0.78	Raw or dried, 5 per cent.	1
	Prohib	ited	2.73	2.99	See Iron manufactnres	5 per cent	2
	Free	Free	Free	Free	Free	Free	3
	Free	Free	Free	Free	Free	Free	4
	10 per	cent	10 per	cent		Free	5
	10 per	cent	10 per	cent	Brass, copper 2.34, other 3.43 per pood.	5 per cent	6
See Household furniture.					See Household furniture.	5 per cent	7
Raw, 100 kilogs Dressed 100 kilogs	Free 15 per	0.487 cent	Free 10 per	0.047 cent	All not specially enumerated, pood. 7.80 Sable, brown fox, skunk, chinchilla, swan, and marten, pood ... 15.60 Muskrat, pood. 3.90.	5 per cent	8
Each	0.29	0.29	10 pe	r cent		5 per cent	9
Each	0.29	0.29	10 per	cent	Pound ... 0.078	5 per cent	10
	15 per	cent	10 per	ceut	35 per cent	5 per cent	11
100 kilogs	29.35	31.20			See Spirits	Hectoliter ...$0.82	12
	Free	Free	Free	Free	Free	Free	13
100 kilogs	Free	0.58	Free	0.48	Free	Free	14
100 kilogs	Free	Free	Free	Free	Free	Free	15
See Gold and silver manufactured.					Gold 25.74, silver 1.72 per pound.	5 per cent	16
100 kilogs	Free	0.78	Free	Free	Free	Free	17
100 kilogs	Free	Free	Free	Free	Free	Free	18
	Free	Free	Free	Free	Free	Free	19
	Prohib	ited	10 per	cent	Pound ... 0.31	5 per cent	20
	Free	Free	Free	Free	Free	Free	21
	Free	Free	Free	Free	Free	Free	22
	Free	Free	Free	Free	Free	Free	23
Per cent	1	1	10	10	Pood ... 9.36	5 per cent	24
See Iron and steel					Pood ... 0.78	5 per cent	25
	Prohib	ited	10 per	cent	Pood ... 17.16	5 per cent	26
	Free	Free	Free	Free	Free	1 per cent	27
	Free	Free	Free	Free	Pood ... 3.43	Free	28
	Free	Free	Free	Free	Free	Free	29
Per cent	1	1	10	10	See Jewelry	5 per cent	30
100 kilogs	Free	0.195	Free	Free	Free	Free	31
100 kilogs	19.50	20.95	3.99	4.29	Pood ... 9.36	5 per cent	32
	Free	Free	Free	Free	Free	5 per cent	33
Each	0.007	0.097	10 per	cent	Over 1 lb, pood. 1.15	5 per cent	34
Each	15 per	cent	10 per	cent	Under 1 lb, pood. 3.51	5 per cent	35

Comparative table of import duties in the United States and European countries.

	ARTICLES.	ITALY.			SPAIN.	PORTUGAL.
			General tariff.	Tariff in treaty with France, &c.		
1	Fruit, green, ripe, or dried..	Preserved in spirits, 100 kilogs.	$3. 90	$1. 65	100 kilogs....$0. 50	Exotic, kilogr. $0. 016 Dry from Europe, kilogr. 0. 03.
2	Frying pans...............	100 kilogs	1. 56	1. 80	100 kilogs.... 1. 50	Kilogramme . 0. 081
3	Fuller's boards	100 kilogs	0. 48	Free	100 kilogs.... 0. 01	Kilogramme . 0. 021
4	earth..............	100 kilogs	0. 48	Free	100 kilogs.... 0. 01	Free ....
5	Fulminates, fulminating powder.	Kilogramme.....	1. 17	Free	Kilogramme 0. 032	For mines free, other per kilogr. 0. 27.
6	Furniture, coach and harness.	100 kilogs	9. 75	9. 75	20 per cent.........	Kilogramme . 1. 08
7	Furniture, household, n. o. p. for.	See Household furniture		......	See Household furniture.	35 per cent ....
8	Furs, dressed, all on the skin.	Furs, raw, 100 kilogs. bear, lion, &c., tanned per 100 kilogs. Manuf. of fur, per 100 kilogs.	0. 78 2. 93 7. 80 9. 75	...... 2. 93 9. 75	100 kilogs.... 1. 50 For ornament per 100 kilog... 0. 10	Furs, raw or prepared, 20 p. cent. Manuf. common, per kilogr. $1. 62. Gloves, pair, 0. 108 Apparel, with its additions, kilogr. 6. 48.
9	Fur, hats or caps of........	Per cent	10	10	Each 0. 40	Kilogramme . 6. 48
10	hat bodies or felt......	100 kilogs.... ..	2. 93	3. 37	Kilogramme . 0. 15	Kilogramme . 0. 27
11	muffs or tippets, and other manufactures, n. o. p. for.	100 kilogs.......	9. 75	9. 75	20 per cent	Kilogramme .. 6. 48
12	Fusil oil, or amylic alcohol.	Hectoliter.......	0. 97	1. 07	Hectoliter ... 3. 75	See Spirits........
13	Fustic.....................	Free	......	......	100 kilogs.... 0. 01	Free...............
14	Galanga, (crude drug,).....	100 kilogs	0. 39	Free	100 kilogs.... 0. 30	5 per cent ....
15	Gallengal or gall-root	100 kilogs	0. 39	Free	100 kilogs.... 0. 30	5 per cent..........
16	Galloons, gold or silver fine or half-fine.	Galloons, cotton, kilogr. See Gold and silver.	0. 117	......	See Silver and gold.	See Gold and silver.
17	Galls, nut	100 kilogs	0. 195	Free	100 kilogs.... 0. 30	Kilogramme . 0. 01
18	Gambia, (Terra Japonica,).	100 kilogs	0. 48	Free	100 kilogs.... 0. 01	Free ....
19	Gamboge, crude or refined.	100 kilogs	1. 95	0. 39	100 kilogs.... 0. 01	....
20	Game bags, leather or twine	Each	0. 39	0. 39	Kilogramme . 0. 50	Double duties, tissue
21	Garanceue, extract or madder, prepared.	....	Free	Free	100 kilogs ... 0. 30	5 per cent..........
22	Garden seeds, n. o. e.......	100 kilogs	0. 195	Free	100 kilogs.... 0. 60	Kilogramme . 0. 027
23	Garnets, a precious stone...	Per cent.........	1	10	Free	½ per cent..........
24	imitation of.......	Per cent.........	1	10	20 per cent	Kilogramme . 0. 54
25	hardware........	100 kilogs.......	1. 56	1. 80	100 kilogs.... 5. 50	See Steel manuf'red
26	Garters, elastic, made of wire, covered with leather.	100 kilogs	9. 75	9. 75	20 per cent.........	Kilogramme . 2. 70
27	Gas-retorts, common earthen or stone-ware, not ornamented.	Crucibles, per 100 kilogs, earthenware 100 kilogs.	0. 195 1. 56	0. 23 1. 56	100 kilogs.... 0. 30	Earthen, klgr 0. 021 Stone, klgr. 0. 0027
28	Gelatine...................	100 kilogs	1. 95	0. 39	Kilogramme . 0. 20	5 per cent ....
29	Gems	Per cent.........	1	10	Free	½ per cent..........
30	set	Per cent.........	1	10	20 per cent.........	1 per cent..........
31	Gentian root...............	100 kilogs	1. 95	0. 39	100 kilogs.... 2. 00	5 per cent..........
32	German silver, manufact'd.	100 kilogs	3. 90	3. 90	100 kilogs.... 7. 50	Kilogramme . 0. 27
33	unmanuf'd.	As Copper	......	......	100 kilogs.... 0. 30	See Copper........
34	Gig harness, (saddlery,)....	100 kilogs.......	9. 75	9. 75	Kilogramme . 0. 50	Kilogramme . 1. 08
35	springs...............	100 kilogs	2. 93	2. 93	100 kilogs.... 5. 50	Kilogramme . 0. 027

(*Duties expressed in gold dollars of the United States.*)—Continued.

BELGIUM.	AUSTRIA.			DENMARK.	SWEDEN.	NORWAY.	
		General tariff.	Tariff in treaty.				
10 per cent	Lemons, citrons, oranges figs, dried, ctr Figs, fresh; chesnuts, &c. cut or pick'd, centner.	$1.262 0.388	......	Green ..... Free	Fresh ...... Free	Fresh ...... Free	1
100 kilogs ..$0.78	Centner	2.88	$2.16	Pound.....$0.017	Centner ...$0.275	Pound $0.082	2
Free	See Manuf. of	mater	ial ...	Pound.....0.0008	Free	....	3
Free	Free.........	......	......	Free	Free	Pound 0.0045	4
100 kilogs... 2.93	Centner	2.40	......	Pound..... 0.017	See Gunpowder..	Free	5
10 per cent	Centner	5.76	......	Pound..... 0.091	See Saddlery	Free	8
10 per cent	See Househol	d furn	iture .	Pound..... 0.017	See Household furniture.	See Household furniture.	7
Furs, large and small, green, dry, Free. Tanned, goat and sheep 0.975; oth's tanned per kil'gs 2.93; otherwise prepared per 100 kilogs 5.85.	Furs, raw, ctr. inside, prepared cent'r articles as: covers, &c., centner. Caps, gloves, lined covers, &c., centner.	0.384 1.26 5.04 36.00	.... 2.16 24.00	Furs, raw, Free prepared, dyed, and for saddlery, pound 0.067 other, lb. 0.03	Furs, prepared or raw, of goats, reindeer, seal, pound... 0.0275 Sheep, lamb, lb. 0.041 Bear, fox, wolf, pound....0.0689 Other furs, lb 0.275	Beaver, chinchilla, cat, leopard, lion, tiger, zobel, lb..0.437 Monkey, muskrat, squirrel, Siberian sheep, fox, rabbit, per pound.... 0.218 Bear, wolf, lb 0.109 Other, lb.. 0.045	8
All manufac. of fur 10 per cent.	Centner	36.00	24.00	Manuf. of 0.091 fur, pound.	Manuf. pay additional duty of 50 per cent. on furs.	Manufac. of not enum. same duty as furs.	9
10 per cent	Centner	5.04	2.16	Pound..... 0.091	See Furs, manuf.	See Fur manuf..	10
....	Centner	1.26	......	Pound..... 0.068	....	....	11
See Spirits........	See Spirits...	......	......	Pot 0.091	Kande..... 0.332	85 to 88 degrees, pound 0.153	12
Free	Free.........	......	......	Pound.....0.0113	Free	Free	13
Free	....	Free	......	Pound.....0.0113	Free	Free	14
Free	....	Free	......	Pound.....0.0113	Free	Free	15
5 per cent	See Gold and silver.	......	......	Pound..... 0.091	See Gold or silver.	Loth...... 0.03	16
Free	....	Free	Free	Free	Free	Free	17
Free	....	Free	......	Free	Free	Free	18
Free	Centner	2.52	1.44	Free	Free	Free............	19
10 per cent	Centner	5.76	......	Pound..... 0.091	Additional 5 per cent of duty on material.	Pound 0.082	20
Free	Centner.....	0.388	......	Pound.....0.0113	Free......	Pound 0.002	21
100 kilogs .. 0.117	Centner	0.388	Free	Free	Free......	Free	22
Free	Centner	0.388	Free	Pound..... 0.091	Free......	Free	23
5 per cent	Centner	5.76	......	Pound. 0.091	10 per cent.......	Pound 0.109	24
100 kilogs .. 0.78	See Cutlery..	......	......	Pound..... 0.017	Pound..... 0.041	Pound 0.048	25
10 per cent.......	Centner	5.76	3.60	10 per cent.......	10 per cent.......	Pound 0.082	26
100 kilogs .. 0.23	Centner	0.12	Free	Free	Free	Free	27
100 kilogs ..11.70	Centner	7.56	4.80	Pound..... 0.04	Pound..... 0.055	Pound 0.061	28
Free	Centner	0.388	Free	Pound..... 0.091	Free............	Free	29
5 per cent	See Jewelry.	......	......	Pound..... 0.091	See Jewelry	See Jewelry	30
Free	....	Free	......	Pound..... 0.043	Free	Free	31
10 per cent	Centner	7.20	5.76	Pound..... 0.045	Pound..... 0.041	Pound 0.047	32
10 per cent	Sheets.......	1.44	1.20	Pound..... 0.017	Free	Sheets, lb. 0.095	33
10 per cent	See Saddlery	......	......	10 per cent.......	See Saddlery	See Saddlery....	34
100 kilogs.. 0.78	See Manuf. of	steel .	......	Pound..... 0.017	10 per cent.......	Pound 0.027	35

Comparative table of import duties in the United States and European countries.

	ARTICLES.	UNITED STATES.	GREAT BRITAIN.	GERNAN ZOLL-VEREIN.	SWITZERLAND.
1	Gig handles	35 per cent	Free	Centner...$1. 92	Centner...$1. 56
2	Gilt-ware	35 per cent	Free	Centner...10. 80	Centner... 2. 93
3	silver or gold-ware	40 per cent	Free	Centner...36. 00	Centner... 2. 93
4	mock jewelry	25 per cent	Free	Centner... 5. 76	Centner... 2. 93
5	watch chains and seals	25 per cent	Free	Centner...10. 80	Centner... 2. 93
6	paper	35 per cent	Free	Centner... 0. 96	Centner... 1. 56
7	Gimlets	45 per cent	Free	Centner... 1. 92	Centner... 0. 68
8	Gimps, cotton	35 per cent	Free	Centner...21. 60	Centner... 1. 56
9	silk	50 per cent	Free	Centner...21. 60	Centner... 1. 56
10	thread linen	40 per cent	Free	Centner...14. 40	Centner... 0. 68
11	wool	See Woolens	Free	See Wool	Centner... 0. 68
12	wire, if a component part of chief value, n. o. p.	35 per cent	Free	Centner...14. 40	Centner... 0. 68
13	Gin, 50 degrees or less, every degree 5 cents additional.	Gallon $2. 05	Gallon...$2. 53	Centner . . 4. 32	Centner . . 1. 56
14	Gin, 70 degrees	Gallon 3. 50			
15	Gin cases with bottles in them, the cases pay.	35 per cent	Free	Free	
16	the bottles pay	35 per cent	Free	Centner . . 0. 12	Centner... 0. 145
17	Ginger, ground	Pound..... 0. 08	Free	Centner . . 0. 36	Centner . . 0. 39
18	roots	Pound..... 0. 05	Free	Centner . . 0. 36	Centner . . 0. 145
19	preserved or pickl'd.	50 per cent	Pound 0. 02	Centner . . 2. 88	Centner . . 0. 39
20	essence of	50 per cent	Free	Centner . . 2. 40	Centner . . 1. 56
21	Ginseng	20 per cent	Free	Centner . . 0. 36	Centner . . 0. 145
22	Girandoles	40 per cent	Free	Centner . . 2. 88	Centner . . 1. 56
23	Glaziers' diamonds	10 per cent	Free	Free	Centner... 0. 39
24	Globes	35 per cent	Free	Free	Centner... 0. 10
	Gloves:				
25	Angora, cotton, linen	35 per cent	Free	Centner... 9. 60	Centner... 2. 93
26	Leather	50 per cent	Free	Centner... 9. 60	Centner... 2. 93
27	Hair	30 per cent	Free	Centner... 5. 76	Centner... 2. 93
28	Glue	20 per cent	Free	Centner... 0. 36	Centner... 0. 058
29	Glycerine	30 per cent	Free	Centner... 2. 40	Centner... 0. 68
30	Goat-skins, raw	10 per cent	Free	Free	Centner... 9. 058
31	tanned	25 per cent	Free	Free	Centner... 0. 39
32	angora, raw	30 per cent	Free	Free	Centner... 0. 058
33	Gold epaulettes	35 per cent	Free	Centner...36. 00	Centner... 2. 93
34	Gold, all articles composed wholly or in part of gold not otherwise specified.	40 per cent	Free	Centner...36. 00	Centner... 2. 93
35	Goldbeaters' brine	Free	Free	Free	

(*Duties expressed in gold dollars of the United States.*)—Continued.

	FRANCE.				RUSSIA.	NETHERLANDS.	
	General tariff.		In treaty with Great Britain, &c.				
	In French vessels.	In other vessels.	In vessels of treaty powers.	In other vessels.			
See Material of manuf..	....	....	....	....	As material manuf...	5 per cent..........	1
100 kilogs..............	$97.50	$100.90	10 per	cent...	Gilt, over 1 lb., pood........$15.60	5 per cent..........	2
See Gold and silver.....	....	....	....	....	Gilt, under 1 lb., pood.........31.20	5 per cent..........	3
See Jewelry	....	....	....	....	Gold-ware, lb..25.74	5 per cent..........	4
As fancy articles 100 klgs	Prohib	ited....	$11.70	$12.76	Silver-ware, lb. 1.72	5 per cent..........	5
See Paper...............	....	....	....	....	Pood........... 6.24	5 per cent..........	6
See Tools...............	....	....	....	....	Pood 0.62	5 per cent..........	7
See Yarn cotton.........	....	....	....	....	Pound......... 0.27	5 per cent..........	8
See Yarn silk	....	....	....	....	Pound......... 0.78	5 per cent..........	9
See Yarn flax...........	....	....	....	....	Pound......... 0.39	5 per cent..........	10
See Yarn wool...........	....	....	....	....	Pound......... 0.39	5 per cent..........	11
See Wire	....	....	....	....	Pood 2.34	5 Fer cent..........	12
100 kilogs..............	4.87	4.87	2.92	2.92	In casks, prohibited.	Hectoliter ...$1.41	13
					Bottle 0.05	Hectoliter ... 1.41	14
....	Free...	Free...	Free...	Free...	Free.................	Free	15
See Manuf. of glass.....	....	....	....	....	Pood 0.85	5 per cent	16
Gingerbread, 100 kilogs.	2.53	2.78	....	....	Pood 1.17	Free	17
Ginger root or ground, 100 kilogs.	0.39	0.42	0.47	0.49	Pood 1.17	Free	18
....	....	....	....	....	Pood 1.17	100 kilogs.... 2.46	19
....	....	....	....	....	Pood.......... 0.85	Free	20
....	Free...	Free...	Free...	Free...	Free	Free	21
....	....	....	10 per	cent.	Pood.......... 0.75	5 per cent	22
....	Free...	Free...	Free...	Free...	Free	5 per cent..........	23
....	30 per	cent.	Free...	Free...	Free	5 per cent..........	24
....	....	....	....	....	Pound......... 1.72	5 per cent..........	25
....	Prohi	bited.	5 per	cent.	Pound......... 1.72	5 per cent..........	26
....	....	....	....	....	Pound......... 1.72	5 per cent..........	27
....	Free...	Free...	Free...	Free...	Fish glue, in balls, lumps, and sheets, pood 3.43	Free	28
Except fish glue, 100 kilogs.	7.81	8.77	7.81	8.77	Str'g glue, pood 0.078		
....	Prohi	bited.	5 per	cent.	Pood 0.85	Free	29
Each, 100 skins, kilogs..	0.487	0.487	0.58	0.58	Free	Free	30
100 kilogs..............	1.95	9.14	1.95	2.14	Free	2 per cent..........	31
Other, 100 kilogs	23.30	24.95	1.95	2.14	Free	Free	32
Gold, mineral, per 100 kilogs.	Free...	0.195	....	......	35 per cent	5 per cent..........	33
Gold, crude, in bars, 100 kilogs.	0.019	0.019	....	......	Pound.........25.74	5 per cent..........	34
Gold, in sheets, 100 kilogs.	4.87	5.35	4.87	5.35			
Gold, spun, (wire,) 100 kilogs.	97.50	100.90	....	......	Free	3 per cent..........	35

Comparative table of import duties in the United States and European countries.

	ARTICLES.	ITALY.			SPAIN.	PORTUGAL.
			General tariff.	Tariff in treaty with France, &c.		
1	Gig handles	100 kilogs	$1.56	$1.80	100 kilogs....$3.50	Kilogramme .$0.162
2	Gilt-ware	100 kilogs	19.50	19.50	Kilogramme . 2.00	Kilogramme . 0.54
3	silver or gold-ware	See Silver and gol	d		Kilogramme . 4.00	See Gold and silver.
4	mock jewelry	Per cent	5	5	Kilogramme . 2.00	Kilogramme . 0.40
5	watch chains and seals	100 kilogs	19.50	19.50	20 per cent	Kilogramme . 0.54
6	paper	100 kilogs	5.85	4,87	100 kilogs.... 10.00	Ordinary, klgr 0.108 Fine, klgr.. 0.216
7	Gimlets	100 kilogs	1.56	1.80	100 kilogs.... 5.50	Kilogramme . 0.081
8	Gimps, cotton	See Cottons			See Cottons	See Cottons
9	silk	See Silk			See Silk	See Silk
10	thread linen	See Linen			See Flax	See Flax
11	wool	See Wool			See Wool	See Wool
12	wire, if a component part of chief value, o. p. n.	See Wire			See Wire	See Wire
13	Gin, 50 degrees or less, every degree 5 cents additional.	Hectoliter	1.95	1.95	Hectoliter .. 3.75	33 degrees, decaliter 1.188
14	Gin, 70 degrees				Hectoliter .. 3.75	Above 33 degrees, decaliter.... 1.62
15	Gin cases with bottles in them, the cases pay.	Free			100 kilogs.... 0.50	Free
16	the bottles pay	100 kilogs	1.56	0.39	100 kilogs.... 1.60	Kilogramme. 0.172
17	Ginger, ground	100 kilogs	1.95	0.39	100 kilogs.... 2.00	Kilogramme. 0.108
18	roots	100 kilogs	0.39	Free.	100 kilogs.... 0.30	Kilogramme. 0.108
19	preserved or pickl'd	100 kilogs	1.56	0.59	Kilogramme . 0.20	Kilogramme. 0.108
20	essence of	100 kilogs	1.95	0.78	See Essences	5 per cent
21	Ginseng	100 kilogs	0.39	Free.	100 kilogs.... 0.30	Kilogramme. 0.108
22	Girandoles	See Material of m	anuf.		10 per cent	Kilogramme. 0.54
23	Glaziers' diamonds			Free.	100 kilogs.... 0.075	½ per cent
24	Globes	100 kilogs	3.90	1.95	10 per cent	5 per cent
	Gloves:					
25	Angora, cotton, linen	As Tissues			Gloves, leather, per kilogs 4.00	Pair......... 0.108
26	Leather	Palr, kilogs Pair, 100 kilogs..	0.029	 9.75	Other, 20 per cent..	Pair......... 0.108
27	Hair	As Tissues of wo	ol or	hair..		Pair......... 0.108
28	Glue	Glue, strong, 100 kilogs. Glue, fish, 100 kilogs.	1.95 1.95	1.95 2.23	Glues, per 100 kilogramme 2.00	Glues: Gelatin and fish glue, per kilogramme ...0.032 Other, kilogs. 0.005
29	Glycerine	100 kilogs	1.95	0.78	Kilogramme . 0.02	Free
30	Goat-skins, raw		Free.		100 kilogs.... 1.50	Kilogramme . 0.005
31	tanned	100 kilogs	7.80	2.93	Kilogramme . 0.95	Kilogramme . 0.005
32	Angora, raw		Free.		100 kilogs.... 1.50	Kilogramme . 0.005
33	Gold epaulettes		1 p. c.	10 p.c.	20 per cent	Kilogramme .21.60
34	Gold, all articles composed wholly or in part of gold not otherwise specified.		1 p. c.	10 p.c.	See Gold manufactures.	Kilogramme .54.00
35	Goldbeaters' brine		Free.		Free	Free

(*Duties expressed in gold dollars of the United States.*)—Continued.

BELGIUM.	AUSTRIA.			DENMARK.	SWEDEN.	NORWAY.	
		General tariff.	Tariff in treaty.				
10 per cent	See Manuf. of	steel.	......	Pound.....$0.039	10 per cent.	Pound $0.048	1
10 per cent	Centner	$7.20	$5.76	Pound..... 0.091	Pound.....$0.082	Pound 0.095	2
5 per cent	See Gold and silver.	......	......	See Gold and silver.	See Jewelry	Pound 0.095	3
10 per cent	See Jewelry	......	......	Pound..... 0.091	Pound..... 0.082	Pound 0.109	4
10 per cent	Centner	48.00	......	Pound..... 0.091	Pound..... 0.084	Pound 0.095	5
100 kilogs ..$0.78	Centner	6.00	5.76	Pound..... 0.045	Pound.....0.0689	Free	6
100 kilogs .. 0.78	Centner	2.88	2.16	Pound..... 0.17	5 per cent	As tools... Free	7
See Cottons manuf't	See Cotton	......	......		See Cotton manuf		8
See Silk manuf	See Silk	......	......	See Manuf. of material.	See Silk manuf..		9
See Flax manuf	See Flax	......	......		See Flax manuf..	See Manuf. of material.	10
See Woolen manuf.	See Wool	......	......	Pound ... 0.091	See Wool		11
100 kilogs .. 0.195	See Wire	......	......		......		12
See Spirits	Centner	3.58	......	Of 8 degrees, quarter. 0.466	Kande... 0.303	Of 85 to 88 per cent., lb. 0.153	13
				Each degree above 8, quarter.....0.0105			14
Free	Free	......	......	Free	Free	Free	15
100 kilogs.. 0.195	Centner	0.36	Free.	Pound.... 0.008	Free	See Glass	16
Free	Centner	3.84	......	Pound.... 0.017	Pound.... 0.019	Pound.... 0.036	17
Free	Centner	2.52	1.44	Pound.... 0.0113	Free	Pound.... 0.036	18
100 kilogs.. 11.70	Centner	3.84	......	Pound.... 0.091	Pound.... 0.11	Pound.... 0.082	19
See Essences	See Essences	......	......	Pound.... 0.0113	See Essences	Free	20
Free	Free	......	......	Pound.... 0.0113	Free	Free	21
6 per cent	Centner	2.52	......	10 per cent	Free	Each 0.137	22
Free	......	Free.	......	Free	Free	Free	23
Free	Centner	4.80	3.60	10 per cent	Free	10 per cent	24
10 per cent	Centner	27.88	21.60	Pound..... 0.189	Pound.....0.2756	Pound 0.073	25
10 per cent	Centner	27.88	21.60	Pound..... 0.409	Pound.....0.2756	Pound 0.327	26
10 per cent	Centner	27.88	21.60	Pound..... 0.182	Pound.....0.096	Pound 0.073	27
Free	Centner	0.36	......	Pound..... 0.017	Free	Free	28
Free	Centner	2.40	......	Pound.....0.0113	Free	Free	29
Free	......	Free.	......	Free	Pound.... 0.0275	Free	30
100 kilogs .. 0.975	Centner	0.48	0.36	Pound..... 0.034	Pound.... 0.055	Pound 0.045	31
Free.	......	Free.	......	Free	Pound.... 0.0275	Free	32
5 per cent	See Gold manufactures...			Manufac's of gold, pound ... 0.091	Gold, crude, and coin .....Free.	Pound 0.319	33
5 per cent	See Gold manufactures...			Of gold wire, pound ... 0.273	Gold leaf, wire, and powder, ort 0.0027	Loth 0.027	34
Free	......	Free	......	Free	Gold manufact's, ort 0.0138	Free	35

Comparative table of import duties in the United States and European countries.

ARTICLES.	UNITED STATES.	GREAT BRITAIN.	GERMAN ZOLL-VEREIN.	SWITZERLAND.
Glass—				
Of antimony	20 per cent	Free	Centner . . $0. 68	Centner . . $0. 68
Old broken, fit only for remanufacture.	Free	Free	Free	
Wares, of cut glass	40 per cent	Free	Green hollow glass, free. White hollow glass not assorted, not cut; window and plate glass in its natural color, cent'r. 0. 48 Massive white glass pressed, cut, assorted; also ornaments for chandeliers, buttons, pearls, enamel of gla's, centner .. 1. 92 Mirrorglass, raw, uncut, centner ...... 0. 36 Mirror glass, fine, silvered, cut, centner .. 2. 88 Glass colored, paint'd, print'd, gilded; articles of glass in combination with other materials, centner .. 2. 88 Toilet and other fancy articles, part glass, centner 10. 80	Green hollow glass; ordinary wine bottles, green or brown, centner .. 0. 145 Massive bars of glass, centner ..... 0. 297 Glass castings, centner .. 0. 39 Window glass, ordinary ware, hollow glass, and tubes, centner .. 0. 68 Fancy articles, crystal glass, cut, painted, and colored, not painted, window glass, centner ...... 1. 56 Mirror glass silvered, of more than 2 sq. feet; also in frames; painted window panes, centner .. 2. 93
Wares, not cut, not specially enumerated	35 per cent	Free		
Apothecaries' vials and bottles, not exceeding 6 ozs. each	35 per cent	Free		
Above 6 ounces, but less than 16 ounces	35 per cent	Free		
Glass bottles, black, not filled	35 per cent	Free		
Glass bottles, black, filled with preserves	40 per cent	Free		
Glass bottles, plain, not filled	35 per cent	Free		
All fluted, rolled, or rough plate glass, not including crown, cylinder, broad, or common window glass, not over 10 by 15 inches	Sq. foot...$0. 00¾	Free		
As above, over 10 by 15 inches, but not over 16 by 24 inches	Sq. foot ... 0. 01	Free		
As above, over 16 by 24 inches, less than 24 by 30 inches	Sq. foot ... 0. 01½	Free		
As above, above 24 by 30 inches	Sq. foot ... 0. 02	Free		
Provided that all, as above, weighing over 1 pound per square foot, shall pay an additional duty on the excess at the same rates herein imposed.				
Glass, all cast, polished plate glass, unsilvered, not over 10 by 15 inches	Sq. foot.... 0. 03	Free		
As above, 10 by 15 inches, less than 16 by 24 inches	Sq. foot.... 0. 05	Free		
As above, over 16 by 24 inches, less than 24 by 30 inches	Sq. foot.... 0. 08	Free		
As above, over 24 by 30 inches, less than 24 by 60 inches	Sq. foot.... 0. 25	Free		
As above, above 24 by 60 inches	Sq. foot.... 0. 50	Free		
Glass, all cast polished plate, silvered, or looking-glass plate, not over 10 by 15 inches	Sq. foot.... 0. 04	Free		
As above, over 10 by 15 inches, less than 16 by 24 inches	Sq. foot.... 0. 06	Free		
As above, over 16 by 24 inches, less than 24 by 30 inches	Sq. foot.... 0. 10	Free		
As above, not over 24 by 60 inches	Sq. foot.... 0. 35	Free		
As above, over 24 by 60 inches	Sq. foot.... 0. 60	Free		

(*Duties expressed in gold dollars of the United States.*)—Continued.

	FRANCE.				RUSSIA.	NETHERLANDS.
	General tariff.		In treaty with Great Britain, &c.			
	In French vessels.	In other vessels.	In vessels of treaty powers.	In other vessels.		
....	....	....	5 per cent.		Pood..........$0.85	Free ....
....	Free...	$0.19	Free...	$0.048	Free	Free ....
Spectacle and watch crystals, raw, 100 kilogs.	$1.95	2.14	10 per cent.		Bottle, green glass, not painted, not cut nor polished, per pood......... 0.39	Glass and glass ware of all sorts, 5 per cent.
As above, cut or polish'd	39.00	41.44				
Bottles (if filled, liquid extra,) liter, they contain.	0.029	0.029	0.25	0.29	Window glass of all kinds, not cut or polished, without painting, pood..... 0.85	
Empty bottles	Prohibited.					
Glassware not enumerated hereafter.	Prohibited.		10 per cent.		Colored or painted, window glass, stained, unpolished, uncut, and without ornaments, gilding, or silvered, pood. 1.56	
Vitrifications:						
In masses or tubes, 100 kilogs.	0.58	0.64	0.72	0.80		
In pierced grains, 100 kilogs.	0.19	0.22	3.90	4.29	Articles of white glass and crystal, cut and polished, but without ornaments, per pood......... 3.12	
Cut for jewelry, 100 kilogs.	1.17	1.29				
Enamel, 100 kilogs	0.39	0.42			Articles of colored glass or double ground milk colored; objects of glass painted, gilded, or silvered, with various and etched designs, and with bronze or other ornaments, pood. 6.24	
Mirror glass not silvered. (In all vessels.)	More than 3 millimeters thick.	3 millimeters or less thick.				
With a surface of:			Mirror glass, less than ½ meter square, square meter.		Mirror glass, size of 100 square vershoks or less, pound. 0.047	
50 square decimeters or less, square meter.	2.92	1.95	3.90	4.29		
50 to 100 sq. decimeters, square meter.	4.38	2.92	½ to 1 meter square, 10 per cent. ad valorem.		Size: 101 to 200 sq. vershoks, square vershoks..... 0.006	
100 to 200 square decimeters, square meter.	5.46	3.64			201 to 200 square vershoks, square vershok 0.0078	
200 to 300 square decimeters, square meter.	7.80	5.20	Raw, 100 kilo., 0.29	0.29		
300 to 500 square decimeters, square meter.	9.75	6.49	Tinn'd, 100 kil., 0.78	0.78	301 to 300 square vershoks, square vershok......... 0.012	
Over 500 sq. decimeters, square meter.	11.70	7.80	All other articles, 10 per ct. ad valorem.			
Silvered:					401 to 400 square vershoks, square vershok......... 0.016	
50 square decimeters or less, square meter.	3.21	2.14				
50 to 100 square decimeters, square meter.	4.82	3.21			501 to 600 square vershoks, square vershok......... 0.017	
100 to 200 square decimeters, square meter.	6.00	4.00			601 to 800 square vershoks, square vershok......... 0.019	
200 to 300 square decimeters, square meter.	8.58	5.72			801 to 1,200 sq. vershoks, square vershok......... 0.021	
300 to 500 square decimeters, square meter.	10.72	7.15			Larger than 1,200 sq. vershoks, each 23.40	
Over 500 sq. decimeters, square meters.	12.87	8.58				
Small mirror glass without regard to thickness, 100 kilogs.	19.50	20.95			Polished looking-glass without amalgam, pays same duties as mirrors, but with a deduction of 30 per cent.	
Window glass, 100 kilogs	Prohibited.		0.67	0.73		

Comparative table of import duties in the United States and European countries.

ARTICLES.—UNITED STATES.—Cont'd.	ITALY.			SPAIN.	PORTUGAL.
		General tariff.	Tariff in treaty with France, &c.		
Glass—Continued.					
Provided that no looking glass plates or plate glass silvered when framed shall pay a less rate of duty than that imposed on similar glass of like description not framed, but shall pay, in addition thereto, 30 per cent. for the frames.	Black bottles, common, 100 kilogs..........	$0.297	$0.39	Glass, common, and hollow, 100 kilogs.......0.35	Glass and crystal, in polished plate of more than 756 square centimeters, tin covered, 6 square centmeters $0.002
	Of 1 liter, 100 kil.	0.39	0.39	Imitation of glass and crystal, 100 kilogs........9.00	
	Larger, 100 kil ..	1.17	0.39		
	Other bottles of any other form or color, 100 kil.	1.56	0.39	Glass and crystal, smooth, 100 kilogrammes ... 3.50	Not covered, 6 sq. centimeters. 0.001
	Window glass, 100 kilogs......	1.56	0.975	Plate overlaid with quicksilver, 100 kilogs 16.00	Polished plate of less size than 756 square centimeters, tinned or not, inclusive of sheet and frames, kilogramme ... 0.054
Glasses, hour, 35 per cent. Looking, with paper and wood frames, (see Glass plate silvered.)	Plate not polish'd if glass, 100 kil.	1.56	1.56		
	If crystal, 100 kil.	2.93	1.56		
Glass, paintings on, not otherwise specified, 40 per cent.	Plate polished if not silvered, 100 kilogs..........	2.93	2.93		
Glass plates or disks, unwrought for optic instruments, 10 per cent.	If silvered, 100 kilogs..........	4.87	4.87		Plate not polished, kilogramme. 0.172
Glass shades for time pieces or mantle ornaments, 35 per cent.	Other articles of crystal polished, but not painted, 100 kilogs......	2.93	2.34		All articles more or less finished, blown, moulded, engraved, of any form or color, kilgramme ... 0.172
Glass, cut, all wares of, 40 per cent.	Also painted, 100 kilogs..........	2.93	2.93		
Glass, all articles not specified, plain or moulded, 35 per cent.	Other articles cut, painted or polished, 100 kilogs.	2.93	1.36		Vessels of ordinary glass, black, or green, kilog. 0.005
Glass weighing under 8 ounces, except tumblers, 35 per cent.	Concave glasses, white, 100 kilogs	1.56	0.975		Jewelry and pieces for jewelry, kilogramme ... 0.054
Glass, cut, ornaments for chandeliers, 40 per cent.	Vitrifications, 100 kilogs..........	1.56	0.73		Artificial gems, kilogramme 0.54
Glass tumblers, and other articles, plain and moulded, 35 per cent.	Vitrifications, cut into false diamonds or crystals, 100 kilogs .	9.75	......		Broken pieces, free.
Glass, watch, or watch crystals, 40 per cent.					
Glass, pressed, 35 per cent.					
Glass, colored, engraved, painted, printed, gilt, stained, silvered, Bohemian, porcelain, spectacles, pebbles, or spectacles, all manufactures of glass not otherwise provided for, 40 per cent.					
Glass bottles filled with preserves; jars filled with preserves, 40 per cent.					

(Duties expressed in gold dollars of the United States.)—Continued.

BELGIUM.	AUSTRIA.			DENMARK.	SWEDEN.	NORWAY.
		General tariff.	Tariff in treaty.			
Glass work, common, 100 kilogrammes.$0.195 Other, 10 per ct. Broken pieces, free.	Glass, common, hollow ware of green, black, and yellow, natural color; not pressed, cut, or polished; mass of glass. centner .... White hollow glass not cut, polished, pressed, or assorted, window and table glass, green, or white, cent'r Medium fine, pressed, cut, polished, assorted, chandeliers, buttons, pearls, cent'r Fine, colored, painted, gilded, or silvered; inlaid paste, artificial diamonds not set, centner .... Mirror glass, cut, silvered, tinned, or not, each piece, not over 284 square meters, centner .... Fancy, all manufactures in connection with other materials, centner.... .... Mirrors, framed or not, of over 284 square ins., centner	$0.36 1.08 3.48 5.04 5.04 7.20 7.20	$0.36 0.72 1.92 2.88 2.44 5.76 5.76	Glass, not cut nor foliated, in plates; window glass; ordinary crown or green hollow glass ware, as bottles, retorts, mirror glass, (not cut.) pound.. 0.0084 In plates, cut, of less than 800 square inches, pound...$0.045 800 to 1,800 sq. inches, lb. 0.068 Over 1,800 square inches, lb. 0.091 Foliated, cut or not, 25 per cent. additional to glass in plates, cut. Glass ware in connect'n with mt'l, pound ... 0.091 All other, lb 0.04 Glass flux, buttons, drops, pound ... 0.091	Glassware, bottles, and vials, plain, cent'r 0.21 Cut and ornament'd, lb. 0.041 Chandeliers, pound .. 0.0138 Window glass, all kinds, lb. 0.0081 Mirror glass not cut, lb.. 0.0081 Mirror glass cut, not silvered, pound .. 0.0138 Mirror glass silvered or tinned, pound .. 0.0275 Watch crystals, pound .. 0.0275 Other articles cut, pressed, &c., pound ... 0.041 Glassy flux cut or not, not set, pound ... 0.165 If set, same as gold, silver, or jewelry.	Glass in plates silvered, lb.$0.031 Not silvered, cut, pound ... 0.018 Painted, gilded, varnished, etched, assorted, pound... 0.018 Other, lb.. 0.009 Glass flux cut, not set, lb ... 0.109 Set in gold, as jewelery, in pearls, lb. 0.054 Other articles of glass; also demijohns, lb. 0.047

Comparative table of import duties in the United States and European countries.

	ARTICLES.	UNITED STATES.	GREAT BRITAIN.	GERMAN ZOLL-VEREIN.	SWITZERLAND.
1	Gold moulds...............	10 per cent......	Free............	Centner..$36.00	Centner...$2.93
2	dust, coin............	Free............	Free............	Free............	....
3	embroideries.........	35 per cent......	Free............	Centner...10.60	Centner... 2.93
4	muriate of............	20 per cent......	Free............	Centner... 2.40	Centner... 0.68
5	paper, in sheets or other form.	40 per cent......	Free............	Centner... 0.96	Centner... 1.56
6	oxide of..............	20 per cent......	Free............	Centner... 2.40	Centner... 0.68
7	shoes or clogs, wood or leather.	35 per cent	Free............	Centner... 2.88	Centner... 0.39
8	Gouges....................	45 per cent......	Free............	Centner... 0.96	Centner... 0.39
9	Grains, tawed or tanned....	25 per cent......	Free	See Leather.....	....
10	Granella, cochineal........	Free............	Free............	Centner... 0.36	Centner... 0.68
11	Grass bags................	30 per cent......	Free............	Centner... 0.48	Centner... 0.145
12	cable, cordage, untarred.	Pound $0.03½	Free............	Centner... 0.12	Centner... 1.56
13	hats or bonnets......	40 per cent......	Free............	Each, cent'r 0.05	Centner... 2.93
14	and cotton cloth......	35 per cent......	Free............	Trimmed, each, centner.. 0.10	Centner... 1.56
15	hopper springs.......	35 per cent......	Free............	Centner... 0.96	Centner... 1.56
16	Sisal................	Ton 15.00	Free............	Free............	Centner... 0.097
17	Grease....................	10 per cent......	Free............	Free............	Centner... 0.097
18	Green turtle..............	20 per cent......	Free............	Centner... 1.44	Centner... 0.145
19	Gridirons.................	35 per cent......	Free............	Centner... 0.96	Centner... 1.56
20	Grindstones, finished.......	20 per cent......	Free............	Free............	Centner... 0.029
21	rough.......	10 per cent......	Free............	Free............	Centner... 0.029
22	Guava jelly or paste.......	50 per cent......	Free............	Centner... 0.36	Centner... 0.68
23	Guano.....................	Free............	Free............	Free............	Free............
24	Guinea grains.............	20 per cent......	Free............	Free............	Centner... 0.027
25	Guitars...................	30 per cent......	Free............	Centner...$2.88	Centner... 1.56
26	strings, (gut).......	30 per cent......	Free............	Centner... 2.88	Centner... 1.56
27	Gum, aloes................	Pound.... 0.06	Free............	All gums, free...	Centner... 0.028
28	benzoin.............	Pound.... 0.10	Free............	....	Centner... 0.145
29	Barbary, Senegal....	....	Free............	....	Others, ctnr 0.68
30	Arabic, tragacanth ..	20 per cent......	....	....	....
31	mastic..............	Pound.... 0.50	Free............	....	....
32	copal and all resinous substances used as copal.	Pound.... 0.10	Free............	....	....
33	shellac.............	Pound.... 0.10	Free............	Free............	....
34				Medicinal use,	Centner... 0.68
35	all not spec'd—crude.	20 per cent......	Free............	centner.. 0.36	Centner... 0.028
36	not crude..........	20 per cent......	Free............	otherwise free.	Centner... 0.145
37	sandarac, damar	Pound.... 0.10	Free............	Free............	....
38	Gum-elastic articles........	35 per cent......	Free............	Centner... 7.20	Centner... 1.56
39	Guns......................	35 per cent......	Free............	Centner... 1.92	Centner... 1.56
40	Gunlocks..................	45 per cent......	Free............	Centner... 2.88	Centner... 1.56
41	Gunpowder .... less than 20 cts. per lb.	20 per cent. and per pound 0.06	Free............ Free............	Centner.. 1.44	Prohibited ......
42	over 20 cts. per lb....	20 per cent. and per pound 0.10	Free............		
43	Gun wadding, of paper	35 per cent......	Free............	Centner... 0.96	Centner... 0.29
44	Guts, sheep, salted.........	20 per cent......	Free............	Centner... 0.36	Centner... 0.058
45	Gutta-percha, unmanufac'd.	10 per cent......	Free............	Free............	Centner... 0.68
46	manufactures of..	40 per cent......	Free............	Thread, also mixed, centner 0.36 See India-rubber.	All manufact's, centner... 1.56

(*Duties expressed in gold dollars of the United States.*)—Continued.

FRANCE.					RUSSIA.	NETHERLANDS.	
	General tariff.		In treaty with Great Britain, &c.				
	In French vessels.	In other vessels.	In vessels of treaty powers.	In other vessels.			
....	....	....	....	....	Free	5 per cent........	1
....	Free...	Free...	Free...	Free...	Free	Free	2
Kilogramme........	$6.04	$6.64	$2.34	$2.38	Pound........$4.29	5 per cent........	3
....	....	....	5 per	cent.	Pood 0.85	Free	4
See Paper........	....	....	....	....	Pood 6.24	3 per cent........	5
....	....	....	5 per	cent.	Pood 0.85	Free	6
....	Prohi	bited.	10 per	cent.	Free	5 per cent........	7
....	....	....	....	....	Free	5 per cent........	8
See Leather	....	....	....	....	See Leather	2 per cent........	9
400 kilogs........	Free...	2.92	Free...	Free...	Free	Free	10
....	15 per	cent.	10 per	cent.	Free	5 per cent........	11
100 kilogs........	4.87	5.36	2.92	3.20	Pood 0.312	100 kilogs....$0.20	12
....	....	....	....	....	Each, pood.... 0.70	5 per cent........	13
....	....	....	....	....	See Cotton........	5 per cent........	14
See Iron and Steel manu	factures	....	....	....	See Iron and Steel manufactures.	5 per cent........	15
....	Free...	Free...	Free...	Free...	Free	Free	16
100 kilogs........	0.39	0.39	Free...	0.048	Free	Free	17
....	Free...	Free...	Free...	Free...	Pood 0.85	Free	18
100 kilogs........	....	....	2.73	2.97	See Iron Manufact's..	5 per cent........	19
100 kilogs........	0.97	0.87	Free...	0.048	Free	Free	20
100 kilogs........	Free...	0.195	Free...	6.048	Free	Free	21
100 kilogs........	8.58	8.58	....	....	Pood 2.34	Free	22
100 kilogs........	Free ..	0.35	Free ..	0.47	Free	Free	23
....	Free ..	Free ..	Free ..	Free ..	Free	Free	24
Each........	0.58	0.58	10 pe	r cent.	Pound 0.117	5 per cent	25
....	15 per	cent.	10 pe	r cent.	Pound 0.08	5 per cent.	26
Gums, pure, 100 kilogs.	Free ..	0.48	Free ..	Free ..			27
							28
....	....	....	....	....			29
....	....	....	....	....			30
....	....	....	....	....			31
....	....	....	....	....	Gums, pood .. 0.23	Free	32
....	....	....	....	....			33
....	....	....	....	....			34
....	Free ..	0.48	Free ..	Free ..			35
....	Free ..	0.48	Free ..	Free ..			36
....	....	....	....	....			37
....	....	....	....	....	Pood........ 2.53	5 per cent	38
Per 100 kilogs........	39.00	41.43	46.80	49.62	Pood........14.04	5 per cent	39
....	....	....	....	....	Pood........14.04	5 per cent	40
							41
....	Prohi	bited.	Prohi	bited.	Prohibited........	100 kilogs ... 2.05	
							42
See paper	....	....	....	....	Pood........ 0.16	5 per cent	43
....	Free ..	Free ..	Free ..	Free ..	Free	Free	44
....	Free ..	Free ..	Free ..	Free ..	Pood........ 0.23	Free	45
Manufactured articles: See India-rubber.	....	....	....	....	Manufactures: See India-rubber.	5 per cent	46

Comparative table of import duties in the United States and European countries.

	ARTICLES.	ITALY.			SPAIN.	PORTUGAL.
			General tariff.	Tariff in treaty with France, &c.		
1	Gold moulds	Gold, in bars, powder, &c. Gold, beaten, kilogr. Gold, laminat'd, kilogr. Gold wire, kil's Articles of gold, hectogram. Jewelry, hecto'e Vermeil, kilogr.	Free. $1. 56 0. 58 1. 17 1. 95 3. 12 4. 68	Free. $1. 80 .... 5 p. cent	Gold, mine'l, Free. Gold, in bars, coin, pieces, powder, or ingots; also useless table service ...... Free. Gold, manufact'd in Spain.. Free. Jewelry, &c., hectogramme $5. 00	Gold, crude, powdered, & broken pieces .... Free. Gold, beaten, laminated, not specified, kilo $0. 5400 Gold, in leaves, kilogr .... 2. 16 Gold wire, kilogramme.. 54. 00 Gold medals, kilogramme.. 0. 054 Gold coin... Free. Gold lace work kilogr .... 21. 60 Gold jewelry, per kilogr 54. 00
2	dust, coin					
3	embroideries					
4	muriate of					
5	paper, in sheets or other form.					
6	oxide of					
7	shoes or clogs, wood or leather					
8	Gouges	100 kilogs	3. 90	1. 95	100 kilogs.... 5. 50	Kilogramme . 0. 002
9	Grains, tawed or tanned	See Leather	......	......	See Leather	Kilogramme . 0. 005
10	Granella, cochineal	100 kilogs	0. 39	Free.	100 kilogs.... 1. 50	20 per cent
11	Grass bags	......	......	......	20 per cent	Kilogramme . 0. 108
12	cable, cordage, untarred.	100 kilogs	0. 39	0. 39	100 kilogs.... 4. 00	Kilogramme . 0. 02
13	hats or bonnets	100 kilogs	4. 87	......	Each 0, 20	Kilogramme . 0. 108
14	and cotton cloth	100 kilogs	9. 75	9. 75	See Cottons	See Cottons
15	hopper springs	100 kilogs	1. 56	1. 80	100 kilogs.... 5. 50	Kilogramme . 0. 162
16	Sisal	......	Free.	Free.	100 kilogs.... 0. 10	Free
17	Grease	100 kilogs	0. 195	0. 195	100 kilogs.... 0. 30	Kilogramme . 0. 054
18	Green turtle	......	Free.	Free.	Free	Free
19	Gridirons	100 kilogs	1. 56	1. 80	100 kilogs.... 1. 60	Kilogramme . 0. 081
20	Grindstones, finished	Each	0. 019	Free	100 kilogs.... 0. 01	Free
21	rough	Each	0. 019	Free.	100 kilogs.... 0. 01	Free
22	Guava jelly or paste	100 kilogs	2. 93	......	100 kilogs.... 2. 80	5 per cent
23	Guano	Free	......	......	100 kilogs.... 0. 01	Free
24	Guinea grains	100 kilogs	0. 48	Free.	100 kilogs.... 0. 60	Kilog 0. 008
25	Guitars	Each	0. 29	0. 39	20 per cent	25 per cent
26	strings, (gut)	Guitar strings, 100 kilogs.	9. 75	9. 75	100 kilogs.... 5. 50	Kilogr 0. 54
27	Gum, aloes	Gums, vegetable, pure: 100 kilogs exotic: 100 kilogs	0. 76 2. 93	....	All gums not specifically enumerat'd 100 kilogs. 2. 00	Gums, kilog. 0. 027 Resin's gums, 5 per cent.
28	benzoin					
29	Barbary, Senegal					
30	Arabic, tragacanth					
31	mastic					
32	copal and all resinous substances used as copal.					
33	shellac					
34	all not spec'd—crude.					
35	not crude					
36						
37	sandarac, damar					
38	Gum-elastic articles	100 kilogs	3. 87	5. 63	Kilog 0. 375	Kilog 0. 027
39	Guns	See Arms	......	......	Prohibited	20 per cent
40	Gunlocks	Each barrel	0. 58	0. 67	Prohibited	30 per cent
41	Gunpowder less than 20 cts. per lb.	Kilog	1. 17	......	Prohibited	Prohibited
42	over 20 cts. per lb					
43	Gun wadding, of paper	......	......	......	Prohibited	......
44	Guts, sheep, salted	100 kilogs	0. 58	......	100 kilogs.... 0. 30	Guts, in leaf.. Free. salted, kilog. 0. 08
45	Gutta-percha, unmanufac'd.	100 kilogs	0. 48	......	100 kilogs.... 1. 00	Free
46	manufactures of	See India-rubber.	......	......	See India-rubber.	See India-rubber.

(*Duties expressed in gold dollars of the United States.*)—Continued.

BELGIUM.	AUSTRIA.			DENMARK.	SWEDEN.	NORWAY.	
		General tariff.	Tariff in treaty.				
Gold, not worked; also gold coin .... Free. Gold, manufactured, 5 per cent. Gold powder, bars, drawn, lamin't'd, spun over silk, free.	Gold, crude, coin, bars, or sheeets, powder, & brok'n pcs. Articles of pure gold, jewelry set in gold, watches of gold and silver, per centner.	Free. 126. 00	Free.	Gold coin, bars, or pieces, free. Gold, manufa'd, pound ..$0. 091 Manufactures of gold wire, per pound .. 0. 273	(See page 101.) Embroideries, 20 per cent. additional to duty on material embroidered. See Paper ...... See Chemicals.. Manufactures of wood, leather, 10 per cent.	Gold, crude, and leaf .... Free. Gold, pressed, not polished, loth ....$0. 027 Gold, manuf'd, loth..... 0. 03 Gold tresses, lace, galloons, and articles of wire, lb. 0. 319	1 2 3 4 5 6 7
10 per cent	See Material,	manuf	act'd .	Pound..... 0. 017	10 per cent.......	Pound 0. 027	8
100 kilogs ..$0. 195	See Leather..	......	......	Pound..... 0. 034	Pound....$0. 0097	Pound 0. 045	9
Free	....	Free.	......	Pound..... 0. 079	Pound.... 0. 0964	Pound 0. 073	10
10 per cent	As Material,	(see M	ats.) .	10 per cent.......	Additio'l to duty on material of which bags are manufactured, 10 per cent.	10 per cent	11
Free	See Cordage .	......	......	Pound..... 0. 056		Pound ... 0. 009	12
10 per cent	See Hats	......	......	Hats, pound 0. 36	Hats, each..0. 21	Hats, each. 0. 109	13
As Cotton tissues..	See Tissues of	cotton	......	See Cotton.......	See Cotton.......	See Cotton	14
100 kilogs .. 0. 78	See Manufac's	of ste	el	Pound..... 0. 017	See Steel manufactured.	Pound 0. 027	15
Free.	....	Free.	......	Free	Free	Free	16
Free	Centner	$0. 388	Free.	Free	Free	Free	17
Free	Centner	Free.	......	Free	Free	Free	18
100 kilogs .. 0. 78	Centner	2. 88	$2. 16	Pound..... 0. 017	Centner... 0. 2756	Pound 0. 027	19
10 per cent	Centner	0. 388	Free.	Pound..... 0. 002	Free	Free	20
Free	....	Free.	......	Free	Free	Free	21
Free	Centner	0. 388	Free.	Free	Free	Pound 0. 018	22
10 per cent	Free..........	......	......	Free	Free	Free	23
Free	Centner	0. 388	Free.	Pound..... 0. 017	Free	Ton 0. 136	24
10 per cent.	Centner	4. 80	3. 60	10 per cent.......	Each 0. 2756	Each 0. 273	25
100 kilogs.. 0. 117	Gut strings, centner.	24. 00	14. 40	metal, lb...0. 0014 gut, lb... 0. 055	metal, lb...0. 0275 other, lb..0. 138	gut, pound. 0. 159 metal 0. 036	26
Gums.... Free...	Gums: aloes, cent... benzoin ..... Arabic, and tragacanth . ammoniac & benzoic, per centner.... resinous, cent. not sp., crude. not crude, cnt. sandarac, damar, centn'r.	 2. 52 Free Free 2. 52 0. 388 Free. 2. 52 2. 52	 1. 44 .... 1. 44 .... 1. 44 1. 44	Pound....6. 0113	Free	Free	27 28 29 30 31 32 33 34 35 36 37
10 per cent.	Centner	5. 76	3. 60	Pound..... 0. 091	Pound.....0. 11	Pound 0. 127	38
Free	Centner	7. 20	7. 20	Pound..... 0. 091	Pound 0. 055	Free............	39
100 kilogs .. 0. 78	See Manufactures of steel.	......	......	Pound..... 0. 091	Pound.....0. 0275	Pound 0. 073	40
100 kilogs .. 2. 93	Centner	12. 60	......	Pound.....0. 0236	all, and cartridges, lb..0. 0138	Free	41 42
100 kilogs .. 0. 78	Centner	0. 36	......	Pound.....0. 0028	Pound.....0. 002	Free	43
Free	Centuer	0. 388	Free.	Free	Free	Free	44
Free	Centner	0. 388	Free.	Free	Free	Free	45
10 per cent	Centner	5. 76	3. 60	Pound..... 0. 091	Pound.....0. 11 tissues, lb.0. 21	Pound 0. 127	46

Comparative table of import duties in the United States and European countries.

	ARTICLES.	UNITED STATES.	GREAT BRITAIN.	GERMAN ZOLL-VEREIN.	SWITZERLAND.
1	Gypsum or plaster of Paris.	Free............	Free............	Free............	Centner... 0.12
2	Hackles, flax or hemp	45 per cent......	Free............	Free............	Centner... 0.058
3	Hair, animal, unmanufact'd.	See Wool, 2d class	Free............	Free............	Centner... 0.29
4	manufactures, all not provided for.	30 per cent......	Free............	Centner... 5.76	Animal, manf'd, centner... 1.56
5	made up into head-dresses; nets (of human hair) and other human hair manufactured.	40 per cent......	Free............	Free............	Centner... 2.93
6	prepared for head-dresses.	35 per cent......	Free............	Free............	Centner... 0.058
7	braids for the head....	35 per cent......	Free............	Free............	Centner... 2.93
8	belts, brooms, bracelets, chains, curls.	35 per cent......	Free............	Free............	Centner... 2.93
9	hogs'	Pound $0.01	Free............	Centner... 0.36	Centner... 0.058
10	human, cleaned	30 Per cent.... }	Free............	Free............	Centner... 1.56
11	not prepared	20 per cent.... }			
12	gloves	30 per cent......	Free............	Centner... 5.76	Centner... 2.93
13	other, cleaned not specified.	10 per cent......	Free............	Free............	Centner... 0.058
14	horse, cleaned	10 per cent......	Free............	....	Centner... 0.29
15	long, for weav'g.	Free............	Free............	....	Centner... 0.29
16	pins	35 per cent	Free............	Centner... 2.58	Centner... 1.56
17	powder, not perfumed.	50 per cent......	Free............	Centner... 1.44	....
18	perfumed....	50 per cent......	Free............	Centner... 2.40	Centner... 2.93
19	other raw..........	Free............	Free............	Free............	Centner... 0.058
20	Hair pencils...............	35 per cent	Free............	Centner... 0.36	Centner .. 2.93
21	Hames, wood..............	35 per cent	Free............	Centner... 0.72	Centner .. 0.39
22	Hammers, blacksmith's	Pound 0.02½	Free............	Centner... 1.92	Centner .. 0.19
23	all oth's, not steel	35 per cent	Free............	Centner... 1.92	Centner .. 0.19
24	Hams, bacon	Pound 0.02	Free............	Centner... 0.36	Centner .. 0.39
25	Handles, for chests.........	35 per cent	Free............	Centner... 0.96	Centner .. 1.56
26	Hangers....................	35 per cent	Free............	Centner... 0.96	Centner .. 1.56
27	Hare's hair or fur..........	20 per cent	Free............	Free............	Centner .. 0.058
28	Hare-skins, undressed	10 per cent	Free............	Free............	Centner .. 0.058
29	dressed	20 per cent	Free............	Free............	Centner .. 0.39
30	Harlem oil	50 per cent	Free............	Centner... 0.60	Centner .. 0.10
31	Harness and furniture......	35 per cent	Free............	Centner... 2.88	Centner .. 1.56
32	Harp strings, gut...........	30 per cent	Free............	Centner... 2.88	Centner .. 1.56
33	wire	35 per cent	Free............	Centner... 2.88	Centner .. 1.56
34	Harps and harpsichords	30 per cent	Free............	Centner... 2.88	Centner .. 1.56
35	Hartshorn, spirits of	40 per cent	Free............	Centner... 2.40	Centner .. 0.68
36	Hatchets	45 per cent	Free............	Centner... 0.96	Centner .. 0.68
37	Hat bodies, cotton	35 per cent	Free............	Centner... 7.20	Centner .. 0.68
38	wool, or chiefly wool.	35 per cent., and per pound.0.50	Free............	Centner... 7.20	Centner .. 0.68
39	Hats, leghorn, hat linings, hats of chip, straw, grass, or cott'n cloth.	40 per cent	Free..........	Hats of straw, not finish'd, ea. 0.05 Finish'd, ea. 0.10 Of paper, not finish'd, cent'r. 0.96 Of paper, finished, centn'r. 2.88 Hats of silk and other tissues, finished, centner ......10.60 Gent's hats of silk, garnished, centner ..21.60 Gent's hats of felt and wool, centner ..10.60 Of leather, centner ...... 2.88 Of leather, varnished, centner 7.20	Hats, all, centner 2.93
40	wool, value over 40c. per lb., not over 60c.	35 per cent., and per pound.0.30	Free..........		
41	from 60c. to 80c. per lb.	35 per cent., and per pound.0.40	Free..........		
42	over 80c. per lb......	35 per cent., and per pound.0.50	Free..........		
43	fur......	35 per cent	Free..........		
44	leather, palm leaf, rattan, japanned.	40 per cent	Free..........		
45	silk (men's)	60 per cent	Free..........		
46	Panama, Manilla, Leghorn, Naples, and others.	40 per cent	Free..........		

* 100 kilogs.

(*Duties expressed in gold dollars of the United States.*)—Continued

FRANCE.					RUSSIA.	NETHERLANDS.	
	General tariff.		In treaty with Great Britain, &c.				
	In French vessels.	In other vessels.	In vessels of treaty powers.	In other vessels.			
....	Free ..	Free ..	Free ..	Free ..	Free	Free	1
....	....	....	....	....	Free	Free	2
Hair, raw or prepared.	Free ..	Free ..	Free ..	Free ..	Pood $1. 716	Hair, spun or manufac'd into wigs or curls, 5 per cent.	3
combed or assorted, 100 kilogs.	$1. 95	$2. 14	....	....	....		4
goats', 100 kil.	....	....	$1. 95	$2. 14	All manufact's of hair not otherwise specified, pound ..0. 468		5
other, 100 kil.	....	....	2. 34	2. 57			
tissues of, cassimeres, not prod. of Europe, 100 kil.	9. 75	10. 72	5 per cent.				
hosiery, castor, 100 k.	78. 00	81. 45	As tissues of wool.		Free		
of other hair..	39. 00	41 43			Pound 0. 468	....	6
all others 100 kil.....	Prohibited.		10 per cent.		....	....	7
....	....	....	....	....	Pound 0. 468	....	8
....	Free ..	Free ..	Free ..	Free ..	Free	Free	9
....	Free ..	Free .	Free ..	Free ..	Free	Free	10
							11
....	....	....	10 per cent.		Pound 0. 468	5 per cent	12
....	Free ..	Free ..	Free ..	Free ..	Free	Free	13
From Europe, 100 kilogs.	Free ..	0. 58	Free ..	0. 047	Free	Free	14
Other, 100 kilogs.......	0. 58	0. 58	Free ..	0. 047	Free	Free	15
100 kilogs..............	....	....	9. 75	10. 72	Pood.......... 2. 34	5 per cent	16
....	Prohibited.		10 per cent.		Pood.......... 2. 34	100 kilogs. .. 0. 41	17
....	Prohibited.		10 per cent.		Pood.......... 9. 36	100 kilogs ... 0. 41	18
....	....	....	....	Free ..	Free	Free	19
....	....	....	10 per cent.		Pood.......... 1. 716	5 per cent	20
....	....	....	10 per cent.		Pood.......... 0. 11	5 per cent	21
See Tools of iron and steel.					Pood.......... 0. 62	5 per cent	22
					Pood.......... 0. 62	5 per cent	23
See Meat...............	....	....	....	....	Pood.......... 0. 51	100 kilogs.... 0. 51	24
See Material of which manufactured.					Pood.......... 2. 34	5 per cent	25
					Pood.......... 2. 34	5 per cent	26
See Hair above—all other.					Free	Free	27
100 kilogs..............	Free.	0. 487	Free ..	0. 048	Free	Free	28
100 kilogs..............	15 per cent.		10 per cent.		Free	2 per cent	29
See Oils................	....	....	....	....	Pood.......... 1. 04	1 per cent	30
....	Prohibited.		10 per cent.		Pound 0. 31	5 per cent	31
....	15 per cent.		10 per cent.		Pound 0. 08	5 per cent	32
See Wire...............	....	....	....	....	Pound 0. 08	5 per cent	33
Each	7. 02	7. 02	10 per cent.		Pound 0. 08	5 per cent	34
....	Prohibited.		5 per cent.		Pood.......... 0. 85	See Chemicals.....	35
See Tools..............	....	....	....	....	Pood.......... 0. 62	5 per cent	36
Each	0. 29	0. 29	....	....	Pound 0. 078	5 per cent	37
Each	0. 29	0. 29	....	....	Pound 0. 078	5 per cent	38
Hats of straw, 100 kilogs. Of felt, each	1. 95 0. 29	2. 14 0. 29	1. 95	2. 14	Hats of felt, silk, each .... 0. 70 Hats of leather, varnished, paper, palm fibres, or other vegetable material, per pound........ 1. 01 Straw hats, not trimmed, per lb... 2. 67 Hats for gents and others, finished and ornamented, 35 per cent. Ordinary farmer's hats, each 0. 27	All hats 5 per cent.	39 40 41 42 43 44 45 46

Comparative table of import duties in the United States and European countries.

	ARTICLES.	ITALY.			SPAIN.	PORTUGAL.
			General tariff.	Tariff in treaty with France, &c.		
1	Gypsum or plaster of Paris.	100 kilogs	$0.48	Free .	Free	Free ....
2	Hackles, flax or hemp......	Free	......	......	100 kilogs....$0.20	Kilog........$0.004
3	Hair, animal, unmanufact'd.					
4	manufactures, all not provided for.	Hair, spun or dyed, 100 kil.	0.39	Free.		Hair, raw.... Free.
5	made up for head-dresses; nets (of human hair) and other human hair manufactured.	curled or twisted: 100 kilogs. coarse articles of hair, 100 kilogs........	0.58 0.78	$0.58 0.78	Hair, horse, and other,	human, prepared, kil.. 0.516 manf'd, kil. 5.40 horse, manfact'd, kil.. 0.26
6	prepared for head-dresses.	other hair, 100 kilogs........	0.195	......	100 kilogs... 0.40	mattresses, incld'g covering, kilo. 0.208
7	braids for the head....	yarn of hair natural, 100 kil.	0.08	0.09	tissues of, kil. 0.50	
8	belts, brooms, bracelets, chains, curls.	dyed, 100 kil ..	0.12	0 14	net'd tissues, kilog 0.80	
9	hogs'.................	tissues of hair,				
10	human, cleaned	see Woollens.				Free ....
11	not prepared..	tissues of horse				Kilog 0.216
12	gloves................	hair by hand,				Kilog 5.40
13	other, cleaned, not specified.	100 kilogs.... other 100 kil..	4.87 7.80	4.87 7.80		Free ....
14	horse, cleaned........					Free ....
15	long, for weav'g.					Free ....
16	pins.................	....	......	......	Kilog......... 0.60	Kilog......... 0.162
17	powder, not perfumed.	Free	......	......	Kilog 0.30	Kilog........ 0.27
18	perfumed.....	100 kilogs........	11.70	10 p.c.	Kilog 0.30	Kilog........ 0.27
19	other raw	100 kilogs	0.195	Free.	100 kilogs.... 0.40	Free ....
20	Hair pencils	5 per cent.......	......	......	20 per cent...	Kilogramme . 1.08
21	Hames, wood	Each	0.097	*9.75	20 per cent........	35 per cent.......
22	Hammers, blacksmith's.....	100 kilogs.......	1.56	1.80	100 kilogs ... 1.60	Kilogramme . 0.081
23	all oth's, not steel.	100 kilogs.......	1.56	1.80	100 kilogs ... 1.60	Kilogramme . 0.081
24	Hams, bacon	100 kilogs.......	3.90	......	100 kilogs ... 1.00	Kilogramme . 0.081
25	Handles for chests	100 kilogs.......	9.75	9.75	100 kilogs ... 3.50	Wood, 35 per cent
26	Hangers	100 kilogs.......	9.75	9.75	100 kilogs ... 3.50	Iron, kilogr'm 0.081
27	Hare's hair or fur..........	100 kilogs.......	0.195	......	100 kilogs ... 0.40	Free ....
28	Hare-skins, undressed......	100 kilogs.......	5.85	2.93	100 kilogs ... 1.50	20 per cent.......
29	dressed	100 kilogs.......	7.80	2.93	100 kilogs ... 1.50	20 per cent.......
30	Harlaem oil.......	Kilog	0.58	......	See Oils..........	Kilogramme . 0.0108
31	Harness and furniture......	100 kilogs.......	9.75	9.75	Kilogramme . 0.50	Kilogramme . 1.08
32	Harp strings, gut	100 kilogs.......	9.75	9.75	20 per cent........	Kilogramme . 0.54
33	wire	100 kilogs.......	3.90	4.50	As metal manuf....	Copp'r, kilog'm 0.054
34	Harps and harpsichords	Each	0.39	0.39	10 per cent........	Each 10.80
35	Hartshorn, spirits of........	100 kilogs.......	1.95	0.78	Kilogramme . 0.02	5 per cent.........
36	Hatchets	100 kilogs.......	1.56	1.80	100 kilogs ... 1.60	Kilogramme . 0.081
37	Hat bodies, cotton	100 kilogs.......	9.75	9.75	See Cotton	Each 0.324
38	wool, or chiefly wool.	100 kilogs.......	2.93	3.37	See Wool..........	Each 0.324
39	Hats, Leghorn, hat linings, hats of chip, straw, grass, or cott'n cloth.					Hats, straw, plain, each 0.972
40	wool, value over 40c. per lb., not over 60c.	Hats of straw, value $1 or less,				Straw, trimmed, each 2.16
41	from 60c. to 80c. per lb.	each..........	0.058	Free.		Straw, common, each 0.108
42	over 80c. per lb......	Value over $1, each..........	0.195	Free.	Hats, straw, kilogramme .. 3.00	Of felt, varnished, each 0.972
43	fur	Other hats, for gents	10 pe	r cent.	Others, each 0.40	Not specified, for men, each.. 0.972
44	leather, palm leaf, rattan, japanned.	For ladies, trimmed, each.....	0.78	0.78		
45	silk, (men's)..........					For ladies, plain, each 1.08
46	Panama, Manilla, Leghorn, Naples, and others.					For ladies, trimmed, each.. 2.16

(*Duties expressed in gold dollars of the United States.*)—Continued.

BELGIUM.	AUSTRIA.			DENMARK.	SWEDEN.	NORWAY.	
		General tariff.	Tariff in treaty.				
10 per cent	Free	......	......	Free	Free	Free	1
Free	Free	......	......	Free	Free	Free	2
							3
Hair, raw.. Free. worked, 10 per cent.	Hair: raw.... prepared, combed, dyed, centn. tissues of hair, also mixed with silk, centner.....	Free. $0.384 28.80	Free. Free. $21.60	Hair, of all kinds, crude or prepared Free. horse hair.. Free. fancy artic's of human hair, lb...$1.092 other manfs. same as manf's of wool.	Hair, horse. pound ...$0.021 oth. animal, & tissues.. Free. articles of human hair, pound 0.069	Hair, and manufct's of human hair ..... Free.	4 5 6 7 8
....	....	......	......	....	Free	Free	9
....	....	......	......	....	Free	Free	10
							11
....	....	......	......	....	Pound.....0.096	See Wool.	12
....	....	......	......	....	Free	Free	13
....	....	......	......	....	Pound.....0.021	Free	
....	....	......	......	....	Pound.....0.021	Free	14
							15
100 kilogs...$0.78	Centner	7.20	5.76	Hair pins, lb 0.017	Pound.....0.069	Pound ...$0.048	16
Free	Free	......	......	10 per cent.......	10 per cent.......	Pound 0.05	17
10 per cent	Centner	0.36	......	10 per cent.......	10 per cent.......	Pound 0.05	18
Free	Free	......	......	Free	Free	Free	19
10 per cent.......	Centner	7.20	5.76	10 per cent	10 per cant	Pound 0.06	20
10 per cent.......	Centner	0.12	Free.	Pound.. ..0.017	Pound 0.0027	Free	21
100 kilogs .. 0.78	Centner	2.88	2.16	Pound 0.0054	Centner ...0.2067	Pound 0.0045	22
100 kilogs .. 0.78	Centner	2.88	2.16	Pound 0.0054	Centner ...0.2367	Pound 0.0045	23
100 kilogs .. 0.23	Centner	1.26	......	Free	Free	Pound 0.009	24
10 per cent.......	See material	manu	fact'd	Pound 0.017	(Wood), lb.0.0027	Pound 0.009	25
10 per cent.......				Pound 0.017	Accord'g to mat'l	Pound 0.027	26
Free	Free	......	......	Free	Free	Free	27
Free	Free	......	......	Free	Free	Free	28
Free	Centner	5.04	2.16	Pound 0.068	Pound 0.055	Pound 0.045	29
Free	See Oils.....	......	......	Pound 0.017	Pound 0.0082	Pound 0.006	30
10 per cent.......	Centner	5.76	3.60	Pound 0.091	Pound 0.055	Pound 0.082	31
10 per cent.......	Centner	24.00	14.40	Pound 0.137	Pound 0.138	Pound 0.036	32
As metal manuf's .	Centner	14.40	14.40	Pound 0.0014	Pound 0.0275	Pound 0.159	33
6 per cent........	Centner	4.80	3.60	Pound 0.091	Each......0.2756	Each 0.273	34
See Chemicals n. e	Centner	0.72	0.36	Pound 0.0113	Free	Free	35
100 kilogs .. 0.78	Centner	2.88	2.16	Pound 0.017	See Tools	Pound 0.027	36
....	See Cotton ..	......	......	Pound 0.068	Pound 0.11	Pound 0.067	37
10 per cent.......	See Wool....	......	......	Pound 0.068	Pound 0.082	Pound 0.067	38
Hats, all, 10 per cent.	Hats, straw, bast & common, centner .... Fancy, centner .... Felt hats, common, centner.... Felt hats, other, centner .... Silk, fine, centner....	4.80 126.00 37.80 75.60 126.00	....	Hats of straw, pound... 0.364 Italian split str'w, ea. 0.226 Of waxed cloth or seal-skin, each .... 0.045 Of silk, ea. 0.226 Others, p'd 0.364 For ladies and children, if trimmed, additional 50 per cent.	Hats of silk and part silk, also ladies' hats, each..... 0.41 Of wool, hair, felt, finished, each ....0.2756 Of straw, (including Panama.) each..... 0.21 Oth's, each 0.11	Bonnets for ladies, silk or other, orna-m't'd, ea 0.409 Japanned hats, pound...0.036 Hats of felt and straw, lb.0.109 Of palm leaf, bast, lb..0.054 Hat forms of chips, lb.0.109	39 40 41 42 43 44 45 46

Comparative table of import duties in the United States and European countries.

	ARTICLES.	UNITED STATES.	GREAT BRITAIN.	GERMAN ZOLL-VEREIN.	SWITZERLAND.
1	Hatter's irons	Pound $0.015	Free	Centner...$0.96	Centner...$0.68
2	Hautboys	30 per cent	Free	Centner... 2.88	Centner .. 1.56
3	Haversacks of leather	35 per cent	Free	Centner... 2.88	Centner... 1.56
4	Hay	20 per cent	Free	Free	Centner... 0.097
5	Hay knives	45 per cent	Free	Centner .. 1.92	Centner... 0.68
6	Headdresses, ornaments for	35 per cent	Free	Accord'g to mat'l	Centner... 2.93
7	Head-pieces for stills	35 per cent	Free	Centner... 0.96	Centner... 0.39
8	Hellebore root	20 per cent	Free	Centner... 0.36	Centner... 0.68
9	Hemlock	20 per cent	Free	Centner... 0.36	Centner... 0.68
10	Hemp seed	Pound 0.00½	Free	Free	Centner... 0.029
11	oil	Gallon 0.23	Free	See Oils	See Oils
12	manufactures of, not over 30c. per sq. yd.	35 per cent	Free	See Manufact'rs of flax or linen.	See Manufact'rs of flax.
13	over 30c	40 per cent	Free		
14	raw	Ton 40.00	Free	Free	Centner... 0.058
15	Manilla	Ton 25.00	Free	Free	Centner... 0.058
16	raw	Ton 15.00	Free	Free	Centner... 0.058
17	Indian	Ton 25.00	Free	Free	Centner... 0.058
18	all manufs. not otherwise provided for.	30 per cent	Free	See Manufact'rs of flax.	Centner... 1.56
19	codilla and tow	Ton 10.00	Free	Free	Centner... 0.058
20	Indian, (crude drug)	20 per cent	Free	Centner... 0.36	Centner... 0.68
21	Henbane	20 per cent	Free	Centner... 0.36	Centner... 0.39
22	Herring, pickled in barrels	Barrel 1.00	Free		
23	in kegs	Barrel 1.00	Free	Ton 0.72	All, centner 0.39
24	smoked or dry	Pound 0.00½	Free		
25	Hides, raw	10 per cent	Free	Free	Centner... 0.058
26	salted or pickled	10 per cent	Free	Free	Centner... 0.058
27	tanned, (sole leather)	35 per cent	Free	Centner... 0.36	Centner... 0.39
28	Hinges, brass, copper	35 per cent	Free	Centner... 1.92	Centner... 0.68
29	silver or gold	40 per cent	Free	Centner...36.00	Centner... 2.93
30	Hobby horses, wood	50 per cent	Free	Centner... 0.72	Centner... 0.29
31	Hods, coal, of iron	35 per cent	Free	Centner... 0.96	Centner... 0.68
32	copper	35 per cent	Free	Centner... 1.92	Centner... 1.56
33	Hoes, steel	45 per cent	Free	Centner... 0.06	Centner... 0.68
34	Hoffmann's anodyne	Pound 0.50	Free	Centner... 2.40	Centner... 0.68
35	Hones	20 per cent	Free	Free	
36	Honey	Gallon 0.20	Free	Centner... 0.24	Centner... 0.29
37	water	50 per cent	Free	Centner... 0.24	Centner... 0.29
38	Hooks, fish	45 per cent	Free	Centner... 0.96	Centner... 1.56
39	Hooks and eyes	35 per cent	Free	Centner... 1.92	Centner... 1.56
40	Hops	Pound 0.05	Free	Centner... 1.80	Centner... 0.39
41	Horn combs	35 per cent	Free	Centner... 2.88	Centner... 1.56
42	tips and plates for lanterns.	10 per cent	Free	Raw .... Free. Polished, per centner.. 2.88	Centner . 1.56
43	Horns	10 per cent	Free	Free	Centner... 0.058
44	Household effects, old, bro't in by families for their own use.	Free	Free	Free	Centner... 0.68

(Duties expressed in gold dollars of the United States.)—Continued.

	FRANCE.				RUSSIA.	NETHERLANDS.	
	General tariff.		In treaty with Great Britain, &c.				
	In French vessels.	In other vessels.	In vessels of treaty powers.	In other vessels.			
See Tools	....	....	....	....	Pood $0.62	5 per cent	1
Each	$0.78	$0.78	10 per	cent.	Pound 0.08	5 per cent	2
....	Prohi	bited.	10 per	cent.	Pound 0.31	5 per cent	3
....	Free ..	Free ..	....	....	Free	Free	4
See Tools	....	....	....	....	Pood 0.62	5 per cent	5
....	Prohi	bited.	10 per	cent.	According to material.	5 per cent	6
See Material of which	made.				Pood 0.62	5 per cent	7
100 kilogs	Free ..	0.97	$0.39	$0.43	Free	Free	8
100 kilogs	Free ..	0.97	Free ..	Free ..	Free	Free	9
100 kilogs	Free ..	0.39	Free ..	0.048	Free	Hectolitre ...$0.04	10
....	See	Oils.			See Oils	100 kilogs.... 0.45	11
See Manufact's of flax..	....	....	....	....	See Manufs. of flax..	All manufactures 5 per cent.	12
See Manufact's of flax..	....	....	....	....	See Manufs. of flax..	....	13
....	Free ..	Free ..	Free ..	Free ..	Free	Free	14
....	Free ..	Free ..	Free ..	Free ..	Free	Free	15
....	Free ..	Free ..	Free ..	Free ..	Free	Free	16
....	Free ..	Free ..	Free ..	Free ..	Free	Free	17
See Manufact's of flax..	....	....	....	....	See Manufs. of flax..	All manufactures 5 per cent.	18
....	Free ..	Free ..	Free ..	Free ..	Free	Free	19
....	Free ..	Free ..	Free ..	Free ..	Free	Free	20
....	Free ..	Free ..	Free ..	Free ..	Free	Free	21
Herring, salt or smoked, 100 kilogs.	Free ..	0.39	....	....	Herring, smok'd, per pood .... 0.16 Salted, per cask of 16 poods.... 0.78 In small kegs, per pood 0.078	Free	22 23 24
100 kilogs	0.487	0.487	Free ..	0.048	Free	Free	25
100 kilogs	0.487	0.487	Free ..	0.048	Free	Free	26
100 kilogs	9.75	10.42	1.95	2.14	Pood 3.43	4 per cent	27
See Manufacture of cop	per.	....	....	....	Pood 2.34	5 per cent	28
See Manufacture of gold	and silv	er.	....	....	See Gold and Silver.	5 per cent	29
....	15 per	cent.	10 per	cent.	Pood 0.19	5 per cent	30
100 kilogs	Prohibi	ted.	2.73	2.99	Pood 0.62	5 per cent	31
100 kilogs	19.50	20.95	3.90	4.29	Pood 2.34	5 per cent	32
100 kilogs	Prohibi	ted.	3.80	4.29	Pood 0.62	5 per cent	33
100 kilogs	Prohibi	ted.	5 per	cent.	Pood 0.85	See Chemicals.	34
....	Free ..	Free ..	Free ..	Free ..	Free	Free	35
....	Free ..	Free ..	Free ..	Free ..	Pood 0.52	100 kilogs.... 1.02	36
....	Free ..	Free ..	Free ..	Free ..	....	Free	37
100 kilogs	39.00	41.43	9.75	10.73	Pood 0.78	5 per cent	38
100 kilogs	....	....	3.90	4.29	Pood 1.17	5 per cent	39
100 kilogs	8.78	9.65	2.43	2.86	Hops, and extract of hops, pood... 0.86	Free	40
100 kilogs	19.50	20.95	10 per	cent.	Pound 0.257	5 per cent	41
100 kilogs	0.58	0.63	....	....	Pound 0.25	5 per cent	42
Raw, 100 kilogs...... Prepared, in plates, 100 kilogs.	Free .. 0.58	0.39 0.63	....	....	Free	Free .... In leaves, 5 per cent	43
....	....	....	....	....	Free	Free	44

Comparative table of import duties in the United States and European countries.

	ARTICLES.	ITALY.			SPAIN.	PORTUGAL.
			General tariff.	Tariff in treaty with France, &c.		
1	Hatters' irons	100 kilogs	$1.56	$1.80	100 kilogs ... $1.60	Kilogramme . $0.081
2	Hautboys	Each	0.39	0.39	10 per cent	25 per cent
3	Haversacks of leather	Each	0.39	0.39	20 per cent	Each 0.216
4	Hay	Free	......	......	100 kilogs ... 0.10	Free, (forage)
5	Hay-knives	100 kilogs	1.56	1.80	100 kilogs ... 5.50	Kilogramme . 0.81
6	Headdresses, ornaments for	10 per cent	......	......	20 per cent	Kilogramme . 0.40
7	Head pieces for stills	See Copper	......	......	100 kilogs ... 14.00	Kilogramme . 0.27
8	Hellebore root	100 kilogs	1.95	0.39	100 kilogs ... 0.30	5 per cent
9	Hemlock	100 kilogs	1.95	0.39	100 kilogs ... 0.30	5 per cent
10	Hemp seed	Free	......	......	100 kilogs ... 0.20	Kilogramme . 0.0016
11	oil	100 kilogs	0.97	1.12	100 kilogs ... 1.60	Kilogramme . 0.0108
12	manufactures of, not over 30c. per sq. yd.	See Manufact'res of flax.			See Manufactures of flax.	See Manufactures of flax.
13	over 30c.	....	......	......	....	....
14	raw	On the stem	Free	Free.	100 kilogs ... 2.00	Kilogramme . 0.004
15	Manillia	100 kilogs, cleaned	0.097	Free.	100 kilogs ... 0.20	Kilogramme . 0.004
16	raw	100 kilogs	0.097	Free.	100 kilogs ... 0.20	Kilogramme . 0.004
17	Indian	100 kilogs	0.097	Free.	100 kilogs ... 0.20	Kilogramme . 0.004
18	all manufs. not otherwise provided for.	See Manufact'res of flax.			See Manufactures of flax.	See Manufactures of flax.
19	codilla and tow	Free	......	......	100 kilogs ... 0.20	Kilogramme . 0.0008
20	Indian, (crude drug)	100 kilogs	1.95	0.39	100 kilogs ... 0.30	5 per cent
21	Henbane	100 kilogs	1.95	0.39	100 kilogs ... 0.30	5 per cent
22	Herrings, pickled in barrels	Herring, all, per 100 kilogs	0.78	0.90	All, 100 kilogs 0.20	All, kilogr'm. 0.075
23	in kegs					
24	smoked or dry					
25	Hides, raw	....	Free.	Free.	100 kilogs 1.50	Raw or prepared green, kilog. 0.005
26	salted	100 kilogs	3.90	2.93	100 kilogs 1.50	Same, dry, k. 0.0075 N. e., 20 per cent
27	tanned, (sole leather)	100 kilogs	7.80	2.93	Kilogramme . 0.25	See Leather.
28	Hinges, brass, copper	100 kilogs	3.90	3.90	100 kilogs 14.00	Kilogramme . 0.27
29	silver or gold	See Silver and	gold.	......	See Silver and gold.	See Silver and gold.
30	Hobby horses, wood	100 kilogs	7.80	10 p.ct	100 kilogs 3.50	35 per cent
31	Hods, coal, of iron	100 kilogs	1.56	1.80	100 kilogs 1.50	Kilogramme 0.162
32	copper	100 kilogs	3.90	3.90	100 kilogs 25.00	Kilogramme . 0.27
33	Hoes, steel	100 kilogs	1.56	1.80	100 kilogs 4.50	Kilogramme . 0.081
34	Hoffmann's anodyne	100 kilogs	1.95	0.78	20 per cent	5 per cent
35	Hones	100 kilogs	0.48	Free.	Free	Free
36	Honey	100 kilogs	0,975	0.975	100 kilogs 0.95	Kilogramme . 0.0054
37	water	100 kilogs	0.195	Free.	100 kilogs 0.95	Kilogramme . 0.0054
38	Hooks, fish	100 kilogs	3.90	4.50	100 kilogs 4.50	Kilogramme . 0.162
39	Hooks and eyes	As Material ma	nufact	ured.	100 kilogs 4.50	Kilogramme . 0.162
40	Hops	100 kilogs	0.59	0.59	100 kilogs 2.00	5 per cent
41	Horn combs	100 kilogs	9.75	9.75	20 per cent	Kilogramme . 3.24
42	tips and plates for lanterns.	10 per cent	......	......	10 per cent	Free
43	Horns	Free	......	......	100 kilogs 0.10	Raw, leaf, or scraping .... Free. Manufac's of deer, rhinoceros, &c., kilog. .... 0.081 Other manuftures, kilog 3.24
44	Household effects, old, bro't in by families for their own use.	....	......	......	....	Free

(Duties expressed in gold dollars of the United States.)—Continued.

BELGIUM.	AUSTRIA.			DENMARK.	SWEDEN.	NORWAY.	
		General tariff.	Tariff in treaty.				
100 kilogs ..$0.78	Centner	$2.88	$2.16	Pound $0.017	See Tools	Pound ...$0.027	1
6 per cent........	Centner	4.80	3.60	Pound 0.091	Each......0.138	Each 0.137	2
10 per cent.......	Centner	5.76	3.60	Pound 0.091	Pound 0.066	10 per cent. more than material.	3
100 kilogs .. 0.78	Free	......	......	Free	Free	Free............	4
10 per cent.......	Centner	2.88	2.16	Pound 0.017	Pound 0.0165	Pound 0.027	5
10 per cent.......	See Clothing.	......	......	Accord'g to mat'l	Accord'g to mat'l	Accord'g to mat'l	6
Free	According to	mater	ial ...	Pound 0.045	Pound 0.041	Pound 0.047	7
Free	Free	......	......	Pound 0.0113	Free	Free............	8
100 kilogs .. 0.117	Free	......	......	Pound 0.113	Free	Free............	9
Free	Centner	0.028	Free.	Free	Free	Ton 0.136	10
See Oils..........	Centner	0.648	Free.	Pound 0.017	Pound 0.0055	Pound 0.006	11
See Manufactures of flax.	See Manufact	ur's of	flax ..	See Manufactur's of flax.	See Tissues of flax.	See Manufact'rs of flax.	12
....	See Manufact	ur's of	flax ..	....	See Tiss. of flax.	See Manfs. of flax	13
Free	Centner	0.0288	Free.	Free	Free	Free............	14
Free	Centner	0.0288	Free.	Free	Free	Free............	15
Free	Centner	0.0288	Free.	Free	Free	Free............	16
Free	Centner	0.0288	Free.	Free	Free	Free............	17
See Manufactures of flax.	See Manufact	ur's of	flax ..	See Manufactur's of flax.	See Manufactur's of flax.	See Manufact'rs of flax.	18
Free	Centner	0.0288	Free	Free	Free	Free............	19
Free	Free	......	......	Pound 0.0113	Free	Free............	20
Free	Free	......	......	Pound 0.0113	Free	Free............	21
All, 100 kilogs 0.195	All, centner.	0.72	0.72	All fish, dried, pickled, and smoked, &c., pound...0.0017	Cubic foot.0.033	See Fish	22 23 24
Free	Raw, green, or dry.	Free .	Free .	Free	Free	Free............	25
Free	....	......	......	Free	Free	Free............	26
....	....	......	......	....	....	....	
100 kilogs .. 0.975	Centner	0.48	0.36	Pound....$0.034	Pound.... 0.0275	Pound ... 0.045	27
10 per cent	See Manuf. o	f copp	er.	Pound.... 0.045	Pound.... 0.041	Pound ... 0.047	28
5 per cent	See Gold and	silver.		See Gold & silver.	See Gold & silver.	See Silver & gold.	29
10 per cent	See Manuf. o	f woo	d.	Pound.... 0.017	Pound.... 0.0027	Pound ... 0.618	30
100 kilogs .. 0.78	See Manuf. o	f iron.		Pound.... 0.017	Centner .. 0.2756	Pound ... 0.027	31
10 per cent	See Manuf. o	f copp	er.	Pound.... 0.045	Pound.... 0.041	Pound .. 0.045	32
100 kilogs .. 0.78	Centner	2.88	2.16	Pound.... 0.017	5 per cent	Pound ... 0.027	33
See Chemicals	Centner	7.20	......	Pound.... 0.0113	Free	Free	34
Free	Free	......	......	Free	Free	Free	35
100 kilogs .. 0.237	Centner	0.504	0.36	Brown, p'd 0.009 White, p'd 0.0018	Pound.... 0.011	Pound 0.018	36
Free	Free	......	......	....	Free	Pound 0.018	37
100 kilogs .. 0.78	See Manuf. o	f steel.		Pound 0.017	Free	Free	38
10 per cent	Centner	7.20	5.76	Pound.... 0.017	Pound.... 0.041	Pound 0.072	49
Free	Centner	1.36	1.20	Pound.... 0.04	Free	Pound 0.061	40
10 per cent	Centner	7.20	5.76	Pound.... 0.091	Pound.... 0.0138	Pound 0.061	41
Free	Centner	0.38	0.36	Free	Pound.... 0.055	Free	42
Free	Free	......	......	Free	Free	Free............	43
Free	Free	......	......	Free	Free	Free	44

Comparative table of import duties in the United States and European countries.

	ARTICLES.	UNITED STATES.	GREAT BRITAIN.	GERMAN ZOLL-VEREIN.	SWITZERLAND.
1	Household furniture........	35 per cent	Free	Centner...$0.72	All new, centner $1.56
2	Hungary water, (cosmetic).	50 per cent	Free	Free	Centner... 0.68
3	Hyacinth roots	30 per cent	Free	Centner... 0.36	Centner... 0.68
4	Hydriodate of potash.......	Pound $0.75	Free	Centner... 2.40	Centner... 0.68
5	Hydrometers of glass	40 per cent	Free	Free	Centner... 0.39
6	Ice........................	Free	Free	Free	....
7	Imitation of precious stones.	40 per cent	Free	Centner... 0.36	Centner...00.39
8	Implements of trade of persons arriving in the United States.	Free	Free	Free	(Implements of agriculture, 5 p. cent.)
9	India grass	Ton 15.00	Free	Free	Centner... 0.058
10	India rubber, unmanufact'd.	10 per cent	Free	Free	Centner... 0.68
11	milk of	20 per cent	Free	Manufactures of India rubber, not varnished, centner. 2.88 Varnish'd, painted, also, if of mix'd material, centner. 7.20 Tissues, elastic, centner. 10.80 Tissues of India rubber thread, centner. 18.00	All manufact'd, centner. 1.56
12	oil cloth, or other articles in part of India rubber, not otherwise provided for.	35 per cent	Free		
13	cloth	35 per cent	Free		
14	silk, or other material, except wool.	50 per cent	Free		
15	shoes and boots, suspenders.	35 per cent	Free		
16	webbing	35 per cent	Free		
17	Indian meal	10 per cent	Free	Centner... 0.36	Centner... 0.097
18	corn	Bushel 0.10	Free	Free	Centner... 0.097
19	hemp, (drug)........	20 per cent	Free	Centner... 0.36	Centner... 0.68
20	Indigo.....................	Free	Free	Free	Centner... 0.097
21	carmine	20 per cent	Free	Free	Centner... 0.68
22	Ink, writing and printing...	35 per cent	Free	Centner... 2.40	....
23					
24	Ink powder.................	35 per cent......	Free............	Centner... 2.40	Centner... 0.68
25	Inkstands, leather..........	35 per cent......	Free............	Centner... 7.20	Centner... 1.56
26	paper, with glass.	40 per cent......	Free............	Centner... 4.32	Centner... 1.56
27	silver	40 per cent......	Free............	Centner...36.00	Centner... 2.93
28	wood	35 per cent......	Free............	Centner... 2.88	Centner... 0.39
29	metal, (iron).....	35 per cent......	Free............	Centner... 0.96	Centner... 0.69
30	glass, plain......	35 per cent......	Free............	Centner... 2.88	Centner... 1.56
31	cut	40 per cent......	Free............	Centner... 4.32	Centner... 1.56
32	Instruments, philosophical.	40 per cent......	Free............	Free............	Centner... 0.39
33	musical	30 per cent......	Free............	Centner.. 2.88	Centner... 1.56
34	brass	30 per cent......	Free............		
35	copper, mat'rl of chief value.	45 per cent......	Free............		
36	Iodine, crude	Pound 0.50	Free............	Free............	Centner.. 0.68
37	salts of	15 per cent	Free............	Centner... 2.40	
38	resublimed	Pound 0.75	Free............	Centner... 2.40	
39	Ipecac.....................	Pound 0.50	Free............	Centner... 0.36	
40	Iridium....................	Free	Free............	Centner... 0.36	
41	Iris root	Free	Free............	Free............	

(*Duties expressed in gold dollars of the United States.*)—Continued.

	FRANCE.				RUSSIA.	NETHERLANDS.	
	General tariff.		In treaty with Great Britain, &c				
	In French vessels.	In other vessels.	In vessels of treaty powers.	In other vessels.			
All new furniture	15 per	cent.	10 per	cent.	Not polished or varnished, pood. $0.195	5 per cent	1
Carved chairs, &c., 100 kilogs.	....	....	$1.36	$1.50	Polished and ornamented, or silvered, pood 0.96		
					With ornaments of bronze, or other material, or reliefs in wood, copper, ivory, &c., pood.... 4.68		
....	See Per	fumery.	....	....	Free	5 per cent.	2
100 kilogs	Free ..	$0.97	Free ..	0.048	Free	Free	3
Hydrochlorate of potash	Free ..	0.048	Free ..	0.048	Pood 1.56	Free	4
100 kilogs	30 per	cent.	Free ..	0.048	Free	5 per cent	5
....	....	....	....	....	Free	Free	6
....	1 per	cent.	10 per	cent.	Free	5 per cent	7
....	....	....	....	....	Free	....	8
....	Free ..	Free ..	Free ..	Free ..	Free	Free	9
100 kilogs.	Free ..	0.78	Free ..	Free ..	Pood 0.23	Free	10
						Free	11
						5 per cent	12
100 kilogrammes: Articles of India rubber simply moulded, pure.	$3.90	4.29	3.90	4.29	Articles of India rubber, pure, p'd. 2.57		
Mixed	9.75	10.72			Mixed 4.68		
Applied on other materials.	39.00	41.43	....	....		5 per cent	13
Tissues, in pieces.	Prohibited.		19.50	20.95	Tissues of India rub'r thread, pood. 17.16	5 per cent	14
Elastic tissued	Prohibited.		39.00	41.43	Shoes, &c., p'd. 7.80		
Hose	Prohibited.		11.70	12.76			
Clothes, made	Prohibited.		23.40	25.06		5 per cent	15
						5 per cent	16
....	Free ..	Free ..	Free ..	Free ..	Pood 0.03	100 kilogs.... $0.20	17
....	Free ..	Free ..	Free ..	Free ..	Free	Hectolitre ... 0.61	18
....	Free ..	Free ..	Free ..	Free ..	Free	Free	19
From India, 100 kilogs	Free ..	5.46	....	....	Pood 2.34	Free	20
Elsewhere, 100 kilogs.	4.25	5.46	....	....	Pood 3.43	Free	21
100 kilogs	11.90	12.76	3.99	4.29	Pood 0.85	Free	22
							23
100 kilogs	1.36	1.36	Free ...	Free ...	Pood 0.85	Free	24
					Pound 0.25		25
As fancy goods, common, 100 kilogs.	19.50	20.95	....	....	Pound 0.25		26
					Pound 1.72		27
Same, fine, 100 kilogs.	39.00	41.43	....	....	Pood 2.87		28
As fancy goods	....	....	....	10 p. c.	Pood 0.62	5 per cent	29
					Pood 1.56		30
					Pood 3.12		31
100 kilogs	30 per	cent.	Free ..	0.048	Free		32
Fife, flageolet, each	....	....	10 per	cent.	Pianos, each .. 31.20	5 per cent.	
Flutes, triangles, each.	....	....			Organs for church, each, ... 31.20		33
Handolines, each	....	....					34
Guitars, violins, each.	....	....			Harmonicas, accordeons, each .. 7.80		35
Organs, each	....	....					
Pianos, square, each	....	....			All other musical instruments, lb. 0.12		
Pianos, others	....	....					
Iodine, crude, 100 kil.	0.97	0.87	Free ..	0.048	Iodine, crude, free	Free	36
refined	0.97	0.87	Free ..	0.048	Salts of and resublimate, pood .. 0.85		37
....	Prohibited.		5 per	cent.		Free	38
....	Prohibited.		5 per	cent.	Free	Free	39
....	Free ..	Free ..	Free ..	Free ..	Free	Free	40
....	Free ..	Free ..	Free ..	Free ..	Free	Free	41

Comparative table of import duties in the United States and European countries.

	ARTICLES.	ITALY.			SPAIN.	PORTUGAL.
			General tariff.	Tariff in treaty with France, &c.		
1	Household furniture	If com'n wood, varnished, 100 kilogs Carved, ornamented, 100 kilogs Of ebony, &c., 100 kilogs	$1.95 9.75 9.75	10 per cent.	All furniture, 100 kilogs .....$0.25 Of common wood, 100 kilogs.. 3.50 Of mahogany, ebony, &c., 100 kilogs....... 7.00 Ornamented, gilded, &c., 100 kilogs.......20.00	Manuf. of wood, 5 per cent. Furniture of wood, having p'ts of metal, e'ch piece 0.216
2	Hungary water, (cosmetic).	100 kilogs	0.195	Free.	See Perfumery.	Kilogramme .0.324
3	Hyacinth roots............	100 kilogs	0.29	Free.	100 kilogs.... 2.00	Free...............
4	Hydriodate of potash.......	100 kilogs	1.95	$0.78	100 kilogs.... 0.02	10 per cent.........
5	Hydrometers of glass.......	100 kilogs	3.90	1.95	10 per cent.........	Kilogramme .0.172
6	Ice........................	....	......	......	....	Free ....
7	Imitation of precious stone .	1 per cent	......	Free.	100 kilogs.... 9.00	Kilogramme .0.54
8	Implements of trade of persons arriving in the United States.	....	......	......	....	....
9	India grass	Free	......	......	100 kilogs.... 0.20	Kilogramme .0.004
10	India rubber, unmanufact'd.	100 kilogs	0.48	......	100 kilogs .. 1.00	Free ....
11	milk of	Manufact's, 100 kilogs. Ribbon and lace, 100 kilogs. Spun, or straps, for machinery, 100 kilogs.	4.87 0.195 0.78	5.63 0.0225 0.90	In pipes, sheets, &c., per k'g 0.15 Manuf., kil'g 0.375 Mixed tissues, kilog........ 0.60 Oth'r artic's, mix'd, kilog..... 0.027	Woven with silk, kilog ......2.16 Woven with other material, kg 1.08 Manufact'd pipes or tubes... Free. Not specified, kilog........0.027
12	oil cloth, or other articles, in part of India rubber, not otherwise provided for.					
13	cloth					
14	silk, or other material, except wool.					
15	shoes and boots, suspenders.					
16	webbing.......					
17	Indian meal	100 kilogs	0.24	......	100 kilogs.... 0.90	Kilogramme .0.054
18	corn...............	100 kilogs	0.145	......	100 kilogs.... 0.60	Kilogramme .0.054
19	hemp, (drug)	100 kilogs	1.95	0.39	Free	5 per cent..........
20	Indigo.....................	100 kilogs	1.17	......	Free	Kilogramme .0.013
21	carmine	100 kilogs	......	......	Free	Free ....
22	Ink, writing and printing...	100 kilogs	11.70	2.25	100 kilogs.... 5.00	Kilogramme .0.054
23						
24	Ink powder................	100 kilogs........	11.70	2.25	100 kilogs.... 5.00	5 per cent..........
25	Inkstands, leather	As merc'ry, common, 100 kilogs Fancy, 100 kil..	9.75 19.50	9.75 19.50	Small ware not specified, 20 per cent.	Fancy goods not spec'fd, kil. 0.40
26	paper, with glass.					
27	silver					
28	wood............					
29	metal, (iron).....					
30	glass, plain......					
31	cut........					
32	Instruments, philosophical..	100 kilogs......	3.90	1.95	10 per cent.........	Surgical, 20 p. ct..
33	musical	Organs, church, 100 kilogs..... Org'ns, portable, each.......... Pianos, each ... Others, 5 per ct.	1.95 0.78 0.39	1.95 0.78 0.39	Pianos, each. 50.00	Matham'tcal, 5 p. c. Musical, pianos, each .....24.84 Harps, each, 10.80 Other, 25 per cent.
34	brass					
35	copper, mat'rl of chief value.					
36	Iodine, crude	Iodine, 100 kilogs	1.95	0.39	20 per cent	Free ....
37	salts of	....	......	......		5 per cent........
38	resublimed	....	......	......		
39	Ipecac.....................	100 kilogs.	5.85	0.39		
40	Iridium....................	Free	......	......	Free...............	Free...............
41	Iris root	Free	......	......	Free...............	Free...............

(*Duties expressed in gold dollars of the United States.*)—Continued.

BELGIUM.	AUSTRIA.			DENMARK.	SWEDEN.	NORWAY.	
		General tariff.	Tariff in treaty.				
10 per cent	Comm'n, not paint'd, c'r. Polished or paint'd, c'r. Upholstered	$0.12 1.20 5.76	Free . $0.72	Pound ..$0.039	Ven'd, p. $0.0082 Mahogany, &c., orn'd, p. .0.0138 Upholstered, additional to duty on material, 20 per cent. Of com'n wood, painted or polished, p. 0.0027	Gilded, p. $0.018 Fine w'd, not upholst'd, p. 0.003 Com'n, p. 0.009 Of foreign wood, pound .. 0.010 Spin'ing wheels, pound .. 0.019 Frames, gilded, pound .. 0.03 Turners' work-handles. Free. Other common, pound .. 0.018 do. fine, p. 0.048	1
See Perfumery....	Centner	3.60	2.40	Pound.... 0.091	Pound.... 0.11	Pound 0.10	2
Free	Free	......	......	Pound.... 0.0113	Free	Free	3
Free	See Chemicals.			Pound.... 0.0113	See Chemicals.	Free	4
Free	Centner	4.80	3.60	Pound.... 0.04	Pound.... 0.041	Pound 0.047	5
Free	Free	......	......	Free	Free	Free	6
5 per cent	Centner	2.64	1.92	Pound.... 0.091	Pound.... 0.165	Pound 0.109	7
....	....	......	......	....	....	....	8
Free	Free	......	......	Free	Free	Free	9
Free	Ind. rubber, raw.	Free .	......	Free	Free	Free	10
Free				Free	Free		11
10 per cent	Manufact'd, centner.	5.76	4.80	Pound.... 0.091			12
10 per cent	Centner	5.76	4.80	Pound.... 0.091	Manuf., p. 0.11 Water pr'f cloth, pound.. 0.21	Plates, rings, tubes, soles, free. All manufact'd, pound .. 0.127	13
10 per cent	Cloth, cen'r	12.00	......	Pound.... 1.041			14
10 per cent	Centner	5.76	3.60	Pound.... 0.091			15
10 per cent	Centner	12.00	......	Pound.... 0.091			16
100 kilogs ..$0.23	Centner	0.388	Free .	Free	Free	Ton....... 0.054	17
100 kilogs .. 0.117	Centner	0.129	Free .	Free	Free	Ton....... 0.054	18
Free	Free	......	......	Pound.... 0.0113	Free	Free	19
Free	Centner	0.388	......	Pound.... 0.079	Pound.... 0.011	Pound 0.073	20
Free	Centner	0.388	......	Pound.... 0.079	Pound.... 0.011	Pound 0.027	21
10 per cent	Centner	7.20	......	Pound.... 0.017	Pound.... 0.0138	Writing . 0.014	22
						Printing. 0.003	23
Free............	Centner	7.20	5.76	Pound..... 0.017	Pound.......0.048	Pound 0.014	24
	Centner	12.00	7.20				25
	Centner	6.00	5.76	Fancy articles, pound....0.091 Or 10 per cent, accord'g to material.			26
	See Silver,						27
10 per cent	centner..	5.76	......		10 per cent	10 per cent......	28
	Centner	7.20	5.76				29
	Centner	1.08	0.72				30
	Centner	3.48	1.92				31
Free............					Pound..... 0.041	Pound 0.091	32
	Scien'fc, &c.,						33
6 per cent	centner....	2.16	2.16	Pound 0.091	Guitars, violins, each ... 0.2756 Flutes, clarin'tes, &c...... 0.138 Pianos ...11.024 Gr'nd p'nos 16.54 Organs, harmoniums, 5 per cent.	Pianos, ea. 10.92 viol's, ea., 0.273 Flutes, hautb's, clarinets, &c., each.....0.137 Bows, ea. 0.054	34
	Music'l, ct'nr	4.80	3.60				35
Free............	....	Free.	......	Free............	Free............	Free............	36
Free.	Centner	2.52	1.44	Pound.....0.0113	Free............	Free............	37
	See Chemicals.		......	Pound.....0.0113	Free............	Free............	38
	Centner	2.52	1.44	Pound.....0.0113	Free............	Free............	39
Free.	....	Free.	......	Free............	Free............	Free............	40
Free.	....	Free.	......	Free............	Free............	Free............	41

Comparative table of import duties in the United States and European countries.

ARTICLES.	UNITED STATES.	GREAT BRITAIN.	GERMAN ZOLL-VEREIN.	SWITZERLAND.
Iron, pig	Ton $9. 00	Free	Pig iron, all sorts, centner, $0. 12. Wrought iron & bar iron, loops, rails, raw and hammer'd steel, cast and refined steel, wire of more than 1-16 inch in diamet'r, parts of machine weighing above, 1 centner, centner, $0. 60. Manuf. iron in bars, wheel tires for rail road cars, wire unpolished of 1-16 inch or less in diameter, centner. . $0. 84. Sheet-iron varnished, polished steel plates, centner, $1. 26. White sheeting, tubes of iron, centner, $1. 80. Manuf. of iron or steel: 1. Heavy castings, stoves, &c., centner, $0. 29. 2. Heavy articles of wrought or cast iron, centner, $0. 96. 3. Articles finished, polished, as axes, sword blades, common knives, centner, $1. 92. 4. Fancy articles & cutlery, centner, $2. 88. 5. Sewing needles, steel pens, watch furnishings, fire arms, centner, $7. 20.	Iron, in pigs or bars, also iron for machines & ship building, rails, sheet-iron of 3 millim. or more thick, centner, $0. 058. Sheet-iron of less than 3 millim. thick, centner, $0. 29. Iron wire and sheet-iron coppered or tinned, centner, $0. 29. Manuf. of iron or steel not polish'd or varn'shd centner, $0. 68. Locksm'th's work not pol'hsd, &c., centner, $0. 68. Iron tubes of more than 9 millimetres diameter, centn'r, $0. 68. Articles of cast and wr'ght iron, the latter predominat'g, centner, $0. 68. All articles of steel or iron, pol'shd, paint-varnished, turned, filed, centner, $1. 56.
andirons, cast	Pound 0. 01½	Free		
anvils	Pound 0. 02½	Free		
anchors and parts of	Pound 0. 02¼	Free		
axles	Pound 0. 02½	Free		
band, hoop, and scroll, from ½ to 6 inches wide, and not less than ⅛-inch thick.	Pound 0. 01¼	Free		
as above, ½ to 6 inches wide, under ⅛ inch thick, and not under No. 20 wire gauge.	Pound 0. 01½	Free		
as above, thinner than No. 20 wire gauge.	Pound 0. 01¾	Free		
bars, rolled or hammered, comprising flats not less than 1 or more than 6 inches wide, nor less than ⅝ or more than 2 inches thick.	Pound 0. 01	Free		
round, not less than ¾ or more than 2 inches in diameter.	Pound 0. 01	Free		
square, not less than ¾ or more than 2 inches in diameter.	Pound 0. 01	Free		
bars, rolled or hammered, comprising flats, less than ⅝ or more than 2 inches thick, or less than 1 inch or more than 6 wide.	Pound 0. 01½	Free		
round, less than ¾ or more than 2 inches in diameter.	Pound 0. 01½	Free		
square, less than ¾ or more than 2 inches square.	Pound 0. 01½	Free		
Provided that all iron in slabs, blooms, loops, or other forms, less finished than bars, and more advanced than pig iron, except castings, shall pay as iron in bars, provided that none of the above iron shall pay a less rate of duty than.	35 per cent	Free		
bars for railroads or inclined planes, made to pattern, ready to lay down.	100 pounds. . 0. 70			
boiler plates or other plate iron, not less than 3-16-inch thick.	Pound.... .0. 01½			
butts, cast; bolts, wrought.	Pound.... .0. 02½			
bed screws	Pound..... 0. 02½			
brads, cut, not over 16 ounces per thous'd.	Millim..... 0. 02½			
brads over 16 ounces per thousand.	Pound......0. 03			

(*Duties expressed in gold dollars of the United States.*)—Continued.

FRANCE.

	General tariff.		In treaty with Great Britain, &c.	
	In French vessels.	In other vessels.	In vessels of treaty powers.	In other vessels.
Iron, ore	Free	Free	Free	Free
pig, 100 kilogs	$0.78	$0.86	$0.39	$0.43
cast, 100 kilogs	1.36	1.50	0.54	0.58
other	Prohibited.		....	....
Stretched in bars and plates, length multiplied by width, being 458 millim. or less, 100 kilogs	1.95	2.14	....	....
213 to 458 millim., 100 kilogs	2.34	2.57	....	....
Less than 213 millim., 100 kilogs	2.73	3.00	....	....
In sq. bars of 22 millim. or more, each, 100 kilogs	1.95	2.14	....	....
15 to 22 millim., 100 kil.	2.34	2.57	....	....
Less than 15 mil., 100 kil.	2.73	3.00	....	....
In round bars of 15 millim., diameter, 100 kilogs	2.34	2.57	....	....
Less than 15 millim., diameter, 100 kilogs	2.73	3.00	....	....
In rails, as above, according to dimens'ns	....	....	....	....
All iron in bars, sq. or round, 100 kilogs	....	....	1.17	1.29
Railroad and T iron, 100 kilogs	....	....	1.17	1.29
Wrought iron, prisms, 100 kilogs	Prohibited.		0.87	0.95
Plates sheet iron, black. 100 kilogs	3.90	4.29	....	....
Same, tinned, 100 kil.	7.80	8.58	....	....
Plates of more than 1 millimeter thick, 100 kilogs	....	....	1.46	1.60
Of less than 1 millim. thick, 100 kilogs	....	....	1.95	2.14
Tinned, copper'd, &c., 100 kilogs	....	....	2.54	2.78
Wire of 5-10 millim. diameter or less, 100 kilogs	....	....	1.95	2.14
Other, wire, &c., &c., 100 kilogs	....	....	1.17	1.29
Wire, also, if cover'd, 100 kilogs	5.85	6.43	....	....
Metalic wire for instruments, 100 kilogs	13.65	14.82	....	....
Steel in bars, all, 100 kilogs	5.85	6.43	....	....
Same, common sheets, 100 kilogs	9.75	10.73	....	....
Sheets more than ½ millim. thick, 100 kil.	....	....	2.19	2.33
Of less thickness than ½ millim., 100 kilogs	....	....	2.92	2.20
Steel plates not polished or tempered, no matter how wide, but of more than 1 millimeter thick, 100 kilogs	9.75	10.73		
1 millim. or less thick, 15 centimeters or more wide, 100 kilogs	14.63	17.94	2.92	3.20
Same, less than 15 centimeters wide, 100 kil.	21.40	22.96		

RUSSIA.

Iron, pig and fragments, pood .. $0.039
In bars, assorted, fit for roll'g, pood $0.27
Plates for armored vess'ls, boilers, kettles, iron plate, and sheet-iron of over 7 in. wide, pood. $0.39
Rails, pood $0.078
Cast-iron articles of more than 3 pounds w'ght, not fin'hd nor pol'shd, pood. $0.39.
Same, finished, not polished or ornamented, pood $0.62
Polish'd cast'gs, with ornaments of other materials, weighing less than 3 pounds, pood $1.95
Cast-steel bells, mortars, tiles, tires, and carriage springs of ov'r 1 pood in w'ght, pood $1.05
Of one pood or less, pood $3.51
Articles of wrought iron, anchors, nails, hooks, frames, cooking stoves, wheels, chains of ov'r ¼-inch thick, articles of untinned sheet-iron, pood $0.78
Iron and steel manf.; locksmiths' work of 1 pood or less weight, unpol'shd, pood, $1.95.
Iron, polished, pood, $3.51.
Blacksmith's w o r k, pood, 0.78.
Iron wire less than ¼-in. diameter, also steel, copper, &c., wire, not tinned or galvanized; wire nails and pegs, covered or not; also wire tackle and submarine cables, pood, $1.17.
Manf. of wire of all sorts not specially enumerated, also of cov'rd wire, frames and bird cag's, pood, $2.34.
Tools for trade and industry, as saws, files, rasps, scrapers, also, if of copper, instruments, boxes, and moulds, pood, by sea, $9.62.
Same by land, $0.39.

NETHERLANDS.

Iron-work found'd, forged, or laminated, not otherwies enumerated; also anvils, 5 per cent.
Anchors, chains, & capstans for ships, 1 per cent.
Cables and nails, 100 kilogs.. $0.30
Iron founded in rough blocks and pieces, bars, pig, hoops, plate, angle, T-iron, wire, spurs, spires for rails; found'd gas tubes, tubes for aqueducts, old iron, shreds & filings, not being finish'd iron-work, free.

FRANCE.—For remainder of tariff on iron, see page 128.

Comparative table of import duties in the United States and European countries.

ARTICLES. United States—Continued.	ITALY.	ITALY. General tariff.	ITALY. Tariff in treaty with France, &c.	SPAIN.	PORTUGAL.
Iron—Continued.					
cables or chains, or parts of, pound, $0.02½.	Iron, ore	Free.	Free.	Iron, pig, 100 kilogs, $0.50.	Iron, raw, k., $0.002.
	Pig and old......	Free.	Free.		Beaten, kil., $0.003.
castings, all not specially enumerated, 30 per cent. chains, trace, halter, fence of wire or rods not less than ¼-inch in diameter, pound, $0.02½.	Simply manufactured; also, with other metals, 100 kilogs.	$0.78	$0.78	Iron in tubes, of all kinds, 100 k., $0.937. Ordinary castings, 100 kil., $1.50.	Cannon ball, free. Laminated: simple, kilogr'mme, $0.003. tinned, kil. $0.0037.
	Same, polished ..	0.78	0.90	Ornament'd cast'ngs, with oth'r met'ls or porcelain, 100 kilogs, $3.50.	Galvanized, zinked, $0.004.
	Iron gates, 100 kilogs.	0.097	0.12		Wire, kilog., $0.037.
chains of less than ¼ of an inch in diameter and not under No. 9 wire gauge, pound, $0.03.	First fusion, bars and rods, 100 kilogs.	0.78	1.12	Bars and rails, 100 kilogs, $2.20.	Wire, covered, kil., $0.324. Wire, in pieces, kil., $0.054.
chains under No. 9 wire gauge, 35 per cent.	Wire-work, 100 kilogs.	1.36	1.58	Wire, 100 kil., $1.60. Nails and screws, also, with brass heads, 100 k., $4.00.	Nails, kilog., $0.108.
	Rails, 100 kilogs.	0.195	0.22		Articles of cast-iron, simple, kil., $0.08.
coated with zinc, or any metal by electric batteries, pound, $0.02½.	Second fusion, simple, 100 kil.	1.95	2.24	Wrought iron tubes, 100 kil., $2.60.	Same, varnished, tinn'd, or emam'ld, kilogra'me, $0.135.
	Beams, bars.....	1.17	1.25		
flues, wrought, per pound, $0.02½.	Same, with other metal, 100 kil.	2.34	2.70	Ordinary articles, of wrought iron laid over with lead, tin, or zinc, painted or varnished, and tubes covered with brass, 100 k., $4.50.	Same, over 135 kil., weight, kil., $0.032.
gas pipe, cast, per pound, $0.01½. gas tubes, wrought, per pound, $0.03½.	Iron anchors, anvils, mallets, ploughs, plo'gh-shares, 100 kil.	1.17	1.56		Wr'ght-iron art'cls: Cables, chains, anchors, kilog., $0.01.
galvanized, pound, $0.02½.	Cannon, 100 kil..	1.17	1.56		Shovels, kil., $0.08.
hatter's, pound, $0.01½. hinges, cast, pound, $0.02½ hollow ware, glazed, per pound, $0.03½.	Iron in plates, 4 millim. thick or more, 100 kilogs.	0.78	1.12	Fancy articles as above 100 k., $5.50. Iron bars, in whatever form, less than 100 millime., 100 kilogs..$2.60	Wrought-iron nails, simple, k., $0.108. Brass heads, kilog., $0.216.
hollow ware, tinned, per pound, $0.03½.	Less thick, also tubes, 100 kil.	1.56	1.79		Other articles, polished or varnished, kilog., $0.27.
	Tinned iron	......	......		
cast, pound, $0.01½. hinges, wrought, per pound, $0.02½.	Not manuf'ed, 100 kilogs.	1.56	1.80	Other bars forged, 100 kilogs .$2.20	Same, tinned and ornament'd, kilog., $0.405.
hammers, blacksmith, pound, $0.02½. malleable casting, not otherwise enumerated, pound, $0.02½.	Manf., also in connect'n with other metals, 100 kilogs.	2.93	2.93	Iron and steel in pieces not yet adapted for use, 100 kilogs..$1.00	Of Flanders sheet-iron, kilog., $0.432.
malleable, pound, $0.02½.	Steel in bars or pieces, 100 kilogs.	2.34	2.80	Needles, pens, and parts of watches and similar articles of iron or steel, kil...$0.60	Pins, clasps, buckl's, kilog., $0.135. Articles not specified, kilog., $0.054.
mill wrought and crank wrought, pound, $0.02.	In plates........	2.34	2.80		
manufactures of all kind not otherwise enumerated, 35 per cent.	Carriage sp'gs, and the like, 100 kilogs.	2.93	2.93	Knives, carving knives, razors, and penknives, kilogs.....$0.20	
nails, cut, pound, 0.01½. nails, wrought, per pound, $0.02½. nails, horseshoe, per pound, $0.05.	Knives, with wooden h'dles, not ornamt'd, for arts, trades, and agricul're, 100 kilogs.	1.56	1.80	Scissors, kil.. 0.45 Side-arms & blades of the same, kilogs........$0.40	
nuts, wrought, per pound, $0.02.	Tools for arts and trad's, &c., 100 kilogs.	1.56	1.80	Fire-arms, kil. 1.00	
old scrap, fit only to be remanufactured, ton, $8.00.					
rivets, wrought, per pound, $0.02¼.					
railroad chairs, wrought, pound, $0.02.					
sad, store, stove, plates.					
steampipes, cast, slit.					
rods not otherwise provided, iron spikes, cut, pound, $0.01½.					
spikes, wrought, per pound, $0.02½.					
sledges, pound, $0.02½.					
steam tubes, wrought, pound, $0.03½.					

UNITED STATES.—For remainder of tariff on iron, see page 126, 127.

(*Duties expressed in gold dollars of the United States.*)—Continued.

BELGIUM.

Iron, ore, free, pig and old, 100 kilogs, $0.097.
Castings manufactur'd, 100 k. $0.39.
Beaten, drawn, or laminated, 100 kilogs, $0.195.
Manufactures of iron or steel, 100 kilogs, 0.78.

AUSTRIA.

	General tariff.	Tariff in treaty.
Iron ore	Free.	Free.
Pig, broken pieces, scrap, filings, c'tnr.	$0.216	$0.192
Pig iron for	0.12	......
Puddled iron, centner.	1.008	0.72
Iron rails, c'tnr	1.20	0.72
Sheet iron, black; plates unp'lshd, c'nr.	1.68	1.20
Tires for wh'ls, centner.	1.68	1.20
Sheets & plat's, polsh'd, tin'd, varn'shd; and wire not polished, cent'nr.	1.92	1.92
Iron prepared for parts of machines or carriages, of above 1 ctn'r weight; anch'rs, pl'ghshares, cable chains, ct'nr.	1.68	1.20
C'st'gs, coarse, as boilers, kettles, stoves, wheels, tubes, grates of over 25 lbs. weight, and parts for machinery of over 100 lbs. weight, c'tnr.	0.48	0.36
Articles not polished or vrn'shd, c'tnr.	2.40	2.16
Axes, saws, scyth's, plan's, files, common knives, large scissors, sieve bottoms, c'tnr.	2.88	2.16
Articles polished or varnished, not gilded or silvered; knives and scissors, wire net-w'rk, centner.	7.20	5.76

DENMARK.

Iron ore, pig, and broken pieces, free.
Hoops, bar, rails, axletrees, wheel-tires, tubes, gas-retorts, plates, sheets, bolts, spik's, nails, wire, steel strings for instr'mts, sheets painted, pound, $0.0014.
Manufactured in other form, lb., $0.0056.
Articles plated, gilded, silvered, cut, connected with ivory or other materials, bronz'd, paint'd, &c., and sheet-ir'n ware, pound, $0.091.
Heavy castings, stoves, cooking utensils, coarse machin'ry, bells, anchors, cables, plou'hshar's, anvils, boilers, gas and water pipes, large hammers, scales, polished or not, pound, $0.0056.
All other articles of iron or steel, pound, $0.017.

SWEDEN.

Iron, unmanufactured, free.
Anchors, casks, hamm'rs, anvils, &c., centner, $0.2067.
Smaller chains, with rings of less than two inches diameter, centner, $1.378.
Cast: bombsh'lls, balls, (of fixed calibre;) can'on, mort'rs, (bored;) also, limbers to various pieces, centner, $0.344.
Cannon, mortars, and other art'lry not bored, c'tnr, $0.1378.
Stoves, kitchen utensils, grates, castings for railroads, and other mach'ry, coarse articles, such as axle-tr'es, scal's, spikes, &c., lb., $0.0082.
Finer art'cls, such as padlocks, coffee-mills, copy-press's, hatr'cks, &c., lb., $0.0165.
F'ncy art'cls, cast: bas-rel'fs, flower vases, baskets, lamps, chandaliers, medals, paper-hold'rs, &c., pound, $0.0275.
Butt'ns, varn'shd, or not, lb. $0.0165
Money ch'sts, bedsteads, 10 p'r ct.
Shoe pegs, cut or pressed, pound, $0.0082.
Spikes, 1.6 inches long or more, centner, $0.41.
Other articles, polished, lb., $0.041.
Not polished, lb., $0.0165.

NORWAY.

Iron ore and pig, cast tubes, bars, bolts, axletrees, can'on, mortars balls, (all;) rails, sheets of $\frac{1}{8}$-inch or more; chains of over $\frac{1}{2}$-inch, diameter; nails, spikes, screws, tinned or coppered, over 1 inch long; wire of steel or iron, also if coppered or tinned; T-iron, anchors, cables, chains, boilers, plates, and all tools not specified, free.
Nails, spikes, screws, also, tinned or coppered, less than 1 inch long, lb., $0.011.
Wire, steel, and other; also, if covered, and wire cordage, pound, $0.036.
Manufacture of wire, lb., $0.109.
Door hinges, coal shovels, coffee-mills, scissors, smooth'g irons, knitt'g needles, awls, &c., lb., $0.027.
Thimbles, sword-blades, cork-screws, table knives, locks, snuffers, spurs, skates, pound, $0.048.
Fire-proof safes, bedsteads, lb., $0.009.

[For remainder of tariff on iron, see page 129.]

Comparative table of import duties in the United States and European countries.

	ARTICLES.	UNITED STATES.	GREAT BRITAIN.	GERMAN ZOLL-VEREIN.	SWITZERLAND.
1	Isinglass	30 per cent	Free	Centner...$0.36	Centner...$0.68
2	Istle	Pound....$0.01	Free	Free	Centner... 0.145
3	Italian cloths, real or imitation, composed wholly or in part of wool, worsted, the hair of the alpaca goat, or other like animals, value not over twenty cents per square yard.	6 cts. per square yd. and 35 per cent.	Free	See Manufactures of wool.	See Manufactures of wool.
	As above, value over twenty cents per sq. yard.	8 cts. per square yard and 40 per cent.			
4	Ivory	10 per cent	Free	Free	
5	black	25 per cent	Free	Free	
6	nuts	10 per cent	Free	Free	
7	manufactures of	35 per cent	Free	Centner... 2.88	Centner... 1.56
8	vegetable, manufactures of.	35 per cent	Free	Centner... 2.88	Centner... 1.56
9	Jack chains and screws	35 per cent	Free	Centner... 0.96	Centner... 0.68
10	Jacks for piano-fortes	35 per cent	Free	Centner... 0.96	Centner... 0.68
11	clothiers	35 per cent	Free	Centner... 0.96	Centner... 0.68
12	Jalap	Pound.... 0.50	Free	Centner... 0.36	Centner... 0.68
13	Japanned wares, not specified otherwise.	40 per cent	Free	Centner...10.80	Centner... 2.93
14	Jellies and similar prepar'tns.	50 per cent	See Succades	Centner... 3.64	Centner... 1.56
15	Jerked beef	Pound.... 0.01	Free	Centner... 0.36	Centner... 0.39
16	Jet, real or composition	35 per cent	Free	Centner... 2.88	Centner... 1.56
17	stones	35 per cent	Free	Centner... 2.88	Centner... 1.56
18	Jewelry	25 per cent	Free	Centner...36.00	Centner... 2.93
19	false, so-called	25 per cent	Free	Centner...10.60	Centner... 2.93
20	Joints, India	35 per cent	Free	Free	Centner... 0.29
21	Juice of oranges	25 per cent	Free	Free	Centner... 1.56
22	lemons and limes	10 per cent	Free	Free	Centner... 1.56
23	Juniper berries	10 per cent	Free	Free	Centner... 0.39
24	plants	30 per cent	Free	Free	Centner... 0.29

United States Tariff on Iron—Continued.

Articles.	United States.	Articles.	United States.
Iron tacks, cut, over 16 ounces per thousand.	Pound.....$0.03	Iron markers, ready punched	Pound.....$0.02
		Iron, wrought, for ships (weight) of 25 pounds or more.	Pound..... 0.02
Iron vessels, cast, not otherwise provided for.	Pound..... 0.01½	Iron, wrought, for locomotive tire, parts of.	Pound..... 0.03
Iron wire, bright, coppered or tinned, drawn and finished, not more than ¼-inch in diameter, nor less than No. 16 wire gauge.	15 per cent., and per pound 0.02	Iron, wrought, for steam engine and parts of, each 25 pounds or more.	Pound..... 0.02
As above, over 16 and not over 25 wire gauge.	15 per cent., and per pound. 0.03½	Iron, rolled or hammered, not otherwise provided for.	Pound..... 0.01¼
Iron wire over No. 25 wire gauge.	15 per cent., and per pound. 0.04	Iron casters	35 per cent
		Iron combs, curry	35 per cent
Iron wire spiral furniture springs.	15 per cent., and per pound. 0.02	Iron cutting knives, for cutting hay or straw.	35 per cent
Provided, wire covered with cotton, silk, or any other material, shall pay 5 cents per pound in addition.		Iron cutting knives, if any steel	35 per cent
		Iron ferrules, piano	35 per cent
		Iron filings	35 per cent
		Iron hoops, made fit for use	35 per cent
Iron water pipe, cast	Pound..... 0.01½	Iron, liquor	10 per cent
Iron water tubes, wrought	Pound..... 0.03½	Iron nails	35 per cent

(*Duties expressed in gold dollars of the United States.*)—Continued.

	FRANCE.				RUSSIA.	NETHERLANDS.	
	General tariff.		In treaty with Great Britain, &c.				
	In French vessels.	In other vessels.	In vessels of treaty powers.	In other vessels.			
......	Free ..	Free ..	Free ..	Free ..	Free	Free	1
100 kilogs......	Free ..	$0.97	Free ..	$0.048	Free	Free	2
See Manufactures of wool.	......	......	......	......	See Manufactures of wool.	5 per cent	3
......	Free ..	0.59	Free ..	0.048	Free	Free	4
......	......	......	......	......	Free	Free	5
......	......	......	......	......	Free	Free	6
......	15 per	cent.	10 per	cent.	Pood......$5.68	5 per cent	7
......	15 per	cent.	10 per	cent.	Pood...... 4.68	5 per cent	8
100 kilogs......	......	......	$1.56	1.80	Pood...... 0.62	5 per cent	9
......	15 per	cent.	10 per	cent.	Pood...... 0.62	5 per cent	10
......	15 per	cent.	10 per	cent.	Pood...... 0.62	5 per cent	11
......	Prohi	bited.	5 per	cent.	Pood...... 0.85	Free	12
See Porcelain	......	......	......	......	Pood......12.48	5 per cent	13
See Comfits	......	......	......	......	Pood...... 3.90	100 kilogs...$10.25	14
See Meat	......	......	......	......	Pood...... 0.51	100 kilogs.... 2.41	15
......	Free...	Free...	Free...	Free...	......	5 per cent	16
......	Free...	Free...	Free...	Free...	......	Free	17
100 kilogs......	$97.50	100.90	97.50	100.90	Pound......25.74	5 per cent	18
......	......	......	10 per	cent.	Pound......25.74	5 per cent	19
......	Free...	Free...	......	......	Free	Free	20
100 kilogs......	......	......	Free...	0.48	Pood...... 0.34 }	Of citrons & lemons,	21
100 kilogs......	......	......	Free...	0.48	Pood...... 0.34 }	per 100 litres 1.23	22
100 kilogs......	0.21	0.21	Free...	0.25	Free	Free	23
......	Free...	Free...	Free...	Free...	Free	Free	24

United States Tariff on Iron—Continued.

Articles.	United States.	Articles.	United States.
Manufactures of iron, partly finished, pay the same rate of duty as if entirely finished.	35 per cent	Iron, all manufactures not otherwise provided for.	35 per cent ......
Iron scythes, part steel......	45 per cent	Iron springs, at not over 16 ounces per thousand.	Millimeter. $0. 02½
Iron shot	30 per cent	Iron springs over 16 ounces per thousand.	Pound 0. 03
Iron shovels, part steel......	45 per cent	Iron sheets, smoothed or polished.	Pound 0. 03
Iron sickles, part steel......	45 per cent	Iron common or black, not thinner than No. 20 wire gauge.	Pound 0. 01¼
Iron spades, part steel......	30 per cent., and per pound $0. 03	Iron, common, less than No. 20, not less than No. 25 wire gauge.	Pound 0. 01½
Iron squares, marked on one side..	30 per cent., and per pound 0. 06	Iron, common, less than No. 25 wire gauge.	Pound 0. 01¾
Iron squares, all other	35 per cent	Iron, screws, wood, 2 inches or over in length.	Pound 0. 08
Iron square wire, used for manufacture of stretchers for umbrellas, and cut in pieces not exceeding the length used therefore.		Iron screws less than 2-ins. long.	Pound 0. 11
		Iron screws, except wood......	35 per cent ......
Iron taggers......	30 per cent	Iron, tailors iron	Pound 0. 01½
Iron wire, annealed	same as iron wire.	Iron tacks, cut not over 16 ounces per thousand.	Millimeter. 0. 02½

Comparative table of import duties in the United States and European countries.

	ARTICLES.	ITALY.			SPAIN	PORTUGAL.
			General tariff.	Tariff in treaty with France, &c.		
1	Isinglass	100 kilogs	$0.48	Free.	100 kilogs. ..$0.10	5 per cent
2	Istle	100 kilogs	0.48	Free.	Free	Free
3	Italian cloth, &c.—Cont'd. Provided, that all goods weighing four ounces and over per square yard, shall pay, 50 cts. per lb. and 35 per cents.	See Manufactures of wool.	......	......	See Manufactures of wool.	See Manufactures of wool.
4	Ivory	100 kilogs	1.95	Free.	Kilogramme. 0.01	Free
5	black	100 kilogs	0.97	$0.39	Kilogramme. 0.01	Free
6	nuts	100 kilogs	0.39	Free.	Kilogramme. 0.01	Free
7	manufactures of	100 kilogs	19.50	19.50	Kilogramme. 2.50	Kilogramme. $5.40
8	vegetable, manufactures of.	100 kilogs	9,75	9.75	Kilogramme. 2.50	Kilogramme. 0.40
9	Jack chains and screws	100 kilogs	1,56	1.80	100 kilogs.... 1.50	Kilogramme. 0.081
10	Jacks for piano-fortes	100 kilogs	1.56	1.80	100 kilogs.... 1.50	Kilogramme. 0.189
11	clothiers	100 kilogs	1.56	1.80	100 kilogs.... 1.50	Kilogramme. 0.189
12	Jalap	100 kilogs	1.95	0.78	Kilogramme. 0.20	Kilogramme. 0.075
13	Japanned wares, not specified otherwise.	100 kilogs	4.87	4.87	20 per cent	Kilogramme. 0.271
14	Jellies and similar prepar'tns.	100 kilogs	7.80	......	Kilogramme. 0.20	Kilogramme. 0.075
15	Jerked beef	100 kilogs	3.90	Free.	100 kilogs.... 0.50	Kilogramme. 0.081
16	Jet, real or composition	1 per cent	......	Free.	100 kilogs.... 9.00	Kilogramme. 0.514
17	stones	1 per cent	......	Free.	100 kilogs.... 0.075	Kilogramme. 0.054
18	Jewelry	Gold, hectog	3.12	5 per cent.	Kilogramme. 4.00	Gold, p. kilog. 51.00
19	false, so-called	Silver, per kilog.	3.90		Kilogramme. 2.00	Silver, kilog. 32.80
		Vermeil, kilog	5.85			Gems, 1 per ct. extra.
20	Joints, India	100 kilogs	0.48	Free.	1 per cent	......
21	Juice of oranges	Hectoliter	1.56	Free.	Hectoliter ... 2.50	Juices, sweet, per kilog ... 0.075
22	lemons and limes	Hectoliter	1.56	Free	Hectoliter ... 2.50	
23	Juniper berries	100 kilogs	0.39	Free.	100 kilogs.... 0.50	5 per cent
24	plants	Free	......	......	100 kilogs.... 0.25	Free

I. French tariff on iron—Continued.

FRANCE.	General tariff.		In treaty with Great Britain, &c.	
	In French vessels.	In other vessels.	In vessels of treaty powers.	In other vessels.
Steel in bands or leaves, polished, blued, temp'd, except saws, 100 kilogs	$0.97	$1.06	....	....
Steel wire, all for instruments, 100 kilogs	13.65	14.82	$3.90	$4.29
Steel filings and flues	Free	Free	Free	Free
Iron, broken articles 100 kilogs	1.56	1.72	0.54	0.59
Cast iron, broken articles, 100 kilogs	0.78	0.86	0.39	0.44
Dross of iron, 100 kilogs	Free	0.156	Free	0.048
Chains, chain cables, 100 kilogs	....	....	1.56	....
See also Machines, Tools, Needles, Steel pens, &c:				
All other manufactures of iron under general tariff prohibited.				
Castings not turned or polished:				
Coussinets for railroads, plates, &c., cast in open air, 100 kilogs	....	....	0.58	0.64
Cylindric tubes, plain or grooved columns; gas retorts and other articles without ornaments, 100 kilogs	....	....	0.72	0.80
Pottery and similar articles, 100 kilogs	....	....	0.87	0.95

(*Duties expressed in gold dollars of the United States.*)—Continued.

Belgium.	Austria.			Denmark.	Sweden.	Norway.	
		General tariff.	Tariff in treaty.				
Free	Free	......	......	Pound ... 0.017	Free	Free	1
Free	Free	......	......	Free	Free	Free	2
See Manufactures of wool.	See Manf. of wool.	......	......	See Manufactures of wool.	See Manufactures of wool.	See Manufactures of wool.	3
Free	Free	......	......	Free	Free	Free	4
Free	Free	......	......	Free	Free	Free	5
Free	Free	......	......	Free	Free	Free	6
10 per cent	Centner	$5.76	......	Pound ...$0.061	Pound... $0.138	Pound...$0.158	7
10 per cent	Centner	5.76	......	Pound.... 0.061	Pound.... 0.138	Pound....0.158	8
See Iron	See Manufactures of iron.			Pound.... 0.0056	See Iron	Pound... 0.0045	9
See Iron	See Manufactures of iron.			Pound.... 0.0056	See Iron	Pound... 0.0045	10
See Iron	See Manufactures of iron.			Pound.... 0.0056	See Iron	Pound... 0.0045	11
100 kilogs..11.70	Centner	2.82	$1.44	Pound.... 0.04	Free	Pound... 0.0061	12
10 per cent	Centner	24.00	14.40	Pound.... 0.091	10 per cent	Pound... 0.095	13
100 kilogs..11.70	See Comfits..	......	......	Pound.... 0.04	Free	Pound... 0.0061	14
100 kilogs.. 0.23	Centner	1.26	......	Free	Free	Pound... 0.009	15
5 per cent	Free	......	......	Pound.... 0.071	Free	Pound... 0.009	16
Free	Free	......	......	Free	Free	Free	17
Gold, &c., 5 p. ct	In gold or silver, centn'r.	126.00	....	Pound... 0.091	Of gold or silver, same as manuf's.	Loth ... 0.03	18
Other, 10 per ct.	Other	48.00	....	Pound... 0.091	Other, lb ..0.0064	Pound.. 0.109	19
Free	Free	......	......	Free	Free	Free	20
Free	See Wine of grapes or fruit			Pound.... 0.018	Free	Pound... 0.009	21
Free	See Wine of grapes or fruit			Pound.... 0.018	Free	Pound... 0.009	22
Free	Free	......	......	Free	Free	Free	23
Free	Free	......	......	Free	Free	Free	24

French tariff on Iron—Continued.

	Vessels of tr'ty pow.	Other vessels.		Vessels of tr'ty pow.	Other vessels.
Tariff in treaty with G. Britain, &c.—Continued.			Nails, by machine, 100 kilogs.	$1.56	$1.72
Castings, polished or turned, 100 kilogs	$1.17	$1.29	Nails, by hand, 100 kilogs....	2.34	2.57
Tinned or varnished, 100 kil..	1.95	2.14	Household and other articles not specially enumerated:		
Wrought: blacksmiths' work, 100 kilogs	1.56	1.72	Of iron, 100 kilogs	2.73	2.99
Locksmiths' work, 100 kilogs.	2.34	2.57	Of sheet-iron, 100 kilogs	3.12	3.43
			Of steel, 100 kilogs	3.90	4.29

Norway tariff on iron—Continued.

II. NORWAY.

Other articles cast; pots, kettles, tinned or glazed, pound	$0.018
Other articles not glazed, pound	0.004
Plate, sheet-iron less than ⅛-inch thick, lacquered, pound...	0.045
Plate, manfacturers, pound	0.0455
Articles of wrought iron, gilded, silvered, or plated, pound	0.095
Articles polished, pound	0.028
Articles, other, pound	0.027

Comparative table of import duties in the United States and European countries.

	ARTICLES.	UNITED STATES.	GREAT BRITAIN.	GERMAN ZOLL-VEREIN.	SWITZERLAND.
1	Junk, old	Free	Free	Free	Centner.. $0. 29
2	Jute, unmanufactured	Ton $15. 00	Free	Free	As linens
3	manufactures of value of 30 cts. per square yard or less.	35 per cent	Free	Centner.. $0. 48	As linens
4	manufactures of value of over 30 cents per square yard.	40 per cent	Free	Centner... 0. 48	See Flax
5	butts	Ton 6. 00	Free	Centner... 0. 48	Centner... 0. 058
6	manufactures not otherwise provided.	30 per cent	Free	Centner... 0. 48	Bagging, pr. centner 0. 145
7	carpeting	Sq. yard.. 0. 08	Free	Centner... 0. 12	Centner... 0. 68
8	Kaleidoscopes	40 per cent	Free	Free	Centner... 1. 56
9	Kaoline	Ton 5 00	Free	Free	Centner... 0. 29
10	Kelp	Free	Free	Free	Centner... 0. 097
11	Kermes, (mineral)	10 per cent	Free	Free	Centner... 0. 29
12	Kettles, brass, in nests	35 per cent	Free	Centner... 1. 92	Centner... 1. 56
13	Keys, watch, gold	25 per cent	Free	Centner...36. 00	Centner... 2. 93
14	silver	25 per cent	Free	Centner...36. 00	Centner... 2. 93
15	all other	40 per cent	Free	Centner... 2 88	Centner... 1. 56
16	Kilmarnock caps	50 per cent	Free	Centner...10. 60	Centner....2. 93
17	Kirschenwasser	See Arrack	Gallon.... $2. 53	Centner....4. 32	Centner....1. 56
18	Knitting-needles	25 per cent	Free	Centner....2. 88	Centner....1. 56
19	Knit goods, of worsted, wholly or part, of alpaca hair without wool, value less than 40 cents per pound.	35 per cent. and per lb... 0. 20	Free		
20	As above, 40 cts. per pound, less than 60 cents.	35 per cent. and per lb....0. 30	Free	Centner...7. 20	Knit by hand p'r cent'r. 2. 93 Otherwise, per centner ..1. 56
21	As above, 60 to 80 cents per pound.	35 per cent. and per lb....0. 40	Free		
22	As above, over 80 cents per pound.	35 per cent. and per lb....0. 50	Free		
23	Knit goods, all or part wool.	35 per cent. and per lb....0. 50	Free		
24	Knives, cutting, curriers', drawing, flesh.	45 per cent	Free	Centner....2. 88	Centner....1. 56
25	silver or gold	40 per cent	Free	Centner...10. 60	Centner....2. 93
26	pen, jack, pocket.	50 per cent	Free	Centner....2. 88	Centner....1. 56
27	Knobs, brass, gilt, plated iron or copper.	35 per cent	Free	Centner....2. 88	Centner....1. 56
28	glass, not cut	35 per cent	Free	Centner....0. 48	Centner....0. 68
29	cut	40 per cent	Free	Centner....2. 88	Centner....1. 56
30	glass, with brass, iron, or composition shanks.	40 per cent	Free	Centner....2. 88	Centner....1. 56
31	Kreosote	40 per cent	Free	Free	Centner....0. 68
32	Labels, printed	25 per cent	Free	Free	Centner....0. 097
33	decanter or other, gilt or plated.	35 per cent	Free	Centner....0. 96	Centner....1. 56
34	gold or other	40 per cent	Free	Centner....0. 96	Centner....1. 56
35	Lac dye	Free	Free	Free	Centner....0. 68
36	marine	20 per cent	Free	Free	Centner....0. 68
37	spirits	Free	Free	Free	Centner....0. 68
38	sulphur	Free	Free	Free	Centner....0. 68

(*Duties expressed in gold dollars of the United States.*)—Continued.

	FRANCE.				RUSSIA.	NETHERLANDS.	
	General tariff.		In treaty with Great Britain, &c.				
	In French vessels.	In other vessels.	In vessels of treaty powers.	In other vessels.			
	Free	Free	Free	Free	Free	Free	1
100 kilogs	Free	$0.58	Free	$0.048	Free	Free	2
For yarns and tissues, see note, pages 142 and 143.					Pood $0.23	All manufactures, 5 per cent.	3
					Pood 0.23		4
					Free		5
					Pound 0.11		6
					Pound 0.11		7
100 kilogs	30 per cent.		Free	0.048	Free	5 per cent	8
	Free	Free	Free	Free	Free	Free	9
	Free	Free	Free	Free	Free	Free	10
	Free	Free	Free	Free	Free	Free	11
100 kilogs	$19.50	20.95	$3.90	4.29	Pood 2.34	5 per cent	12
100 kilogs	97.50	100.95	97.50	100.95	Pound 25.74	5 per cent	13
As watch furniture					Pound 1.72	5 per cent	14
100 kilogs	9.75	10.72	9.75	10.72	Pood 0.62	5 per cent	15
	Prohibited.		10 per cent.		Each 0.27	5 per cent.	16
Hectoliter	29.25	29.25	2.92	2.92	In bottles, each 0.05	Hectoliter $1.23	17
100 kilogs	Prohibited.		3.40	4.29	Pound 0.19	5 per cent.	18
						All manufactures, 5 per cent.	19
See Manufactures of wool					5 per cent.		20
							21
							22
							23
See Cutlery					Knives, ordinary, per pood 9.36	5 per cent.	24
	Prohibited.		10 per cent.		Mounted in silver, gold, ivory, mother of pearl, &c., per pood 18.72	5 per cent	25
See Cutlery						5 per cent	26
See Material of which made					Pood 2.34	5 per cent	27
	Prohibited.		10 per cent.		Pood 1.56	5 per cent	28
	Prohibited.		10 per cent.		Pood 3.12	5 per cent	29
					Pood 2.34	5 per cent	30
	Prohibited.		5 per cent.		Free	Free	31
100 kilogs	58.50	61.90	Free	0.048	Pood 6.24	Paper of all sorts, 5 per cent	32
100 kilogs							33
100 kilogs							34
100 kilogs	Free	1.95	Free	0.048	Pood 1.17	Free	35
100 kilogs	Free	1.95	Free	0.048	Pood 1.17	Free	36
100 kilogs	Free	1.95	Free	0.048	Pood 1.17	Free	37
100 kilogs	Free	1.95	Free	0.048	Pood 1.17	Free	38

Comparative table of import duties in the United States and European countries.

	ARTICLES.	ITALY.			SPAIN.	PORTUGAL.
			General tariff.	Tariff in treaty with France, &c.		
1	Junk, old	Free	......	......	Free	Free
2	Jute, unmanufactured	100 kilogs	$0.48	Free.	100 kilogs....$0.20	100kilogs....$0.08
3	manufactures of value of 30 cents per sq. yard, or less.	Thread measur'g per kilog. 20,000 metres or less, single, bleached or dyed, 100 kilg. Thread measur'g per kilog. 20,000 metres or less, single, twisted and dyed, per 100 kilogs. Measur'g pr. kilg. over 20,000 metres, single, bl. or dyed, per 100 kilogs. Measur'g pr. kilg. over 20,000 metres, sing., twisted and dyed, per 100 kilogs. All manufactures of jute.	1.95 3.90 3.90 5.85 As linen tis's	1.95 2.93 3.90 5.85 15 p. ct.	Manufactures, see Flax.	Manufactures, see Flax.
4	manufactures of value of over 30 cents per square yard.					
5	butts					
6	manufactures not otherwise provided.					
7	carpeting					
8	Kaleidoscopes	100 kilogs	3.90	1.95	10 per cent	5 per cent
9	Kaoline	100 kilogs	0 .48	Free.	100 kilogs.... 0.20	Free
10	Kelp	Free	......	......	Ton......... 0.05	Free
11	Kermes, (mineral)	100 kilogs	1.95	1.39	Ton......... 0.05	Free
12	Kettles, brass, in nests	100 kilogs	3.90	3.90	100 kilogs....14.00	Kilogramme. 0.27
13	Keys, watch, gold	Hectoliter	3.12	......	Kilogramme. 7.00	Kilogramme .54.00
14	silver	100 kilogs	3.90	......	Kilogramme. 1.85	Kilegramme .32.80
15	all other	100 kilogs	9.75	9.75	100 kilogs....25.00	Kilogramme. 0.54
16	Kilmarnock caps	Each	0.097	......	20 per cent	Kilogramme. 1.08
17	Kirschenwasser	Hectoliter	1.95	......	Liter........ 0.20	Decaliter.... 1.62
18	Knitting-needles	100 kilogs	3.90	4.50	Kilogramme. 0.60	Kilogramme. 0.162
19	Knit goods, of worsted, wholly or part, of alpaca hair without wool, value less than 40 cents per pound.	5 per cent	......	......	See Manufactures of wool.	Kilogramme. 1.08
20	As above, 40 cts. per pound, less than 60 cents.					
21	As above, 60 to 80 cents per pound.					
22	As above, over 89 cents per pound.					
23	Knit goods, all or part wool.					
24	Knives, cutting, curriers', drawing, flesh.	Knives not ornamented, per 100 kilogs.	1.56	1.80	Kilogramme. 0.20	Kilogramme. 0.27
25	silver or gold	Others, as mercery, per 100 kilogs.	19.50	19.50	Hectogr'me..0.40	See Gold or silver..
26	pen, jack, pocket.				Kilogramme. 0.20	Kilogramme. 0.324
27	Knobs, brass, gilt, plated, iron or copper.	As Materials man	ufactu	red...	100 kilogs....25.00	Gilt, kilogs .. 0.54
28	glass, not cut.	As Materials man	ufactu	red...	100 kilogs ... 1.60	Kilogramme. 0.172
29	cut	As Materials man	ufactu	red...	100 kilogs ... 3.50	Kilogramme. 0.172
30	glass, with brass, iron, or composition shanks.	As Materials man	ufactu	red...	100 kilogs ... 3.50	Kilogramme. 0.27
31	Kreosote	100 kilogs	1.95	0.39	Kilogramme. 0.02	5 per cent
32	Labels, printed	100 kilogs	11.70	Free.	Kilogramme. 0.25	Kilogramme. 0.05
33	decanter or other, gilt or plated.	100 kilogs	11.70	Free.	Kilogramme. 0.25	Kilogramme. 0.05
34	gold or other	100 kilogs	11.70	Free.	Kilogramme. 0.25	Kilogramme. 0.05
35	Lac dye	100 kilogs	1.95	9.78	100 kilogs ... 2.50	Lac, Brazil
36	marine	100 kilogs	1.95	0.78	100 kilogs ... 2.50	5 per cent
37	spirits	100 kilogs	1.95	0.78	100 kilogs ... 2.50	Lac not specified ..
83	sulphur	100 kilogs	1.95	0.78	100 kilogs ... 2.50	Kilogramme. 0.01

(*Duties expressed in gold dollars of the United States.*)—Continued.

BELGIUM.	AUSTRIA.			DENMARK.	SWEDEN.	NORWAY.	
		General tariff.	Tariff in treaty.				
Free	Free	......	......	Free	Free	Free	1
Free	Centner	0. 0288	Free.	Free	Free	Free	2
Same as manufactures of flax.	Same as manufactures of flax.			See Manufactures of flax.	See Manufactures of flax.	See Manufact'rs of flax.	3
							4
	Free	......	......		Free		5
	Free	......	......		See Manufactures of flax.		6
					Pound.... 0. 0496		7
Free	Centner	4. 80	$3. 60	10 per cent	Pound.... 0. 041	10 per cent	8
Free	Free	......	......	Free	Free	Free	9
Free	Free	......	......	Free	Free	Free	10
Free	Centner	0. 36	0. 36	Free	Free	Free	11
10 per cent	See Copper	......	......	Pound.... 0. 045	Pound.... 0. 041	Pound...$0. 047	12
5 per cent	See Gold and Silver		......	Pound.... 0. 091	See Gold, manf'd.	Loth 0. 03	13
5 per cent	....	......	......	Pound.... 0. 091	See Silver, manf'd.	Loth 0. 03	14
10 per cent	See Copper	......	......	Pound.... 0. 091	Pound.... 0. 095	Loth 0. 095	15
10 per cent	Centner	36. 00	24. 00	Pound 0. 364	10 per cent	Pound.... 0. 109	16
See Liqueurs	See Liqueurs	......	......	Pott 0. 091	Kande 0. 352	Pot....... 0. 218	17
100 kilogs ..$0. 78	Centner	7. 20	5. 76	Pound 0. 017	Pound 0. 0275	Pound.... 0. 027	18
							19
							20
As Tissues according to description.	As clothing of wool, centner.	37. 80	......	Pound 0. 068	Same as manf. of wool.	Pound.... 0. 073	21
							22
							23
100 kilogs .. 0. 78	See Cutlery	......	......	Pound 0. 017	See Cutlery	Pound.... 0. 048	24
5 per cent	See Silver or gold.		......	Pound 0. 091	See G'ld and slv'r.	Loth...... 0. 03	25
100 kilogs .. 0. 78	Centner	7. 20	5. 76	Fancy, lb.. 0. 091	Pound 0. 38	Pound.... 0. 048	26
10 per cent	See Material manf.		......	Pound 0. 091	See Manf. of material.	Pound.... o. 095	27
10 per cent	Centner	1. 08	0. 72	Pound 0. 008	Pound 0. 0138	Pound.... 0. 047	28
10 per cent	Centner	3. 48	1. 92	Pound 0. 04	Pound 0. 0138	Pound.... 0. 047	29
10 per cent	Centner	7. 20	5. 76	Pound 0. 091	Pound 0. 041	Pound.... 0. 054	30
Free	Centner	2. 52	1. 44	Pound 0. 0113	Free	....	31
Free	Centner	2. 64	1. 92	Pound 0. 045	Pound 0. 022	Pound.... 0. 025	32
Free	Centner	2. 74	1. 92	Pound 0. 045	Pound 0. 022	Pound.... 0. 025	33
Free	Centner	6. 00	5. 76	Pound 0. 045	Pound 0. 022	Pound.... 0. 025	34
Free	Centner	0. 72	......	Pound 0. 028	Free	Pound.... 0. 013	35
Free	Centner	0. 72	......	Pound 0. 028	Free	Pound.... 0. 013	36
Free	Centner	0. 72	......	Pound 0. 028	Free	Pound.... 0. 013	37
Free	Centner	0. 72	......	Pound 0. 028	Free	Pound.... 0. 013	38

Comparative table of import duties in the United States and European countries.

	ARTICLES.	UNITED STATES.	GREAT BRITAIN.	GERMAN ZOLL-VEREIN.	SWITZERLAND.
1	Lace cotton, of all kinds, made into wearing apparel.	35 per cent......	Free............	Centner..$21.60	Centner...$2.93
2	Lace, silk.................	60 per cent......	Free............	Centner...21.60	Centner....2.93
3	Lace, all thread...........	30 per cent......	Free............	Centner...28.80	Centner....2.93
4	Lacets or lacings, silk......	50 per cent......	Free............	Centner...21.60	Centner....2.93
5	Ladles, gilt................	35 per cent......	Free............	Centner....2.88	Centner....0.68
	gold or silver.......	40 per cent......	Free............	Centner...36.00	Centner....2.93
6	Lake, (water colors).......	35 per cent......	Free............	Free............	Centner....0.68
7	drop colors..........	35 per cent......	Free............	Free............	Centner....0.68
8	paints..............	25 per cent......	Free............	Free............	Centner....0.68
9	Lampblack................	20 per cent......	Free............	Centner....0.36	Centner....0.29
10	Lamp hooks, pulleys.......	35 per cent......	Free............	Centner....2.88	Centner....1.56
11	Lamps, all except glass, cut.	35 per cent......	Free............	Centner....2.88	Centner....1.56
12	of glass, cut........	40 per cent......	Free............	Centner....2.88	Centner....1.56
13	Lancets..................	35 per cent......	Free............	Free............	Centner....1.56
14	Lancet-cases..............	35 per cent......	Free............	Centner....7.20	Centner....1.56
15	Lantern leaves, or horn plates.	10 per cent......	Free............	Pol. centn'r.2.88 Raw, free	Centner....1.56
16	Lanterns, all..............	35 per cent......	Free............	Centner...10.80	Centner....1.56
17	Lapis caliminaris...........	Free............	Free............	Free............	Centner....0.145
18	infernalis, (nitrate of silver.)	40 per cent......	Free............	Free............	Centner....0.145
19	tutia, (oxide of zinc).	Pound....$0.01¾	Free............	Free............	Centner....0.145
20	Lard.....................	Pound.....0.02	Free............	Free............	Centner....0.097
21	Larding pins..............	35 per cent......	Free............	Centner....0.72	Centner....0.68
22	Lasting, in strips, for buttons, shoes, or bootees.	10 per cent......	Free............	Centner....7.20	Centner....1.56
23	Latches, iron, brass, steel, gilt, plated, &c.	35 per cent......	Free............	Centner....2.88	Centner....1.56
24	Lath.....................	20 per cent......	Free............	....	Centner....0.39
25	Latten, brass..............	35 per cent......	Free............	Centner....2.88	Centner....0.29
26	Laudanum................	40 per cent......	Free............	Centner....2.40	Centner....0.68
27	Lavender, dry, flower of...	20 per cent......	Free............	Free............	Centner... 0.29
28	flower.........	20 per cent......	Free............	Free............	Centner....0.29
29	oil of..........	50 per cent......	Free............	Centner... 2.40	Centner....0.68
30	water.........	50 per cent......	Free............	Centner... 2.40	Centner... 0.68
31	Lead, all manufactures not otherwise provided.	35 per cent......	Free............	Lead, crude, in pigs, molded; old pieces, free. Litharge of lead, pr.centn'r, 0.18 In sheets; also printing type, pr.centn'r, 0.30 Coarse articles of lead, as tubes, shot, wire, &c., pr.centn'r ,2.88 Finer articles; also, if varnished or printed, not properly fancy or toilet articles, pr.centn'r, 2.88	Lead, crude, in pigs, blocks, and old lead, per centner ..0.058 Lead stretched, sheets, tubes, balls, and shot, pr.c'tner, 0.145 White-lead, oxide of lead, per centner....0.29 Articles of lead, not polished or painted, per centner....0.68 Type ......0.68 Articles of lead varnished or painted, per centner .. 1.56
32	in bars............	Pound 0.02	Free............		
33	black..............	Ton.......10.00	Free............		
34	powder of black.....	20 per cent......	Free............		
35	combs.............	35 per cent......	Free............		
36	pots, black, of sand or clay.	25 per cent......	Free............		
37	in pigs.............	Pound 0.02	Free............		
38	old, fit for manufacture only.	Pound 0.01½	Free............		
39	white, dry or ground in oil.	Pound 0.03	Free............		
40	pipes..............	Pound 0.02¾	Free............		
41	ore................	Pound 0.01½	Free............		
42	in any other form not specified.	35 per cent......	Free............		
43	sugar of............	Pound 0.20	Free............	Centner .. 0.72	Centner... 0.29
44	red, dry, or ground in oil.	Pound 0.03	Free............	Centner... 1.08	Centner... 0.68
45	nitrate of...........	Pound 0.03	Free............	Centner... 2.40	Centner... 0.68
46	in sheets...........	Pound 0.02¾	Free............	Centner... 0.36	Centner... 0.145
47	shot..............	Pound 0.02¾	Free............	Centner... 2.88	Centner... 0.145
48	toys..............	50 per cent......	Free............	Centner... 2.88	Centner... 1.56

(*Duties expressed in gold dollars of the United States.*)—Continued.

	FRANCE.				RUSSIA.	NETHERLANDS.	
	General tariff.		In treaty with Great Britain, &c.				
	In French vessels.	In other vessels.	In vessels of treaty powers.	In other vessels.			
....	Prohibited.		10 per cent.		Lace, work of all sorts, pood...$2.34 All wearing apparel 35 per cent.	5 per cent	1
100 kilogs.............	15 per cent.		Free ..	$0.048			2
....	....	....	5 per cent.				3
Kilogramme	$2.12	$2.43	Free ..	....	Pood...........31.20		4
As Copper manufactures	......	......	....	....	....	....	5
See Gold and silver....	....	....	....	....	See Articles of gold and silver.	5 per cent	
....	Free ..	Free ..	Free ..	Free ..	Pood 0.85	Free	6
....	Free ..	Free ..	Free ..	Free ..	Pood 0.85	Free	7
....	Free ..	Free ..	Free ..	Free ..	Pood 0.85	Free	8
100 kilogs	0.195	0.58	Free ..	Free ..	Pood 0.85	Free	9
See Articles of copper, &c		....	....	....	Pood 2.34	5 per cent	10
As Mercery, all	....	....	....	....	Pood 2.34	5 per cent	11
100 kilogs............	19.50	20.95	10 per cent.		Pood 3.12	5 per cent	12
100 kilogs............	10 per cent.		Free ..	0.048	Free..............	5 per cent	13
....	Prohibited.		10 per cent.		Pound 0.25	5 per cent	14
100 kilogs............	0.58	0.63	....	....	Pound......... 0.25	5 per cent	15
As Tinware, 100 kilogs.	Prohibited.		$5. 5	6.43	Pood......... 2.34	5 per cent	16
....	Free ..	Free ..	Free ..	Free ..	Free	Free	17
....	Free ..	Free ..	Free ..	Free ..	Free	Free	18
....	Free ..	Free ..	Free ..	Free ..	Free	Free	19
100 kilogs............	0.39	0.39	Free ..	0.047	Free	Free	20
100 kilogs............	....	....	3.90	4.29	Pound 9.11	5 per cent	21
As Elastic tissues (India-rubber,) 100 kilogs.	Prohibited. ..		11.70	12.76	Pood......... 17.16	5 per cent	22
See Manufactures of iron, steel, and copper				....	Pood......... 2.34	5 per cent	23
....	Free ..	Free ..	Free ..	Free ..	....	Free	24
100 kilogs............	2.92	3.40	....	....	Pood......... 2.34	5 per cent	25
See Chemicals, not enumerated		....	....	....	Pood......... 0.85	Free	26
....	Free ..	Free ..	Free ..	Free ..	Free	Free	27
....	Free ..	Free ..	Free ..	Free ..	Free	Free	28
....	See Oils.		....	....	Pood..............	1 per cent., (if perfumery, 5 pr. ct.)	29
100 kilogs............	19.50	20.95	1.95	2.14	Pood 3.12	Free	30
Lead, ore..........	Free ..	Free ..	Free ..	Free ..	Lead, crude, free	Lead, laminated, not otherwise enumerated, 100 kilogs $0.61	31
Alloyed with antimony, 100 kilogs.	5.07	5.58	0.58	0.64	Lead, in ingots, rolls, sheets, and pieces;		32
Crude, in bars, &c., broken pieces 100 kilogs.	Free ..	0.048	Free ..	0.048	litharge, silver litharge, and all lead		33
					ashes, per pood. 0.03		34
Beaten or stretched into plates, pipes, sheets, &c., 100 kilogs.	4.68	5.15	0.58	0.64	All manufactures of lead, per pood. 0.62		35
							36
All manufactures, 100 kilogs.	4.68	5.15	0.58	0.64		Free	37
						Free	38
						Free	
						Free	39
						All manufactured articles, 5 pr. cent.	40
							41
							42
Chromate of lead, per 100 kilogs.	14.62	15.83	10 per cent.		Pood 0.85	Free	43
Acetate of lead, per 100 kilogs.	13.65	14.82	....	....	Pood 0.195	Free	44
Carbonate of lead......	Free ..	Free ..	Free ..	Free ..	Pood 0.85	Free	45
Oxides of lead..........	Free ..	Free ..	Free ..	Free ..	Pood 0.039	Free	49
100 kilogs.	4.68	5.15	0.58	0.64	Pood 0.624	5 per cent	47
In white-wood, per 100 kilogs.	19.50	20.95	10 per cent.		Pood 0.624	5 per cent	48

Comparative table of import duties in the United States and European countries.

	ARTICLES.	ITALY.			SPAIN.	PORTUGAL.
			General tariff.	Tariff in treaty with France, &c.		
1	Lace, cotton, of all kinds, made into wearing apparel.	As Tissues of cot	ton...	......	Kilogramme. $1. 05	Linen, kilogs. $2. 70 Cotton, kilogs. 0. 756
2	Lace, silk.	Kilogramme	$2. 34	5 p. ct.	Kilogramme. 5. 50	Silk, kilogs.. 5. 40
3	Laces, all thread	As Tissues	......	......	Kilogramme. 2, 50	Kilogramme. 2. 70
4	Lacets or lacings, silk	Kilogramme	2. 34	5 p. ct.	Kilogramme. 5. 50	Kilogramme. 5. 40
5	Ladles, gilt	According to mat	erial..	......	Kilogramme. 1. 85	Kilogramme. 0. 54
	gold or silver	See Gold and silv	er....	......	See Gold and silver.	See Gold and silver.
6	Lake, (water colors)	100 kilogs	11. 70	2. 25	100 kilogs ... 5. 00	5 per cent
7	drop colors	100 kilogs	1. 95	0. 78	100 kilogs ... 5. 00	5 per cent
8	paints	100 kilogs	1. 95	0. 78	100 kilogs ... 5. 00	5 per cent
9	Lampblack.	100 kilogs	0. 97	0. 39	100 kilogs ... 1. 50	Kilogramme. 0. 081
10	Lamp hooks, pulleys	See Manf. of cop	per or	steel..	100 kilogs ...25. 00	Kilogramme. 0. 27
11	Lamps, all except glass, cut.	100 kilogs	19. 50	19. 50	100 kilogs ...25. 00	Accord'g to mat'rial
12	of glass, cut	100 kilogs	2. 92	1. 36	100 kilogs .. 3. 50	Kilogramme. 0. 172
13	Lancets	100 kilogs	3. 90	1. 95	Kilogramme. 0. 20	20 per cent
14	Lancet-cases	100 kilogs	9. 75	6. 75	20 per cent	Kilogramme. 0. 40
15	Lantern leaves, or horn plates.	100 kilogs	9. 75	0. 58	100 kilogs ... 0. 10	Free
16	Lanterns, all	10 per cent	......	......	100 kilogs ...12. 50	Kilogramme. 0. 216
17	Lapis, caliminaris	100 kilogs	1. 17	0. 195	Free	Free
18	infernalis, (nitrate of silver.)	100 kilogs	0. 78	0. 98	20 per cent	10 per cent
19	tutia, (oxide of zinc)	100 kilogs	0. 39	0. 39	20 per cent	10 per cent
20	Lard	100 kilogs	0. 195	0. 195	100 kilogs ... 0. 30	Kilogramme. 0. 054
21	Larding pins	100 kilogs	1. 56	1. 80	100 kilogs ... 4. 50	Kilogramme. 0. 135
22	Lasting, in strips, for buttons, shoes, or bootees.	Kilogramme .... 100 kilogs	0. 195	...... 22. 54	Kilogramme. 0. 375	Kilogramme. 0. 027
23	Latches, iron, brass, steel, gilt, plated, &c.	See Manf. of var	ious m	etals .	See Metals manuf..	See Metals manf...
24	Lath	Free	......	......	Free	Free
25	Latten, brass	100 kilogs	3. 90	3. 90	100 kilogs ...25. 00	Kilogramme. 0. 27
26	Laudanum	100 kilogs	1. 95	0. 78	20 per cent	5 per cent
27	Lavender, dry, flower of	100 kilogs. $0. 97	0. 97	0. 38	5 per cent	5 per cent
28	flower	100 kilogs. 0. 97	0. 97	0. 39	5 per cent	5 per cent
29	oil of	kilog 0. 12	0. 12	Free.	100 kilogs ... 1. 60	.... 0. 54
30	water	....	......	......	100 kilogs ... 1. 60	Kilog 0. 054
31	Lead, all manufactures not	Lead, mineral ...	Free.	Free.	Mineral......free..	Shot.........free..
	otherwise provided.	In leav's or piec's,	0. 097	0. 097	In plate, sheets,	Cast, kilog.. 0. 0027
32	in bars	100 kilogs.			tubes, balls, and	Beaten, canister, 100
33	black	Laminated or	1. 17	0. 58	small shot, per 100	kilogs 0. 0027
34	powder of black	manufactured,			kilogs 0. 30	Alloyed with anti-
35	combs	100 kilogs.			Manufactures, per	mony.......free..
36	pots, black, of sand or	Balls, shot, 100	3. 90	......	100 kilogs... 1. 60	Manufactures not
	clay.	kilogs.				specified, per 100
37	in pigs					kilogs 0. 054
38	old, fit for remanufac-					Small shot, per 100
	ture only.					kilogs 0. 032
39	white, dry or ground in oil.					
40	pipes					Oxide of lead, per
41	ore					kilog 0. 005
42	in any other form not					Carbonate of lead,
	specified.					per kilog .. 0. 027
43	Lead, sugar of	100 kilogs	1. 95	0. 78	Kilogs....... 0. 02	5 per cent
44	red, dry or ground in oil.	100 kilogs	1. 95	0. 78	100 kilogs ... 5. 00	5 per cent
45	nitrate of	100 kilogs	1. 95	0. 78	Kilogs....... 0. 02	10 per cent
46	in sheets	100 kilogs	0. 097	0. 497	100 kilogs ... 0. 30	Kilog 0. 0027
47	shot	100 kilogs	3. 90	......	100 kilogs ... 0. 30	....
48	toys	100 kilogs	1. 17	0. 58	Oxide of lead, 100 kilogs 1. 00	Kilog 0. 154

(*Duties expressed in gold dollars of the United States.*)—Continued.

BELGIUM.	AUSTRIA.			DENMARK.	SWEDEN.	NORWAY.	
		General tariff.	Tariff in treaty.				
See Material of which made.	See Cotton (clothing) ..			Pound $0.273	Pound $0.34	Cotton, lb. $0.407	1
					Pound 0.275	Linen, lb.. 0.236	
	See Silk....	......	......	Pound 1.09	Pound 0.21	Silk, lb... 0.241	2
	See Manf. of flax..		......	Pound 0.273	Pound 0.275	Pound.... 0.236	3
	See Silk and clothing ...			Pound 0.41	See Gold and silver manf.	Pound.... 0.241	4
	See Gold and silver . ..			Pound 0.091	....	Pound.... 0.095	5
	See Jewelry (other).....			Pound 0.091	Free	Loth...... 0.03	
Free	Centner	$0.388	......	Pound 0.028	Free	Pound.... 0.027	6
Free	Centner	0.388	.....	Pound 0.028	Free	Pound.... 0.027	7
Free	Centner	7.20	$5.76	Pound 0.028	Free	Pound.... 0.013	8
Free	Centner	0.388	......	Pound 0.005	Free	Pound....0.0045	9
10 per cent	See Material manf.		......	Pound 0.045	Copper, lb. 0.041	Pound.... 0.047	10
10 per cent	Centner	7.20	5.76	Pound 0.091	As Material manf.	Pound.... 0.095	11
10 per cent	Centner	7.20	......	Pound 0.04	Pound 0.041	Pound.... 0.047	12
Free	Centner	4.80	3.60	Pound 0.017	Pound 0.0680	Pound.... 0.109	13
10 per cent	Centner	5.76	......	10 per cent	10 per cent	10 per cent......	14
Free	Centner	0.38	0.36	Free	Free	Free............	15
10 per cent	Centner	7.20	5.76	Pound 0.045	Accord'g to mat'l.	Pound.... 0.047	16
Free	Free	......	......	Free	Free	Free............	17
Free	See Chemicals.....		......	Free	Pound 0.055	Free............	18
Free	See Chemicals.....		......	Free	Free	Free............	19
Free	Centner	1.26	......	Free	Free	Pound....0.0089	20
100 kilogs... $0.78	Centner	2.88	2.16	Pound 0.017	Pound 0.0165	Pound.... 0.027	21
10 per cent	Centner	12.00	......	Pound 0.091	Pound 0.11	Pound.... 0.127	22
				Iron, pound. 0.017			
100 kilogs.... 0.78	See Material manf.		......	Gilt, pound. 0.091	See Mater'l manf.	Pound.... 0.095	23
Free	Free	......	......	Free	Free	Free............	24
See Copper.......	See Copper..	......	......	Pound 0.045	Free	Pound.... 0.047	25
Free	Centner	2.52	1.44	Pound 0.0113	Free	Free............	26
Free	....	Free.	......	Pound 0.0113	Free	Free............	27
Free	....	Free.	......	Pound 0.0113	Free	Free............	28
Free	(See Oils) ...	......	......	Pound 0.017	Free	Pound ... $.273	29
Free	Centner	7.20	5.76	Pound .. 0.091	Pound.... $0.11	Pound ... 0.10	30
Lead, laminated, free.	Lead, ore....	Free.	Free.	Lead ore in sheets, tubes, shot, and balls, p'nd, 0.0056	Lead, crude or in blocks, sheets, &c., free.	Lead, crude, in bar and sheets, free.	31 32
Manufactures of, pr.centn'r, 10.00	Brok'n piec's, filings, type metal, centner.	0.36	0.36	Manufactured, gilded, silvered, plat'd, p'nd, 0.091	Manufactures of, not painted or varnished, pound.... 0.008	Manufactured into ordinary articles, pound, 0.011.	33 34 35 36
	In sheets, print'g type, stereotpye plates, centner.	1.44	1.20	Other articles, pound, 0.045.	Manufactures of, painted and varnished, pound.... 0.041	Toys and other small ware, not gilded, pound, 0.047.	37 38
	Cast, as boilers, tubes, plates, balls, shot, wire, centner.	1.68	1.20			Gilded, &c., p'nd, 0.095.	39
				White, p'nd, 0.0057	....	White, p'nd, 0.009	40 41
	Toys varnished, painted, centner.	5.76	2.16				42
Free	Lead, oxide of, centner.	1.20	0.72	Pound 0.0113	Free	Free............	43
Free	See Paints...	......	......	Pound.... 0.028	Free	Pound ... 0.007	44
Free.	See Chemic'ls	......	......	Pound.... 0.0113	See Chemicals ...	Free............	45
Free	See Chemic'ls	......	......	Pound.... 0.0056	Free	Free............	46
10 per cent	See Chemic'ls	......	......	Free	Pound.... 0.005	Free............	47
10 per cent	See Chemic'ls	......	......	Pound.... 0.045	Pound.... 0.041	Pound ... 0.047	48

Comparative table of import duties in the United States and European countries.

	ARTICLES.	UNITED STATES.	GREAT BRITAIN.	GERMAN ZOLL-VEREIN.	SWITZERLAND.
1	Lead pencils	Gross ..... $0.50 and 30 per cent.	Free	Centner ... $2.88	Centner ... $1.56
2	Leaders, leather	35 per cent	Free	Centner ... 2.88	Centner ... 1.56
3	worsted	50 per cent	Free	Centner ... 7.20	Centner ... 1.56
4	Leaf, Dutch metal	10 per cent	Free	Free	Centner ... 0.145
5	gold, per package	....	....	Pure gold, centner, 36.00.	....
6	of 500 leaves	Package .. 1.50	Free	Not pure, centner, 10.60.	Centner ... 2.93
7	Leaves, medicinal, in a crude state.	20 per cent	Free	Free	Centner ... 0.68
8	Leaf, silver, of 500 leaves	....	....	Pure, centner, 36.00.	....
	per package	Package .. 0.75	Free	Not pure, centner, 10.60.	Centner ... 2.93
9	Leather, bracelets, elastic	35 per cent	Free	Leather of all kinds, per centner, 1.44.	Leather, raw, red and white, per centner, 0.39.
10	mitts	50 per cent	Free		
11	garters, elastic	35 per cent	Free		
12	and all manufactures thereof not otherwise specifi'd.	35 per cent	Free	Glove leather, (chamois,) per centner, 5.76.	Varnished, and morocco, per centner, 0.68.
13	Leather bend, caps of, bottles, braces, sole, patent.	35 per cent	Free	Ordinary manufactures of leather, per centner, 2.88.	Common articles of leather, shoes, saddlery, per centner, 1.56.
	hats of	40 per cent	Free	Fancy articles of leather, pr. centner, 7.20.	Articles of Corduan, Brussels leather, saddles and harness trimmed, gloves, pr. centner, 2.93
	upper, (tanned calf-skins.)	30 per cent	Free	Gloves, of leather, per centner, 9.54.	
	not otherwise specified.	25 per cent	Free		
14	Leaves, for dyeing crude	Free	Free	Free	Centner .. 0.145
15	not used in dyeing, not otherwise provided for.	20 per cent	Free	Free	Centner .. 0.68
16	boucho	Pound 0.10	Free	Free	Centner .. 0.68
17	Leeches	20 per cent	Free	Free	Centner .. 0.68
18	Lees wine, crystallized or crude, tartar or argols.	Pound 0.06	Free	Centner ... 2.88	Centner .. 1.56
19	Lemons, in bulk	25 per cent	Free	Centner .. 1.44	....
20	in boxes, barrels, &c	25 per cent	Free	Centner .. 1.44	....
21	Lemon juice	10 per cent	Free	Free	Centner .. 0.145
22	oil of	Pound 0.50	Free	....	Centner .. 0.097
23	peel	10 per cent	Free	Centner .. 2.88	Centner .. 0.39
24	essence of	Pound 0.50	Free	Centner .. 2.40	Centner .. 0.68
25	Leopard skins, raw	10 per cent	Free	Free	Centner .. 0.058
26	dressed	20 per cent	Free	Free	Centner .. 0.39
27	Lime	10 per cent	Free	Free	Centner .. 0.028

(Duties expressed in gold dollars of the United States.)—Continued.

	FRANCE.				RUSSIA.	NETHERLANDS.	
	General tariff.		In treaty with Great Britain, &c.				
	In French vessels.	In other vessels.	In vessels of treaty powers.	In other vessels.			
In cedar, per 100 kilogs.	$39. 00	$41. 73	10 per	cent.	Pood $0. 234	5 per cent	1
In White wood, 100 kil..	19. 50	20. 95	10 per	cent.			
....	Prohibit	ed	10 per	cent.	Pound........ 0. 31	5 per cent	2
....	(See Ma	nufactur	e of woo	l.)	Pound........ 0. 39	5 per cent	3
100 kilogs	2. 92	3. 40	$1. 95	$2. 14	Pood 0. 039	Free	4
....	....	....	....	....	....	....	5
100 kilogs	4. 87	5. 35	4. 87	5. 35	Pood 0. 85	3 per cent	6
....	Free ..	Free ..	Free ..	Free ..	Free	Free	7
....	....	....	....	....	....	....	8
100 kilogs	3. 90	4. 29	3. 90	4. 29	Pood 0. 95	3 per cent	
Leather, calf skins, (Russian leather,) per 100 kilogs.	15. 60	16. 86	11. 70	12. 76	Leather, raw and unmanufactured, small skins, tanned or soaked in alum, morocco, dry, chamois skins, per pood, 6. 24 Large skins, tanned, soaked in alum, or tawed, pr. pood, 3. 32 Varnished leather, per pood...... 4. 68 Manufactures, ordinary, shoes, boots, per pound .... 0. 43 Gloves, articles of fancy leather, per pound .... 1. 72 Harness and saddl'ry, valises, hunting bags, fencing-glov's, pock't books, and all articles not enumerated, per pound 0. 31	Leather, tanned, &c., 4 per cent. All manufactures, 5 per cent.	9 10 11
Simply tanned, large, per 100 kilogs.	9. 75	10. 42	1. 95 (bracketed)	2. 14 (bracketed)			12
Simply tanned, small, per 100 kilogs.	23. 30	24. 95					13
Morocco	....	....	11. 70	12. 76			
Colored leather........	....	....	8. 77	9. 64			
Curried leather for boot uppers, per 100 kilogs.	39. 00	41. 40	1. 95 (bracketed)	2. 14 (bracketed)			
Other, per 100 kilogs...	19. 50	20. 95					
In alum, Hungarian, per 100 kilogs.	7. 80	8. 58					
Dressed, per 100 kilogs.	9. 75	10. 72					
All others, per 100 kilogs	Prohib	ited					
Manufactures of leather gloves.	Pro (bracketed)	hibited .	5 per	cent.			
Pocket-books, cases, or other fancy articles, per 100 kilogs.			11. 70	12. 76			
Saddles not trimmed with leather, each.	0. 097	0. 097	10 per (bracketed)	cent.			
Other manufactures ...	Prohib	ited					
Free..................	....	....	....	....	Pood 0. 04	Free	14
Free..................	....	....	....	....	Free	Free	15
Free..................	....	....	....	....	Free	Free	16
Free..................	....	....	....	....	Free	Free	17
5 per cent............	....	....	....	....	Pood 1. 79	Free	18
100 kilogs............	Free ..	0. 78	Free ..	0. 47	Pood 0. 19	Free	19
100 kilogs............	Free ..	0. 78	Free ..	0. 47	Pood 0. 19	Free	20
100 kilogs............	....	....	Free ..	0. 048	Free	100 litres $1. 23	21
100 kilogs............	0. 78	0. 86	0. 175	0. 188	Pood .... [illegible].85	1 per cent	22
Free..................	....	....	....	....	Free	Free	23
5 per cent............	....	....	....	....	....	Free	24
100 kilogs............	0. 487	0. 487	Free ..	0. 047	Free	Free	25
100 kilogs............	0. 487	0. 487	....	0. 047	Free	2 per cent.........	26
All, free	....	....	....	....	Free	Free	27

Comparative table of import duties in the United States and European countries.

	ARTICLES.	ITALY.			SPAIN.	PORTUGAL.
			General tariff.	Tariff in treaty with France, &c.		
1	Lead pencils	100 kilogs	$1.95	......	100 kilogs ...$1.60	Fine, in wood, per kilog...... $0.54 Ordinary, in wood, per kilog .. 0.054
2	Leaders, leather	100 kilogs	9.75	$9.75	Kilog 0.50	Kilog 1.08
3	worsted	Kilog	0.58	0.66	Kilog 0 30	Kilog 1.72
4	Leaf, Dutch metal	100 kilogs	0.097	0.097	100 kilogs ... 0.30	Kilog 0.0027
5	gold, per package					
6	of 500 leaves	Kilog	1.56	1.80	Kilog 1.75	Kilog 2.16
7	Leaves, medicinal, in a crude state.	100 kilogs	0.975	0.39	Free	5 per cent
8	Leaf, silver, of 500 leaves					
	per package	Kilog.	0.78	0.90	Kilog 0.225	Kilog 0.08
9 10 11 12 13	Leather, bracelets, elastic mitts garters, elastic and all manufactures thereof not otherwisespecifi'd. Leather, bend, caps of, bottles, braces, sole, patent. hats of upper, (tanned calf-skins.) not otherwise specified.	Leather, sole, 100 kilogs. Lambskin, 100 kil. Morocco, 100 kil. Varnished, 100 kil. Manufactures of leather, per 100 kilogs. Boots and shoes, per pair. Breeches, each Gloves, per pair	7.80 7.80 13.65 19.50 9.75 0.097 0.78 0.029	2.93 8.77 15.60 15.60 9.75 100 kilogs, 9.75 (boots and shoes, breeches, gloves)	Leather, manufactures, shoes, &c., per kilog., 1.75. Belts and saddlery, per kilog., 0.50. Gloves, per kilog., 4, 00. Patent leather, per kilog., 0.50. For coverings and embellishments, per kilog., 0.10. Tanned leather, per kilog., 0.25.	Leather, sole, per kilog., 0.037. Tanned cowhides, per kilog., 0.054. Tanned in bark, not specified, per kilog., 0.216. Otherwise tanned, not specified, per kilog., 0.216. Colored, morocco, varnished, per kilog., 0.378. Manufactures, simple, pr. kilog., 0.648. Ornaments, per kilog., 1.08. Gloves, per pair, 0.108. Garters, suspenders, trimmed and ornamented, per kilog., 2.70.
14	Leaves, for dyeing, crude	100 kilogs	0.39	Free.	100 kilogs....$2.00	5 per cent
15	not used in dyeing, not otherwise provided for.	100 kilogs	0.97	0.39	100 kilogs.... 2.00	5 per cent
16	buchu	100 kilogs	0.97	0.39	100 kilogs.... 2.00	5 per cent
17	Leeches	100 kilogs	5.85	Free.	100 kilogs.... 1.10	Per mille 0.108
18	Lees, wine, crystallized or crude, tartar or argols.	Hectoliter	0.97	1.12	20 per cent	5 per cent
19	Lemons, in bulk	Hectoliter	0.97	Free.	100 kilogs.... 0.50	Kilogs 0.0027
20	in boxes, barrels, &c	Hectoliter	0.97	Free.	100 kilogs.... 0.50	Kilogs 0.0027
21	Lemon juice	Hectoliter	1.56	Free.	20 per cent	5 per cent
22	oil of	Kilog	0.117	Free.	20 per cent	Decaliter 0.54
23	peel	100 kilogs	1.95	Free.	100 kilogs.... 2.00	5 per cent
24	essence of	100 kilogs	1.95	0.78	20 per cent	5 per cent
25	Leopard skins, raw	100 kilogs	2.93	......	100 kilogs.... 1.50	20 per cent
26	dressed	100 kilogs	3.90	......	Kilogs 0.25	20 per cent
27	Lime	100 kilogs	0.48	Free.	Free	Free

(*Duties expressed in gold dollars of the United States.*)—Continued.

BELGIUM.	AUSTRIA.			DENMARK.	SWEDEN.	NORWAY.	
		General tariff.	Tariff in treaty.				
10 per cent	....	$7. 20	$5. 76	Pound.. .$0. 028	Pound. ..$0. 041	Pound.. .$0. 047	1
10 per cent	See Leather	manu fact's.		Pound.... 0. 091	Pound.... 0. 066	Pound ... 0. 124	2
10 per cent	See Woollen	manu fact's.		Pound.... 0. 068	Pound.... 0. 21	Pound ... 9. 146	3
Free	Same as cop	per ..	......	Pound.... 0. 005	Free	Free	4
Free	....	......	......	....	....	....	5
Free	....	7. 20	5. 76	Pound.... 0. 091	Ort 0. 0027	Free............	6
Free	Free	......	......	Pound.... 0. 0113	Free	Free...	7
Free	....	......	......	....	....	....	8
Free	....	7. 20	5. 76	Pound.... 0. 091	Free	Free............	
Leather, tanned, 100 kilogs., 2. 93. Otherwise prepared, per 100 kilogs., 5. 85. Manufactures of leather, 10 per cent.	Leather, common, centn'r.	2. 64	1. 44	Leath'r, prepar'd, not manufactured, pound, 0.034. Dyed, bronzed, corduan, morocco, parchment, and skins for saddlery, p'nd, 0.068. All manufactur's, pound, 0.091.	Leather, manufactures of, pay ad'ition'l to duty on material, 20 per cent. Leather cut for gloves, pound, 0.082. Leather for soles, pound, 0.0275. See Hats. Leather, sole, prepared, pound, 0.0275. Others, p'nd, 0.056.	Tanned sole leather, pound, 0. 03. corduan, parchment, leather painted, gilded, or otherwise ornamented; saddlers' leather, &c., p'nd, 0. 062. Shoes, silk, pound, 0. 368. Of leather, dyed or lacqueered, pound, 0. 145. Other, lb., 0. 091 Other manuf'es pay double duty of material.	9 10 11 12 13
	Sheep and goat skins tanned, not dyed or prepared, centner.	0. 48	0. 36				
	Dyed in yellow or red, coarse, centner.	0. 48	......				
	Fine leather, for gloves, cordovan, morocco, dyed, varnished, gilded, ornamented, parchment, centner.	6. 24	4. 80				
	Manufactur's:						
	Shoemakers' work, centner.	5. 76	3. 60				
	Saddlery, wallets, &c.	5. 76	3. 60				
	Fancy work, pock'tbooks, hunting b'gs, saddlery ornamented.	12. 00	7. 20				
	Gloves, (also if cut only,) centner.	27. 88	21. 60				
Free	Free	......	......	Free	Free	Free	14
Free	Free	......	......	Free	Free	Free	15
Free	Free	......	......	Free	Free	Free	16
Free	Free	......	......	Free	Free	Free	17
See Wines	See Wines ..	......	......	Pound.... 0. 0113	Medicinal, free...	Free	18
100 kilogs .. 1. 17	Centner	1. 262	......	Free	Free	Pound 0. 027	19
100 kilogs .. 1. 17	Centner	1. 262	......	Free	Free	Pound 0. 027	20
Free	Centner	2. 40	......	Pot 0. 091	Free	Pound 0. 009	21
Free	See Oils	......	......	Pound.....0. 068	Free	See Oils.........	22
Free	Centner	0. 388	......	Pound 0. 004	Free	Pound 0. 027	23
See Essences	See Essences.	......	......	Pound.....0. 0113	Free	Free	24
Free	Free	......	......	Free	Free	Free	25
Free	Centner	1. 26	......	Pound.....0. 068	Pound.... 0. 275	Pound 0. 045	26
Free	Free	......	......	Free	Free	Free............	27

Comparative table of import duties in the United States and European countries.

	ARTICLES.	UNITED STATES.	GREAT BRITAIN.	GERMAN ZOLL-VEREIN.	SWITZERLAND.
1	Lime, borate of	Pound $0.05	Free	Free	Centner ..$0.68
2	chloride of	100 lbs 0.30	Free	Free	Centner .. 0.68
3	white	Pound 0.03	Free	Free	Centner .. 0.68
4	Limes	20 per cent	Free	Centner ..$1.44	Centner .. 0.028
5	Lines, fishing	40 per cent	Free	Centner .. 2.88	Centner .. 1.56
6	Linseed	Bushel 0.16	Free	Free	Centner .. 0.029
7	cakes or meal	20 per cent	Free	Free	Centner .. 0.39
8	Liqueurs or cordials, sweet.	Gallon 2.50	Gallon $2.53	Centner .. 4.32	Centner .. 1.56
9	Liquor, iron	10 per cent	Free	Free	Centner .. 0.68
10	purple	20 per cent	Free	Free	Centner .. 0.68
11	red	20 per cent	Free	Free	Centner .. 0.68
12	tin	20 per cent	Free	Free	Centner .. 0.68
13	Liquorice, paste or rolls	Pound 0.10	Free	Centner .. 0.36	Centner .. 0.68
14	root	Pound 0.02	Free	Centner .. 0.36	Centner .. 0.68
15	Litharge	Pound 0.03	Free	Centner .. 0.72	Centner .. 0.145
16	Lithographic stones	20 per cent	Free	Free	Centner .. 0.029
17	Lithoutriptons	35 per cent	Free	Free	Centner .. 1.56
18	Litmus	20 per cent	Free	Free	Centner .. 0.39
19	Loadstones	20 per cent	Free	Free	Centner .. 0.029
20	Lotions, all cosmetic	50 per cent	Free	Centner .. 2.40	Centner .. 2.93
21	Lozenges, all medicinal	50 per cent	Free	Centner .. 2.40	Centner .. 0.68
22	Locks, brass, wood, and iron.	35 per cent	Free	Centner .. 0.96	Centner .. 1.56
23	wood and steel, gun.	45 per cent	Free	Centner .. 2.88	Centner .. 1.56
24	Long cloth, (linen)	Same as cotton..	Free	Centner .. 7.20	Centner .. 1.56
25	Looking-glass, plates	See Glass	Free	See Glass	See Glass
26	frames, gilt, if metal.	35 per cent	Free	Centner .. 2.88	Centner .. 1.56
27	Lunar caustic	40 per cent	Free	Centner .. 2.40	Centner .. 0.68
28	Lustres glass, cut	40 per cent	Free	Centner .. 2.88	Centner .. 1.56
29	brass and glass.	40 per cent	Free	Centner .. 2.88	Centner .. 1.56
30	Lutes	30 per cent	Free	Centner .. 2.88	Centner .. 1.56
31	Lye, soda	20 per cent	Free	Free	Centner .. 0.058
32	Macaroni	35 per cent	Free	Centner .. 1.44	Centner .. 0.68
33	Mace	Pound 0.40	Free	Centner .. 4.68	Centner .. 0.68

NOTE. FRANCE.—*Duties on*

Articles.	General tariff.		In treaty with Great Britain, &c.	
	In French vessels.	In other vessels.	In vessels of treaty powers.	In other vessels.
Jute yarn pure, measuring per kilogramme—				
Less than 1,400 metres, unbleached ......100 kilogs.	All unbl	eached:	$0.97	$1.06
1,401 to 3,700 metres, unbleached ......do....	$11.70	$12.76	1.17	1.29
3,701 to 4,200 metres, unbleached ......do....	....	....	1.36	1.50
4,200 to 6,000 metres, unbleached ......do....	....	....	1.95	2.14
Over 6,000 metres, unbleached, and bleached and dyed ......do....	....	....	Same as	lin. y'rn.
Less than 1,400 metres, bleached and dyed ......do....	All ble	ached:	1.36	1.50
1,401 to 3,700 metres, bleached and dyed ......do....	15.79	17.05	1.75	1.93
3,701 to 4,200 metres, bleached and dyed ......do....	All	dyed:	1.95	2.14
4,201 to 6,000 metres, bleached and dyed ......do....	15.60	16.86	2.43	3.00
All mixed, jute predominating ......do....	Same	as yarn	of pure	jute.
Tissues of jute, having in the space of five millimetres—				
Less than eight threads, unbleached ......do....	15.01	16.24	....	....
Eight threads, unbleached ......do....	17.55	18.91	....	....
Nine to eleven (inch) threads, unbleached ......do....	25.15	26.88	....	....
Twelve threads or more, unbleached, bleached, and dyed....do....	As tis'ue	s of flax.	....	....

(*Duties expressed in gold dollars of the United States.*)—Continued.

	FRANCE.				RUSSIA.	NETHERLANDS.	
	General tariff.		In treaty with Great Britain, &c.				
	In French vessels.	In other vessels.	In vessels of treaty powers.	In other vessels.			
See Chemicals not enumerated..					Pood $0.85	Free	1
100 kilogs.............			$0.67	$0.70	Pood 0.85	Free	2
					Pood 0.85	Free	3
100 kilogs.............	Free ..	$0.78	Free ..	0.47	Pood 0.19	5 per cent..........	4
15 per cent............					Pood 0.31	5 per cent..........	5
100 kilogs.............	Free ..	0.39	Free ..	0.048	Free	Free	6
					Free	100 kilogs... $0.06	7
Hectoliter.............	$29.25	29.25	2.92	2.92	Bottle 0.50	Liter 0.33	8
Free..................					Pood 0.85	Free	9
Free..................					Pood 0.85	Free	10
Free..................					Pood 0.85	Free	11
Free..................					Pood 0.85	Free	12
100 kilogs.............	9.36	10.20	0.78	9.86	Free	Free	13
100 kilogs.............	Free ..	0.39	Free ..	0.048	Free	Free	14
					Pood 0.039	Free	15
100 kilogs.............	Free ..	0.195	Free ..		Free	Free	16
100 kilogs.............	30 per cent....		Free ..	0.048	Free	5 per cent..........	17
Free..................					Free	Free	18
100 kilogs.............	Free ..	0.195	Free ..		Free	Free	19
See Perfumeries........					Pood 4.29	5 per cent..........	20
See Medicinal preparations not enumerated...					Pood 0.85	Free	21
					Pood 1.95	5 per cent..........	22
					Pood 1.95	5 per cent..........	23
See Manuf. of flax......					30 per cent	5 per cent..........	24
See Glass..............					See Glass............	5 per cent..........	25
					Of wood, gilt... 2.93	5 per cent..........	26
	15 per cent....		10 per cent....		See also Gilt ware ...	5 per cent..........	
100 kilogs.............			1.25	1.36	Pood 0.85	Free	27
See Glass..............					See Glass............	5 per cent..........	28
See Glass..............					See Glass............	5 per cent..........	29
Each	0.58	0.58	10 per cent....		Pound.......... 0.08	5 per cent..........	30
Free..................					Free	Free	31
100 kilogs.............	Free ..	0.78	Free ..	0.48	Pood 0.78	100 kilogs.... 0.82	32
100 kilogs.............	29.25	31.59			Pood 1.95	5 per cent	33

jute yarns and tissues.

Articles.	General tariff.		In treaty with Great Britain, &c.	
	In French vessels.	In other vessels.	In vessels of treaty powers.	In other vessels.
Tissues of jute, having in the space of five millimetres—				
Less than eight threads, bleached and dyed.............100 kilogs.	$20.86	$22.38		
Eight threads, bleached and dyed ....do....	24.57	26.29		
Nine to eleven (inch) threads, bleached and dyed ....do....	37.83	40.21		
Tissues of jute, pure, having in the space of five millimetres—				
Plain, three threads or less, unbleached ....do....			$1.95	$2.14
Pressed, three threads or less, unbleached ....do....			2.34	2.65
Four to five threads, unbleached..........................do....			3.12	2.43
Six to eight threads, unbleached ....do....			4.68	5.15
Over eight threads, unbleached, and bleached or dyed.......do....			As tis'ues of flax.	
Smooth, three threads or less, bleached or dyed ....do....			2.92	3.20
Pressed, three threads or less, bleached or dyed...........do....			3.31	3.64
Four to five threads, bleached or dyed ....do....			4.48	4.93
Six to eight threads, bleached or dyed ....do....			6.82	7.50
Carpet...do....			4.68	5.15
All mixed tissues, jute predominant			15 per cent.	

Comparative table of import duties in the United States and European countries

	ARTICLES.	ITALY.			SPAIN.	PORTUGAL.
			General tariff.	Tariff in treaty with France, &c.		
1	Lime, borate of	100 kilogs	$1. 95	$0. 39	Kilogs $0. 02	10 per cent
2	chloride of	100 kilogs	1. 95	0. 39	100 kilogs.... 0. 50	10 per cent
3	white	100 kilogs	0. 39	Free	Kilogs 0. 02	Free
4	Eimes	100 kilogs	0. 195	......	100 kilogs.... 0. 50	Kilogs $0. 0027
5	Lines, fishing	100 kilogs	2. 34	2. 80	100 kilogs.... 4. 00	As yarn
6	Linseed	100 kilogs	0. 195	Free.	Kilogs 0. 20	Kilogs 0. 001
7	cakes or meal	......	......	......	Kilogs 0. 20	Kilogs 0. 001
8	Liqueurs or cordials, sweet	Hectoliter	11. 70	2. 93	Liter 0. 20	Decaliter 1. 62
9	Liquor, iron	100 kilogs	1. 95	1. 95	100 kilogs.... 2. 50	Kilogs 0. 01
10	purple	100 kilogs	1. 95	1. 95	100 kilogs.... 2. 50	Kilogs 0. 01
11	red	100 kilogs	1. 95	1. 95	100 kilogs.... 2. 50	Kilogs 0. 01
12	tin	100 kilogs	1. 95	1. 95	100 kilogs.... 2. 50	Kilogs 0. 01
13	Liquorice, paste or rolls	100 kilogs	2. 93	0. 78	20 per cent	5 per cent
14	root	100 kilogs	0. 58	Free.	100 kilogs.... 0. 25	5 per cent
15	Litharge	100 kilogs	0. 39	0. 195	100 kilogs.... 1. 00	Free
16	Lithographic stones	5 per cent	......	......	100 kilogs.... 0. 01	Free
17	Lithontriptons	100 kilogs	3 90	1. 95	10 per cent	5 per cent
18	Litmus	100 kilogs	0. 39	Free.	100 kilogs.... 0. 50	5 per cent
19	Loadstones	Each	0. 019	......	100 kilogs.... 0. 01	Free
20	Lotions, all cosmetic	As perfumeries..	......	......	Kilogs 0. 30	20 per cent
21	Lozenges, all medicinal	100 kilogs	1. 95	0. 39	20 per cent	5 per cent
22	Locks, brass, wood, and iron	As manuf. of these metals.			See Manuf. of these materials.	See Manufactures of these materials.
23	wood and steel, gun	Gun locks, each..	0. 58	0. 67		
24	Long cloth, (linen)	See Tissues of flax ...		......	See Manuf. of flax..	See Manuf. of flax..
25	Looking-glass, plates	See Glass	......	......	See Glass	See Glass
26	frames, gilt, on metal.	As manufactures of metals ...			As material manufactured.	35 per cent
27	Lunar caustic	100 kilogs	0. 97	......	20 per cent	5 per cent
28	Lustres, glass, cut	100 kilogs	2. 93	1. 36	100 kilogs.... 3. 50	Kilogs....... 0. 172
29	brass and glass	As mercury	9. 75	9. 75	100 kilogs.... 25. 00	Kilogs 0. 27
30	Lutes	Each	0. 39	0. 39	10 per cent	25 per cent
31	Lye, soda	Free	......	......	5 per cent	10 per cent
32	Macaroni	Free	......	......	100 kilogs.... 2. 80	Kilogs 0. 108
33	Mace	100 kilogs	0. 39	......	Kilogs 0. 10	Kilog....... 0. 108

United States tariff on oils—Continued.

Articles.	United States.	Articles.	United States.
Oil of sassafras	50 per cent	Oil of jasmine or jessamin	50 per cent
spruce	50 per cent	lavender	50 per cent
spike	50 per cent	lemon	Pound $0. 50
spurge	50 per cent	limets, (lisnette,)	50 per cent
valerian	Pound $1. 50	macassar	50 per cent
allspice	50 per cent	neat's foot	20 per cent
ambergris	50 per cent	nerol, or orange flower	50 per cent
almonds, essential	Pound 1. 50	nutmegs	50 per cent
bay leaves	Pound 17. 50	oranges	Pound 0. 50
bergamot	Pound 1. 00	origanum, or thyme, red	Pound 0. 25
cedrat	50 per cent	pimento	50 per cent
Oils of apple, pear, peach, apricot, strawberry, and raspberry.	Pound 2. 50	rhodium	50 per cent
		roses, or otto of roses	Ounce..... 1. 50

(*Duties expressed in gold dollars of the United States.*)—Continued.

BELGIUM.	AUSTRIA.			DENMARK.	SWEDEN.	NORWAY.	
		General tariff.	Tariff in treaty.				
Free	See Chemicals	......	......	Pound....$0.0113			1
Free	See Chemicals	......	......	Pound.....0.0113	See Chem'ls, &c	Free	2
Free	Free	......	......	Free			3
10 per cent	Centner	$2.52	......	Free	Free	Free	4
10 per cent	See Linen yarn		......	Pound..... 0.017	See Yarn of flax	Pound....$0.036	5
100 kilogs..$0.117	Centner	0.0288	Free.	Free	Free	Free	6
Free	Centner	0.0288	Free.	Free	Free	Free	7
Hectoliter..16.53	Centner	6.312	......	Pot....... 0.091	Free	Pot....... 0.218	8
Free	Free	......	......	Pound..... 0.028	Free	Pound.... 0.004	9
Free				Pound..... 0.028	Free	Pound.... 0.004	10
Free	See Chem'ls	......	......	Pound..... 0.028	Free	Pound.... 0.004	11
Free				Pound..... 0.028	Free	Pound.... 0.004	12
Free	Extract, cent.	2.52	$1.44	Pound.....0.0113	Free	Free	13
Free	Centner	0.388	......	Pound.....0.0113	Free	Free	14
Free	Centner	0.48	0.36	Free	Free	Free	15
10 per cent	Free	......	......	Free	Free	Free	16
Free	Centner	4.80	3.60	10 per cent	Pound....$0.041	As mat'l manuf'd.	17
Free	Free	......	......	Free	Free	Free	18
Free	See Stones	......	......	Free	Free	Free	19
10 per cent	Centner	7.20	5.76	Pound..... 0.091	Pound.... 0.041	Pound.... 0.10	20
Free	Centner	7.20	......	Pound..... 0.045	Free	Free	21
100 kilogs, 0.78, or	See Material manufact'd.			Pound..... 0.017	According to mat'l	Pound.... 0.047	22
10 per cent	See Material manufact'd.			Pound..... 0.017	According to mat'l	Pound.... 0.027	23
See Tissues of flax.	See Tissues of flax		......	See Tissues of flax	See Cotton	See Manuf. of flax.	24
10 per cent	See Glass	......	......	10 per cent	Not cut, p'd 0.0081	See Glass	25
10 per cent	See Manufactures of wood.			Pound.....0.0113 Pound..... 0.091	Cut, not silvered, pound....0.0138 Cut and silvered, pound....0.0275	Pound.... 0.03	26
Free	Centner	2.52	1.44	Pound.....0.0113	Free	Free	27
10 per cent	See Glass	......	......	Pound..... 0.091	Pound..... 0.041	Pound.... 0.109	28
10 per cent	See Glass	......	......	Pound..... 0.091	Pound..... 0.041	Pound.... 0.109	29
6 per cent	Centner	4.80	3.60	Pound..... 0.091	Each...... 0.275	10 per cent	30
Free	Free	......	......	Free	Free	Free	31
100 kilogs.. 0.23	Centner	1.26	1.20	Free	Free	Lis. pound. 0.026	32
15 per cent	Centner	7.56	......	Pound..... 0.273	Pound..... 0.11	Pound.... 0.187	33

United States tariff on oils—Continued.

Articles.	United States.	Articles.	United States.
Oil of rosemary, or anthos	50 per cent	Oil, illuminating, from coal, shale, asphaltum, peat, petroleum or rock oil, or other bituminous substances, used for like purposes	Gallon $0.40
sweet marjorum	50 per cent	kerosene	Gallon 0.40
thyme, or origanum, white.	Pound $0.30	linseed	Gallon 0.22
tuberose	50 per cent	rapeseed	Gallon 0.22
vanilla beans	50 per cent	salad	Gallon 1.00
ricini, or palma christe	Gallon 1.00	seal	10 per cent
coal, crude	Gallon 0.15	spermaceti, of foreign fishery.	20 per cent
refined	Gallon 0.40	fish, and all other of American fisheries, all articles the production of said fisheries	Free
castor	Gallon 1.00		
olive, in casks, not salad	Gallon 0.25		
in bottles or flasks	Gallon 1.00		
flaxseed	Gallon 0.23		
hempseed	Gallon 0.23		

Comparative table of import duties in the United States and European countries.

	ARTICLES.	UNITED STATES.	GREAT BRITAIN.	GERMAN ZOLL-VEREIN.	SWITZERLAND.
1	Machinery; models of, and other inventions.	Free	Free	Models.... Free. Machinery; locomotives, tenders, and boilers, centner...$1. 08 Other machinery of wood, per centner... 0. 36 of cast iron, per centner... 0. 36 of steel or wro't iron, per centner....... 0. 60 of other, not precious metals, centner... 0. 96 cylinders for printing of tissues, engraved, centner... 1. 44 not engraved, per centner... 0. 36 Cards for weavers, cent.. 4.32 Railroad cars, 10 per cent. Car'ges, sleighs, &c., each piece, centner.. 36. 00 Sea & river vessels, of wood, 5 per cent. of iron, 8 per ct.	All machinery, centre ...$0. 39
2	Machinery for the manufacture of sugar from beets, including all the preliminary processes requisite therefor.	Free	Free		
3	Other machinery and parts of;				
4	of iron	35 per cent	Free		
5	of steel	45 per cent	Free		

(*Duties expressed in gold dollars of the United States.*)—Continued.

FRANCE.	Gen'l tariff. In French vessels.	Gen'l tariff. In other vessels.		Treaty with G. Brit'n, &c. In vessels of treaty powers.	Treaty with G. Brit'n, &c. In other vessels.
a. Machinery and apparatus complete:					
1. Steam; old, 100 kilogs	$0.97	$1.06		$0.58	$0.64
fixed, 100 kilogs	4.87	5.35		1.17	1.29
for navigation, 100 kilogs	6.82	7.49		......	......
locomotives, 100 kilogs	6.82	7.49		1.95	2.14
			Tenders	1.56	1.72
2. Not steam:					
for weaving, 100 kilogs	2.92	3.20		1.17	1.29
spinning, kilogs	7.80	8.58		1.95	2.14
carding, 100 kilogs	5.85	6.43		1.17	1.29
tull work, 100 kilogs	11.70	12.76		1.95	2.14
paper factory printing, 100 kilogs	5.85	6.43		1.17	1.29
agriculture, 100 kilogs	2.92	3.20		1.17	1.29
railroad cars, (cast wheels,) 100 kilogs	3.90	4.29	All not enumerated, having cast iron 75 per cent. or more, 100 kilog	1.17	1.29
river ships, tenders, boilers, gasometers, apparatus for sugar factories, distilleries, &c.:			50 to 75 per cent., 100 kil.	1.05	2.14
			less than 50 per cent, 100 kilogs	2.92	3.20
a. of iron, 100 kilogs	5.85	6.43	For distilleries, 100 kil	1.95	2.14
b. of copper, 100 kilogs	11.70	12.76	tenders, 100 kil	1.56	1.72
3. Not enumt'd, weigh'g 100 kil. or less, 100 kil	12.67	13.79	boilers, cylindric, iron plate, 100 kil	1.56	1.72
100 to 200 kil., 100 kil	8.77	9.66	tubular iron plate, 100 kilogs	2.34	2.57
201 to 1000 kil., 100 kil	6.82	7.50			
1001 to 2500 kil., 100 kil.	5.85	6.43			
2501 to 5000 kil., 100 kil.	4.87	5.35	tubular steel plate, 100 kilogs	4.87	5.35
over 5000 kil., 100 kil	3.90	4.29	all others, 100 kilog	1.56	1.72
b. Detached portions:					
Plates and bands of cards, 100 kil	39.00	41.43	Plates and bands of cards, 100 kilogs	11.70	12.76
Shuttles and combs for weaving, 100 kil	39.00	41.43	Teeth, (cogs,) iron or copper, 100 kilogs	5.85	6.43
Parts of agricultural machines, per 100 kil	2.92	3.20	Combs for weaving, iron or copper teeth, 100 kil.	5.85	6.43
Detached pieces, cast, or weighing 25 kil. or less, 100 kil	15.60	16.86	Cast pieces, polished and adjusted, 100 kil	1.17	1.29
25 to 50 kil., 100 kil	12.67	13.79	Wrought-iron pieces, polished and adjusted, 100 kilogs	1.95	2.14
51 to 100 kil., 100 kil	10.72	11.74			
101 to 200 kil,, 100 kil	8.77	9.65			
200 to 1000 kil., 100 kil	6.82	7.49	Parts of steel, for carriages, locomotives, &c., 100 kilogs	2.14	3.20
1000 to 2500 kil., 100 kil	4.87	5.35			
2500 to 5000 kil., 100 kil	3.90	4.29	of 1 kil. or more weight, 100 kilogs	2.92	3.20
over 5000 kil., 100 kil	2.92	3.20	of less than 1 kil., 100 kil.	3.90	4.29
Detached pieces of wro't iron weighing 5 kilogs or less, per 100 kilogs	19.50	20.95	Parts of copper pure or alloyed, and plates of leather, India-rubber, &c., destined especially for carding, 100 kilogs	3.90	4.29
5 to 25 kil, 100 kil	15.60	16.86			
25 to 50 kil., 100 kil	13.65	14.82			
over 50 kil., 100 kil	11.70	12.76			
Detached pieces:					
of steel, 100 kil	29.75	30.22			
of copper 100, kil	39.00	41.43			
Cylinders for printing	15 per	cent.	Per 100 kilogs	2.92	3.20
Chemical instruments	10 per	cent.	Per 100 kilogs	Free.	0.048
Optical and mathematical instruments	30 per	cent.	Per 100 kilogs	Free.	0.048

RUSSIA.

Machinery and apparatus: 1
Locomotives: apparatus of copper, imported separately, per pood $0.585 2
All steam machinery,
fire engines, per pood 0.23 3
Detached pieces of 4
mach'y, pood. 0.23 5
Agricult'al machines and outfit to the same .... Free.
Machines for spinning and other work on fibrous substances .... Free.
Machinery for paper factories ...... Free.
Models, all kinds, Free.
Weavers' combs and cards of every description ..... Free.
Sea and river ships, with complete outfit .... Free.
Mathematical, surgical, and optical instruments .... Free.
Chemical apparatus, vessels, &c ... Free.

Comparative table of import duties in the United States and European countries.

	NETHERLANDS.	ITALY.			SPAIN.	PORTUGAL.
			General tariff.	Tariff in treaty with France, &c.		
1 2 3 4 5	Machinery for manufactures and agriculture, paper felt, and metallic gauge, not otherwise enumerated, 1 per cent.	Machines and parts thereof: Weavers' combs and machines on which to make them, per 100 kilogs.......... Cards for weavers and furniture, per 100 kilogs.......... Fixed steam and hydraulic machines, per 100 kilogs...... Agricultural and industrial machinery, per 100 kilogs...... not enumerated ... Steam machinery for navigation, 100 kil..	 $0.975 0.975 0.58 0.39 1 per 0.78	 .... cent. $0.78	Machinery: agricultural, 1 pr. ct. complete machines for any industry, 6 per cent. detached pieces, 10 per cent. Apparatus, insulated, tensors, copper wire, posts, and other pieces for electric telegraphs, 3 per cent.	Machines: Agricultural, complete or in parts, per kilog....$0.002 Cranes, of iron, per kilog .... 0.01 Apparatus for distilling, also of copper, per kilog .... 0.02 Machines for industry, complete or in parts, per kil. 0.01 Others not specified, with declaration of their use, per kilog 0.002

NOTE.—FRANCE. Tariff duties on woolen yarns and

ARTICLES.	SINGLE.				TWISTED FOR WEAVING.				TWISTED FOR TAPESTRY.			
Tariff in treaty with Great Britain and other powers.	Bleached or not.		Dyed.		Bleached or not.		Dyed.		Bleached or not.		Dyed.	
	Treaty vessels.	Other vessels.	Treaty vessels.	Other vessels.	Treaty vessels.	Other vessels.	Treaty vessels.	Other vessels.	Treaty vessels.	Other vessels.	Treaty vessels.	Other vessels.
Woolen yarn, pure, measuring per kilogramme—												
10,000 meters, or less, 100 kilogs....................	$1.95	2.14										
From 10,001 to 15,000 meters, 100 kilogs	2.92	3.20										
From 15,001 to 20,000 meters, 100 kilogs	3.90	4.29	$9.75	$10.72	$6.34	$6.94	$11.21	$12.25	$9.75	$10.72	$14.62	$15.83
From 20,001 to 20,500 meters, 100 kilogs	5.87	6.35										
From 30,501 to 40,500 meters, 100 kilogs	6.82	7.49	11.70	12.76	8.89	9.75	13.74	14.91	13.65	14.82	18.52	19.93
From 40,501 to 50,500 meters, 100 kilogs	8.77	9.61	13.65	14.82	11.41	12.46	16.28	17.57	17.55	18.91	22.42	24.02
From 50,501 to 60,500 meters, 100 kilogs	10.72	11.74	15.60	16.86	13.94	15.11	18.81	20.23	21.45	23.01	26.32	28.12
From 60,501 to 70,500 meters, 100 kilogs	12.67	13.78	17.55	18.91	16.48	17.78	21.34	22.89	25.35	27.10	30.22	32.21
From 70,501 to 80,000 meters, 100 kilogs	14.62	15.83	19.50	20.95	19.01	20.44	23.88	25.56	29.25	31.20	34.12	36.30
From 80,501 to 90,500 meters, 100 kilogs	16.57	17.88	21.45	23.01	21.54	23.10	26.40	28.21	33.15	35.29	38.02	40.40
From 90,501 to 100,500 meters, 100 kilogs	18.52	19.92	23.40	25.05	24.58	25.76	28.95	30.89	37.05	39.38	41.92	44.49
Over 100,500 meters, 100 kilogs....................	19.50	20.92	24.37	26.06	25.35	27.10	30.22	32.21	39.00	41.43	43.87	46.53
Woolen yarn, mixed, wool predominating.*												

* Same as yarns of pure wool.

(Duties expressed in gold dollars of the United States.)—Continued.

BELGIUM.	AUSTRIA.			DENMARK.	SWEDEN.	NORWAY.	
		General tariff.	Tariff in treaty.				
Machinery: cast, 100 kil. $0. 29 of iron or steel, 100 kilogs. 0. 78 of wood, 10 pr. ct. other material, 100 kilogs.. 2. 34 elastic, galvanic, pneumatic machines.... Free.	Machinery of cast iron, centner ... wrought iron or steel, per centner .... other, not prec's metals, centner.	$1. 20 1. 92 3. 60	$0. 96 1. 92 2. 88	Coarse articles of machinery, pound... $0. 0056 All other articles of iron or steel, pound... 0. 017	Machinery or parts of machinery for manufacturing, agricultural purposes, railroads; also, other steam engines, boilers, &c....... Free.	Machinery for industry and agriculture, steam machines, engines, and parts thereof .. Free.	1 2 3 4 5

yarns and tissues not otherwise enumerated, page 251.

Woolen yarn, &c.	General tariff.		Tariff in treaty with Great Britain, &c.	
	French vessels.	Other vessels.	Vessels of treaty powers.	Other vessels.
Yarn of abaca, phormium tenax, and other fibrous substances, unbleached, 100 kilogs	$11. 70	$12. 76	...5 per	cent.
Same, bleached, 100 kilogs	15. 79	17. 05		
Same, dyed, 100 kilogs	15. 60	16. 86		
Yarn of alpaca, lama, and vigonia, pure, mixed with wool to any extent, or with other material	Same as	yarn of	pure wo	ol.
Yarn of hair of the goat, 100 kilogs	3. 90	4. 29	$4. 68	$5. 15
cow, and other cattle, 100 kilogs	1. 75	1. 92	Free.	0. 048
dog, 100 kilogs	0. 19	0. 22	Free.	0. 048
chamois, pure or mixed	Same as	yarn of	wool.	
Other yarns, 100 kilogs	Prohibi	ted.	Free.	0. 048
Tissues of horse hair, pure or mixed—hair cloth, 100 kilogs	7. 99	8. 79	Braids,	tresses.
lace, 100 kilogs	29. 25	31. 20	31. 20	33. 24
All others	Prohibi	ted.	10 per	cent.
Tissues of phormium tenax, abaca, jute, unbleached, having in space of 5 millimeters less than 8 threads, 100 kilogs	15. 01	16. 24	Except of jute. 10 p. ct.	
Same, having in space of 5 millimeters 8 threads, 100 kilogs	17. 55	18. 91		
Same, having in space of 5 millimeters 9 to 11 threads, 100 kilogs	25. 15	26. 88		
Same, having in space of 5 millimeters 12 threads or more, 100 kilogs	As linen	tissues		
Bleached and dyed, less than 8 threads, 100 kilogs	20. 86	22. 38	Except of jute, 10 p. c.*	
8 threads, 100 kilogs	24. 57	26. 29		
9 to 11 threads, 100 kilogs	38. 83	40. 21		
12 threads, or under	As linen	tissues		
Tissues of bark, also mixed with other materials, such as:				
Of palm-tree fibers, 8 threads or more per 5 millimeters, sq. meter, 100 kilogs	0. 087	0. 037	....	
Others	Prohibi	ted.		

* For jute, see note, pages 142 and 143.

Comparative table of import duties in the United States and European countries.

	ARTICLES.	UNITED STATES.	GREAT BRITAIN.	GERMAN ZOLL-VEREIN.	SWITZERLAND.
1	Madder	Free	Free	Free	Centner...$0.058
2	root	Free	Free	Free	Centner....0.058
3	Magic lanterns, and similar articles of tin, glass, wood, brass, copper, &c.	40 per cent	Free	Centner...$2.88	Centner....1.56
4	Magnesia, calcined	Pound....$0.12	Free	Free	Centner....0.68
5	carbonate of	Pound.... 0.06	Free	Centner... 1.44	Centner....0 68
6	Magnesia, sulphate of, (Epsom salts.)	Pound.... 0.01	Free	Centner... 1.44	Centner....0.68
7	Mahogany, unmanufactured.	Free	Free	Free	Centner....0.058
8	manufactures of.	35 per cent	Free	Centner... 0.72	Centner....1.56
9	Mallets, wood	35 per cent	Free	Free	Centner....0.39
10	Malt	20 per cent	Quarter...$6.08	Free	Centner....0.058
11	Manganese	10 per cent	Free	Free	Centner....0.058
12	Mangoes	10 per cent	Free	Centner... 1.44	Centner....0.029
13	Mangroves or shells of	20 per cent	Free	Free	Centner....0.029
14	Manila grass	Ton 25.00	Free	Free	Centner....0.029
15	Manna	Pound.... 0.25	Free	Centner... 0.36	Centner....0.68
16	Mantillas, silk	60 per cent	Free	Centner...28.80	Centner....2.93
17	Manufactured tobacco, n.o.p.	Pound.... 0.50	See Tobacco	Centner... 7.92	Centner....1.56
18	Manuscripts	Free	Free	Free	Free
19	Maps	25 per cent	Free	Free	Centner....0.145
20	Marble, manufactures of	50 per cent	Free	Free	Centner....0.58
21	busts	10 per cent	Free	Free	Centner....0.58
22	Marbles, &c	50 per cent	Free	Free	Centner....0.58
23	Marble table tops	50 per cent	Free	Free	Centner....0.297
24	white, statuary	....	....	....	Centner....0.297
25	Marble, brocatella and antique, in slab or block.	25 per cent; Cubic foot 1.00	Free	Free	Centner....0.145
26	Marble, other, slab or block.	20 per cent; Cubic foot 0.50	Free	Free	Centner....0.145
27	Marbles, toys, baked, &c	Free	Free	Free	Centner....0.29
28	Marine coral	Free	Free	Free	Centner....0.39
29	Marmalade, a sweetmeat	35 per cent	Pound.... 0.02	Centner... 5.04	Centner....1.56
	Mathematical instruments:				
30	specially for schools	15 per cent	Free	Free	
31	of brass	35 per cent	Free	Free	
32	of bone	35 per cent	Free	Free	
33	of gold	40 per cent	Free	Free	Centner...0.39 (30–37)
34	gilt or plated	35 per cent	Free	Free	
35	all of ivory	35 per cent	Free	Free	
36	of silver	40 per cent	Free	Free	
37	of wood	35 per cent	Free	Free	
38	Matches, for pocket, light	35 per cent	Free	Centner... 0.36	Centner....0.29
39	Mats, cocoanuts	30 per cent	Free	Centner... 0.12	Centner....0.68
40	if wool be component part.	As carpet	Free	Centner... 7.20	Centner....0.68
41	Mats, screens, hassocks, and rugs, not exclusively of vegetable material.	45 per cent	Free	Centner... 0.12	Centner....0.68
42	Mats of flax, jute, straw, or grass.	30 per cent	Free	Centner... 0.12	Centner....0.68
43	Mattresses, hair or moss, linen tick.	30 per cent	Free	Centner... 2.88	Centner....1.56
44	Meal, cassava and linseed	20 per cent	Free	Centner... 0.36	Centner....0.10
45	Meats, prepared	35 per cent	Free	Centner... 0.36	Centner....0.39

(Duties expressed in gold dollars of the United States.)—Continued.

France.	General tariff. In French vessels.	General tariff. In other vessels.	In treaty with Great Britain, &c. In vessels of treaty powers.	In treaty with Great Britain, &c. In other vessels.	Russia.	Netherlands.	
Free	....	....	....	....	Pood $0.39	Free	1
Free	....	....	....	....	Free	Free	2
As Mercery, common pr. 100 kilogs.	$19.50	$20.95	10 per	cent.	Pound 0.25	5 per cent	3
....	....	....	....	....	Free	Free	4
100 kilogs	39.00	41.44	Free ..	$0.048	Pood 0.078	Free	5
100 kilogs	13.45	14.82	Free ..	0.048	Pood 0.078	Free	6
See Wood	....	....	....	....	Pood 0.04	Not sawn, 1 pr. ct. Sawn, 3 per cent	7
....	15 per	cent.	10 per	cent.	Pood 0.34	5 per cent	8
....	15 per	cent.	10 per	cent.	Pood 0.20	Fur. wood only, 1 p.c.	9
Free	....	....	....	....	Pood 0.03	Free	10
100 kilogs	Free ..	0.195	Free ..	0.048	Free	Free	11
100 kilogs	Free ..	0.078	Free ..	0.048	Pood 0.39	5 per cent	12
100 kilogs	Free ..	0.48	Free ..	....	Free	Free	13
Free	....	....	....	....	Free	Free	14
100 kilogs	15.60	16.87	$1 56	1.72	Pood 0.23	Free	15
See Manufactures of silk	....	....	....	....	35 per cent	5 per cent	16
....	Prohi	bited.	Prohi	bited.	Pood 20.58	100 kilogs ...$4.92	17
Free	....	....	Free ..	....	Free	Free	18
100 kilogs	....	....	Free ..	0.048	Free	Free	19
Marble, raw. 100 kilogs.	0.19	0.48	Free ..	0.048		5 per cent	20
Slabs, 16 centimeters thick, per 100 kilogs.	0.19	0.48	Free ..	0.048	Marble, raw...Free. Marble, manufactur's of, per pood. 5.35	Free	21
						5 per cent	22
Less than 16 centim'ts. thick, per 100 kilogs.	0.29	0.48	0.29	0.34		5 per cent	23
						5 per cent	24
Modern statues	....	....	Free ..	Free	Free	5 per cent	25
Sculptured, polished, or otherwise manufactured, 100 kilogs.	7.80	8.56	0.29	0.34	Free	5 per cent	26
					Free	5 per cent	27
Free	....	....	....	....	Free	Free	28
100 kilogs	8.19	8.58	....	....	Pood 3.90	100 kilogs ...10.25	29
							30
							31
							32
							33
100 kilogs	30 per	cent.	Free ..	0.048	Pood 4.68	5 per cent	34
							35
							36
							37
....	....	....	5 per	cent.	Pood 0.78	5 per cent	38
Mats and tresses of white wood, coarse, per 100 kilogs.	0.39	0.43	....	....			39
							40
All other of wood, per 100 kilogs.	0.97	1.07	....	....	Pound 0.08	5 per cent	41
Of spartum or bark, 3 ends, for cordage, p'r 100 kilogs.	0.39	0.43	0.195	0.22			
Coarse for mats. 100 kil.	0.39	0.43	0.39	0.43			42
Others.....100 kilogs.	0.97	1.07	0.97	1.07			
....	15 per	cent.	10 per	cent.	Pood 1.71	5 per cent	43
Free	....	....	....	....	Pood 0.03	5 per cent	44
Meats, fresh. 100 kilogs. Salted ....do... Extract of meat	Free .. 0.097 Free ..	Free .. 0.117 Free ..	Free .. 0.118 Free ..	0.047 0.117 Free.	Salted, smoked, or dried, pood. 0.515	Fresh or salted, per 100 kilogs..2.46 Otherwise preserved, 100 kils.3.28 Mut'n, pork, bacon, salt'd, 100 k.0.41 Otherwise preserved, 100 kils.0.51 In airless bxs., per 100 kilogs.10.25	45

Comparative table of import duties in the United States and European countries.

	ARTICLES.	ITALY.			SPAIN.	PORTUGAL.
			General tariff.	Tariff in treaty with France, &c.		
1	Madder	100 kilogs	$0.39	$0.39	100 kilogs....$4.00	5 per cent
2	root	100 kilogs Extract madder	0.39 0.39	0.39 0.39	100 kilogs.... 4.00	Kilogramme..$0.016
3	Magic lanterns, and similar articles of tin, glass, wood, brass, copper, &c.	As Fancy goods, per 100 kilogs.	9.75	9.75	20 per cent	20 per cent
4	Magnesia, calcined	100 kilogs	1.95	0.78	20 per cent	Carbonate and oxide of, kil. 0.054
5	carbonate of	100 kilogs	1.56	......	20 per cent	
6	Magnesia, sulphate of, (Epsom salts.)	100 kilogs	0.23	0.195	20 per cent	Free
7	Mahogany, unmanufactured.	100 kilogs	0.975	0.55	100 kilogs.... 0.10	See Wood
8	manufactures of.	100 kilogs	9.75	10 p.c.	100 kilogs.... 7.00	35 per cent
9	Mallets, wood	100 kilogs	0.58	Free	100 kilogs.... 3.50	35 per cent
10	Malt	Free	......	......	Not enum'd. in tariff.	Kilogramme..0.0054
11	Manganese	100 kilogs	0.195	Free.	20 per cent	Kilogramme..0.0027
12	Mangoes	100 kilogs	0.39	Free.	100 kilogs.... 0.50	Kilogramme..0.0027
13	Mangroves, or shells of	100 kilogs	0.39	Free.	100 kilogs.... 0.50	Kilogramme..0.0027
14	Manilla grass	Free	......	......	100 kilogs.... 0.05	Kilogramme..0.0008
15	Manna	100 kilogs	5.85	0.39	20 per cent	Kilogramme..0.162
16	Mantillas, silk	Kilogramme	1.95	0.58	50 per cent. above duty on material.	Double duty of tissues.
17	Manufactured tobacco, n.o.p.	Prohibited	......	......	Gov'ment monopoly	Kilogramme .0.432
18	Manuscripts	Free	......	......	Free	Free
19	Maps	100 kilogs	5.58	Free.	100 kilogs.... 0.25	Kilogramme .0.108
20	Marble, manufactures of	Raw, squared	Free.	Free	Raw, polished pcs., 100 kilogs. 0.075	Kilogramme 0.0108
21	busts	In slabs of 150 centimtr. long each.	0.039	Free	Squares, stairs, & plates, also, if polished, pr. 100 kilogs.... 0.75	
22	Marbles, &c	Longer slabs	0.058	Free.	Statues, ornam'ts, &c., per 100 kilogs...... 1.50	
23	Marble table tops	Manufactures not enumr'td.	5 p. c.	Free.		
24	white statuary					
25	Marble, brocatella and antique, in slab or block.					
26	Marble, other, slab or block.					
27	Marbles, toys, baked, &c					
28	Marine coral	Free	......	......	100 kilogs.... 0.75	½ per cent
29	Marmalade, a sweetmeat	100 kilogs	7.80	......	Kilogramme . 0.20	Kilogramme .0.075
	Mathematical instruments:					
30	specially for schools	100 kilogs	3.90	1.95	10 per cent	5 per cent
31	of brass					
32	of bone					
33	of gold					
34	gilt or plated					
35	all of ivory					
36	of silver					
37	of wood					
38	Matches, for pocket, light	100 kilogs	9.75	9.75	20 per cent	Kilogramme .0.054
39	Mats, cocoanuts	As Carpet, per 100 kilogs.	0.39	......	See Carpets	Mats, kilog...0.002 Matting of straw: Common, kil. 0.108 Fine ....0.206 Of sparto: Common, kil. 0.001 Finished, kil. 0.0054
40	if wool be a component part.					
41	Mats, screens, hassocks, and rugs, not exclusively of vegetable material.					
42	Mats of flax, jute, straw, or grass.					
43	Mattrasses, hair or moss, linen tick.	All, 100 kilogs	1.95	......	20 per cent	Horsehair, kil. 0.108
44	Meal, cassava and linseed	Free	......	......	100 kilogs.... 1.20	Double duty of grain
45	Meats, prepared	Fresh, 100 kilogs Salt ......do... Extract of. do...	0.975 3.90 1.95	Free. Free. Free.	Corned, salted, or jerked, per 100 kilogs.... 0.50 Otherwise pres'rved, 100 kil. 1.00	Fresh, dry, or prepared, kilo. 0.08

(*Duties expressed in gold dollars of the United States.*)—Continued.

Belgium.	Austria.			Denmark.	Sweden.	Norway.	
		General tariff.	Tariff in treaty.				
Free	Centner	0.0528	Free	Pound....$0.0113	Free	Free	1
Free	Centner	0.0528	Free	Pound.... 0.0113	Free	Free	2
	Extract of...	0.038	......				
10 per cent	Centner	7.20	$5.76	10 per cent	See Toys	10 per cent	3
Free	Centner	2.52	1.44	Pound. 0.0113 (4–6)	Free	Free	4
Free	See Chemicals	......	......		Free	Free	5
Free	Centner	2.52	1.44		Free	Free	6
Free	See Wood	......	......	Free	Free	Free	7
10 per cent	See Manufact	's of w	ood ..	See Household furniture.	Pound....$0.0138	See Manufactur's of wood.	8
10 per cent	See Manufact	's of w	ood ..	Pound.... 0.0008	Pound.... 0.0027	Free	9
100 kilogs ..$0.117	Centner	0.086	Free	Free	Free	Ton $2.53	10
Free	Free	......	......	Pound.... 0.0013	Free	Free	11
10 per cent	Centner	0.388	......	Free	Free	Free	12
Free	Free	......	......	Free	Free	Free	13
Free	Centner	0.0288	Free	Free	Free	Free	14
Free	Centner	2.52	1.44	Pound.... 0.0013	Free	Free	15
10 per cent	See Clothing	......	......	Double duty of material.	See Clothing	10 per cent. above duty on material.	16
100 kilogs .. 8.19	Centner	12.60	......	Pound.... 0.045	See Tobacco	Pound ... 0.109	17
Free	Free	......	......	Free	Free	Free	18
Free	Free	......	......	Free	Free	Free	19
10 per cent	See Manufac (20–27)	tr's of	stone.	Pound .. 0.0028	Free	Free	20
Free				Sculp. lb. 0.091	Free	Free	21
10 per cent				Pound .. 0.0028	Free	Free	22
10 per cent				Pound .. 0.0028	Free	Free	23
Free				Pound .. 0.091	......	......	24
Free				Free	Free	Free	25
Free				Free	Free	Free	26
10 per cent				Free	Free	Free	27
Free	Free	......	......	Free	Free	Free	28
100 kilogs ..11.70	See Comfits	......	......	Pound.... 0.04	Pound.... 0.044	Pound 0.061	29
Free (30–37)	All, centner (30–37)	4.80	3.80	See material manufactured. (30–37)	Pound .. 0.041 (30–37)	See mater'l manufactured. (30–37)	30
							31
							32
							33
							34
							35
							36
							37
10 per cent	Centner	0.36	Free	Pound.... 0.04	Pound.... 0.0055	Free	38
10 per cent (39–42)	Centner	0.12	......	Pound .. 0.0042	......	Pound 0.009	39
	Fast fibr's, per centner.	1.20	0.72	See Carpet	Pound.... 0.008	See Carpet	40
	Wool, centner.	3.28	......				41
	Others, cent'r.	3.28	......	Pound .. 0.0042	Pound... 0.008	Pound.... 0.009	
				......	......	......	42
10 per cent	As tissues of	which	made.	Pound.... 0.017	Same as Cover, (see Tissues.)	Pound 0.019	43
10 per cent	Centner	0.388	Free	Free	Free	Free	44
100 kilogs .. 0.23	Fresh, centr. Prepared, salted, pickled, per centn'r	0.388 ted, pi 1.26	Free ckled, ...	Meats, hermetically sealed, per pound...0.04	Free	Smoked, dried, pickled, per pound . 0.009	45

Comparative table of import duties in the United States and European countries.

	ARTICLES.	UNITED STATES.	GREAT BRITAIN.	GERMAN ZOLL-VEREIN.	SWITZERLAND.
1	Medals and other collections of antiquity.	Free	Free	Free	Centner...$2.93
2	Medicinal preparations, n. o. p	40 per cent	Free	Centner...$2.40	Centner....0.68
3	Medicines, patent	50 per cent	Free	Centner... 2.40	Centner....0.68
4	Medicinal roots and leaves, barks, flowers, plants, and seeds, not otherwise spec'd.	20 per cent	Free	Centner... 0.36	Centner....0.68
5	Metal, plated	35 per cent	Free	Centner... 2.88	Centner....0.29
6	Metallic pens	Gross 0.10, &25p.c	Free	Centner... 7.20	Centner....1.56
7	Metals, unmanufact'r'd, not otherwise provided for.	20 per cent	Free	Crude, free; in sh'ts centner.. 1.26	Centner .. 0.145
8	Melting pots, if earthen	25 per cent	Free	Free	15 centner. 0.12
9	or glue pots	35 per cent	Free	Free	15 centner. 0.12
10	Mercury, or quicksilver	15 per cent	Free	Free	Centner .. 0.68
11	all preparations of	20 per cent	Free	Centner .. 2.40	Centner .. 0.68
12	Merino shawls, body worst'd or combed wool, n. o. p. f.	40 per cent. and pound ...$0.40	Free	Centner ..18.00	Centner .. 2.93
13	Manila hemp	Ton 25.00	Free	Free	Centner .. 0.06
14	Mica, (mineral substance)	20 per cent	Free	Free	Centner .. 0.058
15	Milk of roses	50 per cent	Free	Centner .. 1.24	Centner .. 2.93
16	Millinery of all kinds	35 per cent	Free	Centner ...21.60	Centner .. 2.93
17	Mills, coffee	35 per cent	Free	Centner .. 1.92	Centner .. 1.56
18 19	Miniature cases, ivory } sheets, ivory }	35 per cent	Free	Centner .. 2.88	Centner .. 2.93
20	Miniatures	10 per cent	Free	Free	Free
21	Mineral and bituminous substances in a crude state, not otherwise provided for.	20 per cent	Free	Free	Centner .. 0.058
22	Mineral blue	30 per cent	Free	Free	Centner .. 0.68
23	salt, crude	100 pounds 0.18	Free	Free	Centner .. 0.058
24	water	25 per cent., and bottle.... 0.03 In cask, 30 p. c't.	Free	Free	Centner .. 0.29
25	Mock pearls	40 per cent	Free	Centner ..10.60	Centner .. 2.93
26	Models of invention	Free	Free	Free	Free
27	Molasses and melada	Gallon 0.08	Free	Centner .. 1 80	Centner .. 0.29
28	concentrated	Pound 0.02½	Free	Centner .. 1 80	Centner .. 0.29
29	Moon seed (poppy seed)	20 per cent	Free	Free	Centner .. 0.058
30	Morocco skins	25 per cent	Free	Free	Centner .. 0.39
31	Morphine, (also salts of)	Ounce 2.50	Free	Centner .. 2.40	Centner .. 0.68
32	Mortars, brass	35 per cent	Free	Centner... 1.92	Centner .. 1.56
33	marble	50 per cent	Free	Centner .. 1.92	Centner .. 1.56
34	composition	35 per cent	Free	Centner .. 1.92	Centner .. 1.56
35 36	Moss, Iceland for beds	10 per cent 20 per cent	} Free	Free	Centner... 0.68
37	Mosaics, real, not set	10 per cent	Free	Centner .. 0.36	Centner .. 0.145
38	set	25 per cent	Free	Centner .. 2.88	Centner .. 2.93
39	Mother-of-pearl, shells.	Free	Free	Free	Centner .. 0.39
40	manufactures of	35 per cent	Free	Centner .. 2.88	Centner .. 1.56
41	buttons, metal eyes	30 per cent	Free	....	Centner... 1.56
42	Molds, button	30 per cent	Free	Centner .. 2.88	Centner .. 1.56
43	Mouse-traps, wood and wire	35 per cent	Free	Centner .. 1.92	Centner .. 1.56
44	Muffs, of fur	35 per cent	Free	Centner ..15.84	Centner... 2.93
45	Munjeet, (Indian madder)	Free	Free	Free	Centner .. 0.029
46 47 48 49 50	Muroxide Muriate of barytes gold tin strontium	25 per cent 20 per cent 20 per cent 30 per cent 20 per cent	Free Free Free Free Free	} Centner. 0.36	Centner .. 0.68
51	Music, in sheets or bound	20 per cent	Free	Free	Centner .. 0.09[illegible]

(*Duties expressed in gold dollars of the United States.*)—Continued.

	FRANCE.				RUSSIA.	NETHERLANDS.	
	General tariff.		In treaty with Great Britain, &c.				
	In French vessels.	In other vessels.	In vessels of treaty powers.	In other vessels.			
Free	......	......	......	......	Free	Free	1
}	Prohi	bited.	10 per	cent.	Pood $0.85	Free	2
					Pood 2.34	Free	3
100 kilogs	Free ..	$0.98	Free ..	$0.048	......	Free	4
100 kilogs	$19.50	20.95	$19.50	20.95	......	5 per cent	5
100 kilogs	78.00	86.00	19.50	20.95	Pound 0.23	5 per cent	6
Minerals not enumerated	Free...	Free...	Free...	Free...	Free	Free	7
......	......	......	......	......	Free	......	8
100 kilogs	......	......	Free...	0.048	Free	1 per cent	9
100 kilogs	0.195	0.97	Free...	0.048	Free	Free	10
100 kilogs	Prohi	bited.	10 per	cent.	Pood 0.85	Free	11
See Manuf. of wool	......	......	......	......	Pound 2.34	5 per cent	12
......	Free...	Free...	Free...	Free...	Free	Free	13
......	Free...	Free...	Free...	Free...	Free	Free	14
See Perfumeries	......	......	......	......	Pood 3.12	Free	15
As material	......	......	......	......	35 per cent	5 per cent	16
......	15 per	cent.	10 per	cent.	Pood 2.34	5 per cent	17
			10 per	cent, or	} Pound 0.85	} 5 per cent	18
As fancy articles, 100 kil.	Prohi	bited. }	11.70	12.76		5 per cent	19
......	Free...	Free...	Free...	Free...	Free	Free	20
......	Free...	Free...	Free...	Free...	Free	Free	21
......	Free...	Free...	Free...	Free...	Pood 0.85	Free	22
......	Free...	Free...	Free...	Free...	Free	Free	23
......	Free...	Free...	Free...	Free...	Bottle 0.015	Glass, 100 bot $0.20 Stone, do... 0.10	24
......	Prohi	bited.	10 per	cent.	Pood 1.28	5 per cent	25
......	Free...	Free...	Free...	Free...	Free	Free	26
Molasses of 50 per cent. s	accharin	e, 100 k.	2.15	......	Pood 0.85	Of more than 10 p.c.	27
Over 50 per cent., as ra	w sugar.				Pood 0.85	sugar, 100 k. 6.15	28
						Less than 10 p. cent. sugar, 100 k. 1.64	
100 kilogs	Free...	0.39	Free...	0.018	Free	} Free	29
100 kilogs	Prohi	bited.	11.70	12.76	Free		30
......	Prohi	bited.	5 per	cent.	Pood 7.80		31
100 kilogs	19.50	20.95	3.90	4.29	} Prohibited.	5 per cent	32
100 kilogs	7.80	8.58	0.29	0.24		Free	33
100 kilogs	Prohi	bited.	3.90	4.29		5 per cent	34
{	Free...	Free ..	Free...	Free...	Free	} Free	35
{	Free...	Free ..	Free...	Free...	......		36
......	Free...	Free ..	Free...	Free...	Free		37
......	Prohi	bited.	10 per	cent.	Pound 1.72	5 per cent	38
{ Raw, 100 kilogs { Cleaned	Free... Free...	0.78 1.56	....	....	Free	Free	39
As mercury, 100 kilogs	19.50	20.95	10 per	cent.	Pound 0.85	} 5 per cent	40
As mercury, 100 kilogs	19.50	20.95	10 per	cent.	......		41
100 kilogs	2.53	2.78	2.53	2.78	Pood 0.78		42
As mercury, 100 kilogs	19.50	20.95	10 per	cent.	Pood 2.34		43
......	Prohi	bited.	10 per	cent.	35 per cent		44
100 kilogs	0.97	1.07	0.97	1.07	Free	} Free	45
							46
							47
See Chemicals not enum	erated	......	......	......	Pood 0.85		48
							49
							50
100 kilogs	58.00	61.20	0.39	0.43	Free	5 per cent	51

Comparative table of import duties in the United States and European countries.

	ARTICLES.	ITALY.			SPAIN.	PORTUGAL.
			General tariff.	Tariff in treaty with France, &c.		
1	Medals and other collections of antiquity.	Free............	......	......	Free...............	Free ....
2	Medicinal preparations, n. o. p	100 kilogs......	$1. 95	$0. 39	20 per cent.........	5 per cent........
3	Medicines, patent				Of secret composition... Prohibited.	
4	Medicinal roots and herbs, barks, flowers, plants, and seeds, not otherwise spec'd.	Roots, 100 kilogs Bark, 100 kilogs. Seeds, 100 kilogs	1. 95 1. 95 1. 17	0. 39 0. 39 Free.	100 kilogs..$2. 00	Drugs, crude, and seeds, 5 per cent.
5	Metal, plated	As metal unmanu	factur	ed ...	100 kilogs....10. 00	Kilogramme $0. 0027
6	Metallic pens	100 kilogs.......	9. 75	11. 26	Kilogramme . 0. 60	Kilogramme . 0. 162
7	Metals, unmanufact'r'd, not otherwise provided for.	100 kilogs.......	0. 78	0. 78	Minerals, free...... Bronze, 100 k. 2. 00	Free ....
8	Melting pots, if earthen	....	......	......	100 kilogs .. 0. 30	Kilog......... 0. 216
9	or glue pots	100 kilogs	0. 195	0. 23		Kilogs 0. 216
10	Mercury, or quicksilver....	100 kilogs	3. 90	Free .	20 per cent.........	5 per cent..........
11	all preparations of	100 kilogs	1. 95	0. 78	20 per cent.........	Oxide of, kil'g 0. 054
12	Merino shawls, body worst'd or combed wool, n. o. p. f.	As tissues of wool	......	......	50 per cent. above duty on tissues.	Double duties of tissues.
13	Manilla hemp..............	Free	......	......	100 kilogs.... 2. 00	Kilogs 0. 004
14	Mica, (mineral substance) ..	100 kilogs	0. 48	Free .	100 kilogs.... 0. 50	Free ....
15	Milk of roses	100 kilogs	11. 70	10 p.c.	See Perfumery.....	20 per cent..........
16	Millinery of all kinds	As material of wh	ich m	ade ..	50 per cent. above duty on material.	Double duties of material.
17	Mills, coffee................	100 kilogs	1. 56	1. 80	100 kilogs.... 1. 50	Kilogs 0. 081
18	Miniature cases, ivory......	As mercury	......	......	Kilog......... 2. 50	20 per cent.........
19	sheets, ivory......	As mercury	......	......	Kilog......... 2. 50	20 per cent.........
20	Miniatures.................	Free	......	......	Free	Free ....
21	Mineral and bituminous substances in a crude state, not otherwise prov'd for.	Free	......	......	Ton......... 0. 05	Free ....
22	Mineral blue...............	100 kilogs	1. 95	0. 78	100 kilogs.... 1. 50	Kilogs 0. 0054
23	salt, crude.........	100 kilogs	0. 39	......	100 kilogs.... 0. 65	Free ....
24	water	100 kilogs	0. 195	Free .	Free...............	Kilog......... 0. 01
25	Mock pearls...............	Per cent.........	1	10	100 kilogs.... 9. 00	Kilogs 0. 54
26	Models of invention........	Free	......	......	Free...............	Free ....
27	Molasses and melada.......	100 kilogs	1. 17	1. 36	Not enumerated in this tariff.	Kilogs 0. 0216
28	concentrated	100 kilogs	2. 93	0. 39		Kilog........ 0. 0216
29	Moon seed, (poppy seed) ...	100 kilogs	0. 195	Free .	100 kilogs.... 0. 32	Kilogs....... 0. 0016
30	Morocco skins	Raw, free	......	......	100 kilogs.... 1. 50	Kilogs....... 0. 0075
31	Morphine, (also salts of) ...	100 kilogs	1. 95	0. 39	20 per cent	5 per cent..........
32	Mortars, brass	100 kilogs	3. 90	3. 90	100 kilogs....25. 00	Kilogs 0. 27
33	marble	5 per cent........	......	Free .	100 kilogs.... 1. 50	Kilogs 0. 0108
34	composition	100 kilogs	2. 93	3. 38	100 kilogs....25. 00	Kilogs 0. 27
35	Moss, Iceland..............	Free	......	......	100 kilogs.... 2. 00	5 per cent..........
36	for beds	Free	......	......	100 kilogs.... 2. 00	5 per cent..........
37	Mosaics, real, not set.......	Per cent.........	1	Free .	100 kilogs.... 0. 075	½ per cent.........
38	set................	Per cent.........	1	Free .	See Jewelry	1 per cent..........
39	Mother of pearl, shells	Free	......	......	100 kilogs.... 0. 01	Free ....
40	manufactures of...	100 kilogs	19. 50	19. 50	Kilog......... 2. 50	Kilogs 0. 81
41	buttons, metal eyes	100 kilogs	19. 50	19. 50	Kilog......... 0. 40	Kilogs 0. 54
42	Moulds, button.............	As material man	ufactu	red ..	According to mate'l.	Kilogs 0. 054
43	Mouse traps, wood or wire..	100 kilogs	1. 36	1. 58	20 per cent.........	Kilogs 0. 054
44	Muffs, of fur...............	Common, kilog .. Fancy, kilog.....	0. 39 0. 78	100 k. 9. 75	20 per cent.........	Kilogs 0. 648
45	Munjeet, (Indian madder) ..	Free	......	......	100 kilogs.... 0. 50	5 per cent..........
46	Muroxide	100 kilogs	1. 95	0. 78	Kilog......... 0. 02	10 per cent.........
47	Muriate of barytes.........					
48	gold............					
49	tin					
50	strontium					
51	Music in sheets or bound....	100 kilogs	2. 93	2. 93	See Paper, printed .	Kilogs....... 0. 032

(*Duties expressed in gold dollars of the United States.*)—Continued.

Belgium.	Austria.			Denmark.	Sweden.	Norway.	
		General tariff.	Tariff in treaty.				
Free	Free			Free	Free	Free	1
Not alcoholic, free.	Centner	$7.20		Pound....$0.0013	Free	Free	2
							3
Free	Free			Pound.... 0.0013	Free	Free	4
Free	Free			Pound.... 0.091	Free	Pound $0.095	5
10 per cent	Centner	7.20	$7.20	Pound.... 0.091	Pound....$0.0689	Pound 0.082	6
Free	Free			Free	Free	Free	7
100 kilogs ..$0.29	Centner	0.12	Free.	Pound.... 0.0014	Free	Free	8
100 kilogs .. 0.29	Centner	0.12	Free.	Pound.... 0.0014	Free	Free	9
Free	Centner	7.20		Pound.... 0.0113	Free	Free	10
Free	Centner	7.20		Pound.... 0.0113	Free	Free	11
As tissues of wool.	See Clothing.			Double d'y of w'l'n tissues, p.. 0.364	See Clothing.	10 per cent. above duty on mater'l.	12
Free	Free			Free	Free	Free	13
Free	Free			Free	Free	Free	14
See Perfumeries.	See Perfumeri	es.		Pound.... 0.091	Pound.... 0.11	Free	15
10 per cent.	Same as cloth	ing.		Double duty of material.	See Clothing.	10 p. c. more than d'ty on material.	16
10 per cent.	Centner	2.40	2.16	Pound.... 0.017	10 per cent	Pound 0.027	17
10 per cent.	See Ivory ma	nufac	tured.	Pound.... 0.091	Pound..... 0.138	Pound 0.158	18
10 per cent				Pound.... 0.091		Pound 0.158	19
Free	Free			Free	Free	Free	20
Free	Free.			Free	Free	Free	21
Free	Free			Pound.... 0.028	Free	Pound 0.0045	22
Free	Free			Free	Free	Free	23
Free	Free			Free	Free	Free	24
10 per cent	Centner	5.76		10 per cent	(Glass) p'd. 0.041	Pound 0.054	25
Free	Free			Free	Free	Free	26
For distil'ries, free.	Centner	1.512		Not above 25 p. c.	Pound..... 0.011	Pound 0.009	27
Of 50 p. c. saccharine, 100 k 2.92 Above 50 per c't. sugar as raw sug.	Centner	1.512		Pound.... 0.0098	Pound..... 0.011	Pound 0.009	28
100 kilogs.. 0.117	Free			Free	Free	Free	29
Free	Free			Free	(Prepar'd) p 0.055	Free	30
Free	Centner	7.20		Pound.... 0.0113	Free	Free	31
10 per cent	See Copper or	brass		Pound.... 0.045	Pound..... 0.041	Pound 0.045	32
10 per cent	See Manufactu	res of	stone.	Pound.... 0.0028	Free	Free	33
10 per cent	See Copper or	brass		Pound.... 0.045	As brass	Pound 0.045	34
							35
Free	Free			Free	Free	Free	36
							37
5 per cent	See Jewelry			Pound.... 0.091	Pound..... 0.138	Pound 0.109	38
Free	Raw, free .. Cut, centner	 0.388		Free Pound.... 0.091	Free	Free	39
10 per cent	Centner	24.00	14.40	Pound.... 0.091	Pound 0.0964	Pound 0.109	40
10 per cent	Centner	24.00	14.40	Free	Pound..... 0.138	Pound 0.109	41
10 per cent	See Lead			Pound.... 0.017	Accord'g to mat'l.	Pound 0.045	42
100 kilogs. 0.78 or 10 per cent.	Centner	3.60	2.16	Pound.... 0.091	10 per cent	Pound 0.017	43
10 per cent	Centner	36.00	24.00	Free	50 p. c. additional to duty on fur.	Pound 0.109	44
Free	Free			Pound.... 0.0113	Free		45
					Free		46
							47
Free	See Chemicals			Pound.... 0.0113	See Chemicals	Free	48
							49
							50
Free	Free			Free	Free		51

Comparative table of import duties in the United States and European countries.

	ARTICLES.	UNITED STATES.	GREAT BRITAIN.	GERMAN ZOLL-VEREIN.	SWITZERLAND.
1	Musical instruments	30 per cent	Free	Centner . . $2.88	Centner . . $1.56
2	Musical instruments, strings of gut.	30 per cent	Free	Centner ... 0.36	Centner . . 1.56
3	part metal	35 per cent	Free	Centner ... 0.36	Centner ... 1.56
4	Mushrooms prepared	35 per cent	Free	Centner ... 5.04 raw, free.	Centner . . 2.93 raw 0.145
5	Musk	50 per cent	Free	Centner ... 0.36	Centner ... 0.68
6	Musket bayonets and barrels	45 per cent	Free	Centner ... 1.92	Centner . . 0.39
7	Muskets, bullets, rods, stocks	35 per cent	Free	Centner ... 1.92	Centner . . 0.39
8	Mustard, manufactured	Pound $0.16	Free	Centner ... 5.04	Centner ... 0.68
9	ground, in bulk	Pound 0.12	Free	Centner ... 5.04	Centner ... 0.145
10	seed	Pound 0.03	Free	Free	Centner ... 0.145
11	Myrrh, gum, crude	20 per cent	Free	Free	Centner ... 0.68
12	refined	20 per cent	Free	Free	Centner . . 0.68
13	Myrobolan, nut for dyeing	Free	Free	Free	Centner ... 0.057
14	Nails, brass, and composit'n.	35 per cent	Free	Centner ... 0.96	Centner ... 0.68
	Copper, pure or chief mat'l.	45 per cent	Free		
15	Nails, iron, cut	Pound 0.01½	Free	Centner ... 0.96	Centner ... 0.68
16	wrought	Pound 0.02½	Free	Centner ... 0.96	Centner . . 0.68
17	Naphtha, refined	Gallon 0.40	Free	Free	Centner . . 0.68
18	Naples soap	25 per cent., and per pound. 0.10	Free	Centner ... 2.40	Centner ... 0.145
19	Narcotine, (medical preparation.)	40 per cent	Free	Free	Centner . . 0.68
20	Natron, (carbonate of soda.)	Pound 0.00½	Free	Centner . . 0.36	Centner ... 0.057
21	Needles	25 per cent	Free	For sewing, centner.. 7.20	Centner ... 1.56
22	crochet, knitting and sewing machine.	35 per cent., and mille . .. 1.00	Free	All others, centner 2.88	Centner ... 1.56
23	Nets, fishing, seines	Pound 0.06½	Free	Unbleached, centner .. 0.36	Centner ... 1.56
24	dip or scoop	35 per cent	Free	Bleached, centner 2.88	Centner ... 1.56
25	Nickel	15 per cent	Free	Free	Centner ... 0.68
26	Nippers, iron	35 per cent	Free	Centner ... 2.88	Centner . . 0.68
27	Nitrate of potash or saltpeter, unrefined.	Pound 0.02½	Free	Free	Centner . . 0.057
28	As above, refined	Pound 0.03	Free	Free	Centner . . 0.057
29	partly refined	Pound 0.02	Free	Free	Centner . . 0.057
30	Nitrate of barytes	20 per cent	Free	Centner . . 0.36	Centner . . 0.68
31	iron	20 per cent	Free	Free	Centner . . 0.145
32	silver	40 per cent	Free	Centner . . 0.72	Centner . . 0.68
33	strontium	20 per cent	Free	Centner . . 2.40	Centner . . 0.68
34	tin	20 per cent	Free	Centner . . 0.40	Centner . . 0.145
35	lead	Pound 0.03	Free	Centner . . 0.72	Centner ... 0.68
36	Nitre, mur., tin	20 per cent	Free	Centner ... 0.48	Centner . . 0.145
37	refined soda	Pound 0.01	Free	Centner ... 0.48	Centner . . 0.058

(*Duties expressed in gold dollars of the United States.*)—Continued.

FRANCE.					RUSSIA.	NETHERLANDS.	
	General tariff.		In treaty with Great Britain, &c.				
	In French vessels.	In other vessels.	In vessels of treaty powers.	In other vessels.			
Fifes, flageolets, each Flutes, triangles, each Tamborines, each Trumpets & violins, e. Clarionets Bass, each Harmonicas and transportable organs, each Pianos, square, each other Church organ, each	$0.12 0.145 0.29 0.58 0.97 1.45 3.51 58.50 78.00 78.00	$0.12 0.145 0.29 1.58 0.78 1.45 3.51 58.50 78.00 78.00	Free... 10 per	$0.48 cent.	Piano-fortes and organs not portable, each .... $31.20 Ordinary and church organs, and harps each .... 7.80 All not specially enumerated, p'nd. 0.117	5 per cent	1
....	15 per	cent.	10 per	cent.	Pound 0.08	5 per cent	2
....	15 per	cent.	10 per	cent.	Pound 0.08	5 per cent	3
100 kilogs .... green	0.58 Free...	0.64 Free...	0.58 Free...	0.64 Free...	In vinegar, pood 3.12 Oil or salted, or dried, pood 0.31	Pickled, 5 per cent. Hermetically sealed, like confect'y.	4
100 kilogs	0.39	0.43	0.39	0.43	Pood 9.36	Free	5
See Arms and ammunition ..					Prohibited	5 per cent	6
						5 per cent	7
100 kilogs	4.87	5.35	0.97	1.06	Pood 2.34	Free	8
....					Pood 2.34	Free	9
....	Free...	Free...	Free...	Free...	Free	Artificial mustard, 100 kilogs.. 10.25	10
100 kilogs	Free...	0.39	0.39	0.39	Pood 0.23	Free	11
....					Pood 0.23	Free	12
Dry, not comfit	Free...	0.78			Pood 0.04	Free	13
Myrobolan, Indian plum, 100 kilogs.	12.09	13.18					
Nails, by machine, 100 kil	Prohi	bited.	1.56	1.72	Pood 0.78	5 per cent	14
Nails, by hand, 100 kil..	Prohi	bited.	2.34	2.57	Pood 0.78	100 kilogs.... 0.30	15
....					Pood 0.78	100 kilogs.... 0.30 Zinc, 100 kil 0.12	16
See Oils, (petroleum)...					Pood 0.12	Free	17
See Soap					Pood 4.29	100 kilogs.... 2.46	18
....	Prohi	bited.	10 per	cent.	Pood 0.85	See Chemicals and other preparations.	19
....	Prohi	bited.	10 per	cent.	Pood 0.07	Free	20
Sewing, less than 5 centimeters in length, 100 kilogs.	97.50	106.00	39.00	41.43	Sewing, pound. 0.39	5 per cent	21
Over 5 centimeters in length, 100 kilogs.	39.00	43.00	19.50	20.95	Others, pound.. 0.195	5 per cent	22
100 kilogs	4.87	5.32	3.90	4.29	Pood 0.31	5 per cent	23
100 kilogs	4.87	5.32	3.90	4.29	Pood 0.31	5 per cent	24
Ore and speiss, pure or alloyed.	Free...	Free...	Free...	Free...	Free	Free	25
Rolled or drawn, 100 kil.	19.50	20.95	1.95	2.14			
100 kilogs	24.37	26.27	2.92	3.20	Pood 0.62	5 per cent	26
100 kilogs	Free...	0.78	Free...	0.048			27
100 kilogs	Free...	0.78	Free...	0.048	Pood 0.039	Free	28
....			Free...				29
Nitrate of lime, 100 kil..			Free...	0.048	Pood 0.39	Free	30
100 kilogs			Free...		Pood 0.16	Free	31
100 kilogs			1.25	1.36	Pood 0.23	Free	32
....			1.25		Pood 0.36	Free	33
....			1.25		Pood 0.31	Free	34
....			1.25		Pood 0.31	Free	35
See Chemicals not enum	erated .				Pood 0.85	Free	36
100 kilogs	5.16	5.77			Pood 0.156	Free	37

Comparative table of import duties in the United States and European countries.

	ARTICLES.	ITALY.			SPAIN.	PORTUGAL.
			General tariff.	Tariff in treaty with France, &c.		
1	Musical instruments........	Organs for ch's, 100 kilogs. Others, portable, each, or Pianos, each ... Other instrum'ts not enum'd, e'h.	$1.95 0.78 5 per 1.36 0.39 or 5 p	$1.95 0.78 cent. 1.36 0.39 er ct.	Pianos, each $50.00 Other scientific instrum'ts, 10 p. ct.	Harps, each $10.80 Pianos, e'h 24.84 All not specified, 25 per cent.
2	Musical instruments, strings of gut.	100 kilogs	9.75	9.75	20 per cent	Kilogramme . 0.54
3	part metal............	100 kilogs	9.75	9.75	20 per cent	Kilogramme . 0.324
4	Mushrooms prepared.......	100 kilogs .... 100 kilogs	2.93 2.93	Free. Free.	100 kilogs.... 0.25	5 per cent.......... Raw, free.
5	Musk	Kilogramme.....	5.85	100 k. 0.39	Kilogramme . 0.30	Kilogramme .16.20
6	Muskets, bayonets, barrels..	See Arms	......	......	Kilogramme . 1.00	30 per cent.........
7	bullets, rods, stocks	See Arms	......	......	100 kilogs.... 1.50	30 per cent.........
8	Mustard, manufactured.....	100 kilogs	2.92	0.975	100 kilogs.... 2.00	Kilogramme . 0.27
9	ground, in bulk...	100 kilogs	2.92	0.975	100 kilogs.... 0.32	Kilogramme . 0.086
10	seed..............	100 kilogs	1.17	Free.	100 kilogs.... 0.32	Kilogramme . 0.054
11	Myrrh, gum, crude	100 kilogs	2.93	0.39	100 kilogs.... 2.00	Free...............
12	refined	100 kilogs	2.93	0.39	100 kilogs.... 2.00	Free...............
13	Myrobolan, nut for dyeing..	100 kilogs	0.39	Free.	100 kilogs.... 0.32	20 per cent.........
14	Nails, brass, copper, and composition.	100 kilogs	2.34	2.34	100 kilogs....10.00	Kilogramme . 0.216
15	Nails, iron, cut.............	100 kilogs	0.195	0.22	100 kilogs.... 4.00	Kilogramme . 0.108
16	wrought.............	100 kilogs	0.195	0.22	100 kilogs.... 4.00	Kilogramme . 0.108
17	Naphtha, refined...........	Free	......	......	100 kilogs.... 0.05	Kilogramme .0.0108
18	Naples' soap...............	100 kilogs	11.70	1.17	100 kilogs.... 3.75	Kilogramme . 0.027
19	Narcotine, (medical preparation.)	100 kilogs	1.95	0.78	20 per cent.........	5 per cent..........
20	Natron, (carbonate of soda.)	100 kilogs	0.097	0.097	Kilogramme . 0.02	Free ....
21	Needles	Sewing, 100 kil..	9.75	11.26	Kilogramme . 0.60	Kilogramme . 0.054
22	crochet, knitting, and sewing machine.	100 kilogs	3.90	4.50	Kilogramme . 0.60	Kilogramme . 0.054
23	Net, fishing, seines.........	100 kilogs	2.34	2.80	100 kilogs.... 5.50	See Yarn of flax..
24	dip and scoop.........	100 kilogs	2.34	2.80	100 kilogs.... 5.50	
25	Nickel	In ingots, 100 kil. Wire, 100 kilogs. Manufactures of, 100 kilogs......	0.78 5.85 19.50	0.78 1.95 19.50	Crude, free .... Plate, &c., 100 kilogrammes .. 0.30	Cast and ball, free; otherwise as brass.
26	Nippers, iron	100 kilogs	1.56	1.80	100 kilogs.... 1.50	Kilogramme . 0.189
27	Nitrate of potash or saltpeter, unrefined.	100 kilogs	1.95	Free.	100 kilogs.... 0.75	Kilogramme . 0.013
28	As above, refined..........	100 kilogs	1.95	Free.	100 kilogs.... 0.75	Kilogramme . 0.013
29	partly refined ...	100 kilogs	1.95	Free.	100 kilogs.... 0.75	Kilogramme . 0.013
30	Nitrate of barytes	See Chemicals n	ot enu	mera-	Kilog 0.02	10 per cent ....
31	iron	ted.				
32	silver	100 kilogs	0.78	......		
33	strontium	See Chemicals n	ot enu	mera-		
34	tin..............	ted.				
35	lead					
36	Nitre, mur., tin............					
37	refined soda.........	Free	......	......	100 kilogs.... 0.20	Kilogramme . 0.02

(Duties expressed in gold dollars of the United States.)—Continued.

BELGIUM.	AUSTRIA.			DENMARK.	SWEDEN.	NORWAY.	
		General tariff.	Tariff in treaty.				
6 per cent	Centner	$4.80	$3.60	Pianos, organs, accordeons, and similar, 10 p. c. Others, p. $0.091	Guitars, violins, drums, trump'ts, &c., each 0.2756; Flutes, clar'n't's, &c., each 0.138; Pianos, e. 11.024; Gr'd do., e. 16.54; Musical boxes, each ... 0.138; Org'ns, harmoniums, 5 per cent.	Pianos, guitars, violins, violincellos, contrabassos, e. 0.273; Flutes, clarionets, hautboys, &c., each 0.137; Bows for instruments, e. 0.054	1
10 per cent	Of gut, covered, cent'r.	24.00	14.40	Pound.... 0.091	Pound.... 0.138	Pound ... 0.159	2
10 per cent	Steelwire, cen Others, cent'r.	2.40 14.40	1.92 14.40	Pound.... 0.0056	Pound.... 0.0275	Pound ... 0.036	3
100 kilogs .. 1.95	Centner	0.388	Free.	Free .... Hermetic, sealed, pound... 0.04	Free	Free .... Hermetic, sealed, pound ... 0.05	4
Free.............	Centner	2.52	1.44	Pound.... 0.0113	Free	Free	5
Free	Centner	7.20	7.20	Pound.... 0.091	Pound.... 0.055	Pound ... 0.073	6
As metal manuf'd.	Centner	1.68	1.20	Pound.... 0.017	See material manufactures.	Rods, &c., pound .. 0.027	7
....	Centner	3.88	3.60	Pound.... 0.04	Pound.... 0.0689	Pound ... 0.054	8
15 per cent	Centner	3.88	3.60	Pound.... 0.04	Pound.... 0.0689	Pound ... 0.063	9
100 kilogs.. 0.117	Centner	0.38	Free.	Pound.... 0.017	Pound.... 0.0082	Pound ... 0.009	10
Free	Centner	2.52	1.44		Free...........	Free	11
Free	Centner	2.52	1.44	Pound .. 0.0113	Free...........	Free	12
Free	Free	......	......		Free...........	Free	13
10 per cent	Centner	2.88	1.92	Pound.... 0.017	Pound.... 0.041	Pound ... 0.095	14
100 kilogs .. 0.78	Centner	1.92	1.92	Pound.... 0.0014	See Iron.........	Pound ... 0.011	15
100 kilogs .. 0.78	Centner	1.92	1.92	Pound.... 0.0014	See Iron.........	Pound ... 0.011	16
Free	Centner	0.36	0.36	Pound.... 0.017	Free	Free	17
100 kilogs .. 1.17	Centner	7.56	......	Pound.... 0.091	Pound.... 0.033	Pound ... 0.013	18
Free	Centner	7.20	......	Pound.... 0.0113	Free	Free	19
Free	Free	......	......	Free	Free	Free	20
Free	Sewing, cent'r	12.00	7.20	Pound.... 0.017	Pound.... 0.0275	Pound ... 0.027	21
10 per cent	Centner	7.20	5.36	Pound.... 0.017	Pound.... 0.0275	Pound ... 0.027	22
10 per cent	See Fishing nets ...		......	Pound .. 0.091	Free	10 per ct. above duty on mat'l.	23
				Pound .. 0.091	Free		24
10 per cent	Free	......	......	Free, manufactured as copper.	Free	Free	25
Free	Centner	2.88	2.16	Pound.... 0.017	Pound.... 0.041	Pound ... 0.027	26
100 kilogs .. 0.78	Free	......	......	Pound.... 0.0028	Free		27
Free	Centner	0.36	0.36	Pound.... 0.0028	Free		28
Free	Centner	0.36	0.36	Pound.... 0.0028	Free		29
							30
							31
						Free	32
Free	See Chemic'ls	......	......	Pound. .. 0.0113	See Chemicals ...		33
							34
							35
							36
Free	Free	......	......	Free	Free		37

Comparative table of import duties in the United States and European countries.

	ARTICLES.	UNITED STATES.	GREAT BRITAIN.	GERMAN ZOLL-VEREIN.	SWITZERLAND.
1	Nitre, unrefined soda	Pound $0. 01	Free	Centner .. $0. 18	Centner .. $0. 058
2	Nitric ether, spirits of	Pound 0. 50	Free	Centner ... 2. 40	Centner ... 0. 68
3	Nobs or knobs, glass, with shanks or rivets.	40 per cent	Free	Centner ... 1. 88	Centner ... 1. 56
4	As above, of steel	45 per cent	Free	Centner ... 2. 88	Centner ... 0. 68
5	Norfolk latches	35 per cent	Free	Centner ... 2. 88	Centner .. 0. 68
6	Noyeau	Gallon 2. 50	Free	See Spirits	Centner ... 0. 68
7	Nut-galls	Free	Free	Free	Centner .. 0. 68
8	Nutmegs	Pound 0. 50	Free	Centner .. 4. 68	Centner .. 0. 68
9	Nuts, not otherwise provided for.	Pound 0. 02	Free	Free	Centner .. 0. 057
10	Nuts for dyeing, crude	Free	Free	Free	Centner .. 0. 057
11	Newspapers	25 per cent	Free	Free	Free
12	Nux vomica	Free	Free	Centner ... 2. 40	Centner .. 0. 68
13	Oakum and junk	Free		Free	Centner ... 0. 058
14	Oats	Bushel 0. 10		Free	Centner ... 0. 039
15	Oatmeal	10 per cent		Centner ... 0. 36	Centner ... 0. 097
16	Ochres, dry, n. o. p	100 lbs 0. 50		Free	Centner ... 0. 145
17	in oil	100 lbs 1. 50		Free	Centner ... 0. 68
18	Ochrey earths, dry	100 lbs 0. 50		Free	Centner ... 0. 145
19	in oil	100 lbs 1. 50		Free	Centner ... 0. 68
20	Odors or perfumes	50 per cent	Free	Centner ... 2. 40	Centner ... 2. 93
21	Oil cakes	20 per cent		Free	Centner ... 0. 97
22	cloth, table mats	45 per cent		Centner ... 0. 48	Centner ... 1. 56
23	lined with woollen	45 per cent		Centner ... 1. 44	
24	silk	60 per cent		Centner ... 1. 44	Centner .. 1. 56
25	floor, painted, &c	35 per cent		Centner ... 1. 44	
26	Oil, Harlaem	50 per cent		Oil of all kinds in bottles, &c., centner .. 0. 60	Oil, fish, centner 0. 058
	allspice	50 per cent		In barrels, centner 0. 36	Not medicinal, centner .. 0. 097
	absynthe, or wormwood	50 per cent		Palm and cocoanut oil, centner.. .... 0. 12	Etherial, centner 2. 93
	of almonds, fixed or expressed	Pound 0. 10		Fish oil, centner 0. 36	
	essential	Pound 1. 50		Medicinal oil and perfumed, centner 2. 40	
	of amber, or amber crude	Pound 0. 10			
	rectified	Pound 0. 20			
	animali	20 per cent			
	of aniseed, essential or essence of	Pound 0. 50			
	bear's	50 per cent	Free		
	bay, fixed or expressed	Pound 0. 20			
	cajaput	Pound 0. 25			
	camomile	50 per cent			
	of cassia	Pound 1. 00			
	caryophil	Pound 2. 00			
	of caraway	Pound 0. 50			
	cinnamon	Pound 2. 00			
	cloves	Pound 2. 00			
	cocoanuts	10 per cent			
	croton, fixed or expressed	Pound 1. 00			
	citronella	Pound 0. 50			
27	petroleum, crude	Gallon 0. 20	Free	Free	Centner ... 0. 097
	refined	Gallon 0. 40			
28	Olives, in oil	30 per cent	Free	Centner ... 1. 44	Centner ... 2. 93
29	Onions	10 per cent	Free	Free	Centner ... 0. 029
30	Opium	Pound 2. 50	Free	Centner ... 0. 36	Centner ... 0. 68
31	prepared for smoking	100 per cent	Free	Centner ... 2. 40	Centner ... 0. 68
32	extract of	100 per cent	Free	Centner ... 2. 40	Centner ... 0. 68

(*Duties expressed in gold dollars of the United States.*)—Continued.

	FRANCE.				RUSSIA.	NETHERLANDS.	
	General tariff.		In treaty with Great Britain, &c.				
	In French vessels.	In other vessels.	In vessels of treaty powers.	In other vessels.			
100 kilogs	$3.70	$4.08			Pood $5.078	Free	1
artificial soda of 60 degrees, 100 kilogs.			$0.36	$0.42			
Less than 60 degrees, 100 kilogs.			1.14	1.25			
See Chemicals not enum	erated				Pood 0.85	Ether, liter $0.51	2
Fancy goods, 100 kilogs	19.50	20.95	10 per	cent.	Pood 3.02	5 per cent	3
100 kilogs	Prohi	bited.	3.90	4.29	Pood 3.51	5 per cent	4
					Pood 0.62	5 per cent	5
See Liqueurs					See Liqueurs	Liter 0.51	6
100 kilogs	Free	0.78	Free	0.048	Free		7
In shell, 100 kilogs	19.50	21.45			Pood 1.95	5 per cent	8
without shell, 100 kil.	29.25	31.20					
	Free	Free	Free	Free	Pood 0.39	Free	9
	Free	Free	Free	Free	Pood 0.04	Free	10
	Free	Free	Free	Free	Free	Free	11
See Chemicals not enum	erated				Pood 0.16	Free	12
	Free	Free	Free	Free	Free	Free	13
	Free	Free	Free	Free	Free	Free	14
	Free	Free	Free	Free	Pood 0.02	100 kilogs 0.16	15
100 kilogs	Free	0.195			Pood 0.04	Free	16
					Pood 0.85	Free	17
100 kilogs	Free	0.195			Pood 0.04	Free	18
					Pood 0.85	Free	19
See Perfumery					Pood 3.12	5 per cent	20
	Free	Free	Free	Free	Free	100 kilogs 0.06	21
See Material, (silk,)					Pound 0.08	5 per cent	22
See Material, (flax,)					Pound 0.08	5 per cent	23
					Pound 0.78	5 per cent	24
					Pound 0.08	5 per cent	25
Oil, fish, 100 kilogs	1.56	1.56	1.17	1.28	Olive or wood oil, and all vegetable oils not specially enumerated, pood 1.40 Essent'l oils, oils used in medicine and perfumery, pood 9.36 Cocoanut and palm oil, pood 0.39 Volatile oils, for lighting purposes, per pood 0.43 Oil of turpentine, pood 0.23 Oil of bitter almonds, prohibited.	Oil, salad; oil, beech; poppy oil, and all table oils; olive, photogene oil, and all sorts of rock oil; petroleum, 100 kilogs 0.23 All sorts of seed oil, sesam oil, and patent oil, 100 kilogrammes 0.51 Bergamot & lemon oil, oleum neroli, lavender, rose, and all oils for perfumery in original state, 1 per cent.	26
Fixed, pure, 100 kilogs.							
Fixed, pure olive	0.58	0.78	0.58	0.64			
Fixed pure palm, cocoanut	0.195	0.58	0.58	0.58			
Fixed pure other	1.17	1.36	1.17	1.28			
Fixed aromatic	0.19	0.21					
Volatile or essential, kilogramme							
Rose or rhodes wood	7.80	8.58	9.36	10.30			
Muscate, mace, cassia lignea, sassafras, cajaput, chamomile, valerian, and bitter almond, kilogramme	0.97	1.07					
All other	0.145	0.156	0.175	0.188			
Incl. rhodes wood, 100 kilogs			19.50	20.95			
100 kilogs	0.58	0.97			Pood 0.43	100 kilogs 0.23	27
100 kilogs	7.02	7.74	1.56	1.92	Pood 0.78	100 kilogs 10.25	28
100 kilogs	Free	0.048	Free	0.048	Free	Free	29
100 kilogs	39.00	41.43			Pood 7.80	Free	30
						Free	31
						Free	32

Comparative table of import duties in the United States and European countries.

	ARTICLES.	ITALY.			SPAIN.	PORTUGAL.
			General tariff.	Tariff in treaty with France, &c.		
1	Nitre, unrefined	Free	......	......	100 kilogs....$0.20	Free
2	Nitric ether, spirits of	100 kilogs	$0.78	$0.195	Kilogramme . 0.02	Kilogramme. $0.027
3	Nobs or knobs, glass, with shanks or rivets.	100 kilogs	9.75	9.75	100 kilogs.... 3.50	Kilogramme . 0.172
4	As above, of steel	100 kilogs	3.90	4.50	100 kilogs.... 3.50	Kilogramme . 0.162
5	Norfolk latches	100 kilogs	1.56	1.80	100 kilogs.... 1.50	Kilogramme . 0.162
6	Noyeau	Hectoliter	0.97	1.07	Liter 0.20	Decaliter 1.62
7	Nut-galls	100 kilogs	0.195	Free.	100 kilogs.... 0.30	Free
8	Nut-megs	In shell, 100 kil..	6.82	......	100 kilogs.... 0.50	Kilogramme . 0.108
		Not in shell, 100 k.	0.39	......		
9	Nuts, not otherwise provided for.	100 kilogs	0.195	Free.	100 kilogs.... 0.32	Free
10	Nuts for dyeing, crude	100 kilogs	0.195	Free	100 kilogs.... 0.32	Free
11	Newspapers	Free	......	......	Free	Free
12	Nux vomica	Free	......	......	100 kilogs.... 2.00	5 per cent
13	Oakum and junk	Free	......	......	100 kilogs.... 0.05	Free
14	Oats	100 kilogs	0.145	0.145	100 kilogs.... 0.52	100 kilogs.... 0.043
15	Oatmeal	100 kilogs	0.24	0.24	100 kilogs.... 1.04	100 kilogs.... 0.054
16	Ochres, dry, n. o. p	100 kilogs	0.45	Free.	100 kilogs.... 1.50	Kilogramme . 0.005
17	in oil	100 kilogs	1.95	0.78	100 kilogs.... 5.00	5 per cent
18	Ochry earths, dry	100 kilogs	0.48	Free.	100 kilogs.... 1.025	Kilogramme . 0.005
19	in oil	100 kilogs	1.95	0.78	100 kilogs.... 5.00	5 per cent
20	Odors or perfumes	See Perfumes	......	......	Kilogramme . 0.30	20 per cent
21	Oil cakes	....	......	......	100 kilogs.... 0.20	Kilogramme . 0.001
22	cloths, table mats	100 kilogs	9.75	9.75	Oil cloth for packing, 100 kilogrammes . 6.50 Other, kilogramme .. 0.20	Oil cloth, silk, 100 kilogs. 0.54 Other, floor, 100 kilogs. 0.054 Not enumerated, 100 kilogs. 0.81
23	lined with woolen	5 per cent	......	......		
24	silk	10 per cent	......	......		
25	floor, painted, &c.	10 per cent	......	......		
	Oils—Cont'd. (United States.)					
26	Oil, all essential, or essence, n. o. p., 50 per cent. of cogniacs, or ananthic ether, ounce....$4.00 of cubebs, pound.. 1.00	Oils, fixed olives, 100 kilogs	1.95	0.58	Oils of cocoa-nut, palm, linseed, and all of grains, or seeds, 100 kilogrammes.... 1.60 Train oil, per kilogramme .... 0.01 Table oils, 100 kilogrammes.... 5.00	Oil, codfish, and other fish oils, kilogramme .... 0.01 Others, not specifi'd, kilogramme 0.005 Oils fixed: liquid of Florence, kilogramme ....0.108 Not specified, decaliter .... 0.54 Of almonds, kilogramme .. 0.108 Of purifi'd rosin, kilogramme ...0.216 Of linseed, kilogramme ....0.043 Concrete, free. Volatile: of turpentine, kilog...0.005 Not specified, kilogramme 0.54
	of fennel, pound.. 0.50 of hartshorn, 50 per ct.	Fixed sesame and oth's for domestic use and burning, 100 kilogs..	1.95	1.17		
	of juglandium, 50 per ct. of juniper, pound.. 0.25 of laurel, fixed or expressed, pound.. 0.20	Linseed, palm, cocoa-nut, and beech, seal, &c., 100 kilogs	0.97	1.12		
	of mace, fixed or expressed, pound.. 0.50	Volatile of canella, cloves, rose, sassafras, kilog.	0.58	......		
	of mint, 50 per cent. of nuts, 50 per cent.	Of camphor, 100 kilogs	7.80	0.39		
	of palm-bean, 10 per ct. of palm, 10 per cent.	Of caoutchouc, 100 kilogs	3.90	......		
	of poppies, 20 per cent. of rue, 50 per cent. of rock, crude, gallon .... 0.20 of sage, 50 per cent. of savin, 50 per cent.	Others, n. e., kilogramme	0.12	Free.		
27	of petroleum, crude, gallon .... 0.20 *of petroleum, refined, gallon 0.40	100 kilogs	1.95	0.58	100 kilogs... 0.05 100 kilogs... 1.10	100 kilogs.. 0.005
28	Olives, in oil	100 kilogs	2.93	1.56	Kilogramme.. 0.20	Kilogramme . 0.037
29	Onions	Free	......	......	100 kilogs 0.25	Free
30	Opium	100 kilogs	0.487	......	20 per cent	Kilogramme . 0.648
31	prepar'd for smoking.	100 kilogs	0.487	......		Kilogramme . 0.648
32	extract of	100 kilogs	1.95	0.78		5 per cent

* For remainder of United States tariff on oil see note, pages 144 and 145.

(*Duties expressed in gold dollars of the United States.*)—Continued.

BELGIUM.	AUSTRIA.			DENMARK.	SWEDEN.	NORWAY.	
		General tariff.	Tariff in treaty.				
Free	Free	......	......	Free	Free	Free	1
See Ethers	See Ethers	......	......	Pound....$0.091	See Ethers	Free	2
10 per cent	Centner	$3.48	$1.92	Pound.... 0.091	Pound....$0.041	Pound ...$0.047	3
100 kilogs ..$0.78	Centner	7.20	5.76	Pound.... 0.017	Pound.... 0.068	Pound ... 0.027	4
100 kilogs .. 0.78	Centner	7.20	5.76	Pound.... 0.017	See Iron	Pound ... 0.027	5
See Spirits	See Spirits	......	......	Pot....... 0.061	See Spirits	Pot 0.218	6
....	Free			Free	Free	Free	7
Free	Centner	7.56	......	Pound.... 0.273	Pound.... 0.11	Pound ... 0.182	8
Free	Centner	0.388	Free.	Free	Free	Free	9
Free	Free	......	......	Free	Free	Free	10
Free	Free	......	......	Free	Free	Free	11
Free	Centner	0.388	Free.	Pound.... 0.0113	Free	Free	12
Free	Free	......	......	Free	Free (rows 13–19)	Free	13
100 kilogs .. 0.117	Centner	0.086	Free.	Free		Free	14
100 kilogs .. 0.23	Centner	0.388	Free.	Free		Free	15
Free	Free	......	......	Pound..... 0.005		Free	16
Free	Centner	0.388	Free.	Pound..... 0.028		Pound 0.027	17
Free	Free	......	......	Free		Free	18
Free	Centner	0.388	Free.	Pound..... 0.028		Pound 0.027	19
10 per cent	Centner	3.60	2.40	Pound..... 0.091	Pound..... 0.11	Free	20
Free	Centner	0.0288	Free.	Free	Free	Free	21
10 per cent (rows 22–25)	Fine, centner.	5.76	4.80	Pound ... 0.091	Same as tissue (rows 22–25)	All, pound. 0.056 (rows 22–25)	22
	Coarse, for packing, not print'd, centner	0.72	0.48	Pound ... 0.091			23
				Pound ... 0.273			24
				Pound ... 0.091			25
Oils, medicinal, and for perfumery, 10 per cent. Whale oil, sperm and other animal oils, free.	Oils: train oil, centner Oil in bottles or in jars, centner Oil of olives, centner Oil of cocoa-nut, centner Oil of palm, centner Oth's, not perfumed, centner Amber, caoutchouc, laurel oil, centner Oils, ethereal, n. o. e., centner	0.254 6.312 1.212 0.388 0.388 0.648 2.52 3.60	.... 0.36 1.44 2.40	Oils perfumed, pound ....0.068 All others, pound 0.017	Oils, mineral and medicinal, free. Olive, in barrels, pound ...0.0027 Olive, in bottles, pound ...0.0055 Oil of hemp, cocoa, palm, sp'rmaceti, pound... 0.0055 Other oils, not medicinal, pound ...0.0082 Oils volatile, vegetable essences, pound ...0.0689 Mineral oils, rectified, p'nd. 0.0055 Oil of turpentine, pound ...0.0082 Train oil, pound ...0.0027	Oils, ethereal, pound...0.0067 Oils perfumed, pound....0.273 Olive oil, in barrels, p'nd. 0.009 Palm, hemp, and cocoa-nut oil, pound...0.0067 Of linseed, rape, and spermaceti, pound....0.009 Camphene, paraffine, petroleum, pound...0.0067 Oleum ricini, free.	26
Free	Centner	0.36	......	Pound 0.017	Free Pound .. 0.0055	Pound .. 0.0067	27
100 kilogs .. 1.95	Centner	0.388	Free.	Pound 0.04	Pound 0.04	Pound.... 0.054	28
Free	Free	......	......	Free	Free	Free	29
Free	Centner	2.52	1.44	Pound.....0.0113	Free	Free	30
Free	Centner	2.52	1.44	Pound.....0.0113	Free	Free	31
See Extracts	See Extracts	......	......	Pound.....0.0113	Free	Free	32

Comparative table of import duties in the United States and European countries.

	ARTICLES.	UNITED STATES.	GREAT BRITAIN.	GERMAN ZOLL-VEREIN.	SWITZERLAND.
1	Orange crystals	20 per cent		Free	Centner ... $0.68
2	flowers	10 per cent		Centner ... $0.36	Centner ... 0.68
3	Oranges	25 per cent		Centner ... 1.44	Centner ... 0.12
4	in boxes, barrels, and casks.	25 per cent		Centner ... 1.44	Centner ... 0.12
5	Orange peel	10 per cent		Centner ... 2.88	Centner ... 0.145
6	issue peas	40 per cent		Centner ... 0.36	Centner ... 0.145
7	flower water	50 per cent	Free (1–12)	Free	Centner ... 2.93
8	Orchille, or orchello	10 per cent		Free	Centner ... 0.68
9	Ore, specimens, n. o. p	10 per cent		Free	Centner ... 0.028
10	copper	5 per cent		Free	Centner ... 0.028
11	silver and gold	Free		Free	Centner ... 0.028
12	Organs	30 per cent		Centner ... 2.88	Centner ... 0.058
	Ornaments:				
13	gilt wood	35 per cent	Free	Centner .. 10.80	Centner ... 1.56
14	gold paper	40 per cent	Free	Centner .. 16.80	Centner ... 1.56
15	for ladies' head-dresses,	50 per cent	Free	Centner .. 21.60	Centner ... 2.93
16	of silk.				
17	cut glass, chandeliers	40 per cent	Free	Centner ... 2.88	Centner ... 1.56
18	Ornamental feathers, manufactured.	50 per cent	Free	Centner ... 0.36	Centner ... 2.93
19	Orpiment	20 per cent	Free	Free	Centner ... 1.45
20	Orris root, or Iris root	Free	Free	Free	Centner ... 1.45
21	Osiers, for basket makers' use.	30 per cent	Free	Free	Free
22	Ostrich plumes, raw	25 per cent	Free	Centner ... 0.36	Centner ... 2.93
23	Oxymuriate of lime	20 per cent	Free	Free	Centner ... 0.68
24	Oxymuriate of chlorate of potasse.	Pound ... $0.06	Free	Free	Centner ... 0.68
25	Oysters	Free	Free	Centner ... 1.44	Centner ... 0.68
26	Packthread	40 per cent	Free	Centner ... 2.88	Centner ... 1.56
27	Paddy	Pound 5	Free	Centner ... 0.48	Centner ... 0.028
28	Pad screws	35 per cent	Free	Centner ... 1.92	Centner ... 0.39
29	Paint brushes	40 per cent	Free	....	....
30	Paintings	10 per cent	Free	Free	Centner ... 0.097
31	Paintings by Amer'n artists.	Free	....	....	....
32	Paints, dry, or ground in oil, not otherwise prov'd for.	25 per cent	Free	Free	Centner ... 0.68
33	Paints, (water colors)	35 per cent	Free	Free	Centner ... 0.68
34	French green, mineral green.	30 per cent	Free	Free	Centner ... 0.68
35	terra umbra	100 pounds 0.50	Free	Free	Centner ... 0.097
36	white lead	Pound 0.03	Free	Centner ... 0.72	Centner ... 0.68
37	all others	25 per cent	Free	Free	Spanish brown, pound ... 0.145
38	Palm leaves, unmanufact'd.	Free	Free	Free	Centner ... 0.097
39	leaf hats	40 per cent	Free	Each 0.05	Centner ... 2.93
40	leaf baskets	35 per cent	Free	Centner ... 2.88	Centner ... 1.56
41	oil	10 per cent	Free	See Oil.	....
42	Pamphlets	25 per cent	Free	Free	....
43	Pannel saws	45 per cent	Free	Centner .. 1.92	Centner ... 0.68
44	Papers, illustrated	25 per cent	Free	Gray blott'g and packing paper, pasteboard, artificial parchment, paper for polishing, slate paper....Free.	Pasteboard, centner 0.39
45	Paper, antiquarian, drawing, and writing.	35 per cent	Free		
46	Paper, bank folio and quarto post, letter and bank note.	35 per cent	Free		Printing & writing paper, glued or not glued, white or one colored, centner...... 0.68
47	Paper for books and newspapers.	20 per cent	Free		

(*Duties expressed in gold dollars of the United States.*)—Continued.

FRANCE.					RUSSIA.	NETHERLANDS.	
	General tariff.		In treaty with Great Britain, &c.				
	In French vessels.	In other vessels.	In vessels of treaty powers.	In other vessels.			
Free					Free	Free	1
Free					Free	Free	2
100 kilogs	$1.95	$2.14	$0.39	$0.43	Pood $0.195	5 per cent	3
					Pood 0.195	5 per cent	4
Free					Free	5 per cent	5
Free					Free	Free	6
See Perfumery					Pood 3.12	See Perfumery	7
Free					Free	Free	8
Free					Free	Free	9
Free					Free	Free	10
Free					Free	Free	11
Portable, each Church organs, each	3.50 78.00	3.51 78.00	10 per cent.		Ch'ch organs, ea. 31.20	5 per cent	12
As fancy articles	Prohibited.		10 per cent.		Pood 2.93	5 per cent	13
					Pood 6.24		14
							15
					35 per cent		16
					Pood 6.24		17
					Pood 4.38		18
	Free.	Free.	Free.	Free.	Free	Free	19
100 kilogs	Free.	0.97	0.39	0.43	Free	Free	20
	Free.	Free.	Free.	Free.	Free	Free	21
	Free.	Free.	Free.	Free.	Pood 4.38	Free	22
	Prohibited.		10 per cent.		Free	Free	23
	Prohibited.		6.31	6.92	Free	Free	24
Fresh, French fisheries, 100 kilogs.	Free.	Free.	Free.	Free.	Pood 4.85	Free	25
Fresh, foreign fisheries, 100 kilogs.	0.29	0.97	0.29	1.17			
Pickled, all, 100 kilogs	1.17	1.29	1.95	2.14			
See Linen yarn, (Flax)					Pood 0.31	100 kilogs $1.33	26
100 kilogs	0.048	0.33			Pound 0.07	Free	27
					Pood 0.42	5 per cent	28
			10 per cent.		Pood 1 72	5 per cent	29
					Free	Free	30
					Free	Free	31
Paints, not enumerated	Free.	Free.	Free.	Free.	Copper paints, arsenical, cobalt, antim'al, chrome, and cinnabar paints, per pood 1.56 All other, per pood 0.85	5 per cent 5 per cent	32
Orseille, 100 kilogs	39.00	41.43	5 per cent.			Free	33
Orseille, blue paste, 100 kilogs.	19.50	26.95				5 per cent	34
Extr'ts of dye-woods, 100 kilogs: black	Prohibited.		3.90	4.29		Free	35
violet						5 per cent	36
yellow			5.85	6.43			
and red.							
	Prohibited.		5 per cent.			5 per cent	37
	Free.	Free.	Free.	Free.	Free	Free	38
100 kilogs	1.95	2.14	1.95	2.14	See Hats	5 per cent	39
					Pound 0.62	5 per cent	40
See Oil					Pood 0.39	100 kilogs 0.51	41
	Free.	Free.	Free.	Free.	Free	Free	42
					Pood 0.62	5 per cent	43
Pasteboard in leaves, single cast, 100 kilogs.	29.25	31.20	1.50	1.72	All sorts of unsized paper, pood 1.56	Paper, all sorts: Music, hanging, &c., and pasteboard, 5 per cent.	44
Glossy, 100 kilogs	15.60	16.86			All sorts of sized paper, white or colored, not enumerated, pood 2.34		45
Other, 100 kilogs	29 25	31.20					46
Papier maché, 100 kilogs	39.00	41.40	10 per cent.				
Pasteboard, cut and assorted.	19.50	20.95					47

Comparative table of import duties in the United States and European countries.

	ARTICLES.	ITALY.			SPAIN.	PORTUGAL.
			General tariff.	Tariff in treaty with France, &c.		
1	Orange crystals............	100 kilogs	$2.93	$2.93	100 kilogs $0.50	100 kilogs....$0.30
2	flowers......	100 kilogs	0.39	Free.	100 kilogs 2.00	Free ....
3	Oranges....................	100 kilogs	0.97	Free.	100 kilogs 0.50	Kilogramme. 0.0027
4	in boxes, barrels, and casks.	100 kilogs	0.97	Free.	100 kilogs 0.50	Kilogramme. 0.0027
5	Orange peel	100 kilogs	1.95	Free	100 kilogs 0.50	Free ....
6	issue peas..........	100 kilogs	1.17	Free	100 kilogs 0.30	Kilogramme . 0.054
7	flower water.......	See Perfumery..	......	......	Kilogramme.. 0.30	20 per cent ....
8	Orchille, or ochello.........	Free	......	......	100 kilogs 1.50	20 per cent ....
9	Ore, specimens, n.o.p......	Free	......	......	Free	Free ....
10	copper.....	Free	......	......	Free	Free ....
11	silver and gold........	Free	......	......	Free	Free ....
12	Organs	Portable, each.. / Church, 100 kil.	0.78 / 1.95	0.78 / 1.95	10 per cent	25 per cent ....
	Ornaments:					
13	gilt wood..............	Ornaments, as fancy goods, if common, 100 kilogs			100 kilogs....20.00	35 per cent.........
14	gold paper				Kilogramme . 0.20	Kilogramme . 0.40
15	for ladies' head-dresses,				....	....
16	of silk..		9.75	9.75	Kilogramme . 0.20	Kilogramme . 0.40
17	cut glass, chandaliers ..	If fine	19.50	19.50	100 kilogs.... 3.50	Kilogramme. 0.172
18	Ornamental feathers, manufactured.	100 kilogs	0.195	Free.	20 per cent	Kilogramme . 0.70
19	Orpiment.................	....	Free.	Free.	.... Free	5 per cent..........
20	Orris root, or iris root	100 kilogs	0.39	Free.	100 kilogs 2.00	5 per cent ....
21	Osiers, for basket makers' use.	....	Free.	Free.	100 kilogs.... 0.10	.... Free.
22	Ostrich plumes, raw	100 kilogs	0.195	Free.	20 per cent.........	5 per cent..........
23	Oxymuriate of lime........	Oxide of iron, lead, zinc, 100 kilogs.	0.39	0.39	100 kilogs.... 0.50	10 per cent ....
24	Oxymuriate of chlorate of potasse.				100 kilogs.... 0.10	.... Free
25	Oysters	100 kilogs	0.78	0.90	.... Free.	.... Free.
26	Pack thread	100 kilogs	1.95	2.24	100 kilogs.... 4.00	Kilogramme . 0.324
27	Paddy	100 kilogs	0.39	Free.	100 kilogs.... 0.80	Kilogramme . 0.009
28	Pad screws................	100 kilogs	1.56	1.80	100 kilogs.... 1.50	Kilogramme . 0.189
29	Paint brushes..............	100 kilogs	9.75	9.75	Kilogramme . 0.40	Fine......... Free. Common, per kilogramme ... 0.40
30	Paintings.................	....	Free.	Free.	.... Free.	.... Free.
31	Paintings by Amer'n artists	....	Free.	Free.	.... Free.	.... Free.
32	Paints, dry, or ground in oil, not otherwise prov'd for.	Paints in boxes, bladders, &c., 100 kilogs.	1.95	0.78	100 kilogs.... 5.00	5 per cent..........
33	Paints, (water colors)	100 kilogs	1.95	0.78	100 kilogs.... 5.00	5 per cent..........
34	French green, mineral green.	100 kilogs	1.95	0.78	100 kilogs.... 1.50	Kilogramme .0.0054
35	terra umbra	100 kilogs	0.48	Free.	100 kilogs.... 1.025	Kilogramme .0.0054
36	white lead..........	100 kilogs	1.95	0.78	100 kilogs.... 1.50	5 per cent..........
37	all other............	100 kilogs	1.95	0.78	See Varnishes......	5 per cent..........
38	Palm leaves, unmanufact'd.	....	Free.	Free.	.... Free.	.... Free.
39	leaf hats............	Each............	0.097	0.097	20 per cent.........	Each 0.972
40	leaf baskets	100 kilogs	0.975	0.975	20 per cent.........	Kilogramme . 0.001
41	oil..................	100 kilogs	0.975	1.12	100 kilogs.... 1.60	Kilogramme .0.0108
42	Pamphlets.................	....	Free.	Free.	.... Free.	.... Free.
43	Panel saws................	100 kilogs	1.56	1.80	100 kilogs.... 3.50	Kilogramme . 0.081
44	Papers, illustrated	Paper, white or colored, per 100 kilogs.	1.95	1.95	Paper, printing, 100 kilogs.. 2.00	Paper, writing, all kinds and colors, kilogs 0.108
45	Paper, antiquarian, drawing and writing.				Writing, and for lithographs, 100 kilogs.. 5.00	
46	Paper, bank folio and quarto post, letter and bank note.	Painted, gilded, 100 kilogs.	5.85	4.87		Printing, kilogramme 0.032
47	Paper for books and newspapers.	Wall paper, 100 kilogs.	5.85	......		Drawing, kilogramme 0.037

(*Duties expressed in gold dollars of the United States.*)—Continued.

BELGIUM.	AUSTRIA.			DENMARK.	SWEDEN.	NORWAY.	
		General tariff.	Tariff in treaty.				
Free	Centner	$0. 388	Free.	Free	Free	Free	1
Free	Free	......	......	Free	Free	Free	2
100 kilogs..$1. 17	Centner	1. 262	......	Pound....$0. 0079	Free	Pound....$0. 027	3
100 kilogs .. 1. 17	Centner	1. 262	......	Pound.....0. 0079	Free	Pound.... 0. 022	4
Free	Centner	0. 388	......	Pound.....0. 0045	Free	Pound.... 0. 027	5
100 kilogs .. 0. 117	Centner	0. 388	......	Free	Free	Free	6
See Perfumery...	Centner	2. 52	$1. 44	Pound.....0. 0113	Pound $0. 02	Pound..... 0. 10	7
Free	Free	......	......	Free	Free	Free	8
Free	Free	......	......	Free	Free	Free	9
Free	Free	......	......	Free	Free	Free	10
Free	Free	......	......	Free	Free	Free	11
6 per cent	Centner	4. 80	3. 60	10 per cent	5 per cent	Each 0. 273	12
10 per cent.	Centner	5. 76	......	Pound..... 0. 091	10 per cent	Pound 0. 048	13
	Centner	6. 00	5. 76	Pound..... 0. 091	10 per cent	Pound 0. 082	14
	....	......	......	....	10 per cent	....	15
	See silk	......	......	Pound..... 0. 041	Pound..... 0. 41	Pound 0. 47	16
	Centner	3. 48	1. 92	Pound..... 0. 04	Pound ... 0. 0138	Pound 0. 047	17
	Centner	5. 76	......	Pound..... 1. 092	Pound..... 0. 827	Pound 0. 496	18
Free	Centner	0. 388	Free.	Free	Free	Free	19
Free	....	Free.	......	Free	Free	Free	20
Free	....	Free.	......	Free	Free	Free	21
Free	Centner	0. 38	Free.	Pound..... 1. 092	Free	Pound 0. 51	22
Free	Centner	0. 72	......	Pound.... 0. 0113	See Chemicals ...	Free	23
Free	Centner	0. 72	......	Pound.... 0. 0113	See Chemicals ...	Free	24
100 kilogs .. 0. 195	Centner	0. 36	Free.	Free	Free	Free	25
See Yarns	See Yarns	......	......	Pound..... 0. 017	See Linen yarn ..	Pound 0. 019	26
100 kilogs .. 0. 195	Centner	0. 129	......	Free	Free	Free	27
100 kilogs .. 0. 78	See Manufacture of metal.			Pound..... 0. 017	See Material manufactured.	Pound 0. 027	28
10 per cent	Centner	2. 04	1. 44	Pound.... 0. 022	5 per cent	Pound 0. 018	29
Free	Centner	0. 388	Free.	Free	Free	Free	30
Free	Centner	0. 388	Free.	Free	Free	Free	31
Free	Paints and colors for painting, centner.	7. 20	n. 76	Pound.... 0. 0056	Free	Pound.... 0. 027	32
Free				Pound.... 0. 0056	Free	Free	33
Free	Centner	0, 38	Free.	Pound.... 0. 0056	Free	Free	34
Free	....	Free.	......	Pound.... 0. 0056	Free	Free	35
Free	Centner	0. 388	Free.	Pound.... 0. 0056	Pound.... 0. 0082	Free	36
Free	All other p'ts centner.	7. 20	5. 76	Pound.... 0. 028	Free	Free	37
Free	....	Free.	......	Free	Free	Free	38
10 per cent	See Hats	......	......	Pound.... 0. 364	See Hats	Pound ... 0. 054	39
10 per cent	See Baskets	......	......	10 per cent	Pound.....0. 0689	Pound. .. 0. 013	40
Free	See Oils	......	......	Pound..... 0. 017	See Oils	Pound.... 0. 0067	41
Free	....	Free.	......	Free	Free	Free	42
100 kilogs... 0. 78	See Manufac's of steel			Pound..... 0. 017	See Manuf. of steel	Pound ... 0. 048	43
Paper, for medicinal use; gilded and printed paper.......Free. For cigarettes, cut for artific'l flowers, ornaments, &c., 10 per cent.	Paper, very comm'n, for blotting, pack'g, tarred, pasteboard, asphaltic felt, fibr's mass, centner.	0. 36	......	Paper acts, manuscripts, paper money, and other papers of value ....Free.	Paper for roofing...... Free. For packing and polishing, per pound.. 0. 0027 Blotting, printing, and wall paper, pound .. 0. 011	Paper for printing, white or oth'r; also blotting and filtering paper, free. Paper for writi'g, drawing, ruled note, lb.. 0. 025	44 45 46 47

Comparative table of import duties in the United States and European countries.

	ARTICLES.	UNITED STATES.	GREAT BRITAIN.	GERMAN ZOLL-VEREIN.	SWITZERLAND.
1	Paper, all other	35 per cent	Free	Fly-paper, centner ......$0. 36 Paper, not glued, centner .. 0. 48 Gold and silver paper; with ornaments; all manufactures of paper only; wall paper, &c., centner ...... 0. 96 All other paper, centner . 0. 72 Articles of paper and other materials, centr 2. 88	Paper of various colors, gilded or silvered, and all other, per centner $1. 56
2	Paraffine	Pound $0. 10	Free	Centner... 0. 36	Centner... 0. 097
3	Parasols, silk	60 per cent	Free	Centner...10. 60	Centner... 2. 93
4	of other material	50 per cent	Free	Centner... 10. 60	Centner... 2. 93
5	Parasol sticks or frames	35 per cent	Free	Iron, steel, &c., centner, 0. 92 Wood, centner, 0. 72.	Centner... 1. 56
6	Parchment	30 per cent	Free	Centner... 1. 44 Artificial, free...	Centner... 0. 39
7	Paris white, dry	100 pounds. 1. 00	Free	Free	Centner... 0. 145
8	in oil	100 pounds. 1. 50	Free	Free	Centner... 0. 145
9	Paris green	30 per cent	Free	Free	Centner... 0. 145
10	Parts of still of copper	45 per cent	Free	Centner... 2. 88	Centner... 1. 56
11	Pasteboard	35 per cent	Free	Free	Centner... 0. 39
12	Paste, giggers	35 per cent	Free	Centner... 2. 40	Centner... 1. 56
13	almond	50 per cent	Free	Centner... 2. 40	Centner... 1. 56
14	perfumed	50 per cent	Free	Centner... 2. 40	Centner... 2. 93
15	pasta do Brazil	10 per cent	Free	Free	Centner... 0. 68
16	Paste work, set in gold or silver jewelry.	35 per cent	Free	Centner...36. 00	Centner... 2. 93
17	Pastel, or woad	Free	Free	Free	Centner... 0. 057
18	Paving stones	10 per cent	Free	Free	Free
19	tiles	20 per cent	Free	Free	15 c'tners . 0. 029
20	Pearl, mother of	Free	Free	Free	Centner... 0. 39
21	Pearls, not set	10 per cent	Free	Centner... 0. 36	Centner... 2. 93
22	mock	40 per cent	Free	Centner...10. 60	Centner... 2. 93
23	set, (composition)	35 per cent	Free	Centner...36. 00	Centner... 2. 93
24	Peas, for seed	30 per cent	Free	Free	Centner... 0. 145
25	Peas, green or dried, (not for seed.)	10 per cent	Free	Free	Centner... 0. 145
26	Peanuts, (ground beans)	Pound 0. 01	Free	Free	15 c'tners . 0. 12
27	shelled	Pound 0. 01½	Free	Free	Centner... 0. 12
28	Pellitory root	20 per cent	Free	Centner... 0. 36	Centner... 0. 14
29	Pelts, salted	10 per cent	Free	Free	Centner... 0. 39
30	Pencils, wood, filled with lead or other material.	30 per cent. and 0.50 per gross.	Free		
31	Pencils, camel's hair	35 per cent	Free	All—	All—
32	chalk	35 per cent. and 0.50 per gross.	Free	Centner... 2. 88	Centner... 1. 56
33	slate	40 per cent	Free	Centner... 0. 12	....
34	Pencil cases, gold and silver.	40 per cent	Free	Centner...36. 00	Centner... 2. 93
35	gilt or plated	35 per cent	Free	Centner...10. 60	Centner... 2. 93
36	Penknives	50 per cent	Free	Centner... 2. 88	Centner... 1. 56

(*Duties expressed in gold dollars of the United States.*)—Continued.

FRANCE.					RUSSIA.	NETHERLANDS.	
	General tariff.		In treaty with Great Britain, &c.				
	In French vessels.	In other vessels.	In vessels of treaty powers.	In other vessels.			
Paper, white, or ruled for music, 100 kilogs. Colored, 100 kilogs Wrapping, 100 kilogs Printed, for shades, 100 k. Silk paper, 100 kilogs Albums, 100 kilogs	$29.25 17.55 15.60 24.37 19.50	$31.20 18.91 16.86 26.96 20.95	$1.56 11.70	$1.72 12.76	Wall paper, per pood .... $3.31 Writing and printing paper, pood.. 6.24 Paper, ornamented, edged; cigarette paper, silk paper, pood......... 4.68 Counting-house and copying books, bound, pood.. 8.58	Paper of all sorts, 5 per cent.	1
Free	....	....	....	....	Pood.......... 0.43	Free	2
Each	0.39	0.39	10 per	cent.	Each.......... 0.17	5 per cent	3
Each	0.39	0.39	10 per	cent.	Each.......... 0.17	5 per cent	4
....	....	....	10 per	cent.	Each set 0.23	5 per cent	5
Free	....	....	....	....	Free	2 per cent	6
Free	....	....	....	....	Pood.......... 0.85	Free	7
Free	....	....	....	....	Pood.......... 0.85	Free	8
Free	....	....	....	....	Pood.......... 0.85	Free	9
100 kilogs	Prohi	bited.	3.90	4.29	Pood.......... 2.34	5 per cent	10
100 kilogs	29.25	31.20	1.56	1.72	Pood.......... 0.16	5 per cent	11
					Pood.......... 0.195	Free	12
Liquid paste, perfumed, per 100 kilogs.	4.87	5.35	1.95	2.14	....	Free	13
					....	See Perfumery	14
					....	Free	15
See Jewelry	....	....	....	....	Pound 1.72	5 per cent	16
Free	....	....	....	....	Pood.......... 0.85	Free	17
100 kilogs	Free...	0.95	Free...	Free...	Free	Free	18
100 kilogs	1.95	1.95	Free...	Free...	Free	Free	19
100 kilogs	Free...	0.78	Free...	Free...	Free	Free	20
Free	....	....	....	....	Free	Free	21
100 kilogs	1.17	1.29	3.90	4.29	Pood.......... 1.28	5 per cent	22
See Jewelry	....	....	....	....	Pound 0.25	5 per cent	23
Free	....	....	....	....	Free	Free	24
Free	....	....	....	....	Free	Free	25
Free	....	....	....	....	Pood.......... 0.78	Free	26
Free	....	....	....	....	Pood.......... 0.78	Free	27
100 kilogs	Free...	0.97	0.39	0.43	Pood.......... 0.19	Free	28
100 kilogs	0.487	0.487	Free...	0.048	Free	Free	29
							30
							31
Fancy goods, per 100 kilogs.	19.50	20.95	10 per	cent.	All, per lb.... 0.23	5 per cent	32
							33
See Gold and silver, man	ufacture	d.......	....	....	See Gold and silver ..	5 per cent	34
Fancy goods, fine, per 100 kilogs.	39.00	41.43	10 per	cent.	Pood... ......15.60	5 per cent	35
See Cutlery	....	....	....	....	Ordinary, pood. 9.36 Silver-m'ted, p. . 18.72	5 per cent	36

Comparative table of import duties in the United States and European countries.

	ARTICLES.	ITALY.			SPAIN.	PORTUGAL.
			General tariff.	Tariff in treaty with France, &c.		
1	All other paper	Lithogr'd, printed, 100 kilogs. Wrapping, 100 kilogs. Manuscripts	$11.70 {.... 1.56 Free.	Free. $1.56 *Free. Free.	Paper, cut, prepared, and ruled, 100 kilogs ....$10.00 Wall paper, ordinary, 100 kilo's 5.50 Enamelled, 100 kilogramme... 10.00 With gold, silver, wool, or crystal, 100 kilogs..40.00 For blotting and packing, per 100 kilogs ..... 2.50 All other not enu'd, 100 kilogs.. 8.00	Wrappi'g, per kilogramme $0.054 Silvered, per kilogramme 0.01 Gilded, ordinary, kilog 0.01 Gilded, fine, kilogramme 0.021 Waste paper. Free. Pasteboard, kilogramme 0.008
2	Paraffine	Free	......	......	100 kilogs.... 0.05	Free
3	Parasols, silk	Each	0.195	0.195	Each 0.50	Each 1.404
4	of other material	Each	0.097	0.097	Each 0.30	Each 0.972
5	Parasol sticks or frames	100 kilogs	3.90	3.90	100 kilogs.... 3.50	Each set .. 0.864 or, per kil. 1.90
6	Parchment	100 kilogs	2.56	......	Kilog........ 0.25	20 per cent
7	Paris white, dry	100 kilogs	1.95	0.78	100 kilogs.... 1.50	5 per cent
8	in oil	100 kilogs	1.95	0.78	100 kilogs.... 5.00	5 per cent
9	Paris green	100 kilogs	1.95	0.78	100 kilogs.... 1.50	5 per cent
10	Parts of still of copper	100 kilogs	3.90	3.90	100 kilogs....14.00	Kilog....... 0.27
11	Pasteboard	100 kilogs	1.56	1.56	100 kilogs.... 8.00	Kilog....... 0.008
12	Paste, giggers	Free	......	......		Kilog....... 0.0081
13	almond	Free	......	......		Kilog....... 0.0081
14	perfumed	Free	......	......	Kilog 0.30	20 per cent
15	pasta de Brazil	Free	......	......		Kilog....... 0.0081
16	Paste work, set in gold or silver jewelry.	5 per cent	......	......	Kilog 0.50	Kilog.......54.00
17	Pastel, or woad	Free	......	......	100 kilogs.... 0.05	5 per cent
18	Paving stones	Free	......	......	100 kilogs.... 0.01	Free
19	tiles	100 kilogs	0.58	Free.	100 kilogs.... 0.50	Kilog....... 0.001
20	Pearl, mother of	Free	......	......	Kilog 0.01	Free
21	Pearls, not set	Per cent	1	Free	Free	1 per cent
22	mock	100 kilogs	9.75	9.75	100 kilogs.... 9.00	Kilog....... 0.54
23	set, (composition)	Per cent	1	Free.	Kilog........ 4.00	1 per cent
24	Peas, for seed	100 kilogs	0.195	Free.	100 kilogs.... 0.60	Free
25	Pea, green or dried, (not for seed.)	Free	......	......	100 kilogs.... 0.60	Kilog....... 0.008
26	Peanuts, (ground beans)	100 kilogs	0.97	Free.	100 kilogs.... 0.50	Kilog....... 0.01
27	shelled	100 kilogs	1.95	Free.	100 kilogs.... 0.50	Kilog....... 0.01
28	Pellitory root	100 kilogs	0.39	Free.	100 kilogs.... 0.60	Free
29	Pelts, salted	100 kilogs	0.97	Free.	100 kilogs.... 0.20	Kilog....... 0.005
30	Pencils, wood, filled with lead or other material.					Kilog....... 0.054
31	Pencils, camel's hair	All, per 100 kilogs			20 per cent	Free
32	chalk		1.95	1.95		Kilog....... 0.057
33	slate					Free
34	Pencil cases, gold and silver.	According to material manufactured.			100 kilogs.... 0.01	Kilog.......54.00
35	gilt or plated				Hectogramme. 0.40 Kilog........ 1.85	Kilog.......16.20
36	Penknives	100 kilogs	1.56	1.80	Kilog........ 0.20	See Cutlery

* Switzerland, free.

(*Duties expressed in gold dollars of the United States.*)—Continued.

Belgium.	Austria.			Denmark.	Sweden.	Norway.	
		General tariff.	Tariff in treaty.				
Wall paper, 100 kilogs....$1.56 All other, 100 kilogramme.. 0.78	All common paper not glued, centner. Paper glued, color'd, lithographed, print'd, ruled, medicinally prepar'd, oil'd, wax'd, p'nter's paste, centner. Paper gilded, silv'd, pressed, perforated, centner. Wall paper, centner. Articles not fancy goods centner.	$1.32 2.64 6.00 6.00 6.00	$0.72 1.92 5.76 5.76 5.76	Paper for printing, drawing, or writing; packing and other covered with asphal'm, glass, &c., po'd $0.0028 Paper, all other, also colored in mass, varnished or oiled, per pound ... 0.021 Paper, colored, gilded, or silvered; printed labels, envelo's, pound ... 0.045 Articles manufactured of paper, pound 0.91	Paper, all other, pound ...$0.022 All manufactures of paper not varnished, per pound ... 0.04 Paper varnished, & papier maché, pound .. 0.0689	Paper for packing and cartri's, p und ...$0.009 Paper for roofi'g, tarred, sand paper, lb.. 0.0022 Colored paper, wall paper, engravings, envelopes, per pound ... 0.025 Paper bound, per pound ... 0.036 Articles of papier maché, lb 0.082	1
						Pound ... 0.0067	2
Free	Centner	0.648	Free.	Pound.... 0.017	Free	Each 0.205	3
10 per cent	Not enumerated in tariff.			Each 0.344	Each 0.206	Each 0.065	4
10 per cent				Each 0.136	Each 0.0068	Pound ... 0.047	5
10 per cent				Pound.... 0.045	Pound.... 0.051		
Free	Centner	6.24	4.80	Pound.... 0.068	Pound.... 0.055	Pound ... 0.062	6
Free	Centner	0.388	Free	Pound... 0 0113	Free	Pound ... 0.027	7
Free	Centner	0.388	Free.	Pound.... 0.0113	Free	Pound ... 0.027	8
Free	Centner	0.388	Free.	Pound.... 0.0113	Free	Pound ... 0.027	9
10 per cent	See Articles of copper			Pound.... 0.045	Pound.... 0.041	Pound ... 0.047	10
See Paper	Centner	0.36	......	Pound.... 0.0028	Pound.... 0.022	Pound ... 0.032	11
For toilet, 10 p'r cent.	Centner	0.36	......	Free	Free	Free	12
	Centner	0.36	......	Free	Free	Free	13
Sugar'd pastes, 100 kilogs, $11.70.	See Perfumery		......	Pound.... 0.091	Pound.... 0.11	Free	14
	Centner	0.36	......	Free	Free	Free	15
5 per cent	See Jewelry	......	......	Pound.... 0,091	Pound.... 0.0964	Pound ... 0.109	16
Free	Free	......	......	Free	Free	Free	17
Free	Free	......	......	Free	Free	Free	18
Free	Free	......	......	Free	Free	See Tiles	19
Free	Free	......	......	Free	Free	Free	20
10 per cent	Cut, centner	5.76	5.76	Free	Free	Free	21
10 per cent	Centner	5.76	......	Pound.... 0.091	10 per cent	Pound ... 0.158	22
5 per cent	As jewelry	......	......	Pound.... 0.091	Pound.... 0.0964	As material of setting.	23
100 kilogs . 0.117	Centner	0.167	Free.	Free	Free	Free	24
100 kilogs . 0.117	Centner	0.129	Free.	Free	Free	Free	25
100 kilogs . 0.117	Centner	0.388	Free.	Free	Free	Free	26
100 kilogs . 0.117	Centner	0.388	Free	Free	Free	Pound ... 0.022	27
Free	Free	......	......	Free	Free	Free	28
Free	Centner	1.26	......	Free	Free	Free	29
10 per cent	Centner	7.20	5.76	Pound.... 0.028	Pound.... 0.041	Pound ... 0.047	30
10 per cent	Centner	7.20	5.76	Pound.... 0.028	Pound.... 0.041	Pound ... 0.047	31
10 per cent	Centner	0.388	Free.	Pound.... 0.028	Pound.... 0.041	Pound ... 0.047	32
10 per cent	Centner	0.388	Free.	Free	Free	Free	33
5 per cent	See Gold and silver.		......	Pound.... 0.091	See Gold & silver	Loth 0.03	34
10 per cent	See Jewelry	......	......	Pound.... 0.091	Pound.... 0.082	Pound ... 0.095	35
10 per cent	Centner	7.20	5.76	Fancy, lb. 0.091 Others, lb. 0.017	Pound.... 0.138	Pound ... 0.048	36

Comparative table of import duties in the United States and European countries.

	ARTICLES.	UNITED STATES.	GREAT BRITAIN.	GERMAN ZOLL-VEREIN.	SWITZERLAND.
1	Penholders	35 per cent	Free	According to material.	Centner...$1.56
2	Pens, metallic	25 per cent. and $0.10 per gross.	Free	Centner...$7.20	Centner... 1.56
3	Pepper, black	Pound $0.15	Free		
4	ground	Pound 0.18	Free		
5	white	Pound 0.15	Free		
6	ground	Pound 0.18	Free	Centner.. 4.68	Centner.. 0.68
7	Cayenne	Pound 0.15	Free		
8	ground	Pound 0.18	Free		
9	red	Pound 0.15	Free		
10	Perfumery vials and bottles	35 per cent	Free	Centner... 2.40	Centner... 0.68
11	Percussion caps	40 per cent	Free	Centner... 2.88	Centner... 0.68
12	Perfumed soap, &c	Pound 0.10	Free	Centner... 2.40	Centner... 0.145
13	Perfumes	50 per cent	Free	Centner... 2.40	Centner... 2.93
14	Perfumes containing alcohol.	50 per cent. and $3.00 p'r gallon.	Gallon....$3.41	Centner... 2.40	Centner... 2.93
15	Persian berries, (a dye)	Free	Free	Free	Centner... 0.68
16	Peruvian bark	20 per cent	Free	Free	Centner... 0.029
17	Pewter, old, fit only to be re-manufactured.	Pound 0.02	Free	Free	Centner... 0.29
18	Pewter, manufactures of	35 per cent	Free	Ordinary, centner, $0.72. Fancy, centner, $2.88.	Centner... 1.56
19	Phosphate of lime	20 per cent	Free	Free	Centner... 0.68
20	soda	20 per cent	Free	Centner... 2.40	Centner... 0.68
21	Phosphorus lights in glass bottles with paper cases.	35 per cent	Free	Centner... 2.40	Centner... 0.68
22	Phosphorus	20 per cent	Free	Centner... 2.40	Centner... 0.68
23	Phosphuret of lime	20 per cent	Free	Centner... 2.40	Centner... 0.68
24	Piano-fortes	30 per cent	Free	Centner... 2.88	Centner... 1.56
25	Piano-forte ferules, (iron)	35 per cent	Free	Centner... 2.88	Centner... 1.56
26	Pickled fish, other than mackerel and salmon in barrels.	Barrel 1.50	Free	All, centn'r 0.36	All, centn'r 0.39
27	Pickled herring in barrels and kegs.	Barrel 1.00	Free		
28	Pickled mackerel	Barrel 2.00	Free		
29	Pickled salmon	Barrel 3.00	Free		
30	Pickles	35 per cent	In vinegar, gallon 0.02	Free	Centner... 0.68
31	Picrotoxine, (an extract)	40 per cent	Free	Centner... 2.40	Centner... 0.68
32	Pimento	Pound 0.15	Free	Centner... 4.68	Centner... 0.68
33	ground	Pound 0.18	Free	Centner... 4.68	Centner... 0.68
34	Pin or needle cases of gold or silver.	40 per cent	Free	Centner .10.60	Centner... 2.93
35	All others	35 per cent	Free		
36	Pincushions, cotton	35 per cent	Free	Centner ..10.60	Centner... 2.93
37	silk	50 per cent	Free	Centner...10.60	Centner... 2.93
38	Pincers of iron	35 per cent	Free	Centner... 2.88	Centner... 0.68
39	Pine-apples	25 per cent	Free	Centner... 1.44	15 centner. 0.097
40	Pink root	20 per cent	Free	Free	Centner... 0.39
41	Pins, rest, iron, or pound	35 per cent	Free	Centner... 2.88	Centner... 1.56
42	silver jewelry	25 per cent	Free	Like silverware	Centner... 1.56
43	Pipe, clay, unwrought	Ton 5.00	Free	Free	15 centner. 0.029
44	Pipes, clay, smoking	35 per cent	Free	Centner... 1.26	Centner... 0.145
45	Pipes, meerschaums, and other tobacco smoking and pipe bowls, not otherwise provided for.	75 per cent. and gross ... 1.50	Free	Centner... 2.88	Centner... 2.93

(Duties expressed in gold dollars of the United States.)—Continued.

FRANCE.					RUSSIA.	NETHERLANDS.	
	General tariff.		In treaty with Great Britain, &c.				
	In French vessels.	In other vessels.	In vessels of treaty powers.	In other vessels.			
Fancy goods, per 100 kilogs.	$19.50	$20.95	10 per	cent.	Pound.........$0.23	5 per cent	1
Kilog	0.78	0.86	....	....	Pound 0.23	5 per cent	2
							3
							4
							5
100 kilogs............	9.75	11.89	....	....	Pood......... 1.17	100 kilogs ..$0.61	6
							7
							8
							9
Bottles, 100 kilogs	Prohib	ited.	$0.15	$0.29	See Glass............	5 per cent	10
....	10 per	cent.	....	....	Prohibited...........	5 per cent	11
100 kilogs..............	31.98	34.07	1.17	2.14	Pood.......... 4.29	100 kilogs.... 2.46	12
Liquid paste, 100 kilogs.	4.87	5.35	1.95	2.14	Pood..........23.40	5 per cent	13
100 kilogs..............	29.25	31.20	2.92	2.92	Pood..........23.40	Liter. 0.51 to 0.82	14
Not containing alcohol, 100 kilogs.	19.50	20.95	1.95	2.14	....	....	
Odorous pastils, 100 kil.	Free...	2.53	1.87	2.14	....	....	
Free....................	....	....	....	....	Free	Free	15
Free....................	....	....	....	....	Free	Free	16
100 kilogs..............	....	....	0.97	1.06	Pood.......... 0.47	Free	17
Ordinary	19.50	20.95	5.85	6.43	Pood.......... 9.36	5 per cent	18
Pottery, fine	39.00	41.43	5.85	6.43	....	....	
Other, prohibited.......	....	....	....	....	....	....	
....	Prohi	bited.	5 per	cent.	Pood 0.31	Free...............	19
....	Prohi	bited.	5 per	cent.	Pood 0.85	Free...............	20
....	Prohi	bited.	10 per	cent.	Pood 0.85	Free...............	21
White, 100 kilogs.......	Prohi	bited.	7.80	8.58	Pood 7.80	Free...............	22
red	....	....	10 per	cent.			
Phosphoric acid, 100 kil.	12.09	13.18	....	....	Pood 0.85	Free...............	23
Square, each...........	58.50	58.50	10 per	cent.	Each 31.20	5 per cent	24
others	78.00	78.00	10 per	cent.			
See Material manufact'd	....	....	....	....	Pound 0.08	5 per cent..........	25
							26
All except codfish, 100 kilogs.	7.80	8.58	0,97	1.06	All, pood.... 0.85	Free.............	27
							28
							29
100 kilogs..............	0.58	0.64	0.58	0.64	Pood 0.39	Free...............	30
....	Prohi	bited.	See Pa	ints.	Pood 0.85	Free...............	31
100 kilogs..............	7.80	19.50	....	....	Pood 1.17	100 kilogs.... 0.41	32
....	....	....	....	....	Pood 1.17	100 kilogs.... 0.41	33
						5 per cent	34
As fancy articles	Prohi	bited.	10 per	cent.	Pound 0.25	5 per cent	35
....	Prohi	bited.	10 per	cent.	Pound 0.27	5 per cent..........	36
....	Prohi	bited.	10 per	cent.	Pound 0.78	5 per cent..........	37
....	Prohi	bited.	10 per	cent.	Pood 0.62	5 per cent..........	38
100 kilogs..............	9.75	10.72	1.95	2.14	Pood 0.39	5 per cent..........	39
100 kilogs..............	Free...	0.48	....	....	Free..................	Free...............	40
As fancy articles	Prohi	bited.	10 per	cent.	Pound 0.39	5 per cent..........	41
As jewelry.............	....	....	....	....	Pound 1.72	5 per cent..........	42
100 kilogs..............	Free...	0.48	Free...	0.048	Free..................	Free...............	43
100 kilogs..............	Prohi	bited.	Free...	0.048	Pood 0.16	5 per cent..........	44
....	15 per	cent.	10 per	cent.	Pood 0.19	5 per cent..........	45

Comparative table of import duties in the United States and European countries.

	ARTICLES.	ITALY.			SPAIN.	PORTUGAL.
			General tariff.	Tariff in treaty with France, &c.		
1	Penholders	100 kilogs	$9.75	$9.75	20 per cent	Kilog $0.40
2	Pens, metallic	100 kilogs	9.75	11.26	Kilog $0.60	Kilog 0.162
3	Pepper, black					
4	ground					
5	white					
6	ground	100 kilogs	7.80	......	Kilog 0.05	Kilog ..... 0.081 Guinea pepper, per kilog. 0.027
7	Cayenne					
8	ground					
9	red					
10	Perfumery vials and bottles.	100 kilogs	1.56	0.39	100 kilogs.... 1.60	Kilog 0.172
11	Percussion caps	Not enumerated	......	......	100 kilogs....35.00	Kilogs 0.27
12	Perfumed soap, &c	100 kilogs	11.70	1.70		Aromatic spirits, kilog, $0.27. Pastils and sticks, free. Not specified, 20 per cent.
13	Perfumes	100 kilogs	11.70	10 p.c.		
14	Perfumes containing alcohol.	Civet cat and amber, per 100 kilogs	11.70	0.39	Kilog 0.30	
15	Persian berries, (a dye)	Free	......	......	100 kilogs.... 0.05	Free
16	Peruvian bark	100 kilogs	0.39	Free.	100 kilogs.... 0.05	Kilog 0.01
17	Pewter, old, fit only to be remanufactured.	100 kilogs	0.195	......	Free	Old pieces, free
18	Pewter, manufactures of	Vessels, 100 kils	1.56	Free.	100 kilogs....25.00	Beaten, laminated, kilog, $0.0027. Manufact'ed, kilog, $0.6216.
19	Phosphate of lime	100 kilogs	1.95	0.78		
20	soda	See Chemical preparations not enumera'd.			See Chemicals not enumerated.	See Chemicals not enumerated.
21	Phosphorus lights in glass bottles with paper cases.					
22	Phosphorus	100 kilogs	1.56	1.56	Kilogramme . 0.10	Kilogramme . 0.108
23	Phosphuret of lime	100 kilogs	1.95	0.78	See Chemic'ls n. e.	See Chemic'ls n. e.
24	Piano-fortes	Each	1.36	1.36	Each 50.00	Each 24.84
25	Piano-forte ferules (iron)	100 kilogs	1.56	1.80	See Mat'l manufac'd	See Mat'l manufac'd
26	Pickled fish, other than mackerel and salmon in barrels.					
27	Pickled herring in barrels and kegs.	100 kilogs	0.78	0.90	100 kilogs.... 1.60	Kilogramme . 0.036
28	Pickled mackerel					
29	Pickled salmon					
30	Pickles	100 kilogs	1.56	0.59	Kilogramme . 0.20	Kilogramme . 0.037
31	Picrotoxine, (an extract)	100 kilogs	1.95	0.78	20 per cent	10 per cent
32	Pimento	100 kilogs	7.80	......	Kilogramme . 0.05	Kilogramme . 0.081
33	ground	100 kilogs	7.80	......	Kilogramme . 0.05	Kilogramme . 0.081
34	Pin or needle cases of gold or silver.	See Manuf. of gold, &c.		......	20 per cent	See Gold or silver..
35	All others	100 kilogs	19.50	19.50	20 per cent	
36	Pincushions, cotton	As manuf. of cotton ...		......	20 per cent	As fancy goods not specified, kilog ... 0.40
37	silk	As manuf. of silk	.....	.....	20 per cent	
38	Pincers of iron	100 kilogs	1.56	1.80	100 kilogs.... 1.50	Kilogramme. 0.081
39	Pine-apples	100 kilogs	0.195	Free.	100 kilogs.... 0.50	Kilogramme 0.0027
40	Pink root	100 kilogs	0.39	Free	100 kilogs.... 2.00	Free
41	Pins, rest, iron, or pound...	100 kilogs	9.75	9.75	Kilogramme . 0.60	Kilogramme . 0.135
42	silver jewelry	See Jewelry	.....	.....	Hectogramme 0.40	Kilogramme . 5.40
43	Pipe clay, unwrought	100 kilogs	0.48	Free	100 kilogs.... 0.01	Free
44	Pipes, clay, smoking	100 kilogs	1.56	1.56	100 kilogs.... 0.01	Kilogramme . 0.001
45	Pipes, meerschaums, and other tobacco smoking and pipe bowls, not otherwise provided for.	100 kilogs	19.50	19.50	20 per cent	Kilogramme . 0.40

(*Duties expressed in gold dollars of the United States.*)—Continued.

BELGIUM.	AUSTRIA.			DENMARK.	SWEDEN.	NORWAY.	
		General tariff.	Tariff in treaty.				
10 per cent	According to material.			10 per cent	According to material.	10 per cent	1
10 per cent	Centner	$7. 20	$7. 20	Pound....$0. 017	Pound....$0. 0689	Pound ...$0. 081	2
							3
							4
							5
15 per cent	Centner	3. 84	......	Pound .. 0. 017	Pound .. 0. 03	Cayenne, per lb., $0. 375. All other, per lb., $0. 036.	6
							7
							8
							9
100 kilogs . 0. 195	See Glass....	......	......	Pound.... 0. 008	Pound.... 0. 041	Pound ... 0. 089	10
10 per cent	Centner	7. 68	5. 76	Pound.... 0. 0227	Pound.... 0. 138	Pound ... 0. 182	11
100 kilogs . 1. 17	Centner	7. 56	......	Pound.... 0. 091	Pound.... 0. 033	Pound ... 0. 013	12
10 per cent	Centner	7. 20	5. 76	Pound.... 0. 091	Pound.... 0. 11	10 per cent	13
10 per cent	Centner	7. 20	5. 76	Pound.... 0. 091	(50 p. c.,) kande, $0.352.	Pound ... 0. 10	14
Free	Free	......	......	Free	Free	Free	15
Free	Free	......	......	Free	Free	Free	16
Free	Free	......	......	Free	Free	Free	17
10 per cent	Centner	2. 40	2. 16	Ordinary, lb. 0. 045 Gilded, lb. 0. 091	Pound.... 0. 041	Ordinary, lb. 0. 047 Gilded, lb. 0. 095	18
					See Chemicals..	Free	19
					See Chemicals..	Free	20
Free	See Chemic'ls	......	......	Pound . .. 0. 0113	See Chemicals..	Free	21
					Free	Free	22
					See Chemicals..	Free	23
6 per cent	Centner	4. 80	3. 60	10 per cent.......	Each .....11. 024 Grand, ea. 16. 54	Each..... 10. 92	24
10 per cent.......	As material manuf'd		......	Pound.... 0. 045	5 per cent........	Pound ... 0. 048	25
					Centner . 0. 2067		26
100 kilogs. 0. 195	Centner	0. 72	0. 72	Pound .. 0. 0017	Cubic ft . 0. 033	Free	27
					Centner . 0. 2067		28
					Centner . 0. 2067		29
100 kilogs .. 1. 95	Centner	0. 388	Free.	Free.............	Free.............	Pound ... 0. 027	30
See Extracts.	Medic'es prepared, cent'r	7. 20	......	Pound.... 0. 0113	Free.............	Free	31
15 per cent.	Centner	3. 84	......	Pound.... 0. 017	Pound.... 0. 03	Pound ... 0. 036	32
15 per cent.	Centner	3. 84	......	Pound.... 0. 017	Pound.... 0. 03	Pound ... 0. 036	33
5 per cent	See Gold or silver .		......	Pound.... 0. 091	See Gold and silver.	10 per cent	34
10 per cent	Fancy goods, leather, &c., centner	5. 76	......	10 per cent.......	10 per cent.......	10 per cent	35
10 per cent	Centner	5. 76	......	10 per cent.......	10 per cent.......	10 per cent	36
10 per cent	Centner	28. 80	21. 60	10 per cent.......	10 per cent.......	10 per cent	37
Kilogramme. 0. 78	Centner	2. 88	2. 16	Pound.... 0. 017	See Iron manufac.	Pound ... 0. 027	38
10 per cent	Centner	2. 52	......	Free.............	Free.............	Pound ... 0. 027	39
Free	Free	......	......	Free.............	Free	Free	40
100 kilogs .. 0. 78	Centner	7. 20	......	Pound.... 0. 091	Pound.... 0. 0689	Pound ... 0. 109	41
5 per cent	See Jewelry	......	......	Pound.... 0. 091	See Silver manuf.	Pound ... 0. 109	42
Free	Free	......	......	Free.............	Free.............	Free	43
100 kilogs .. 0. 23	Centner	0. 12	Free	Pound.... 0. 0056	Pound.... 0. 11	Pound ... 0. 004	44
10 per cent	Centner	5. 76	......	10 per cent.... ..	Pound.... 0. 2756	10 per cent	45

Comparative table of import duties in the United States and European countries.

	ARTICLES.	UNITED STATES.	GREAT BRITAIN.	GERMAN ZOLL-VEREIN.	SWITZERLAND.
1	Pipe cases, stems, mountings, and all parts of pipe and pipe fixtures, and all smokers' articles.	75 per cent	Free	Centner...$2.88	Centner...$2.93
2	Pistols	35 per cent	Free	Centner... 7.20	Centner... 0.39
3	Pitch	20 per cent	Free	Free	Centner... 0.058
4	Plantain or Manila grass, (Manila hemp.)	Ton $25.00	Free	Free	Centner... 0.058
5	Plaster of Paris, unground	Free	Free	Free	15 cent'rs . 0.145
6	ground	20 per cent	Free	Free	15 cent'rs . 0.145
7	calcined	20 per cent	Free	Free	15 cent'rs . 0.145
8	Plaster busts, casts of, statue.	40 per cent	Free	Free	Free
9	Plaster ornaments	40 per cent	Free	Centner... 0.36	Centner... 1.56
10	Planks, wrought or rough	20 per cent	Free	Free	Centner... 0.058
11	Plants, medicinal	20 per cent	Free	Centner... 0.36	Centner... 0.68
12	other	30 per cent	Free	Free	15 cent'rs . 0.058
13	Plantains	25 per cent	Free	Centner... 1.44	15 cent'rs . 0.12
14	Planes	45 per cent	Free	Centner... 1.92	Centner... 0.68
15	Plata pina	Free	Free	Free	Centner... 0.29
16	Plate, silver	40 per cent	Ounce, troy $0.36	Centner...36.00	Centner... 2.93
17	gold	40 per cent	Ounce, troy 4.14	Centner...36.00	Centner... 2.93
18	Plated ware of all other kinds.	35 per cent	Free	Centner...10.60	Centner... 2.93
19	Platina, unmanufactured	Free	Free	Free	Centner... 0.29
20	manufactured	40 per cent	Free	Centner...31.00	Centner... 2.93
21	vases or retorts	Free	Free	Free	Centner... 0.145
22	Playing cards, value 25 cts. or less, per pack.	Pack...... 0.25	Doz. packs, free	All, cent'r. 7.20	All, cent'r. 2.93
23	Playing cards, value over 25 cents.	Pack...... 0.35			
24	Plier's iron	35 per cent	Free	Centner... 1.92	Centner... 0.68
25	Ploughs, iron	35 per cent	Free	Centner... 1.06	Centner... 0.39
26	plane	45 per cent	Free	Free	Centner... 0.39
27	Plumbago	Ton 10.00	Free	Free	Centner... 0.058
28	Plums	Pound 0.05	French prunella, centner .. 1.75 Dried or preserved, cent'r 1.70 All not otherwise enumerated per pound ... 0.02	Free	Centner... 0.145
29	Plumes, ornamental, manufactured.	50 per cent	Free	Centner... 0.36	Centner... 2.93
30	Plush, wool, not o. p. for	35 per cent, per pound $0.50.	Free	Centner...14.40	Centner... 1.56
31	cotton	See Cottons	Free	Centner...11.50	Centner... 1.56
32	hair	See Worsted	Free	Centner... 5.76	Centner... 1.56
33	Pocket-books, leather	35 per cent	Free	As fancy goods, centner. 10.60	Centner... 2.93
34	paper	35 per cent	Free		Centner... 1.56
35	Pocket bottles, green glass	35 per cent	Free	Centner...10.60	Centner... 1.56
36	Pole caps, and ferules	35 per cent	Free	Centner... 0.96	Centner... 0.68
37	carriage hooks	35 per cent	Free	Centner... 0.96	Centner... 0.68
38	Polishing stones	Free	Free	Free	Centner... 0.029
39	powders	25 per cent	Free	Free	Centner... 0.029
40	Polypodium (drug)	20 per cent	Free	Centner... 0.36	Centner... 0.68
41	Pomatum	50 per cent	Free	Centner... 2.40	Centner... 2.93
42	Pomegranates	10 per cent	Pound 0.02	Centner... 1.44	Centner... 0.68
43	Pomegranate-peel	20 per cent	Free	Centner... 2.88	Centner... 0.39
44	Poppy heads	20 per cent	Free	Free	Centner... 0.058
45	oil	50 per cent	Free	Centner... 0.36	Centner... 0.68
46	seed	20 per cent	Free	Free	Centner... 0.058

(*Duties expressed in gold dollars of the United States.*)—Continued.

France.					Russia.	Netherlands.	
	General tariff.		In treaty with Great Britain, &c.				
	In French vessels.	In other vessels.	In vessels of treaty powers.	In other vessels.			
....	15 per	cent.	10 per	cent.	Pood $0.19	5 per cent..........	1
See Arms	....	....	....	....	Pood 14.04	5 per cent..........	2
....	Free...	Free...	Free...	Free...	Free..................	Free...............	3
....	Free...	Free...	Free...	Free...	Free..................	Free...............	4
Plaster, all raw or prepared.	Free.	Free...	Free...	Free...	Free	Free...............	5
	Free.	Free...	Free...	Free...	Free	Free...............	6
	Free.	Free...	Free...	Free...	Pood 0.85	Free...............	7
....	Free...	Free...	Free...	Free...	Free	Free...............	8
....	Free...	Free...	Free...	Free...	Free	5 per cent..........	9
See Wood	....	....	....	....	Free	3 per cent..........	10
....	Free...	Free...	Free...	Free...	Free	Free...............	11
....	Free...	Free...	Free...	Free...	Free	Free...............	12
100 kilogs..............	Free...	$0.78	Free...	$0.47	Pood 0.78	5 per cent..........	13
As tools, 100 kilogs.....	$24.37	26.27	$2.92	3.20	Pood 0.62	5 per cent..........	14
....	Free...	Free...	Free...	Free...	Free	Free...............	15
See Silver	....	....	....	....	Pound 1.72	5 per cent..........	16
See Gold	....	....	....	....	Pound 25.74	5 per cent..........	17
100 kilogs..............	Prohi	bited.	19.50	20.95	Gold, silver, and platina plated, per pood ....15.60 Articles of less than 1 lb., pood...39.60	5 per cent..........	18
Platina, mineral, 100 kilogs.	Free...	0.195	....	....	Free	Free...............	19
Crude, in bars, 100 kil..	0.019	0.019	....	....	Pound 12.87	Kilogramme .$0.04 (also wire.)	20
In sheets, 100 kilogs	4.87	5.35	4.87	5.35	Free	1 per cent..........	21
Wire, 100 kilogs........	97.50	100.90	....	....			
Manufactures, as manuf.	of gold .	....	....	....			
....	....	....	15 per ce	nt and			22
Pack	Prohibi	ted.....	0.09	0.09	Prohibited	5 per cent..........	23
See Iron tools..........	....	....	....	....	Pood 0.62	5 per cent..........	24
100 kilogs..............	2.92	3.20	1.17	1.29	Free	5 per cent..........	25
100 kilogs..............	2.92	3.20	1.17	1.29	Free..................	5 per cent..........	26
....	Free	Free	Free	Free	Free..................	Free	27
100 kilogs..............	3.12	3.43	1.56	1.72	Pood 0.78	5 per cent..........	28
As fancy goods.........	Prohibi	ted.....	10 per	cent...	Pound 4.68	5 per cent..........	29
See Wool	....	....	....	....	Pound 0.39	5 per cent..........	30
See Cotton.............	....	....	....	....	Pound......... 0.35	5 per cent..........	31
See Hair...............	....	....	....	....	Pood 1.72	5 per cent..........	32
100 kilogs..............	Prohibi	ted.....	11.70	12.76	Pound......... 1.72	5 per cent..........	33
100 kilogs..............	Prohibi	ted.....	10 per	cent...	Pound......... 0.85	5 per cent..........	34
100 kilogs..............	Prohibi	ted.....	0.25	0.29	Pood 6.24	5 per cent..........	35
100 kilogs..............	19.50	20.95	3.90	4.29	Pood 0.62	5 per cent..........	36
100 kilogs..............	19.50	20.95	3.90	4.29	Pood 0.78	5 per cent..........	37
....	Free	Free	Free	Free	Free	Free	38
....	Free	Free	Free	Free	Free	Free	39
....	Free	Free	Free	Free	Pood 0.47	Free	40
All sorts, 100 kilogs	23.98	25.66	1.95	2.14	Pood 9.36	5 per cent..........	41
100 kilogs..............	1.95	2.14	0.39	0.43	Pood 0.39	5 per cent..........	42
....	Free	Free	Free	Free	Free	5 per cent..........	43
....	Free	Free	Free	Free	Free	Free	44
See Oils	....	....	....	....	Pood 1.40	See Oil	45
100 kilogs..............	Free	0.39	Free	0.048	Free	Free...............	46

Comparative table of import duties in the United States and European countries.

	ARTICLES.	ITALY.			SPAIN.	PORTUGAL.
			General tariff.	Tariff in treaty with France, &c.		
1	Pipe cases, stems, mounting, and all parts of pipe and pipe fixtures, and all smokers' articles.	100 kilogs	$9.75	$9.75	20 per cent.........	As mat'l manufac'd.
2	Pistols	Each barrel	0.07	0.07	Kilogramme .$1.00	30 per cent.........
3	Pitch.....................	Free	......	......	100 kilogs.... 0.05	Free ....
4	Plantain or Manilla grass, (Manilla hemp.)	Free	......	......	100 kilogs.... 2.00	Kilogramme $0.0008
5	Plaster of Paris, unground .	100 kilogs	0.48	Free.	100 kilogs.... 0.01	Kilog 0.0001
6	ground....	100 kilogs	0.48	Free.	100 kilogs.... 0.01	
7	calcined...	100 kilogs	0.48	Free.	100 kilogs.... 0.01	
8	Plaster busts, cast of, statue.	5 per cent	......	......	100 kilogs.... 1.50	Kilogramme 0.01
9	Plaster ornaments	5 per cent	......	......	100 kilogs.... 1.50	Kilogramme 0.01
10	Planks, wrought or rough..	Free	......	......	Cubic meter . 0.30	See Wood sawed...
11	Plants, medicinal	Free	......	......	Free	5 per cent..........
12	other	Free	......	......	Free	Free ....
13	Plantains..................	100 kilogs	0.195	Free	100 kilogs.... 0.50	Kilogramme . 0.002
14	Planes	100 kilogs	1.56	1.80	100 kilogs.... 1.50	Kilogramme . 0.081
15	Plata pina..................	Free	......	......	100 kilogs.... 0.01	100 kilogs.... 0.01
16	Plate, silver	See Silver.......	......	......	Kilogramme . 1.85	Kilogramme .16.20
17	gold......	See Gold.........	......	......	Kilogramme . 7.00	Kilogramme .54.00
18	Plated ware of all other kinds.	5 per cent	......	......	As plate, gold or silver.	See Plated silver or gold.
19	Platina, unmanufactured...	Free	......	......	In bars, pieces, powder, ingots, and useless table service, free. Manufactured in Spain, free. Otherwise, hectogramme ... 0.40	Sponge or powder, free. Drawn or spun, kilog ...... 2.70 Manufactured, per kilog 21.60
20	manufactured	As manuf. of silver....		......		
21	vases or retorts....	As manuf. of silver....		......		
22	Playing cards, value 25 cts. or less, per pack.	Pack..........	0.04	0.04	As prints, maps, &c., kilog. 0.25 (See Books.)	Playing cards, kilog..... 0.108
23	Playing cards, value over 25 cents.					
24	Plier's iron	100 kilogs	1.56	1.80	100 kilogs.... 1.50	Kilogr 0.081
25	Ploughs, iron	100 kilogs	1.17	1.56	100 kilogs.... 1.50	Kilogr 0.081
26	plane	100 kilogs	1.17	1.56	100 kilogs.... 1.50	Kilogr 0.081
27	Plumbago	100 kilogs	0.78	Free	Ton 0.05	Kilogr 0.081
28	Plums......................	100 kilogs	0.19	Free	100 kilogs.... 0.50	Fresh, kilogr 0.0108 Dry, kilogr 0.03
29	Plumes, ornamental, manufactured.	100 kilogs........	5.85	......	20 per cent.........	Kilogr 2.70
30	Plush, wool, not o. p. for ..	See Wool	......	......	See Wool..........	See Wool..........
31	cotton	See Cotton	......	......	See Cotton.........	See Cotton ....
32	hair	See Wool	......	......	See Wool..........	See Hair ....
33	Pocket books, leather......	100 kilogs	9.75	9.75	20 per cent.........	Kilogr 0.40
34	paper.......	100 kilogs	9.75	9.75	20 per cent.........	Kilogr....... 0.40
35	Pocket bottles, green glass .	100 kilogs	1.56	0.39	20 per cent.........	Kilogr. 0.172
36	Pole caps and ferules	100 kilogs	3.90	3.90	Copper,100kls25.80	Copper, kilogr 0.27
37	carriage hooks........	100 kilogs	1.56	1.80	Iron, 100 klgs 4.50	Iron, kilogr.. 0.162
38	Polishing stones............	Free	Free	......	Free..............	Free ....
39	powders..........	Free	Free	......	100 kilogs.... 0.01	Free ....
40	Polypodium, (drug)........	100 kilogs	0.39	Free	100 kilogs.... 1.10	5 per cent..........
41	Pomatum	100 kilogs	11.70	1.95	100 kilogs.... 0.30	Kilogs 0.54
42	Pomegranates	100 kilogs	0.195	Free	100 kilogs.... 0.50	Kilogs 0.002
43	Pomegranate-peel	100 kilogs	1.95	Free	100 kilogs.... 0.50	See Fruit ....
44	Poppy heads	Free	Free	......	100 kilogs.... 0.20	Kilogr 0.0016
45	oil	See Oil..........	......	......	See Oil.............	Kilogr 0.0108
46	seed...............	100 kilogs	0.29	Free	100 kilogs.... 0.20	Kilogr 0.0016

(*Duties expressed in gold dollars of the United States.*)—Continued.

BELGIUM.	AUSTRIA.			DENMARK.	SWEDEN.	NORWAY.	
		General tariff.	Tariff in treaty.				
10 per cent	Centner	$5.76		10 per cent	Pound....$0.0689	10 per cent	1
Free	Centner	7.20	$5.76	Pound....$0.091	Pound.... 0.055	Free	2
Free	Free			Free	Free	Free	3
Free	Free			Free	Free	Free	4
Free	Free			Free	Free	Free	5
Free	Free			Free	Free	Free	6
Free	Free			Free	Free	Free	7
Free	Free			Pound.... 0.0056	Free	Free	8
100 kilogs .. 0.195	Centner	0.388	Free.	Pound.... 0.0056	Free	Free	9
See Wood	Free			Cubic foot. 0.021	Free	Free	10
Free	Free			Pound.... 0.0113	Free	Free	11
Free	Free			Free	Free	Free	12
10 per cent	Centner	2.52		Free	Free	Pound ... 0.027	13
100 kilogs .. 0.78	Centner	2.88	2.16	Pound.... 0.019	5 per cent	Pound ... 0.028	14
Free	Free			Free	Free	Free	15
5 per cent	See Silver			Pound ... 0.091	See Silver	Loth.... 0.03	16
5 per cent	See Gold			Pound ... 0.091	See Gold		17
5 per cent	See Gold or silver			Pound ... 0.091	Pound.... 0.082	Pound ... 0.095	18
Free	Free			Free	Free	Free	19
15 per cent	As jewelry			Pound ... 0.091	Same os of gold	Pound ... 0.095	20
5 per cent	See Instruments, scientific.			Free	Free	Free	21
10 per cent	Centner (Stamp duties extra.)	15.12		Pack.....0.0113 and stamp duty	Playing cards; all, gross, (12 dozen packs, 4.96.	Prohibited	22
				Pack..... 0.045			23
100 kilogs .. 0.78	Centner	2.88	2.16	Pound..... 0.017	5 per cent	Pound 0.027	24
100 kilogs .. 0.78	Centner	1.68	1.20	Pound..... 0.017	5 per cent	Pound 0.027	25
100 kilogs .. 0.78	Centner	1.68	1.20	Pound..... 0.017	5 per cent	Pound 0.027	26
Free		Free		Free	Free	Free	27
100 kilogs .. 2.93		Free		Fresh ..... Free Dried, lb 0.0045	Pound.....0.0165	Pound 0.022	28
100 per cent	See Feathers			Pound..... 1.092	Pound..... 0.827	Pound 0.51	29
As wool	See Wool			See Woolen tissues	See Wool manuf.	See Wool manuf.	30
As cotton	See Cotton			See Cotton tissues	See Cotton manuf.	See Cotton, man.	31
As wool	See Hair			See Hair tissues	See Hair manuf.	See Hair manuf.	32
10 per cent	Centner	12.00	7.20	10 per cent	10 per cent	10 per cent	33
10 per cent	Centner	6.00	5.76	Pound..... 0.091	10 per cent	Pound 0.082	34
100 kilogs .. 0.195	See Glass			Pound..... 0.04	Pound..... 0.041	Pound 0.047	35
10 per cent	As material manufact'd			Copper, lb. 0.045	See Material manufactured.	Copper, lb 0.047	36
Steel, 100 kgs 0.78				Steel, lb... 0.017		Steel, lb .. 0.027	37
Free		Free		Free	Free	Free	38
Free	Centner	0.206	Free	Free	Free	Free	39
Free		Free		Pound.....0.0113	Free	Free	40
10 per cent	See Perfumery			Pound..... 0.091	Pound..... 0.11	Pound 0.005	41
10 per cent	Centner	2.52		Free	Free	Free	42
Free	Centner	0.388		Pound.....0.0045		Pound 0.027	43
Free		Free		Free	Free	Kree	44
Free	See Oils			Pound..... 0.017	See Oils	Pound 0.009	45
100 kilogs .. 0.117	Centner	0.388	Free	Free	Free	Free	46

Comparative table of import duties in the United States and European countries.

	ARTICLES.	UNITED STATES.	GREAT BRITAIN.	GERMAN ZOLL-VEREIN.	SWITZERLAND.
1	Porcelain and Parian ware, not ornamented.	45 per cent	Free	All porcelain, white, centner $1.26	Centner...$1.56
2	ornamented	50 per cent	Free		Centner... 1.56
3	glass..........	40 per cent	Free	All other, centner 2.88	Centner... 1.56
4	slates..........	45 per cent	Free		Centner... 1.56
5	Pork	Pound $0.01	Free	Centner... 0.36	Centner... 0.39
6	Porphyry	45 per cent......	Free	Free	Centner... 0.029
7	Portable desks............	35 per cent......	Free	Centner... 0.72	Centner... 1.56
8	Porter, in bottles	Gallon 0.35	All, barrel.....$4.87	All, centner. ... 0.48	All, centner.... 0.68
9	otherwise	Gallon 0.20			
10	Potasse, (potash) prussiate of red.	Pound 0.10	Free	Free	Centner... 0.058
11	yellow	Pound 0.05	Free	Free	Centner... 0.058
12	Potassium	Pound 0.20	Free	Centner... 2.40	Centner... 0.68
13	Potash, bi-chromate of.....	Pound 0.03	Free	Centner... 0.36	Centner... 0.68
14	chromate of	Pound 0.03	Free	Centner... 0.36	Centner... 0.68
15	chlorate of.........	Pound 0.06	Free	Centner... 2.40	Centner... 0.68
16	hydriodate of	Pound 0.75	Free	Centner... 2.40	Centner... 0.68
17	pure	20 per cent......	Free	Free	Centner... 0.058
18	iodide of...........	Pound 0.75	Free	Centner... 2.40	Centner... 0.68
19	acetate of	Pound 0.75	Free	Centner... 2.40	Centner... 0.68
20	Potatoes..................	Bushel 0.25	Free Potato flour, free	Free	15 centner. 0.028
21	Pots, black lead...........	25 per cent	Free	Centner... 0.72	Centner... 0.68
22	cast iron.............	Pound 0.01½	Free	Centner... 0.96	Centner... 0.68
23	melting, earthen	25 per cent......	Free............	Free............	Centner .. 0.68
24	Poultry or game, dressed...	10 per cent......	Free............	Free............	15 centner 0.58
25	prepared .	35 per cent......	Free............	Centner... 0.36	Centner .. 0.39
26	Pounce....................	20 per cent......	Free............	Free............	Centner .. 0.058
27	Powder, black lead	20 per cent......	Free............	Centner... 0.36	Centner... 0.68
28	blue	20 per cent......	Free............	Centner... 0.36	Centner... 0.68
29	of brass...........	20 per cent......	Free............	Free............	Centner... 0.145
30	of bronze	20 per cent......	Free............	Free............	Centner... 0.145
31	Powder, gun, and all explosive substances for blasting, value less than 20 cents per pound.	20 per cent., and per pound. 0.06	Free	Centner... 1.44	Prohibited ......
32	as above, over 20 cts. per pound.	20 per cent., and per pound. 0.10	Free	Centner... 1.44	Prohibited ......
33	Powder, hair	50 per cent......	Free............	Centner... 2.40	Centner... 2.93
34	teeth and skin, subtile.	50 per cent......	Free............	Centner... 2.40	Centner... 2.93
35	puffs	35 per cent......	Free............	Centner... 2.88	Centner... 2.93
36	pastes, balsams, &c.	50 per cent......	Free............	....	....
37	Precious stones, set	25 per cent......	Free............	Centner...36.06	Centner... 2.93
38	not set	10 per cent......	....	Centner... 0.36	Centner... 0.39
39	Ditto, of glass, imitations.	35 per cent......	....	Centner... 5.76	Centner... 2.93
40	imitations of, set	40 per cent......	....	Centner... 0.36	Centner... 0.39
41	Prepared clay	Ton 5.00	Free	Free............	15 centners 0.029
42	Prepared vegetables, meats, poultry, game, fish, &c.	35 per cent......	Free............	Centner... 0.26	Centner... 0.39
43	Preparations, chemical, not otherwise enumerated.	20 per cent......	Free............	Centner... 2.40	Centner... 0.68

(*Duties expressed in gold dollars of the United States.*)—Continued.

	FRANCE.				RUSSIA.	NETHERLANDS.	
	General tariff.		In treaty with Great Britain, &c.				
	In French vessels.	In other vessels.	In vessels of treaty powers.	In other vessels.			
Pocelain, not from Europe, 100 kilogs.	10 per	cent...	10 per	cent...	Porcelain, white, one-colored, gilded, not ornamented, per pood $3.12	All porcelain, 5 per cent.	1
Other common, 100 klgs.	$31.98	$34.07	10 per	cent...		....	2
Other fine, 100 kilogs...	63.70	67.07	10 per	cent...		....	3
....	....	....	....	....	Porcelain, gilded, ornamented, vases, statuettes, &c., also, with bronze ornaments, per pood 12.48	....	4
100 kilogs ....Fresh	....	....	Free	$0.048	Pood $0.50	100 kilogs....$0.41	5
Salt	0.097	0.097	$0.117	0.117			
....	Free	Free	Free	Free	Free	Free	6
....	15 per	cent...	10 per	cent ..	See Househ'd fur'ture	5 per cent..........	7
} Hectoliter............	1.17	1.17	0.86	0.86	Bottle 0.12	100 liters..... 1.20	8
					Pood 0.78	100 liters..... 1.29	9
100 kilogs..............	40.95	43.48	5.85	6.43	Pood 1.56	Free	10
100 kilogs..............	40.95	43.48	3.90	4.29	Pood 1.56	Free	11
100 kilogs..............	0.39	0.78	....	....	Pood 1.56	Free	12
....	Prohibi	ted.....	10 per	cent...	Potash, tartrate of, pood. 0.156	Free	13
100 kilogs..............	29.25	31.20	10 per	cent...	Pood 1.53	Free	14
100 kilogs..............	....	....	6.31	6.92.	Pood 0.85	Free	15
See Chemicals n. e	....	....	....	....	Pood 0.85	Free	16
See Chemicals u. e	....	....	....	....	Free	Free	17
See Chemicals n. e	....	....	....	....	Pood 0.85	Free	18
See Chemicals n. e	....	....	....	....	Pood 0.85	Free	19
....	Free	Free	Free	Free	Free	Free .... Potato-flour, 100 kilogs $0.81.	20
100 kilogs	4.68	5.15	3.90	4.29	} Pots for chemical purposes. Free	1 per cent..........	21
100 kilogs	Prohibi	ted.....	3.12	3.43		5 per cent..........	22
100 kilogs	....	....	Free	0.048	Pood 0.156	1 pes cent..........	23
....	Free	Free	Free	Free	Free	5 per cent..........	24
....	....	....	....	....	Pood 0.51	5 per cent..........	25
....	Free	Free	Free	Free	Free	Free	26
....	....	....	....	....	Pood.......... 0.85	Free	27
....	....	....	....	....	Pood.......... 0.85	Free	28
100 kilogs..............	Free ..	0.048	Free ..	Free ..	....	Free	29
100 kilogs..............	Free ..	0.048	Free ..	Free ..	....	Free	30
Prohibited	....	....	....	....	Prohibited..........	100 kilogs.... 2.05	31
Prohibited	....	....	....	....	Prohibited..........	100 kilogs.... 2.05	32
100 kilogs..............	4.87	5.25	1.95	2.14	Pood.......... 9.36	5 per cent	33
100 kilogs..............	35.88	38.16	1.95	2.14	Pood.......... 9.36	5 per cent	34
100 kilogs..............	31.98	34.07	1.17	1.29	Pood.......... 9.36	5 per cent	35
....	....	....	....	....	....	....	36
See Jewelry	....	....	....	....	Pound 0.85	5 per cent	37
....	Free ..	Free ..	Free ..	Free ..	Free	Free	38
See Jewelry	....	....	....	....	Pound 0.85	5 per cent	39
See Jewelry	....	....	....	....	Free	5 per cent	40
100 kilogs..............	Free ..	0.48	Free ..	0.049	Free	Free	41
....	Free ..	Free ..	Free ..	Free ..	Pood.......... 0.51	5 per cent	42
....	Prohi	bited...	5 per	cent.	Pood.......... 0.85	If containing alcohol per liter, 0.37 to 0.82, otherwise, free.	43

Comparative table of import duties in the United States and European countries.

	ARTICLES.	ITALY.			SPAIN.	PORTUGAL.
			General tariff.	Tariff in treaty with France, &c.		
1	Porcelain and Parian ware, not ornamented.	Porcelain, white, 100 kilogs.	$3.12	$2.34	Porcelain, per 100 kilogs..$10.50	Porcelain, kilogramme....$0.324
2	ornamented	Porcelain, gilded or painted, 100 kilogs.	4.87	4.87	......	......
3	glass		......	......	......	......
4	slates		......	......	......	......
5	Pork	100 kilogs	0.97	Free	100 kilogs.... 1.00	Kilogr....... 0.081
6	Porphyry	Free	Free	......	100 kilogs.... 0.01	Free
7	Portable desks	100 kilogs	9.75	10 p. ct	100 kilogs.... 7.00	35 per cent
8	Porter, in bottles	Each bottle	0.019	0.019	Hectoliter.. 2.50	Decaliter... 0.734
9	otherwise	Hectoliter	0.39	0.39		
10	Potasse, (potash) prussiate of red.	100 kilogs	0.975	Free	See Chemicals n. e.	See Chemicals n. e.
11	yellow	......	......	......		
12	Potassium	100 kilogs	0.975	Free		
13	Potash, bi-chromate of	100 kilogs	1.95	0.78		Potash:
14	chromate of	100 kilogs	1.95	0.78		Tartrate of.. Free
15	chlorate of	100 kilogs	1.95	0.39	100 kilogs.... 0.10	Acetate of, klgr 0.27
16	hydriodate of	100 kilogs	1.95	0.78	See Chemicals n. e.	Chromates of, kilogr....... 0.01
17	pure	100 kilogs	0.975	Free		Ferro-cyanide of.......... Free
18	iodide of	100 kilogs	1.95	0.78		Oxalate of, kgr 0.135
19	acetate of	100 kilogs	1.95	0.78		......
20	Potatoes	......	Free	......	100 kilogs.... 0.25	Kilogr....... 0.005
21	Pots, black lead	......	......	......	100 kilogs.... 1.60	Kilogr....... 0.054
22	cast iron	100 kilogs	1.56	1.80	100 kilogs.... 1.50	Kilogr....... 0.081
23	melting, earthen	100 kilogs	0.195	0.22	100 kilogs.... 0.30	Kilogr....... 0.021
24	Poultry or game, dressed	100 kilogr	0.975	Free	Small game 100 kilogs. 0.05	Kilogr....... 0.081
25	prepared	100 kilogs	0.975	Free		Kilogr....... 0.181
26	Pounce	100 kilogs	0.39	Free	100 kilogs.	Free
27	Powder, black lead	Free	......	......	100 kilogs ... 1.50	Free
28	blue	Free	......	......	100 kilogs ... 1.50	Free
29	of brass	Free	......	......	100 kilogs ... 0.30	Free
30	of bronze	Free	......	......	100 kilogs ... 0.30	Free
31	Powder, gun, and all explosive substances for blasting, value less than 20 cents per pound.	Kilogramme	1.17	......	Powder, blasting, kilog..... 0.062 Gun powder, kilogramme .. 0.25 Explosive mixt're, kilogramme 0.032	Powder, gun, prohibited. Blasting powder for mines, free.
32	as above, over 20 cts. per pound.	......	......	......		Other, per kilogramme ... 0.27
33	Powder, hair	As perfumery	......	......	Kilogramme . 0.30	20 per cent
34	teeth and skin, subtile.					100th per kilogramme.. 0.27
35	puffs					Kilogramme 1.08
36	pastes, balsams, &c.					20 per cent
37	Precious stones, set	Per cent	1	10	See Jewelry	1 per cent
38	not set	1 per cent	......	Free.	100 kilogs ... 0.075	½ per cent
39	Ditto, of glass, imitations	See Glass	......	......	See Jewelry	Kilogramme. 0.054
40	imitations of, set.	See Glass	......	......	100 kilogs ... 9.00	Kilogramme. 0.54
41	Prepared clay	100 kilogs	0.48	Free	100 kilogs ... 0.01	Free
42	Prepared vegetables, meats, poultry, game, fish, &c.	100 kilogs	1.56	0.59	See meat	See Vegetables .... See Meat
43	Preparations, chemical, not otherwise enumerated.	100 kilogs	1.95	0.78	Kilogramme . 0.02	10 per cent

(Duties expressed in gold dollars of the United States.)—Continued.

BELGIUM.	AUSTRIA.			DENMARK.	SWEDEN.	NORWAY.	
		General tariff.	Tariff in treaty.				
Porcelain and faience, 10 p. cent.	Porcelain, white, colored or			Plain, lb...$0.045	Porcelain, white or colored, not	Porcelain, white, not gilded or	1
....	gilded			Gilded&c.lb 0.091	painted:	ornamented, p.	2
....	border, cent'r	$2.88	$2.16	....	Plates, l b. $0.0082	pound ..$0.031	3
....	Porcelain, painted, printed, gilded, centner.....	7.20	5.76	....	Other articles, pound....0.0138 Painted: Plates, lb..0.0165 Other articles, pound.... 0.022 White, one color'd ed, pound 0.0275 Figured, gilded pound.... 0.055	Gilded or ornamented, per pound .. 0.062	4
100 kilogs ..$0.23	Centner	1.26	......	Free	Free	Pound 0.009	5
Free	....	Free	......	Free	Free	Free	6
10 per cent	See Manufac.	of wood	...	Pound.....0.0398	See Furniture....	Pound 0.009	7
Hectoliter .. 1.36	Centner	2.40	......	Pot 0.091	Kande..... 0.055	Pot 0.064	8
Hectoliter .. 1.17	Centner	0.72	......	Pound gross 0.0028	Kande..... 0.055	Pound 0.0228	9
Free	Centner	1.20	0.72				10
Free	Centner	1.20	0.72				11
Free	....	Free	......				12
Free							13
Free	See Chemicals	....	......	Medicinal salts, free. Other chemicals, pound 0.0113	See Chemicals not enumerated.	Free.	14
Free							15
Free							16
Free	....	Free	Free				17
Free	See Chemicals	......	......				18
Free	See Chemicals	......	......				19
Free	....	Free	......	Free	Free	Free	20
10 per cent	See Lead	......	......	Pound..... 0.045	Pound..... 0.008	Pound 0.011	21
100 kilogs .. 0.78	See Iron.....	......	......	Pound..... 0.017	Centner ... 0.275	Glazed, lb. 0.018 not gla'd, lb0.0045	22
100 kilogs .. 0.195	Centner	0.12	Free	Pound.....0.0014	Free	Free	23
100 kilogs .. 0.23	Centner	0.388	Free	Free	Free	Free	24
100 kilogs .. 1.95	Centner	1.26	......	Free	Free	Free	25
Free	....	Free	......	Free	Free	Free	26
Free	Centner	0.36	......	Free	Free	Free	27
Free	Centner	0.36	......	Free	Free	Free	28
Free	Centner	7.20	5.76	Free	Free	Free	29
Free	Centner	7.20	5.76	Free	Free	Free	30
Powder, gun or fulminating, 100 kilogs.	Centner	12.60	......	....	Pound 0.0138	Free	31
	Gun cotton, oxides and fulminating gold, centner.	126.00		Pound 0.026	Pound 0.0138	Free	32
10 per cent	Centner	0.36	......	Pound..... 0.079	Pound 0.11	Free	33
10 per cent	Centner	0.36	......	Pound..... 0.005	10 per cent	Free	34
10 per cent	Centner	5.76	......	Pound..... 0.091	10 per cent	10 per cent......	35
10 per cent.......	Centner	0.36	......	Pound.....0.0113	Free	Free	36
5 per cent	See Jewelry.	......	......	Pound 0.091	See Jewelry.....	Not gold, lb 0.109	37
Free	(Cut,) centner	5.76	5.76	Pound 0.091	Free	Free	38
10 per cent	See Glass....	......	......	Pound 0.091	Pound 0.0964	As material of setting, lb 0.109	39
10 per cent	See Glass....	......	......	Pound 0.091	Pound 0.041		40
Free	Free	......	......	Free............	Free	Free	41
....	Vegetables—centner....	0.36	......	....	....	Pound.... 0.002	42
100 kilogs .. 1.95	Meat, centner	1.26	......	If hermetically sealed, lb. 0.04	Free .... If medicinal, Free other, 5 per cent.	Hermetical 0.082 sealed vessels, lb	
If not alcoholic, free.	Centner	2.40	......	Pound 0.0113		Eree............	43

Comparative table of import duties in the United States and European countries.

	ARTICLES.	UNITED STATES.	GREAT BRITAIN.	GERMAN ZOLL-VEREIN.	SWITZERLAND.
1	Prints or engravings	25 per cent	Free	Free	Centner...$0.29
2	Prisms, cut glass	40 per cent	Free	Centner...$2.88	Centner... 0.29
3	Protractors, ivory-mounted	35 per cent	Free	Free	Centner... 0.39
4	Prunes	Pound....$0.05	Cwt......$1.70	Centner...$1.44	Centner... 0.145
5	Prussian blue	30 per cent	Free	Free	Centner... 0.68
6	Prussiate of potash, red	Pound.... 0.10	Free	Free	Centner... 0.68
7	Pucheri, (earthen pots for chemical use.)	20 per cent	Free	Free	15 centners 0.145
8	Pumice	Free	Free	Free	Centner... 0.058
9	Pumpkins	10 per cent	Free	Free	15 centners 0.015
10	Purple brown	25 per cent	Free	Free	Centner... 0.68
11	tin liquor	20 per cent	Free	Centner... 2.40	Centner... 0.68
12	Putty	Pound.... 0.01½	Free	Centner... 0.36	Centner... 0.68
13	Quadrants and sextants	35 per cent	Free	Free	Centner... 0.39
14	Quality binding worsted	50 per cent	Free	Centner... 7.20	Centner... 1.56
15	Quassia wood	20 per cent	Free	Centner... 0.36	Centner... 0.058
16	Quicksilver	15 per cent	Free	Free	Centner... 0.29
17	Quill baskets	30 per cent	Free	Centner... 5.76	Centner... 2.93
18	Quilla bark	20 per cent	Free	Medicinal—centner 0.36	Centner... 0.68
19	Quills, prepared	30 per cent	Free	Free	Centner... 1.86
20	unprepared	30 per cent	Free	Free	Centner... 0.68
21	Quiltings, or bed quilts	35 per cent	Free	Centner	Centner... 2.93
22	Quinine	45 per cent	Free	Centner... 2.40	Centner... 0.68
23	sulphate of	45 per cent	Free	Centner... 2.40	Centner... 0.68
24	salts of	45 per cent	Free	Centner	Centner... 0.68
25	Radix, or angelica root	20 per cent	Free	Free	Centner... 0.08
26	Roncou, or Orleans	Free	Free	Free	Centner... 0.08
27	Rag stones	10 per cent	Free	Free	Free
28	Rags of any kind, except wool.	Free	Free	Free	Centner... 0.058
29	Rags, wool	Pound.... 0.12	Free	Free	Centner... 0.058
30	Raisins, in boxes or jars, and other.	Pound.... 0.05	Cwt...... 1.70	Centner... 2.88	Centner... 0.145
31	Rakes, iron or wood	35 per cent	Free	Centner... 1.92	Centner... 0.68
32	steel	45 per cent	Free	Centner... 1.92	Centner... 0.68
33	Rape seed	Pound.... 0.01	Free	Free	Centner... 0.29
34	oil	Gallon.... 0.23	Free	Centner... 0.36	Centner... 0.097
35	Rappers, brass	35 per cent	Free	Centner .. 1.92	Centner .. 1.56
36	iron	35 per cent	Free	Centner .. 2.88	Centner .. 1.56
37	Rass, cornu cervi	20 per cent	Free	Free	Centner .. 0.29
38	Rasps, not over 10 inches long.	30 per cent., and per pound, 0.10.	Free	Centner .. 1.92	Centner .. 5.68
39	over 10 inches long	30 per cent., and per pound, 0.06.	Free	Centner .. 1.92	Centner .. 0.68
40	Rattans, unmanufactured	Free	Free	Free	Centner .. 0.058
	manufactured	25 per cent	Free	Centner .. 0.72	Centner .. 0.39
41	Rattles, of wood, ivory, &c., with bells.	50 per cent	Free Free	Centner .. 10.60	Centner .. 1.56
42	Ravens duck, hemp or flax	30 per cent	Free	Centner .. 0.48	Centner .. 1.56
43	Razors	35 per cent	Free	Centner .. 2.88	Centner .. 1.56
44	cases and strops	35 per cent	Free	Centner .. 2.88	Centner .. 1.56
45	Ready-made clothing, wool	See Wool	Free	Silk, cent. 28.80	Centner .. 2.93
46	other	35 per cent	Free	Other, cent. 21.60	Centner .. 2.93
47	Reaping hooks, iron	35 per cent	Free	Centner .. 1.92	Centner .. 0.68
48	steel	45 per cent	Free	Centner .. 1.92	Centner .. 0.68
49	Red chromate of potash	Pound 0.03	Free	Centner .. 0.36	Centner .. 0.68
50	sanders	Free	Free	Free	Centner .. 0.058
51	or crude tartar, (wine lees.)	Pound 0.06	Free	Centner .. 0.36	Centner .. 0.68
52	liquor	20 per cent	Free	Free	Centner .. 0.68
53	precipitate	20 per cent	Free	Centner .. 0.36	Centner .. 0.68

(*Duties expressed in gold dollars of the United States.*)—Continued.

	FRANCE.				RUSSIA.	NETHERLANDS.	
	General tariff.		In treaty with Great Britain, &c.				
	In French vessels.	In other vessels.	In vessels of treaty powers.	In other vessels.			
....	Free ..	Free ..	Free ..	Free ..	Free	Free	1
See Glass	....	....	....	....	Pood..........$3.12	5 per cent	2
100 kilogs.............	30 per	cent.	Free ..	$0.008	Free	5 per cent	3
100 kilogs.............	$3.12	$3.43	$1.56	1.72	Pood.......... 0.85	Not fresh: 100 kilogs..$0.61	4
....	Free ..	Free ..	Free ..	Free ..	Pood.......... 1.56	Free	5
100 kilogs.............	40.95	43.48	5.85	6.43	Pood.......... 1.56	Free	6
100 kilogs.............	1.17	1.29	Free ..	0.048	Free	Free	7
....	Free ..	Free ..	Free ..	Free ..	Free	....	8
....	Free ..	Free ..	Free ..	Free ..	Free	Free	9
....	Free ..	Free ..	Free ..	Free ..	Pood.......... 1.56	Free	10
....	Free ..	Free ..	Free ..	Free ..	Pood.......... 0.85	Free	11
....	....	....	....	....	Pood.......... 0.195	Free	12
100 kilogs.............	30 per	cent.	Free ..	0.048	Free	5 per cent	13
See Wollens	....	....	....	....	See Woollens........	5 per cent	14
See Wood	....	....	....	....	Free	Free	15
100 kilogs.............	0.195	0.97	Free ..	0.048	Pood.......... 0.85	Free	16
100 kilogs.............	3.90	4.68	10 per	cent.	Pood.......... 1.72	5 per cent	17
100 kilogs.............	Free ..	0.97	Free ..	0.048	Free	Free	18
....	Free ..	Free ..	Free ..	Free ..	Pood.......... 0.234	5 per cent	19
....	Free ..	Free ..	Free ..	Free ..	Pood.......... 0.234	Free	20
As material of which ma	de......	....	....	....	35 per cent	5 per cent	21
....	Prohi	bited.	5 per	cent.	Pood.......... 0.85	Free	22
....	Prohi	bited.	5 per	cent.	Pood.......... 0.85	Free	23
....	Prohi	bited.	5 per	cent.	Pood.......... 0.85	Free	24
100 kilogs.............	Free ..	0.97	0.29	0.43	Free	Free	25
....	....	....	....	....	Free	Free	26
100 kilogs.............	Free ..	0.0019	Free ..	Free ..	Free	Free	27
100 kilogs.............	Free ..	0.195	Free ..	Free ..	Free	Free	28
100 kilogs.............	Free ..	0.195	Free ..	Free ..	Free	Free	29
100 kilogs.............	0.048	0.39	0.058	0.106	Pood.......... 0.78	100 kilogs ... 0.10	30
See Tools..............	....	....	....	....	Pood.......... 0.62	5 per cent	31
See Tools..............	....	....	....	....	Pood.......... 0.62	5 per cent	32
....	Free ..	Free ..	Free ..	Free ..	Free	Hectoliter ... 0.04	33
100 kilogs.............	1.17	1.36	1.17	1.28	Pood.......... 1.40	See Oil............	34
See Tools..............	....	....	....	....	Pood.......... 0.62	5 per cent	35
See Tools..............	....	....	....	....	Pood.......... 0.62	5 per cent	36
Free..................	....	....	....	....	Free	Free	37
Ordinary, per 100 kilogs.	14.62	15.83	3.90	4.29	Free	5 per cent	38
Polished, length of 17 centimeters or more, per 100 kilogs.	35.10	37.53					
Less than 17 centimeters, 100 kilogs.	43.87	46.58					
Free..................	....	....	....	....	Free	Free	39
Prohibited	....	....	10 per	cent....	Pood.......... 0.19	5 per cent	40
100 kilogs.............	15.60	16.86	10 per	cent....	Pound.......... 0.25	5 per cent	41
See Manufactures of flax.	....	....	....	....	Pound.......... 0.11	5 per cent	42
See Cutlery...........	....	....	....	....	Pood.......... 9.36	5 per cent	43
100 kilogs.............	19.50	20.95	10 per	cent....	Pood.......... 0.31	5 per cent	44
As material	....	....	....	....	35 per cent	5 per cent	45
30 per cent............	....	....	....	....	35 per cent	5 per cent	46
100 kilogs.............	15.60	16.86	1.95	2.14	Pood 0.62	5 per cent	47
100 kilogs.............	15.60	16.86	3.90	4.29	Pood 0.62	5 per cent	48
See Chemicals not enum	erated..	....	....	....	Pood 0.68	Free	49
Free..................	....	....	....	....	Free	Free	50
See Chemicals not enum	erated..	....	....	....	Pood 0.156	Free	51
Free..................	....	....	....	....	Pood 0.156	Free	52
Free..................	....	....	....	....	Pood 0.85	Free	53

Comparative table of import duties in the United States and European countries.

	ARTICLES.	ITALY.			SPAIN.	PORTUGAL.
			General tariff.	Tariff in treaty with France, &c.		
1	Prints or engravings	Free			Kilogramme. $0.25	Kilogramme. $0.054
2	Prisms, cut glass	100 kilogs	$2.93	$1.36	100 kilogs ... 9.00	See Glass
3	Protractors, ivory-mounted	100 kilogs	3.90	1.95	10 per cent	5 per cent
4	Prunes	100 kilogs	0.39	Free.	100 kilogs.... 0.50	Kilogramme. 0.03
5	Prussian blue	100 kilogs	1.95	Free.	100 kilogs.... 5.00	Free
6	Prussiate of potash, red	100 kilogs	1.95	1.95	Kilogramme. 0.02	5 per cent
7	Pucheri, (earthen pots for chemical use.)	100 kilogs	0.195	0.23	100 kilogs ... 0.30	Kilogramme. 0.001
8	Pumice	Free			Free	Free
9	Pumpkins	Free			100 kilogs.... 0.25	Free
10	Purple brown	100 kilogs	1.95	0.78	100 kilogs ... 1.50	5 per cent
11	tin liquor	100 kilogs	1.95	0.78	100 kilogs ... 5.00	5 per cent
12	Putty	100 kilogs	0.39	0.39	100 kilogs.... 1.50	5 per cent
13	Quadrants and sextants	100 kilogs	1.90	1.95	10 per cent	5 per cent
14	Quality binding worsted	See Wool			See Manufactures of wool.	See Manufactures of wool.
15	Quassia wood	Free			100 kilogs ... 0.50	5 per cent
16	Quicksilver	100 kilogs	3.90	Free.	Kilogramme. 0.20	10 per cent
17	Quill baskets	100 kilogs	3.90	3.90	20 per cent	Kilogramme. 0.40
18	Quilla bark	100 kilogs	0.39	Free.	100 kilogs.... 2.00	5 per cent
19	Quills, prepared	100 kilogs	9.75	9.75	20 per cent	Kilogramme. 0.054
20	unprepared	100 kilogs	9.75	9.75		
21	Quiltings, or bed quilts	As Material of manufacture.			50 per cent. above duty on material.	Double duty on material.
22	Quinine	100 kilogs	2.93	0.39	20 per cent	5 per cent
23	sulphate of	100 kilogs	1.95	0.78	90 per cent	Free
24	salts of	100 kilogs	1.95	0.78	20 per cent	5 per cent
25	Radix, or angelica root	100 kilogs	1.95	Free.	100 kilogs ... 2.00	5 per cent
26	Roncou, or Orleans	Free			100 kilogs ... 2.00	5 per cent
27	Rag stones	Free			Free	Free
28	Rags of any kind, except wool.	Free			Free	Free
29	Rags, wool	100 kilogs	9.70	11.26	Free	Free
30	Raisins, in boxes or jars, or other.	100 kilogs	1.56	1.56	100 kilogs ... 0.50	Kilogramme. 0.016
31	Rakes, iron or wood	100 kilogs	1.56	1.80	100 kilogs ... 1.50	Iron, kilog... 0.081
32	steel	100 kilogs	1.56	1.80	100 kilogs ... 1.50	Steel, kilog.. 0.081
33	Rape seed	100 kilogs	0.19	Free.	100 kilogs ... 0.32	Kilogramme. 0.0016
34	oil	100 kilogs	0.975	1.12	100 kilogs ... 1.60	Kilogramme. 0.0108
35	Rappers, brass	100 kilogs	3.90	3.90	100 kilogs.... 25.00	Kilogs 0.27
36	iron	100 kilogs	1.56	1.80	100 kilogs.... 1.50	Kilogs 0.189
37	Rass, cornu cervi	Free			100 kilogs.... 0.10	5 per cent
38	Rasps, not over 10 inches long.	100 kilogs	1.56	1.80	100 kilogs.... 0.50	Kilogs 0.081
39	over 10 inches long	100 kilogs	1.56	1.80	100 kilogs.... 1.50	Kilogs 0.081
40	Rattans, unmanufactured	Free			100 kilogs.... 0.10	Free
41	manufactured	100 kilogs	0.95		100 kilogs.... 5.00	Kilogs 0.108
42	Rattles, of wood, ivory, &c., with bells.	100 kilogs	9.75	9.75	Kilogs 0.30	Kilogs 0.27
43	Ravens duck, hemp or flax	See Manuf. of flax.			See Manuf. of flax	See Manuf. of flax
44	Razors	100 kilogs	1.56	1.80	Kilog 0.20	Kilog 0.162
45	cases and strops	100 kilogs	9.75	9.75	20 per cent	20 per cent
46	Ready-made clothing, wool	50 per ct. above duty on material.			Addit'l to duty on material, 50 per ct.	Double duty on material.
47	other					
48	Reaping hooks, iron	100 kilogs	1.56	1.80	100 kilogs.... 1.50	Kilogs 0.081
49	steel	100 kilogs	1.56	1.80	100 kilogs.... 1.50	Kilogs 0.081
50	Red chromate of potash	100 kilogs	1.95	0.78	Kilogs 0.02	Kilogs 0.0108
51	sanders	Free			100 kilogs.... 1.02	5 per cent
52	or crude tartar, (wine lees.)	Free			Kilogs 0.02	5 per cent
53	liquor	100 kilogs	1.95	1.95	20 per cent	Kilogs 0.0108
54	precipitate	100 kilogs	1.95	0.78	20 per cent	10 per cent

(Duties expressed in gold dollars of the United States.)—Continued.

BELGIUM.	AUSTRIA.			DENMARK.	SWEDEN.	NORWAY.	
		General tariff.	Tariff in treaty.				
Free	Free	......	......	Free	Free	Free	1
10 per cent	Centner	$3.48	$1.92	Pound $0.04	Pound $0.041	Pound $0.018	2
Free	Centner	4.80	3.60	Pound 0.091	Pound 0.041	10 per cent	3
10 per cent	Centner	0.388	Free.	Pound 0.0045	Pound 0.0165	Pound.... 0.022	4
Free	Centner	1.20	0.72	Pound 0.028	Free	Free	5
Free	Centner	0.36	......	Pound 0.0113	Free	Free	6
100 kilogs ..$0.195	Centner	0.12	Free	Free	Free	Free	7
Free	Free	......	......	Free	Free	Free	8
Free	Free	......	......	Free	Free	Pound.... 0.002	9
Free	Centner	0.388	Free.	Pound 0.0056	Free	Pound.... 0.009	10
Free	Centner	0.36	......	Pound 0.0056	Free	Pound.... 0.009	11
Free	Centner	0.36	Free	Free	Free	Free	12
Free	Centner	2.88	2.16	Accord'g to mat'al	Pound 0.041	10 per cent	13
See Manufactures of wool.	See Manufac	t's of	wool.	Pound 0.008	See Manufac. of wool.	Pound.... 0.146	14
Free	Free	......	......	Free	Free	Pound.... 0.109	15
Free	Free	......	......	Pound 0.0113	Free	Free	16
10 per cent	Centner	4.80	......	10 per cent	Pound 0.0689	Pound.... 0.072	17
Free	Free	......	......	Free	Free	Pound.... 0.072	18
Free	Centner	0.384	Free	Pound 0.028	Pound ...0.0689	Free	19
					.... Free	Free	20
10 per cent	As material m	anuf.	......	Double duty on material.	10 per cent	10 p. cent. above duty on materi'l.	21
Free	Medicines, ctr	7.20	......	Pound 0.0113	Free	Free	22
Free	See Chemic'ls	......	......	Pound 0.0113	Free	Free	23
Free	See Chemic'ls	......	......	Pound 0.0113	Free	Free	24
Free	......	Free	......	Free	Free	Free	25
Free	......	Free	......	Free	Free	Free	26
Free	......	Free	......	Free	Free	Free	27
Free	......	Free	......	Free	Free	Free	28
Free	......	Free	......	Free	Free	Pound.... 0.027	29
100 kilogs .. 2.93	Centner	2.52	......	Pound 0.0045	Pound 0.0165	Free	30
10 per ct., (wood)..	Centner	1.68	1.20	Wood.... Free	5 per cent	Wood .... Free	31
100 kilogs .. 0.78	Centner	1.68	1.20	Ir'n, steel. lb 0.017	5 per cent	On iron. lb 0.027	32
100 kilogs .. 0.117	Centner	0.028	Free	Free	Free	Ton 0.136	33
Free	Centner	0.648	0.36	Pound..... 0.017	See Oils	Pound.... 0.009	34
10 per cent	Centner	3.60	2.16	Pound..... 0.045	Pound..... 0.041	Pound 0.047	35
100 kilogs .. 0.78	Centner	2.88	2.16	Pound..... 0.017	Pound.....0.0165	Pound 0.027	36
Free	Free	......	......	Free	Free	Free	37
100 kilogs .. 0.78	Centner	2.88	2.16	Pound..... 0.017	5 per cent	Pound 0.027	38
100 kilogs .. 0.78	Centner	2.88	2.16	Pound..... 0.017	5 per cent	Pound 0.027	39
Free	Free	......	......	Free	Free	Free	40
10 per cent	Centner	1.20	0.72	Free	Pound..... 0.32	Pound 0.014	41
10 per cent	Centner	5.76	......	See Manuf. of wood, ivory. &c	Pound.....0.0689	See Wood, ivory, &c.	42
See Tissues of flax.	See Tissues of	flax ..	......	See Tissues of flax	See Manuf. of flax.	See Tissues of fiax	43
10 per cent	See Cutlery	......	......	Pound..... 0.017	See Cutlery	Pound 0.027	44
10 per cent	According to	mater	ial ...	10 per cent	10 per cent	10 per cent	45
10 per cent	See Clothing	......	......	Double duties of material.	See Clothing. ..	10 per ct.; embroidered, 20 per ct. above material.	46
10 per cent	See Clothing	......	......				47
100 kilogs .. 0.78	Centner	2.88	2.16	Pound..... 0.017	5 per cent	Pound 0.027	48
100 kilogs .. 0.78	Centner	2.88	2.16	Pound..... 0.017	5 per cent	Pound 0.027	49
Free	See Chemicals	......	......	Pound.....0.0113	See Chemicals ...	......	50
Free	Free	......	......	Free	Free	Free	51
Free	Free	......	......	Pound.....0.0113	Free		52
Free	Centner	0.36	......	Pound..... 0.028	Free		53
Free	See Chemicals	......	......	Pound.....0.0113	Free		54

Comparative table of import duties in the United States and European countries.

	ARTICLES.	UNITED STATES.	GREAT BRITAIN.	GERMAN ZOLL-VEREIN.	SWITZERLAND.
1	Red wood	Free	Free	Free	Centner . . $0. 058
2	wool or fur for hatters	20 per cent	Free	Free	Centner . . 3. 058
3	Reeds, unmanufactured	Free	Free	Free	Centner . . 0. 058
4	manufactured	25 per cent	Free	Centner . . $0. 72	Centner . . 0. 68
5	weavers	35 per cent	Free	Free	Centner . . 0. 058
6	Regulus of antimony	10 per cent	Free	Free	Centner . . 0. 68
7	Reindeer skins, undressed	10 per cent	Free	Free	Centner . . 0. 058
8	dressed	20 per cent	Free		Centner . . 0. 39
9	tanned	25 per cent	Free	Centner . . 0. 48	Centner . . 0. 39
10	tongues	20 per cent	Free	Centner . . 0. 36	Centner . . 0. 39
11	Rennets, raw	10 per cent	Free	Free	Centner . . 0. 058
12	Resin	20 per cent	Free	Free	Centner . . 0. 058
13	of jalap	40 per cent	Free	Free	Centner . . 0. 058
14	nux vomica	40 per cent	Free	Centner . . 2. 40	Centner . . 0. 68
15	Rhodium, oil of	50 per cent	Free	See Oil	See Oil
16	Rhubarb	Pound $0. 50	Free	Centner . . 0. 36	Centner . . 0. 68
17	Rice, clean	Pound 0. 02½	Free	Centner . . 0. 72	Centner . . 0. 097
18	unclean	Pound 0. 02	Free	Centner . . 0. 48	Centner . . 0. 028
19	Rifles	35 per cent	Free	Centner . . 7. 20	Centner . . 0. 39
20	Rivets, brass	35 per cent	Free	Centner . . 0. 96	Centner . . 1. 56
21	iron	Pound 0. 02½	Free	Centner . . 0. 96	Centner . . 1. 56
22	steel	45 per cent	Free	Centner . . 0. 96	Centner . . 1. 56
23	Rock moss	10 per cent	Free	Free	Centner . . 0. 029
24	Rods and eyes for stairs	35 per cent	Free	Centner . . 1. 92	Centner . . 1. 56
25	wood	35 per cent	Free	Free	
26	composition and copper	35 per cent	Free	Centner . . 2. 88	Centner . . 1. 56
27	steel	45 per cent	Free	Centner . . 1. 92	Centner . . 1. 56
28	Roman cement	20 per cent	Free	Free	Centner . . 0. 029
29	vitriol	Pound 0. 05	Free	Centner . . 0. 36	Centner . . 0. 057
30	Rope, made of hides, cut in strips.	20 per cent	Free	Centner . . 0. 48	Centner . . 0. 29
31	of grass, bark, or clar, and cordage of cocoanut hulls.	Pound 0. 03½	Free	Centner . . 0. 48	Centner . . 0. 29
32	Roots, arrow	30 per cent	Free	Centner . . 1. 44	Centner . . 0. 68
33	madder	Free	Free	Free	Centner . . 0. 058
34	medicinal, crude, not otherwise enumerated.	20 per cent	Free	Centner . . 0. 36	Centner . . 0. 058
35	all bulbous, not otherwise enumerated.	30 per cent	Free	Free	Centner . . 0. 058
36	Rose leaves	Pound 0. 50	Free	Centner . . 0. 36	Centner . . 0. 68
37	water	50 per cent	Free	Centner . . 2. 40	Centner . . 2. 93
38	Rosin	20 per cent	Free	Free	Centner . . 0. 058
39	Rosolio, (a cordial)	Gallon 2. 50	See Spirits	Centner . . 1. 32	Centner . . 1. 56
40	Rotten stone	Free	Free	Free	Free
41	Rouge	50 per cent	Free	Centner ... 2. 40	Centner ... 2. 93
42	Rubrum, bark	20 per cent	Free	Free	Centner ... 0. 145
43	Rubies	10 per cent	Free	Free	Centner ... 0. 39
44	set	25 per cent	Free	Centner ... 5. 76	Centner ... 2. 93
45	Rules, of bone, brass, ivory, &c., &c.	35 per cent	Free	According to material.	Centner ... 0. 39
46	Rum	See Gin	Gallon ...$2. 47 to.. 2. 53	Centner.. 4. 32	Centner ... 1. 56
47	essence, or oil of	Ounce 2. 00		Centner ... 4. 32	Centner ... 1. 56
48	Rust of iron	20 per cent	Free	Free	Centner ... 0. 058
49	Rye	Bushel 0. 15	Free	Free	Centner ... 0. 03
50	flour	10 per cent	Free	Free	Centner ... 0. 097
51	Sabres	35 per cent	Free	Centner ... 1. 92	Centner ... 0. 39
52	Saddlery, all n. o. s	35 per cent	Free	Centner ... 7. 20	Common, centner .... 1. 56; Silver plated, centn'r. 2. 93

(*Duties expressed in gold dollars of the United States.*)—Continued.

FRANCE.	General tariff.		In treaty with Great Britain, &c		RUSSIA.	NETHERLANDS.	
	In French vessels.	In other vessels.	In vessels of treaty powers.	In other vessels.			
Free					Free	Free	1
Free					Free	Free	2
Reeds, exotic, raw, 100 k.	Free ..	$0. 39	$0. 39	$0. 39	Free	Free	3
Other, 100 kilogs	Free ..	0. 195	Free ..	Free ..	Free	5 per cent	4
Prepared 100 kilogs	$1. 95	2. 92			Free	5 per cent	5
Free					Pood $0. 16	Free	6
					Free	Free	7
See Skins					Free	Free	8
					Pood 3. 43	2 per cent	9
See Meat					Pood 0. 50	100 kilogs $3. 28	10
Free					Not enumerated	Free	11
100 kilogs	Free ..	0. 195	Free ..	0. 048	Pood 0. 078	Free	12
Resinous extracts					Pood 0. 234	Free	13
100 kilogs	Free ..	2. 53			Pood 0. 234	Free	14
See Oil					Pood 0. 47	See Oil	15
					Free	Free	16
100 kilogs	0. 097	0. 39			Pood 0. 39	Free	17
100 kilogs	0. 048	0. 33			In the straw, imported into St. Petersburg, pood 0. 16	Free Rice meal: 100 kilogs .. 0. 16	18
100 kilogs	39. 00	41. 43	46. 80	49. 62	Pood 14. 04	5 per cent	19
100 kilogs			3 90	4. 29	Pood 0, 62	5 per cent	20
100 kilogs	Prohibited		3. 12	3. 43	Pood 0. 62	5 per cent	21
100 kilogs			3. 90	4. 29	Pood 0. 62	5 per cent	22
Free					Free	Free	23
100 kilogs	Prohibited		3. 90	4. 29	Pood 2. 34	5 per cent	24
See Wood					Free	5 per cent	25
See Copper					Pood 2. 34	5 per cent	26
See Steel					Pood 0. 19	5 per cent	27
Free					Free	Free	28
See Vitriol					Pood 0. 16	Free	29
100 kilogs	4. 87	5. 36	2. 92	3. 20	Pood 0. 31	100 kilogs 0. 20	30
100 kilogs	0. 97	1. 06	1. 17	3. 20	Pood 0. 31	100 kilogs 0. 20	31
100 kilogs	0. 097	0. 097			Pood 0. 78	Free	32
Free					Free	Free	33
100 kilogs	Free ..	0. 39	Free ..	0. 048	Free	Free	34
Free					Free	Free	35
Free					Free	Free	36
See Perfumery					Pood 3. 12	See Perfumery	37
100 kilogs	Free ..	0. 195	Free ..	0. 048	Free	Free	38
100 kilogs	29. 25	29. 25	2. 92	2. 92	Bottle 0. 50	Liter 0. 22	39
Free					Free	Free	40
100 kilogs	19. 11	20. 55	1. 95	2. 14	Pood 9. 36	As perfumery	41
100 kilogs	Free ..	0. 97	Free ..	0. 048	Free	Free	42
Free					Free	Free	43
See Jewelry					Pound 0. 85	5 per cent	44
See Instruments—mathematical.					According to material.	5 per cent	45
Hectolitre, of pure alcohol.	4. 87	4. 87	2. 92	2. 92	Pood 6. 63 Bottle 0. 50	Litre 0. 22	46
See Essences					Pood 6. 63	See Oil	47
					Free	Free	48
Free					Free	Hectoliter 0. 61	49
					Pood 0. 03	100 kilogs 0. 16	50
100 kilogs	78. 00	81. 40	7. 80	8. 58	Pood 14. 04	5 per cent	51
Saddles not trimmed with leather, each... Other saddlery	0. 97 Prohibited.	0. 97	10 per cent.		Pound 0. 31	5 per cent	52

Comparative table of import duties in the United States and European countries.

	ARTICLES.	ITALY.			SPAIN.	PORTUGAL.
			General tariff.	Tariff in treaty with France, &c.		
1	Red wood	100 kilogs	$0.39	Free.	100 kilogs....$2.00	5 per cent
2	wool or fur for hatters.	See Wool			100 kilogs.... 0.40	See Wool
3	Reeds, unmanufactured	Free			100 kilogs.... 0.10	Free
4	manufactured	100 kilogs	0.195	Free.	20 per cent	Kilogr $0.108
5	weavers	100 kilogs	0.195	Free.	100 kilogs.... 3.50	100 kilogr.... 2.00
6	Regulus of antimony	100 kilogs	2.93	1.17	100 kilogs.... 0.30	Kilogr 0.02
7	Reindeer skins, undressed	Free			100 kilogs.... 1.50	20 per cent (7–9)
8	dressed	100 kilogs	1.95		100 kilogs.... 1.50	
9	tanned	100 kilogs	3.90	2.93	Kilogr 0.25	
10	tongues	100 kilogs	3.90		100 kilogs.... 0.50	Kilogr 0.081
11	Rennets, raw	Free			100 kilogs.... 0.10	
12	Resin	Resin indigenous,				Copal, kilogr. 0.027
13	of jalap	crude, 100 kil..	0.19	0.195	100 kilogs.... 2.00	Not specified, kilogr 0.013
14	nux vomica	Purified, 100 kil.	0.97	0.39	20 per cent	Colophonium turpentine, free.
15	Rhodium, oil of	See Oils			100 kilogs.... 1.60	Decaliter 0.54
16	Rhubarb	100 kilogs	1.95	0.39	20 per cent	5 per cent
17	Rice, clean	Free			100 kilogs.... 1.60	Kilogr 0.016
18	unclean	Free			100 kilogs.... 0.80	Kilogr 0.009
19	Rifles	See Arms			Kilogr 1.00	30 per cent
20	Rivets, brass	100 kilogs	3.90	3.90	100 kilogs....25.00	Kilogr 0.27
21	iron	100 kilogs	1.56	1.80	100 kilogs.... 1.50	Kilogr 0.189
22	steel	100 kilogs	1.56	1.80	100 kilogs.... 1.50	Kilogr 0.162
23	Rock moss	Free			100 kilogs.... 0.10	5 per cent
24	Rods and eyes for stairs	100 kilogs	3.90	3.90	100 kilogs....25.00	Kilogs 0.27
25	wood	100 kilogs	0.58	Free	See Wood	See Wood
26	composition and copper	100 kilogs	3.90	3.90	100 kilogs....25.00	Kilogr 5.27
27	steel	100 kilogs	1.56	1.80	100 kilogs.... 1.50	Kilogr 0.162
28	Roman cement	100 kilogs	0.48	Free	100 kilogs.... 0.01	Kilogr 0.0001
29	vitriol	100 kilogs	0.195	0.195	Kilogr 0.02	10 per cent
30	Rope, made of hides, cut in strips.	100 kilogs	0.58	0.58	100 kilogs.... 4.00	Kilogr 0.072
31	of grass, bark, or ciar, and cordage of cocoanut hulls.	100 kilogs	0.29	0.29	100 kilogs.... 4.00	Kilogr 0.086
32	Roots, arrow	100 kilogs	1.35	0.39	100 kilogs.... 2.00	5 per cent
33	madder	Free			100 kilogs.... 4.00	Kilogr 0.013
34	medicinal, crude, not otherwise enumerated.	100 kilogs	1.35	0.39	100 kilogs.... 2.00	All 5 per cent ....
35	all bulbous, not otherwise enumerated.	100 kilogs	1.35	0.39	100 kilogs.... 2.00	For dyeing, free ..
36	Rose leaves	100 kilogs	0.97	0.39	100 kilogs.... 2.00	20 per cent
37	water	As perfumery			See Perfumery and Essences.	20 per cent
38	Rosin	100 kilogs	0.195	0.195	100 kilogs.... 2.00	Kilogr 0.013
39	Rosolio, (a cordial)	Hectoliter	1.95	1.95	Liter 0.20	Decaliter 1.62
40	Rotten stone	Free			Free	Free
41	Rouge	As Perfumery			100 kilogs 1.50	5 per cent
42	Rubrum, bark acu	100 kilogs	1.95	0.39	100 kilogs.... 2.00	5 per cent
43	Rubies	Per cent	1	Free.	Free	½ per cent
44	set	Per cent	1	10	See Jewelry	1 per cent
45	Rules, of bone, brass, ivory, &c.	100 kilogs	9.75	9.75	See Material manufactured.	See Material manufactured.
46	Rum	Hectoliter Bottle	1.95 0.12		Liter 0.20	Decaliter 1.62
47	essence, or oil, of	See Oil			20 per cent	Decaliter 0.54
48	Rust of iron	Free			100 kilogs.... 0.50	Free
49	Rye	100 kilogs	0.145	0.145	100 kilogs.... 0.52	10 kilogs..... 0.043
50	flour	100 kilogs	0.24		100 kilogs ... 0.78	10 kilogs..... 0.054
51	Sabres	See Arms			Kilogramme.. 0.40	15 per cent
52	Saddlery, all n. o. s.	Saddles, not trimm'd, each Other articles, 100 kilogs	0.097 9.75	 9.75	Kilogramme.. 0.50	Kilogramme 0.648 Ornamented, kilogramme .. 1.08 Trunks, each 1.836

(*Duties expressed in gold dollars of the United States.*)—Continued.

BELGIUM.	AUSTRIA.			DENMARK.	SWEDEN.	NORWAY.	
		General tariff.	Tariff in treaty.				
Free	Free			Free	Free		1
Free	See Wool			Free	Free	Free	2
Free	Free			Free	Free		3
10 per cent	Centner	$1.20	$0.72	Free	Pound $0.32	Pound $0.014	4
10 per cent	Centner	0.12	Free.	Free	Free	Free	5
Free	Free			Pound $0.0113	Free	Free	6
Free	See Hides and skins.			Free	Free	Free	7
Free	See Hides and skins.			Pound 0.068	Pound 0.055	Pound 0.045	8
100 kilogs ..$2.93	See Leather			Pound 0.068	Pound 0.055	Pound 0.045	9
100 kilogs .. 0.23	See Meat			See Meat	Free	Dried and smok'd, pound ... 0.009	10
Free	Free			Free	Free	Free	11
Free	Centner	0.388					12
Free	Centner	0.388		Pound ...0.0013	Free	Free	13
Free	Centner	0.388					14
Free	See Oils			Pound 0.017	See Oils	Pound 0.0067	15
Free	Centner	2.52	1.44	Pound 0.0113	Free	Free	16
100 kilogs .. 0.29	Centner	0.388		Pound 0.0113	Shelled, p'd 0.0027	Pound 0.011	17
100 kilogs .. 0.195	Centner	0.129		Pound 0.0367	Not shelled, free	Pound .... 0.006 In ships: Ton 1.09	18
Free	Centner	7.20	5.76	Pound 0.091	Pound 0.055	Free	19
10 per cent	See Manuf. of copper			Pound 0.045	Pound 0.041	Pound 0.047	20
100 kilogs .. 0.78	See Manuf. of iron			Pound 0.017	See Iron and steel manuf's.	Pound 0.027	21
100 kilogs .. 0.78	See Manuf. of iron			Pound 0.017		Pound 0.027	22
Free	Free			Free	Free	Free	23
10 per cent	See Material manufact'd.			According to mat'l	Pound 0.041	Pound 0.047	24
10 per cent	Centner	0.12	Free.	Free	Free	Free	25
10 per cent	See Copper			Pound 0.045	Pound 0.041	Pound 0.047	26
100 kilogs .. 0.78	See Steel			Pound 0.017	Pound 0.027	Pound 0.027	27
Free	Free			Free	Free	Free	28
Free	Free			Pound 0.0113	Free	Free	29
(See Cordage,) free.	See Cordage.			Pound 0.0056	Pound 0.008	Pound 0.009	30
(See Cordage,) free.	See Cordage.			Pound 0.0056	Pound 0.008	Pound 0.009	31
Free	Free			Free	Free	Free	32
Free	Centner	0.0528	Free.	Free	Free	Free	33
Free	Free			Free	Free	Free	34
Free	Free			Free	Free	Free	35
Free	Free			Free	Free	Free	36
Free	Centner	7.20	5.76	Pound 0.091	Pound 0.11	Pound 0.10	37
Free	Centner	2.52		Free	Free	Free	38
See Liqueurs	See Liqueurs.			Pot 0.091	Kande 0.303	Pot 0.218	39
Free	Free			Free	Free	Free	40
	Centner	0.36				Free	41
Free	Free			Free	Free	Free	42
	Centner	5.76	5.76			Free	43
5 per cent	See Jewelry.			Pound 0.091	See Jewelry	Pound 0.109	44
Free	Centner	4.80	3.60	See Materials manufactured.	Pound 0.041	See Manufactur's of ivory, &c.	45
See Spirituous Liquors.	Centner	3.88		Pot 0.091	Kande 0.303	As Spirits	46
See Essences	See Essences.			Pound 0.091	See Essences	Free	47
Free	Free					Free	48
100 kilogs .. 0.117	Centner	0.129	Free.	Free	Free	Ton 0.054	49
100 kilogs .. 0.23	Centner	0.388	Free.			Ton 0.054	50
Free	Centner	7.20	5.76	Pound 0.017	See Manfs. of steel.	Pound 0.073	51
10 per cent	Centner	5.76	3.60	Pound 0.091	Mounted, gilded, &c., p'nd 0.0689 Other, p'nd 0.055	Pound .. 0.062	52

Comparative table of import duties in the United States and European countries.

	ARTICLES.	UNITED STATES.	GREAT BRITAIN.	GERMAN ZOLL-VEREIN.	SWITZERLAND.
1	Safflour	10 per cent	Free	Centner ...$0.36	Centner ...$0.145
2	extract of	20 per cent	Free	Centner ... 0.36	Centner ... 0.68
3	Saffron, (including cake,)	10 per cent	Free	Centner ... 4.68	Centner ... 0.68
4	Sago, and flour of sago	Pound $0.01½	Free	Free	Centner ... 0.029
5	Salacine, (medic. prep.,)	40 per cent	Free	Centner ... 2.40	Centner ... 0.68
6	Sail duck	30 per cent	Free	Centner ... 0.48	Centner ... 0.39
7	Sal ammoniac	10 per cent	Free	Centner ... 0.36	Centner ... 0.68
8	diuretic	20 per cent	Free	Centner ... 2.40	Centner ... 0.68
9	succinic	20 per cent	Free	Centner ... 2.40	Centner ... 0.68
10	Salad oil	Gallon 1.00	Free	See Oil	See Oil
11	Salmon, preserved	30 per cent	Free	Centner ... 0.36	Centner ... 0.39
12	in oil	30 per cent	Free	Centner ... 3.60	Centner ... 1.56
13	pickled in barrels	Barrel..... 3.00	Free	Centner ... 0.36	Centner ... 0.39
14	dry or smoked	Pound 0.00½	Free	Centner ... 0.36	Centner ... 0.39
15	Saleratus	Pound 0.01½	Free	Free	Centner ... 0.68
16	Salt, in bulk	100 lbs 0.18	Free	Prohibit'd, except by spec'l permit.	Centner.. 0.029
17	otherwise	100 lbs 0.24	Free		Centner.. 0.029
18	Saltpetre, or sal nitre, or nitrate of potash, crude.	Pound 0.02½	Free	Free	Centner ... 0.058
19	Saltpetre, refined	Pound 0.03	Free	Free	Centner ... 0.58
20	partially refined	Pound 0.02	Free	Free	Centner ... 0.58
21	Salts, brown	20 per cent	Free	Centner ... 1.44	Centner ... 0.68
22	Epsom	Pound 0.01	Free	Centner ... 1.44	Centner ... 0.68
23	Glauber	Pound 0.00½	Free	Centner ... 0.12	Centner ... 0.68
24	Rochelle	Pound 0.15	Free	Centner ... 1.44	Centner ... 0.68
25	all other chemical	20 per cent	Free	Centner ... 2.40	Centner ... 0.68
26	Sand	10 per cent	Free	Free	Centner ... 0.145
27	Sandarach, refined	Pound 0.10	Free	Free	Centner ... 0.68
28	Santonin	Pound 5.00	Free	Free	Centner ... 0.68
29	Sarcocolla, crude	20 per cent	Free	Free	Centner ... 0.68
30	Sardines, in oil, bbls. or kegs	50 per cent	Free	See Fish	See Fish
31	Sarsaparilla	20 per cent	Free	Centner ... 0.36	Centner ... 0.68
32	Sash fasteners	35 per cent	Free	Iron, centn'r 1.92	Centner ... 0.68
33	Sassafras	20 per cent	Free	Centner ... 0.36	Centner ... 0.68
34	oil of	50 per cent	Free	Centner ... 0.60	Centner ... 0.68
35	Satin, white	Pound 0.03	Free	See Silk	Centner ... 1.65
36	Sauces, all kinds	35 per cent	Free	Centner ... 5.04	Centner ... 2.93
37	Sausages	35 per cent	Free	Centner ... 0.36	Centner ... 0.39
38	Saws, cross cut	Lineal foot. 0.10			
39	mill pit, not over 9-in. wide.	Lineal foot. 0.12½			
40	drag, not over 9-in. wide.	Lineal foot. 0.12½			
41	mill pit, over 9-inches wide.	Lineal foot. 0.20			
42	drag, over 9-inches wide.	Lineal foot. 0.20	Free	Centner.... 1.92	Centner.... 0.68
43	hand, not over 24-in. long.	30 per cent. and per dozen. 0.75			
44	hand, over 24-inches long.	30 per cent. and per dozen. 1.00			
45	back, not over 10-in. long.	30 per cent. and per dozen. 0.75			
46	back, over 10-inches long.	30 per cent. and per dozen. 1.00			
47	sets, steel	45 per cent			
48	Scagliola tables or slabs	35 per cent	Free	Free	Centner... 0.058
49	Scale beams	35 per cent	Free	Centner... 0.96	Centner... 0.68
50	Scales, bone	35 per cent	Free	Centner... 2.88	Centner... 0.68

(*Duties expressed in gold dollars of the United States.*)—Continued.

FRANCE.					RUSSIA.	NETHERLANDS.	
	General tariff.		In treaty with Great Britain, &c.				
	In French vessels.	In other vessels.	In vessels of treaty powers.	In other vessels.			
					Free	Free	1
					Pood $0.85	Free	2
100 kilogs	Free	$0.58	Free	$0.048	Pood 6.24	5 per cent	3
100 kilogs	$0.195	0.48			Pood 0.78	Free	4
	Prohib	ited	5 per	cent	Pood 0.85	Free	5
See Manufactur's of flax					Pound 0.12	Roll $0.12	6
Crude, 100 kilogs	0.097	0.097			All, pood 0.16		7
Refined, 100 kilogs	0.195	0.21				All, free	8
	Prohib	ited	5 per	cent			9
See Oil					See Oil	See Oil	10
100 kilogs	0.97	1.06	$0.97	1.07	Pood 2.34	See Fish	11
100 kilogs	4.87	5.36	1.95	2.14	Pood 2.34		12
Salt'd or smok'd, 100 kils	7.80	8.54	0.97	1.06	Pood 0.85		13
Dry, 100 kilogs	0.97	1.06	0.97	1.06	Pood 0.85		14
Prohibited					Free	Free	15
Salt, not white, by Atlantic and Channel, 100 kilogs	0.335	0.43			Salt, by sea or land, pood 0.30	Salt, refined and residue, 100 kilogs. 4.92	16
By Mediterranean, 100 kilogs	0.097	0.195			Into Archangel, pood 0.17		17
White refined, by Atlantic and Channel, 100 kilogs	0.535	0.63					
By Mediterranean, 100 kilogs	0.097	0.195					
100 kilogs	Free	0.78	Free	0.048	Pood 0.31	All, free	18
100 kilogs	Free	0.78	Free	0.048	Prohibited		19
100 kilogs	Free	0.78	Free	0.048	Pood 0.31		20
					Pood 0.85		21
					Pood 0.078		22
	Prohib	ited	5 per	cent	Pood 0.078		23
					Pood 0.85		24
					Pood 0.85		25
Common sand	Free	Free	Free	Free	Free	All, free	26
For glass manf., 100 kilos	Free	0.195			Pood 0.85		27
See Chemicals, not enumerat'd.					Free		28
100 kilogs	Free	0.39	0.39	0.39	Free		29
See Fish					See Fish	See Fish	30
100 kilogs	Free	0.78	0.39	0.43	Free	Free	31
	15 per	cent.	10 per	cent.	Pood 0.62	5 per cent	32
100 kilogs	Free	0.97	Free	0.048	Free	Free	33
See Oil					Pood 1.40	See Oil	34
Kilogramme	3.12	3.43	Free	0.048	See Silk	5 per cent	35
100 kilogs	4.87	5.35	4.87	5.35	Pood 2.34	100 kilogs 10.24	36
Free					Pood 0.51	100 kilogs 1.26	37
							38
							39
							40
Saws, circular, diameter over 20 centimetres	100 kilogr'mes. 34.12	36.30	All of iron & steel 2.92	3.20	All, pood 0.62	5 per cent	41
20 centimetres or less	39.00	41.43					42
Others of length, 146 centimetres or more	21.40	22.96	Of steel only				43
146 to 50 centimeters	34.12	36.30	3.90	4.29			44
50 or less centimeters	39.00	41.43					45
							46
							47
Free					Free	5 per cent	48
100 kilogs	9.75	10.72	1.95	2.14	Pood 0.62	5 per cent	49
As fancy goods	9.75	10.72	1.95	2.14	Pood 0.62	5 per cent	50

Comparative table of import duties in the United States and European countries.

	ARTICLES.	ITALY.			SPAIN.	PORTUGAL.
			General tariff.	Tariff in treaty with France, &c.		
1	Safflour.....................	100 kilogs.......	$0.97	$0.39	100 kilogs....$0.50	5 per cent..........
2	extract of..........	100 kilogs.......	1.95	0.78	20 per cent.........	5 per cent..........
3	Saffron, (including cake,)..	100 kilogs.......	0.487	......	100 kilogs.... 0.50	Kilogramme .$0.03
4	Sago, and flour of sago.....	Free............	......	......	100 kilogs.... 0.60	Kilogramme . 0.016
5	Salacine, (medic. prep.) ...	100 kilogs.......	1.95	0.39	20 per cent.........	5 per cent..........
6	Sail duck..................	See Manufactur's	of flax	......	See Tissues of flax.	Unbl'ch'd, kil. 0.162
7	Sal ammoniac............	100 kilogs.......	1.95	0.78	100 kilogs.... 0.75	Kilogramme . 0.054
8	diuretic..............	100 kilogs.......	1.95	0.78	100 kilogs.... 0.75	5 per cent..........
9	succinic	100 kilogs.......	1.95	0.78	100 kilogs.... 0.75	5 per cent..........
10	Salad oil..................	See Oil	......	......	100 kilogs.... 5.00	Kilogramme.. 0.108
11	Salmon, preserved.........				100 kilogs.... 0.20	Kilogramme . 0.037
12	in oil....	See Fish	......	......	100 kilogs... 1.60	In oil, kilogrm 0.075
13	pickled, in barrels				100 kilogs... 0.20	Kilogramme . 0.037
14	dry or smoked				100 kilogs... 0 20	Kilogramme . 0.037
15	Saleratus..................	100 kilogs.......	0.73	Free.	100 kilogs.... 0.02	Kilogramme . 0.02
16	Salt, in bulk...............	Sea Salt	Prohi	bited.	Salt, common, per 100 kilogs. 0.65	Free ....
17	otherwise	Miner'l salt, per 100 kilogs....	7.80	7.80		
18	Saltpeter, or sal niter, or nitrate of potash, crude.	100 kilogs.......	1.95	Free.	100 kilogs... 0.75	Free ....
19	Saltpeter, refined....	100 kilogs.......	1.95	Free.		
20	partially refined..	100 kilogs.......	1.95	Free		
21	Salts, brown..............	100 kilogs.......	0.195	0.195	Alkalies, carbonates, caustics, and ammonia salts, 100 kilogs.. 0.75	5 per cent.... ....
22	epsom	100 kilogs.......	0.23	0.195		5 per cent ....
23	glauber	100 kilogs.......	0.195	0.195		Free ....
24	Rochelle	100 kilogs.......	1.95	0.78		5 per cent.... ....
25	all other chemical....	100 kilogs.......	1.95	0.78		5 per cent ....
26	Sand	Free............	......	......	Free	Free...............
27	Sandarach, refined.........	100 kilogs.......	1.95	0.39	100 kilogs.... 2.00	5 per cent..........
28	Santonin..................	100 kilogs.......	0.97	0.39	Kilogramme.. 0.02	5 per cent..........
29	Sarcocolla, crude	100 kilogs.......	2.39	0.39	100 kilogs.... 2.00	5 per cent..........
30	Sardines, in oil, bbls. or kegs	See Fish........	......	......	100 kilogs.... 1.60	Kilogramme . 0.075
31	Sarsaparilla...............	100 kilogs.......	0.195	Free.	100 kilogs.... 2.40	5 per cent..........
32	Sash fasteners............	100 kilogs.......	3.90	3.90	Iron, 100 kilos 1.50	Kilogramme . 0.189
33	Sassafras..................	100 kilogs.......	1.95	0.39	Vegetable matter not enumerated, 100 kilogs. 2.00	5 per cent ....
34	oil of.............	See Oil	......	......	100 kilogs.... 1.60	Kilogramme . 0.01
35	Satin, white...............	See Silk	......	......	See Silk	See Silk ....
36	Sauces, all kinds...........	100 kilogs.......	5.85	4.88	Meat preserved, 100 kilogs. 1.00	Kilogramme 0.081
37	Sausages	100 kilogs.......	3.90	......		
38	Saws, cross-cut	All Tools of iron or steel, per 100 kilogs.....	1.56	1.80	As Articles of steel not otherwise specifi'd 100 kil. 5.50	Tools of iron or steel, kilog. 0.081
39	mill-pit, not over 9 in. wide.					
40	drag, not over 9 in. wide.					
41	mill-pit, over 9 inches wide.					
42	drag, over 9 inches wide.					
43	hand, not over 24 in. long.					
44	hand, over 24 inches long.					
45	back, not over 10 in. long.					
46	back, over 10 inches long.					
47	sets, steel............					
48	Scagliola tables or slabs....	Each.... 0.03 to	0.05	Free.	100 kilogs ... 1.50	Kilogramme .0.0108
49	Scale beams...............	100 kilogs.......	1.56	1.80	100 kilogs ... 4.50	Kilogramme. 0.162
50	Scales, bone...............	100 kilogs.......	9.75	9.75	Kilogramme. 0.01	Kilogramme. 3.24

(*Duties expressed in gold dollars of the United States.*)—Continued.

Belgium.	Austria.			Denmark.	Sweden.	Norway.	
		General tariff.	Tariff in treaty.				
Free	Centner	0.0528	Free.	Free	Free	Free	1
Free	See Extracts.	......	......	Pound... $0.0113		Free	2
15 per cent	Centner	7.56	......	Free		Free	3
100 kilogs	Centner	2.52	......			Pound.. $0.011	4
Free	Centner	7.20	......	Pound.... 0.0113		Free	5
See Tissues of flax.	See Tissues of flax		......	See Tissues of flax.	See Tissues of flax.	See Tissues of flax	6
Free	Centner	0.388	Free.	Free	Free	Free	7
						Free	8
						Free	9
Free	See Oils	......	......	Pound.... 0.017	See Oils	Pound.... 0.009	10
100 kilogs ..$1.95	See Fish	......	......	Pound...0.0017	See Fish	Pound .. 0.027	11
100 kilogs .. 1.95				Pound.... 0.04		Pound .. 0.027	12
100 kilogs .. 1.95				Pound...0.0017		Pound .. 0.027	13
100 kilogs .. 1.95				Pound...0.0017		Pound .. 0.027	14
Free	Free	......	......	Free	Free	Free	15
Salt, raw, free.. Refined, 100 kilogram's. 7.94	Salt, for cooking, centner.	0.2016	......	Pound.... 0.023	Salt, not refin'd; also Glauber salts, free. For cooking, cubic foot. 0.027 Refined, per pound.. 0.008 Medicinal, pound.. 0.008	Ton.... 0.1366 Refin'd, for table use, p'nd 0.0045 (Salt, crude, entered at ports Vardo, Vadso, and Hammerfest, ton 0.068)	16 17
Free	Free	......	......	Pound.... 0.0028	Free	Free	18
	Centner	0.36	0.36	Pound.... 0.0028		Free	19
	Centner	0.36	0.36	Pound.... 0.0028		Free	20
Free	Medicines, centner...	2.52	1.44	Free	See Chemicals and medicinal articles.	Free	21
	Or see Chemicals		......			Free	22
						Free	23
						Free	24
						Free	25
Free	Free	......	......			Free	26
Crude, free..... 10 per cent	Centner	2.52	1.44	Pound.... 0.0113	Free	Free	27
See Chemicals n. e.	Centner	2.52	1.44	Pound.... 0.0113		Free	28
Free	Free	......	......	Free		Free	29
100 kilogs .. 1.95	See Fish	......	......	Pound.... 0.0017	See Fish	Pound.... 0.027	30
Free	Centner	2.52	1.44	Free	Free	Free	31
10 per cent	According to	material	..	Brass, p'nd. 0.045	Accord'g to mat'l.	Accord'g to mat'l.	32
Free	Free	......	......	Pound.... 0.0113	Free	Free	33
Free	See Oils	......	......	Pound 0.017	See Oils	Pound.... 0.009	34
See Silk	See Silk	......	......	See Silk	See Silk	See Silk	35
15 per cent	Centner	1.26	......	Free	Pound 0.044	Free	36
100 kilogs. 0.23	Centner	3.88	......	Free	Pound 0.027	Pound.... 0.009	37
							38
							39
							40
							41
							42
All saws, per 100 kilogs. 0.78	Saws, cent'r.	2.88	2.16	Pound 0.017	All Tools 5 p. cent.	Pound 0.027	43
							44
							45
							46
							47
10 per cent	See Manf. of	stone.	......	Pound 0.0056	Free	Free	48
100 kilogs .. 0.78	Centner	2.88	2.16	Pound 0.017	Pound 0.0165	Pound.... 0.027	49
10 per cent	Centner	1.20	0.72	Pound 0.039	Pound 0.068	Pound.... 0.05	50

Comparative table of import duties in the United States and European countries.

	ARTICLES.	UNITED STATES.	GREAT BRITAIN.	GERMAN ZOLL VEREIN.	SWITZERLAND.
1	Scales, ivory with steel joints.	45 per cent......	Free............	Centner...$1.92	Centner...$0.68
2	all ivory	35 per cent......	Free............	Centner... 2.88	Centner... 0.68
3	Scantling and sawed timber not planed or wrought.	20 per cent......	Free............	Free............	Centner... 0.058
4	Scammoniate, medic. gum..	20 per cent......	Free............	Centner... 0.36	Centner... 0.68
5	Scilla or squills	10 per cent......	Free............	Free............	Centner... 0.68
6	Scissors....................	35 per cent......	Free............	Not pol., cen. 1.92 Polish'd, cen. 2.88	Centner.. 1.56
7	Scoop nets	35 per cent...... (See fishing nets)	Free............ Free............	Unblch'd, cen. 0.36 Bleached, cen. 2.88	Centner.. 1.56
8	Scythes....................	45 per cent......	Free............	Not sh'p'd, cen. 0.96 All finsh'd, cen. 1.92	Centner.. 0.68
9	Sealing wax	35 per cent......	Free............	Centner... 2.40	Centner... 1.56
10	Sea weed and other vegetable substances used for mattresses.	20 per cent......	Free............	Free............	Centner... 0.145
11	Seeds, garden and agriclt'ral.	30 per cent......	Free............	Free............	Centner... 0.029
12	medicinal...........	20 per cent......	Free............	Centner... 0.36	Centner... 0.68
13	anise................	Pound....$0.05			
14	anise, star..........	Pound.... 0.10			
15	canary (60 lbs.=1 bus.)	Bushel.... 1.00			
16	caraway	Pound.... 0.03			
17	cardamom	Pound.... 0.50			
18	coriander	Pound.... 0.03	Free..........	Free............	All others per centner. 0.029
19	fennel	Pound.... 0.02			
20	fenugreek	Pound.... 0.02			
21	hemp....	Pound.... 0.00½			
22	mustard	Pound.... 0.03			
23	rape	Pound.... 0.01			
24	castor (50 lbs per bus.)	Bushel.... 0.60			
25	Seed and stick lac..........	Pound.... 0.10	Free............	Centner... 0.36	Centner... 0.68
26	Seines	Pound.... 0.06½	Free............	Centner... 2.80	Centner... 1.56
27	Segars.....................	50 p.ct. & lb. 2.50	Pound....$1.22	Centner...14.40	Centner... 2.93
28	Seltzer water.............	30 per cent......	Free............	Free............	Centner... 0.29
29	Seneca root.............	20 per cent......	Free............	Free............	Centner... 0.68
30	Senna	20 per cent......	Free............	Free............	Centner... 0.68
31	Sepia (cuttle fish)..........	Pound.... 0.05	Free............	Free............	Centner... 0.39
32	Sextants..................	35 per cent......	Free............	Free............	Centner... 0.39
33	Shaddocks................	10 per cent......	Free............	See Oranges	See Fruit.......
34	Shawls, cotton	35 per cent......			
35	cashmere, silk	60 per cent......			
36	camel's hair	40 p. c. & lb. 0.50			
37	lace, sewed	35 per cent......			
38	worsted, costing less than $2 per yard, weighing over 8 ounces per yard.	40 per cent. and per pound. 0.50	Free........	Shawls, silk, per centner... 28.80 Wool, cen'r 21.60	All, cen.. 2.93
39	worsted, costing ov'r $2, weighing over 8 ounces per yard.	40 per cent. and per pound. 0.50			
40	worsted, costing ov'r $2, weighing under 8 ounces per yard.	40 per cent. and per pound. 0.50			
41	silk	60 per cent......			
42	Shears	35 per cent......	Free............	Centner... 2.88	Centner... 0.68
43	Sheathing, copper	45 per cent......	Free............	Free............	Centner... 0.29
44	part copper	45 per cent......	Free............	Free............	Centner... 0.29
45	Sheathing paper	10 per cent......	Free............	Free............	Centner... 0.39
46	Sheets, willow............	30 per cent......	Free............	....	....
47	Sheetings, linen, hemp, or Russia, brown or white, &c.	35 per cent......	Free............	See Manufactur's of flax.	....
48	Shell gold, or silver for painting	40 per cent......	Free............	Free............	Centner... 0.68
49	Shell baskets, boxes, &c....	35 per cent......	Free............	Centner... 2.85	Centner... 2.93

(*Duties expressed in gold dollars of the United States.*)—Continued.

FRANCE.					RUSSIA.	NETHERLANDS.	
	General tariff.		In treaty with Great Britain, &c.				
	In French vessels.	In other vessels.	In vessels of treaty powers.	In other vessels.			
As Fancy goods					Pood $0.62	5 per cent	1
As fancy goods, 100 kilo's	$19.50	$20.95	10 per cent.		Pood 0.62	5 per cent	2
100 kilogs	Free	0.019	Free	$0.022	Free	3 per cent	3
100 kilogs	Free	0.39	$0.39	0.39	Pood 0.23	Free	4
Free					Free	Free	5
100 kilogs	24.37	26.27	2.92	3.20	Pood 0.62	5 per cent	6
100 kilogs	4.87	5.32	3.90	4.29	Pood 0.31		7
100 kilogs	23.40	25.05	2.92	3.20	Pood 0.34	5 per cent	8
100 kilogs	19.50	20.95	5.85	6.43	Pood 1.56	5 per cent	9
Free					Free	5 per cent	10
Free					Free	Free	11
					Free	Hectoliter .. $0.04	12
							13
							14
							15
							16
							17
All other seeds, 100 kil.	Free	0.97	Free	0.048	Free	All seeds not spec'ly enum'd, heclt'r. 0.04	18
							19
							20
							21
							22
							23
							24
100 kilogs	Free	1.95	Free	0.048	Pood 0.85	Liter 0.37	25
100 kilogs	4.87	5.32	3.90	4.29	Pood 0.31	5 per cent	26
For gov't account only	Free	2.92			Pound 1.72	100 kilogs 16.40	27
Free					Bottle 0.016	100 bottles .. 0.20	28
100 kilogs	Free	0.97	0.39	0.43	Free	Free	29
100 kilogs	Free	0.97	Free	0.048	Free	Free	30
Free					Free	Free	31
100 kilogs	30 per cent.		Free	0.048	Free	5 per cent	32
100 kilogs	Free	0.78	Free	0.47	Pood 0.195	See Fruit	33
							34
							35
							36
							37
							38
Cashmere, 100 kilogs Silk, See silk See Manf. of wool	9.75	10.72	5 per cent.		Shawls of silk or wool, pound.. 2.34	Shawls, 5 per cent.	39
							40
							41
100 kilogs	15.60	16.86	2.92	3.20	For she'ri'g sh'p, free	5 per cent	42
100 kilogs	2.92	3.40	1.95	2.14	Pood 0.47	100 kilogs 0.40	43
100 kilogs	2.92	3.40	1.95	2.14	Pood 0.47		44
100 kilogs			1.56	1.72	Pood 0.16	5 per cent	45
	Free		Free	Free	Free	5 per cent	46
					30 per cent	5 per cent	47
100 kilogs	4.87	5.35	4.87	5.35	Pood 3.43	Free	48
As fancy articles	Prohibited.		10 per cent.		Pound 0.85	5 per cent	49

Comparative table of import duties in the United States and European countries.

	ARTICLES.	ITALY.			SPAIN.	PORTUGAL.
			General tariff.	Tariff in treaty with France, &c.		
1	Scales, ivory with steel joint.	100 kilogs.......	$9.75	$9.75	Kilogramme. $2.50	Kilogramme. $5.40
2	all ivory	100 kilogs.......	19.50	19.50	Kilogramme. 2.50	Kilogramme. 5.40
3	Scantling and sawed timber not planed or wrought.	Free............	......	......	100 kilogs ... 0.50	Kilogramme. 0.027
4	Scammoniate, medic. gum..	100 kilogs.......	2.93	......	100 kilogs ... 2.00	Kilogr'mme. 0.0027
5	Scilla or squills............	100 kilogs.......	0.39	Free.	20 per cent	Kilogramme. 0.054
6	Scissors.......	100 kilogs.......	1.56	1.80	Kilogramme. 0.45	Kilogramme. 0.081
7	Scoop nets	100 kilogs.......	2.34	2.80	See Yarns of flax..	See Fishing nets ...
8	Scythes	100 kilogs.......	1.56	1.80	100 kilogs ... 5.50	Kilogramme. 0.081
9	Sealing wax..............	See Wax	......	3 p. c.	Kilogramme. 0.15	Kilogramme. 0.137
10	Sea weed and other vegetable substances used for mattresses.	Free............	......	......	100 kilogs ... 2.00	5 per cent ....
11	Seeds, garden and agriclt'ral	....	......	......	100 kilogs ... 0.32	....
12	medicinal	....	......	......	100 kilogs ... 0.32	....
13	anise...............					
14	anise, star..........					
15	canary (60 lbs.=1 bus.)					
16	caraway					
17	cardamom					Garden, kilog. 0.027
18	coriander	Seeds, various, 100 kilogs.....	0.195	Free.	Seeds not enum'd, 100 kilogs.. 0.32	For Agricul. free..
19	fennel	Oleous, 100 kil..	0.20	0.20		Oleous seeds, per kilogramme. 0.0016
20	fenugreek					For distilling per kilogramme. 0.054
21	hemp					
22	mustard............					
23	rape					
24	castor (50 lbs. per bus.)					
25	Seed and stick lac..........	100 kilogs.......	1.95	1.95	100 kilogs ... 2.50	Kilogramme. 0.0108
26	Seines...................	100 kilogs	3.90	4.58	See Yarn of flax...	See Yarn of flax...
27	Segars	....	Prohi	bited.	Gov't monopoly ...	Kilogramme. 0.432
28	Seltzer water..............	100 kilogs.......	0.165	Free	Free	Kilogramme. 0.0108
29	Seneca root...........	100 kilogs.......	1.95	0.29	100 kilogs ... 2.00	5 per cent.........
30	Senna...................	100 kilogs.......	0.97	0.39	100 kilogs ... 2.00	5 per cent ....
31	Sepia, (cuttle fish)..........	See Fish........	......	......	100 kilogs ... 1.60	Kilogramme. 0.036
32	Sextants	100 kilogs.......	3.90	1.95	10 per cent	5 per cent.........
33	Shaddocks	100 kilogs.......	1.95	0.39	100 kilogs ... 0.50	Kilogramme. 0.0162
34	Shawls, cotton					Shawls of cashmere, one color, kilogr'me.. 1.752
35	cashmere, silk					One or more col'rs, merino, kil. 4.07
36	camel's hair........					Shawls not specified, one or more colors, per kilogr'me.. 3.52
37	lace, sewed					Shawls of cashmere or other hair, kilogr'me.. 2.70
38	worsted, costing less than $2 per yard, weighing over 8 ounces per yard.	See Manuf. of cotton, silk, wool, and hair.			See Tissu's of silk, wool, &c.	Shawls of silk-lace or thread, per kilogr'me.. 5.40
39	worsted, costing ov'r $2, weighing over 8 ounces per yard.		......	......		Other silk shawls, kilogr'me.. 1.70
40	worsted, costing ov'r $2, weighing under 8 ounces per yard.					
41	silk......					
42	Shears	100 kilogs.......	1.56	1.80	100 kilogs ... 5.50	Kilogramme. 0.081
43	Sheathing, copper	100 kilogs.......	2.34	2.34	100 kilogs ...14.00	Kilogramme. 0.0027
44	part copper....	100 kilogs.......	2.34	2.34	100 kilogs ...14.00	Kilogramme. 0.0027
45	Sheathing paper...........	100 kilogs.......	1.56	1.56	Kilogs 1.0081	Kilogs...... 0.0081
46	Sheets, willow............	Free............	......	......	20 per cent	Kilogs...... 0.108
47	Sheetings, linen, hemp, or Russia, brown or white, &c.	See Manuf. of flax.	......	......	See Tissues of flax.	Kilogs...... 0.54
48	Shell gold, or silver for painting.	Free............	......	......	See Gold	Kilogs...... 2.16
49	Shell baskets, boxes, &c....	100 kilogs.......	9.75	9.75	20 per cent	Kilogs...... 0.10

(*Duties expressed in gold dollars of the United States.*)—Continued.

Belgium.	Austria.			Denmark.	Sweden.	Norway.	
		General tariff.	Tariff in treaty.				
10 per cent	Centner	$7.20	$5.76	Pound ... $0.091	Pound ... $0.138	Pound ... $0.158	1
10 per cent	Centner	7.20	5.76	Pound ... 0.091	Pound ... 0.138	Pound ... 0.158	2
Free	Centner	2.52	1.44	Pound ... 0.0113	Free	Free	3
Above 5 centimeters thick, cubic meter ... $1.17; 5 centimeters or less thick, cubic meter .. 1.75 or 5 per cent.	Free	......	......	Cubic foot. 0.034	Free	Free	4
Free	Centner	0.388	Free.	Free	Free	Free	5
For trades, 100 kilogs 0.78; Fancy, 10 p. cent.	Large, centn'r.	2.88	2.16	Pound ... 0.017	Not pol. lb. 0.027; Pol. lb ... 0.0689	Not pol., lb. 0.027; Pol., lb ... 0.048	6
Free	See Fishing..	nets..	......	Pound ... 0.0027	Free	Pound ... 0.072	7
100 kilogs . $0.78	Centner	2.88	2.16	Pound ... 0.017	5 per cent	Pound ... 0.027	8
10 per cent	Centner	2.40	......	Pound ... 0.045	10 per cent	Pound ... 0.063	9
Free	Free	......	......	Free	Free	Free	10
....	Centner	0.129	Free.	....	Free	Free	11
....	Centner	0.388	Free.	....	Free	Free	12
							13
							14
					Canary, lb. .0.011	Canary, lb. .0.018	15
							16
Seeds, per 100 kil ... 0.117	Other seeds, centner.	0.388	Free.	Seeds, oleous and medicinal, free.	All seeds n. o. e .. Free	All seeds no. .e .. Free	17
							18
							19
							20
						Hemp, ton. 0.136	21
							22
						Rape, ton .. 0.136	23
							24
Not alco'lic, free ..	Centner	7.20	5.76	Pound ... 0.028	Free	Pound ... 0.009	25
As Yarn	As Yarn	......	......	Pound ... 0.0027	As Yarn	Pound ... 0.079	26
100 kilogs .. 50.30	Centner	12.60	......	Pound ... 0.182	Pound ... 0.50	Pound ... 0.182	27
Free	Free	......	......	Pound ... 0.0057	Free	Free	28
Free	Centner	2.52	1.44	Free	Free	Free	29
Free	Free	......	......	Free	Free	Free	30
See Fish	See Fish	......	......	Pound ... 0.0017	Free	Pound ... 0.027	31
Free	Centner	2.88	2.16	10 per cent	Pound ... 0.041	10 per cent	32
Free	Free	......	......	Pound ... 0.0079	Free	Pound ... 0.027	33
							34
							35
							36
							37
							38
10 per cent	See Clothing.	......	......	Pound ... 0.182	See Clothing	Embroidered with silk and wire, lb. 0.319; Others, lb. 0.146	39
							40
							41
100 kilogs ... 0.78	Centner	2.88	2.16	Pound ... 0.017	5 per cent	Pound ... 0.027	42
10 per cent	See Copper..	......	......	Pound ... 0.017	Free	Pound ... 0.047	43
10 per cent	See Copper..	......	......	Pound ... 0.017	Free	Pound ... 0.047	44
100 kilogs ... 0.78	Centner	0.36	......	Pound ... 0.0028	Pound ... 0.0027	Pound ... 0.002	45
10 per cent	Free	......	......	....	10 per cent	Free	46
See Manuf. of flax.	See Manuf. of flax.	......	......	Pound ... 0.034	See Manuf. of flax.	See Tissues of flax.	47
Free	Centner	7.20	5.76	Pound ... 0.028	Free	Free	48
Free	Centner	5.76	......	10 per cent	10 per cent	10 per cent	49

Comparative table of import duties in the United States and European countries.

	ARTICLES.	UNITED STATES.	GREAT BRITAIN.	GERMAN ZOLL-VEREIN.	SWITZERLAND.
1	Shells, all except cocoa	Free............	Free............	Free............	Centner...$0.39
2	cocoa shells..........	Pound..$0.02			
3	Shellac.................	Pound.... 0.10	Free............	Free............	Centner... 0.68
4	Shingles..................	35 per cent......	Free............	Free............	15 centner 0.12
5	Shirts, not otherwise provided for.	35 per cent......	Free............	Centner..$21.60	Centner... 2.93
6	woolen	35 per cent., and per pound. 0.50	Free............	Centner... 7.20	Centner... 2.93
7	made on frame......	35 per cent., and per pound. 0.50	Free............	Centner... 7.20	Centner... 1.56
8	Shoe binding, cotton.......	35 per cent......	Free............	Centner... 2.16	Centner... 1.56
9	silk	60 per cent......	Free............	Centner...28.80	Centner... 1.56
10	thread	40 per cent......	Free............	Centner... 2.16	Centner... 0.68
11	Shoes or slippers...........	35 per cent......	Free............	Centner... 2.88	Com'n, cen. 1.56
12	of silk....	35 per cent......	Free............	Centner... 7.20	Fan'y, cen. 2.93
13	Shot bags and belts	35 per cent......	Free............	Centner... 7.20	Centner... 2.93
14	Shovels, wood and iron	35 per cent......	Free............	Centner... 0.96	Centner... 0.68
15	iron and steel.....	45 per cent......	Free............	Centner... 0.96	Centner... 0.68
16	Shrubs	30 per cent......	Free............	Free............	Centner... 0.68
17	Shumac, or sumac	10 per cent......	Free............	Centner... 0.36	Centner... 0.68
18	Shuttlecocks and battledore.	35 per cent......	Free............	Centner... 2.88	Centner... 1.56
19	if toys........	50 per cent......	Free............	Centner... 2.88	Centner... 1.56
20	Sickles, iron................	35 per cent......	Free............	Centner... 1.92	Centner... 0.68
21	steel	45 per cent......	Free............	Centner... 1.92	Centner... 0.68
22	Side arms	35 per cent......	Free............	Centner... 2.88	Centner... 0.39
23	Sieves, lawn................	35 per cent......	Free............	Centner... 2.88	Centner... 1.56
24	wire	35 per cent......	Free............	Centner... 2.88	Centner... 1.56
25	hair.................	35 per cent......	Free............	Centner... 2.88	Centner... 1.56
26	Skins, pickled, (in casks)...	10 per cent......	Free..........	Skins, raw. Free Prepared for fur, centner.. 0.18 Dressed, not tanned. cent'r 0.48 Tanned goat or lamb skins, per centner.. 0.36 Tanned Angora, dyed, &c., per centner.. 2.16 See also Leather.	Skins, seal and other, raw, centn'r. 0.058 Prepared, centner.... 0.39 Tanned, centner.... 0.68 Tanned and finished centner.... 1.56
	tanned, not otherwise enumerated.	25 per cent......	Free..........		
	of all kinds, dried....	....	....		
	raw or unmanufactur'd, not otherwise enumerated.	10 per cent......	Free..........		
	calf, tanned and dressed.	30 per cent......	Free..........		
	glazed as patent leather.	35 per cent......	Free..........		
	fish, for saddlers, &c.	20 per cent......	Free..........		
	fur, raw or undressed	10 per cent......	Free..........		
	dressed	20 per cent......	Free..........		
	white, for druggists..	25 per cent......	Free..........		
	dressed with alum only.	25 per cent......	Free..........		
	sheep, tanned and dressed.	25 per cent......	Free..........		
	goats' or morocco, tanned and dress'd.	25 per cent......	Free..........		
	kid, tanned and dressed or not.	25 per cent......	Free..........		
	goat and sheep, all tanned, not dressed.	25 per cent......	Free..........		
	all other, tanned and dressed.	25 per cent......	Free..........		
27	Slates of all kinds, except roofing.	40 per cent......	Free............	Free............	Centner... 0.12
28	Slate pencils................	40 per cent......	Free............	Free............	....
29	Slates, roofing...........	35 per cent......	Free............	....	....
30	Sledges	Pound.... 0.02½	Free............	Centner... 0.72	Centner... 0.29
31	Smalts	20 per cent......	Free............	Centner... 0.12	Centner... 0.097
32	Snails....................	10 per cent......	Free............	Centner... 1.44	Centner... 0.39

(*Duties expressed in gold dollars of the United States.*)—Continued.

	FRANCE.				RUSSIA.	NETHERLANDS.	
	General tariff.		In treaty with Great Britain, &c.				
	In French vessels.	In other vessels.	In vessels of treaty powers.	In other vessels.			
100 kilogs	Free	$0.97			Free	Free	1
							2
100 kilogs	Free	9.58	Free	$0.048	Pood $0.08	Free	3
1,000	$0.019	0.29	Free	0.34	Pood 0,34	5 per cent	4
As material					All 35 per cent	5 per cent	5
As material						5 per cent	6
As material					Pound 0.39	5 per cent	7
See Cotton					Pound 0.39	5 per cent	8
See Silk					Pound 0.78	5 per cent	9
See Thread or Yarn					Pood 0.31	3 per cent	10
	Prohi	bited.	10 per	cent.	Pound 0.43	5 per cent	11
	Prohi	bited.	10 per	cent.	Pound 0.85	5 per cent	12
	Prohi	bited.	10 per	cent.	Pound 0.43	5 per cent	13
	15 per	cent.	10 per	cent.	Pood 0.62	5 per cent	14
100 kilogs	15.60	16.86	$2.92	3.20	Pood 0.62	5 per cent	15
	15 per	cent.	10 per	cent.	Pood 1 72	Free	16
	Free		Free		Free	Free	17
					Pound 0.25	5 per cent	18
100 kilogs	15.60	16.86	10 per	cent.	Pound 0.25	5 per cent	19
100 kilogs	15.60	16.86	2.92	3.20		5 per cent	20
100 kilogs	15.60	16.86	3.90	4.29		5 per cent	21
100 kilogs	78.00	81.40	7.80	8.58		5 per cent	22
	15 per	cent.	10 per	cent.	Pound 0.17	5 per cent	23
	15 per	cent.	10 per	cent.	Pood 2.34	5 per cent	24
	15 per	cent.	10 per	cent.	Pood 1.72	5 per cent	25
					Skins of all kinds, not dressed, fish skins...... Free. Dressed, small calf skin and other, pood ...... 6.24 Large, ox, horse, and other, pood. 3.43 Skins (furs) not enumerated, per pood ...... 7.80 Muskrat, pood 3.90 Fox, pood ... 3.90 Sable, blue fox, chinchilla, marten, and swan skin, pood. 15.60	Skins, raw, free. Tanned, 2 per cent Pelts tanned, tawed, or dres'd, 5 per cent.	26
Skins of lamb or goat dressed, 100 kilogs.	0.487	0.487	0.58	0.58			
Tanned, 100 kilogs	0.58	0.58	0.70	0.70			
Of swan or goose, for fans, 100 kilogs.	11.934	122.74					
Prepared calf skins, (Russian leather,) 100 kilogs.	15.60	16.86	11.70	12.76			
Tanned of goat, 100 k's	1.95	2.14					
of hog, 100 kil's	39.00	41.40					
Other, large, 100 kilogs	9.75	10.42					
Other, small, 100 kilogs	23.30	24.95					
Colored lamb, 100 kil's			8.77	9.64			
Other, 100 kilogs			11.70	12.76			
Morocco, 100 kilogs			11.60	12.76			
All others not enumerated, 100 kilogs.			1.95	2.14			
Curried for boot-legs, 100 kilogs.	39.00	44.40					
Other, 100 kilogs	19.50	20.95					
In alum, Hungarian style, 100 kilogs.	7.80	8.58					
Dressed, 100 kilogs	9.75	10.72					
All others	Prohib	ited.					
For building	Free		Free	Free	Free	5 per cent	27
Roofing, 100 kilogs	0.78	0.78	0.78	0.78		5 per cent	28
For writing, 100 kilogs			0.72	0.80		Free	29
In squares or slabs, 100 kilogs.	0.78	0.78	Free	1.048			30
See Tools					Pood	5 per cent	31
100 kilogs	0.39	0.39	Free	0.048	Pood	Free	32
Free			Free		Pood In hermetically sealed vessels, pood. 2.34	Free	33

Comparative table of import duties in the United States and European countries.

	ARTICLES.	ITALY.			SPAIN.	PORTUGAL.
			General tariff.	Tariff in treaty with France, &c.		
1	Shells, all except cocoa	Free			100 kilogs ...$0.10	Free
2	cocoa shells					
3	Shellac	100 kilogs	$2.93		100 kilogs ... 2.00	Free
4	Shingles	Free			100 kilogs ... 0.50	Each $0.02
5	Shirts, not otherwise provided for.	As material manufactured.			See Clothing	Needlework, lin'n, kilogs ..... 1.18 Other double duty on material.
6	woolen	See Wool			See Clothing	
7	made on frame	See Wool			See Clothing	
8	Shoe binding, cotton	See Cotton yarn			See Yarn of cotton	See Yarns
9	silk	See Silks			See Silks	See Yarns
10	thread.				See Yarn of flax	See Yarns
11	Shoes or slippers	Pair	0.09	$0.09	Kilogs 1.75	Shoes, unfinished, pair 0.864
12	of silk	100 kilogs	9.75	9.75	Kilogs 1.75	
13	Shot bags and belts	100 kilogs	9.75	9.75	Kilogs 0.50	Each 0.216
14	Shovels, wood and iron	100 kilogs	1.56	1.80	100 kilogs 1.50	Kilogs 0.081
15	iron and steel	100 kilogs	1.56	1.80	100 kilogs 1.50	Kilogs 0.189
16	Shrubs	100 kilogs	9.75	9.75	Free	Free
17	Shumac, or sumac	100 kilogs	1.95	0.39	100 kilogs 0.10	Kilogs 0.027
18	Shuttlecocks and battledore.	100 kilogs	1.56	10 p.c.	100 kilogs 3.50	35 per cent
19	if toys	100 kilogs	9.75	10 p.c.	100 kilogs 3.50	35 per cent
20	Sickles, iron	100 kilogs	1.56	1.80	100 kilogs 5.50	Kilogs 0.081
21	steel	100 kilogs	1.56	1.80	100 kilogs 5 50	Kilogs 0.081
22	Side-arms	See Arms			Kilog 0.40	15 per cent
23	Sieves, lawn	10 per cent	10 p.c.	10 p.c.	Kilog 0.25	Kilogs 1.18
24	wire	100 kilogs	1.36	1.58	Kilog 0.20	Kilogs 0.054
25	hair	100 kilogs	7.80	7.80	Kilog 0.80	Kilogs 5.40
26	Skins, pickled, (in casks) tanned, not otherwise enumerated. of all kinds, dried raw or unmanufactur'd, not otherwise enumerated. calf, tanned and dressed. glazed, as patent leather. fish, for saddlers, &c. fur, raw or undressed. dressed white, for druggists dressed with alum only. sheep, tanned and dressed. goat, or morocco, tanned and dressed. kid, tanned and dressed, or not. goat and sheep, all tanned, not dressed all other, tanned and dressed.	Skins, raw, green, or dry. Furs, raw, per 100 kilogs. Lion, bear, panther, &c., skins, with hair, 100 kil'gs. Tanned skins, 100 kilogs. Not tanned, 100 kilogs.	Free. 0.78 2.93 7.80 3.90	 2.93 2.93	Skins, untanned, 100 kilogs, 1.50 Tanned, kil. 0.25 Articles for beit and harness making, kilogramme . 0.50	Skins, raw, or in any way prepared, not enumerated, 20 per cent.
27	Slates of all kinds, except roofing.	Free	Free.		100 kilogs 0.01	Free
28	Slate pencils	Free	Free.		100 kilogs 0.30	Kilogs 0.001
29	Slates, roofing	1000	0.58		100 kilogs 0.30	Free
30	Sledges	5 per cent			100 kilogs 1.50	Kilogs 0.081
31	Smalts	100 kilogs	0.195	0.195	100 kilogs 0.30	Kilogs 0.054
32	Snails	Free	Free.		Free	Free

(*Duties expressed in gold dollars of the United States.*)—Continued.

BELGIUM.	AUSTRIA.			DENMARK.	SWEDEN.	NORWAY.	
		General tariff.	Tariff in treaty.				
10 per cent	Free	......	......	Free	Free	Free	1
							2
Free	Centner	$0.388	......	Pound ...$0.0113	Free	Free	3
5 per cent	See Manuf. of	wood.	......	Free	Free	Free	4
							5
10 per cent	See Clothing.	......	......	See Clothing	See Clothing	10 p.cent above duty on material.	6
							7
See Cotton	See Cotton	yarn.	......	See Cotton yarn	See Cotton	Pound...$0.091	8
See Silk	See Silk yarn.	......	......	See Silks	See Silk	Pound... 0.127	9
See Yarns of mat'l.	See Linen	yarn.	......	See Yarn of flax	See Flax (yarn)	Pound... 0.091	10
10 per cent	Centner	5.76	$3.60	Pound 0.182	Pound ...$0.165	Pound... 0.145	11
10 per cent	Centner	12.00	7.20	Pound 0.273	Pound 0.275	Pound... 0.318	12
10 per cent	As material	manu	fact'd.	Pound 0.091	Additional to leather, 20 p.cent.	Pound... 0.082 Pound... 0.027	13
100 kilogs...$0.78	Centner	2.88	2.16	Pound 0.017	5 per cent	Pound... 0.027	14
100 kilogs... 0.78	Centner	2.88	2.16	Pound 0.017	5 per cent	Free	15
Free	Free	......	......	Free	Free	Free	16
Free	Centner	0.388	Free.	Pound 0.0113	Free	Pound... 0.018	17
10 per cent	See Manuf. of	wood.	......	Pound 0.039	10 per cent	Pound... 0.018	18
10 per cent	See Manuf. of	wood.	......	Pound 0.039	Pound 0.0689	Pound... 0.018	19
100 kilogs... 0.78	Centner	2.88	2.16	Pound 0.017	5 per cent	Pound... 0.027	20
100 kilogs... 0.78	Centner	2.88	2.16	Pound 0.017	5 per cent	Pound... 0.027	21
Free	Centner	7.20	7.20	Pound 0.017	See Manufactures of steel.	Pound... 0.073	22
10 per cent	Centner	7.20	5.76	Pound 0.039	5 per cent	Pound... 0.071	23
10 per cent	Centner	2.04	1.44	Pound 0.039	5 per cent	Pound... 0.071	24
10 per cent	Centner	7.20	5.76	Pound 0.039	5 per cent	Pound... 0.071	25
Skins, large and small, raw, green salted, or dry, free. Of goat and lamb, tanned, 100 k'gs. 0.975 Other, tanned and finished, 100 k'gs. 2.93 Otherwise prepar'd & finish'd, 100 kilogs 5.85 All manufactu's 10 per cent.	Hides and skins, raw, green, dry, common... Others, centner Prepared, tann'd, dy'd, centner	Free. 0.384 1.26	Free. Free.	Skins, raw, prepared, and for saddlery, pound. 0.068	Skins, raw, free. Prepared, per pound 0.055 See Leather.	Raw, free. Prepared, pound. 0.055 Manufactures, pound. 0.062	26
Mille 0.75	Centner	0.388	0.36	Free	Free	Free	27
10 per cent	Centner	0.388	0.36	Free	Free	Free	28
Mille 0.78	Centner	......	......	Free	Free	Free	29
100 kilogs .. 0.78	Each	1.26	......	Pound.... 0.017	Centner.. 0.2067	Pound ... 0.027	30
Free	Centner	0.388	0.36	Free	Free	Free	31
Free	Free	......	......	Free	Free	Free	32

Comparative table of import duties in the United States and European countries.

ARTICLES.	UNITED STATES.	GREAT BRITAIN.	GERMAN ZOLLVEREIN.	SWITZERLAND.
Silk cocoons, raw and waste.	Free	Free	Free	Centner ..$0.058
Silks in the gum, not more advanced than single, tram, or organzine.	35 per cent	Free	Silk floss, comb'd, spun, or thread, not dyed; waste of all silk, free.	Silk and floss silk combed and spun in single thread, centner 0.39
Si k spun, for filling in skeins.	35 per cent......	Free		
Silk floss..................	35 per cent......	Free	Silk and floss silk dyed, centner $2.88	
Silk, sewing	40 per cent......	Free		Silk, bleached, dyed; silk for sewing, crocheting, &c., centner 0.68
Silk, all dress and piece	60 per cent......	Free		
Silk velvet, or of which silk is chief value.	60 per cent......	Free	Manufactures of silk or floss silk, also with metallic thread, centner 28.80	
Silk aprons, bonnets, braids, caps, chemisettes, cords, drawers, fringes, gloves, galloons, handkerchiefs, hats, hose, laces, mantillas, mits, pongees, pelerines, ribbons, shawls, scarfs, shirts, stockings, suspenders, turbans, tassels, trimmings, vestings, veils, watch chains, webbing.	60 per cent...... 60 per cent......	Free .... Free	Manufactures of silk or floss silk mixed with cotton, flax, or wool, and other hair, centner 21.60	All manufact'res of silk, centner ...... 1.56 Fringework and lace of silk, also tissues mixed with gold and silver, hats and gloves of silk, centner .. 2.93
Silk buttons, button cloth ..	40 per cent......	Free		
Silk, ready-made clothing, or of which silk is the component material of chief value.	60 per cent......			
Silk, cotton vesting, bobbin, hat bands.	50 per cent......			
Silk gaiters with wire and clasps, ornaments for head dresses, oil cloth stocks, and all articles not otherwise specified, made up by hand, in whole or part, if no wool or worsted, to be worn.	60 per cent......			
Silk bolting cloth	Free			
All manufactures of silk, or of which silk shall be a component material of chief value, not otherwise provided for.	50 per cent......			

(*Duties expressed in gold dollars of the United States.*)—Continued.

FRANCE.

	Gen'l tariff.		Treaty with G. Britain, &c.	
	In French vessels.	In other vessels.	In vessels of treaty powers.	In other vessels.
....	Free...	....	Free...	....
Silk, unbleached	Free...	....	Free...	....
dyed all sorts, 100 kilo.	Free...	$0.047	....	....
Dyed in mass	Free...	....	....	....
Combed, 100 kilogs......	$1.05	2.14	....	....
Spun, single, bleached, or dyed, measuring per kilogr. 80,500 metres or less, 100 kilogs.	14.62	15.83	....	....
Over 80,500 metres, 100 kilogs.	23.40	25.05	....	....
Thread of waste silk, measuring per kilogs. 30,000 metres single, 100 kilogs.	4.87	5.36	....	....
Over 30,000 metres, 100 kilogs.	Same as	raw silk	thread.	
Tissues of silk, per kilogramme:				
Handkerc'fs, (India foulards.)	Free...	....	Free...	$0.048
H'dk'fs, other unbl'ch'd.	1.36	1.56	Free...	0.048
H'dk'fs, other, printed..	2.73	2.92	Free...	0.048
Crape, plain	3.90	4.87	} Free .	0.048
Crape embroidered, figured.	6.63	7.80		
Other tissues, not made in Europe and imported directly.	Free ..	0.048	Free...	0.048
Other tissues pure, plain.	3.12	3.43	Free...	0.048
figured	3.70	4.07	....	....
embroidered with silk	3.70	4.07	....	....
embroidered with gold or silver.	6.04	6.64	....	....
ditto, imitation	Prohi	bited.	....	....
mixed thread	2.53	2.78	....	....
ditto, gold or silver ...	3.31	3.64	....	....
ditto, imitation	Prohi	bited.	....	....
Silk covers, 100 kilogs ..	39.78	42.26	....	....
carpet mixed with thread, 100 kilogs.	59.67	63.07	....	....
Tissues of silk or floss silk unbleached, white, dyed, or printed, 100 kilogs.	....	....	$39.00	41.43
ditto, mixed with gold or silver fine, 100 kilogs.	....	....	234.00	237.40
ditto, imitation, 100 kilogs.	....	....	68.25	71.15
Gauze per 1 kilog.:				
Gauze of pure silk......	6.04	6.64	Free...	0.048
mixed with thread....	3.31	3.64	Free...	0.048
ditto, gold and silver .	12.09	13.18	Free...	0.048
ditto, imitation	Prohi	bited.	Free...	0.048
Silk fringe 100 kilogs...	234.00	237.40	....	....
Lace work, per kilog.:				
of gold or silver, fine .	5.83	6.43	....	....
ditto, imitation	0.58	0.63	....	....
of silk, pure..........	2.12	2.43	Free...	0.048
ditto, mixed with gold or silver, fine.	4.87	5.35	....	....
ditto, imitation	1.56	1.72	....	....
or mixed with other materials.	156.00	159.40	....	....
Velvet, ribbons of silk, pure or mixed, 100 kilogs.	156.00	159.40	97.50	100.90

RUSSIA.

Pood $0.39

Twist, tram, and organzine; sewing silk, and silk wound for woof or warp, dyed or not dyed, p'd. 3.90

Yarn of silk (bourre de soie) and all yarn of wool or hair mixed with silk, dyed and printed or not, pood..... 3.51

Scarfs, shawls, handkerchiefs, and ribbons of pure silk, also foulards, plain or printed, in the warp, velvet, plush, per pound 3.90

Foulards printed in the cloth, lb .. 2.34

Scarfs, shawls, &c., of mixed silk, lb. 1.72

Trimmings of pure or mixed silk printed goods, lb 0.78

Wax and oil cloth of silk, pound ... 0.78

Silk buttons, lb . 0.23

Lace or blonde, per pound 2.24

Ready-made articles of clothing, 35 per cent.

NETHERLANDS.

Free ....

Silk manufactured for sewing, stitching, and farret silk, 3 per cent.

All manufactures of silk, 5 per cent.

FRANCE: For remainder of tariff on silk see page 209.

Comparative table of import duties in the United States and European countries.

ARTICLES.	ITALY.			SPAIN.	PORTUGAL.
		General tariff.	Tariff in treaty with France, &c.		
Silk cocoons, raw and waste.	....	......	......	Silk in cocoons and waste of cocoons, free.	Silk, cocoons..free.
Silk in the gum, not more advanced than single, tram, or organzine.	Silkworm eggs ..	Free.	Free.		Silk, single, raw, kilog.. ......$0.081
	Cocoons.........	Free.	Free		
Silk spun, for filling in skeins.	Silk, crude, single, or twisted.	Free.	Free.	Spun, not twisted, kilog $0.30	Dyed, kilog .. 1.08
					Twisted, kilo. 2.70
Silk floss.	Silk, dyed, kilog	$0.58	Free.	Twisted to four threads, kilo. 1.25	Waste........free.
Silk, sewing.	Remains of silk spun or dyed, kilog.	0.39	Free.		Tissues:
Silk, all dress and piece.				5 threads or more, kilog 1.75	Lace and tulle, kilog 5.40
Silk velvet, or of which silk is chief value.	Other remains...	Free	Free.	Waste silk, spun not twisted, kilo. 0.10	Velvets, kilog. 8.10
Silk aprons, bonnets, braids, caps, chemisettes, cords, drawers, fringes, gloves, galloons, handkerchiefs, hats, hose, laces, mantillas, mits, pongees, pelerines, ribbons, shawls, scarfs, shirts, stockings, suspenders, turbans, tassels, trimmings, vestings, veils, watch chains, webbing.	Tissues pure silk or mixed gold or silver, fine or imitation, kilog.	1.95	$0.58	Ditto, twisted to 4 threads, kilog 0.30	Ribbon, kilog. 6.80
					Bolting-cloth..free.
				Ditto, 5 threads or more, kilog.. 0.90	Handk'rch'fs pocket, kilog 1.16
	Linen mixed with silk, kilog.	1.56	0.58		Do., not specified, kilog 5.40
	Waxed, kilog....	0.78	10 p.c.	Tissues, plain and figured, kilogramme 3.50	Tissues not classified, plain, k 6.804
	Mixed with other material, kilog.	0.58	10 p.c.		
	Ribbons, of velvet, kilog.	1.95		Satin and plush, kilog 5.25	Do., figured, kilog 8.10
Silk buttons, button cloth.	Other silk, kilog .	1.95	10 per cent	Of waste silk, half or so called crude silk, kilog... 1.80	Mixed, *see note* p. 61.
Silk, ready-made clothing, or of which silk is the component material of chief value.	Mixed, kilog. 0.58	to 1.56			Other manuf's of silk:
	Laces, &c., in gold or silver, fine, kilog.	1.95	2.14	Tulle, kilog .. 4.50	
				Laces, edgings, kilog 5.50	Girdles, kilog. 6.804
Silk, cotton vesting, bobbin, hat bands.	Ditto, imitation, kilog.	1.95	0.67	Point lace, kilo. 3.00	Mesh or net work, kilog 6.804
Silk gaiters with wire and clasps, ornaments for head dresses, oil-cloth, stocks, and all articles not otherwise specified, made up by hand, in whole or part, if no wool or worsted, to be worn.	Handk'ch'fs, foulards, raw, kilog.	0.975	0.58	Articles of trimmings, kilog. 2.50	Fringe-work not specifi'd, kilog 5.40
	Pressed, dyed, kilog.	1.36	0.58		
	Buttons of gold or silver thread, kilog.	1.95	2.14		
Silk bolting cloth.	of silk, pure, kilog.	1.17	......		
All manufactures of silk, or of which silk shall be a component material of chief value, not otherwise provided for.	of silk, mixed, kilog.	0.39	......		
	Tulle, lace, &c., pure or mixed, kilog.	2.34	5 p. ct.		

(*Duties expressed in gold dollars of the United States.*)—Continued.

BELGIUM.	AUSTRIA.			DENMARK.	SWEDEN.	NORWAY.
		General tariff.	Tariff in treaty.			
Silk, cocoons. free.	Silk cocoons .	Free.	......	Silk, crude....... pound ...$0. 273	Silk, raw, not dyed, lb...... free.	Silk, single or twisted, dyed or not, lb...$0. 127
Lace, tulle, &c., centner 5	Silk, raw, not spun, also waste, centner.	$0. 388	......	Oil cloth of silk, pound ... 0. 273	Do., dyed, lb $0. 11	Manufactu's bobbinet, lace, tulle, pure or mixed, pound....o. 241
All tissues, 100 kilogs $58. 50	Silk, raw, spun, organzine, tram, sewing silk; also, if mixed, centner.	3. 88	......	Yarn and cords ½ inch or less, pound 0. 41	Tissues of pure silk, or silk velvet, lb .. 0. 2756	Velvet and other figured tissues, pound .. 0. 473
	Silk waste, spun, also if mixed, centner.	3. 88	......	Tissues, as button-maker's g'ds and fringework, pound ... 0. 546	Other, mixed with gold or silver, pound 0. 41	Plush, mixed or unmixed, per pound .. 0. 319
	Silk, white or dyed, waste spun & dyed, also if mixed, centner.	7. 56	......	Other tissues of pure silk, lb 1.092	Of part silk, also silk felt, lb 0.2756	Other articles of pure silk or mixed with metal or glass thread, lb. 0. 473
	Tissues of silk, pure or mixed, *a.* fine of pure silk, or mixed with gold or silver thread, lace embroideries, centner.	126. 00	......	Ditto, part of silk, pound ... 0. 728	Ribbons, silk and silk velvet, pound ... 0. 41	Others of silk mixed with other materials, pound... 0. 319
	Ditto, *b.* common, mixed, and all other, centner.	49. 44	$33. 60		Half silk ribbons, pound .. 0. 2756	
					Tassels, cord, and trimmings, pure or part silk, pound ... 0. 827	
					Other tassels, pounds ... 0. 21	

FRANCE.—Tariff on silk—Continued.

France.	General tariff.		Treaty with G. Britain, &c.	
	In French vessels.	In other vessels.	In vessels of treaty powers.	In other vessels.
Other manufactures of silk..........	....	....	10 per	cent.
Tissues of mixed material, silk or floss silk predominating, 100 kilogs....	....	....	$58. 50	$61. 90
Manufactures of floss silk:				
Cashmeres	Prohi	bited.	....	....
Tissues pure, kilogr..........	$1. 36	$1. 50	....	....
Ditto, mixed, gold or silver, kilogr..........	1. 95	2. 14	....	....
Ditto, mixed, gold or silver imitation, kilogr	Prohi	bited.	....	....
Covers, 100 kilogs	39. 78	42. 25	....	....
Carpet, (also mixed with thread,) 100 kilogs..........	59. 67	63. 07	....	....
Fringe-work, kilogr..........	1. 17	1. 29	....	....
Lace ribbons, 100 kilogs..........	156. 00	159. 40	....	....

Comparative table of import duties in the United States and European countries.

	ARTICLES.	UNITED STATES.	GREAT BRITAIN.	GERMAN ZOLL-VEREIN.	SWITZERLAND.
1	Silver, bullion, coin, and old silver.	Free	Free	Free	Free
2	epaulettes and wings.	35 per cent	Free	Centner . $36. 00	Centner...$2. 93
3	leaf, of 500 leaves in 1 package.	Package ..$0. 75	Free	Centner . . 0. 96	Centner... 1. 56
4	nitrate of	40 per cent	Free	Centner . . 2. 40	Centner... 0. 68
5	all manufactures not otherwise specif'd.	40 per cent	Free	Centner . .36. 00	Centner... 2. 93
6	German, in sheets	35 per cent	Free	Centner . . 1. 26	Centner... 1. 56
7	manuf's of.	40 per cent	Free	Centner . . 2. 88	Centner... 1. 56
8	Silvered wire	35 per cent	Free	Centner . .36. 00	Centner... 1. 56
9	Sisal grass, unmanufactured.	Ton...... 15. 00	Free	Free	Centner... 0. 058
10	manufactures of.	30 per cent	Free	Centner . . 1. 92	Centner... 0. 68
11	Skates, costing 20 cents per pair.	Pair 0. 08	Free	Centner . . 0. 96	Centner... 1. 56
12	costing over 20 cents per pair.	35 per cent	Free	Centner . . 0. 96	Centner... 1. 56
13	Snake root	20 per cent	Free	Centner... 0. 36	Centner... 0. 68
14	Snaps, snap bits	35 per cent	Free	Centner... 0. 96	Centner... 1. 56
15	Snuff	Pound 0. 50	Pound.... 0. 90 to 1. 09	Centner... 7. 92	Centner... 1. 56
16	Snuffers, silver or gold	40 per cent	Free	Centner...36 00	Centner... 2. 93
17	all other	35 per cent	Free	Centner... 1 92	Centner... 0. 68
18	Soap, castile	30 per cent., and per pound, 0. 01	Free	Soap, soft, centner..... 0. 60 Soap, ordinary, centner . 0. 60 Soap, fine, centner ..... 1. 44 Soap, perfumed, centner . 2. 40	Soap, all, centner 0. 145
	fancy, all	25 per cent., and per pound, 0. 10	Free		
	hard, all other	30 per cent., and per pound, 0. 01	Free		
	Naples	25 per cent., and per pound, 0. 10	Free		
	perfumed, all	25 per cent., and per pound, 0. 10	Free		
	shaving, wash balls	25 per cent., and per pound, 0. 10	Free		
	Windsor	25 per cent., and per pound, 0. 10	Free		
	soft, all, and turpentine	30 per cent., and per pound, 0. 01	Free		
19	Soap stocks and stuffs	10 per cent	Free	Free	Centner... 0. 145
20	Soda, ash	Pound 0. 00½	Free	Centner... 0. 48	Soda, raw, carbonate, and sulphate of, centner. 0. 058 Caustic, centner. .... 0. 145 All other preparations, centner 0. 68
	bicarbonate of	Pound 0. 01½	Free	Centner... 0 60	
	carbonate of	Pound 0. 00½	Free	Centner... 0. 60	
	iodate of	20 per cent	Free	Centner... 2. 40	
	caustic	Pound 0. 01½	Free	Centner... 0. 72	
	hydriodate of	20 per cent	Free	Centner... 2. 40	
	hyposulphate of	20 per cent	Free	Centner... 2. 40	
	lye	20 per cent	Free	Centner... 2. 40	
	powders	20 per cent	Free	Centner... 0. 60	
	sal	Pound 0. 00½	Free	Centner... 0. 18	
	salts of	Pound 0. 00½	Free	Centner... 0. 18	
	all carbonates of, except soda-ash, barilla kelp.	20 per cent	Free	Centner... 2. 40	
21	Solanine, (medic. prep.)	40 per cent	Free	Centner... 2. 40	Centner... 0. 68

(Duties expressed in gold dollars of the United States.)—Continued.

FRANCE.					RUSSIA.	NETHERLANDS.	
	General tariff.		In treaty with Great Britain, &c.				
	In French vessels.	In other vessels.	In vessels of treaty powers.	In other vessels.			
Silver, ore, 100 kil	Free ..	$0.195	....	....	Free........	Free........	1
Crude or broken, 100 kil.	$0.0019	0.0019	....	....	Pound $1.72	5 per cent........	2
In sheets, 100 kilogs	3.90	4.29	$3.90	$4.29	Pound......... 0.85	3 per cent........	3
Wire, 100 kilogs........	97.50	100.90	97.50	100.90	Pound......... 0.85	Free........	4
100 kilogs........	97.50	100.90	97.50	100.90	Pound......... 1.72	5 per cent........	5
100 kilogs........	5.07	5.58	0.58	0.64	Pood......... 0.47	Free........	6
100 kilogs........	Prohib	ited.	19.50	20.95	Pood......... 9.36	5 per cent........	7
See above........	....	....	....	....	Pound......... 4.28	3 per cent........	8
Free........	Free ..	....	....	....	Free........	Free........	9
100 kilogs........	3.90	4.68	10 per	cent.	Free........	5 per cent........	10
100 kilogs........	Prohib	ited.	3.90	4.29	Pood......... 0.78	5 per cent........	11
100 kilogs........	Prohib	ited. ...	3.90	4.29	Pood......... 0.78	5 per cent........	12
100 kilogs........	Free...	0.97	0.29	0.43	Free........	Free........	13
See tools........	....	....	....	....	Pood......... 0.85	5 per cent........	14
For private account	Prohib	ited	....	....	Pound......... 0.69 In jars and rolled, per pood..... 20.25	100 kilogs....$4.92	15
100 kilogs........	97.50	100.90	97.50	100.90	See Gold and silver manufactures.	5 per cent........	16
100 kilogs........	34.12	36.30	3.90	4.29	Pood......... 0.62	5 per cent........	17
Soap, not perfumed, 100 kilogs.	Prohib	ited	1.17	1.29	Soap, perfumed, per pood .... 4.29 All other, pood 0.78	Soap, hard and soft, and soap powder, 100 kilogs...$1.74 Soap, perfumed, 100 kilogs... 2.46	18
Of alkali and oil of olives, 100 kilogs.	....	....	1.69	1.72			
Balm and cocoa nut, 100 kilogs.	....	....	0.78	0.78			
Perfumed, 100 kilogs....	31.98	34.07	1.17	1.29			
....	....	....	....	....	Pood......... 0.156		19
Soda, crystallized, 100 kilogs.	3.70	4.08	....	....	Pood......... 0.85		20
Other, 100 kilogs........	5.16	5.67	....	....	Soda, boracic, sulphate and crystalized, pood .. 0.078 sillicate, bicarbonate and calcined, pood....... 0.156 caustic, pood. 0.234 nitrate, pood. 0.039 acetate and phosphate, pood. 0.85 powd'rs, pood 2.34		
Carbonate of soda, crystalized, 100 kilogs.	....	....	0.36	0.42			
Caustic, 100 kilogs......	....	....	1.25	1.36			
Nitrate of soda, 100 kilogs.	Free...	0.78	Free...	0.48			
Hyposulphate of soda, 100 kilogs.	....	....	0.73	0.80			
Artificial soda, 100 kilogs.	....	....	0.36	0.42		Free.	
Salt of 60 deg., 100 kilogs.	....	....	0.80	0.87			
Less than 60 degrees 100 kilogs.	....	....	2.73	3.00			
Bicarbonate of soda, 100 kilogs.	....	....	0.82	0.90			
Salts, not enumerated, kilogs.	....	....	0.67	0.73			
....	Prohib	ited....	5 per	cent ...	Pood......... 0.85		21

Comparative table of import duties in the United States and European countries.

	ARTICLES.	ITALY.			SPAIN.	PORTUGAL.
			General tariff.	Tariff in treaty with France, &c.		
1	Silver, bullion, coin, and old silver.	Free............	......	......	....	....
2	epauletts and wings.					
3	leaf, of 500 leaves in 1 package.				Silver, ore, free.	Silver, crude or broken pieces........ Free
4	nitrate of...........	Silver, in mass..	......	Free.	In bars, coin, pieces, powder, ingots, and useless table service free.	
5	all manufactures not otherwise specified.	In plates, per kilog.	$0.78	$0.90		Plates or sheets not specified, kilog.....$5.40
6	German, in sheets...	Wire, kilog....	1.17	......		
7	manuf's of.	Articles of, kil'g	2.34	......	Manufactured in Spain, free.	In leaf, k'g, . 1.08
8	Silvered wire..............	Jewelry, kilog.. Vermeil, kilog..	3.90 5.85	....	In Jewelry, hectoliter......$0.70	Wire, kilog.. 5.40 Lace, kilog..10.80 Jewelry, k'g.32.80
9	Sisal grass, unmanufactured	Free............	Free.	......	100 kilogs.... 0.05	Free..............
10	manufactures of	100 kilogs.......	0.39	0.39	20 per cent.........	Kilogs...... 0.002
11	Skates, costing 20 cents per pair.	100 kilogs.......	3.90	4.50	100 kilogs.... 5.50	Kilogs...... 0.162
12	costing over 20 cents per pair.	100 kilogs.......	3.90	4.50	100 kilogs.... 5.50	Kilogs...... 0.162
13	Snake root................	100 kilogs.......	1.95	0.39	100 kilogs.... 2.00	5 per cent..........
14	Snaps, snap bits...........	100 kilogs.......	1.56	1.80	100 kilogs.... 5.50	Kilogr....... 0.162
15	Snuff.....................	Of Spain, 100klgs; other, prohibit'd	2.34	......	Government monopoly.	Kilogr....... 0.432
16	Snuffers, silver or gold.....	....	......	......	See Gold and silver.	Gold, kilogr..54.00 Silver, kilogr.32.80
17	all other.........	....	......	......	100 kilogs... 25.00	Other, kilogr. 0.547
18	Soap, castile...............	Soap, ordinary, 100 kilogs....	1.95	1.17	Soap, 100 klgs 3.75	Soap. kilogr. 0.02 wash-balls, per kilogr...... 0.16
	fancy, all............	Soap, perfumed, 100 kilogs....	11.70	1.17		
	hard, all other.......					
	Naples..............					
	perfumed, all........					
	shaving, wash balls..					
	Windsor............					
	soft all, and turpentine					
19	Soap stocks and stuffs......					
20	Soda, ash..................	Soda:			Sulphate of soda,	Carbonate of soda,
	bi-carbonate of......	pure, 100 kilogs	0.975	......	100 kilogs .. 0.10	(natural)... Free
	carbonate of.........	caustic, 100 klgs	0.975	......	100 kilogs.... 0.50	Crude, artficial or
	iodate of............	artificial, 100 ki-				refined, dry, per
	caustic..............	logs..........	0.097	0.097	See Chemicals n. e.	kilogr...... 0.021
	hydriodate of........	chloride of, 100				Of crystallized so-
	hyposulphate of.....	kilogs.........	0.39	0.39	100 kilogs.... 0.75	da, kilogr . 0.013
	lye..................	nitrate of......	......	Free	See Chemicals n. e.	Salts of soda. Free
	powders.............	sulphate of, 100				All others as chem-
	sal..................	kilogs.........	0.195	0.195		icals n. o. e. 10 per
	salts of.............	carbonate of, 100				cent.
	all carbonates of, except soda-ash, barillas kelp.	kilogs.........	0,097	0.097		
					Nitrate of soda, per 100 kilogs .. 0.20	Borate of soda, free
21	Solanine, (medic. prep.)....	100 kilogs.......	1.95	0.39	20 per cent.........	5 per cent..........

(*Duties expressed in gold dollars of the United States.*)—Continued.

BELGIUM.	AUSTRIA.			DENMARK.	SWEDEN.	NORWAY.	
		General tariff.	Tariff in treaty.				
....	Free	......	......	Free	....	Free	1
Silver, crude, in powder, bars, and in mass; in sheets or drawn, (wire) spun on thre'd, free. All articles of manufacture, 5 per cent. Coin, free.	In bars, or sheets .... Jewelry, of gold or silver, centner ...... Gold and silver sheet, leaf or articles of metal gil'd or silvered fine, centner.	Free 126.00 $48.00	....	Manufactures and leaf, pound. $0.091 Wire and embroideries, pound.. 0.273	Silver, crude, coin, and in sheets, free. Manufactured, Ort... $0.0082 In leaves, free. Wire: pound.. 0.041 Lace, ort. 0.0027	Plates or sheets, not polished, Loth. $0.027 All articles manufactur'd Loth.. 0.03	2 3 4 5 6 7 8
Free	Free	......	......	Free	Free	Free	9
5 per cent........	Centner	4.80	......	Pound ... 0.004	Pound..... 0.005	Pound 0.005	10
10 per cent	Centner	2.88	2.16	Pound ... 0.017	10 per cent.......	Pound 0.027	11
10 per cent	Centner	2.88	2.16	Pound ... 0.017	10 per cent.......	Pound 0.027	12
Free	Centner	2.52	1.44	Pound.....0.0113	Free..........	Free	13
100 kilogs .. 0.78	Centner	2.88	2.16	Pound.....0.017	See Manuf. of steel.	Pound 0.027	14
100 kilogs .. 8.19	Centner	12.00	......	Pound.....0.045	Pound..... 0.15	Pound 0.109	15
5 per cent	See Siver and gold.	......	......	Pound.....0.091	See Gold or silver.	Loth...... 0.03	16
10 per cent	Centner	7.20	5.76	Pound.....0.045	Pound..... 0.041	See Manf. of copper, &c.	17
Soap of all kinds, 100 kilogs .1.17	Soap, not perfumed, cent'r Italian, centner......... Perfumed, centner.....	1.512 1.26 7.56	....	All, pound 0.091	Soap: perfumed, lb 0.033 Other, lb...0.0138 Green or black, pound....0.0082	Soap: green or white, pound ..0.0045 all other, per pound .. 0.013	18
Free	Soda, raw, ct'r	0.202	0.192	Soda, carbonate of, calcined or crystallized, Free.	Free..........	Free..........	19
	Centner	0.202	0.192		See Chemical and medicinal preparations.		20
	See Chemicals			Others, as chemicals n. o. e., per pound....0.0113			
	Centner	0.202	0.192				
	See Chemic'ls	......	......				
	See Chemic'ls	......	......				
	....	Free	......				
	....	Free	......				
	Centner	0.202	0.192				
	Centner	0.202	0.192				
	Centner	0.202	0.192	Pound.....0.0113	Free..........		21

Comparative table of import duties in the United States and European countries.

	ARTICLES.	UNITED STATES.	GREAT BRITAIN.	GERMAN ZOLL-VEREIN.	SWITZERLAND.
1	Soles, felt or cork	50 per cent	Free	Felt, centn'r $7. 20 Cork, cent'r 0. 26	Centner... $0. 68
2	Soy, (sauce)	35 per cent	Free	Centner... 5. 04	Centner... 2. 93
3	Spanish flies, (cantharides)	Pound $0. 50	Free	Centner... 0. 36	Centner... 0. 68
4	Spars	20 per cent	Free	Free	Centner... 0. 058
5	Spartaria	30 per cent	Free	Centner... 1. 92	Centner... 0. 68
6	Spa, or spa ware	30 per cent	Free	Centner... 11. 60	Centner... 1. 56
7	Spectacle glasses and pebbles, not set.	40 per cent	Free	Free	Centner... 1. 56
8	Spectacles, steel	45 per cent	Free	If not gold or silver, cent. 11. 60	Centner... 1 56
9	all other	40 per cent	Free		....
10	Spelter, in pigs or blocks	Pound 0. 01½	Free	Centner... 1. 26	Centner... 0. 145
11	in sheets	Pound 0. 02¼	Free	Centner... 1. 26	Centner... 0. 145
12	manufactures of	35 per cent	Free	Centner... 2. 88	Not polished, per centner... 0. 68 Polished, centner 1. 56
13	Spermaceti oil, foreign fisheries.	20 per cent	Free	Centner... 0. 36	Centner... 0. 58
14	Spices, all not otherwise provided for.	20 per cent	Free	Centner... 4. 68	Centner... 0. 68
15	Spirituous liquors, not otherwise provided for.	100 per cent	Gallon.... $2. 53	Centner... 4. 32	Centner... 1. 56
16	Spirits of turpentine	Gallon 0. 30	Free	Free	Centner... 0. 68
17	Spokes	35 per cent	Free	Centner... 0. 36	Centner... 0. 39
18	Spokeshaves	45 per cent	Free	Centner... 0. 96	Centner... 0. 39
19	Sponges	20 per cent	Free	Free	Centner... 0. 058
20	Springs, for wigs	45 per cent	Free	Centner... 7. 20	Centner... 1. 56
21	Spy-glasses	40 per cent	Free	Free	Centner... 0. 39
22	Starch, made of potatoes or corn.	20 per cent., and per pound, 0. 01	Free	Centner... 1. 44	Centner... 0. 058
23	other	20 per cent., and per pound, 0. 03	Free	Centner... 1. 44	Centner... 0. 058
24	Statues and statuary, not merchandise.	10 per cent	Free	Free	Centner... 1. 56
25	Statues and statuary, articles of commerce.	10 per cent	Free	Free	
26	(brass)	35 per cent	Free	Free	Centner . 1. 56
27	(metal)	35 per cent	Free	Free	
28	(plaster)	40 per cent	Free	Free	
29	(wood)	10 per cent	Free	Free	
30	Staves, for pipes, casks, &c.	10 per cent	Free	Free	Centner .. 0. 058
31	for hogsheads	20 per cent	Free	Free	Centner .. 0. 058
32	Stave bolts	Free	Free	Free	Centner .. 0. 058

(*Duties expressed in gold dollars of the United States.*)—Continued.

	FRANCE.				RUSSIA.	NETHERLANDS.	
	General tariff.		In treaty with Great Britain, &c.				
	In French vessels.	In other vessels.	In vessels of treaty powers.	In other vessels.			
100 kilogs	$19.50	$20.95	10 per	cent	Pood $2.92	100 kilogs $4.10	1
	15 per	cent	10 per	cent	Pood 2.34	100 kilogs 10.25	2
100 kilogs	0.39	0.43	$0.39	$0.43	Free	Free	3
	Free	Free	Free	Free	Free	½ per cent	4
100 kilogs	3.90	4.68	10 per	cent	Free	5 per cent	5
See Porcelain					See Porcelain	5 per cent	6
Raw, 100 kilogs Cut and polished, 100 kilogs.	1.95 39.00	2.14 41.44	10 per	cent	Free	5 per cent	7
	15 per	cent	10 per	cent	Set in common material, pood 4.68	5 per cent	8
					Costly, pound 0.85	5 per cent	9
100 kilogs	Free	0.048	Free	0.048	Pood 0.47	Spelter, sheets,	10
100 kilogs	4.68	5.15	0.58	0.64	Pood 0.47	plates and leaves,	11
100 kilogs	19.50	20.95	3.90	4.29	Pood 9.36	wire, and nails, 100 kilogs 0.12 Utensils, varnished, painted or not, 5 per cent.	12
Raw, 100 kilogs Pressed, 100 kilogs Refined, 100 kilogs	0.39 3.90 9.75	0.78 3.27 10.72	0.39	0.43	Free	See Oil Candles, 5 per cent.	13
	15 per	cent	10 per	cent	Pood 1.17	5 per cent	14
Hectolitre	4.87	4.87	2.92	2.92	Bottle 0.50 or pood 6.63 N. B.—The importation of spirits, from grain, in casks is prohibited.	Hectoliter 1.43	15
Not enumerated					Pood 0.85	Liter 0.51	16
Mille	0.048	0.048	0.048	0.058	Free	1 per cent	17
Mille	0.048	0.048	0.048	0.058	Free	5 per cent	18
100 kilogs	9.75	10.72	9.75	10.72	(Greek) pood 1.29	Free	19
See Manuf. of steel					Pood 3.51	5 per cent	20
	30 per	cent	10 per	cent	Free	5 per cent	21
100 kilogs	4.09	4.50	0.28	0.33	Pood 0.43	100 kilogs 0.41	22
100 kilogs	4.09	4.50	0.78	0.33	Pood 0.43	100 kilogs 0.41	23
	Free	Free	Free	Free	Free	Free	24
See Marble, stone, &c.					Free	Free	25
					Free		26
							27
							28
							29
Millimeter	0.019	0.29	Free		Free	Pipe, 100 kil. 1.64	30
Millimeter	0.019	0.29	Free		Free	Cask, 100 kil. 0.41	31
Free					Free	1 per cent	32

Comparative table of import duties in the United States and European countries.

	ARTICLES.	ITALY.			SPAIN.	PORTUGAL.
			General tariff.	Tariff in treaty with France, &c.		
1	Soles, felt or cork	Felt, 100 kilogs .. cork, 100 kilogs	$0. 97 1. 95	$1. 12 1. 95	20 per cent	Kilogr $0. 432
2	Soy, (sauce)	100 kilogs	5. 85	4. 88	20 per cent	20 per cent
3	Spanish flies, (cantharides)	100 kilogs	0. 39	0. 39	Free	5 per cent
4	Spars	......	Free	......	1 per cent	See Wood
5	Spartaria	100 kilogs	1. 93	0. 39	20 per cent	Kilogr 0. 002
6	Spa, or spa ware	See Porcelain	......	......	100 kilogs ... $10. 50	See Porcelain
7	Spectacle glasses and pebbles, not set.	100 kilogs	2. 93	2. 93	100 kilogs 3. 50	Kilogr 0. 172
8	Spectacles, steel	100 kilogs	9. 75	9. 75	20 per cent	Accord'g to materi'l.
9	all other	100 kilogs	9. 75	9. 75	20 per cent	......
10	Spelter, in pigs or blocks	100 kilogs	0. 195	0. 195	100 kilogs 0. 30	Free
11	in sheets	100 kilogs	1. 17	9. 78	100 kilogs 0. 30	Free
12	manufactures of	Manuf. 100 kilogs	5. 85	1. 56	100 kilogs 7. 50	Manufac. as copper.
13	Spermaceti oil, foreign fisheries.	See Oil	......	......	......	Kilogr 0. 005
14	Spices, all not otherwise provided for.	100 kilogs	19. 50	......	Not enumerated	Kilogr 0. 108
15	Spirituous liquors, not otherwise provided for.	22 degrees, hectoliter over 22 degrees, hectoliter	0. 97 1. 95	1. 07 1. 95	Hectoliter 3. 75	33 degrees, decaliter .... 1. 188 Above 33 degrees, decaliter 1. 62
16	Spirits of turpentine	100 kilogs	1. 95	0. 78	See Chemicals n. e.	10 per cent
17	Spokes	100 kilogs	0. 58	Free	100 kilogs 0. 10	See Wood
18	Spokeshaves	100 kilogs	0. 58	Free	100 kilogs 0. 10	See Wood
19	Sponges	Common, 100 klgs fine, 100 kilogs	3. 90 19. 50	3. 90 9. 75	100 kilogs 2. 00	Kilogr 0. 108
20	Springs, for wigs	100 kilogs	3. 90	4. 50	100 kilogs 5. 50	Kilogr 0. 162
21	Spy-glasses	100 kilogs	3. 90	1. 95	20 per cent	5 per cent
22	Starch, made of potatoes or corn.	100 kilogs	1. 95	0. 297	100 kilogs 2. 00	All, kilogr .. 0. 008
23	other	100 kilogs	1. 95	0. 297	100 kilogs 2. 00	
24	Statues and statuary, not merchandise.	......	Free	......	100 kilogs 1. 50	Kilogr 0. 01
25	Statues and statuary, articles of commerce.	Per cent	1	Free	Stone, 100 klgs 1. 50	Kilogr 0. 01
26						
27	(brass)	......	......	......		
28	(metal)	......	......	......	As material	......
29	(plaster)	......	......	......		
30	(wood)	......	......	......		
31	Staves, for pipes, casks, &c.	1,000	0. 58	Free.	Millimeter ... 1. 50	See Wood
32	for hogsheads	1,000	0. 58	Free.	Millimeter ... 1. 50	See Wood
33	Stave bolts	100 kilogs	0. 58	Free	Millimeter ... 1. 50	See Wood

(*Duties expressed in gold dollars of the United States.*)—Continued.

BELGIUM.	AUSTRIA.			DENMARK.	SWEDEN.	NORWAY.	
		General tariff.	Tariff in treaty.				
10 per cent	Centner	$1. 20	$0. 72	Pound.....$0. 017	Cork, lb...$0. 138	Free	1
15 per cent	Centner	1. 26	......	10 per cent.......	Pound..... 0. 044	Pot $0. 109	2
Free	Centner	2. 52	1. 44	Pound.....0. 0113	Free	Free	3
Free	See Wood ...	......	......	Free	Free	Free	4
5 per cent	Centner	4. 80	......	Pound..... 0. 004	Pound..... 0. 005	Pound..... 0. 005	5
10 per cent	See Porcelain	......	......	See Porcelain....	See Porcelain	Pound 0. 04	6
10 per cent	Centner	3. 48	1. 92	Pound..... 0. 04	Pound..... 0. 041	Pound 0. 047	7
10 per cent.......	Centner	7. 20	5. 76	10 per cent.......	20 per cent.	Not gold cases,	8
10 per cent	As material manuf.	......	......	10 per cent.......	20 per cent	pound..0. 0047	9
Free	....	Free	......	Free............	Free............	Free	10
Free	Centner	0. 388	Free	Free............	Free	Free	11
10 per cent	Centner	2. 40	2. 16	Pound..... 0. 045	Pound..... 0. 041	As Copper manuf.	12
Free	Centner	1. 26	......	Pound..... 0. 017	See Oils	Pound 0. 009	13
15 per cent	Centner	2. 52	......	Free............	Free	Free	14
Spirituous liquors, Dutch fabricat'n, 50 degrees or less, hectoliter. . 9. 25 Other fabricat'ns, 50 degrees or less, hectoliter.. 8. 275 Dutch fabrication, all above 50 degrees — each degree above—per hectoliter .. 0. 19 Other fabrication, all above 50 degrees — for each degree above— hectoliter.. 0. 17 Liquors in bottles, hectoliter..16. 58 Other alcoholic liquors, hectoliter 11. 70	Centner	3. 88	......	Of 8 degr's (Spendrup's alcoholometer,) quarter .... 0. 466 Each degree ab've 8, quarter. 0.0115	Spirit'ous liquors of 50 per cent. alcohol, temperture 15 degrees Celsius, pr. kande .... 0. 303 French brandies of grape, 50 per cent, 15 degrees per kande 0. 206 If in bottle, per kande.... 0. 248 Other than French of grape, and all of other fruit, 50 per cent and 15 degrees, per kande 0. 303	Of 100 per cent., pound ... 0. 153 80 to 90 per cent. less, lb...0. 0009 60 to 79 less, pound ...0. 0008 Below 60 p. cent. less, lb...0. 0007 All spirituous liquors in bottles, pot 0.218	15
Hectoliter ..11. 70	See Chemical	prepa	rat'ns.	Free............	Free	Free	16
5 per cent	See Wood ...	......	......	Free............	Free	Free	17
5 per cent	See Wood ...	......	......	Free	Free	Free	18
Free	....	Free	......	Washing, lb 0. 182 others, lb. 0. 017	Free	Washing, lb 0. 364 other .... Free	19
10 per cent	Centner	2. 88	2. 60	Pound..... 0. 017	Manuf. of steel...	Pound 0. 027	20
15 per cent	Centner	7. 20	5. 75	10 per cent.......	5 per cent........	10 per cent......	21
100 kilogs .. 0. 23	Centner	0. 36	......	Free............	Pound.....0. 0165	Dextrine, per	22
						pound .. 0. 0045	23
100 kilogs .. 0. 23	Centner	0. 36	......	Free............	Pound.....0. 0165	other.... Free	
							24
Free	All stone, ct'r	0. 48	Free	Pound..... 0. 091	Free	Weighing over	
						50 lb .... Free	25
Free	....	......	......	Pound..... 0. 091	Free	As material manufactured.	26
							27
Free	Free.........	......	......	As material......	Free	As material	28 29
							30
Free	See Wood ...	......	......	Free	Free............	Free............	31
Free	See Wood ...	......	......	Free	Free............	Free............	32
Free	See Wood ...	......	......	Free	Free	Free............	33

Comparative table of import duties in the United States and European countries.

	ARTICLES.	UNITED STATES.	GREAT BRITAIN.	GERMAN ZOLL-VEREIN.	SWITZERLAND.
1	Steel, in bars, ingots, sheets, coils, valued at 7 cents or less per pound.	Pound....$0. 02¼	Free............	Raw, cement, cast, and refined, per centner, $0.60. Raw, in blocks, per centner, $0.36. In sheets, raw, per centner, $0.84. Same, polished, per centner, $1.26. For manufactures, see Iron.	See Iron ......
2	Same, valued over 7 cents per pound.	Pound.... 0. 03	Free............		
3	Same, valued over 11 cents per pound.	10 per cent. and $0. 03½ per lb.	Free............		
4	Steel wire, not less than ¼ inch in diameter, valued at 7 cts. or less per pound.	Pound.... 0. 02¼	Free............		
5	Same, not less than ¼ inch in diameter, valued from 7 to 11 cents per pound.	Pound.... 0. 03	Free............		
6	Same, not less than ¼ inch in diameter, valued over 11 cents per pound.	10 per cent. and $0. 03½ per lb.	Free............		
7	Same, less than ¼ inch in diameter, not less than No. 16, wire gauge.	20 per cent. and $0. 02½ per lb.	Free............		
8	Same, less than ¼ inch in diameter, less than No. 16, wire gauge.	20 per cent. and $0.03 per lb.	Free............		
9	Steel in any form, not otherwise provided for.	30 per cent......	Free............		
10	Steel plates, engraved	25 per cent......	Free............		
11	Steel, all manufactures of, not otherwise provided for.	45 per cent......	Free............		
12	Steelyards.................	35 per cent......	Free............		
13	Stereotype plates..........	25 per cent......	Free............	Centner .. 0. 72	Centner ..$1. 56
14	Stoneware, common	25 per cent......	Free...	Stone, raw or cut, flint, millstones, whetstones, and coarse manufactures, free. Precious stones, imitations, articles of serpentine, centner, $0.36. Articles of precious stones or imitations of jewelry, centner, $36.00. Articles of other stone, centner, $0.12. If combin'd w'th other materials, centner $2.88.	Stone, building, free. Articl's of st'ne, fancy, centner, $1. 56. Ordinary, centner, $0.145. Millstones, 2 p'r cent.
15	Same, all other, gilt, painted, printed, or glazed.	40 per cent......	Free............		
16	Same, exceeding the capacity of 10 gallons, not ornamented.	25 per cent......	Free............		
17	Same, gas retorts, not ornamented.	25 per cent......	Free............		
18	Stones, Bristol.............	10 per cent......	Free............		
	polishing, burr, unw'ght or wrought.	Free............	Free............		
	building	20 per cent......	Free............		
	carnelian	10 per cent......	Free............		
	garnet, grind, paving, precious, ray, and sand.	10 per cent......	Free............		
	marbles	50 per cent......	Free............		
	load, mill, (burr,) oil, touch, whet.	20 per cent......	Free............		

(*Duties expressed in gold dollars of the United States.*)—Continued.

	FRANCE.				RUSSIA.	NETHERLANDS.	
	General tariff.		In treaty with Great Britain, &c.				
	In French vessels.	In other vessels.	In vessels of treaty powers.	In other vessels.			
In bars, 100 kilogs....	$5.85	$6.43	$1.75	$1.92	Steel, not wrought, per pood, $0.62. Cast-steel, manuf'd, as bells, mortars, carriage springs, weigh'g more than 1 pood, pood, $1.05. Weighing less than 1 pood, pood, $3.51. Locksmith's work, small articles, not polished, pood, $1.95. Polished, pood, $3.51. Larger articles, per pood, $0.78. Wire, pood, $1.17. Manufact'res of steel in combinat'n with other materials, pound, $0.25.	In bars, wire, sheets, and rails, free. All manufactures, 5 per cent.	1
In sheets, common, 100 kilogs.	9.75	10.73	....	....			2
In bands or leaves, not polish'd or tempered, not of more thickness than 1 millimeter, 100 kilogs.	9.75	10.73	....	....			3, 4
Same, 1 millimeter or less thick, 15 centimeters or more wide, 100 kilogs.	14.63	17.94	....	....			5
Same, less than 15 centimeters wide, 100 kilogs.	21.40	22.90	....	....			6
Same, of more than ½ millimeter in thickness.	....	....	2.19	2.33			7
Same, of ½ millimeter or less in thickness.	....	....	2.92	3.20			8
All steel in bands or plates, polished, tempered, blued, except saws, 100 kilogs.	0.97	1.06	....	....			9
Household articles of steel, 100 kilogs.	....	....	3.90	4.29			10, 11
For other manufactures of steel, see Iron, Machinery, Tools, &c.							12
100 kilogs.............	....	....	1.56	1.72	Pood..........$0.23	5 per cent.........	13
							14
							15
							16
							17
							18
Stone, cut or sawn.	Free ..	Free ..	Free ..	Free ..	All stone, raw, free. Pumice stone, per pood, $0.19. Stoneware, not gilded, p'r pood, $0.16. Gilded, per pood, $0.78. Millstones, oilstones, &c., free.	Stone, freestone, marble; alabaster in lumps, not manufact'ed any way; millstones, pumice stones, lithographers' stones, bricks, flint, pebbles, slates for roofing, limestone, and marble statues, free. Stones, hewn, polished, carved, marble or alabaster, 5 per cent. Cement, 100 kils., $0.30.	
Articles of stone, for chemical use	Free ..	Free ..	Free ..	Free ..			
Common ware, 100 kilogs.	....	....	0.97	....			
Modern statues, 100 kilogs.	....	....	Free ..	0.048			
All other work in stone.	....	....	15 per cent.				
Millstones, free	....	....	....	....			
Whetstones, rough, 100 kilogs.	Free ..	0.195	Free ..	Free ..			
Same, cut, 100 kilogs.	0.97	0.97	Free ..	0.048			

Comparative table of import duties in the United States and European countries.—

	ARTICLES.	ITALY.			SPAIN.	PORTUGAL.
			General tariff.	Tariff in treaty with France, &c.		
1	Steel, in bars, ingots, sheets, coils, valued at 7 cents or less per pound.	In b'rs or pieces, per 100 kilogs. In plates, p'r 100 kilogs. Wire, or manufactures, per 100 kilogs.	$2.34 2.34 3.90	$2.80 2.80 4.50	In bars, plates, & carriage springs, 100 kilogs, $3.00 Man'factur's; also with other metal, ordinary, 100 kilogs, $4.50. Fine, 100 kilogs, $5.50.	Bars, kilog., $0.004. Springs for vehicles, kilog., $0.027. Plates, not specified, kilog., $0.162. Wire, kilog, $0.054. Cutlery, with handles of mother-of-pearl, ivory, tortoise, &c., kilog. $0.378. Same, other animal material, kilog, $0.324. Same, wood or metal, (except gold and silver,) kilog. $0.27. Same, inlaid gold and silver, kilog, $0.54. Claspknives, wood handles, kilog, $0.108. Scissors, kilog, $0.54. Iron tools, kilog., $0.081. Articles not specified, kilog, $0.162.
2	Same, valued over 7 cents per pound.					
3	Same, valued over 11 cents per pound.					
4	Steel wire, not less than ¼ inch in diameter, valued at 7 cts. or less per pound.					
5	Same, not less than ¼ inch in diameter, valued from 7 to 11 cents per pound.					
6	Same, not less than ¼ inch in diameter, valued over 11 cents per pound.					
7	Same, less than ¼ inch in diameter, not less than No. 16, wire gauge.					
8	Same, less than ¼ inch in diameter, less than No. 16, wire gauge.					
9	Steel in any form, not otherwise provided for.					
10	Steel plates, engraved......					
11	Steel, all manufactures of, not otherwise provided for.					
12	Steelyards.................					
13	Stereotype plates..........	As metal manuf.	......	......	100 kilogs.... 3.00	Kilog........ 0.162
14	Stoneware, common.......	Stone and clay, per 100 kilogs. Whetstones, ea. Millstones, each. Vessels, 100 kilogs. Stoneware, white, 100 kilogs. Gilded, &c., 100 kilogs. Modern statues, Marble and all alabast'r sculptured, 100 kilogs. Slabs, &c., each, 100 kilogs.	0.48 0.019 0.195 0.156 1.56 2.34 5 p. ct. 5 p. ct. 0.039 to 0.058	Free. Free. Free. 0.175 1.56 2.34 Free. 0.297 0.195	Marble, precious stones, alabaster, coarse, or in polished pieces, 100 kilogs, $0.075. Cut in squares, polished or not, 100 kilogs, $0.75. Articles of stone and statues, 100 kilogs, $1.50. Stone, all other employed in the arts, 100 kilogs, $0.01.	Stoneware ordinary, kilog, $0.0027. Fine, kilog, $0.081. Stones for millstn's, kilog, $0.0001. All others not enumerated, free. Manufactures of alabaster, &c., kilog, $0.0108. Not specified, kilog, $0.001.
15	Same, all other, gilt, painted, printed, or glazed.					
16	Same, exceeding the capacity of 10 gallons, not ornamented.					
17	Same, gas retorts, not ornamented.					
18	Stones, Bristol............. polishing, burr, unw'ght or wrought. building........... carnelian.......... garnet, grind, paving, precious, ray, and sand. marbles............ load, mill, (burr,) oil, touch, whet.					

(*Duties expressed in gold dollars of the United States.*)—Continued.

BELGIUM.	AUSTRIA.			DENMARK.	SWEDEN.	NORWAY.	
		General tariff.	Tariff in treaty.				
Cast, raw, 100 kilogs, $0.097. Castings, work'd, 100 kils., $0.39. Bars, leaves, or wire, 100 kilos., $0.195. Artic'l's manuf'd, 100 kil., $0.78.	Raw or cement steel, cast & refined steel, centner.	$1.20	$0.72	In bars, per lb., $0.0014. For manufact's, see Iron.	Steel, not manufactured, free. Manufactures of steel, not polished, per lb., $0.0275. Same, polished, p'r lb., $0.0689.	Same as iron.	1 2 3 4 5 6 7 8 9 10 11 12 13
	Steel wire, polish'd, & strings, centner.	2.40	1.92				
	Manufact's, see Iron.	......	......				
	Steel pearls, centner.	7.20	5.76				
10 per cent	Centner......	1.44	1.20	Pound.... 0.017	Free	Free	14
Common, 100 kilogs, $0.29. All other, gilt, printed, painted, or glazed, 10 per cent. Raw, cut, or sawed, free. Polish'd or sculptured, 10 per cent.	Centner....	2.16	1.20	Stoneware, common, pound, $0.017. Gilded, silver'd, ornamented, pound, $0.045. Stone, pulv'riz'd, pound, $0.0056. Millstones, each, diameter to 14 inches, $0.0113. Same, 14 to 20 inches, $0.0226. Same, 20 to 32 inches, $0.045. Same, 32 to 41 inches, $0.091. Same, over 41 inches, per cubic foot, $0.091. Sculptur'd w'rk, such as toilet articles, vases, ch'ndeliers, &c. pound, $0.091. Other manufactures, pound, $0.0028.	Plates, per lb., $0.0082. All other, not gilded, per lb., $0.055. Pound.. 0.0138 Stone, and manufact'res of, not otherwise specified, free.	Stoneware, ordinary, free. White, per lb., $0.018. Building stones, and all manufactures of stone not oth'rwise specified, free. Statues weighing over 50 lbs., free.	15
	Centner....	2.88	2.16				16
	Centner....	0.12	Free.				17
	Centner....	0.12	Free.				18
	Centner....	0.388	Free.				
	Stone, n. o. e., cut or polish'd, centner.	0.388	0.36				
	Others, centner.	0.388	Free.				
	Models, ornaments, diamonds, (cut,) centner.	5.76	5.76				
	Statues over 10 pounds weight, centner.	0.48	Free.				
	Other stat's, centner.	0.48	0.36				
	Stone-ware, fancy, centner.	5.76	5.76				
	Same, painted, gilded, printed, centner.	2.88	2.16				
	One color, white, centner.	2.16	1.20				

Comparative table of import duties in the United States and European countries.

	ARTICLES.	UNITED STATES.	GREAT BRITAIN.	GERMAN ZOLL-VEREIN.	SWITZERLAND.
1	Storax or styrax, (balsam) .	30 per cent......	Free............	Free............	Centner ..$0. 68
2	Straw baskets..............	35 per cent......	Free............	Centner ..$2. 88	Centner .. 1. 56
3	carpets and carpeting.	See Matting.....	....	Not colored, per centner, 0. 12. Colored, p'r centner, $2.16.	Centner .. 1. 56
4	Strings, bow, if gut........	30 per cent......	Free............	Centner .. 0. 36	Centner .. 1. 56
5	of musical instruments, if gut.	30 per cent......	Free............	Centner .. 0. 36	Centner .. 1. 56
6	Strontian..................	20 per cent......	Free............	Free............	Centner ..0. 145
7	Strychnine and its salts	Ounce $1. 50	Free............	Centner .. 0. 36	Centner .. 0. 68
8	Studs, all gold or silver	25 per cent......	Free............	Centner ..11. 60	Centner .. 1. 56
9	ivory, &c...........	35 per cent......	Free............	Centner ..11. 60	Centner .. 1. 56
10	Succory root	Pound.... 0. 04	Free............	Centner .. 0. 48	Centner .. 0. 68
11	Same, ground, burnt, or prepared.	Pound.... 0. 05	Free............	Centner .. 0. 48	Centner .. 0. 68
12	Sugars, all not above No. 12, Dutch standard in color. all above No. 12 and not above No. 15. all above No. 15, not stove-dried, and not above No. 20. all refined in form of loaf, lump, crushed, powdered, pulverized, granulated. all stove-dried or other sugars above No. 20. refined, when tinctured, colored, or adulterated, valued at 30 cts. per pound or less. as above, valued over 30 cts. per pound, (candy.) sirup of .... sirup of cane	Pound .... 0. 03 Pound .... 0. 03½ Pound .... 0. 04 Pound .... 0. 05 Pound .... 0. 05 Pound .... 0. 15 50 per cent ...... Pound .... 0. 02½ Pound 0. 02½	Succades, including all fruits and vegetables preserved in sugar, lb. $0. 02 Sugar, candy, brown, white, refined or equal to refined and manufactures of refined sugar per cwt...2. 93 White clarified sugar, or equal to it, not refin'd, per cwt...2. 75 Yellow Muscovado sugar or sugar equal to it, per cwt...2. 55 Brown Muscovado or sugar equal to it, per cwt.......2. 33 Any other sugar not equal to brown Muscovado, per cwt 1. 94	Sugar, loaf and hat, centner 5. 28 Sugar, raw and farina, centner 4. 32 Sugar, raw for inland refineries by special permit, centner...... 3. 06	Sugar, all, centner...... 0. 68
13	Sulphate of ammonia.......	20 per cent	Free	Centner ... 0. 72	Centner... 0. 68
14	quinine	45 per cent	Free	Centner ... 2. 40	Centner... 0. 68
15	zinc	20 per cent	Free	Centner ... 2. 00	Centner... 0. 68
16	iron	Pound.... 0. 00½	Free	Centner ... 0. 72	Centner... 0. 68
17	rhubarb	20 per cent	Free	Centner ... 0. 72	Centner... 0. 68
18	Sulphur, flour	15 per cent., and ton 20 00.	Free	Free	Centner... 0. 145
19	Sulphuric ether............	Pound.... 1. 00	Free	Centner ... 2. 40	Centner... 0. 68
20	Sumac	10 per cent	Free	Free	Centner... 0. 068

(*Duties expressed in gold dollars of the United States.*)—Continued.

FRANCE.					RUSSIA.	NETHERLANDS.	
	General tariff.		In treaty with Great Britain, &c.				
	In French vessels.	In other vessels.	In vessels of treaty powers.	In other vessels.			
100 kilogs	Free	$0.48	$0.39	$0.39	Pood $0.85	Free	1
100 kilogs	$2.34	2.73	10 per	cent.	All manufactures of straw, mixed or unmixed, per lb., $0.62.	5 per cent	2
100 kilogs	0.97	1.07	0.97	1.07		Straw, in ropes, for hats, 5 per cent.	3
	15 per	cent.	10 per	cent.	Pound 0.08	5 per cent	4
	15 per	cent.	10 per	cent.	Pound 0.08	5 per cent	5
Free					Pound 0.85	Free	6
	Prohib	ited	5 per	cent.	Pound 0.85	Free	7
100 kilogs	97.50	100.90	97.50	100.90	Pound 4.68	5 per cent	8
Kilog	0.78	0.86	1.117	0.128	Pound 4.68	5 per cent	9
See Chiccory					Pound 1.17	Free	10
See Chiccory					Pound 1.17	Free	11
Sugar, raw, below No. 13, 100 kilogs.	8.19	8.58			Sugar, crude, broken, and powdered by sea, pood 2.34	Succades, 100 kilogrammes $1.23	12
From England and Belgium.			8.19	8.58	By land, pood 1.95	Sugar, bastard, refined, and mixed, 100 kilogs 14.25	
From oth'r treaty powers			8.58	8.58	Lump, candy, loaf, and refined, and sugar molasses by sea, pood 3.59	Sirup of more than 10 per cent. sugar, 100 kilogs 6.15	
No. 13 to No. 20, 100 kil.	8.58	8.97			By land, pood 3.02	Of less than 10 per cent. sugar, 100 kilogs 3.28	
From Engl'nd & Belgium			8.58	8.97			
From oth'r treaty powers			8.97	8.97			
Refined, similar to refined, powdered, and above No. 20, 100 kilos.	Prohib	ited	10.73	11.74			
Candies from England and Belgium, 100 kilos.			10.19	11.18			
All other, 100 kilogs			9.53	10.46			
Sulphate of baryte, 100 kilogs.	Free	0.195	5 per	cent	Pood 0.16	Free	13
Iron, 100 kilogs	1.17	1.27	5 per	cent	Pood 0.85	Free	14
Copper, 100 kilogs	6.04	6.64	5 per	cent	Pood 0.31	Free	15
Zinc, 100 kilogs	6.04	6.64	5 per	cent	Of baryte, pood 0.39	Free	16
Iron, double and copper.	3.60	3.96	5 per	cent	Of alumina, p'd. 0.16 Of magnesia, per pood 0.078 Of soda, pood 0.078	Free	17
	Free	Free	Free	Free	Free	Free	18
	Prohib	ited	5 per	cent	Ether, pood 3.43	Litre 0.51	19
	Free	Free	Free	Free	Free	Free	20

Comparative table of import duties in the United States and European countries.

	ARTICLES.	ITALY.			SPAIN.	PORTUGAL.
			General tariff.	Tariff in treaty with France, &c.		
1	Storax or styrax, (balsam)	100 kilogs	$2.39	$0.39	20 per cent	5 per cent
2	Straw baskets	Tissues of straw for hats or other objects, per 100 kilogs.	4.87	......	20 per cent	Kilog $1.08
3	carpets and carpeting.				See Matting	Kilog 0.002
4	Strings, bow, if gut	100 kilogs	9.75	9.75	100 kilogs $1.50	Kilog 0.54
5	of musical instruments, if gut.	100 kilogs	9.75	9.75	20 per cent	Kilog 0.54
6	Strontian	Free	......	......	100 kilogs 0.01	5 per cent
7	Strychnine and its salts	See Chemicals	......	......	Kilog 0.02	5 per cent
8	Studs, all gold or silver	As gold or silv'r, per 100 kilogs.	19.50	19.50	See Gold and silver.	See Gold and silver.
9	ivory, &c				See Ivory	See Ivory
10	Succory root	100 kilogs	0.39	Free.	100 kilogs 2.00	As vegetable material, not classified, 5 per cent.
11	Same, ground, burnt, or prepared.	As chiccory	......	......	See Chiccory	
12	Sugars, all not above No. 12, Dutch standard in color.	Sugar refined, pr. 100 kilogs.	4.87	5.63	Raw from Spanish provinces 100 kilogs 3.80	Sugar, raw: kilogr 0.081
	all above No. 12 and not above No. 15.	Not refined, per 100 kilogs.	3.51	4.06	Other, 100 ki. 4.725	Refined, klgr. 0.135
	all above No. 15, not stove-dried, and not above No. 20.	Sugar of tin, per 100 kilogs.	3.51	Free	Refined and candy from Spanish colonies, 100 ki. 5.40	
	all refined in form of loaf, lump, crushed, powder'd, pulverized, granulated.				Other, 100 ki. 6.45	
	all stove-dried or other sugars above No. 20.					
	refined, when tinctured, colored, or adulterated, valued at 30 cts. per pound or less.					
	as above, valued over 30 cts. per pound, (candy.)					
	syrup of					
	syrup of cane					
13	Sulphate of ammonia	Sulphate of alumina and potasse, 100 kil'gs	0.39	0.39	Sulphate of soda 100 kilogs .. 0.10	Sulphates, n. e.: kilogr 0.0027
14	quinine	Of barytes, per 100 kilogs.	0.195	0.195	Kilogramme . 0.02	Sulphurates, n. e. free.
15	zinc	Of iron and manganese, copper, zinc, and double iron, 100 kilogs.	0.39	0.39	100 kilogs 0.30	
16	iron				20 per cent	
17	rhubarb					
		Of magnesia, per 100 kilogs.	0.23	0.95		
		Of soda, per 100 kilogs.	0.195	0.195		
18	Sulphur, flor	100 kilogs	4.04	Free	Sulphur, crude, per ton 0.05	Sulphur, crude, free refined, kil., 0.001.
		Sulphur of mercury, kilogs.	0.195	......		
19	Sulphuric ether	100 kilogs	1.95	0.78	Kilogramme . 0.02	....
20	Sumac	....	Free	......	Free	Free

(*Dutics expressed in gold dollars of the United States.*)—Continued.

BELGIUM.	AUSTRIA.			DENMARK.	SWEDEN.	NORWAY.	
		General tariff.	Tariff in treaty.				
Free	Centner	$2.52	$1.44	Pound....$0.0113	Free	Free	1
10 per cent	Centner	1.20	0.72	Pound.... 0.056	Pound....$0.0689	Pound ...$0.127	2
10 per cent	Centner	0.12	......	Pound.... 0.004	See Mats	See Mats	3
10 per cent	Of gut, covered with silk, per centner.	24.00	14.40	Gut, lb ... 0.017	Pound.... 0.138	Of gut; also if spun over, per lb., $0.159.	4
10 per cent				Steel, lb .. 0.0056	Pound.... 0.138		5
	Others, per ct.	14.40	14.40				
Free	See Ch'micals	......	......	Pound.... 0.0113	Free	Free	6
Free	See Ch'micals	......	......	Pound.... 0.0113	Free	Free	7
5 per cent	See Gold and silver.		......	Pound.... 0.091	See Gold & silver.	See G ld & silver.	8
10 per cent	See Gold and silver.		......	Pound.... 0.091	Pound.... 0.138	See Ivory	9
Free	Sub-titutes of coffee, per centner.	3.84	......	Pound.... 0.0056	Pound.... 0.005	Pound ... 0.039	10
Free				Pound.... 0.023	As coffee	If prepared as coffee, prohibited.	11
Sugar, raw, under No. 18, free. Refined candy, 100 kilos $10.67 Refined, loaf, 100 kilogs. 9.97 Raw, No. 18, and above, sugar, 100 kils., 9.97. Syrup for distilleries, free. Syrup of more than 50 per ct., 100 kilogs. 2.93 Other syrup, free.	Sugar, raw, centner. Sugar for refining, cent. Refined, cent.	4.526 3.024 6.312	....	Sugar, pulveriz'd below Dutch No. 9, lb. 0.02 Above, No. 9. pound .... 0.021 Candy and other, in hats or loaf, equal to Dutch No. 18, lb. 0.0314 Syrup, not above 25 per ct. sugar pound .. 0,0098	Sugar not refin'd, not darker than Dutch stand'rd No. 18, lb. 0.03[illegible] Refined, lb. 0.03[illegible] Darker than Dutch No. 18, or liquid, lb. 0.022	Sugar, brown, pound... 0.04 White, in loaf, candy, and all other, lb. 0.047 Syrup, pound .0.009	12
Free	Sulphate of baryte, c'r.	0.36	......	Pound.....0.0113	See Chemicals	Free	13
Free	See Chemicals	......	......	Pound.....0.0113	See Chemicals	Free	14
	See Chemicals	......	......	Pound.....0.0113	See Chemicals	Free	15
	See Chemicals	......	......	Pound.... 0.0113	See Chemicals	Free	16
Free	....	Free	Free	Free	Free	Free	17
Free	....	Free	Free	Free	Free	Free	18
See ether	Centner	2.40	......	Pound.... 0.091	See Ether	Free	19
Free	....	Free	Free	Pound.....0.0113	Free	Free	20

Comparative table of import duties in the United States and European countries.

	ARTICLES.	UNITED STATES.	GREAT BRITAIN.	GERMAN ZOLLVEREIN.	SWITZERLAND.
1	Superacetate of lead, (sugar of)	Pound.... $0. 20	Free	Centner ...$0. 72	Centner...$0. 145
2	Surgeons' instrum'ts, iron..	35 per cent	Free	Free	Centner ... 1. 56
3	silver.	40 per cent	Free	Free	Centner ... 1. 56
4	steel .	45 per cent	Free	Free	Centner ... 1 56
5	Sweetmeats, n. o. s	35 per cent	Pound.....$0. 02		
6	Sword blades..............	45 per cent	Free	Unpolished, centner...... 1. 92	Centner .. 0. 39
7	for canes	45 per cent	Free	Polished, centner...... 2. 88	Centner... 0. 39
8	Sword knots, lace..........	35 per cent	Free	Centner ...10. 60	Centner ... 2. 93
9	gold and silver fine.	35 per cent	Free	Centner ...36, 00	Centner... 2. 93
10	gold and silver half fine.	35 per cent	Free	Centner ...36. 00	Centner ... 2. 93
11	Swords....................	35 per cent	Free	Centner ... 2. 88	Centner ... 0. 39
12	Table cloths, linen covers..	See cotton, linen, wool, &c.			
13	Table fasteners	35 per cent	Free	See household furniture.	
14	knives and forks.....	35 per cent	Free	See cutlery......	
15	tops, composition	35 per cent	Free	Centner ... 2. 88	Centner ... 0. 68
16	scagliola	35 per cent	Free	See household furniture.	
17	Tables, wood..............	35 per cent	Free	See household furniture.	
18	Tailors' chalk	10 per cent......	Free............	Free............	Centner... 0. 29
29	Talc, mineral..............	20 per cent......	Free............	Free............	Centner... 0. 058
20	Tallow....................	Pound.... 0. 01	Free............	Free............	Centner... 0. 097
21	candles...............	Pound.... 0. 02½	Free............	Centner... 1. 08	Centner... 0. 39
22	Tamarinds	10 per cent......	Free............	Centner... 1. 44	Centner... 0. 145
23	preserved in sugar ..	35 per cent......	See Succades....	Centner... 5. 04	Centner... 1. 56
24	Tambourines..............	30 per cent......	Free............	Centner...11. 60	Centner... 1. 56
25	Tannin and tannic acid	Pound.... 2. 00	Free............	Tan'n. cent 0. 36 Acid, cent. 2. 40	Centner... 0. 145 Centner... 0. 68
26	Tapers, paper, cotton wick.	35 per cent......	Free............	Centner... 1. 08	Centner... 1. 56
27	adamantine	Pound.... 0. 05			
28	spermaceti	Pound.... 0. 08			
29	stearine	Pound.... 0. 05	Free...........	Centner... 1. 44	....
30	wax...............	Pound.... 0. 08			
31	paraffine	Pound.... 0. 08			
32	all other.........	Pound.... 0. 02½	Free............	Centner... 1. 08	Centner... 1. 56
33	Tapioca..................	20 per cent......	Free............	Centner... 1. 44	Centner... 0. 68
34	Tar, Barbadoes, crude	20 per cent......	Free............	Free............	Centner... 0. 058
35	coal	20 per cent......	Free............	Free............	Centner... 0. 058
36	Tares	10 per cent......	Free............	Free............	Centner... 0. 029
37	Tarpaulings	20 per cent......	Free............	Centner... 0. 36	Centner... 0. 68
38	Tartaric acid	Pound.... 0. 20	Free............	Centner... 2. 40	Centner... 0. 68
39	Tartar, crude, (Argol)	Pound.... 0. 06	Free............	Centner... 0. 36	Centner... 0. 68
40	emetic, or tartrite of antimony.	Pound.... 0. 15	Free............	Centner... 2. 40	Centner... 0. 68
41	Tea, all direct from country where produced.	Pound.... 0. 25	Till Aug. 1, '67, pound.. 0. 12	Centner.. 5. 76	Centner... 2. 93
42	other.................	Pound.... 0. 25			

(Duties expressed in gold dollars of the United States.)—Continued.

	FRANCE.				RUSSIA.	NETHERLANDS.	
	General tariff.		In treaty with Great Britain, &c.				
	In French vessels.	In other vessels.	In vessels of treaty powers.	In other vessels.			
....	Prohib	ited	5 per	cent ..	Pood $0.85	Free................	1
						5 per cent..........	2
100 kilogs............	10 per	cent ...	Free ..	$0.048	Pood 4.68	5 per cent..........	3
						5 per cent..........	4
Sweetmeats, 100 kilogs .	....	....	....	....	Pood.......... 3.90	100 kilogs...$10.25	5
Syrups and bonbons....	$6.19	$8.58	....	....			
Comfits................	8.19	8.58	....	....			
Confectionery..........	4.09	4.28	....	....			
Confectionery, not with sugar or honey.	1.95	2.14	....	....			
See Side-arms..........	....	....	....	....	Pood 14.04	5 per cent..........	6
See Side-arms..........	....	....	....	....	Pood 14.04	5 per cent..........	7
	15 per	cent ...	10 per	cent ...	Gold, pood ...25.74 Silver, pood.. 1.72	5 per cent	8
See Gold manufactured .	....	....	....	....	Silk, pood ... 0.78	5 per cent	9
Same as gold..........	....	....	....	....	Lace, gold, p'd 8.28 Worsted, pood 0.39	5 per cent	10
See Side-arms..........	....	....	....	....	Pood 14.04	5 per cent..........	11
See Manufacture of flax.	....	....	....	....	Pound......... 0.507	5 per cent..........	12
See Iron and steel, household articles.	....	....	....	....	....	5 per cent..........	13
See Cutlery............	....	....	....	....	....	5 per cent..........	14
100 kilogs..............	19.50	20.95	$3.90	4,90	....	5 per cent..........	15
See Household furniture.	....	....	....	....	....	5 per cent..........	16
See Household furniture.	....	....	....	....	....	5 per cent..........	17
....	Free ..	Free ..	Free ..	Free ..	Free	Free	18
100 kilogs..............	Free ..	0.195	Free ..	0.195	Free	Free	19
....	Free ..	Free ..	Free ..	Free ..	Free	Free	20
....	5 per	cent.	5 per	cent.	Pood.......... 0.78	100 kilogs ... 1.23	21
100 kilogs..............	Free ..	0.39	Free ..	0.47	Pood 0.39	5 per cent	22
100 kilogs..............	4.09	4.29	4.29	4.29	Pood 0.78	100 kilogs ... 7.38	23
Each	0.29	0.29	10 per	cent.	Pound......... 0.08	5 per cent	24
....	Free ..	Free ..	Free ..	Free ..	Free	Free	25
....	Free ..	Free ..	Free ..	Free ..	Pood.......... 0.85	....	
....	5 per	cent.	5 per	cent.	Pood 0.78	5 Per cent	26
							27
							28
....	5 per	cent.	5 per	cent.	Pood 0.78	5 per cent..........	29
							30
							31
....	5 per	cent.	5 per	cent.	Pood 0.78	5 per cent	32
....	Free ..	Free ..	Free ..	Free ..	Pound......... 0.78	Free	33
....	Free ..	Free ..	Free ..	Free ..	Free................	Free	34
....	Free ..	Free ..	Free ..	Free ..	Free	Free	35
....	Free ..	Free ..	Free ..	Free ..	Free	Free	36
....	Free ..	Free .	Free ..	Free ..	Pood.......... 0.31	Free	37
100 kilogs..............	13.65	14.82	1.95	2.14	Pood 0.85	Free	38
....	Free ..	Free ..	Free ..	Free ..	Pound......... 0.146	Free	39
....	Free ..	Free ..	Free ..	Free ..	Pound......... 0.85	Free	40
Tartrate of potasse.....	13.65	14.85	Free ..	0.048			
of soda & potasse	13.65	14.82	Free ..	0.048			
100 kilogs............	7.80	19.50	....	....	Tea, flower, green & yellow, pood.17.76	100 kilogs ..10.25	41
100 kilogs............	19.50	19.50	....	....	ordinary black, stem & brick, pood.12.00		42

Comparative table of import duties in the United States and European countries.

No.	ARTICLES.	ITALY.			SPAIN.	PORTUGAL.
			General tariff.	Tariff in treaty with France, &c.		
1	Superacetate of lead, (sugar of.)	100 kilogs	$1.95	$0.78	Kilogramme. $0.02	Kilogram's. $0.0027
2	Surgeons' instrum'ts, iron ..	100 kilogs	3.90	1.95	10 per cent.........	20 per cent.........
3	silver.	100 kilogs	3.90	1.95	10 per cent.........	20 per cent.........
4	steel .	100 kilogs	3.90	1.95	10 per cent.........	20 per cent.........
5	Sweetmeats, n. o. s	100 kilogs	7.80	......	Kilogramme . 0.20	In juice, klgr. 0.075 Dry, kilogr .. 0.135
6	Sword blades...............	Sword blades, ordinary, per 100 kilogs.	4.68	5.40	Kilogramme . 0.40	15 per cent ....
7	for canes	Gilded, Damas., each.	0.087	0.097	Kilogramme.. 0.40	15 per cent ....
8	Sword knots, lace..........	Knots, 100 kilo.	1.95	0.58	20 per cent.......	Lace work of gold, kilogram's . 21.60 Silver, klgr. 10.80
9	gold and silver fine.	Swords mounted in ornament of steel, each	0.44	0.51	20 per cent.......	
10	gold and silver half fine.	Silver, each....	1.17	1.35	20 per cent.......	
		Gilded, each ...	1.75	2.03		
		Simple	0.29	0.67		
11	Swords....................	Other gilded ...	0.58	0.67	Kilogramme . 0.40	15 per cent.........
12	Table cloths, linen covers..	See Linen, &c...	......	......	See Tissues of flax.	See Manuf. of flax according to mat'l.
13	Table fasteners	100 kilogs	1.56	1.80	See Iron manufac..	....
14	knives and forks.....	100 kilogs	1.56	1.80	See Cutlery........	See Cutlery........
15	tops, composition....	Per cent.........	1	Free	100 kilogs....25.00	Kilogramme . 0.277
16	scagliola	Per cent.........	1	Free	100 kilogs.... 1.50	Kilogramme .0.001
17	Tables, wood...............	See Household fur	niture	......	See Household furniture.	See Household furniture.
18	Tailors' chalk	100 kilogs.......	0.78	Free.	Ton......... 0.05	100 kilogs.. 0.00027
19	Talc, mineral..............	100 kilogs.......	0.48	Free.	Ton......... 0.05	Free ....
20	Tallow....................	100 kilogs	0.195	0.195	100 kilogs.... 0.30	Raw or str'd, free.
21	candles............	100 kilogs.......	0.975	0.975	Not enumerated ...	Kilogramme 0.032
22	Tamarinds	100 kilogs.......	5.85	......	100 kilogs ... 0.50	Kilogramme .0.0027
23	preserved in sugar ..	100 kilogs.......	5.85	......	100 kilogs.... 0.20	Hermet'l, kil. 0.135
24	Tambourines	Each	0.39	0.39	10 per cent	25 per cent........
25	Tannin and tannic acid	100 kilogs.......	0.78	Free.	Kilogramme . 0.02	Kilogramme . 0.216
26	Tapers, paper, cotton wick.	....	......	......	20 per cent........	Not enumerated....
27	adamantine........	....	......	......	100 kilogs ...10.00	Not enumerated....
28	spermaceti	....	......	......	100 kilogs ...10.00	Kilogramme. 0.054
29	stearine	100 kilogs.......	1.95	1.95	100 kilogs ...10.00	Kilogramme. 0.054
30	wax...............	100 kilogs.......	7.80	3 p. c.	Kilogramme. 0.15	Kilogramme. 0.054
31	paraffine	....	......	......	20 per cent........	Kilogramme. 0.054
32	all others..........	....	......	......	20 per cent........	Not enumerated....
33	Tapioca...................	100 kilogs.......	0.24	......	100 kilogs ... 2.00	Kilogramme .0.0054
34	Tar, Barbadoes, crude	100 kilogs......	1.95	1.95	100 kilogs ... 0.05	Free ....
35	coal					
36	Tares	Free.............	......	......	100 kilogs ... 0.60	5 per cent.........
37	Tarpaulings	Free.............	......	......	100 kilogs ... 0.60	5 per cent.........
38	Tartaric acid	100 kilogs......	1.56	1.56	Kilogramme . 0.54	Kilogramme .0.216
39	Tartar, crude, (Argol)	Free.............	......	......	20 per cent...	5 per cent.........
40	emetic, or tartrate of antimony.					
41	Tea, all direct from the country where produced.	Kilog	0.58	......	Tea, all, kil. 0.30	Kilogrammo . 0.496
42	other.................	....	......	......		

(*Duties expressed in gold dollars of the United States.*)—Continued.

BELGIUM.	AUSTRIA.			DENMARK.	SWEDEN.	NORWAY.	
		General tariff.	Tariff in treaty.				
Free	See Chemicals	......	......	Pound....$0. 0113	Free	Free	1
Free	Centner	$2. 88	$2. 16	As mater'l manuf.	Pound.... $0. 041	In cases, lb. $0. 109	2 3
Sweetmeats prepar'd with brandy or sugar, per 100 kilogs 11 70 Other, 10 per cent.	See Comfits..	......	......	Pound..... 0. 04	Pound..... 0. 041	Pound 0. 061	4 5
Free	Centner	7. 20	7. 20	See Manuf. of iron and steel.	See Manufactures of iron.	Free	6
10 per cent	Centner	7. 20	7. 20	....	....	Pound 0. 073	7
10 per cent ..... 5 per cent	Silk lace, ctnr	126. 00	......	Pound.... 0. 091	10 per cent..... See Gold Manufactures.	Pound .... 0. 24 Pound 0. 319	8 9
5 per cent	Centner	126. 00	......		Pound... 0. 0964	Pound 0. 319	10
Free	Centner	7. 20	7. 20	See Iron manufs..	See Iron manufs	Free	11
See Tissues.......	See Tissues of cotton, &c., according to material.	......	......	As tissues of flax.	See Tissues of flax, &c.	See Manufs. of flax.	12
10 per cent	....	......	......	Pound..... 0. 017	See Manu. of iron or wood.	Pound 0. 027	13
10 per cent	See Cutlery..	......	......	See Cutlery......	See Cutlery......	See Cutlery	14
10 per cent	Centner	3. 60	2. 16	Pound..... 0. 045	Pound..... 0. 041	Pound 0. 047	15
10 per cent	See Stone m'nufactured.	......	......	Free	Free	Free	16
10 per cent	See Househ'ld furniture.	......	......	Pound.....0. 0027	Pound.....0. 0027	See Manufac. of wood.	17
Free	Free	......	......	Free	Free	Free	18
Free	Free	......	......	Free	Free	Free	19
Free	Centner	0. 388	......	Pound.....0. 013	Free	Pound 0. 007	20
10 per cent	Centner	1. 512	......	Pound.....0. 017	Pound.....0. 0082	Pound 0. 018	21
10 per cent	Centner	2. 52	......	Pound.....0. 0079	Pound..... 0. 011	Pound 0. 027	22
100 kilogs ..11. 70	See Comfits..	......	......	Pound.....0. 04	In brandy, p. 0. 082	Pound 0. 082	23
6 per cent	Centner	4. 80	3. 60	Pound.....0. 091	Each 0. 275	Each 0. 137	24
Free	See Chemicals	......	......	Pound.....0. 0113	Free	Free	25
10 per cent	Same as Candles ...		......	Pound.... 0. 034	Pound ... 0. 0138	Pound 0. 018	26 27 28 29 30 31
100 kilogs .. 0. 23	Centner	2. 52	......	Free	Free	Pound 0. 018	32 33
Free	Free	......	......	Free	Centner ...0. 0689	Free	34 35
Free	Free	......	......	Free	Free	Free	36
Free	Free	......	......	Free	Free	Free	37
Free	See Chemicals	......	......	Pound.....0. 0113	See Chemicals....	Free	38
Free	Free .... Centner	...... 2. 52	...... 1. 44	Pound... 0. 0113	Free	Free	39 40
100 kilogs ..17. 55	Centner	7. 56	......	Pound.....0. 0683	Pound.... 0. 1378	Pound 0. 191	41 42

Comparative table of import duties in the United States and European countries.

	ARTICLES.	UNITED STATES.	GREAT BRITAIN.	GERMAN ZOLL-VEREIN.	SWITZERLAND.
1	Teazles, (carding thistles)..	10 per cent......			Centner.. $0. 145
2	Teeth, elephants'	10 per cent......			Centner.. 0. 39
3	manufactured	20 per cent......			Centner.. 0. 39
4	Telescopes	40 per cent......			Centner.. 0. 39
5	Terra alba	20 per cent......	Free..........	Free............	Centner.. 0. 145
6	japonica............	Free............			Centner.. 0. 145
7	de sienna, dry	100 lbs....$0. 40			Centner.. 0. 145
8	in oil......	100 lbs.... 1. 50			Centner.. 0. 78
9	umbra	100 lbs.... 0. 50			Centner.. 0. 145
10	Teutenegue, in sheets......	Pound.... 0. 02¼			
11	in pigs and blocks.	Pound.... 0. 01½	Free..........	Centner...$0. 36	Centner... 0. 29
12	in boxes..........	35 per cent......			
13	Thermometers.............	40 per cent......	Free............	Free............	Centner ... 0. 39
14	Thor, marine..............	Pound.... 0. 00½	Free............	Free............	Centner... 0. 058
15	Thread, escutcheons	35 per cent......	Free............	See under Yarns	Centner.. 0. 68
16	packing...........	40 per cent......	Free............	Centner... 2. 58	
17	Thridace	20 per cent......	Free............	Free............	Centner... 0. 29
18	Tiles, encaustic...........	35 per cent......			
19	marble..............	50 per cent......	Free..........	Free............	15 centner. 0. 12
20	paving and roofing ..	20 per cent......			
21	Timber, hewn and sawed...	20 per cent......	Free............	Free............	15 centner. 0. 029
22	Timepieces	35 per cent.....	Free............	Astronom'l, free. Wooden, centner...... 2. 88 Tower clocks, centner .. 2. 88 Gold or silver watches, centner..... 36. 00	Centner... 2. 93
23	Tin, Banca, in bars, block, and pigs.	15 per cent	Free	Tin, block, bars, and old broken tin...... Free. Tin in sheets per centner ..0. 36 Ordinary manufactures of tin, centner ..0. 72 Varnished articles, &c., per centner ..2. 88 Oxide of tin Free. Chloride of tin, centner.. 2. 10 Tagger, per centner ......0. 36 Liquor.... Free.	Tin, crude, in block, per centner. ... 0. 145 Tin in bars and sheets, p'r centner ..... 0. 39 Manufactures of tin not polished or varnished, centner . 0. 68 Articles of tin varnished or polished, per centner ..... 1. 56 Oxide of tin and muriate of tin, centner . 0. 68
24	boxes	35 per cent	Free		
25	crystals of, foil........	30 per cent	Free		
26	muriate of, oxide of....	30 per cent	Free		
27	granulated, grain, liquor.	20 per cent	Free		
28	in plates and sheets....	25 per cent	Free		
29	in plates, galvanized by electric batteries.	Pound 0 02½	Free		
30	salts of................	30 per cent	Free		
31	tagger	25 per cent	Free		
32	all manufactures, not enumerated, wholly or part tin.	35 per cent	Free		
33	Tincal, or borax, crude	Pound 0 05	Free	Free	Centner... 0. 68
34	Tinctures, odoriferous......	50 per cent	Free	Centner ... 2. 40	Centner... 2. 93
35	bark and medicinal.	40 per cent	Free	Centner ... 2. 40	Centner... 0. 68
36	Tobacco, unmanufact'd and not stemmed.	Pound 0 35	10 lbs. moisture in 100 lbs.. $0 72 per lb 0 84	Centner.. 2. 88	Centner... 0. 68
37	leaves, stemmed...	Pound 0 50	Less the 10 lbs. moisture..0 72 per lb 0 84	....	....
38	stems............	Pound 0 15	Cavendish per lb........1 09	All manufact'd, centner . 7. 92	All manufact'd, centner . 1. 56
39	manufactured, not otherwise provided for.	Pound 0 50	Other, p'r lb. 0 97		

(*Duties expressed in gold dollars of the United States.*)—Continued.

	FRANCE.				RUSSIA.	NETHERLANDS.	
	General tariff.		In treaty with Great Britain, &c.				
	In French vessels.	In other vessels.	In vessels of treaty powers.	In other vessels.			
....	Free ..	Free ..	Free ..	Free ..	Free	Free	1
100 kilogs.	Free ..	$0.58	Free ..	$10.047	Free	Free	2
....	....		....	....	Free	5 per cent..........	3
....	30 per	cent.	Free ..	0.048	Free	5 per cent	4
....	Free ..	Free ..	Free ..	Free ..	Pood $0.04	Free	5
....	Free ..	Free ..	Free ..	Free ..	Pood 0.04	Free	6
....	Free ..	Free ..	Free ..	Free ..	Pood 0.04	Free	7
....	Free ..	Free ..	Free ..	Free ..	Pood 0.85	Free	8
....	Free ..	Free ..	Free ..	Feer ..	Pood 0.04	Free	9
							10
See Lead	....	....	....	....	Pood 0.47	Free	11
							12
100 kilogs.	30 per	cent.	Free ..	0.048	Free	5 per cent	13
....	Free ..	Free ..	Free ..	Free ..	Free	Free	14
See under Yarns	....	....	....	....	Pood 0.31	3 per cent	15
						100 kilogs ..$1.21	16
....	Free ..	Free ..	Free ..	Free ..	Free	Free	17
Tiles, flat, 100 kilogs..	$0.78	$0.78	Free ..	0.048	Pood 0.156	Free	18
arched, 100 kilogs..	1.95	1.95	Free ..	0.048	Free	Free	19
Ridge tiles, 100 kilogs.	4.87	4.87	Free ..	0.048	Free	Free	20
....	....	....	....	....	Free	See Wood..........	21
Time pieces:					Time pieces:	All, 5 per cent	22
Watches, silver case or metal, simple movement, *each*—					gold and gilt, each 1.01		
balance wheel..........	0.29	0.29	$0.195	0.19[illegible]	others, each.. 0.507		
all others	0.35	0.35			wooden each. 0.234		
repeating watches....	0.35	0.35	0.195	0.19[illegible]	clocks for towers, each....12.87		
Gold case, *each*—							
simple movement, balance wheel..........	0.60	0.60					
others	0.86	0.86					
Rept'g watches, each—			5 per cent., or				
balance wheel..........	0.86	0.86					
others	1.17	1.17	each	0.97			
Pocket chronometers, each	1.17	1.17					
Tin, mineral	Free ..	Free ..	Free ..	Free ..	Tin in blocks, bars, sheets, and scraps, per pood 0.156	Tin in blocks, bars, sheets, and scraps, free.	23
Tin filings, broken pieces, per 100 kilogs.	Free ..	0.048	Free ..	0.048			24
Tin beaten and stretched, per 100 kilogs.	11.70	12.76	1.17	1.29			25
							26
							27
Tin alloyed with antimony.	....	....	0.97	1.06	Oxidized and muriate per pood 0.85	Lacquered, paint'd, or not, 5 per ct.	28
Tin, manufactures:							29
Pottery, ordinary, per 100 kilogs.	19.50	20.95			Manufactures not polished per pood 0.78	All manufactur's of tin, 5 per cent.	30
Pottery, fine, per 100 kilogs.	39.00	41.43	5.85	6.43	Manufact'es polished and painted per pood 1.95	Free	31
Pottery, other, per 100 kilogs.	Prohibi	ted.				5 per cent	32
....	Free ..	Free ..	Free ..	Free ..	Free	Free	33
See Perfumeries..........	....	....	....	....	Per pood 3.12	See Perfumery	34
100 kilogs	Free ..	0.39	Free ..	Free ..	Free	Free	35
100 kilogs.	Free ..	1.95	....	....	Tobacco in leaf and bundles, pood 3.43	100 kilogs.... 0.29	36
For government account	....	....	....	....	Manufactured per pood........ 20.59	Unstemmed per 100 kilogs 0.61	37
Prohibited to private	account	....	....	....	....	See Snuff & cigars.	38
							39

Comparative table of import duties in the United States and European countries.

	ARTICLES.	ITALY.			SPAIN.	PORTUGAL.
			General tariff.	Tariff in treaty with France, &c.		
1	Teazles, (carding thistles)..	Free............	......	......	100 kilogs ...$2. 00	5 per cent..........
2	Teeth, elephants'	100 kilogs.......	$1. 95	Free.	Kilogramme . 0. 01	Kilogramme .$0. 216
3	manufactured	100 kilogs.... ..	19. 50	$19 50	Kilogramme . 2. 50	Kilogramme . 5. 40
4	Telescopes	100 kilogs.......	3. 90	1. 95	10 per cent........	5 per cent..........
5	Terra alba	Kilog...........	0. 48	Free.	100 kilogs .. 5. 50	Kilogramme .0. 0054
6	japonica............	Kilog...........	0. 48	Free.		
7	de sienna, dry	Kilog...........	0. 48	Free.		
8	in oil	Kilog.	1. 92	0. 78		
9	umbra	Kilog	0. 48	Free.		
10	Teutenegue, in sheets......	As lead and its manufactures.	See	Lead.	See Lead..........	See Lead ....
11	in pigs and blocks.					
12	in boxes..........					
13	Thermometers..............	100 kilogs.......	3. 90	1. 95	10 per cent........	5 per cent..........
14	Thor, marine	Free............	......	......	100 kilogs ... 0. 05	Free ....
15	Thread, escutcheons	See Yarns	......	......	See Yarns.........	Hemp, for cord'ge, and sails, kil. 0.108
16	packing					
17	Thridace	Free............	......	......	100 kilogs ... 1. 50	....
18	Tiles, encaustic............	Tiles, all, 1000.	0. 58	Free.	100 kilogs ... 0. 30	Dutch, kilog 0. 054
19	marble					Kilog 0. 091
20	paving and roofing ...					Kilog 0. 001
21	Timber, hewn and sawed...	See Wood	......	......	See Wood..........	Kilogramme. 0. 0027
22	Time-pieces	Pocket watches, simple, gold case, each..... other met'l, each repeat'g watches, each....... Parlor clocks...	 0. 39 0. 195 0. 78 5 per	 0. 29 0. 29 0. 90 cent.	20 per cent .... Gold watches, each ... 1. 50 Silver watches, each.... 0. 40	Time - pieces, of wood, part metal, each ... 0. 216 See Watches .....
23	Tin, Banca, in bars, block, and pigs.	Tin in bars or pieces, 100 kils.	0. 195	Free.	Tin in bars & plat's, 100 kilogs ..0 .35	Tin in bars and sheets, kil . 0.0027
24	boxes	Tin in strips, 100 kilogs.	0. 975	Free.	Tin in sheets, 100 kilogs 3. 75	
25	crystals of, foil.........					
26	muriate of, oxide of....	Tin laminated and in sheets, 100 kilogs.	1. 56	1. 17	Tin worked, 100 kilogs .12. 50	Tin, manufactured, kilog 0. 216
27	granulated, grain, liquor.				Tin in ingots, 100 kilogs . 5. 00	Broken pieces, free.
28	in plates and sheets....					
29	in plates, galvanized by electric batteries.				Tin manufactures, 100 kils....10. 00	
30	salts of...............	....	......	......	....	Oxide of tin, kilog...... 0. 027
31	tagger					
32	all manufactures not enumerated, wholly or part tin.	Tin vessels, and other coarse articles also alloyed, 100 kils.	2. 93	3. 38	....	Kilog 0. 216
33	Tincal, or borax crude.....	100 kilogs.......	0. 39	Free.	Kilog 0. 02	Free ....
34	Tinctures, odoriferous......	100 kilogs.......	1. 95	0. 78	Kilog 0. 30	20 per cent ....
35	bark, and medicinal.	100 kilogs.......	1. 95	0. 39	20 per cent	5 per cent ....
36	Tobacco, unmanufact'd and not stemmed.	Tobacco in leaf..	......	....	Government monopoly.	Tobacco, leaf or rolls, from Cape Verde, kil.. 0. 108
37	leaves stemmed...	Prohibited	......	....		Tobacco, leaf or from Brazil, kilog...... 0, 162
38	stems	Prohibited	......	....		Other tobacco, kilog 0. 216
39	manufactured, not otherwise provided for.	Prohibited	......	....		All manufactures pay double duties as leaf tobacco.

(*Duties expressed in gold dollars of the United States.*)—Continued.

BELGIUM.	AUSTRIA.			DENMARK.	SWEDEN.	NORWAY.	
		General tariff.	Tariff in treaty.				
Free	Free	......	......	Free	Free	Free	1
Free	Free	......	......	Free	Free	Free	2
10 per cent	Centner	$7.20	$5.76	Pound.....$0.091	Pound.....$0.138	Pound....$0.158	3
Free	Centner	2.16	2.16	10 per cent	Pound..... 0.141	10 per cent	4
							5
							6
Free	Free	......	......	Free	Free	Free	7
							8
							9
Free Free 10 per cent	Free	......	......	Free	Free	Free	10 11 12
Free	Centner	2.88	2.16	Free	Pound..... 0.041	10 per cent	13
Free	Free	......	......	......	Free	Free	14
See Yarns	See Yarns	......	......	Pound ... 0.045 Pound ... 0.017	See Yarn	Pound 0.091	15 16
Free Millimeter .$0.78 Free Millimeter . 0.78	Free	......	......	Free	Free	Free Free Not glazed, free. Glazed, M 2.185	17 18 19 20
See Wood	See Wood	......	......	Cubic foot . 0.02'	Free	Free	21
Time-pieces and watches, 10 p.c.	Watches: gold and silver, centner others, cent clocks, cent.	 126.00 48.00 24.00	 .... 14.00	Chronometers, each .... 0.273 Parlor clocks, pound... 0.091 Tower clocks, as chief material. others, lb. 0.045	Watches, pocket, and chrnm's, each .... 0.2756 Clocks, frame of bronze or other metal, lb. 0.082 frame of alabaster or porcelain, lb .. 0.082 frame of wood or other material, lb... 0.055 Watch material, lb.... 0.21	Watches and chronometers, each .... 0.273 Parlor clocks, fancy, each 2.18 Ditto, common, each .... 1.365 Tower clocks, same as chief material.	22
Tin, raw or laminated.....free	Tin, crude ..	Free.	Free.	Tin in sheets, plates, or tubes, pound.. 0.0056	Tin, crude, sheets, &c.......free.	Free	23
							24
							25
Articles of manufacture, 10 pr. ct. Free	Tin in sheets, wire, and tin cast, per centner.	1.44	1.20	Manufactures of tin, not gilded, pound... 0.045	Manufactures of tin, not varnis'd or painted, per pound.. 0.041	Articles not gilded, pound 0.047	26 27
	Common articles, c'tner.	2.40	2.16	Gilded, lb.. 0.091	Varnished or painted, lb 0.082	Articles gilded, pound .. 0.095	28 29
Free	Fancy articles, c'tner.	7.20	5.76	Oxide and salts of tin, lb. 0.0113	Tin liquor, lb 0.041	Chemical preparations...free.	30 31
10 per cent	Gilded, ornamented.						32
Free	....	Free.	......	Pound ... 0.0113	Free	Free	33
See Chemicals, n.e.	Centner	7.20	5.76	Pound ... 0.091	See Chemicals...	Free	34
See Chemicals, n.e.	Centner	7.20	......	Pound ... 0.0113	Free	Free	35
100 kilogs .. 1.64	Tobacco, leaf and stems, centner.	5.04	......	Leaf and stem, pound... 0.028	Tobacco leaves and stems not prepared, per pound.. 0.0698	Leaves & stems, pound .. 0.091	36
100 kilogs .. 2.57	All manufactures, including cigars, snuff, &c., centner.	12.60	......	Manufactured tobacco, lb. 0.045	Cut, pound 0.138	Smoking tobacco and snuff, per pound .. 0.109	37
100 kilogs .. 8.19				Cigars, lb.. 0.082	For chewing, pressed, lb. 0.096 Cigars, lb.. 0.50 Cheroots, lb 0.165 Snuff, lb... 0.15	Cigars, lb . 0.132	38 39

Comparative table of import duties in the United States and European countries.

	ARTICLES.	UNITED STATES.	GREAT BRITAIN.	GERMAN ZOLL-VEREIN.	SWITZERLAND.
1	Toilet vials, or bottles, exceeding 4 oz. and not 16 oz. each.	40 per cent	Free	As fancy goods, cent'r. $11 60	Centner.. $2.93
2	Toilet vials, or bottles, not exceeding 4 oz.	40 per cent	Free		
3	Tongues, reindeer	20 per cent	Free	Centner... 0.36	Centner... 0.39
4	sounds (fish)	20 per cent	Free	Centner... 0.36	Centner... 0.39
5	neats' (smoked)	20 per cent	Free	Centner... 0.36	Centner... 0.39
6	Tonca beans	20 per cent	Free	Free	15 centner. 0.029
7	Tools	See Iron and steel.	Free	See Manufactures	of iron and steel.
8	Tooth brushes	40 per cent	Free	Centner... 2.88	Centner... 1.56
9	powders	50 per cent	Free	Centner... 2.40	Centner... 2.93
10	picks, all	35 per cent	Free	Centner... 2.88	Centner... 1.56
11	except gold and silver.	40 per cent	Free	Centner...36.00	Centner... 2.93
12	Topaz, real	10 per cent	Free	Centner... 0.36	Centner... 0.39
13	imitation	40 per cent	Free	Centner... 0.36	Centner... 0.39
14	Tortoise shell	Free	Free	Free	Centner... 0.09
15	Touchstones	20 per cent	Free	Free	Centner... 0.058
16	Tow of hemp	Ton ... $10 00	Free	Free	Centner... 0.29
17	flax	Ton ... 5 00	Free	Free	Centner... 0.29
18	Toys of every description except dolls.	50 per cent	Free	Centner...11.60	Centner... 1.56
19	Treacle, molasses	Gallon 0 08	Cwt...... $0.87	Centner... 1.80	Centner... 0.29
20	Trees	30 per cent	Free	Free	15 centner. 0.058
21	Truffles, preserved	35 per cent	Free	Centner ... 5.04	Centner... 1.56
22	earthen, common	25 per cent	Free	Free	Centner... 0.145
23	Tubes, cast	40 per cent	Free	Centner.. 0.96	Centner... 0.39
	wrought	See Iron	Free		
24	Turmeric	Free	Free	Free	Centner... 0.145
25	Turquoises	10 per cent	Free	Centner... 0.36	Centner... 0.39
26	Turpentine, spirits of	Gallon 0.30	Free	Free	Centner... 0.145
27	Turtles, green	20 per cent	Free	Centner... 1.44	Centner... 0.39
28	Types				
29	new	25 per cent	Free	Centner... 0.72	Centner... 0.145
30	old, fit only for remanufacture.	Free	Free	Centner... 0.72	Centner... 0.145
31	metal	25 per cent	Free	Centner... 0.72	Centner... 0.145
32	Ultramarine	25 per cent	Free	Centner... 1.44	Centner... 0.68
33	Umber	Per pound. 0.00½	Free	Free	Centner... 0.029
34	Umbrellas, not silk	50 per cent	Free	Centner... 2.88	Centner... 1.56
35	silk	60 per cent	Free	Centner... 2.88	Centner... 2.93
36	Umbrella furniture	35 per cent	Free	Iron or steel, centner. 1.92	Centner. 1.56
37	(of silver)	40 per cent	Free	Other metal centner. 2.88	
38	Vandyke, brown	20 per cent	Free	Centner... 0.36	Centner... 0.68
39	Valonia, (a nut for dyeing)	Free	Free	Free	Centner... 0.029
40	Vanilla, plants	30 per cent	Free	Free	15 centner. 0.058
41	beans	Pound 3.00	Free	Centner... 4.68	Centner... 0.68
42	Varnishes of all kinds, value not over $1 50 per gallon.	20 per cent. and gallon ... 0.50	Varnishes containing any quantity of spirit, gal 2.92	Centner.. 0.36	Centner... 0.68
43	value over $1 50 per gallon.	25 per cent. and gallon ... 0.50	Others free		

(*Duties expressed in gold dollars of the United States.*)—Continued.

FRANCE.					RUSSIA.	NETHERLANDS.	
	General tariff.		In treaty with Great Britain, &c.				
	In French vessels.	In other vessels.	In vessels of treaty powers.	In other vessels.			
							1
Fancy goods	Prohibited		10 per cent.		Pound $0.85	5 per cent	
							2
See meat	....	....	....	....	Pood 0.51	100 kilogs $3.28	3
See meat	....	....	....	....	Pood 0.51	100 kilogs 3.28	4
See meat	....	....	....	....	Pood 0.51	100 kilogs 3.28	5
....	....	....	Free	Free	Free	Free	6
....	Free	Free	....	....	Pood 0.62	5 per cent	7
Flax combs, points of iron and copper.	100 kilogr's. $15.66	$16.86					
Flax combs, points of steel.	39.00	41.43					
Other tools of pure iron.	9.75	10.72	$1.95	$2.14			
Other tools of iron and steel.	24.37	26.27	2.92	3.20			
Other tools of pure steel.	34.12	36.30	3.90	4.27			
100 kilogs	19.50	20.95	10 per cent.		Pound 0.85	5 per cent.	8
100 kilogs	35.88	38.16	1.95	2.14	Pood 9.36	5 per cent	9
100 kilogs	19.50	20.95	10 per cent.		Pound 0.85	5 per cent	10
100 kilogs	97.50	100.90	97.50	100.90	Pound 25.74	5 per cent	11
....	Free	Free	Free	Free	Free	Free	12
100 kilogs	1.17	1.29	0.039	0.0429	Free	5 per cent	13
100 kilogs	Free	0.97	....	....	Free	Free	14
100 kilogs	Free	Free	Free	Free	Free	Free	15
100 kilogs	4.87	5.36	2.92	3.20	Pood 0.31	5 per cent	16
100 kilogs	4.87	5.36	2.92	3.20	Pood 0.31	5 per cent	17
100 kilogs	15.60	16.86	10 per cent.		Pound 0.26	5 per cent	18
See Molasses	....	....	....	....	Pood 0.85	100 kilogs 1.64	19
Free	....	....	....	....	Free	Free	20
100 kilogs	0.58	0.64	0.58	0.64	Pood 3.90	100 kilogs 10.25	21
Free	....	....	....	....	Free	Free	22
			9 mill. or more.				
100 kilogs. Tubes, iron, of 25 mill. diameter or less.	6.82	7.49	2.14	2.45	Pood 0.62	Free	23
			Less than 9 mill.				
100 kilogs. Tubes, iron, of less than 25 mill. diameter or more.	9.75	10.72	3.90	4.29			
100 kilogs. All others	Prohibited.		....	....			
Free	....	....	....	....	Free	Free	24
100 kilogs	Free	0.97	....	....	Free	Free	25
See Chemicals n. e.	....	....	....	....	Pood 0.23	Litre 0.23	26
Free	....	....	....	....	Live, free	Free	27
....	....	....	....	....	....	....	28
							29
New French, 100 kilogs.	39.00	41.43	1.56	1.92	Pood 0.23	100 kilogs .. 2.87	30
New German, 100 kilogs.	9.75	10.72				100 kilogs .. 2.87	
Other, 100 kilogs	19.50	20.95				Free	31
100 kilogs	0.48	0.52	3.05	3.55	Pood 1.56	Free	32
Free	....	....	....	....	Pood 0.04	Free	33
Each, (oil-cloth)	0.145	0.145	10 per cent.		Wood, each 0.47	5 per cent	34
Each	0.39	0.39			Silk, each 1.17	5 per cent	35
							36
....	15 per cent.		10 per cent.		All others, each. 0.23	5 per cent	37
Free	....	....	....	....	Free	Free	38
100 kilogs	Free	0.78	....	....	Free	Free	39
....	Free	....	....	....	Free	Free	40
Vanilla, 100 kilogs	39.09	41.73	Free	Free	Pood 6.24	Free	41
							42
Varnishes, vermeil, 100 kilogs.	7.89	8.89	10 per cent.		Pood 5.15	Litre 0.37	
Other, 100 kilogs	15.99	17.28					43

Comparative table of import duties in the United States and European countries.

	ARTICLES.	ITALY.			SPAIN.	PORTUGAL.
			General tariff.	Tariff in treaty with France, &c.		
1	Toilet vials, or bottles, exceeding 4 oz. and not 16 oz. each.	100 kilogs	$1.56	$0.29	100 kilogs ...$0.60	Kilog $0.172
2	Toilet vials, or bottles, not exceeding 4 oz.					
3	Tongues, reindeer	See Meat	......	......		
4	sounds (fish)				100 kilogs ... 0.50	Kilog 0.081
5	neats' (smoked)					
6	Tonca beans	Free	Free.	Free.	100 kilogs ... 0.60	5 per cent
7	Tools	Tools, 100 kilogs.	1.56	1.80	See Iron	Kilog 0.081
8	Tooth brushes	100 kilogs	9.75	9.75	Kilog 0.40	Kilog 1.08
9	powders	As perfumery	......	......	Kilog 0.30	Kilog 0.27
10	picks, all	100 kilogs	9.75	9.77	20 per cent	Kilog 0.40
11	except gold and silver.		1 p. c.	10 p.c.	Kilog 5.00	Kilog 5.40
12	Topaz, real	Per cent	0.01	Free.	100 kilogs.... 0.075	½ per cent
13	imitation	Per cent	0.01	0.10	100 kilogs.... 9.00	Kilog 0.54
14	Tortoise shell		Free.	Free.	Kilog 0.01	Kilog .... 0.216; Manufactures of, kilog. .. 5.40
15	Touchstones		Free.	Free.	100 kilogs.... 0.01	Free
16	Tow of hemp	Tow of all kinds.	Free.	Free.	100 kilogs.... 4.00	Raw, kilog.. 0.0008
17	flax	Tow of all kinds.	Free.	Free.	100 kilogs.... 4.00	Twisted, kil. 0.324
18	Toys of every description except dolls.	100 kilogs	7.80	7.80	Except of gold, ivory, &c., kil. 0.30	Kilog 0.27
19	Treacle, molasses	100 kilogs	1.17	1.36	Kilog 0.0216	Kilog 0.021
20	Trees	Free	......	......	Free	Free
21	Truffles, preserved	100 kilogs	7.80	......	Kilogramme . 0.20	Kilogramme .0.037
22	earthen, common	100 kilogs	2.93	Free.	100 kilogs.... 0.25	Free
23	Tubes, cast	100 kilogs	1.56	1.79	100 kilogs .. 0.937	Kilogramme .0.081
	wrought				100 kilogs .. 2.60	Kilogramme .0.189
24	Tumeric	100 kilogs.	0.39	Free.	Ton.......... 0.05	5 per cent
25	Turquoises	Free	......	......	100 kilogs.... 0.10	5 per cent
26	Turpentine, spirits of	100 kilogs.	1.95	0.78	100 kilogs.... 1.60	Kilogramme .0.005
27	Turtles, green	Free	......	......	Free	Free
28	Types		......	......		Type and ornaments for printing, kilog. 0.027
29	new	100 kilogs.	......	1.12	100 kilogs.... 1.50	
30	old, fit only for remanufacture.	100 kilogs	0.975	0.58	100 kilogs.... 1.50	
31	metal	100 kilogs	0.975	0.58	100 kilogs....25.00	
32	Ultramarine	100 kilogs	1.95	0.39	100 kilogs.... 1.50	Kilogramme .0.054
33	Umber	100 kilogs.	1.95	0.39	100 kilogs.... 1.50	Kilogramme .0.0054
34	Umbrellas, not silk	Each	0.097	0.097	Each 0.30	Each 0.972
35	silk	Each	0.185	0.195	Each 0.50	Each 1.404
36	Umbrella furniture	100 kilogs	3.90	3.90	As material manufactured.	Frames, complete, each.... .0.864
37	(of silver)					Frames, in parts, kilog......1.90
38	Vandyke brown	100 kilogs.	1.95	0.78	100 kilogs.... 1.50	Kilogramme .0.0054
39	Valonia, (a nut for dyeing).	100 kilogs	0.39	Free.	100 kilogs.... 0.05	20 per cent
40	Vanilla, plants	Free	......	......	Free	Free
41	beans	Kilogramme	0.487	......	100 kilogs....20.00	Free
42	Varnishes of all kinds, value not over $1 50 per gallon.	100 kilogs	1.95	1.95	100 kilogs.... 2.50	Kilogramme ..0.01
43	value over $1 50 per gallon.					

(Duties expressed in gold dollars of the United States.)—Continued.

BELGIUM.	AUSTRIA.			DENMARK.	SWEDEN.	NORWAY.	
		General tariff.	Tariff in treaty.				
							1
10 per cent	See Glass....	......	......	Pound $0.04	See Glass........	Pound $0.047	2
							3
100 kilogs ..$0.23	See Meat....	......	......	Free	Free	Pound 0.009	4
							5
100 kilogs .. 0.117	Centner	$2.52	$1.44	Free	Free	Free...........	6
100 kilogs .. 0.78	Centner	2.88	2.16	Pound 0.17	5 per cent	Pound 0.027	7
10 per cent	Centner	7.20	5.76	10 per cent	Pound ....$0.05[illegible]	Pound 0.636	8
See Perfumery...	Centner	0.36	......	Pound 0.079	10 per cent	Free...........	9
10 per cent	Centner	7.20	5.76	As material manufactured.	10 per cent	According to material.	10
5 per cent	Centner	126.00	......		See Gold & silver.		11
Free	Cut, centner	5.76	......	Free	Free	Free...........	12
10 per cent	Cut, centner.	5.76	......	Pound 0.09	Pound 0.04	Pound.... 0.109	13
Free	Free	......	......	Free	Free	Free...........	14
Free	Centner	0.388	Free	Free	Free	Free...........	15
Free	Free	......	....	Free	Free	Free...........	16
Free	Free	......	......	Free	Free	Free...........	17
10 per cent	Centner	5.76	.....	As material manufactured.	Pound ... 0.068	Turners' work, exclusively.	18
100 kilogs .. 2.93	Centner	1.512	.....	Pound.... 0.0098	Pound ... 0.022	Pound.... 0.082	19
Free..............	Free	......	....	Free..........	Free............	Free	20
10 per cent	Centner	0.388	Free	Hermetically sealed, lb. 0.04	In brandy, per pound ... 0.082	Pound.... 0.082	21
Free..............	Free	......	......	Free.............	Free............	Free	22
100 kilogs ..0.097 100 kilogs .. 0.39	See Iron and	lead .	......	Pound .. 0.0056 Pound... 0.017	See Iron .... See Iron	Pound... 0.0045 Pound... 0.027	23
Free..............	Free	......	......	Free.............	Free.............	Free	24
Free..............	Free........	......	....	Free.............	Free	Free	25
See Chemicals n. e.	Centner	0.2916	Free	Pound.... 0.0014	Pound ... 0.0082	Free	26
Free..............	Free	......	......	Free.............	Free	Free	27
....	....	......	.....	....			28
10 per cent.	Centner	1.44	1.20	Pound.... 0.017	Pound 0.027	Pound... 0.0045	29
Free..............	Free	......	......	Pound.... 0.017	Free	Pound... 0.0045	30
Free..............	Centner	0.36	0.36	Pound.... 0.017	Free	Pound... 0.0045	31
Free	Free	......	.....	Pound.... 0.0056	Free	Pound... 0.009	32
Free	Free	......	.....	Pound.... 0.0056	Free	Pound... 0.009	33
10 per cent	N. e., centner	5.76	.....	Each.... 0.136	Each 0.0689	Each 0.086	34
10 per cent	N. e., centner	5.76	.....	Each 0.344	Each 0.206	Each 0.205	35
10 per cent.	N. e., centner	5.76	......	As material......	Pound ... 0.051	Pound... 0.047	36 37
Free	Centner.	0.388	......	Pound.... 0.0056	Free	Pound... 0.009	38
Free	Free	......	......	Free.............	Free	Free	39
Free	Free.........	......	......	Free.............	Free	Free	40
15 per cent	Centner.	7.56	.....	Pound.... 0.273	Vanilla, lb . 1.51	Pound... 1.748	41
Alcoholic. See Spirituous liq. Others, 10 per ct.	Centner....	7.20	7.56	Pound.... 0.028	Varnishes, all, per pound .. 0.0275	Pound... 0.036	42 43

Comparative table of import duties in the United States and European countries.

	ARTICLES.	UNITED STATES.	GREAT BRITAIN.	GERMAN ZOLL-VEREIN.	SWITZERLAND.
1	Vases, porcelain	50 per cent	Free	Centner...$2.88	Centner...$1.56
2	Vegetables, prepared	35 per cent	Free	Free Preserved, centner...... 3.60	Centner... 1.56
3	Vegetables used in dyeing	Free	Free	Centner... 0.36	Centner... 0.68
4	Vegetable substances for cordage.	Per ton ..$15.00	Free	Free	Centner... 0.058
5	Vellum	30 per cent	Free	Centner... 5.76	Centner... 0.145
6	Velvet, cotton and other	35 per cent	Free	Centner... 11.60	Centner... 1.56
7	silk	60 per cent	Free	Centner... 21.60	Centner .. 1.56
8	Venetian red, dry	25 per cent	Free	Free	Centner... 0.68
9	in oil	25 per cent	Free	Free	Centner... 0.68
10	Venison hams	Pound 0.02	Free	Centner... 0.36	Centner... 0.39
11	Veratrine, (medical prep.)	40 per cent	Free	Centner... 2.40	Centner... 0.68
12	Verdigris	Pound..... 0.06	Free	Centner... 0.48	Centner... 0.68
13	Verditure	20 per cent	Free	Free	Centner... 0.145
14	Vermicelli	35 per cent	Free	Centner... 1.44	Centner... 1.56
15	Vermilion	25 per cent	Free	Centner... 2.40	Centner... 0.058
16	Vessels, cast iron, n. o. s.	Pound 0.15	Free	Centner... 0.28	Centner... 0.39
17	copper	45 per cent	Free	Centner... 1.92	Centner... 0.68
18	Vinegar	Gallon 0.10	Free	Centner... 0.96	Centner... 0.145
19	Violins	30 per cent	Free	Centner... 2.88	Centner... 1.56
20	Violin strings, gut	30 per cent	Free	Centner... 0.36	Centner... 1.56
21	wire	35 per cent	Free	Centner... 0.82	Centner... 1.56
22	Vetches, dried for feed	10 per cent	Free	Free	Centner... 0.145
23	for seed	30 per cent	Free	Free	15 centner. 0.029
24	Vitriol, green	Pound 0.00½	Free	Free	} Centner. 0.039
25	white, or sulphate of zinc	20 per cent	Free	Centner... 0.36	
26	Wadding paper	35 per cent	Free	Centner 0.36	Centner 0.29
27	Wafers	35 per cent	Free	Centner 2.40	Centner 1.56
28	Wagon boxes	35 per cent	Free	Free	Centner 0.39
29	Walnuts, all	Pound......0.03	Free	Free	15 centner ..0.29
30	Walking sticks, or canes	35 per cent	Free	Mounted, centner.......2.88 Unmounted, per centner...0.72	Centner 1.56
31	Wash, blue	25 per cent	Free	Free	Centner 0.68
32	Washes, cosmetic or dentrifice.	50 per cent	Free	Centner 2.40	Centner 2.93
33	Wash-balls	25 per cent., and pound.... 0.10	Free	Centner 0.60	Centner ...0.145
34	Watches, gold and silver	25 per cent	Free	Centner...36.00	Centner 2.93
35	and parts of oth'r	20 per cent	Free	Centner....1.92	Centner 2.93
36	Watch crystals	40 per cent	Free	Cut, centner.1.92	Centner 1.56
37	Watch materials	20 per cent	Free	Centner 7.20	Centner 2.93
38	Water-proof cloth, not otherwise provided for.	45 per cent	Free	Centner ...10.60	Centner 1.56
39	Water, Hungary	50 per cent	Free	Free	Centner 2.93
40	lavender	50 per cent	Free	Centner 2.40	Centner 2.93
41	orange flower	50 per cent	Free	Centner 2.40	Centner 2.93
42	rose	50 per cent	Free	Centner 2.40	Centner 2.93
43	colors	35 per cent	Free	Centner 2.40	Centner 0.68

(*Duties expressed in gold dollars of the United States.*)—Continued.

	FRANCE.				RUSSIA.	NETHERLANDS.	
	General tariff.		In treaty with Great Britain, &c.				
	In French vessels.	In other vessels.	In vessels of treaty powers.	In other vessels.			
100 kilogs	$63.76	$67.17	10 per	cent.	Pood ... $12.48	5 per cent	1
Preserved in salt, 100 kil.	0.58	0.64	$0.58	$0.64	Pood ... 0.39	5 per cent	2
Green, free					Hermetically sealed, pood ... 2.34		
Free					Free	Free	3
Free					Free	Free	4
See Parchment					Pood ... 4.68	Free	5
Unbleached, 100 kilogs.	Prohibited.		11.70	12.76	Pound ... 0.35	5 per cent	6
Dyed or printed, 100 kil.	Prohibited.		16.57	17.88	Pound ... 3.90	5 per cent	7
Free					Free	Free	8
Free					Pood ... 0.85	Free	9
See Meat					Pood ... 0.51	5 per cent	10
	Prohibited.		5 per cent.		Pood ... 0.85	Free	11
{ dry, 100 kilogs.	2.53	2.78	{		Pood ... 1.95	Free	12
{ wet, 100 kilogs.	6.04	6.63	}				
Free					Pood ... 0.04	Free	13
Free					Pood ... 0.78	100 kilogs ... $0.82	14
Free					Pood ... 0.85	Free	15
100 kilogs.	Prohibited.		0.72	0.80	Pood ... 0.62	5 per cent	16
100 kilogs	19.50	20.95	3.90	4.29	Pood ... 2.34	5 per cent	17
{ Hectolitre	0.39	0.39	0.39	0.39	In casks, pood .. 0.78	{ 2 degrees or less, 100 litres. 1.23	18
{ Perfumed, hectolitre	19.50	20.95	1.95	2.14	Bottle ... 0.078	{ Higher strength, 100 litres. 8.20	
Each	0.58	0.58	10 per	cent.	Pound ... 0.12	5 per cent	19
	15 per	cent.	10 per	cent.	Pound ... 0.12	5 per cent	20
See Steel wire					Pound ... 0.12	5 per cent	21
100 kilogs	3.12	3.43	1.56	1.72	Pood ... 0.78	Hectolitre ... 0.61	22
Free					Free	Hectolitre ... 0.04	23
{ Free					Pood ... 0.156	Free	24
{ 100 kilogs	6.04	6.64	5 per cent.		Pood ... 0.31	Free	25
See Paper					Pood ... 0.16	5 per cent	26
	15 per	cent...	10 per	cent...	Pound ... 0.23	5 per cent	27
100 kilogs	6.04	6.63	10 per	cent...	Free	5 per cent	28
	Free ..	Free ..	Free ..	Free ..	Free	Free	29
100 kilogs	1.95	2.92	5 per	cent...	Pound ... 0.25	5 per cent	30
	Free ..	Free ..	Free ..	Free ..	Pood ... 1.56	Free	31
See Perfumeries					Pood ... 4.29	See Perfumery	32
See Soap					Pood ... 0.78	See Soap	33
See Time-pieces					Each ... 1.06	5 per cent	34
			5 per	cent...	Pound ... 0.062	5 per cent	35
Raw, 100 kilogs	1.95	2.14	10 per	cent...	} Pound ... 0.062	5 per cent	36
Cut, 100 kilogs	39.00	41.44	10 per	cent...	}		
	10 per	cent...	5 per	cent...	Pound ... 0.062	5 per cent	37
See India-rubber tissues					Pood ... 17.16	5 per cent	38
}					}	{ 100 bottles ... 0.20	39
}					} Alcoholic, pood 7.80	{ Free	40
} See Perfumeries					} Perfum., pood 23.40	{ Free	41
}					}	{ Free	42
}					} Pood ... 3.43	{ Free	43

Comparative table of import duties in the United States and European countries

	ARTICLES.	ITALY.			SPAIN.	PORTUGAL.
			General tariff.	Tariff in treaty with France, &c.		
1	Vases, porcelain	100 kilogs.	$4.87	$4.87	100 kilogs...$10.50	Kilogramme $0.324
2	Vegetables, prepared	Dissected, 100 kil Green Preserv'd, 100 kil	2.93 Free. 1.56	0.39 Free. 0.59	100 kilogs.... 0.25 ... Kilogramme . 0.20	Green........Free ... Dry, kilog...0.016
3	Vegetables used in dyeing	100 kilogs	0.39	Free.	100 kilogs.... 2.00	20 per cent
4	Vegetable substances for cordage.	100 kilogs.	Free.	Free.	100 kilogs.... 0.20	Free
5	Vellum	As Zinc	......	......	As Zinc	See Zinc
6	Velvet, cotton and other	Kilogramme	0.145	0.164	Kilogramme . 0.70	Cotton, kilog 0.486
7	except silk	Kilogramme	1.95	0.58	Kilogramme . 5.25	Silk, kilog....8.10
8	Venetian red, dry	100 kilogs	1.95	0.78	100 kilogs.... 1.50	5 per cent
9	in oil	100 kilogs	1.95	0.78	100 kilogs.... 5.00	5 per cent
10	Venison hams	Free	......	......	100 kilogs.... 0.50	Kilogramme . 0.081
11	Veratrine, (medical prep'n)	100 kilogs	1.95	0.39	20 per cent	5 per cent
12	Verdigris	100 kilogs	1.95	0.78	100 kilogs.... 1.50	5 per cent
13	Verditure	100 kilogs	1.95	0.78	100 kilogs.... 1.50	5 per cent
14	Vermicelli	Free	......	......	100 kilogs.... 2.80	Not enumerated
15	Vermilion	100 kilogs	1.95	0.78	100 kilogs.... 1.50	5 per cent
16	Vessels, cast iron, n. o. s.	100 kilogs	1.17	1.56	100 kilogs.... 1.50	Kilogramme . 0.081
17	copper	100 kilogs	3.90	3.90	100 kilogs....25.00	Kilogramme ..0.27
18	Vinegar	Hectolitre	0.643	......	Not enumerated	Decalitre...0.377 Arom'tic, kil 0.324
19	Violins	Each or, 5 per cent.	0.39	0.39	10 per cent	25 per cent
20	Violin strings, gut	100 kilogs	9.75	8.75	20 per cent	See Strings
21	wire	100 kilogs	3.90	4.50	Copper, 100 kil 10.00	See Strings
22	Vitches, dried for feed	Free	......	......	100 kilogs.... 0.10	Free
23	for seed	Free	......	......	100 kilogs.... 0.60	Free
24	Vitriol, green	100 kilogs	0.39	0.39	See Chemicals n. e	See Chemicals n. e.
25	white, or sulphate of zinc.	100 kilogs	0.39	0.39		
26	Wadding paper	100 kilogs	1.56	1.56	100 kilogs 2.00	See Paper
27	Wafers	Free	......	......	Not enumerated	Kilog 1.08
28	Wagon boxes	100 kilogs	1.17	10 p.c.	Manuf. of wood	35 per cent
29	Walnuts, all	Raw, 100 kilogs . Shell'd, 100 kilogs	0.10 0.58	Free Free	100 kilogs ... 0.50	Kilog 0.01
30	Walking sticks, or canes	Free	......	......	20 per cent	Kilog 0.108
31	Wash, blue	100 kilogs	1.95	0.78	100 kilogs 1.50	Free
32	Washes, cosmetic or dentifrice.	As Perfumery	......	......	Kilog 0.30	Kilog 0.27
33	Wash balls	See Soap	......	......	100 kilogs 2.00	20 per cent
34	Watches, gold and silver	See Timepieces	......	......	Gold, each....1.50 Silver, each...0.40	Gold, each....1.188 Silver, and others, each 0.648
35	and parts of oth'r.	100 kilogs or 5 per cent.	9.75	11.26	20 per cent	Watch furnit're not specified, 20 p. c.
36	Watch crystals	......	......	......	100 kilogs....16.00	Kilogr 0.1728
37	Watch materials	100 kilogs	9.75	11.26	20 per cent	Each set......0.216
38	Water-proof cloth, not otherwise provided for.	See India-rubber cloth.	......	......	Kilog 0.60	Kilog 1.08
39	Water, Hungary					
40	lavender	Medicinal waters, 100 kilogs.	1.95	0.39	As Perfumery, per kilog 0.30	Kilog ....0.27 or 20 per cent.
41	orange flower					
42	rose					
43	colors	100 kilogs	11.70	2.25	100 kilogs 5.00	5 per cent

(*Duties expressed in gold dollars of the United States.*)—Continued.

BELGIUM.	AUSTRIA.			DENMARK.	SWEDEN.	NORWAY.	
		General tariff.	Tariff in treaty.				
10 per cent	See Porcelain			Pound....$0. 091	Pound $0. 055	Pound...$0. C8	1
10 per cent Green, free	Centner	$0. 388	Free.	Hermet. lb. 0. 04 Otherwise, free	Vegetabl's, fresh, centner. 0. 133 Preserved in vinegar or brandy, pound.. 0. 086 Dried, lb. 0. 016	Pound. 0. 0045 Hermet. sealed, pound. 0. 082	2
Free	Free			Free	Freo	Free	3
Free	Free			Free	Free	Free	4
Free	See Leather, (parchment)			Free	Free	Free	5
See Cotton	See Manf. of cotton & silk			Pound.... 0. 182	See Silk or cotton	See Cotton	6
See Silk	See Silk			Pound.... 1. 092	See Silk or cotton	Pound... 0. 473	7
Free	Centner	0. 388	Free.	Pound.... 0. 0056	Free	Pound... 0. C09	8
Free	Painting, cent	7. 20		Pound.... 0. 0055	Free	Pound... 0. 009	9
Free	See Meat			Free	Free	Pound... 0. 009	10
100 kilogs ..$0. 23	Centner	7. 20		Pound.... 0. 0113	Free	Pound... 0. 009	11
Free	Medical prep.	0. 72	$0. 72	Pound.... 0. 0056	Free	Pound... 0. 018	12
Free	Free			Pound.... 0. 0056	Free	Pound... 0. 009	13
Free	Centner	1. 26	1. 20	Free	Free	Pound .. 0. 0045	14
100 kilogs. 0. 097	Centner	0. 72	0. 72	Pound.... 0. 028	Free	Pound... 0. 047	15
10 per cent	See Iron			Pound.... 0. 0014	See Iron	See Iron	16
10 per cent	See Copper			Pound.... 0. 045	See Copper	See Copper	17
Of wood ..Free Of wine, &c, per hectolitre.1. 17	Bottles, cent. Barrels, cent.	3. 88 0. 388		In bottles, pot ... 0. 0284 Otherwise, pound. 0. 004 Perfumed, pound. 0. 091	Pound. 0. 01C5	Bbls., lb. 0. 009 Bottl's, pot 0. 018	18
6 per cent	Centner	4. 80	3. 60	Pound.... 0. 091	Each 0. 2756	Each 0. 273	19
10 per cent	See Strings			10 per cent	Pound ... 0. 138	Pound ... 0. 159	20
10 per cent	See Wire			Brass, lb .. 0. 017 Steel, lb. 0. 0056	Pound ... 0. 0275	Pound ... 0. C47	21
Free	Centner	0. 388	Free.	Free	Free	Free	22
100 kilogs. 0. 117	Centner	0. 388	Free.	Free	Free	Free	23
Free	Centner	0. 72		Free	Centner. 0. 138	Free	24
					Centner. 0. 36	Free	25
See Paper	See Paper			Pound....0. 0028	Pound.....0. 0275	Pound 0. 0022	26
10 per cent	Centner	0. 26		Pound....0. C91	Pound.....0. 165	Pound ... 0. 109	27
10 per cent	See Manufactures of wood			Pound....0. 00085	Manuf. of wood	10 per cent	28
10 per cent	Centner	0. 388	Free	Pound....0. 0056	Free	Free	29
10 per cent	See Manufactures of wood			Pound....0. 0042	Pound.....0. 32	Pound 0. C47	30
	Centner	3. 088	Free	Pound....0. 0056	Free	Pound 0. 009	31
See Perfumery	See Perfum'y			Pound....0. 091	Pound.... 0. 023	Pound 0. 10	32
100 kilogs ...1. 17	See Soap			Pound....0. 091	Pound.....0. 0138	Pound 0. 013	33
5 per cent	See Time-pieces			Each 0. 273	Each 0. 2756	Each......0. 273	34
10 per cent				Pound....0. 091	Pound.....0. 20	As mat'l manuf..	35
10 per cent	See Glass, (articles cut)			Pound....0. 04	Pound.....0. 0275	Pound 0. 047	36
10 per cent	Centner	7. 20	5. 76	Pound....0. 091	Pound.....0. 21	Each set ..0. 32	37
10 per cent	See Tiss'es of wool, cotton, &c.			Pound....0. 091	Pound.....0. 21	Pound 0. 127	38
							39
See Perfumery	See Perfum'y			Pound....0. 091	Pound.....0. 11	Pound 0. 10	40
							41
							42
Free	Centner	0. 384		Pound....0. 028	Free	Pound 0. 009	43

Comparative table of import duties in the United States and European countries.

	ARTICLES.	UNITED STATES.	GREAT BRITAIN.	GERMAN ZOLL-VEREIN.	SWITZERLAND
1	Wax beads	50 per cent	Free	Centner ..$10. 60	Centner ...$2. 93
2	bees' bleached or unbleached.	20 per cent	Free	Centner 0. 36	Centner ... 0.145
3	sealing	35 per cent	Free	Centner 2. 40	Centner 0. 68
4	shoemakers'	20 per cent	Free	Free	Centner 0.145
5	tapers	Pound.... $0. 08	Free	Free	Centner 1. 56
6	Wearing apparel in use by persons arriving in United States.	Free	....	....	....
7	Web, or webbing	See Manufactur's of cotton, wool, &c.	....	....	....
8	Webbing, India-rubber	35 per cent	Free	Centner 2. 88	Centner 1. 56
9	Wedgewood-ware, white	40 per cent	Free	See Wood'n ware	Centner 1. 56
10	Weld	Free	Free	Free	Centner 0.145
11	Wet blue	25 per cent	Free	Free	Centner 0. 39
12	Whalebone, foreign fishing	20 per cent	Free	Free	Centner 0. 29
13	Amer. fishing	Free	Free	Free	Centner 0. 29
14	Whale-oil, foreign fishing	20 per cent	Free	Centner 0. 36	Centner 0.058
15	Americ'n fishing	Free	Free	Centner 0 36	Centner 0.058
16	Wheat	Bushel 0. 20	Free	Free	Centner 0.029
17	flour	20 per cent	Free	Free	Centner 0. 14
18	Whetstones	20 per cent	Free	Free	Centner 0.029
19	Whips	35 per cent	Free	Centner 2. 88	....
20	Whiting, dry	Pound......0. 01	Free	Free	....
21	in oil	Pound......0. 02	Free	Centner 2. 40	Centner 0. 68
22	Wick, cottons	35 per cent	Free	Centner 4. 32	Centner 0. 68
23	Wigs	35 per cent	Free	Centner ...10. 60	Centner 2. 93
24	Willow sheets, for hats, baskets, &c.	30 per cent	Free	Free	....
25	Willows, coopers', split	20 per cent	Free	....	....
26	Window glass, crown and common cylinder, unpolished, not above 10 by 15 inches.	Pound 0. 01½	Free	Window glass in its natural color, per centner.......0. 48	Window glass, centner...0. 68
27	As above, over 10 by 15, not over 16 by 24.	Pound......0. 02	Free	Other, per centner.......2. 88	
28	As above, over 16 by 24, not over 24 by 30.	Pound 0. 02½	Free		
29	As above, all above 24 by 30 inches.	Pound......0. 03	Free		
30	Window-glass, polished, cylinder and crown, not over 10 by 15 inches.	Square foot. 0. 02½	Free		
31	As above, over 10 by 15, not over 16 by 24.	Square foot. 0. 04	Free		
32	As above, over 16 by 24, not over 24 by 30.	Square foot. 0. 06	Free		
33	As above, over 24 by 30, not over 24 by 60.	Square foot. 0. 20	Free		
34	As above, over 24 by 60 inches.	Square foot. 0. 40	Free		
35	Wines, value not over 50 cents per gallon.	25 per cent., and per gallon. 0. 20	Of 26 degrees, gallon ...$0. 25	Centner ... 2. 88	Wine of fruit, per centner...0.145
36	value over 50 cents per gallon.	25 per cent, and per gallon. 0. 50	Of 42 degrees, gallon 0. 62	Centner 2. 88	Wine in bottles, centner...0. 68
37	value over $1 per gallon.	25 per cent, and per gallon. 1. 00	For every deg. above 42, add'l, gallon 0. 06		
38	all other	50 per cent			

(*Duties expressed in gold dollars of the United States.*)—Continued.

	FRANCE.				RUSSIA.	NETHERLANDS.	
	General tariff.		In treaty with Great Britain, &c.				
	In French vessels.	In other vessels.	In vessels of treaty powers.	In other vessels.			
......	......	......	......	......	Free	5 per cent	1
Wax, yellow, brown, or white, from prod'cing country, raw.	$0.195	$0.58	$0.195	$0.24	Free	Free	2
As above, assorted	0.58	0.58	0.195	0.24			
As above, elsewhere	0.78	0,86	0.78	0.86			
100 kilogs	19.50	20.95	5.85	6.42	Pood $1.56	5 per cent	3
See Wax	......	......	......	......	Free	5 per cent	4
See Candles	......	......	......	......	Pood 0.78	5 per cent	5
......	......	......	......	......	......	......	6
See Various tissues	......	......	......	......	For machinery, per pood 0.234	5 per cent	7
See India-rubber	......	......	......	......	Pood 4.32	5 per cent	8
......	15 per cent		10 per cent		Free	5 per cent	9
......	Free	Free	Free	Free	Free	Free	10
......	Free	Free	Free	Free	Free	Free	11
100 kilogs	Free	0.39	Free	0.048	Raw, free	Free	12
For corsets, 100 kilogs	1.95	2.92	......	......	Split, pood 1.56	Free	13
100 kilogs	1.56	1.56	1.17	1.28	Pood 1.404	See Oil	14
100 kilogs	1.56	1.56	1.17	1.28	Pood 1.404	See Oil	15
100 kilogs	0.097	0.097	......	......	Free	Hectolitre $0.61	16
100 kilogs	0.195	0.195	......	......	Pood 0.55	100 kilogs 0.16	17
Cut, 100 kilogs	0.97	0.97	Free	0.048	Free	Free	18
Raw, 100 kilogs	Free	0.195	......	......			
100 kilogs	19.50	20.95	10 per cent		Pound 0.212	5 per cent	19
......	Free	Free	Free	Free	Free	Free	20
......	Free	Free	Free	Free	Pood 0.85	Free	21
See Cotton yarn	......	......	......	......	Pood 2.53	5 per cent	22
As hair, prepared	Free	Free	Free	Free	Pound 0.46	5 per cent	23
......	Free	Free	Free	Free	Free	Free	24
......	Free	Free	Free	Free	Free	Free	25
Window glass	Prohibited		10 per cent		Window glass, not cut or polished, per pood 0.85 All polished, cut, paint'd, stain'd, &c., per pood 1.56	All articles of glass, 5 per cent.	26
							27
							28
							29
							30
							31
							32
							33
							34
All fermented ordinary wines, in barrels, per hectoliter.	0.048	0.048	0.058	0.058	In casks or barrels, per pood 1.79	Free	35
					Greek sirup, p'd. 1.12	Free	36
					Not effervescing, per bottle 0.26	Free	37
					Efferves'g, bot. 0.78	Free	38

Comparative table of import duties in the United States and European countries.

	ARTICLES.	ITALY.			SPAIN.	PORTUGAL.
			General tariff.	Tariff in treaty with France, &c.		
1	Wax beads	Wax, white, raw, 100 kilogs.	$3.90	3 p.c.	Crude, kilog. $0.02	Wax, raw, clean, or residue, yellow, kilog $0.01
2	bees', bleached or unbleached.	Yellow, 100 kil ..	2.19	3 p.c.	Manufactured, per kilog 0.15	As above, white, kilog 0.03
		Worked, and all manufactures, yellow, per 100 kilogs.	4.38	3 p.c.		Manufactures of, kilog 0.054
3	sealing					
4	shoemakers'	White, 100 kilogs.	7.80	3 p.c.		
5	tapers	See Candles	......	......		
6	Wearing apparel in use by persons arriving in United States.	....	......	......	....	....
7	Web, or webbing	See Material manufactured.	......	......	10 per cent	See Material manuf.
8	Webbing, India-rubber	100 kilogs	4.87	$5.63	Kilog 0.60	Kilog 1.08
9	Wedgewood-ware, white ...	100 kilogs	1.17	10 p.c.	20 per cent	35 per cent ....
10	Weld	Free	......	......	100 kilogs 0.01	100 kilogs 0.01
11	Wet blue	100 kilogs	1.95	0.78	100 kilogs 1.50	5 per cent ....
12	Whalebone, foreign fishing .	Crude, free	......	......	100 kilogs 0.10	Raw, kilog ...0.005
13	Amer. fishing ..	Cut, 100 kilogs ...	11.70	......	100 kilogs 0.10	Cut, or prepared, kilog 0.432
14	Whale-oil, foreign fishing ...	White of whale, 100 kilogs.	0.47	0.39	100 kilogs 0.30	Kilog 0.054
15	Americ'n fishing.	Refined, 100 kil ..	1.17	0.39	100 kilogs 0.30	Kilog 0.054
16	Wheat	100 kilogs	0.145	0.145	100 kilogs 0.60	Regulated by special laws; in Lisbon, 10 kil.. 0.54
17	flour	100 kilogs	0.24	0.24	100 kilogs 0.90	10 kil., 0.059 to 0.08
18	Whetstones	Each	0.019	Free	100 kilogs 0.01	Free ....
19	Whips	100 kilogs	9.75	9.75	20 per cent	Accord'g to material
20	Whiting, dry	Free	......	......	100 kilogs 1.50	5 per cent ....
21	in oil	100 kilogs	1.95	0.78	100 kilogs 5.00	5 per cent ....
22	Wick, cotton	See Cotton yarn.	......	......	As Cotton yarn....	As Cotton yarn....
23	Wigs	Kilog	0.58	0.66	20 per cent	Hair prep., kil. 0.216
24	Willow sheets, for hats, baskets, &c.	100 kilogs	0.39	0.39	100 kilogs 0.10	See Wood ....
25	Willows, coopers', split	100 kilogs	0.30	0.39	100 kilogs 0.10	See Wood ....
26	Window glass, crown and common cylinder, unpolished, not above 10 by 15 inches.	Window glass, 100 kilogs. Plate, not polished, 100 kilogs.	1.56 1.56	0.975 1.56	Common, per 100 kilogs ......1.50 Cryst'l, 100 kil 3.50	See Glass ....
27	As above, over 10 by 15, not over 16 by 24	Polished, not silvered, 100 kil.	2.93	2.93		
28	As above, over 16 by 24, not over 24 by 30.	Silvered or tinned.	4.87	4.87		
29	As above, all above 24 by 30 inches.					
30	Window glass, polished, cylinder and crown, not over 10 by 15 inches.					
31	As above, over 10 by 15, not over 16 by 24.					
32	As above, over 16 by 24, not over 24 by 30.					
33	As above, over 24 by 30, not over 24 by 60.					
34	As above, over 24 by 60 inches.					
35	Wines, value not over 50 cents per gallon.	Wine in casks, hectolitre.	0.975	1.125	Wines, sparkling, liter........0.20	Decaliter.....1.08
36	value over 50 cents per gallon.	In bottles, each..	0.29	......	All other, liter. 0.10	
37	value over $1 per gallon.					
38	all other	....	......	......	....	....

(*Duties expressed in gold dollars of the United States.*)—Continued.

BELGIUM.	AUSTRIA.			DENMARK.	SWEDEN.	NORWAY.	
		General tariff.	Tariff in treaty.				
10 per cent	Centner	$24.00	$14.40	Wax, animal and vegetable, per pound $0.017	10 per cent.......	Pound ... $0.091	1
Free	Centner	1.44	1.20	All manufactures of wax, per pound .. 0.091	Free	Wax, raw or bleached, pound .. 0.007	2
10 per cent	Centner	2.40	......		10 per cent.......	Pound 0.063	3
Free	Centner	1.44	1.20		Free	Pound 0.009	4
10 per cent	Centner	3.84	......		Pound.... $0.0138	Pound 0.018	5
....	....	......	......	....	....	....	6
See Tissues......	See Tissues of flax, &c.	......	......	As Tissues	See Manuf. of cotton, &c.	For machinery, free.	7
10 per cent	Centner	12.00	......	Pound.... 0.091	Pound..... 0.11	Pound 0.127	8
10 per cent	See Wooden	ware.	......	Pound.... 0.017	Pound..... 0.0689	See Wood, turner work.	9
Free	Free	......	......	Free	Free	Free	10
Free	Centner	0.388	Free	Pound.... 0.0056	Free	Pound 0.009	11
Free	Whalebone, split.	1.20	0.72	Pound.... 0.0056	Free	Whalebone, also split, free.	12
Free				Pound.... 0.0056	Free		13
Free	See Oils	......	......	Pound.... 0.017	Pound..... 0.0027	Pound 0.0067	14
Free	See Oils	......	......	Pound.... 0.017	Pound..... 0.0027	Pound 0.0067	15
100 kilog ... 0.117	Centner	0.167	Free	Free	Free	Ton 0.218	16
100 kilogs .. 0.23	Centner	0.388	Free	Free	Free	Ton 0.218	17
Free	Centner	0.388	Free	Free	Free	Free	18
10 per cent	Centner	12.00	7.20	Pound.... 0.091	10 per cent.......	10 per cent	19
Free	Centner	0.388	Free	Pound.... 0.0056	Free	Pound 0.009	20
....	Centner	0.388	......	Pound.... 0.028	Free	Pound 0.009	21
See Cotton yarn .	See Cotton	yarn .	......	As Yarns	See Cotton yarn	As Yarn	22
10 per cent	Not enumera	ted...	......	10 per cent.......	Pound..... 0.096	10 per cent	23
5 per cent	Free	......	......	Free	Free	Free	24
5 per cent	Free	......	......	Free	Free	Free	25
Window glass, 10 per cent.	Wind. glass, green, white, centner.	1.08	0.72	Window glass, ordinary, pound .. 0.0084	Window glass, all kinds, lb . 0.0081	See Glass; all other, lb . 0.009	26
	Painted, colored, &c., centner.	5.04	2.88				27
				In plates cut, of less than 800 square inches, pound .. 0.045			28
				800 to 1,800 sq. in., pound .. 0.068			29
				Over 1,800 sq. in., pound .. 0.091			30
							31
							32
							33
							34
In casks, per hectolitre.... 0.097	In bottles, centner.	6.312	......	Bot's, pot 0.091 Other, pot. 0.021	21 per cent. alcohol, in barrels, pound ... 0.019	Bottl's, pot . 0.0054 Bbls, lb.... 0.002	35
In bottles, hectolitre...... 0.29	In barrels, centner.	5.04	......				36
					Over 21 per cent. alcohol in bbls., pound .. 0.039		37
....	....	......	......	....	21 per cent. in bottles, lb ... 0.151		38
					Over 21 per cent. in bot., lb . 0.482		

Comparative table of import duties in the United States and European countries.

	ARTICLES.	UNITED STATES.	GREAT BRITAIN.	GERMAN ZOLL-VEREIN.	SWITZERLAND.
1	Wire bonnet or cap cover'd with gold or silk.	See Iron	Free...........	Covered, centner ....$11.60 All other, centner 2.88	All, cent'r. $0.29
2	Covered with gold or silver.	40 per cent......			
3	Covered with brass	35 per cent......			
4	Cover d with copper......	45 per cent......			
5	All other	35 per cent......			
6	Wood, bar, box, Brazil, Brazilette, camwood, carmaguey, dye-wood in sticks, fustic, lignum-vitæ, lance, log, Nicaragua, Pernambuco, queen's, red sanders, red, Rio de la Hache, Santa Martha, and other dye-woods; sandal in sticks; ebony and granadilla; ebony, green, (dye;) jacaranda, rose, satin, cedar, and mahogony—all cabinet wood.	Free	Free........	All wood, unmanufact'd, free. Wood in veneers, cen'r. 0.36 Furniture, centner ...... 0.72 Fancy work, per centner .. 2.88 All cabinet wood, free.	All cabinet wood, 15 cent'r. 0.029 Wood'nware, free. Manufactur's not specially enumerated, 10 per cent. Dyewood, centner...... 0.145
	Wood, awl hafts..........	35 per cent	Free	Centner... 0.72	10 per cent.....
	balls, gilt or not......	35 per cent	Free	Centner... 2.88	
	backgammon men ...	35 per cent	Free	Centner... 2.88	
	chessmen	35 per cent	Free	Centner... 2.88	
	casters with rivets ...	35 per cent	Free	Centner... 2.88	
	casters, otherwise ..	35 per cent	Free	Centner... 2.88	
	fire	20 per cent	Free	Free	
	goncallo	20 per cent	Free	Free	
	jacks	35 per cent	Free	Centner... 0.72	
	lake................	25 per cent	Free	Free	
	ornaments, gilt	35 per cent	Free	Centner... 2.88	
	rules	35 per cent	Free	Centner... 2.88	
	unmanufactured, of any kind not enum.	20 per cent	Free	Free	15 centner. 0.029
	Wood quassia, (drug)......	20 per cent	Free	Centner... 0.36	Centner .. 0.68
	manufactures of, not otherwise enumer'd.	35 per cent	Free	Centner... 2.88	10 per cent......
7	Wood screws	See Iron screws..	Free	Centner... 0.96	Centner... 0.68

(Duties expressed in gold dollars of the United States.)—Continued.

	FRANCE.				RUSSIA.	NETHERLANDS.	
	General tariff.		In treaty with Great Britain, &c.				
	In French vessels.	In other vessels.	In vessels of treaty powers.	In other vessels.			
							1
Iron wire, 100 kilogs....	$5.85	$6.43	$1.17	$1.29	All wire, pood..$1.17	All wire, 5 per ct.	2
Metallic wire, 100 kilogs.	13.65	14.82	1.95	2.14	Covered, pood.. 2.34		3
Brass wire, 100 kilogs ..	19.50	20.95	1.95	2.14			4
							5
Wood for fuel..........	Free...	Free...	Free...	Free...	All wood, not otherwise provided for, free.	Wood for building, not sawn, 1 per ct. Sawn, 3 per cent.	6
Wood for building, raw, 100 cubic meters.	Free...	0.19	Free...	0.022			
Wood for building, of 80 millimeters thick, 100 cubic meters.	Free...	0.19	Free...	0.022	Precious woods, as guaiac, ced'r, cypre's, mahogany, nutwo'd,	Wainscot and unsound pieces: 100 kilogs ..$3.07	
As above, of less than 80 millimeters thick, cubic meter.	0.009	1.195	Free...	0.23	rosewood, palmtree, &c., &c., pood. 0.04	Pipestaves: 100 kilogs .. 1.64	
Oak for building	Free...	Free...	....	....	All in leaves or veneers, pood... 0.33	Caskstaves: 100 kilogs .. 0.41	
Masts spars, cub. meter.	Free...	Free. .	Free...	Free...	Ordinary ware, free. Carved manufactures, pood 2.90	Spars, poles, and oars, ½ per cent. Furniture wood not sawn, 1 per cent.	
Charcoal, cubic meter ..	Free...	0.009	Free...	0.0117		Sawn, 3 per cent.	
Wood in splinters, per mille.	0.019	0.39	0.019	0.46		All articles of wood, except shoes, 5 per cent.	
In leaves, 1,000 leaves..	0.019	0.29	Free...	0.34			
Wood shelv's, poles, &c., mille.	0.048	0.048	0.048	0.058			
Wood staves, mille.....	0.019	0.29	....	....			
Willow in fagots, roots for hoops, brush for brooms.	Free...	Free...	Free...	Free...			
Heath, 100 kilogs.......	0.097	0.97	0.097	0.145			
Cabinet wood in planks, over 2 decimeters thick:							
Box tree, 100 kilogs....	0.195	0.195	....	....			
Other, 100 kilogs.......	Free...	1.17	....	....			
Sawn, less than 2 decimeters thick:							
Box tree, 100 kilogs	0.19	0.39	....	....			
Other, 100 kilogs.......	0.19	1.36	....	....			
Fragrant wood, 100 kil.	Free...	0.58	....	....			
Dye wood in fagots:							
Barbary wood	Free...	Free...	Free...	Free...			
Fustic	Free...	Free...	Free...	Free...			
Other, 100 kilogs	Free..	0.58	Free...	0.048			
Ground, 100 kilogs ...	0.58	0.58	Free...	0.048			
100 kilogs	Prohi	bited.	1.56	1.72	See Iron	See Iron	

Comparative table of import duties in the United States and European countries.

	ARTICLES.	ITALY.			SPAIN.	PORTUGAL.
			General tariff.	Tariff in treaty with France, &c.		
1	Wire bonnet or cap cover'd with gold or silk.	Steel, 100 kilogs	$3.90	$4.50		
2	Covered with gold or silver.				See under the vari- metals.	See under the various metals.
3	Covered with brass	Copper, 100 kil..	3.34	2.34		
4	Covered with copper.......	Iron, 100 kilogs..	1.36	1.56		
5	All other..................					
6	Wood, bar, box, Brazil, Brazilette, camwood, carmaguey, dye-wood in sticks, fustic, lignum-vitæ, lance, log, Nicaragua, Pernambuco, queen's, red sanders, red, Rio de la Hache, Santa Martha, and other dye-woods; sandal in stick; ebony and granadilla; ebony, green, (dye;) jacaranda, rose, satin, cedar, and mahogony—all cabinet wood.	Wood for fuel,	Free.		Wood staves, per mille ....$1.50 Boards, planks, beams, per cubic meter ...... 0.30 Masts and ship timber, 1 per cent. Cabinet wood in pieces, 100 k. 0.10 In boards: 100 kilogs... 0.50 Hogsheads & staves for the same: 100 kilogs .. 2.00 Manufactures, common, 100 kil. 3.50 Of precious woods, 100 kilogs... 7.00 Of precious woods ornamented in metal, pearls, &c., 100 kilogs.. 20.00 For fuel, ton. 0.10	Wood, timber, raw, kilog .....$0.0027 Squared, common, sawed, thickness: 2.75 centimeters—meter ...... 0.01 2.75 to 5.50 centimeters, meter. 0.021 5.50 to 8.25 centimeters, meter 0.032 Above 8.25 centimeters, meter. 0.043 Boards, for cabinet work, kilog. 0.162 Not specified, kilogramme .... 0.01 Rafter beams—meter ...... 0.02 Small beams and pieces, met'r 0.108 Staffs for casks—100 pieces. 0.108 Other, of various length, per 100 from 0.108 to 1.57 Spars, from 5 meters to above 26 meters length, per 100 from 0.108 to 1.728. Boards of ordinary wood, kilog. 0.02 Small articles for table use, instruments, &c., kilogramme .... 0.54 Articles complete or not, not specially enumerat'd, 35 per cent. Fire-wood, ki. 0.001
		Cabinet wood not sawed, 100 kil..	0.39	......		
		Sawed in tables or slabs, of 1 centimeter or less thick, 100 kilogs	2.34	0.56		
		In larger slabs, 100 kilogs......	0.97	0.55		
		Wood, joined and inlaid, for flooring, 100 kilogs..	0.39	......		
	Wood, awl hafts........... balls, gilt or not .... backgammon men .. chessmen .... castors with rivets .. castors, otherwise... fire .... goncallo............ jacks............... lake................ ornaments, gilt ..... rules .... unmanufactured .... of any kind not enum. Wood, quassia, (drug) .... manufactures of, not otherwise enum'd.	Building wood,	Free.			
		Staves for barrels, &c., 100 kil	0.58	Free.		
		Articles of wood not specially enumerated:				
		Common, 100 kil.	1.17	10 p.ct		
		Other, 100 kilogs.	1.56	10 p.ct		
		See Furniture:				
		Fancy articles, 100 kilogs	7.80	7.80		
7	Wood screws..............	See Iron..	......	......	See Iron...........	See Iron ....

(*Duties expressed in gold dollars of the United States.*)—Continued.

BELGIUM.	AUSTRIA.			DENMARK.	SWEDEN.	NORWAY.
		General tariff.	Tariff in treaty.			
All wire, per kilogrammes. $0.195	Tin, centner.	$1.44	$1.20	Copper or brass, also covered, pound ...$0.017 Steel, lb .. 0.0014	Wire, gold or silver, ort. $0.0027 Wire, copper, gilded, silvered, or plated, per pound .. 0.2756	Wire, spun, per pound ..$0.0455 Steel, lb. 0.027 Copp'r, lb 0.047
	Copper, cent'r	2.88	1.92			
	Iron not polished, cent'r	1.92	0.92			
Wood, common, free. Oak for staves, free. For masts, spars, &c., free. Dye-wood, free. For building and furniture, oak, beech, &c., cub. meter.... 0.195 Other, cubic memer ...... 0.58 For building and cabinet furnit're over 5 centimeters thick, cub. meter .... 1.17 As above, of 5 centimeters th'k or less, cubic meter .... 1.76 Various kinds, 5 per cent. All articles manufactured of wood, 10 per ct.	Wood for fuel, 100 cubic ft.	0.2016	Free.	Wood, not at all worked, for fuel; oak, ebony, beach, free. Timber in ships, commercial last...... 1.775 Other, cubic foot ..... 0.0217 Ship timber for building, cubic foot ..... 0.034 Common, carpenters' work, not conveniently measured: pound .. 0.0008 Turners' work, furniture, parts of machinery, massive articles of fine wood, pound .. 0.0398 Other, lb. 0.017 Fancy work of wood, amber, ivory, horn, bone, me'rsch'm, mother-of-pearl, tortoise shell, butt'ns, & canes, pound ... 0.091	Wood, all, not manufactured: Staves, masts, spars, boards & planks, blocks for rifle stocks, handspikes, fuel, willow, veneers of ¼-inch or less thick, free. Manufactured: Turners' work not otherwise specified: pound .. 0.0689 Articles of common wood, paint'd, polish'd, pound .. 0.0027 Furniture, veneer'd, lb. 0.0082 Same, mahogany, &c., ornament'd, &c., lb . 0.0138 Same, upholst'd, 20 per ct. more than duty on material.	Wood not manufactured: veneers, planks, over ½-in. thick, spokes, staves, bars, manufactures not specified, wooden shoes, free. Vene'rs of foreign wood, ¼ inch thick or less; also if inlaid with mother-of-pearl, lb. 0.031 Pegs for shoes, pound... 0.009 Frames, &c., gilded, not over 3 pounds a piece, pound.... 0.03 Spinning wheels, table feet, per pound... 0.019 Cabinet work, gilded, lb. 0.018 Not upholstered, of fine wood, pound... 0.003 Of beach and other, lb 0.009 Of walnut, mahogany, and other foreign wood, lb. 0.018 Handles for tools, free. Articles, comm'n, pound... 0.018 Fancy, lb. 0.045
	Wood for manufactures:					
	Common, in trunks of 1 meter leng'h or more, in doubes and oth'r roughly prepared work, 100 cubic feet...	0.388	Free.			
	Foreign wood in blocks, boa'ds, posts,	Free.	Free.			
	Manufactur's:					
	Coopers' and other common work not painted, centner.....	0.12	Free.			
	Veneers, cen'r	0.36	0.36			
	Cabinet and other work, printed, polished, &c., centner.....	1.20	0.72			
	Fancy work and upholstered furniture, centn'r	5.76				
10 per cent.......	See Iron.....	......	......	Pound 0.019	See Iron	Pound.... 0.027

Comparative table of import duties in the United States and European countries.

ARTICLES.	UNITED STATES.	GREAT BRITAIN.	GERMAN ZOLL-VEREIN.	SWITZERLAND.
Wool, 1st class:				
Clothing, wools, value at last port whence exported, excluding charges in such port, 32 cents or less per pound.	11 per cent. and per lb....$0.10	Free	Free	Wool, raw or combed, dyed or undyed, refuse of wool, centner..$0.058
Wool, as above, value over 32 cents per pound.	10 per cent. and per pound 0.12	Free	Free	Yarn, bleached, not dyed, centner 0.39
Wool, 2d class:				
Combing wools, value as above, 32 cents or less.	11 per cent. and per pound 0.10	Free	Free	Yarn, bleached, or dyed, centner 0.68
As above, value over 32 cents per pound.	10 per cent. and per pound 0.12	Free.	Woolen yarn, pure or mixed, not with cotton:	Cloth, woolen, not dyed, centner....... 0.68
Wool, 3d class:				
Carpet wools, value as above, 12 cents or less per pound.	Pound..... 0.03	Free.	1. Single, dyed, or undyed, double, not dyed, centner ..$0.36	All other manufact's bleached, dyed, or print'd, including carpets, cen'r. 1.56
As above, value over 12 cents per pound.	Pound..... 0.06	Free.	2. Double, dyed, and triple, all, centner .. 2.88	
Wool, all manufactures of wool, or of which wool shall be a component material, not otherwise provided for.	35 per cent. and per pound 0.50	Free.	Manufactures: Embroide's, lace, tulle, cent. 21.60	
Woolen bags	35 per cent. and per pound 0.50	Free.	Printed goods, centner.. 18.00	
cloth	35 per cent. and per pound 0.50	Free.	Not printed, also with metallic thread, per centner 14.40	
cassimere..........	35 per cent. and per pound 0.50	Free.	Not printed, cloth, felt, hosiery, carpets, per centner .. 7.20	
embroideries.......	35 per cent. and per pound 0.50	Free.		
hosiery	35 per cent. and per pound 0.50	Free.		
flocks	Pound..... 0.12	Free.		
listings	35 per cent. and per pound 0.50	Free.		
Wool, mungo.............	Pound..... 0.12	Free.		
Woolen shawls	35 per cent. and per pound 0.50	Free.		
Yams.....................	10 per cent......	Free............	Centner....0.36	Centner 0.68
Yarn, coir	Pound 0.01½	Free............	For all yarns, see Cotton, hemp, flax, jute, silk, and wool.	For all yarns, see Cotton, hemp, flax, jute, silk, and wool.
cotton............	35 per cent......	Free............		
flax or linen, for carpeting, not over No. 8 lea, and valued at 24 cts. or less per lb.	30 per cent......	Free............		
ditto, over 24 cts. per pound.	35 per cent......	Free............		
jute	25 per cent......	Free............		
hemp................	Pound......0.05	Free............		
worsted and woolen, valued not over 40 cts. per lb.	35 per cent., and per pound 0.20	Free............		
ditto, over 40 cts. per lb. to 60 cts.	35 per cent., and per pound 0.30	Free............		
ditto, over 60 cts. per lb. to 80 cts.	35 per cent., and per pound 0.40	Free............		
ditto, over 80 cts. per pound.	35 per cent., and per pound 0.50	Free............		
untarred, hemps......	Pound......0.05	Free............		

(*Duties expressed in gold dollars of the United States.*)—Continued.

	FRANCE.				RUSSIA.	NETHERLANDS.
	General tariff.		In treaty with Great Britain, &c.			
	In French vessels.	In other vessels.	In vessels of treaty powers.	In other vessels.		
Wool, raw, from Europe in French vessels, 100 kilogs	$0.58	$0.58	Free...	$0.048	Wool, raw, pood $0.17 Shoddy, pood .. 0.34 Yarn, mixed or unmixed, pood .. 3.51 Manufactures: Felted materials, per pound .... 0.66 Cloth, cassimeres, tricot, &c., lb ... 0.94 Blankets, lb.... 0.31 Not felted materials of wool, goats' hair, plain, figured, or embroidered, mixed with cotton or unmixed, having in 1 pound 5 arschines or less, pound.... 0.39 5 to 9 arschines, per pound .... 0.66 9 or more arschines, pound .... 0.86 The same, dyed, an addition of 30 per cent.	Wool, raw, free.... Woolen yarn, 3 per cent. Yarn for disks, per 100 kilogs ..$0.20 All tissues and manufactures of wool, 5 per cent.
Wool, combed, 100 kil.	13.65	15.60	$4.87	5.36		
Dyed, all, 100 kilogs...	19.50	22.42	4.87	5.36		
Waste, wool, hair, 100 kilogs..........	0.58	0.58	....	....		
Flock wool..........	Free...	Free...	....	....		
Woolen yarn, combed, long, unbleached, twisted, scoured, and broiled, 100 kilogs	136.59	150.15	See note on pages 148 and 149.			
All other woolen yarn .	Prohibited.		....	....		
Manufactures of wool:						
Socks of list..........	....	....	10 per cent.			
Fringes, ribbons, pure, white, 100 kilogs......	37.05	39.39	10 per cent.			
Mixed, wool and hair, dyed, 100 kilogs	42.90	45.52	10 per cent.			
Blankets, fringe, lace, other tissues and all articles not enumerated	Prohibited.		10 per cent.			
Clothing, ready-made, new	....	....	10 per cent.			
Old, 100 kilogs.........	....	....	3.90	4.29		
Mixed tissues, wool predominant	Same as wool..		....	....		
Tissues of alpaca	Same as wool..		....	....		
100 kilogs	Free ..	0.97	0.39	0.43	Free	Free ....
For yarns not otherwise specified, see note pages 148 and 149.	....	....	....	....	See Cotton, flax, silk, and wool.	All yarns, 3 per ct.

Comparative table of import duties in the United States and European countries.

<table>
<tr><th rowspan="2">ARTICLES.</th><th colspan="3">ITALY.</th><th rowspan="2">SPAIN.</th><th rowspan="2">PORTUGAL.</th></tr>
<tr><th></th><th>General tariff.</th><th>Tariff in treaty with France, &c.</th></tr>
<tr><td>United States tariff on wool—Continued.

Woolen cloth'g, ready-made, 40 per ct. and per lb. $0.50
Woolen endless belts for paper machines, 35 per cent. and per pound, 0.20.
Woolen blanketing for printing machines, 35 per cent. and per pound, 0.20.
Wool on the skin, raw, 30 per cent.
Woolen tippets, wove, 35 per cent. and per lb. 0.50
Worsted shawls, hemmed, not otherwise enumerated, 40 per ct. and per lb. 0.50
Worsted, all manufactures, value not over 40 cents per pound, not otherwise enumerated, 35 per cent. and per pound, 0.20.
Worsted, value 40 to 60 cts. per pound, 35 per ct. and per pound, 0.30.
Worsted, value 60 to 80 cts. per pound, 35 per ct. and per pound, 0.40.
Worsted, value over 80 cts. per pound, 35 per ct. and per pound, 0.50.
Worsted caps wove on frame, 35 per cent.
Worsted hose, draw's, gloves, mits, and shirts, 35 per ct.
As above, composed in part of wool, 35 per cent. and per pound, 0.50.</td><td>Wool, natural...
Wool, dyed, per 100 kilogs .....
Yarn, natural, kilog ....
Yarn, dyed: kilogs ....
All tissues of wo'l pressed or carded, kilog.......
Embroidered in cotton or wool, kilogs..........
Other articles, cravats, &c., kil. or 5 per cent.</td><td>Free.
$0.58
0.078
0.12
...... 0.27
0.58
0.58</td><td>Free.
$0.67
0.09
0.14
....
0.66
0.66</td><td>Wool, raw, comm'n, 100 kilogs...$5.60
For worsted, per 100 kilogs .. 2.50
Combed and prepared, 100 k. 6.00
Yarns: worsted thread, crude or oily, kilog . 0.375
Cleaned & bleach'd, kilog 0.52
Dyed, kilog.. 0.60
Tissues, pure, mix'd, also flannels, felts, plushes, kil. 1.00
Cassimeres and fine cloth, kilog. 1.60
Common cloth and drapery, kil. 1.25
Textures, coarse & hairy, mixed or not, kilog... 0.30</td><td>Wool, raw, washed or not, kil. $0.0005
Dyed, kilog. 0.54
Yarns for embroidery, white, kilogramme 1.62
Dyed, kilog.. 2.70
Other, white, kilogramme ... 0.729
Other, dyed, kilogramme ... 1.188
Tissues, transparent thread and lace work, kilog. 1.08
Merinos, kil.. 2.70
Other, transparent, kilog 1.62
Closely woven:
Baizes, one color, kilog 0.486
Stamped, kil. 0.432
Linsey, white, kilogramme ... 0.81
Colored, kil . 0.486
Others of short wo'l, kilog 0.486
Of long wool:
Velvets, kilog. 0.81
Damasked, ki. 1.08
Not specified, kilogramme 1.62
Lustre shorn, kilogramme..... 0.48
Other, kilog.. 1.08

Mixed tissues, see note page 61.</td></tr>
<tr><td>Yams......................
Yarn, coir ....
cotton ....
flax or linen, for carpeting, not over No. 8 lea. and valued at 24 cts. or less per lb.
ditto, over 24 cts. per pound.
jute ....
hemp................
worsted and woolen, valued not over 40 cts. per lb.
ditto, over 40 cts. per lb. to 60 cts.
ditto, over 60 cts. per lb. to 80 cts.
ditto, over 80 cts. per pound.
untarred, hemp ......</td><td>100 kilogs ....
Yarns of hemp or flax, single, raw, smooth or bleached, per 100 kilogs.
As above, dyed, 100 kilogs.
As above, twist'd, raw or bleached, 100 kilogs.
As above, dyed, 100 kilogs.
See, also, Cotton, jute, &c.</td><td>0.95
1.95
3.90
3.90
5.85</td><td>0.78
2.24
4.58
4.58
6.75</td><td>100 kilogs.....2.00
Yarns, all kinds, 100 kilogs ....0.25</td><td>5 per cent..........
Yarns, see in connection with Cotton, flax, jute, silk, wool, &c.</td></tr>
</table>

(Duties expressed in gold dollars of the United States.)—Continued.

BELGIUM.	AUSTRIA.			DENMARK.	SWEDEN.	NORWAY.
		General tariff.	Tariff in treaty.			
Wool in mass, carded, combed, dyed, and waste, free. Yarn not twisted or dyed, per 100 kilogs. 3.90 Twisted and dyed, 100 kilogs. 5.86 Tissues, shawls, scarfs, cassimeres of India, 5 per cent. All other, 5 per cent., or at the option of importer, per 100 kilogs. 50.70	Wool, raw, c waste ...... Wool, bleach centner .... Yarn: carded dyed, or twi centner .... Combed, raw, or twist'd, c'r Dyed, double centner .... Tissues of wo animal hair; with India-r not with silk *a.* Very comm sieve-cloth, cloth, carpet dog or cow h felt, felt soles unble'h'd, c'r *b.* Common: n not velvety not printed, sive,) and ot centner .... *c.* Medium: al close tissues, included, n stockings, bu centner .... *d.* Close wo printed, c'r. *e.* Fine: all lo not before in shawls, ce'r. *f.* Fancy: lac eries mixed or silver thre centner	omb'd Free. ed or $0.388 , raw, sted, s 0.48 not 2.16 , or m 6.312 ol and also ubber : on oil- horse- s of air; t and s 3.88 ot pr . felt (hatse her ca 17.28 l velv not b ot pri tton c 25.92 ven 36.00 ose ti clud'd 43.20 e, emb with ad or 126.00	or Free. dyed, Free. not ingle, 0.36 dyed ...... ore, ... other mix'd thr'd, cloth, hair calf, arred hoes, ... inted, goods xclu- rpets, 12.00 etry, efore nted; loth, 21.60 goods 25.60 ssues ; also 33.60 roid- gold glass, ...	Wool, all kinds, free. Yarn, thread, and cords of 1 line diameter or less, not dyed, per pound..$0.0227 As above, dyed, pound ... 0.045 Tissues or knitted work, also if mix'd with other hair; felt not dyed, carpet, pound . . 0.068 Loose tissues, also with metal or gla's thre'd, lac's, crochet, fringe, button makers' work, lb. 0.273 All other manufactured goods, pound ... 0.182	Wool, all kinds, and wool'n felts, free. Yarn, not dyed, pound ..$0.0275 Bleached or dyed, pound ... 0.041 Tissues, mixed, (not with silk,) felt, and carpets, pound .. 0.082 Pressed cloth, per pound .. 0.0275 Other tissues, per pound 0.21	Wool, raw, free. Yarn, not dyed, pound...$0.036 Dyed, lb.. 0.045 Tissues: felt not dyed or printed, free. Tricot, knit, woven, gloves, pound... 0.073 Other tricots, pound... 0.159 Fringe work: pound... 0.236 Ribbon and other mixed with India-rubber: pound... 0.159 Fringes, tulle, and oth'r loose go'ds, pound... 0.236 Closely woven, embroideries of silk or wire: pound... 0.319 All others closely woven: pound... 0.146 Carpets, lb. 0.082
Free .... Yarns, see Cotton, flax, silk, and wool.	Centner	0.36	Free.	Pound.....0.0113 Yarns and thread, not dyed, 1 line thick, lb..0.017 Dyed and all other, pound. 0.045 See, also, in connection with Cotton, flax, silk, wool, &c.	Free .... Yarns, cotton, all not dyed, per pound....0.022 Dyed ......0.0385 Woolen, not dyed, pound....0.0275 Bleached or dyed, pound....0.041 Linen, not bleached or dyed, per pound....0.0275 Bleached or dyed, pound....0.055 Pack thread, per pound....0.0275 See, also, in connection with Silk and wool.	Free .... Yarn of cotton, not twisted nor dyed, lb..0.016 Other of cotton, also wire-spun, pound....0.045 Of flax, hemp, manila, jute, linen, not dyed, pound ... 0.019 Dyed, not twisted, pound. 0.061 Dyed, twisted, pound....0.091
	Cotton yarn, not bleach'd or dyed, per centner.	2.52	1.92			
	All bleached, not dyed, per centner.	5.04	2.88			
	All dyed, per centner.	6.312	......			
	Linen, not bleached or dyed, centn.	0.36	Free.			
	Bleached, dyed, not twisted, per centner.	3.88	2.16			
	All twisted, centner.	6.312	......			
	Wool, single, not dyed, corded, cent.	0.48	0.36			
	Ditto, combed, centner.	2.16	......			
	Dyed, double or twisted, centner.	6.312	......			

Comparative table of import duties in the United States and European countries.

	ARTICLES.	UNITED STATES.	GREAT BRITAIN.	GERMAN ZOLL-VEREIN.	SWITZERLAND.
1	Yellow, king's patent......	25 per cent......	Free............	Free............	Centner ...$0. 68
2	berries, (dyeing) ...	Free............	Free............	Free............	Centner 0.145
3	chromate of potash.	Pound.....$0. 03	Free............	Centner ...$2. 40	Centner 0. 68
4	citric acid..........	Pound......0. 10	Free............	Centner 2. 40	Centner 0. 68
5	salt of chrome	20 per cent......	Free............	Centner 2. 40	Centner 0. 68
6	ochre, dry	100 pounds..0. 50	Free............	Free............	Centner 0.145
7	in oil........	100 pounds..1. 50	Free............	Free............	Centner 0. 68
8	spirits	20 per cent	Free............	Free............	Centner 0. 68
9	Zaffre	20 per cent	Free............	Free............	Centner 0.145
10	Zinc, nails.................	35 per cent	Free............	Centner 0. 72	Centner ... 0. 68
11	in pigs, blocks	Pound 0. 01½	Free............	Free............	Centner 0.145
12	in sheets	Pound 0. 02¼	Free............	Centner 0. 36	Centner 0.145
13	sulphate of...........	20 per cent	Free............	Centner 2. 40	Centner 0. 68
14	oxide of..............	Pound 0. 01¾	Free............	Centner 0. 72	Centner 0. 68
15	manufactures of......	35 per cent	Free............	Coarse, cen'r 0. 72 Fancy, cen'r 2. 88	Not polished, per centner...0. 68 Polished, per centner.......1. 56
16	valerianate of.........	20 per cent	Free............	Centner.... 2. 40	Centner 0. 68

TURKEY.

Turkey has not been included in the preceding comparison, as the tariff duty under treaty with the United States and other countries amounts to 8 per cent. ad valorem on all articles imported.

OBSERVATIONS.

A.—WEIGHTS AND MEASURES.

1. *United States.*—"Proof" strength of spirits, 50 per cent. alcohol. The measures of length and the weights of the United States are the same as those of Great Britain; but the measures of volume are different—the measures of volume in the United States being the wine gallon and the Winchester bushel, formerly in use in England—not the imperial measures which are now the standards.

2. *Great Britain.*—"Proof" strength of spirits, 57 per cent. alcohol. 1 imperial gallon = 1. 2 gallon U. S. 1 imperial gallon of British proof-strength = 1. 368 U. S. gallons of U. S. proof-strength.

3. *German Zollverein.*—1 centner = 50 kilogrammes = 100 Zoll. pounds = 110. 231 lbs. U. S. (avoirdupois.)

4. *Switzerland.*—1 quintal (centner) = 50 kilogs. =110.231 lbs. U. S.

5. *France.*—1 kilogramme = 10 hectogrammes = 100 decagrammes = 1,000 grammes = 2.204621 lbs. U. S. (avoirdupois) = 15432.3488 grains U. S. 1 meter = 10 decimeters = 100 centimeters = 1000 millimeters = 3.280867 feet U. S. 1 cubic meter = 35.3155 cubic feet U. S. = 1.30798 cubic yard U. S. 1 cubic meter = 1 kiloliter = 10 hectoliters = 100 decaliters = 1,000 liters. 1 liter = 1.0567 quart U. S. liquid measure. 1 decaliter = 2.6417 gallons U. S. 1 hectoliter = 26.417 gallons U. S

(*Duties expressed in gold dollars of the United States.*)—Continued.

FRANCE.					RUSSIA.	NETHERLANDS.	
	General tariff.		In treaty with Great Britain, &c.				
	In French vessels.	In other vessels.	In vessels of treaty powers.	In other vessels.			
....	Free ..	Free ..	Free ..	Free ..	Free	Free	1
....	Free ..	Free ..	Free ..	Free ..	Free	Free	2
100 kilogs	$29.25	$31.20	$6.82	$7.49	Pood..........$1.56	Free	3
See Chemicals not enumerated		....	....	....	Pood...........0.85	Free	4 5
....	Free ..	Free ..	Free ..	Free ..	Pood...........0.04	Free	6
....	Free ..	Free ..	Free ..	Free ..	Pood...........0.85	Free	7
....	Free ..	Free ..	Free ..	Free ..	Pood...........0.85	Free	8
....	Free ..	Free ..	Free ..	Free ..	Free	Free	9
Zinc, ore	Free ..	Free ..	Free ..	Free ..	Zinc in pieces, per	Zinc, crude ..Free.	10
in pigs, 100 kilogs.	Free ..	0.048	Free ..	Free ..	pood ...0.23	In plates and leaves,	11
in sheets..100 kil.	9.75	10.72	0.78	0.86	in sheets, per	wire and nails, per	12
filings and broken ware.	Free ..	Free ..	Free ..	Free ..	pood ...0.47	100 kilogs...$0.12 All articles o tin,	
100 kilogs	6.04	6.64	5 per ct.	5 per ct.	Pood...........0.31	5 per cent	13
....	Prohibited		10 p. ct.	10 p. ct.	Pood...........0.85		14
Manufactures of zinc and copper, 100 kil.	Prohibited		3.90	4.29	Not polished, pd. 0.78		15
Pure zinc	Prohibited		1.56	1.72	Polished and ornamented, pood..1.95		
See Chemicals not enumerated		....	....	....	Pood...........0.85	Free	16

OBSERVATIONS—Continued.

6. *Russia.*—1 pood = 40 funti (pounds) = 36.113 lbs. U. S. (avoirdupois.) 1 funti (pound) = 0.90282 lb. U. S. 1 arsheen = 28 inches U. S.

7. *Netherlands.*
8. *Italy.*
9. *Spain.*
10. *Portugal.*
11. *Belgium.*

(7–11) French weights and measures.

12. *Austria.*—1 centner = 50 kilogrammes = 110.231 lbs. U. S. (avoirdupois.) 1 foot = 1.03713 feet U. S.

13. *Denmark.*—1 pund (pound) = ½ kilogramme = 1.1023 lbs. U. S. (avoirdupois.) 1 lispund = 16 pund = 17.637 lbs. U. S. 1 pot = 0.25522 gallon U. S. 1 kande = 0.51044 gallon U. S. 1 ton (grain) = 3.948 bushels U. S.

14. *Sweden.*—1 pund (pound) = 0.93697 lbs. U. S. (avoirdupois.) 1 centner = 100 pund. 1 ort = 65.588 grains (troy) U. S. 1 kande = 0.69139 gallon U. S.

15. *Norway.*—1 pund (pound) = 1.08813 lbs. U. S. (avoirdupois.) 1 pund = 32 lod. 1 ton = 3.94 bushels U. S. 1 pot = 0.2550 gallon U. S. 1 kande = 2 pots = 0.5100 gallon U. S.

Comparative table of import duties in the United States and European countries.

	ARTICLES.	ITALY.			SPAIN.	PORTUGAL.
			General tariff.	Tariff in treaty with France, &c.		
1	Yellow, king's patent......	100 kilogs	$1. 95	$0. 78	100 kilogs....$1. 50	5 per cent ....
2	berries, (dyeing) ...	100 kilogs	0. 39	Free.	100 kilogs.....2. 00	Free ....
3	chromate of potash	100 kilogs	1. 95	0. 78	100 kilogs.....0. 02	5 per cent ....
4	citric acid	100 kilogs	1. 56	1. 56	100 kilogs.....0. 02	5 per cent ....
5	salt of chrome.....	100 kilogs	0. 95	0. 78	100 kilogs.....0. 75	Kilog $0. 0108
6	ochre, dry	100 kilogs	0. 39	Free.	100 kilogs.....1. 025	20 per cent ....
7	in oil........	100 kilogs	1. 95	0. 78	100 kilogs.....5. 00	20 per cent ....
8	spirits.............	100 kilogs	1. 95	0. 78	100 kilogs.....2. 50	Kilog 0. 0108
9	Zaffre	Free	......	......	Free	Free ....
10	Zinc, nails	Zinc, mineral....	Free.	Free.	Zinc, in bars, per	Zinc, cast, broken
11	in pigs, blocks........	bars, 100 kil.	0. 19	0. 19	100 kilogs....1. 20	pieces, free.......
12	in sheets	Sheets and plates,	1. 17	Free.	In sheets, wire, nails,	Plates and sheets,
		100 kilogs.			100 kilogs....3. 00	kilog 0. 01
		Coarse articles...	1. 17	0. 78	....	Manufactured, per
13	sulphate of...........	Other manufact's	5. 85	1. 56	Kilog 0. 02	Kilog 0. 075
14	oxide of..............	not gilded.			Manufactured, per	Kilog 0. 005
15	manufactures of......	Gilded	9. 75	11. 27	100 kilogs....5. 00	Kilog 0. 075
16	valerianate of........	See Chemicals...	......	......	Kilog 0. 02	5 per cent..........

OBSERVATIONS—Continued.

B.—SOURCES.

The following documents have furnished the basis for the preceding tabular arrangement:

Great Britain.—The imperial tariff of Great Britain, 1866 and 1867. General order of May 31, 1869.

*Germany.**—Customs tariff of the German Zollverein of July 1, 1865; general list of articles classified for tariff purposes; amendments by law in force from June 1, 1868. Annals of the North German Union of Oct. 14, 1868.

Switzerland.—Swiss customs tariff of July 1, 1865.

France.—Table of import and export duties, Paris, 1864, as amended by subsequent legislation to January 31, 1869, inclusive. This document contains the general tariff and the tariffs under commercial treaty with Great Britain, Belgium, Italy, Sweden and Norway, Switzerland, German Zollverein, Netherlands, Turkey, Austria, Portugal, and the Pontifical States. The discriminating duties on foreign vessels under the tariffs terminated June 12, 1869.

Russia.—Tariff of customs duties levied on the European frontier of the empire of Russia, from January 1, (13th,) 1869. St. Petersburg, 1868.

Netherlands.—The tariff of the Netherlands. The Hague, 1862.

Italy.—General tariff of customs for Italy. Turin, 1864. No. 221—Document of the Chamber of Deputies, session of 1867 and 1868. Treaty of commerce concluded between Italy and Switzerland, July 22, 1868.

Spain.—Decree of July 12, 1869. Gaceta de Madrid, No. 202.

* The German Zollverein, or Customs Union, includes the following States: Prussia, Lauenburg, Lubec, Hamburg and Bremen, Saxony, Upper Hessen, Thuringia, (Saxon principalities,) Mecklenberg, Oldenburg, Brunswick, (these forming the North German Union,) and Luxemburg, Bavaria, Wurtemburg, Baden, and Lower Hessen, in South Germany.

(*Duties expressed in gold dollars of the United States.*)—Continued.

BELGIUM.	AUSTRIA.			DENMARK.	SWEDEN.	NORWAY.	
		General tariff.	Tariff in treaty.				
Free	Centner	$0.388	......	Pound....$0.028	Free	Pound....$0.009	1
Free	Free	......	......	Free	Free	Free	2
Free							3
Free	See Chemicals		......	Pound.....0.0113	See Chemicals	Free	4
Free							5
Free	Free	......	......	Free	Free	Free	6
Free	Centner	0.388	....	Free	Free	Pound.....0.009	7
Free	Centner	0.388	Free.	Pound.....0.028	Pound ...$0.0082	Free	8
Free	Centner	0.72	0.72	Free	Free	Free	9
Free	Zinc, crude or broken pcs.	Free.	Free.	Zinc in sheets, plates, tubes, bolts, nails, per pound ...0.0065	Zinc, mineral, in blocks, sheets, &c.......Free.	Zinc, crude, free.	10
Free	In sheets, per centner.	0.69	0.72			Nails, lb...0.013	11
Free	In tubes, wire, and coarse articles.	1.20	0.72	Manufactures, see Tin.	Manufactured articles, not painted or varnished, pound...0.0082	Articles gilded, pound....0.095	12
Free						Articles bronzed, varnished, per pound....0.047	13
Free	Articles, common, centner	2.40	2.16		Painted or varnished, lb 0.011	Cast, over 25 lbs., pound....0.018	14
10 per cent	Ditto, gilded, &c., centner.	7.20	5.76		Gilded, plated, &c., lb....0.082	All other articles, pound....0.036	15
Free	See Chemicals	.....	......	Pound....0.0113	Free	Free	16

OBSERVATIONS—Continued.

Portugal.—General tariff of customs for the continent of Portugal and adjacent islands. Lisbon, 1865.

Belgium.—General tariff of customs of Belgium, approved by royal decree of March 30, 1866. Brussels, June, 1866.

Austria.—General customs tariff of December 5, 1853, as amended by law of June 30, 1865. Tariff in treaty with the German Zollverein of April 11, 1865. (No copy of the treaty with Great Britain has been received.)

Denmark.—General tariff of imports and exports, law of July 4, 1863, in force since April 1, 1864; amended by law of March 11, 1865.

Sweden.—General tariff. Law of March 24, 1865; in force since April, 1865.

Norway.—Tariff of imports and exports of February 25, 1863, as amended by treaty with France of March 18, 1865, and by law of March 6, 1869.

C.—*Discriminating duties in Spain.*

The decree of July 12, 1869, contains this provision: No discrimination will be made in duties on goods, whether arriving under national or foreign flag or by land. The extra duties on the following goods will be levied till January 1, 1872, only:

1. Five cents ($0.05 gold U. S.) per 100 kilogrammes on abacca, olives, sulphuric acid, muriatic acid, alum, sulphur, carbonate of soda, beeswax in combs, chloride of lime, glass and earthenware, pig iron, cast-iron tubes, iron scythes, plowshares, cable chains, flax, butter, muriate of potassium, machinery of all kinds, and nitrate of soda.
2. Twenty-five cents ($0.25 gold U. S.) per 100 kilogrammes on brandy, hemp, tin, copper, and brass, in bars and plates, iron not otherwise specified, thread of all kinds, furniture of all classes, saltpeter, and tissues of all kinds.
3. Fifty cents ($0.50 gold U. S.) per 100 kilogrammes on raw cotton, sugar, cod-fish, cocoa, coffee, cinnamon, beeswax out of combs, and hides.

ABSTRACT.—*Comparative table of minimum and maximum rates of import duties on various measurements and gold*

	Commodities.	Measurements.	United States.		Great Britain.		German Zoll-Verein.		Switzerland.	
			Min.	Max.	Min.	Max.	Min.	Max.	Min.	Max.
	I. Raw Materials.									
1	Earth, clay, chalk	Ton	$3.00	$10.00		Free		Free		Free
2	Coal	Ton	0.40	1.25		Free		Free		$0.037
3	Stone, marble, &c {	Per ct. *ad val.*	20	25		Free		Free		
	}	Cubic foot	0.50	1.00						
		Ton								0.54
4	Ores	Per ct. *ad val.*	Free	10		Free		Free		
		Pound	0.015	0.03					0.00001	0.00002
5	Wood, (timber)	Per ct. *ad val*	Free	35		Free		Free		
		Ton								0.037
		Cubic foot								
6	Flax	Ton	15.00	40.00		Free		Free		1.16
7	Cotton	Ton		Free		Free		Free		1.16
8	Wool {	Pound	0.03	0.12		Free		Free		0.0008
	}	Per ct. *ad val.*	10	11						
9	Silk	Pound		Free		Free		Free		0.00052
10	Other raw material	Per ct. *ad val.*	10	50		Free		Free		
		Cwt								0.0006
	II. Breadstuffs.									
11	Cereals	Bushel	0.10	0.20		Free		Free		
		Pound								0.00026
12	Flour	Pound				Free		Free		0.00088
		Per ct. *ad val.*	10	20						
	III. Medicinal, &c.									
13	Drugs, crude	Pound	0.01	0.50		Free	Free	$0.0032	0.0005	0.00617
		Per ct. *ad val.*		20						
14	Ethers, essences, &c	Pound	0.25	64.00			Free	0.0218		0.00617
		Gallon			$0.73	$5.07				
		Per ct. *ad val.*								
15	Prepared medicines	Pound	2.40	40.00		Free	Free	0.0218		0.00617
		Per ct. *ad val.*	40	50						
16	Perfumeries, (alcoholic) {	Per ct. *ad val.*		50		Free				
	}	Gallon		3.00						
		Pound						0.0218	0.006	0.026
17	Chemical preparations	Pound	0.003	2.00		Free	Free	0.0218	0.00053	0.0061
		Per ct. *ad val.*	10	45						
	IV. Beverages.									
18	Wines {	Per ct. *ad val.*		25						
	}	Gallon	0.20	1.00	0.208	0.516				
		Cwt						2.62		0.51
19	Spirits	Per ct. *ad val*	50	100						
		Proof gallon	2.50	3.00	1.827	1.842				
		Cwt						3.92		1.50
	V. Colonial Produce.									
20	Coffee	Pound		0.05	0.06	0.08		0.031		0.0026
21	Pepper	Pound	0.15	0.18		Free		0.042		0.0061
22	Sugar, raw	Pound	0.03	0.05	0.01	0.022		0.028		0.0061
23	refined	Pound		0.15	0.025	0.026		0.048		0.0061
24	Tea	Pound		0.25		0.12		0.052		0.026
25	Tobacco	Pound	0.35	0.50	0.97	1.09	0.026	0.072		0.015
26	Cigars {	Pound		2.50		1.21		0.13		0.026
	}	Per ct. *ad val*		50						

NOTE.—The *braces* in this supplementary table indicate that under the United States tariff the articles are subject to a joint specific and *ad valorem* duty. *Single* rates of duty are placed in the maximum column.

M E N T.

classes of commodities in the tariffs of the United States and European countries, (reduced to values of the United States.)

FRANCE.				RUSSIA.		NETHERLANDS.		ITALY.				
General tariff.		Treaty tariff.						General tariff.		Treaty tariff.		
Min.	Max.	Min.	Max.	Min.	Max.	Min.	Max.	Min.	Max.	Min.	Max.	
	Free		Free		Free		Free	Free	$0.96		Free	1
	$0.20		$0.29		Free		Free		Free		Free	2
												3
	2.90		2.90		Free		Free		Free		Free	
	Free		Free		Free		Free		Free		Free	4
	Free		Free			1	3					5
				Free	$2.40			Free	23.40	Free	$5.50	
	Free		Free		Free		Free		Free		Free	6
	4.87		Free		Free		Free		Free		Free	7
	0.0026		0.0002		0.0047		Free		Free		Free	8
	Free		Free		0.0108		Free		Free		Free	9
	Free		Free		Free		Free		Free		Free	10
					Free		$0.215					11
Free	0.0004		Free						0.00065		0.00065	
Free	0.00088		Free	$0.00063	0.0015		0.00072		0.00108		0.00108	12
Free	0.0017	Free	0.0017		Free		Free	$0.0026	0.004		Free	13
Prohi	bited.				0.095			0.009	0.09	$0.009	0.09	14
						Free	1.40					
			5									
Prohi	bited.			0.0003	0.216		Free	0.009	0.09	0.009	0.09	15
			5									
							5				10	16
						1.93	3.10					
$0.021	0.13	$0.009	0.013		0.086				0.053		0.0017	
Free	0.17	Free	0.035	0.001	0.047	Free	1.40†	Free	0.35	Free	0.035	17
Prohi	bited.		5									
				0.26*	0.78*				0.29*			18
	0.0018		0.0022				Free		0.037		0.047	
				3.47	5.55							
					0.50*							19
	0.184		0.115				0.054	0.037	0.074	0.041	0.074	
					20.62							
0.044	0.05		0.05		0.032		Free		0.044		0.044	20
0.044	0.054				0.032		0.0028		0.037			21
0.032	0.04	0.037	0.04		0.065		Free		0.016		0.018	22
Prohi	bited.	0.043	0.049		0.096		0.065		0.022		0.027	23
0.035	0.088			0.33	0.475		0.04		0.027			24
Govern	ment	mono	poly.	0.095	0.057	0.0012	0.0027	Govern	ment	mono	poly.	25
Govern	ment	mono	poly.		1.89		0.074	Prohi	bited.	Prohi	bited.	26

* Per bottle.

† If containing alcohol.

SUPPLE

Abstract.—*Comparative table of minimum and*

	Commodities.	Measurements.	United States.		Spain.		Portugal.		Belgium.	
			Min.	Max.	Min.	Max.	Min.	Max.	Min.	Max.
	I. Raw Materials.									
1	Earth, clay, chalk	Ton	$3.00	$10.00		$0.02		Free		Free
2	Coal	Ton	0.40	1.25		0.25		Free		Free
3	Stone, marble, &c	Per ct. *ad val.*	20	25				Free		Free
		Cubic foot	0.50	1.00						
		Ton				$0.75				
4	Ores	Per ct. *ad val*	Free	10		Free		Free		Free
		Pound	0.015	0.03						
5	Wood, (timber)	Per ct. *ad val.*	Free	35	Free	1				
		Ton			Free	1.00		$2.70		
		Cubic foot							Free	$0.065
6	Flax	Ton	15.00	40.06						
7	Cotton	Ton		Free		5.00	Free	4.30		Free
8	Wool	Pound	0.03	0.12		0.0024		0.0024		Free
		Per ct. *ad val.*	10	11						
9	Silk	Pound		Free		Free		Free		Free
10	Other raw material	Per ct. *ad val.*	10	50		Free		Free		Free
		Cwt								
	II. Breadstuffs.									
11	Cereals	Bushel	0.10	0.20						
		Pound			0.00108	0.0027		0.00367		0.0005
12	Flour	Pound			0.0016	0.004		0.00367		0.001
		Per ct. *ad val.*	10	20						
	III. Medicinal, &c.									
13	Drugs, crude	Pound	0.01	0.50	0.009	0.049	$0.0024	0.073		Free
		Per ct. *ad val.*		20						
14	Ethers, essences, &c	Pound	0.25	64.00						Free
		Gallon								
		Per ct. *ad val*				20		20		5
15	Prepared medicines	Pound	2.40	40.00				0.294		Free
		Per ct. *ad val*	40	50		20		5		
16	Perfumeries, (alcoholic)	Per ct. *ad val*		50		20		20		5
		Gallon		3.00			or			
		Pound					0.12	0.75		
17	Chemical preparations	Pound	0.003	2.00	0.00048	0.04		0.001	Free	0.0026
		Per ct. *ad val.*	10	45						
	IV. Beverages.									
18	Wines	Per ct. *ad val.*		25						
		Gallon	0.20	1.00	0.39	0.77		0.40		0.0037
		Cwt								
19	Spirits	Per ct. *ad val*	50	100						
		Proof gallon	2.50	3.00	0.056	0.142		0.61	0.321	0.642
		Cwt								
	V. Colonial Produce.									
20	Coffee	Pound		0.05	0.017	0.022	0.005	0.03	0.007	0.0155
21	Pepper	Pound	0.15	0.18		0.022	0.01	0.037		0.012
22	Sugar, raw	Pound	0.03	0.05	0.017	0.019		0.037		Free
23	refined	Pound		0.15	0.024	0.029		0.06	0.0468	0.05
24	Tea	Pound		0.25		0.135		0.225		0.08
25	Tobacco	Pound	0.35	0.50	Govern	ment	0.049	0.098	0.0074	0.037
26	Cigars	Pound	2.50		mono	poly.	0.098	0.198		0.23
		Per ct. *ad val.*	50							

MENT.

maximum rates of import duties, &c.—Continued.

AUSTRIA.				DENMARK.		SWEDEN.		NORWAY.		
General tariff.		Treaty tariff.								
Min.	Max.	Min.	Max.	Min.	Max.	Min.	Max.	Min.	Max.	
	Free		Free		Free		Free		Free	1
	Free		Free		$0.40		Free		Free	2
	Free		Free				Free		Free	3
				Free	0.082					
					0.40					
	Free		Free		Free		Free		Free	4
							Free		Free	5
				Free	0.72					
Free	$0.0038		Free	Free	0.01					
										6
Free	0.28		Free		Free		Free		Free	7
	Free		Free		Free		Free		Free	8
Free	0.0035				0.24	Free	$0.11		$0.11	9
	Free		Free		Free		Free		Free	10
										11
$0.0007	0.0015		Free		Free		Free	Free	0.0002	
	0.0035		Free		Free		Free	Free	0.003	12
Free	0.02	Free	0.0013	Free	0.0103		Free		Free	13
	0.032		0.021		0.067		0.067		Free	14
	0.065		0.052		0.0103		Free		Free	15
										16
0.02	0.03	0.013	0.02		0.091		0.11		0.10	
Free	0.02	Free	0.013		0.0103				Free	17
							5			
										18
					0.36	0.22	0.71		0.21	
5.13	6.45				2.19	2.43	4.86		2.24	
										19
					0.36	0.35	0.44		0.78*	
3.95	6.43				2.19				7.84	
	0.034			0.022	0.023	0.029	0.044		0.041	20
	0.034				0.016		0.03	0.033	0.30	21
	0.037				0.02	0.026	0.032		0.03	22
	0.057			0.02	0.03		0.032		0.041	23
	0.068				0.062		0.147		0.17	24
0.045	0.11			0.025	0.041	0.07	0.176	0.073	0.10	25
Special	permit.	Special	permit.		0.165		0.53		0.17	26

* If in bottles.

SUPPLE

ABSTRACT.—*Comparative table of minimum and*

	COMMODITIES.	MEASUREMENTS.	UNITED STATES.		GREAT BRITAIN.		GERMAN ZOLL-VEREIN.		SWITZERLAND.	
			Min.	Max.	Min.	Max.	Min.	Max.	Min.	Max.
	VI. MANUFACTURES.									
27	1. Earthenware	Per ct. *ad val.*	25	40	......	Free..	......	......	......	......
		Pound	......	......	......	......	$0.011	$0.013	0.0013	0.014
28	Porcelain	Per ct. *ad val.*	40	50	......	Free..	......	......	......	......
		Pound	......	......	......	......	0.011	0.024	......	0.014
	2. *Metals.*									
29	Gold	Per ct. *ad val.*	35	40	......	......	......	......	......	......
		Pound	......	......	......	49.63*	......	0.32	......	0.026
30	Silver	Per ct. *ad val.*	35	40	......	......	......	......	......	......
		Pound	......	......	......	4.38*	......	0.32	......	0.026
31	Copper................	Per ct. *ad val.*	......	45	......	Free..	......	......	......	......
		Pound	......	......	......	......	0.0175	0.026	0.0026	0.014
32	Iron, pig	Ton	......	$9.00	......	Free..	......	2.40	......	1.16
33	castings............	Pound	$0.01¼	0.02½	......	Free..	0.0026	0.0087	......	0.0017
		Per ct. *ad val.*	......	......	......	......	......	......	......	......
34	Other articles of iron or steel	Per ct. *ad val.*	35	45	......	Free..	......	......	......	......
		Pound	......	......	......	......	0.0026	0.0087	0.0035	0.014
35	Machinery	Per ct. *ad val.*	40	45	......	Free..	......	Free..	......	......
		Pound	For be	et su-	......	......	0.003	0.013	0.0035	0.0061
			gar,	free.						
	3. *Yarns.*									
36	Cotton	Per ct. *ad val.*	35	40	......	Free..	......	......	......	......
		Pound	......	......	......	......	0.013	0.039	0.0035	0.0061
37	Linen	Per ct. *ad val.*	30	35	......	Free..	......	......	......	......
		Pound	......	......	......	......	Free..	0.01	......	0.0061
38	Woolen .... {	Per ct. *ad val.*	25	35	......	Free..	......	......	......	......
		Pound	0.20	0.50	......	......	0.003	0.026	0.0035	0.0661
39	Silk spun..............	Per ct. *ad val.*	40	60	......	Free..	......	......	......	......
		Pound	......	......	......	......	......	0.026	0.0035	0.0061
	4. *Tissues, including lace.*									
40	Cotton .... {	Per ct. *ad val.*	......	15	......	Free..	......	......	......	......
		Square yard	0.01¼	0.07½	......	......	......	......	......	......
		Pound	......	......	......	......	0.065	0.196	......	0.014
41	Linen	Per ct. *ad val.*	30	40	......	Free..	......	......	......	......
		Pound	......	......	......	......	0.026	0.13	......	0.014
42	Woolen .... {	Per ct. *ad val.*	30	35	......	Free..	......	......	......	......
		Pound	0.20	0.50	......	......	0.065	0.196	......	0.014
43	Silk	Per ct. *ad val.*	40	60	......	Free..	......	......	......	......
		Pound	......	......	......	......	0.196	0.261	0.014	0.0266
44	India-rubber............	Per ct. *ad val.*	35	50	......	Free..	......	......	......	......
		Pound	......	......	......	......	......	0.096	......	0.0014
	5. *Other manufactures.*									
45	Of India-rubber	Per ct. *ad val.*	10	35	......	Free..	......	......	......	......
		Pound	......	......	......	......	0.026	0.045	0.0061	0.014
46	Prepared leather.........	Per ct. *ad val.*	25	35	......	Free..	......	......	......	......
		Pound	......	......	......	......	0.013	0.032	0.0035	0.0032
47	Articles of leather	Per ct. *ad val.*	25	35	......	Free..	......	......	......	......
		Pound	......	......	......	......	0.026	0.087	0.011	0.026
48	Articles of wood.........	Per ct. *ad val.*	......	35	......	Free..	......	......	......	10
		Pound	......	......	......	......	Free..	0.026	......	......
49	Glass manufactures	Per ct. *ad val.*	35	40	......	Free..	......	......	......	......
		Square foot..	0.0075	0.60	......	......	......	......	......	......
		Pound	......	......	......	......	Free..	0.096	0.0013	0.026
50	Fancy goods	Per ct. *ad val.*	35	100	......	Free..	......	......	......	......
		Pound	......	......	......	......	0.099	0.32	......	0.026

* Only plate.

M E N T.

maximum rates of import duties, &c.—Continued.

FRANCE.				RUSSIA.		NETHERLANDS.		ITALY.				
General tariff.		Treaty tariff.						General tariff.		Treaty tariff.		
Min.	Max.	Min.	Max.	Min.	Max.	Min.	Max.	Min.	Max.	Min.	Max.	
Prohi	bited.		15				5					27
$0.005	$0.009		Free	$0.0044	$0.054			$0.0018	$0.01	Free	$0.01	
	10		10			1	5					28
				0.089	0.346			0.014	0.021	$0.01	0.021	
						3	5				5	29
	0.442		$0.442		28.51				8.84			
						3	5				5	30
	0.442		0.442		1.90				1.06			
							5					31
0.088	0.188	$0.017	0.019	0.013	0.065	$0.007		0.013	0.088	0.015	0.088	
	7.80		3.90		2.375		Free		Free		Free	32
Prohi	bited.	0.005	0.019	0.02	0.054	Free		0.00043	0.007	0.0005	0.008	33
							5					
Prohi	bited.		15				5					34
0.013	0.19	0.0088	0.019	0.02	0.52			0.007	0.018	0.008	0.02	
				Ind'stry	Free		1		1		1	35
0.0044	0.16	0.0028	0.023	0.0064	0.016			0.0017	0.0044	0.0017	0.0044	
Prohi	bited.						3					36
0.62	0.78	0.013	0.383	0.07	0.09			0.013	0.026	0.021	0.0306	
							3					37
0.033	0.241	0.013	0.16		0.0086			0.0088	0.026	0.01	0.0306	
							3					38
0.62	0.68	0.0088	0.21		0.099			0.035	0.053	0.042	0.063	
							3					39
0.066	0.11			0.097	0.108				0.177		Free	
	5		15				5					40
Prohi	bited.											
	0.086	0.044	0.30	0.24	1.14			0.044	0.176	0.102	0.25	
							5					41
0.053	0.87	0.024	0.37	0.43	0.55			0.018	0.022	0.033	0.08	
	15		10				5		5		5	42
0.168	0.458			0.73	2.59			0.12	0.26		0.39	
							5		5		5	43
Free	0.035		Free	0.88	4.30			0.263	0.886	0.263	0.886	
							5					44
Prohi	bited.	0.088	0.19		0.475			0.022	0.088	0.025	0.101	
							5					45
0.018	0.187	0.0175	0.195	0.071	0.21			0.0035	0.022	0.004	0.025	
						1	5					46
0.0087	0.187	0.0087	0.058	Free	0.175				0.035		0.013	
Prohi	bited.		10				5					47
				0.012	0.0475			0.01	0.044		0.044	
Free	15	Free	10				5	Prohi	bited.		10	48
				Free	0.08			0.005	0.022			
Prohi	bited.		10				5					49
0.27	1.20	0.36	0.49	0.28	1.00							
0.0088	0.18	0.003	0.019	0.02	0.162			0.007	0.022	0.0017	0.022	
Prohi	bited.	5	10			3	3					50
0.88	0.442	0.05	0.058	0.30	0.94			0.044	0.088	0.044	0.088	

SUPPLE

ABSTRACT.—*Comparative table of minimum and*

	COMMODITIES.	MEASUREMENTS.	UNITED STATES.		SPAIN.		PORTUGAL.		BELGIUM.	
			Min.	Max.	Min.	Max.	Min.	Max.	Min.	Max.
	VI. MANUFACTURES.									
27	1. Earthenware	Per ct. *ad val.*	25	40	......	......	......	......	......	......
		Pound	......	......	$0.0013	$0.034	$0.001	$0.049	......	$0.0013
28	Porcelain	Per ct. *ad val.*	40	50	......	......	......	......	......	10
		Pound	......	......	......	0.048	......	0.148	......	......
	2. *Metals.*									
29	Gold	Per ct. *ad val*	35	40	......	......	......	......	......	5
		Pound	......	......	......	22.68	9.80	24.54	......	......
30	Silver	Per ct. *ad val*	35	40	......	......	......	......	......	5
		Pound	......	......	......	3.18	2.45	14.88	......	......
31	Copper	Per ct. *ad val.*	......	45	......	......	......	......	......	10
		Pound	......	......	......	0.045	0.10	0.98	......	......
32	Iron, pig	Ton	......	9.00	......	5.00	......	0.02	......	0.975
33	castings	Pound	0.01¼	0.02½	......	0.007	0.038	0.063	......	0.0018
		Per ct. *ad val*	......	......	......	......	......	......	......	......
34	Other articles of iron or steel	Per ct. *ad val*	35	45	......	......	......	......	......	10
		Pound	......	......	0.0068	0.09	0.004	0.24	......	0.0035
35	Machinery	Per ct. *ad val.*	40	45	1	10	......	......	......	......
		Pound	For beet sugar,	free.	......	......	0.0009	0.0045	$0.0018	0.0035
	3. *Yarns.*									
36	Cotton	Per ct. *ad val*	35	40	......	......	......	......	......	......
		Pound	......	......	0.11	0.22	0.068	0.145	0.0095	0.44
37	Linen	Per ct. *ad val.*	30	35	......	......	......	......	......	......
		Pound	......	......	0.025	0.11	0.122	0.981	0.0095	0.028
38	Woolen	Per ct. *ad val.*	25	35	......	......	......	......	......	......
		Pound	0.20	0.50	0.17	0.27	0.327	1.23	0.018	0.028
39	Silk, spun	Per ct. *ad val.*	40	60	......	......	......	......	......	......
		Pound	......	......	0.045	0.08	0.036	1.23	......	Free..
	4. *Tissues, including lace.*									
40	Cotton	Per ct. *ad val*	......	15	......	......	......	......	......	......
		Square yard	0.01¼	0.07½	......	......	......	......	......	......
		Pound	......	......	0.27	0.57	0.049	1.22	0.044	0.265
41	Linen	Per ct. *ad val*	30	40	......	......	......	......	5	10
		Pound	......	......	0.011	1.13	0.031	1.27	......	......
42	Woolen	Per ct. *ad val.*	30	35	......	......	......	......	5	10
		Pound	0.20	0.50	0.137	0.73	0.02	1.27	......	0.23
43	Silk	Per ct. *ad val*	40	60	......	......	......	......	......	......
		Pound	......	......	0.818	2.50	0.72	3.72	......	0.265
44	India-rubber	Per ct. *ad val.*	35	50	......	......	......	......	......	10
		Pound	......	......	......	0.275	0.49	0.98	......	......
	5. *Other manufactures.*									
45	Of India-rubber	Per ct. *ad val.*	10	35	......	......	......	......	......	10
		Pound	......	......	0.068	0.185	......	0.012	......	......
46	Prepared leather	Per ct. *ad val*	25	35	......	......	......	......	......	......
		Pound	......	......	......	0.11	0.022	0.10	0.0044	0.265
47	Articles of leather	Per ct. *ad val*	25	35	......	......	......	......	......	10
		Pound	......	......	0.045	0.80	0.30	1.22	......	......
48	Articles of wood	Per ct. *ad val.*	......	35	......	......	......	35	......	10
		Pound	......	......	0.016	0.09	0.022	......	......	......
49	Glass manufactures	Per ct. *ad val*	35	40	......	......	......	......	......	10
		Square foot	0.0075	0.60	......	......	0.01	0.02	......	......
		Pound	......	......	0.0016	0.072	0.024	0.078	......	0.0039
50	6. Fancy goods	Per ct. *ad val*	35	100	......	......	......	......	......	10
		Pound	......	......	0.01	1.81	0.18	5.89	......	......

MENT.

maximum rates of import duties, &c.—Continued.

Austria.				Denmark.		Sweden.		Norway.		
General tariff.		Treaty tariff.								
Min.	Max.	Min.	Max.	Min.	Max.	Min.	Max.	Min.	Max.	
$0.001	$0.065	Free	$0.052	$0.0012	$0.041	Free	$0.0088	Free	$0.004	27
0.026	0.065	$0.009	0.052	0.041	0.082	$0.0088	0.06	$0.028	0.0637	28
0.43	1.14			0.082	0.248	0.29	1.47	0.106	0.806	29
0.43	1.14			0.082	0.248		0.87	0.106	0.806	30
0.032	0.065	0.009	0.052	0.041	0.082	0.044	0.087	Free	0.10	31
1.20	2.01		1.92		Free		Free		Free	32
	0.021		0.019	0.0012	0.002	0.005	0.029	Free	0.016	33
										34
0.026	0.109	0.019	0.065	0.005	0.015	0.01 Free	0.073 10	Free	0.066 Free	35
0.01	0.032	0.008	0.026		0.015					
0.022	0.057	0.017	0.026	0.015	0.041	0.024	0.042	0.016	0.041	36
0.003	0.057	Free	0.019	0.015	0.041	0.029	0.058	0.016	0.083	37
0.004	0.057	0.003	0.003	0.025	0.041	0.029	0.043	0.033	0.041	38
0.035	0.068				0.37		0.041		0.11	39
										40
0.157	1.145	0.109	0.30	0.01	0.24	0.058	0.36	0.016	0.22	
0.0065	1.145	0.003	0.30	0.01	0.24	0.043	0.22	0.016	0.21	41
0.035	1.145	0.109	0.30	0.062	0.248	0.029	0.22	0.07	0.21	42
0.45	1.145	0.30	1.36	0.37	1.00	0.29	0.43	0.24	0.43	43
	0.109		0.109		0.082		0.22		0.115	44
0.052	0.109	0.032	0.065	0.025	0.082	Free	0.12	Free	0.115	45
0.004	0.056	0.003	0.043	0.031	0.062	0.029	0.058	0.029	0.046	46
0.052	0.253	0.032	0.196		0.082	0.035	0.07	0.08	0.13	47
0.001	0.052	Free	0.052	0.0008	0.082	0.0029	0.073	Free 6	0.047 10	48
										49
0.003	0.065	0.003	0.052	0.0076	0.082 10	Free	0.178	Free	0.047	
0.043	1.145	0.043	1.145	0.082	0.50	0.029	0.88	0.04	1.00	50

O

www.ingramcontent.com/pod-product-compliance
Lightning Source LLC
LaVergne TN
LVHW020937110826
845150LV00004B/891

* 9 7 8 1 4 2 5 5 5 1 6 6 7 *